Knowledge Management for the Information Professional

Edited by
T. Kanti Srikantaiah, Ph.D.
Director, Center for Knowledge Management
Dominican University

and

Michael E. D. Koenig, Ph.D.
Dean
Long Island University

asis

ASIS Monograph Series

Published for the
American Society for Information Science by

 **Information Today, Inc.**

Medford, New Jersey

Library of Congress Cataloging-in-Publication Data

Knowledge management for the information professional/edited by
   T. Kanti Srikantaiah and Michael E. D. Koenig.
      p.   cm. -- (ASIS monograph series)
   Includes bibliographical references and index.
   ISBN 1-57387-079-X (hardbound)
   1. Knowledge management. 2. Organizational learning.
I. Srikantaiah, T. Kanti. II. Koenig, Micheal E. D. III. American
Society for Information Science.   IV. Series.
HD30.2.K6369 1999
658.4'038--dc21

                         99-16446
                         CIP

Publisher: Thomas H. Hogan, Sr.
Editor-in-Chief: John B. Bryans
Managing Editor: Janet M. Spavlik
Copy Editor: Michelle Sutton-Kerchner
Production Manager: M. Heide Dengler
Cover Designer: Jacqueline Walter
Book Designers: Patricia F. Kirkbride
               Jeremy M. Pellegrin
Indexer: Laurie Andriot

Table of Contents

Part I: Overview

Part II: Background & Issues

Part III: Knowledge Management—Creating the Culture of Learning & Knowledge Sharing in the Organization

Part IV: Knowledge Management—The Tools

Part V: Knowledge Management—Application

Part VI: Appendices

Preface and Acknowledgments

Knowledge Management for the Information Professional unfolded in stages from several concerns and perceptions on the part of the authors and editors.

The first concern, the first stage, was the practical requirement of introducing and teaching a course on knowledge management to students already enrolled in graduate programs of library and information science, business schools, information/records management, information technology and similar disciplines who not unnaturally believe that all of their courses were already devoted to various aspects of information and knowledge management. To these students, an elective course on knowledge management tended to appear as would an elective course titled simply "medicine" might appear to a medical student in medical school.

The topic is clearly relevant, but questions arise such as: What does knowledge management consist of; where does it fit in; and what will I learn that I don't already know or can't acquire elsewhere to pursue a career in knowledge management? The first section of this book, particularly the chapters by the editors, directly addresses these issues.

The next stage was the realization in assembling material for the course that while there is a large and rapidly burgeoning literature on knowledge management (see Appendix B) there are two significant and overlapping gaps. The first gap is that although there is substantial literature written from the viewpoint of general, and particularly senior management, and from the viewpoint of information technologists, very little has been written from the viewpoint of those who need to be the central actors in the unfolding of this drama—the information professionals. The second gap was the realization that although the literature is already indeed very large, there is no one good textbook or sourcebook on which to base a knowledge management course either in the context of information science/information management, or in the context of undergraduate business education.

The next stage was the attempt to address this gap. The authors concluded that in this rapidly evolving field the attempt to write an up-to-date textbook was a task that would be heroic to say the least, and likely futile. We decided upon a multi-authored book, not a "key papers in" approach, as the field is changing too rapidly for that, but a collection of simultaneously written components by authors who are active and experienced in the field. This book will be useful, not only as a course book, but also as an updated background on the field of knowledge management for information professionals and managers.

The editors would like to acknowledge the contributions of the authors, without whose speedy cooperation the book would have been infeasible. We would like to thank them not only for their individual chapters, but also for insights, suggestions, and the education that they have provided to the editors. We would also like to thank Information Today, Inc. for its support and for handling the book in so expeditious a fashion. Finally, we would like to thank Panya Worawichawong for his help on the mechanics of keeping everything under control.

T. Kanti Srikantaiah   Michael E. D. Koenig

Dominican University   Long Island University

Part I :

Overview

CHAPTER 1

An Introduction to Knowledge Management

T. Kanti Srikantaiah
Director, Center for Knowledge Management
Dominican University

Knowledge management is a concept that has emerged explosively in the business community over the last few years. What is it? The Gartner Group's definition—"A discipline that promotes an integrated approach to identifying, capturing, evaluating, retrieving, and sharing all of an enterprise's information assets. These assets may include databases, documents, policies, procedures, and previously uncaptured expertise and experience in individual workers"—is a good description, relatively brief and yet fairly inclusive.[1]

The chapters "Knowledge Management: A Faceted Overview" and "The Evolution of Knowledge Management" explain in more detail what is now meant by the increasingly inclusive term, knowledge management, and how it evolved into having very broad connotations. Also, see the chapter "Components of a Knowledge Strategy: Keys to Successful Knowledge Management" for even further details.

This book will explore knowledge management from the perspective of the information professional whose job it is to make knowledge management an operational reality, not just a platitude. Furthermore, unlike most works on knowledge management, which address it almost exclusively in the context of a firm or an organization to help gain a competitive advantage, this book looks at knowledge management in a broader transorganizational context.

The book is divided into five major areas:

- Overview of knowledge management
- Background and issues in knowledge management
- Knowledge management—Creating the culture of learning and knowledge sharing in the organization

- Knowledge management—The tools
- Knowledge management—The application

The contents of each section are sketched below; however, each section opens with a more detailed set of introductory notes, particularly for the benefit of the reader who wants to dip into the book, not necessarily in sequential order.

The first section provides an overview of knowledge management, including this introduction, along with a faceted approach to the topic.

The second section, "Background & Issues," explores the background and some major issues in knowledge management and attempts to define this rapidly evolving area. The chapter on the evolution of knowledge management not only traces the history of knowledge management, but also presents an operational definition of it and how the meaning of the term has changed substantially, even in its very brief lifetime. In addition, several of the chapters in subsequent sections also contain excellent operational definitions. The chapter by Short, "Components of a Knowledge Strategy: Keys to Successful Knowledge Management," develops the notion of "knowledge levers," the mechanisms by which one puts knowledge management to work. This chapter sets forth a clear cohesive vision of what the conceptual components of knowledge management are. It is placed in section five because it is so germane to the applications of knowledge management, and for the reader who is casually browsing the book, it should be there. However, for the reader who is approaching this book as an introduction to knowledge management or who is using this as a textbook, that chapter should be considered part of the introductory material.

The third section, "Knowledge Management—Creating the Culture of Learning and Knowledge Sharing in the Organization," is given priority in placement after the introductory sections because of the editors' belief that knowledge management is fundamentally more an issue of corporate cultural transformation than it is of information technology and its deployment. The latter is, of course, also a fundamental issue, but the former is the more difficult, yet subtler problem that demands greater management attention and involvement. It also requires greater organization of one's management by the information professionals involved in knowledge management. These professionals must educate their management-level employees if they are to be successful.

This section of the book explores some of the issues in transforming the corporate culture both to help information professionals understand the context in which they will be introducing cultural change and to understand some of the complexities and issues involved. It also assists in educating the organization's management about those issues and stresses the need for management's involvement.

The fourth section, "Knowledge Management—The Tools," contains some of the tools and technologies involved in setting up a knowledge management undertaking. The attempt here is to provide tool information that will be of some enduring utility to the information professional. Deliberately avoided are comparisons of particular knowledge management products because they are evolving so rapidly that a chapter in a monograph is bound to be dated before it publishes.

Sahasrabudhe's "Information Technology in Support of Knowledge Management" in the fourth section, provides an excellent delineation of how information technology typically is deployed in the knowledge management context. In the process, it provides an information technology view of knowledge management issues.

The fifth and final section, "Knowledge Management—The Application," discusses and describes the application of knowledge management in a number of contexts. Here it is emphasized that knowledge management is not merely a corporate phenomenon, but that it is in principle and in practice a broad-based phenomenon of utility and applicability in information-intensive organizations of all types.

This book also includes several appendices. The first is a course syllabus developed by the editors for a course in knowledge management taught at the Graduate School of Library and Information Science at Dominican University. It is included with the hope that other educators in the information field may find it useful. Feedback, improvements, additions, and comments from other academics and knowledge management practitioners are appreciated. The last two appendices include a thematic model of information-driven management, which is followed by a list of contributors to this publication.

Also included is a bibliography, now exceeding 600 items related to knowledge management that the editors, together with Morgen Macintosh, graduate assistant at the Dominican University, prepared in part as preparation for this book and in part as preparation for developing the course syllabus in knowledge management.

Endnote

1. Quoted in Duhon, Bryant, "It's All in Our Heads," *Inform* 12 (8):10, September, 1998.

CHAPTER 2

Knowledge Management: A Faceted Overview

T. Kanti Srikantaiah

Director, Center for Knowledge Management

Dominican University

INTRODUCTION

Currently, knowledge management (KM) is the hot topic in the business world, and many practitioners in different disciplines have become active partners in embracing this new field. The degree of interest, the view, and the interpretation of KM of these practitioners depend on their environment and are reflected in their professional literatures and in the content of professional conventions. Currently, three groups dominate the articulation of the newly emerged field of KM: vendors promoting hardware and software technologies and services promising to improve the bottom line in corporations; information purveyors providing information services (also utilizing technologies such as Intranet, Internet, and online systems) to clients through explicit knowledge; and organization learning specialists analyzing tacit and explicit knowledge systems in corporations and making recommendations to enhance their performance levels. Additionally, there are the ancillary views of scientists, sector specialists, and the general public, viewing KM more from the consumer viewpoint and voicing their concerns. General opinion is that KM is the re-amalgamation of earlier experiments, such as management information systems, business process reengineering, and information resources management, and has benefited from the lessons learned in those earlier, more limited initiatives.

Throughout this book, a relatively straightforward account of the development of KM is traced. That account is, by necessity, also a definition of what has been and is now meant by the term KM. However, the reality of what KM actually is and what various individuals think it to be, is nothing quite that simple. KM has become a potpourri term and a bandwagon on which many partners have jumped for various and sundry reasons. In this chapter, I will sketch some of those viewpoints and illustrate their notion of what KM is.

A recent World Bank report compared knowledge to light, weightless and intangible, which can easily travel the world, enlightening the lives of people everywhere.[1] While this notion seems reasonable, it is too vague. And, there is almost as much of a variety of definitions for KM in the KM professional literature. Obviously, the perceptions of knowledge management depend on the person and his/her specialty. Information professionals such as librarians, record managers, and archivists emphasize document management. Information technologists such as software developers, programmers, and similar technologists stress hardware, software, network, and telecommunications. Sector specialists such as those in agriculture, education, and industry and organization learning specialists have their own perceptions of KM. Similarly, while discussing KM, scientists, federal/state/local governments, health specialists, legal specialists, business and finance analysts, and the general public have their own viewpoints reflecting their interests.

KM has become a new way of capturing an institution's full expertise addressing factors such as: databases, Web site interfaces and documents; knowledge infrastructure for just-in-time knowledge and global access; enhancing the visibility of knowledge in an institution; sharing knowledge not only within an institution but also with external clients; an institution's knowledge culture; capturing tacit knowledge and experience of staff; and information collected in libraries, record centers, administrative units, operational units, and with individual staff.

INVOLVEMENT

As a major issue of the 1990s, almost every company is concerned with pursuing KM to reap the benefits from its implementation. Consulting firms such as Arthur Andersen, Andersen Consulting, Booz Allen & Hamilton, Price Waterhouse, the Gartner Group, KPMG Peat Marwick, and Coopers & Lybrand are all involved in KM. Professional organizations such as American Productivity and Quality Center, Special Libraries Association, American Society for Information Science, and Association for Information and Image Management offer seminars, conferences, and publications and facilitate consultations in the area of KM. Private corporations such as Ford, Chrysler, Amoco, Dow, GM, Monsanto, Columbia/Healthcare, and Texas Instruments have all experimented with KM and are reportedly benefiting from the outcomes.

Central Themes

Three central themes dominate the field of KM as discovered through communications with field specialists and surveys of the professional literature. These themes are: organizational learning; document management; and technology.

Organizational learning (OL) specialists point out the heavy investment in technology by institutions to transfer information and knowledge and make them available at the institutional level. OL specialists point out that the technology approach is a purely mechanistic solution to information issues. They should consider these solutions as naively promoting software and hardware packages to resolve KM problems. OL experts claim that information technology has never addressed the tacit knowledge, which includes not only the actions, expertise, and ideas of staff, but also the values and emotions of staff. OL emphasizes that the efficiency and effectiveness of knowledge workers depends mostly on how workers communicate and collaborate in their efforts and expose themselves to communities of practice within the institution as well as outside the institution.

Document management specialists point to their information systems such as libraries, information centers, record centers, and archives, and emphasize collections and policies. According to them, the effectiveness of those information systems relies on factors like response time, throughput, quality of information, accuracy of information, completeness of information, relevancy of information, and operating costs. Obviously the focus of those specialists is on the explicit knowledge component.

Technology experts view KM with systems analysis, design, and implementation in mind. Their approach may emphasize one or several of the following areas: knowledge storage and access; "push" and "pull" approaches; networks; customer satisfaction; institutional culture; telecommunications; application software packages; and cost recovery. As the costs of technology are plummeting everywhere and, at the same time, processing capacity is increasing exponentially with an accompanying increase in portability, computer technology has drastically changed over the last decade, helping users in terms of CPU, memory, hard disks, system software, image display, and costs. (For instance, in 1988 we had PCs with 16 MHz with 2 Mbytes memory whereas in 1999 we have 300-400 MHz with 64 Mbytes and still often feel that is not adequate.)

In the area of KM alone, the professional literature indicates that the U.S. paid $1.5 billion to consultants in 1996. This figure is expected to rise to $5 billion by 2001. Impressive returns reported by many corporations are making the KM field even more popular. Some well-publicized examples of profiting by KM include Dow Chemical, Texas Instruments, and Chevron.

KMS Business Cases

Over the years, corporations have experimented with various initiatives (to improve their productivity and effectiveness) such as database management systems, management information systems, decision support systems, business process reengineering, just-in-time inventory management, total quality management, electronic data interchange, selective dissemination of information, and information resource management. These initiatives have prospered at different times and some of them are still relevant and very much in use. Experts in those fields, because of their strong interest and commitment, are integrating intellectual capital and social capital (tacit knowledge) with those areas, and frequently marketing the new products as knowledge management systems (KMS).

In general, KMS business cases may revolve around: establishing intranet systems; setting up help desks for providing referral services; publishing yellow pages or directories of companies; providing demographic information; providing opportunity for staff to have online conversations; facilitating access to internal and external information; and providing rewards for staff who are participating in the KM program. KMS business cases also attempt to track all types of KM activities in organizations, for instance: budget resources; time recording systems; help desks; statistical systems; and GroupWare participation. KMS can track all input, output, and effects of managing knowledge in organizations.

A review of KM Internet/Web sites demonstrates that KM has a heavy technology orientation. Those sites fall into three general categories. First, there are many polished KM sites offered that are hosted by consulting firms. These sites are heavily used as marketing tools, promoting services and products. Second, there are KM sites of educational institutions that are geared towards course support and academic research. Third, there are several sites covering professional literature such as online forums, newsletters, and listservs.

A thorough understanding of these sites (for example, through surveys) will also help in developing appropriate business cases and implementations.

Another important and very welcoming aspect of current KMS doctrine is that people must be treated as assets. People are the embodiment of tacit knowledge. Staff in the company should be able to understand the short- and long-term business goals and objectives of the corporation. The company should understand employee perceptions of work conditions and workforce diversity. Corporations should allocate a certain percentage of their total expenditures on KM initiatives for the training of their employees. They should recognize and respect self-knowledge and the growth of individual staff. Corporations should put people first and learn from external sources, industry, customers, and competitors. Last but not least, the role of information technology should be to serve as an important infrastructure, helping staff to perform better.

KM Model

In terms of a general model for KM, a descriptive model is proposed integrating explicit knowledge, tacit knowledge, and the infrastructure. Explicit knowledge and tacit knowledge have a symbiotic relationship whereby tacit knowledge contributes to explicit knowledge and vice versa. Some examples of explicit knowledge are found in the following: commercial publications; organizational business records; email; Web; GroupWare; Intranets; databases; and self-study material. Similarly, some examples of tacit knowledge are reflected in: face to face conversations, both formal and informal; telephone conversations, both formal and informal; the knowledge that individuals possess in their heads as well as in their desk drawers and file cabinets.

To make KM effective, bringing explicit knowledge and tacit knowledge together in an infrastructure is absolutely essential. The type of infrastructure is dependent on the company's complexity and its available resources for supporting KM, and upon the company's goals and objectives. The infrastructure may include simple or sophisticated information technology, top management support, social capital, and a basis of trust, mentoring, benchmarking, training, and employee development, along with the allocation of sufficient budget to invest in KM initiatives. The salient point here is that infrastructure is much broader than information technology. Information technology is only a substrate, the connective tissue, for the infrastructure.

Several figures are provided for an understanding of explicit knowledge, tacit knowledge, and technology infrastructure and their relationships. The first schematic diagram in Figure 2.1 establishes a general model for KM. It emphasizes the relationships between explicit knowledge, tacit knowledge, and their current dependency on the infrastructure. Each of the key themes in this illustration can be explored in a finer level of detail. The most basic is perhaps explicit knowledge as illustrated in the "supplier" model (Figure 2.2) and the "forms" model of explicit knowledge in Figure 2.3.

Explicit knowledge is relatively straightforward, even though still underrecognized. However, it is with tacit knowledge that KM enters largely unexplored territory, enthusiasm for expert systems notwithstanding. Some of the components of tacit knowledge are shown in the illustration in Figure 2.4 (see page 14). KM does depend upon and is enabled by a technology infrastructure, which is depicted in Figure 2.5 (see page 14).

Another way to view KM is as the contribution of existing information systems and enthusiasms with two relatively new insights: the awareness of the importance of intellectual capital; and the awareness of the importance of social capital

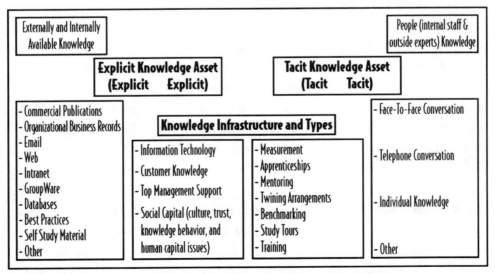

Figure 2.1   Knowledge Management Model (T. Kanti Srikantaiah 1/18/1999)

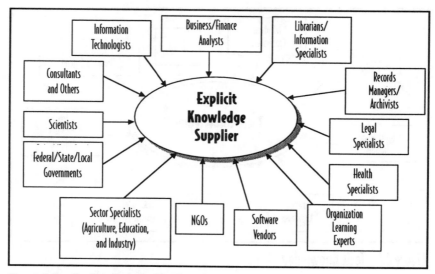

Figure 2.2   Explicit Knowledge: Supplier

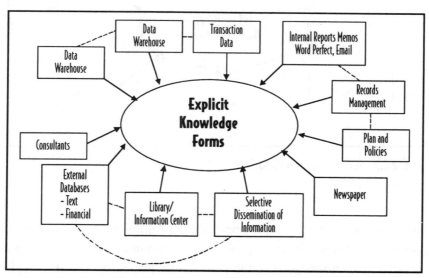

Figure 2.3   Explicit Knowledge: Forms

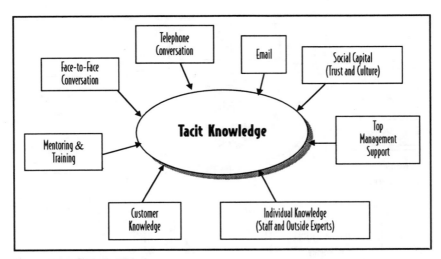

Figure 2.4   Tacit Knowledge

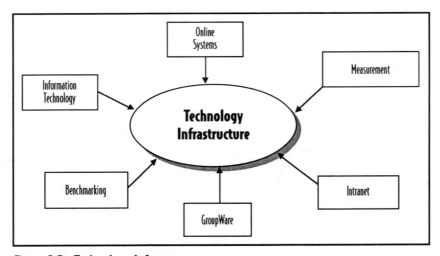

Figure 2.5   Technology Infrastructure

to enable and encourage the deployment and utilization of intellectual capital. In other words, there is a shift in emphasis away from information technology, still vital nonetheless, to recognizing the crucial role played by social capital. This view is selected graphically in Figure 2.6.

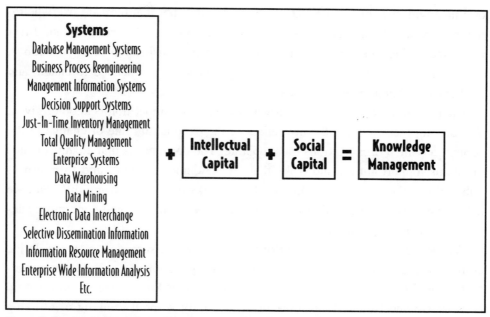

Figure 2.6   Evolution of Knowledge Management Integrating Intellectual Capital

What does one do to establish KM? In a sense, this entire book addresses this question. However, in terms of a KM overview, two diagrams provided in chapter 3 and chapter 13 can be useful.

Why Knowledge Management?

The obvious answer to "Why knowledge management?" is to make the organization more productive, more effective, and more successful. A more useful response to the question is to categorize the reasons. Tom Short (personal communication, November 2, 1998) of IBM indicates that the reasons people and organizations prepare for KM all appear to fall into four categories. KM is introduced to enhance collaboration, to improve productivity, to enable and encourage innovation, and to cope with information overload and deliver only the essentials. Two of those reasons are "means," enhancing collaborations and coping with information overload. The other two are "ends" to those means, improving productivity and enabling innovation (Hibbard, 1997).

The "enhancement of collaboration" motivation is driven not only by the perceived need to work smarter and by the realization that most innovations do not originate with the solitary inventor in his/her garret, but that they are overwhelmingly the result of collaboration and rich information flow. The concomitant driver is the increasing internationalization and geographic dispersion of organizations, and the realization that some compensating mechanism is needed to enable and facilitate collaboration at a distance.

The need to innovate more effectively than one's competition is another given. The driving factor here is the awareness of the exponential rate of change in the context in which organizations must operate. The corollary is that change creates problems, opportunities, and tasks that are new and different, and to return to Hibbard (1997), "If we apply knowledge to tasks that are new and different, we call it innovation." Innovation is how we cope with change, and cope more successfully than the competition.

The desire for the improvement of productivity is assumed. It may not define competitiveness and success, but it is certainly a great enabler. As we are entreated to work smarter, as more industrial work becomes knowledge work, it would be perverse and foolhardy to think of productivity without thinking of utilizing knowledge more efficiently and more effectively.

Coping with information overload is a need that is to a large extent created by information technology. However, it has been argued in an article entitled "The Information Controllability Explosion" (Koenig, 1982) that while the information explosion (the awareness of the exponential growth of information, popularized by Fremont Rider (1944) and Derek Price (1963)) is hardly abating, only in recent years have we been in the situation where the tools of information technology are growing faster than the problem is. One can, with considerable justification, view KM as the intuitive awareness that such is the case and that the time has come to address the problem in new and innovative fashions that take advantage of the opportunities provided by the capabilities of information technology.

Endnote

1. The World Bank. "*World Development Report*" 1998/99 Washington D.C. P.1

References

Davenport, T. H. and Prusak, L. (1998) *Working Knowledge: How Organizations Manage What They Know*. Boston, Harvard Business School Press.

Davenport, T. H. (1997) *Information Ecology: Mastering the Information and Knowledge Environment*. New York, Oxford University Press.

Hibbard, J. (1997) "Knowing What We Know." *Information Week*. 20:46-64.

Koenig, M. E. D. (1982) "The Information Controllability Explosion." *Library Journal*: 107(19): 2052-2054.

Price, D. J. de Solla (1963) *Little Science, Big Science*. New York, Columbia University Press.

Rider, F. (1944) *The Scholar and the Future of the Research Library: A Problem and Its Solution*. New York, Hadham Press.

The World Bank, *World Development Report 1998/99*. Washington D.C.

Stewart, T. A. (1997) *Intellectual Capital: The New Wealth of Organizations*. New York, Doubleday/Currency.

O'Dell, C. and Grayson, C. J. Jr. (1998) *If Only We Knew What We Know*. New York, The Tree Press.

Part II :

Background & Issues

Background & Issues
Introductory Notes

This section addresses both the development and the evolution of the concept of knowledge management and some of the issues surrounding its implementation. The section commences with a chapter on "The Evolution of Knowledge Management" by Koenig and Srikantaiah examining the immediate antecedents of knowledge management and tracing how and, to some degree, why the concept of knowledge management has evolved as it has. In the process, it also describes how the meaning and the extent of all that is included and involved in the increasingly broad concept of knowledge management has changed over a comparatively brief period of time, and what the business community now generally understands the term to mean. This sets the stage for the subsequent chapters.

A complementary approach is provided by Malhotra's "From Information Management to Knowledge Management: Beyond the 'Hi-Tech Hidebound' Systems," which also looks at the development of knowledge management, but from a more theoretical viewpoint, and which places knowledge management in the broader domain of information and knowledge handling. Albert's "Is Knowledge Management Really the Future for Information Professionals?" provides a from-the-trenches view of what constitutes knowledge management, what is new, what isn't, and what are some of the real issues in implementing knowledge management.

The chapter "Information Services and Productivity: A Background" by Koenig presents a review of what is known substantively and with some degree of rigor about the relationship between the provision and the use of information services and the organization's information environment on the one hand and the productivity of the organization on the other. Knowledge management is too new yet to have an analytical literature of its own relating to the efficacy of knowledge management in any fashion other than in an anecdotal or snapshot fashion. There is, however, a significant but very scattered body of literature documenting a very positive relationship between the provision and use of information services in an appropriate climate, and a more productive and competitive performance by the organization supported.

This literature is not just a background to, but also a justification for, knowledge management and its investment. Knowledge management indeed can be thought of as the logical response to the relationships revealed and to the previous under-investment in information services implied by that literature. The reader interested in this topic should also see the chapter by Nelke, "Knowledge Management in Swedish Corporations—The Value of Information and Information Services." This chapter appears in section five because it discusses implementation and applications, but it also gathers useful value data. Mazzie's, "Key Challenges Facing the Evolution of Knowledge Management" not only (as the title implies) reviews key issues, but also reviews what is currently underway in attempts to value knowledge management and who is undertaking the work. The attempts to place a value on shared knowledge are still very underdeveloped, but they represent some of the most exciting areas for research and development in the field of information science.

The chapter "Ethics for Knowledge Management" by Schmidt argues that in such a rapidly evolving area as knowledge management, a conventional normative style of ethics may not be an adequate guide. Normative ethics have weak points in any case, which will be particularly the situation in knowledge management where the context is rapidly changing and where the complexity of issues—involving not only issues such as copyright, but issues such as employee privacy rights within and outside of the organization—are deep, broad, and intricately interwoven. The author argues for a more discerning, more nuanced, more metaphysical view of ethics as necessary for the complex, issue-rich domain of knowledge management.

CHAPTER 3

The Evolution of Knowledge Management

Michael E. D. Koenig
Dean
Long Island University

and

T. Kanti Srikantaiah
Director, Center for Knowledge Management
Dominican University

Knowledge management, as we now know it, is a relatively recent phenomenon. Developed in the mid-1990s, it may perhaps succinctly be described in the equestrian tradition as by the Intranet out of intellectual capital.

THE DAM: INTELLECTUAL CAPITAL

Intellectual capital became popular in the early and mid-1990s. It is necessary to indicate that knowledge management has exploded so rapidly that we can already speak of its predecessor of only a few years ago in the past tense. "Intellectual Capital represents the awareness that information is a factor of production, as economists would phrase it, in a category with land, labor, capital, and energy" (Talero and Gaudette, 1995). In the early and mid-1990s, there was an increasing awareness in the business community that knowledge was an important organizational resource that needed to be nurtured, sustained, and accounted for, if possible. Peter Drucker phrases it most compellingly:

> We now know that the source of wealth is something, specifically human knowledge. If we apply knowledge to tasks that we obviously know how to do, we call it productivity. If we apply knowledge to tasks that are new and different, we call it innovation. Only

knowledge allows us to achieve those two goals. (Hibbard, 1997).
The notion that an organization's knowledge and expertise is
immensely valuable is not new. In the 1960s, a perhaps apocryphal
story circulated about Edwin H. Land, developer of the camera,
CEO of the Polaroid corporation, and second only to Thomas
Edison in the number of patents received. The setting of the story
was a tax dispute between Polaroid and the Internal Revenue
Service that centered on how Polaroid valued its inventory and its
assets. Land was alleged to have left one meeting with the IRS representatives muttering to his aides, "Those guys don't have the
slightest idea what an asset is, ninety percent of Polaroid's assets
get in their cars and drive home at night."

Intellectual capital was first defined as having two major components:
information/knowledge capital and structural capital. Information and knowledge capital was the organization's information and knowledge, but the informal and unstructured as well as the formal. The structural capital was the
mechanisms in place to take advantage of the information and knowledge capital, the mechanisms to capture, store, retrieve, and communicate that information and knowledge.

What was new with the intellectual capital movement was the attempt to
not just reorganize the importance of knowledge, but also to quantify and
measure it in some utilitarian fashion. The attempt to quantify knowledge and
information proved very difficult. Information and knowledge are extraordi-
narily amorphous and diffuse notions to measure. Relatively little progress
was made in that direction. A few companies, Skandia Corporation with its
intellectual capital supplement to its annual report being the most famous
example (Edvinsson, 1994), made and still make noble efforts to quantify or
to chart progress and changes in the organization's intellectual capital, but
very few other companies have followed their lead, particularly Skandia's, for
external reporting.

However, the intellectual capital movement was very successful in gaining
publicity demonstrating the importance of valuing and nurturing intellectual
capital. Thomas Stewart authored a number of prominently featured articles
(Stewart, 1991, 1991, 1994, 1995, 1997) in *Fortune*, of which probably the
most compelling was "Your Company's Most Valuable Assets: Intellectual

Capital" (Stewart, 1994). In the same period, the conference board organized a number of meetings at which intellectual capital was a central theme.

The Sire, the Internet

In that same period, the Internet, hitherto solely an academic and not-for-profit enthusiasm, burst into the consciousness of the business community. Soon came the realization that Internet technology could be used to link an organization together, using the Internet and its conventions for data display and access, but limiting access to the members of one's own organization. Companies used LANs (local area networks) and WANs (wide area networks) for some time, but Internet-based Intranets were far easier to set up and administer, and the tools for employees to put information on the Net and to access it were far superior.

The Merger

One immediate consequence of the appearance of Intranets was the awareness that they could be used to facilitate communications with one's customers, as well as within the organization itself (an Intranet extended to include customers and or supplies is an Extranet). Of course, electronic communications with suppliers and customers had been increasing since the 1970s, electronic data interchange (EDI) and just-in-time inventory (JIT) are examples, but the Intranet very much accelerated that process. One consequence of this was an expanded definition of intellectual capital to include the customer's knowledge and input, i.e., customer capital. The inclusion of customer capital was also not unrelated to the popularity of total quality management (TQM), in which responding to customers' needs and demands was a key element.

Concurrent with intellectual capital, and very much reinforcing it, was the notion of the "balanced score card" (Kaplan and Norton, 1992). The idea was that traditional financial reporting was too narrow in its outlook, and that it focused only on the present and on the past, with no thought of the future. It was argued that there would be instead a balanced score card that included the traditional financial measures, but also measured other things such as comparative product quality, customers' satisfaction, and customer turnover—things that were more indicative of current performance and better indicators of likely future performance. Regarding traditional financial indicators, if the current balance sheet looks good, but customers have begun to take interest in the competition, there is nothing in those figures to reveal that the situation is unhealthy. The idea of the balanced score card is intended to resolve that anomaly.

Intellectual capital is one of the obvious items that should be included on the balanced score card. One should be aware that the enthusiasm for the balanced score card arose partly as a consequence of the perception in Anglo countries that their financial systems and the market's interest in short-term financial gain forced corporations to focus too much on the short term, with not enough thought for the long term. This is in contrast with the banking and financial reporting procedures in Japan and Germany and the East Asian tigers where corporations and their banks customarily enjoyed long-term relationships that presumably fostered long-term thinking and strategy. The recent downturn in Japan and Southeast Asia, attributed in large part to the close relationships between companies and banks, has made that thesis rather less compelling.

THE NEW PARADIGM: KNOWLEDGE MANAGEMENT

The first organizations to fully realize the potential of Intranets were typically the larger, worldwide consulting firms who had long realized that the commodity they dealt in was information and knowledge. An example of a primary concern to such organizations is: How can a consultant in Valparaiso, Chile, working for a company headquarted in Chicago be made aware of work by another consultant in Stockholm, which the Valparaiso consultant could use to respond authoritatively and convincingly to a request for a proposal and be awarded the contract?

These firms saw the Intranet as an ideal tool with which to share and disseminate knowledge throughout their organization's scattered offices. They recognized that the confluence of the Intranet with information and knowledge as an asset was substantially more than just an expansion of the concept of intellectual capital. The phrase they chose to describe this new confluence and, in particular, the Intranet-based systems they were developing was "knowledge management."[1]

From there the concept of knowledge management continued to expand. Senge's (1990) *The Fifth Discipline: The Art and Practice of the Learning Organization* had appeared in the early 1990s and had established a "cult" following, but it had not made a major impact. With the Intranet-driven knowledge management, however, it meshed perfectly. The learning organization is the belief that what ultimately creates and distinguishes a successful organization is its success in creating and sharing information and knowledge. In short, it is success at learning. The obvious corollary is that to be successful, an organization must create a culture that fosters learning. One can say, to summarize perhaps too briefly, that the concept of the learning organization focuses on the creation of knowledge, while knowledge management, as it was originally construed, focuses on the acquisition, structuring, retention, and dissemination of that knowledge. Knowledge management has expanded to include the concept of the learning organization, and to include knowledge creation.

A new term that has recently emerged, representing an extension of knowledge management further in that same direction, is the Faster Learning Organization (FLO). This is the goal of knowledge management, to create a FLO that will thereby have a major competitive advantage over other organizations. In the words of Skip LeFauve (1998), senior vice-president of General Motors Corporation, president of General Motors University, and previously chairperson of General Motor's Saturn division: "The only long-term competitive advantage that a company has is how effectively it manages its company knowledge."

Another important perception that has accelerated the enthusiasm for knowledge management has been the richness versus reach thesis of Evans and Wurster (1997). They point out that the nature of communications has drastically changed. Their observation is that, until now, one had a choice of richness or reach in communication, but one could not achieve both simultaneously. A face-to-face conversation for example was rich in content, nuance, and interactivity, but its reach was small, touching one or at most a few persons. A mass mailing or radio or TV broadcast had great reach, but was thin on content, nuance, and interactivity. Communication strategies were always an either-or choice.

Now with the Internet, the argument exists that we can craft systems that simultaneously provide both richness and reach, and this transforms not only how we think about communications, but also how we think about organizations and how they do business. This thesis, which is an instantiation of Gibson and Jackson's (1987) *Domain III* and Koenig's (1992) *Entering Stage III*, has been incorporated into the canon of knowledge management as a very persuasive argument explaining why the time is right for a thorough rethink of how information and knowledge are shared in the organization. Further, it can be argued that the removal of the richness or reach dichotomy means that changes will not be gradual and incremental, but that they will be major and dramatic, and that the organization that does not persist will not only risk being left behind, but risk being quickly put out of business.

Those dramatic changes reflect back to the vision of business process reengineering.

KNOWLEDGE MANAGEMENT—THE PORTMANTEAU TERM

Subtle and fascinating describes the relationship between knowledge management and business process reengineering. The latter, stripped to its essentials, simply meant redesigning the operations and workflow of organizations to take advantage of the capabilities of information technology and electronic communications. Business process reengineering has gradually developed a secondary use as not only making organizations more efficient and more effective, but also leaner and meaner. The negative side to that, at least for the employees, is downsizing, euphemistically referred to as rightsizing.

Both knowledge management and business process reengineering derive from the same foundation—that we are no longer bound by the constraints of print-on-paper technology. In a response to the argument that there was a "productivity paradox" (Banks, 1989), the economist David (1990) indicated that there is a fascinating parallel between information technology and the introduction of electric power and the electric motor. He reveals how surprisingly long it took for that technology to have a measurable impact on industrial productivity.

Koenig and Wilson (1996) extend David's observation and link it to business process reengineering. The reason that David (1990) posits that the dynamo and the grid took so long to have an effect was that major industrial redesign and manufacturing process redesign had to be accomplished first. New factories that were not built around pulleys and shafts, but factories that were built to take advantage of unit-drive capability (machines being driven directly by an electric motor, rather than connected to a central mechanical power source) had to be constructed before a dramatic effect was seen. Koenig and Wilson (1996) argue that business process redesign is the factory rebuilding of the computer age, the corollary being when that is accomplished, we will then enter an era of noticeably improved productivity. They draw the analogy that business process reengineering is at the limitations of delivering information via print-on-paper technology. This parallels the manufacturing process redesign, which was necessary to take advantage of electric motors and the electric process distribution network to avoid the limitation of delivering power by shafts, gears, pulleys, and belts.

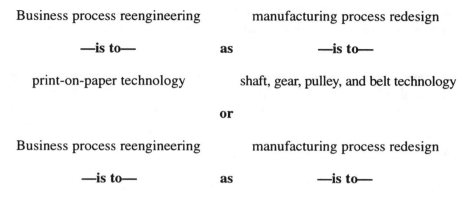

Business process reengineering   manufacturing process redesign

—is to—   **as**   **—is to—**

print-on-paper technology   shaft, gear, pulley, and belt technology

or

Business process reengineering   manufacturing process redesign

—is to—   **as**   **—is to—**

computer and information technology   the dynamo and electrical technology

Similarly, knowledge management came about because of the same awareness concerning the limitations of previous communication technologies, particularly print-on-paper. The "richness and reach" observations of Evans and Wurster (1997) make precisely that point. Despite their joint parentage, however, a key thrust of what knowledge management has come to mean in the business community is that knowledge management is, to a large degree, a rejection (or at least a partial rejection) and a reaction to the excesses of business process reengineering, the corporate downsizing with its combination of human suffering among those downsized and insecurity among those remaining. The word now being mentioned, often simultaneously with knowledge management, is "trust."

This is perhaps a trifle surprising, but it is also in fact quite logical. Good communication and extensive knowledge sharing are not likely to happen unless there is an atmosphere of trust and some commitment to the employee. Knowledge management is being presented as the antidote to the trust lost and to the knowledge lost in ill-conceived and ill-executed rightsizings when valuable employees were "let go," with their knowledge going with them, and with a reservoir of mistrust and insecurity left behind. As Larry Prusak (1998) bluntly puts it "reengineering is the enemy of knowledge."

Social capital is another frequently mentioned concept with the same recognition. In this business context, social capital is operationally defined as those behavioral norms that lower transaction costs and enable cooperation. What norm better to enhance communications, transactions, and cooperation than trust? It is interesting to observe that at the same time there is an increasing recognition at the macroeconomic level of the importance of trust and consistency in facilitating international trade and for inducing foreign direct investment.

In another sense, social capital is what has been added to intellectual capital to create knowledge management. Prusak (1998) of IBM employs the following graphic:

Knowledge Resources	Social Capital	Infrastructure
Explicit	Culture	Processes
Tacit	Trust	Resources
Formal	Knowledge Behavior	Technology
Informal	Human Capital Issues	Metrics

It is now assumed that customer capital is included in all, with the infrastructure extended to include the customer, the knowledge resources including the customer, and the social capital embracing the relationships, not just within the organization, but with the customer (and the supplier to whom one is a customer) as well. It is not too strong to say that knowledge management has

Knowledge Management Framework

expanded to become a portmanteau term intended to include all of the positive aspects of the management fads of the last decade and a half, while avoiding the excesses.

Another very useful graphic visualization of the expanded concept of knowledge management is shown on page 30.

This is intended to represent knowledge management as it enhances knowledge sharing and collaboration. The results achieved are:

- Innovation   in areas of high interaction and individual knowledge
- Competency   in areas of low interaction and individual knowledge
- Responsiveness   in areas of high interaction and group knowledge
- Productivity   in areas of low interaction and group knowledge

This idea, promoted by IBM, conveys particularly well how broad the concept of knowledge management has become in the business community. Another useful aid to thinking about knowledge management is the knowledge management progression.

THE KNOWLEDGE MANAGEMENT PROGRESSION
Knowledge Management, GroupWare, Email

The idea here is that typically the first extensive use of information technology to enhance knowledge sharing is the widespread use of email. Then comes the broad use of GroupWare, software designed to help teams work together in an electronic environment, and then the apex is true knowledge management, including transformation in the culture of the organization to encourage and reward information creation and sharing.

Knowledge management has grown into a far broader, more pervasive, more powerful notion than it started out to be or than its name would suggest. In fact, there is beginning to be a reaction in some circles that the term knowledge management is not the appropriate phrase. It is argued that it is too specific for a concept that is really much broader, and also that it is perhaps somewhat impolitic—that users, employees, and customers don't particularly relish the implication that their knowledge is being managed, rather they would prefer terminology that would imply that they are being supported in their undertakings. One of many phrases that has been suggested to replace knowledge management is "knowledge sharing," another is "knowledge networking." Both terms are certainly more descriptive of what knowledge management has evolved to become.

Whether or not any substitute term will replace knowledge management, even if substantially more descriptive, is another matter. It may be that the term knowledge management will be replaced by a more descriptive term, just as the term management information systems (MIS) was replaced by decision support systems. This, however, only resulted because MIS got something of a "black eye." The author suspects that a more intuitive parallel is that of the term "word processing," which we now take for granted, but which aroused much discussion and numerous suggested alternative terms in its nascent period. The term word processing became the standard through IBM's promotion of the term. A similar standardization is likely to unfold for knowledge management.

Knowledge Management Themes

Now that we have tried to sketch the domain of knowledge management, we will discuss some of the major themes running through what the business community understands knowledge management to be.

Silos

Silo is the latest buzzword. The silo here is a metaphor for the too self-contained unit into which stuff gets dumped into and extracted from, but which has no communication with the other silos (products, regions, divisions, units, etc.) that constitute the organization. The solution to the silo problem is to create communities and, thereby, further collaboration. This is part of the reaction against the excesses of business process reengineering. The silos are what were left after business process reengineering removed much of middle management and "flattened" the organization. That middle management provided much of the connective tissue of the organization. They provided the communication channels that kept the units from becoming silos. Knowledge management is now seen as the repair mechanism for business process reengineering, presumably both more effective and less expensive than replacing those middle management staff positions.

Communities and Collaboration

Most of the concrete applications of knowledge management described to date consist of creating and supporting communities of shared interest and information need. These communities might be sales representatives in pharmaceutical companies or those people at the World Bank and their clients interested in road transport and logistics. In some cases, as in the former, the community already exists formally and hierarchically, or as in the latter, it exists informally and horizontally. At the World Bank, for example, there are now 70-some "knowledge areas" grouped into 15 large sections; at IBM there are 49 "competency networks." The intended consequence of these communities is not only knowledge sharing, but also collaboration, and, of course, enhanced productivity.

Tacit Knowledge

Tacit knowledge is now the term for the knowledge that is in people's hands or in their own files, as distinguished from explicit knowledge, which exists in documents or databases. Current knowledge management thinking is almost entirely about establishing the structure and the climate to enable and encourage those who have knowledge to share it. There is the encouragement and the establishment of systems to enable the employee to submit a "best practices" description of how he/she accomplishes something so that others can use it. The information may be edited before it goes on the system, but the user inputs the knowledge, not a "knowledge engineer" or "knowledge manager."

This is an important point for information professionals to recognize. There has been substantial disillusionment in the business community with the very much over-hyped "artificial intelligence" and "expert systems," and with the software packages and consulting firms that promised to set up "AI" systems for companies. There certainly have been AI successes, but they have been at the tactical and near clerical level, monitoring credit card transactions for plausibility or likely misuse, for example. They have not been at the strategic level envisioned by the proponents of knowledge management, nor have they been of the collaborative synergistic kind, yielding new knowledge or faster learning. Information professionals can make a contribution toward capturing tacit knowledge, but they must be careful to phrase their proposed contributions in terms of making tacit knowledge accessible. They must be careful about suggesting that they are going to capture it and structure it.

Incentives and Rewards

Effective knowledge sharing requires rewarding those who input information into the system and who contribute something useful. Otherwise, what motivation do employees have to contribute information that will, for example, improve the performance of other sales representatives with whom they are competing? Changing cooperation and incentive systems is not something that organizations do readily, or lightly. It is an undertaking fraught with peril and with unintended, and often unfortunate, consequences. A frequent complaint among knowledge management system implementers is how slow and difficult it is to get upper management to make such changes.

This does not impact information professionals directly—after all, information sharing is the reason they are hired. However, as the importance of information creation and sharing is better recognized in the organization, then there is hope for some spillover recognition to those who facilitate and make possible that information creation and sharing. For that positive spillover to take effect, however, we must have achieved recognition as key players in the knowledge management process.

CUSTOMER KNOWLEDGE

A pervasive theme in business discussion of knowledge management is the importance of including the customer in the scope of knowledge management systems so as to include and leverage this expertise. This is considered key for a number of reasons, some examples of which follow.

- Better and more timely design of new products and services
- Early warning and competitive intelligence
- Customer commitment and loyalty
- The synergy of collaboration

The emphasis here is upon the exchange of knowledge, ideas, and opinions, not just the transaction data currently exchanged with just-in-time inventory or supply chain management systems.

TOP MANAGEMENT SUPPORT AND CHANGE AGENTS

Another major theme is that knowledge management is about a whole new way of operating, indeed the transformation of the organization. As such, knowledge management requires knowledge management professionals to be change agents, and that in turn requires upper management support and direct involvement. The obvious insight here is that knowledge management is an exciting concept, something in which we must be involved.

One concern is whether or not the trend of knowledge management will continue: Is it simply a buzzword or will it be a classical term for all times? For those of us in the information profession, perhaps the most compelling indicators of the business communities' perception of knowledge management's importance are these:

- In IBM's 1997 annual report, Lou Gerstner, the president of IBM, said that his goal was "to turn IBM into the world's premier knowledge management company."
- The president of Donaldson, Lufkin & Jenrette (DLJ) stated recently that not only do knowledge management systems add value to a company, but that DLJ analysts specifically look for the existence of knowledge management systems when analyzing a company's worth and its stock value.

These are anecdotal points, but they are certainly strong indications that knowledge management is a big presence, and is likely here to stay.

Endnote

1. Don Marchland apparently was the first to use the term knowledge management as the final stage in his stage hypothesis on the development of information systems (Marchland, 1985), but the term languished for many years. Whether the recoiners of the term were aware of Marchland's earlier use is not clear.

References

Banks, H. (1989) The Productivity Paradox. *Forbes*: 144 (2), 15.

David, P. A. (1990) The Dynamo and the Computer: An Historical Perspective on the Modern Productivity Paradox. *American Economic Review*: 80 (2), 355-361.

Edvinsson, L. (1994) Developing Intellectual Capital at Skandia. *Long Range Planning*: 30, 366-373.

Evans, P. B. and Wurster, T. S. (1997) Strategy and the New Economics of Information. *Harvard Business Review*: 75 (15), 70-82.

Gibson, C. F. and Jackson, B. B. (1987) *The Information Imperative: Managing the Impact of Information Technology on Business and People.* Lexington, Mass.: D.C. Heath.

Hibbard, J. (1997) Knowing What We Know. *Information Week*: Oct. 20, 46-64.

Kaplan, R. S. and Norton, D. P. (1992) The Balanced Scorecard—Measures that Drive Performance. *Harvard Business Review*: 70 (1), 71-79.

Koenig, M. E. (1992) Entering Stage III —The Convergence of the Stage Hypotheses. *Journal of the American Society for Information Science*: 43, 204-207.

Koenig, M. E. and Wilson, T. D. (1996) Productivity Growth, The Take-Off Point. *Information Processing and Management*: 32 (2), 247-254.

LeFauve, S. (1998) The 1998 Conference on Knowledge Management and Organization Learning. Presentation to the Conference Board Conference, Chicago (April 15).

Marchland, D. A. (1985) Information Management: Strategies and Tools in Transition. *Information Management Review* 1 (1) 27-37.

Prusak, L. (1998) The 1998 Conference on Knowledge Management and Organizational Learning. Managing Principal, IBM Global Services, Consulting Group Presentation to the Conference Board Conference, Chicago (April 16).

Senge, P. M. (1990) *The Fifth Discipline: The Art and Practice of the Learning Organization.* New York: Doubleday/Currency.

Stewart, T. A. (1997) *Intellectual Capital: The New Wealth of Organizations.* New York: Doubleday/Currency.

Stewart, T. A. (1995). Getting Real about Brainpower. *Fortune*: 132, 201-203.

Stewart, T. A. (1994) Your Company's Most Valuable Asset: Intellectual Capital. *Fortune*: 130, 68-74.

Stewart, T. A. (1991) Brainpower. *Fortune*: 123, 44-60.

Stewart, T. A. (1991) Now Capital Means Brains, Not Just Bucks. *Fortune*: 123, 31-32.

Talero, E. and Gaudette, P. (1995) Harnessing Information for Development: World Bank Group Vision and Strategy. Draft Document: The World Bank, Washington D. C.

CHAPTER 4

From Information Management to Knowledge Management: Beyond the "Hi-Tech Hidebound" Systems

Yogesh Malhotra

Faculty of Business Administration

Florida Atlantic University

Chairperson and CKO

BRINT Research Institute

To conceive of knowledge as a collection of information seems to rob the concept of all of its life... Knowledge resides in the user and not in the collection. It is how the user reacts to a collection of information that matters. —Churchman (1971)

INTRODUCTION

Most extant knowledge management systems are constrained by their overly rational, static, and non-contextual view of knowledge. Effectiveness of such systems is constrained by the rapid and discontinuous change that characterizes new organizational environments. The prevailing knowledge management paradigm limits itself by its emphasis on convergence and consensus-oriented processing of information. Strategy experts have underscored that the focus of organizational knowledge management should shift from "prediction of future" (which cannot be computed) to "anticipation of surprise." Such systems may be enabled by leveraging the divergent interpretations of information based upon the meaning-making capability of human beings. By underscoring the need for synergy between innovation and creativity of humans and the advanced capabilities of new information technologies, this chapter advances current thinking about knowledge management.

The current conceptualization of information technology (IT) enabled knowledge management suffers from the fallibility of imposing the traditional information-processing model on the strategic needs of contemporary organizations. The traditional knowledge management model emphasizes convergence and compliance to achieve pre-specified organizational goals. The knowledge management systems were modeled on the same paradigm to ensure adherence to organizational routines built into information technology. Optimization-based routinization of organizational goals with the objective of realizing greater efficiencies was suitable for an era marked by a relatively stable and predictable environment.

However, this model is increasingly inadequate for an era characterized by an increasing pace of discontinuous environmental change (Arthur, 1996; Nadler et al., 1995). The new era requires continual reassessment of routines embedded in organizational decision-making processes to ensure that underlying assumptions are aligned with the changing environment. Hence, the primary focus is not as much on *doing things right* as it is on *doing the right things* (Drucker, 1994b). Convergence and consensus-oriented nature of traditional information systems is relevant for "freezing" the meaning of information for achieving optimization-based efficiencies. However, "unfreezing" of meaning embedded in information is critical for reassessing and renewing the routines embedded in organizational decision-making processes.

The proposed model of knowledge management attempts to achieve simultaneous "freezing" and "unfreezing" of meaning to ensure that effective decision-making (doing the right things) is not sacrificed for the sake of increased efficiencies (doing things right). It does so by proposing a balance between the optimization-based predictive capacity of information-processing systems and the divergence of meaning (of information) based on innate common sense-making capabilities.

By providing the theoretical and conceptual fundamentals for the proposed model, this chapter provides the basis for organizational deployment and further refinement by practitioners and scholars. This chapter also provides the basis for developing measures and methodologies for understanding and deploying "enhanced" knowledge management models in contemporary organizations.

The next section discusses the prevailing information-processing view of knowledge management and provides the background for the proposed model. Subsequent discussion on contemporary thinking about organizational strategy highlights the limitations of the predominant information-processing view of knowledge management. Thereafter, the theoretical basis of the proposed model is reviewed, the model is presented in definitional terms, and its key implementation characteristics are discussed. At the closing of the chapter, an explanation is provided as to how the explicit emphasis of the proposed model on the creation of new knowledge builds upon the strengths of the information-processing capabilities of computer-based knowledge management systems.

INFORMATION-PROCESSING PARADIGM OF KNOWLEDGE MANAGEMENT

Growing interest in knowledge management stems from the realization that in the knowledge era, organizational knowledge is a strategic corporate asset that needs to be garnered, retained, updated, disseminated, and applied to future

Table 1.1 Knowledge Management: The Information-Processing Paradigm

The process of collecting, organizing, classifying, and disseminating information throughout an organization, so as to make it purposeful to those who need it. (Albert, 1998)

Policies, procedures, and technologies employed for operating a continuously updated linked pair of networked databases. (Anthes, 1991) Partly as a reaction to downsizing, some organizations are now trying to use technology to capture the knowledge residing in the minds of their employees so it can be easily shared across the enterprise. Knowledge management aims to capture the knowledge that employees really need in a central repository and filter out the surplus. (Bair, 1997)

Ensuring a complete development and implementation environment designed for use in a specific function requiring expert systems support. (Chorafas, 1987) Knowledge management IT concerns organizing and analyzing information in a company's computer databases so this knowledge can be readily shared throughout a company, instead of languishing in the department where it was created, inaccessible to other employees. (CPA Journal, 1998)

Identification of categories of knowledge needed to support the overall business strategy, assessment of current state of the firm's knowledge and transformation of the current knowledge base into a new and more powerful knowledge base by filling knowledge gaps. (Gopal and Gagnon, 1995)

Combining indexing, searching, and push technology to help companies organize data stored in multiple sources and deliver only relevant information to users. (Hibbard, 1997)

Knowledge management in general tries to organize and make available important know-how, wherever and whenever it's needed. This includes processes, procedures, patents, reference works, formulas, "best practices," forecasts, and fixes. Technologically, intranets, GroupWare, data warehouses, networks, bulletin boards, and videoconferencing are key tools for storing and distributing this intelligence. (Maglitta, 1996)

Mapping knowledge and information resources both online and off-line; training, guiding, and equipping users with knowledge access tools; monitoring outside news and information. (Maglitta, 1995) Knowledge management incorporates intelligent searching, categorization, and accessing of data from disparate databases, e-mail, and files. (Willett and Copeland, 1998)

Understanding the relationships of data; identifying and documenting rules for managing data; and assuring that data are accurate and maintain integrity. (Strapko, 1990)

Facilitation of autonomous coordinability of decentralized subsystems that can state and adapt their own objectives. (Zeleny, 1987)

Knowledge management is the strategic application of collective company knowledge and know-how to build profits and market share. Knowledge assets—either ideas or concepts and know-how—are created through the computerized collection, storage, sharing, and linking of corporate knowledge pools. Advanced technologies make it possible to mine the corporate mind. (Zuckerman and Buell, 1998)

organizational problems (Drucker, 1994a; Stewart, 1997). Recent advances in information technology such as Lotus Notes, Internet, and the World Wide Web have offered the means to organize various types of information into organizational "knowledge repositories." Popular examples of such repositories include Andersen's Knowledge Xchange, Booz Allen & Hamilton's Knowledge Online, CAP Gemini's Knowledge Galaxy, Ernst & Young's Center for Business Knowledge, and Monsanto's Knowledge Management Architecture. The principal motivation for development of such knowledge repositories is that information technology can enable the sharing of information between various employees, thus preventing duplication of information work while offering the advantage of immediate access to information. Such repositories of organizational knowledge are expected to serve as enablers of access to company-wide information at any time, at any place, and in whatever form (Davidow and Malone, 1992). These repositories are even expected to enable adaptive functioning and survival of the firm long after the original purveyors of information have departed (Applegate et al., 1988; italics added for emphasis):

Information systems will maintain the corporate history, experience and expertise that long-term employees now hold. The information systems themselves—*not the people*—can become the stable structure of the organization. People will be free to come and go, but the value of their experience will be incorporated in the systems that help them and their successors run the business.

A review of mainstream scholarly and trade publications similarly suggests the centrality of the computer in most mainstream explanations of knowledge management. The concept of information technology as the key enabler of knowledge management (Maglitta, 1995) is not a new idea. Over the last decade, this concept has been discussed in various forms. Proponents of artificial intelligence and machine learning have emphasized the key role of such technologies in the process of knowledge generation (Ford, 1989). Considering numerical data as the basis for decision making, decision support systems have also been depicted as encompassing knowledge management (Shen, 1987). Other computer-based technologies, such as expert systems (Candlin and Wright, 1992; Chorafas, 1987; Strapko, 1990) and networked databases (Anthes, 1991), have been described as central to an organization's knowledge management objectives. Illustrative examples of the conception of knowledge management based on the computer-based, information-processing paradigm are given in Table 1.1.

Paradoxically, it was also suggested that a firm's capacity for knowledge creation may even become unduly impaired by a heavy reliance on IT-based knowledge management (Gill, 1995). It has also been argued that such solutions often specify the "minutiae of machinery" while disregarding how people in organizations actually go about acquiring, sharing, and creating new knowledge: "They glorify information technology and ignore human psychology" (Davenport, 1994). Based primarily upon a static and "syntactic" view of knowledge, such solutions consider only a partial perspective of the organizational knowledge creation process. By considering the meaning of knowledge as "unproblematic, predefined, and prepackaged" (Boland, 1987), they ignore the human dimension of organizational knowledge creation (Manville and Foote, 1996). Such restricted perspective of the IT-enabled organizational knowledge management may even have detrimental influence on the firm's learning and adaptive capabilities (Drucker, 1994b). This perspective is increasingly problematic given the dynamically changing organizational environments that demand multiple interpretations of information, as well as their ongoing evaluation.

The alternative model of knowledge management—based upon the synergy of innovation and creativity of humans and the advanced capabilities of new information technologies—which is delineated in this chapter, seems to ameliorate the weaknesses inherent in the mechanistic nature of the information-processing model.

The section that follows describes how changing organizational environments limit the effectiveness of the information-processing model of knowledge management. The proposed model of knowledge management is explained in the subsequent section.

New Organizational Environments and Changing Knowledge Needs

More than three decades ago, Emery and Trist (1965) observed that the organizational environments were changing at an ever-increasing rate, and toward an ever-increasing complexity. More recently, increased significance of environmental change for an organization's knowledge creation needs is apparent in the suggested need for more flexible and adaptive organizations (Malone and Crowston, 1991).

Organizational change is generally described as a response to the increasing environmental complexity and environmental turbulence. While environmental complexity is a function of the numerosity, diversity, and interdependence of other entities in the organization's environment, environmental turbulence is a consequence of the decreasing cycle-time of the individual events (such as new product introduction, customer response, etc.). It has been suggested that the levels of both environmental complexity and turbulence, as well as their absolute rates of growth, will be significantly greater in the future than in the past (Huber and Glick, 1993). Hence, future environmental change is expected to be more rapid and more discontinuous in nature (Handy, 1990).

Increasing complexity and turbulence of the external environment impose upon the organization with a greater demand for processing information and making quick decisions (Huber, 1984). Within this scenario, organizational response to environmental change is the crucial determinant of its effectiveness (Bennis, 1974). Radically changing organizational environments that demand ever-faster rates of information-processing, information-renewal, and knowledge creation have motivated contemporary managers' interest in retrieving, archiving, storing, and disseminating their organization's information by using advanced information technologies. Organizations are devising means to accumulate employees' knowledge in electronic databases to use them as repositories of the shared, company-wide "structural intellectual capital" (Stewart, 1997).

However, for most post-industrial organizations, characterized by dynamically complex and uncertain environments, more and more knowledge *utilization* as well as knowledge *creation* is needed at the interface of the organization and the environment. The information-processing model of knowledge management is overwhelmed by the intense information flows required for:

(a) keeping the centralized knowledge base and its custodians (managers) continuously current with the discontinuously changing external environment, and

(b) continually updating the employees on the latest changes in their outputs (goals) and changes in procedures to achieve those outputs (Bartlett and Ghoshal, 1995).

Furthermore, increasing hyperturbulence and discontinuous change are not conducive for the sustained role of managers as custodians of organizational knowledge (Landau and Stout, 1979): "...control is a function of knowledge (of managers), and in uncertain environments, knowledge (of managers) often does not exist." Within such environments, it is more efficient to handle complexity wherever and whenever it first enters the organization—efficient operations in the new environment require a more equitable distribution of knowledge and authority (Zuboff, 1995). Such environments impose the need for *anticipating the future* based on multiple interpretations instead of predicting the "right forecast" (Brown and Eisenhardt, 1997). Members of such organizations would need to be "effective anticipators" (Nadler and Shaw, 1995) who can carry out the mandate of a faster cycle of knowledge creation and action based on new knowledge. However, the prevailing information-processing view of knowledge management that is tuned to optimization-based efficiency is unable to provide the organizational agility and adaptability that is necessary for radically changing environments.

"Hi-Tech Hidebound" Knowledge Management

The current thrust of organizational knowledge management efforts is on archiving "best practices" for later reference by other employees. It is a popular belief that archival and subsequent observance of such practices would facilitate efficient problem-solving and prevent unnecessary allocation of sources to inefficient search processes. Incidentally, in due course, archived "best practices" tend to define the dominant logic (Bettis and Prahalad, 1995) or the "company way." Knowledge management solutions, characterized by memorization of best practices, tend to define the assumptions that are embedded not only in information databases, but also in the organization's strategy, reward systems, and resource allocation systems. However, most such solutions represent "a temporary event, specific to a context, developed through the relationship of persons and circumstances" (Wheatley, 1994). Such recipes for specific problem-based situations (with the implicit assumption of *ceteris paribus*) may turn out to be recipes for disaster when future solutions need to be either thought afresh or in discontinuation from past solutions (Landau, 1973).

The dominant logic often persists even after the underlying assumptions have fundamentally changed. Hardwiring of underlying assumptions on an organizational knowledge basis may lead to "perceptual insensitivity" (Hedberg and Jonsson, 1978) of the organization to the changing environment. Due to the changing business environment, such organizations may find themselves doing more of the same but better and better, however, with diminishing marginal returns (Drucker, 1994b). These locked-in behavior patterns lead to decreasing sensitivity to the obsolescence of yesterday's best practices archived in knowledge repositories. Just like the boiling frog that is unable to sense the gradual change in temperature and ultimately boils to death (Senge, 1990a), the cycle of doing more of the same leads to the organizational death spiral.

Yesterday's core capabilities embedded in information technologies could become tomorrow's core rigidities (Gill, 1995; Leonard-Barton, 1995). Institutionalization of best practices by embedding them in information technology might facilitate efficient handling of routine, linear, and predictable situations during stable or incrementally changing environments. However, when change is radical and discontinuous, there is a persistent need for continual renewal of the basic premises underlying the practices archived in the knowledge repositories. Often, effective knowledge management in such an environment may need imaginative suggestions more than it does concrete, documented answers (Hedberg et al., 1976).

Unfortunately, the information-processing paradigm of knowledge management is devoid of capabilities that are essential for continuous learning *and* unlearning processes mandated by radical and discontinuous change. To ensure that yesterday's "core capabilities" do not become tomorrow's "core rigidities" (Leonard-Barton,

1995), organizations' capacity to *unlearn* ineffective "best practices" assumes increased significance (Bettis and Prahalad, 1995; Hedberg, 1981; and Hedberg et al., 1976). However, the mechanistic and rigid nature of the routines embedded in information-processing-based knowledge management is incapable of keeping pace with dynamic knowledge-creation needs for wicked environments.

In contrast, the proposed model of knowledge management is based upon more proactive involvement of human imagination and creativity (March, 1971) to facilitate greater internal diversity (of the organization) to match the variety and complexity of the dynamically discontinuous environmental change (Ashby, 1956).

BEYOND "HI-TECH HIDEBOUND" KNOWLEDGE MANAGEMENT SYSTEMS

Churchman (1971) had explicated that knowledge does not reside in the collection of information, and underscored the importance of humans in the process of knowledge creation. More recently, Nonaka and Takeuchi (1995) argued that "knowledge, unlike information, is about *beliefs* and *commitment*." Davenport and Prusak (1998) have also defined knowledge as deriving from minds at work:

> Knowledge is a fluid mix of framed experience, values, contextual information, and expert insight that provides a framework for evaluating and incorporating new experiences and information. It originates in the minds of knowers. In organizations, it often becomes embedded not only in documents or repositories but also in organizational routines, processes, practices, and norms. Churchman's (1971) emphasis on the human nature of knowledge creation seems more pertinent now than it was three decades ago given the increasingly wicked environment characterized by discontinuous change (Nadler and Shaw, 1995) and a wide range of potential surprise (Landau and Stout, 1979). The new business environment defeats the traditional organizational response of *predicting* and *reacting* based on pre-programmed heuristics. Instead, it demands more *anticipatory* responses from the organization's members who need to play a more proactive role in the faster cycle of knowledge creation and action (Brown and Eisenhardt, 1997; Nadler and Shaw, 1995).

The information-processing model of knowledge management (and knowledge repositories) discussed above is suitable for a predictable environment characterized by incremental and continuous change. As noted above, such technology-based conceptualizations of knowledge management, based upon heuristics—embedded in procedure manuals, mathematical models, or programmed logic—capture the preferred solutions to the given repertoire of an organization's problems. Such computer-centric systems of organizational knowledge management have "implicitly assumed...a well-structured problem, a data or model basis, an operational control-hierarchical authority organizational context and an impersonalistic [sic] computer printout mode of presentation" (Mason and Mitroff, 1973).

Following Churchman (1971), such systems are best suited for:

(a) "well-structured problem situations for which there exists a strong consensual position on the nature of the problem situation," and

(b) "well-structured problems for which there exists an analytic formulation with a solution" (Mason and Mitroff, 1973).

Type (a) situations are known as Lockean systems and type (b) situations are known as Leibnitzian systems. Current conceptualization of organizational knowledge repositories is motivated by projected efficiencies that would follow from (almost) impassive acceptance of institutionalized and archived best practices. Based primarily upon the above consensus-building models, such knowledge repositories tend to institutionalize the status quo. Organizational routines that were originally embedded in the standard operating procedures and policies, practices, rules, and norms become embedded in the shared knowledge databases in the form of best practices "Formalized information systems tend to be mechanistic and inflexible, and they incorporate assumptions that their designers have already identified the organizational and environmental properties deserving attention" (Hedberg and Jonsson, 1978)

As evident, the information-processing view of knowledge management is primarily based upon a Lockean and Leibnitzian logic of consensus building. This view of knowledge management seems to be an extension of the decades-old predisposition of information systems designers for Leibnitzian and Lockean inquiry systems (Churchman, 1971). However, such consensus building systems are generally capable of providing "only one view of the problem," and, hence, are not very suitable for discontinuously changing environments (Mason and Mitroff, 1973). Dynamic environments not only require multiple perspectives of solutions to a given problem, but also diverse interpretations of the problem based upon multiple views of the future. Two other types of inquiring systems discussed by

Churchman (1971) may facilitate understanding, development, and deployment of such divergence-oriented systems.

Churchman's (1971) two other kinds of inquiry systems that are more conducive to ill-structured environments are as follows. Kantian systems attempt to give multiple *explicit* views of "complementary" nature and are best suited for "moderate" ill-structured problems (Mason and Mitroff, 1973). In contrast, Hegelian systems provide multiple, completely antithetical representations that are characterized by "intense conflict" because of the contrary underlying assumptions, and are best suited for wickedly ill-structured problem domains (Mason and Mitroff, 1973).

The proposed model of knowledge management based upon Kantian and Hegelian systems is expected to facilitate multiple interpretations of archived best practices. This divergence-oriented process would ensure that the best practices and their underpinning assumptions are subjected to continual re-examination and modification. Continuously challenging the current "company way," such systems are expected to prevent the "core capabilities" of yesterday from becoming "core rigidities" of tomorrow (Leonard-Barton, 1995).

PROPOSED MODEL OF KNOWLEDGE MANAGEMENT

Drawing upon the previous discussion, the proposed model of knowledge management takes a strategic view of organizational information processes and knowledge creation activities. It attempts to synthesize the information-processing capabilities afforded by new information technologies with the innovative and creative capabilities of human and social elements of the organization. By doing so, it develops the basis for achieving simultaneous "freezing" and "unfreezing" of meaning to ensure that effectiveness of decision making (doing the right things) is not sacrificed at the altar of increased efficiencies (doing things right). The proposed model of knowledge management is defined in the following terms:

Knowledge management caters to the critical issues of organizational adaption, survival, and competence in face of increasingly discontinuous environmental change. Essentially, it embodies organizational processes that seek a synergistic combination of data and information-processing capacity of information technologies, and the creative and innovative capacity of human beings (Malhotra 1998).

The proposed model addresses the knowledge creation and dissemination processes that are both *participative* and *anticipative* (Bennis and Nanus, 1985). Instead of a formal, step-by-step rational guide, this model favors a set of guiding principles for helping people understand not "how it should be done" but "how to understand what might fit the situation they are in" (Kanter, 1984). This model assumes the existence of only a few rules, some specific information, and a lot of freedom (Wheatley, cited in Stuart, 1995).

An illustration of such a model is that of the retailer Nordstrom, which earned a reputation for unequalled customer service quality. Surprisingly, this organization uses a two-sentence policy manual: "Use your good judgment in all situations. There will be no additional rules." (Taylor 1994) The primary responsibility of most supervisors is to continuously coach the employees about this philosophy for obtaining the organizational pursuit of serving the customer better (Peters 1989).

The proposed model builds upon the strengths of the extant conceptualizations based on the archival, retrieval, and dissemination capabilities afforded by advanced information technologies. However, its key contribution lies in overcoming the weaknesses of the information-processing view by explicit integration of the human and social creative and innovative capacities in the knowledge creation and dissemination processes.

The next section discusses the key characteristics of the proposed model of knowledge management that distinguish it from the information-processing model. Subsequent sections explain how these characteristics integrate individual and organizational innovation and creativity with the strengths of the information-processing view.

Key Characteristics of the Proposed Model

The proposed model of knowledge management may be distinguished from the information-processing view discussed earlier based on four key characteristics of all organizational processes and activities. These characteristics are the playfulness in organizational choices, the shift from error avoidance to error detection and correction, the strategic planning as "anticipation of surprise," and the creative chaos through organizational vision.

Playfulness in Organizational Choices

The information-processing model of knowledge management is constrained by its overemphasis on consistency that is often institutionalized in the form of "best practices." The proposed model of knowledge management is expected to break this cycle of institutionalized knowledge reinforcement. Instead of emphasizing unquestioning adherence to pre-specified goals or procedures, it encourages the use of intuition through playfulness. "Not requiring consistency in behavior may be achieved by encouraging playfulness in the choice process in organizations, allowing intuition to guide action without sanction" (Cooper et al., 1981).

Playfulness in organizational choice processes enables internal diversity that can match the variety and complexity of the dynamically changing environment (Ashby, 1956). It can be facilitated by treating goals as hypotheses, treating intuition as real, treating organizational memory as enemy, and treating experience as a theory that requires ongoing reassessment (Landau, 1973; March, 1971). Playfulness creates an environment conducive to the subjective, interpretative, and constructive aspects of knowledge creation that are guided by individual and organizational "sense making" (Weick, 1990).

Within the proposed model, the designers of organizational knowledge management systems can, at best, facilitate the organization's self-designing. Not only would the organization's members define problems for themselves and generate their own solutions, the members would also evaluate and revise their solution-generating processes (Hedberg et al., 1976). By explicitly encouraging experimentation and rethinking the premises, one promotes reflection-in-action and creation of tacit knowledge.

Shift from Error Avoidance to Error Detection and Correction

The information-processing model of knowledge management is based on avoidance of errors by meticulous obedience of pre-specified plans, goals, procedures, and rules. Characterized by *over-definition* of rules and *over-specification* of tasks (Landau and Stout, 1979), this model nurtures those who conform to the rules regardless of the results. While errors are informational, compliance is not. Knowledge management systems designed to ensure compliance might ensure that the rules and procedures are followed exactly (i.e., the variance between the pre-specified rules and the actual execution is minimized). However, they do not ensure the detection of error (Landau and Stout, 1979). Unquestioning obedience to rules is synonymous with avoidance of errors: It motivates an organization's members to reduce "the risk of error through conformance to existing patterns of meaning" (Landau, 1973). In this model, "information is selectively processed so as to minimize the rate and extent of change required, [and] the repertoire of response remains impervious to experience" (Landau, 1973).

The current conception of knowledge repositories, with its emphasis on replicating archived best practices, suffers from this frailty. In absence of explicit recommendation for providing contrary (or complementary) alternatives, legitimization of any kind of practices by embedding them in technology is expected to result in the above outcome. It is essentially a negative activity since it defines what cannot be done (Stout, 1980). Hence, such practices reinforce a process of single loop learning with its primary emphasis on error avoidance (Argyris, 1994). The explicit bias for seeking compliance makes such systems inadequate for motivating divergence-oriented interpretations that are necessary for ill-structured and complex environments.

In contrast, the proposed model of knowledge management deploys "unprogrammed processes for monitoring errors [which] utilize discontent and emit signals through dissent, complaint, discontent, and controversy" (Hedberg et al., 1976). It facilitates a process of error detection and error correction, which seeks to identify what can be done (Stout, 1980) within the constraints imposed by the task environment. These distinguishing features of the proposed model facilitate development of a large repertoire of responses that reify alternative (complementary and contradictory) solutions, as well as diverse approaches for implementing such solutions.

Strategic Planning as "Anticipation of Surprise"

The information-processing model of knowledge management focuses on the reduction of variance between planned and actual performance. The decision rules embedded in knowledge repositories assume the character of predictive proclamations, which draw their legitimacy from vested authority in best practices, not necessarily because they provide desirable solutions (Hamel and Prahalad, 1994). Challenges to such rules tend to be often perceived as challenges to the authority embedded in best practices (Landau, 1973).

In contrast, the proposed model of knowledge management is more conducive to a future marked by wicked environments characterized by a wide range of potential surprise (Landau and Stout, 1979). An illustrative example of knowledge management based on anticipation of surprise is provided by the chief learning officer of General Electric, who has underscored the need for emphasizing anticipation over prediction of the future when he stated, "The future is moving so quickly that you can't anticipate it...We have put a tremendous emphasis on quick response instead of planning. We will continue to be surprised, but we won't be surprised that we are surprised. We will anticipate the surprise" (Kerr, 1995).

Within the proposed model of knowledge management, organizational planning activities are not eliminated. However, organizational plans are seen not as a set of instructions for what will take place, but rather as an ideological device that functions to build constituency, and to define the limits of responsible opinion. In this view, the organization plans for its future, but does not rely on its plans (Hedberg et al., 1976). The primary objective of this process is a faster cycle of knowledge creation and action based on the new knowledge, by enabling continuous and rapid detection and correction of any discrepancies between the plan and the dynamically changing business environment.

In this model, access to an organizational information base, authority to take decisive action, and the requisite skills are embedded at the frontlines where real action takes place. An organization's members devise their objectives based on the organization's vision, they measure their own performance against those objectives, and they take their own corrective actions. The dialectical approach (Mason, 1969) could be adopted for this purpose by infusing it into the organization members in the frontline. Contrary to the traditional role of reinforcing the embedded knowledge through policy statements of "the company way," emphasis is on maintaining a "dynamic imbalance" by "challenging conventional wisdom, questioning the data behind accumulating knowledge, and recombining expertise to create new capabilities" (Ghoshal and Bartlett, 1996).

How can the organization ensure that its long-term goals are fulfilled while allowing the subjective, interpretative, constructive, and social interactive processes of knowledge creation? This is the most important role of senior management—as the architect of the organizational vision. The most critical task of top management in this respect is "to conceptualize a vision about what kind of knowledge should be developed and to operationalize it into a management system for implementation" (Nonaka and Takeuchi, 1995).

CREATIVE CHAOS THROUGH ORGANIZATIONAL VISION

Within the proposed model, the organization's vision serves a dialectical purpose: It binds the organization's members together with relatively flexible goal and task definitions. The primary obligation of employees is *not* the fulfillment of pre-specified goals and tasks given in detail, but devising whatever goals and tasks are best to realize the shared vision of the organization. In other words, "autonomous individuals and groups in knowledge-creating organizations set their task boundaries by themselves to pursue the ultimate goal expressed in the higher intention (vision) of the organization" (Nonaka and Takeuchi, 1995).

Organizational vision is a picture of what might be, which generates a "creative tension" necessary for moving toward tomorrow's opportunities from the current reality (Senge, 1990b). This shared picture ("hologram") of the future possibilities emerges from a collection of personal visions of the various organization members and typifies an ever-evolving product of a continuous process (Senge, 1990b).

In this view, top management creates a knowledge vision that defines the world in which they live and the general direction of knowledge they ought to create. The knowledge vision fosters personal commitment of middle managers and frontline workers by providing meaning to their daily tasks. The knowledge vision is purposefully equivocal and open-ended to allow diversity of multiple personal perspectives. The strategic equivocality of the top management's vision encourages an active investigation of the alternatives to established procedures (Nonaka and Takeuchi, 1995). At the level of the implementing staff, ambiguity of the knowledge vision translates into interpretive equivocality, which facilitates reflection-in-action (Schön, 1983), resulting in creative chaos (Nonaka and Takeuchi, 1995).

The information-processing model of knowledge management assumes problems as a given and the solution as based upon a "preset algorithm" (Nonaka and Takeuchi, 1995). In contrast, the proposed model constructs the definition of the problem from the knowledge available at a certain point in time and context (Nonaka and Takeuchi, 1995). While the individual autonomy in the proposed model facilitates the divergence of individual personal perspectives, the organizational vision facilitates the various views to converge in a given direction. This process avoids premature closure or convergence.

The distinguishing characteristics of the proposed model of knowledge management, therefore, provide means for balancing the optimization-based, consensus-oriented focus on efficiency with divergence of meaning that continuously assesses the validity of fundamental assumptions. Given the emphasis on constructive conflict, the proposed model of knowledge management is better suited to detecting changes in external environment and taking corrective action. Since organizational mission is shared across all members in terms of the broad vision, the detection and correction of error occurs where it is first encountered—on the frontline. Diversity of perspectives provides interpretive flexibility to organization members who are better tuned to multiple views of the future and are better prepared for adapting to changing circumstances.

These characteristics of the proposed model integrate the sense-making capabilities that are human and social, with the information-processing capabilities of archival, retrieval, and dissemination, which are the forte of the new computer-based technologies.

Toward Knowledge Management that Makes Sense

Knowledge management includes various processes such as acquisition, creation, renewal, archiving, dissemination, and application (conversion of new knowledge into action or behavior modification) of knowledge. The processes of collecting, organizing, classifying, and disseminating information (Albert, 1998) are served well by the searching, indexing, collating, archiving, and transmission capabilities of new technologies.

However, the prevailing information-processing focus of knowledge management systems doesn't address the creation of new knowledge, the ongoing reassessment and re-framing of existing and new information given the dynamically changing context of application. As discussed earlier, the proposed model is expected to address this critical shortcoming with the understanding of knowledge management for new organizational environments. Within the proposed model, creation of new knowledge is central to the organization's knowledge management activities. Explicit focus on knowledge creation also aims to address the existing "virtual neglect" of this crucial aspect of knowledge management in extant theory, practice, and research (Nonaka and Takeuchi, 1995).

The creative aspect of knowledge management accounts for some key processes that are critical for a richer understanding and practice of knowledge management. They are as follows:

- Tacit dimension of knowledge creation
- Subjective, interpretative, and sense-making bases of knowledge

- Construction of meaning in knowledge creation
- Social, interactive nature of knowledge

Tacit Dimension of Knowledge Creation

The current conception of information technology-enabled knowledge reposi-tories misses the creative aspect of knowledge processing—especially the pro-cessing of tacit knowledge, which is deeply rooted in an individual's action and experience, ideals, values, or emotions (Nonaka and Takeuchi, 1995). Although tacit knowledge lies at the very basis of organizational knowledge creation, its nature renders it highly personal and hard to formalize, making it difficult to communicate or to share with others (Nonaka and Takeuchi, 1995). The current conception of knowledge management is capable of handling explicit knowledge that is transmittable in formal, systematic language and can be stored in specifi-cations, reference manuals, and company handbooks (Nonaka and Takeuchi, 1995). However, it is not capable of transferring the associated emotions and spe-cific contexts in which that information is embedded (Nonaka and Takeuchi, 1995). By explicitly taking into consideration the innovative and creative aspects of knowledge creation, the proposed model integrates aspects of knowledge (such as intuition and insight) that are difficult to formalize or communicate by com-puter-based, information-processing mechanisms.

Nonaka and Takeuchi (1995) have suggested that knowledge is created through the interaction between tacit and explicit knowledge through four different modes. These modes are: socialization, which involves conversion from tacit knowledge to tacit knowledge; externalization, which involves conversion from tacit knowl-edge to explicit knowledge; combination, which involves conversion from explic-it knowledge to explicit knowledge; and internalization, which involves conver-sion from explicit knowledge to tacit knowledge.

The information-processing view of knowledge management is limited in its support of knowledge creation through socialization since it cannot provide the "shared experience" (Nonaka and Takeuchi, 1995) necessary for relating to anoth-er individual's thinking process. In knowledge creation through externalization, the information-processing view of knowledge management is limited since it doesn't explicitly address the process of dialogue or collective reflection. The pro-posed model, by integrating these aspects of knowledge creation, seems to over-come the limitations of the information-processing view.

Subjective, Interpretative, and Sense-Making Basis of Knowledge

Dynamically changing environments call for interpretation of new events and re-interpretation of extant practices (Boland et al., 1994). Daft and Weick (1984) defined interpretation as the process through which people give meaning to information. However, the information-processing view generally ignores the critically important construct of meaning, which is essentially a function of human interpretative and constructive activities (Boland, 1987; Holland, 1995 personal communication). It fosters an image of the knowledge base in which "the human meaning of knowledge and action are unproblematic, predefined, and prepackaged" (Boland, 1987) and the process of the "continuous human problem of accomplishing meaning is replaced by a technology of packaging data" (Boland, 1987).

Prepackaged or assumed interpretation of knowledge, residing in archived best practices, works against the generation of multiple and contradictory viewpoints that is necessary for ill-structured environments. Simplification of contextual information for storage in computer-based repositories doesn't preserve the complexity of multiple viewpoints (Davenport, 1994). Institutionalization of definitions and interpretations of events and issues work against the exchanging and sharing of diverse perspectives. It hampers the trial-and-error process that can enhance the capacity for effective action (Senge cited in Koch and Fabris, 1995).

The proposed model explicitly addresses multiple and diverse interpretations (Eisenhardt, 1989, 1992) that are necessary for preventing oversimplification or premature decision closure (Imai et al., 1985; Senge, 1990a). The proposed model of knowledge management is expected to facilitate diverse views within a framework that is broad enough to encompass individual differences (Fiol, 1994).

Construction of Meaning in Knowledge Creation

In the computational metaphor that is characteristic of computer-based repositories of best practices, "information is [considered] indifferent with respect to the message...meaning is preassigned to messages" (Bruner, 1990). However, this assumption is questionable because construction of meaning and the processing of information are profoundly different matters (Bruner, 1990). These meanings would not exist if human beings had not originally created the objects and entities in them (Strombach, 1986). The syntactic dimension of information, which has been the primary focus of the information-processing view, is only a carrier for semantic and pragmatic dimensions (Morris, 1938).

Something makes sense only if it can be related or connected to the existing frameworks or schemas: "To grasp the meaning of a thing, an event, or a situation is to see it in its *relation* to other things..." (Dewey, 1933). New experiences are interpreted with reference to the existing mental models, which, in turn, are modified by newer experiences. The process is highly individualized and based on one's existing system of personal constructs (frames of reference), and is aimed at finding meaning and making sense of situations (Kelly, 1963). Individuals respond to what they interpret the stimulus to be, which is a function of the constructs they detect or impose upon their world (Bannister and Fransella, 1971, 1986).

Hence, for most ill-structured situations, it is difficult to ensure a unique interpretation of best practices residing in computer-based repositories since knowledge is created by the *individuals* in the process of using that data. Also, because individuals adjust their constructs (to better match the environment) to improve predictions of their actions "all of our present interpretations of the universe are subject to revision or replacement" (Kelly, 1963). The constructive aspect of knowledge creation embraced by the proposed model is expected to enable the organization's (desirable) anticipatory response to discontinuous change (Brown and Eisenhardt, 1997).

Social Interactive Nature of Knowledge

New knowledge may be facilitated by divergence of meanings and perspectives based upon Hegelian and Kantian inquiry. The diversity of interpretations—of extant and new information—may be motivated by the social interactive process of continuous dialog (Senge, 1990a). Dialog is important for surfacing and challenging existing assumptions and continually renewing the pool of common meaning (Bohm cited in Senge, 1990a). This is the very essence of the process of dialogue: "meaning passing or moving through...a free flow of meaning between people..." (Bohm cited in Senge, 1990a). It is the flow of meaning, and not the flow of information, that constitutes knowledge flow. "Meanings express personal views of reality" (Stamper, 1987), therefore, diversity of meanings and conflicts between various interpretations are not unexpected. The current organizational thrust on information technology-enabled knowledge repositories ignores the critical social and interactive nature of knowledge creation. "Information is not a resource to be stockpiled as one more factor of production. It is meaning, and it can only be achieved through dialogue in a human community" (Boland, 1987).

Discontinuously changing hyper-turbulent environments impose upon the organization a need for creative synthesis resulting from a dialectical confrontation of opposing interpretations (Mason and Mitroff, 1973). Davenport (1995) also asserted the relevance of social interaction in the creation of new knowledge when he stated, "successful knowledge transfer involves neither computers nor documents but rather interactions between people."

The characteristics of the proposed model leverage the tacit knowledge of individuals, the subjective and interpretative biases of diverse perspectives, and dynamism of meaning with changing contextual conditions based on the social interactive process of dialog. The proposed model recommends the synthesis of these characteristics and related processes with the information-processing emphasis of the mainstream notion of knowledge management systems.

CONCLUSION

The mainstream model of knowledge management based on the information-processing view is problematic because of its focus on premature convergence of problem definitions and related solutions. The theoretical, conceptual, and pragmatic basis for building upon the strengths of the information-processing model, while minimizing its limitations, was discussed. The need for better synergy between the human innovation and creativity and the existing information-processing focus on knowledge management was underscored. The theoretical basis of the proposed model was reviewed, and the model was presented in definitional terms, and its key implementation characteristics were discussed. It was also explained how the explicit emphasis of the proposed model on the creation of new knowledge builds upon the strengths of the information-processing capabilities of computer-based knowledge management systems.

In sum, this chapter underscores how organizations' strategic needs for creating (and recreating) new knowledge can be met by a synergy between data- and information-processing capabilities of advanced information technologies and innovative and creative capabilities latent in their human members. While providing the theoretical, conceptual, and pragmatic basis for advancing practice and research, the chapter ameliorates the weaknesses of the existing model by proposing an enhanced model of knowledge management.

The information-processing model is apparent in the knowledge management practice of a major U.S.-based global communications company: "What's important is to find useful knowledge, bottle it, and pass it around" (Stewart and Kaufman, 1995). In contrast, the model proposed in this chapter is illustrated in practice by an alternative approach taken by the Pfizer company (Dragoon, 1995): "There's a great big river of data out there. Rather than building dams to try and bottle it all up into discrete little entities, we just give people canoes and compasses."

References

Albert, S. "Knowledge Management: Living Up to the Hype?" *Midrange Systems,* September 7, 1998, 11(13), p. 52.

Anthes, G.H. "A Step Beyond a Database," *Computerworld,* 25(9), 1991, p. 28.

Applegate, L., Cash, J., Mills, D.Q. "Information Technology and Tomorrow's Manager," In McGowan, W.G. (ed.), *Revolution in Real Time: Managing Information Technology in the 1990s,* pp. 33-48, Boston, Harvard Business School Press, 1988.

Argyris, C. "Good Communication that Blocks Learning," *Harvard Business Review,* July-August 1994, 72 (4), pp. 77-85.

Arthur, W. B. "Increasing Returns and the New World of Business." *Harvard Business Review,* July-August 1996, 74(4), pp. 100-109.

Ashby, W.R. *An Introduction to Cybernetics,* New York, Wiley, 1956.

Bair, J. "Knowledge Management: The Era of Shared Ideas," *Forbes,* 1(1) (The Future of IT Supplement), Sep 22, 1997, p. 28.

Bannister, D., Fransella, F. *Inquiring Man: The Theory of Personal Constructs,* New York, Penguin, 1971.

Bannister, D., Fransella, F. *Inquiring Man: The Psychology of Personal Constructs,* 3rd ed., London, U.K., Croom Helm, 1986.

Bartlett, C.A., Ghoshal, S. "Changing the Role of the Top Management: Beyond Systems to People," *Harvard Business Review,* May-June 1995, 73 (3), pp. 132-142.

Bennis, W. "A Funny Thing Happened on the Way to the Future," In Leavitt, H., Pinfield, L., Webb, E. (eds.), *Organizations of the Future: Interaction with the External Environment,* New York, Praeger, 1974.

Bennis, W., Nanus, B. *Leaders: The Strategies for Taking Charge,* New York, Harper & Row, 1985.

Bettis, R., Prahalad, C.K. "The Dominant Logic: Retrospective and Extension," *Strategic Management Journal,* January 1995, 16, pp. 5-14.

Boland, R.J. "The In-formation of Information Systems," In Boland, R.J., Hirschheim, R. (eds.), *Critical Issues in Information Systems Research,* pp. 363-379, Chichester, U.K., Wiley, 1987.

Boland, R.J., Tenkasi, R.V., Te'eni, D. "Designing Information Technology to Support Distributed Cognition," *Organization Science,* August 1994, 5(3), pp. 456-475.

Brown, S. L, Eisenhardt, K. M. "The Art of Continuous Change: Linking Complexity Theory and Time-Paced Evolution in Relentlessly Shifting Organizations," *Administrative Science Quarterly,* March 1997, 42(1), pp. 1-34.

Bruner, J. *Acts of Meaning,* Cambridge, Harvard University Press, 1990.

Chorafas, D.N. "Expert Systems at the Banker's Reach," International Journal of Bank Marketing, 1987, 5(4), pp. 72-81.

Candlin, D.B., Wright, S. "Managing the Introduction of Expert Systems," *International Journal of Operations and Production Management,* 1992, 12(1), pp. 46-59.

Churchman, C.W. *The Design of Inquiring Systems*, New York, Basic Books, 1971.

Cooper, D.J., Hayes, D., Wolf, F. "Accounting in Organized Anarchies: Understanding and Designing Accounting Systems in Ambiguous Situations," *Accounting, Organizations and Society*, 1981, 6(3), pp. 175-191.

"Knowledge Management Consulting Gives CPAs a Competitive Edge," *CPA Journal*, August 1998, 68(8), p. 72.

Daft, R.L, Weick, K.E. "Toward a Model of Organizations as Interpretation Systems," *Academy of Management Review*, 9, pp. 284-295.

Davenport, T.H. "Saving IT's Soul: Human-Centered Information Management," *Harvard Business Review*, March-April 1994, 72 (2), pp. 119-131.

Davenport, T.H. "Think Tank: The Future of Knowledge Management," *CIO*, December 15, 1995.

Davenport, T.H., Prusak, L. *Working Knowledge: How Organizations Manage What They Know*, Boston, Harvard Business School Press, 1998.

Davidow, W.H., Malone, M.S. *The Virtual Corporation*, New York, HarperCollins, 1992.

Dewey, J. *How We Think*, Boston, D.C. Heath and Company, 1933.

Dragoon, A. "Knowledge Management: Rx for Success," *CIO*, July 1995, 8(18), pp. 48-56.

Drucker, P.F. *Post-Capitalist Society*, New York, Harper-Business, 1994a.

Drucker, P.F. "The Theory of Business," *Harvard Business Review*, September-October 1994b, 72 (5), pp. 95-104.

Eisenhardt, K.M. "Making Fast Strategic Decisions in High-Velocity Environments," *Academy of Management Journal*, 1989, 32(3), pp. 543-576.

Eisenhardt, K.M. "Speed and Strategic Choice: Accelerating Decision-Making," *Planning Review*, September-October 1992, 20(5), pp. 30-32.

Emery, F.E., Trist, E.L. "The Causal Texture of Organizational Environments," *Human Relations*, 1965, 18, pp. 21-32.

Fiol, C.M. "Consensus, Diversity, and Learning in Organizations," *Organization Science*, August 1994, 5(3), pp. 403-420.

Ford, N. "From Information to Knowledge-Management," *Journal of Information Science Principles and Practice*, 1989, 15(4,5), pp. 299-304.

Ghoshal, S., Bartlett, C.A. "Rebuilding Behavioral Context: A Blueprint for Corporate Renewal," *Sloan Management Review*, Winter 1996, pp. 23-36.

Gill, T.G. "High-Tech Hidebound: Case Studies of Information Technologies that Inhibited Organizational Learning," *Accounting, Management and Information Technologies*, 1995, 5(1), pp. 41-60.

Gopal, C., Gagnon, J. "Knowledge, Information, Learning and the IS Manager," *Computerworld (Leadership Series)*, 1995, 1(5), pp. 1-7.

Hamel, G., Prahalad, C.K. *Competing for the Future*, Boston, Harvard Business School Press, 1994.

Handy, C. *The Age of Unreason*, Boston, Harvard Business School Press, 1990.

Hedberg, B. "How Organizations Learn and Unlearn," In Nystrom, P., Starbuck, W. (eds.), *Handbook of Organizational Design*, pp. 1-27, New York, Oxford University Press, 1981.

Hedberg, B., Jonsson, S. "Designing Semi-Confusing Information Systems for Organizations in Changing Environments," *Accounting, Organizations and Society*, 1978, 3(1), pp. 47-74.

Hedberg, B., Nystrom, P.C., Starbuck, W.H. "Camping on Seesaws: Prescriptions for a Self-Designing Organization," *Administrative Science Quarterly*, 1976, 21, pp. 41-65.

Hibbard, J. "Ernst & Young Deploys App for Knowledge Management," *Information Week*, July 28, 1997, p. 28.

Huber, G.P. "The Nature and Design of Post-Industrial Organizations," *Management Science*, 1984, 30(8), 928-951.

Huber, G.P., Glick, W.H. *Organizational Change and Redesign: Ideas and Insights for Improving Performance*, New York, Oxford University Press, 1993.

Imai, K., Nonaka, I., Takeuchi, H. "Managing the New Product Development Process: How Japanese Companies Learn and Unlearn," In Clark, K., Hayes, R., Lorenz, C. (eds.), *The Uneasy Alliance*, Boston, Harvard Business School Press,1985.

Kanter, R.M. *The Change Masters: Innovation and Entrepreneurship in the American Corporation*, New York, Simon & Schuster, 1984.

Kelly, G.A. *A Theory of Personality: The Psychology of Personal Constructs*, New York, W.W. Norton & Company, 1963.

Kerr, S. "Creating the Boundaryless Organization: The Radical Reconstruction of Organization Capabilities," *Planning Review*, September-October 1995, pp. 41-45.

Koch, C., Fabris, P. "Fail Safe," *CIO*, December 1, 1995, 9(5), pp. 32-36.

Landau, M. "On the Concept of Self-Correcting Organizations," *Public Administration Review*, November/December 1973, pp. 533-542.

Landau, M., Stout, R., Jr. "To Manage Is Not to Control: Or the Folly of Type II Errors," *Public Administration Review*, March/April 1979, pp. 148-156.

Leonard-Barton, D. *Wellsprings of Knowledge: Building and Sustaining the Sources of Innovation*, Boston, Harvard Business School Press, 1995.

Maglitta, J. "Smarten Up!," *Computerworld*, June 5, 1995, 29(23), pp. 84-86.

Maglitta, J. "Know-How, Inc." *Computerworld*, January 15, 1996, 30(1).

Malhotra, Y. "Tools@work: Deciphering the Knowledge Management Hype," *Journal for Quality and Participation*, July/August 1998, 21(4), pp. 58-60.

Malone, T.W., Crowston, K. "Toward an Interdisciplinary Theory of Coordination," *Technical Report 120*, Center for Coordination Science, MIT, 1991.

Manville, B., Foote, N. "Harvest Your Workers' Knowledge," *Datamation*, July 1996, 42 (13), pp. 78-80.

March, J.G. "The Technology of Foolishness" *Civilokonomen*, May 1971, pp. 7-12.

Mason, R.P. "A Dialectical Approach to Strategic Planning," *Management Science*, April 1969, 15(8), pp. B 403-414.

Mason, R.O., Mitroff, I.I. "A Program for Research on Management Information Systems," *Management Science*, January 1973, 19(5), pp. 475-487.

Morris, C.W. *Foundations of the Theory of Signs*, Chicago, University of Chicago Press, 1938.

Nadler, D.A., Shaw, R.B. "Change Leadership: Core Competency for the Twenty-First Century," In Nadler, D.A., Shaw, R.B., and Walton, A.E. (eds.) *Discontinuous Change: Leading Organizational Transformation*, San Franscisco, Jossey-Bass, 1995.

Nadler, D.A., Shaw, R.B., Walton, A.E. (eds.). *Discontinuous Change: Leading Organizational Transformation*, San Francisco, Jossey-Bass, 1995.

Nonaka, I., Takeuchi, H. *The Knowledge-Creating Company*, New York, Oxford University Press, 1995.

Peters, T. *Thriving on Chaos: Handbook for a Management Revolution*, London, U.K., Pan Books, 1989.

Schön, D.A. *The Reflective Practitioner: How Professionals Think in Action*, New York, Basic Books, 1983.

Senge, P.M. *The Fifth Discipline: The Art and Practice of the Learning Organization*, New York, Doubleday, 1990a.

Senge, P.M. "The Leader's New Work: Building Learning Organizations," *Sloan Management Review*, Fall 1990b, 32(1), pp. 7-23.

Shen, S. "Knowledge Management in Decision Support Systems," *Decision Support Systems*, 1987, 3(1), pp. 1-11.

Stamper, R. "Semantics," In Boland, R.J., Hirschheim, R. (eds.), *Critical Issues in Information Systems Research*, pp. 43-78, Chichester, Wiley, 1987.

Stewart, T.A., Kaufman, D.C. "Getting Real about Brainpower," *Fortune*, December 11, 1995

Stewart, T.A. *Intellectual Capital: The New Wealth of Organizations*, New York, Doubleday/Currency, 1997.

Stout, R., Jr. *Management or Control?: The Organizational Challenge*, Bloomington, Indiana University Press, 1980.

Strapko, W. "Knowledge Management," *Software Magazine*, 1990, 10(13), pp. 63-66.

Strombach, W. "Information in Epistemological and Ontological Perspective," In Mitcham, C. Huning, A. (eds.), *Philosophy and Technology II: Information Technology and Computers in Theory and Practice*, Dordrecht, Holland, D. Reidel Publishing Company, 1986.

Stuart, A. "Elusive Assets," *CIO*, November 15, 1995, pp. 28-34.

Taylor, W.C. "Control in an Age of Chaos," *Harvard Business Review*, November-December 1994, 72 (6) p. 72.

Weick, K.E. "Cognitive Processes in Organizations," In Cummings, L.L., Staw, B.M. (eds.), *Information and Cognition in Organizations*, Greenwich, JAI Press, 1990.

Wheatley, M.J. *Leadership and the New Science*, San Francisco, Berett-Koehler, 1994.

Willett, S., Copeland, L. "Knowledge Management Key to IBM's Enterprise Plan," *Computer Reseller News*, July 27, 1998, pp. 1, 6.

Zeleny, M. "Management Support Systems," *Human Systems Management*," 1987, 7(1), pp. 59-70.

Zuboff, S. "The Emperor's New Workplace," *Scientific American*, September 1995, 273(3), pp. 202-204.

Zuckerman, A., Buell, H. "Is the World Ready for Knowledge Management?" *Quality Progress*, 31(6), pp. 81-84.

CHAPTER 5

Is Knowledge Management Really the Future for Information Professionals?

Judith Albert

Research Coordinator

Ernst & Young LLP

INTRODUCTION

Current knowledge management literature tends to emphasize access to and organization of internal data, ignoring the contributions of information professionals who primarily access and organize external data. In this chapter, the roots and biases of major schools of knowledge management are explored to see why this is so. The ways information professionals are most likely to encounter knowledge management initiatives that do not begin with the information center are described critically, and the prospects of increased status for information professionals who adopt knowledge management are assessed.

WHAT KNOWLEDGE MANAGEMENT IS...AND ISN'T

Everyone's first question is still: "Just what is knowledge management?" Here's my favorite discussion:

> Quick—in 25 words or less, define knowledge management. Can't do it? You're not alone. Many managers would be hard pressed to explain, precisely and concisely, what this evolving business trend means. What they probably do know is that knowledge management has been billed

as a critical tool for the 21st Century Corporation. They know it's the subject of a recent torrent of books, magazine articles, conferences, business-school classes, WWW sites, and even an executive position, chief knowledge officer (CKO)... And they know it's something they just have to get to—even if they don't know exactly what it is. The confusion's understandable. Even experts and practitioners disagree on something as fundamental as exactly what to call concerted efforts to capture, organize, and share what employees know. With some semantic quibbling, you're as likely to hear such efforts referred to as managing "intellectual capital," "intellectual assets," or "knowledge resources" as knowledge management.

Whatever it's called, proponents generally agree about why it's important. Because of downsizing, frequent job jumping, constant change, globalization and the transition from an industrial to a knowledge-based economy, they say, companies feel more pressure than ever to maintain a well-informed workforce, boost productivity, and gain competitive advantage. By creating an inclusive, comprehensive, easily accessible organizational memory, knowledge management helps meet all these goals. But even the concept's champions acknowledge the questions continue to evolve along with the trend itself. Among them, "How is it possible to manage something as intangible as knowledge? How do you determine its value? And how do the benefits fit into the balance sheet?" (Stuart, 1997).

While some of the most successful and visible players in this area have information professional backgrounds (Lois Remeikis of Booz Allen & Hamilton and Jill Maserian of Arthur D. Little come to mind), most well-known knowledge management theorists and practitioners have backgrounds either in information technology or management (human resources, strategic planning, organizational management). As a result there are two basic flavors of knowledge management: technological and cultural.

The technological element is the new version of the premise that we can somehow get automatic indexing, intelligent agents, document management software, or data mining—whatever the latest artificial intelligence toy is—to do most of our thinking for us. Here the premise is that, if studied the right way, what we do can be broken into small enough standardized pieces that the blue-collar efficiency techniques of industrial automation—Taylorism—will do their wonders for the thought work of the white-collar professional. This is always a particular threat to information professionals, since our job is to do the thinking for others in our companies, but it's not a new nor a particularly more timely threat.

The technologists tend to avoid what we do in retrieving external data and focus on developing structures for sharing and reuse of internal information. It's easier to show the value of creating a structure for confidential customer information that has never been organized than demonstrate the value of creating a structure to put *The New York Times* online on everyone's desk instead of providing access through the library. As a result the invaluable data we can provide may disappear in the torrent of databases gathered, organized, and deployed totally outside the information center.

If what we do seems trivial to the technology-focused knowledge management camp, this does not mean that their opponents are our allies. As Philip Murray, editor-in-chief of *Knowledge Management Briefs*, describes the cultural camp:

> ...business managers (and knowledge management consultants who sell services to them) tend to adopt a **top-down viewpoint of knowledge management**. They are concerned with what managers have to know and do in order to help themselves and with how to push organizations toward leveraging corporate intellectual assets. They often emphasize "new thinking" about work roles and responsibilities, and they sometimes exhibit an anti-technology, anti-rationalist attitude. After all, knowledge management is really a "people problem," isn't it? (Murray, 1998).

A lot of the cultural elements appearing under the guise of "knowledge management" have little to do with knowledge. Much of it is business process reengineering, total quality management, virtual organizations, learning organizations, visioning, and other recent management fads reappearing in a sexier guise. How can you decipher? If you can take the description of the concept involved, substitute words like "process," "cooperation," or "quality" in place of "knowledge" or "information" and it still makes sense, then it's probably not really knowledge management.

If the technological camp dismisses our databases in favor of data warehouses, the cultural camp tends to avoid what we do in favor of what is often called "tacit" or "informal" knowledge. This "intellectual capital" exists in the minds of employees but is seldom articulated—and without knowledge management, almost never formalized. (A copy of a customer's contract would be explicit knowledge; details of the negotiation process would be tacit knowledge held by the client's account representative. Access to that information would disappear with the departure or reassignment of the representative unless steps were taken to articulate and classify the details.)

Obviously, as mediated researchers we have a great deal of tacit knowledge about how our organizations employ information, even if the end product we hand out and measure is explicit information. Depending on our level of involvement with how our research is used, we may even have the best view in our organizations of how information is really employed. Besides, our users are, by definition, information-seekers and form a natural interest group for managers trying to develop a knowledge culture. These points are frequently made in upbeat assessments of the promise of knowledge management for our field.

Unfortunately, no one is making this point in print outside of the library literature. To the cultural camp, information professionals appear too technical, over-relying on computer technology, and too focused on details rather than the organization as a whole. It's not a given that everyone needs formal secondary research derived from outside sources. (By contrast, everyone needs human resources and budget planning.)

Another common stumbling block to understanding knowledge management is grasping the difference between knowledge management as a process and knowledge management as an end product. As Tom Davenport et al. describe in their "Successful Knowledge Management Projects," an absolutely key article on this topic:

> A lot of the energy in knowledge management has been spent on treating knowledge as an 'it'—an entity separate from the people who create and use it. The typical goal is to take documents with knowledge embedded in them—memos, reports, presentations, articles—and store them in a repository where they can be retrieved easily (Davenport, DeLong, and Beers, 1998).

Even the most successful system can only reflect the knowledge base at a single point in time unless it has an evolving organic structure. Replenishing and updating whatever knowledge management system develops allows it to become the "working memory" of an organization rather than a high-tech photo album full of increasingly dated snapshots. To quote another Tom Davenport piece:

> It is tempting to create a hierarchical model or architecture for knowledge, similar to the *Encyclopedia Britannica's* Propedia (or, I might add, the Dewey Decimal system), that would govern the collection and

categorization of knowledge. But most organizations are better off letting the knowledge market work, and simply providing and mapping the knowledge its consumers seem to want. The dispersion of knowledge in a map may seem illogical, but it is still more useful to a user than a hypothetical knowledge model that is best understood by its creators and rarely fully implemented. Mapping organizational knowledge is the single activity most likely to yield better access.

Knowledge managers can learn from the experience of data managers, whose complex models of how data would be structured in the future were seldom realized. Firms rarely created maps of (existing) data, so they never had any guides to where the information was in the present (Davenport, 1997).

To summarize in one sentence, as Ellen Knapp, CKO of Coopers & Lybrand, has put it, "Remember you need to understand how people think, not just what they know" (Knapp, 1997).

The last point I want to make about confusion in defining knowledge management is that it leads to greater confusion in measuring knowledge management. The best summary of current approaches is a link on the Special Libraries Association (SLA) page subsection on knowledge management. This page summarizes twelve techniques used to value intangible assets, adopted from a longer piece entitled "CEO's Guide to Intellectual Capital, " authored by the Montague Institute. Without going into great detail, let me just say that only one of the dozen approaches involves dollar amounts that could be easily and objectively obtained, and that approach is appropriate only for certain subsystems of a knowledge management program!

Forbes ASAP did an intellectual capital issue in 1997. As you can judge from this issue's title, "Is Intellectual Capital the New Wealth or the Latest Consulting Wank?" it is even more skeptical about this field than I am. One humorous column (Rutledge, 1997) suggests that measuring intellectual capital is a conspiracy of left-leaning social engineers to destroy this country's accounting standards.

To judge success in knowledge management projects, Davenport and his colleagues from the Ernst & Young Center for Business Management used four indicators of success:

- Growth in the resources attached to the project, including people, money, and so on

- Growth in the volume of knowledge content and usage (i.e., the number of documents or accesses for repositories or participants for discussion-oriented projects
- The likelihood that the project would survive without the support of a particular individual or two, i.e., the project is an organizational initiative, not an individual project
- Some evidence of financial return either for the knowledge management activity itself (i.e., it was a profit center) or for the larger organization; this linkage need not be rigorously specified and may be only perceptual (Davenport et al., 1998)

Even by these relatively forgiving standards, eighteen of thirty-one projects were successful, eight were too new to determine success, and five were unsuccessful. While these criteria tended to track together, so successful projects met most of them and unsuccessful ones met few, even some successes failed to demonstrate clear financial benefit.

Common Knowledge Management Tools and Techniques

Now that we have an idea of what knowledge management means in the general corporate environment, let's turn to the ways information professionals are most likely to encounter knowledge management in their professional lives. Basically, these tools and techniques are:

- Benchmarking and best practices
- Information or knowledge audits
- Intranets
- Notes and other GroupWare

You may be lucky enough to be the prime mover behind these technologies... but odds are that even if you are part of the group implementing these tools and techniques, you or your department will be the subject (I nearly said victim) of scrutiny, and not solely the objective scrutinizer. As a result, my take on these is a little more skeptical and critical than most of what you are likely to read in the business press.

Benchmarking, or best practices as it is often known, has often struck me as simplistic. Of course it's useful to have a snapshot of what your employees, or your best competitors, or the entire American public sees as the way they would handle a given situation. But just because some people, or many people, or many successful people do something doesn't make it the best practice in that situation—just the best existing practice.

If you know what the absolute best practice is outside of what is currently in your survey, then why survey all those people in the first place? And if you can't tell what the absolute best practice is, how can you identify and rate the relative best practices from the existing choices made by your respondents? Benchmarking seems to me to ignore professional judgment in favor of a mechanical solution.

The real problem with this approach is that best practices are a response to changing situations, and no user is in a position to tell you about the options—in our case, the sources or access points—they don't know to use. An example of this paradox:

> A railroad company, in deciding whether to put a train station in a town that lacks one, sends market researchers to the town to see if there is any demand for a station. Arriving in the town, the researchers find absolutely no one waiting for a train, and therefore conclude there is no demand (Artz, 1997).

Your users are not waiting for a train they don't know is coming: it's your job as a professional to decide where to lay the track and how to get passengers onboard. Unfortunately many information professionals see this as danger rather than opportunity, fearing "information malpractice" or the appearance of telling end users how to do their jobs. Hiding behind our role as information middlemen means never taking control of the knowledge management process.

As Jerry Ash summarizes in "State of Knowledge Management Practice among Early Adopters,"

> The demonstrations of management of explicit knowledge generated by twenty years of benchmarking and best practices barely scratches the surface of the brainpower of our employees…the early knowledge management efforts focus on **what is**, not **what could be**. Best practices is a valuable component of knowledge management but it only copies knowledge currently in action. Creating value from existing intellectual property is a valuable component of knowledge management, but it only capitalizes on old ideas. Neither leads to innovations. Neither digs below the surface of our knowledge resources. A vast majority of knowledge resources lies in the untapped tacit knowledge

of our employees. The real power of knowledge management will unfold when it steps beyond the explicit to the tacit (Ash, 1997).

Another way librarians first encounter or implement knowledge management within their companies is through the information audit. Mary Ellen Bates opens her recent article on this topic as follows:

> When doing a search on the Net for the phrase "information audit,"...there were Web sites for how to get information from within your company out onto the Web for customers. There were MIS articles about managing files and information within a company and articles describing how to manage sales lead-tracking systems. There were articles about how a company tracks its internal databases—keeping the right hand informed of what the left is doing and preventing the construction of multiple customer or vendor databases, for example—essentially, audits of information systems. There is information on ISO 900 certification of quality management, which of course involved tracking processes and maintaining databases of information regarding quality systems. But there isn't much on the related concept of how we analyze what information sources an organization needs, how it acquires them, how it manages them, and how it uses them (Bates, 1997; Berkman, 1997).

Even within the library literature, the most frequently cited piece involves auditing information policy, not actual information use and content (Cortez and Kazlauskas, 1996). The information audit or knowledge audit derives from the communications audit. Advertisers, public relations firms, lobbyists, and other professional communicators to identify information flows to a client's key audiences use this research technique. Then they tailor their client's message to take account of the background of existing perceptions and conflicting messages from competing sources.

Communications firms look primarily at the *content*: What messages are coming through *The New York Times* or CNN on a given topic. The means they have to disseminate their intended messages are mass media—reaching much more than the intended audience—so there is little value to determining exactly the preferences of any individual in the target population.

An information or knowledge audit seeks instead to study the effectiveness of *information flow* within an organization. It does not analyze or judge the information content, except possibly to compare competing channels for the same information. While an information audit hopes to examine information needs throughout the organization, the unit it examines is the individual, and here, the analogy with a communications audit begins to break down.

An example will make this clearer. Although no *Wall Street Journal* reader reads every word of every issue, over time a group of readers will obtain pretty much the same content. But one person's Nexis may always be very different from another's, and the portion of data that each individual accesses over time will always be dwarfed by the enormity of the whole available database. It is much harder to generalize meaningfully from an information audit than the communications audit analogy would suggest.

The good news is that as information professionals, we have much more control over the source our clients receive than communications professionals have over the media. Of course your clients will always have additional, sometimes unauthorized, sources of information to which they can refer. But you control the content selection (choosing not to subscribe to a particular system, for example). You control the means of access (whether through your department as intermediaries, or through your decision to put a source on the LAN or Intranet). And most likely you control the cost (whether through bill backs or by negotiating the overall contract). The bad news, as embodied in the term knowledge audit rather than information audit, is that the flow of information that is mediated through information professionals may be totally dwarfed and overshadowed by the flows of internal information over which you have no control.

Intranets are another tool that leads to demand for knowledge management, as they radically improve access to data and erode internal corporate boundaries. But I think it's crucial to separate the goal of an Intranet—company-wide seamless access to a variety of resources through one interface—from the technology issues on one side, and the access and application issues on the other.

The goal of an Intranet fits into everything you've read or heard about knowledge management, since it has become, in many ways, the poor person's GroupWare. There are all kinds of HTML conversion tools that allow Intranet publishing of existing documents by employees with little technical expertise but a strong desire to share knowledge. I welcome the concept of an Intranet; I am less than thrilled with the reality.

On the technology front, the Web is the cheapest, easiest way to connect employees in many locations to both internally and externally produced data in a secure fashion. But I suspect one reason Intranets are growing so fast is that they reduce ongoing maintenance demands on MIS as well as reducing the variety of pieces of hardware they need to purchase and support and software packages to configure, especially when compared to LANs and WANs. In the long run, Intranets need architecture too, but you truly can post a site that looks and functions adequately to begin with in a single day. Then it takes considerable growth before the dangers of a lack of infrastructure become obvious to users and decision-making executives.

The access and application front is more problematic because uniformity of using the Web comes with a high price that perhaps only we who specialize in the quirks of information retrieval can fully grasp. While browsers are the most widely available universal search engines, they are not the most accurate and, despite many claims to the contrary, are far from the easiest search tools to use well. It's a shame to see deeply structured, well-designed internal databases handed over to the surfers for the sake of consistency. Shockingly, few users understand how inefficiently their search engines work, and why indexing still exists in a world of full-text searching.

Meta-engines, bots, and the class of knowledge management software that organizes retrieved results only exacerbate the problem. More results, or even more accessible results, are just not as valuable as better results. Relevance algorithms help but cannot make up for poorly designed or poorly deployed search engines. The attitude of the developers is simple: Users won't need training because if they can't get results from our system the first time they surf there, they'll never come back. (The CEO of Northern Light actually said this to explain why they offer training and support only to information professionals rather than all subscribers.) As a result, few users even know how little they know about the full capability of the tools that they now use every day.

The premier technology for encountering and fostering the principles of knowledge management has been Lotus Notes. Describing the benefits of Notes in print is a lot like watching television ads that showed a color picture as seen on a Quasar TV. If you didn't have one, you couldn't see how good it was; and if you had one, you could see the picture great, but you didn't need the ad! Many consultants now claim that aggressive use of e-mail or an Intranet can nearly replace Notes. Personally, having worked both with and without it, I cannot agree. Some functions are replaceable: widespread e-mail can replace discussion groups; with Java, an Intranet can make all pieces of the network appear uniform and accessible to the lightly trained end user.

However, the main advantage of Notes over an Intranet or aggressive use of email, the real transformational power of Notes, is this: Everything you have can run from one platform; it can be individualized, indexed, notated, and reorganized by each individual, and those changes either updated throughout the network or held privately; and it passively stores everything produced. Therefore, it builds its own knowledge database as it's used. Notes is not in itself enough to create a knowledge culture...but I cannot imagine developing one without it.

INFORMATION PROFESSIONALS: WHERE'S THE FIT?

Now we know the major concepts of knowledge management, and its major tools and techniques we are likely to encounter. Where's the fit with what we do as information professionals? Why are so many people so excited about a movement that ignores what we do every day, and requires massive technological and cultural investment without a clearly defined bottom-line payback?

One reason is the hope that we will be elevated from managing the corporate information center into managing corporate knowledge, that we will become the chief knowledge officers and chief learning officers of the future. I would love such a job myself. Most of us do not have the operational knowledge and visible profile in our companies to hold such a position even though we have the technical skills it requires in abundance. A quote from Brian Newman on the difference between knowledge management and knowledge engineering will reinforce my point.

> ...If you were to ask either a manager or an engineer if their jobs were the same, I doubt you would get them to agree...to manage is to exercise executive, administrative, and supervisory direction, while to engineer is to lay out, construct, contrive, or plan out, usually with subtle skill and craft.

> The main difference seems to be that the (knowledge) manager establishes the direction the process should take, where as the (knowledge) engineer develops the means to accomplish that direction....

> We should find knowledge managers concerned with the knowledge needs of the enterprise. We should see them doing the research to understand what knowledge is needed to make what decision and enable what actions. They should be taking a key role in the design of the enterprise and from the needs of the enterprise establishing

enterprise level knowledge management policies. It is to the knowledge managers that the user should go with their "need to know."

…We should find knowledge engineers working on such areas as data and information representation and encoding technologies, data repositories and retrieval, GroupWare technologies, etc. The knowledge engineers would most likely be researching the technologies needed to meet the enterprise's knowledge management needs. The knowledge engineers should also be establishing the processes by which knowledge requests are examined, information assembled, and knowledge returned to the requestor (Newman, 1996).

Most of us function in neither of these positions on a daily basis. If I assigned our function a title, it would be "knowledge technician," a technician being someone with "special and usually practical knowledge of a particular subject, especially one organized on scientific principles." Knowledge technicians do the actual knowledge work, using the means laid out by knowledge engineers to accomplish the goals set by knowledge managers. As librarians begin developing Intranets, deploying Notes applications, or moving into records management or other large database management techniques that are all corollaries to the knowledge management movement, we are only moving towards knowledge engineering, not knowledge management.

All our use of computers and new technologies, all our trappings of graduate training, professionalism, and core competencies—the whole movement from library to information center, still has not gotten most of us up to the corporate level of the knowledge engineers we commonly know as "systems." It has trapped us as technicians trying to educate users about more of our jobs than they want to know. It is the possibility that knowledge management will be the means to moving our jobs around the roadblock of the knowledge engineers to become a core function like financial management or operations management that has people in our profession saying, "Gee, I need to know about this," even if nothing they read comes close to the reality of their own short-staffed, GroupWare-less, paper-oriented companies that never hire management consultants.

Knowledge Management will not succeed if there are no workers and managers whose primary duties involve gathering and editing knowledge from those who have it, paving the way for the operation of knowledge networks, and setting up and managing knowledge technology infrastructures (Davenport, 1997).

Knowledge technologist is not a role I'm denigrating. This new role is valuable to our employers, to our profession, and to us personally. I'm just not convinced that it's a step up in the corporate hierarchy. To many in our field, it seems axiomatic that knowledge work is a step up for us, and that we will be tapped as candidates to guide others in our organizations in the transition to a knowledge culture. To understand how tenuous this possibility is, ask yourself, "Who will be a knowledge worker? The CIO and the Webmaster? The people formerly known as information professionals? Or everyone, from the sales force to the secretaries, now accessing internal data on their desktops?" If your answer is anything less than "everyone," you are out of step with the vendors and theorists driving this trend.

Unless we can insinuate ourselves into the management structure of knowledge management, we will lose a position that ought to be our birthright. However, I have yet to see the professional literature that addresses what knowledge management means below the corporate management level, which concentrates on professionalizing what we already do in the context of knowledge management, rather than trying to leverage knowledge management into making us a different profession.

References

Artz, J. (1997, Third Quarter). The Ghost of Socrates. *Strategy and Business*, vol. 1, no. 8, pp. 4-6.

Ash, J. (1997, August). State of Knowledge Management Practice Among Early Adopters. *Knowledge Inc.*

Bates, M. E. (1997, Fall). Information Audits: What Do We Know and When Do We Know It? *Library Management Briefings*, online at: www.libraryspecialists.com.

Berkman, R. (1997, September). The Steps to Take for Conducting an Information Audit. *Information Advisor Knowledge Management Quarterly Supplement*, vol. 1, no. 3, pp. 1-4.

Cortez, E., Kazlauskas, E. (1996, Spring). Information Policy Audit: A Case Study of an Organizational Analysis Tool. *Special Libraries*, pp. 85-88.

Davenport, T., DeLong, D., Beers, M. (1998, Winter). Successful Knowledge Management Projects. *Sloan Management Review*, pp. 43-57.

Davenport, T. (1997, June 15). Known Evils: Common Pitfalls of Knowledge Management. *CIO*, pp. 34-36.

Davenport, T. (1997, First Quarter). Some Principles of Knowledge Management. *Strategy and Business*, online at: www.bus.utexas.edu/kman/kmprin.htm.

Knapp, E. (1997, March 17). Know-How's Not Easy: How to Keep Knowledge Management from Flickering Out. *Computerworld Leadership Series*, vol. 3, no. 3, pp. 2-11.

Murray, P. (1998). New Language for New Leverage: The Terminology of Knowledge Management, online at: www.ktic.com/topic6/13_TERM1.HTM.

Newman, B. (1996). Knowledge Management vs. Knowledge Engineering, online at: http://revolution.3-cities.com/~bonewman/kmvske.htm.

Rutledge, J. (1997, April 7). You're A Fool If You Buy This. In *Is Intellectual Capital the New Wealth, or the Latest Consulting Wank? Forbes ASAP*, online at: www.forbes.com/asap/97/0407/042.htm.

Special Libraries Association. (No date). Measuring Intellectual Capital, online at: www.sla.org/membership/irc/knowledg.html.

Stuart, Ann. (1997, June 1). Five Uneasy Pieces, Part Two: Knowledge Management. *CIO.*

Seuss, David. (1998, October 13). Remarks made during CEO panel presentation. Online World, Washington D.C., October 12-14, 1998.

CHAPTER 6

Information Services and Productivity: A Backgrounder

Michael E. D. Koenig

Dean

Long Island University

INTRODUCTION

A good operational description of knowledge management is the deliberate modification of an organization to improve its information and knowledge creation and sharing. In short, knowledge management improves an organization's information environment in order to improve organizational performance and productivity. While knowledge management is too recent for any rigorous analyses of its success, there is extensive but very scattered literature on the relationship between the information services and information environment of an organization and the productivity of that organization. When that scattered literature is analyzed, it argues strongly that there is a positive relationship between the provision of information and information services with organizational productivity, and that organizations substantially under-invest in information services. Indeed, knowledge management can be seen as the logical response to that awareness. This chapter will review the state of our knowledge and the relationship between the information environment and organizational productivity, and attempt to extract from that knowledge some lessons and directions for knowledge management.

INFORMATION SERVICES AND PRODUCTIVITY: A BACKGROUND

A major factor in implementing a knowledge management system is making a convincing case for it. Knowledge management is too new to have any substantive documentation as to its efficacy, other than the purely anecdotal. There is, however, a scattered but substantial body of literature already existing on the relationship between the provision of information support and organizational productivity. That literature is remarkably consistent in showing a positive relationship between the provision of information services and organizational productivity. More than that, it reveals characteristics of the information environment that are conducive to organizational productivity. Thus, the literature can serve both as a justification for knowledge management and as a guide to the factors to consider in designing and implementing knowledge management systems.

The relationship between the information environment of an organization and its productivity is an important one, but it is an exceedingly difficult phenomenon to quantify. Productivity and effectiveness themselves are difficult things to measure and evaluate, particularly in a context relevant to knowledge management. Across the spectrum of blue-collar work to white-collar work, from traditional production work to knowledge work, it is the knowledge work for which it is hardest to measure or evaluate productivity, and it is precisely the knowledge workers who are the most likely participants in knowledge management. If it is difficult to measure productivity and effectiveness, it is even more difficult to measure the effect of something upon productivity and effectiveness. This is particularly the case when, as in the case of information support services, the relationship is loose and indirect, and occurs amidst numerous other factors (a statistician would call them confounding variables) that can and do also have an effect.

Most of the literature on the relationship between an organization's information environment and its productivity is episodic snapshot reporting, of the sort that is reported in trade journals to the effect that mega corporation introduced _____ (you fill in the blank) and programmer productivity, or customer satisfaction, or _____ increased threefold. Such material is not only highly suspect (the failures never get reported) but it is only temporarily useful. Nevertheless, there is a non-trivial body of literature that addresses this topic in a fashion that has some permanent utility. The literature is, however, scattered and even somewhat obscure, as a glance at the bibliography to this piece will reveal. One reason for that scatter is that the topic is so very interdisciplinary; it engages the interest of economists, librarians, engineers, social scientists, research administrators, and others. This chapter will try to recapitulate that literature briefly, summarize its major themes and findings, and analyze them for lessons to be applied to knowledge management.

Studies Attempting to Calculate the Value of Information Services

Perhaps the most obvious way to demonstrate the worth of libraries and information services is to attempt to derive a value for the information services. The seminal work on attempting to value and evaluate the effect of providing information services was conducted by Margaret Graham and Ben Weil at the Exxon Research Center in the mid-1970s (Weil, 1980). Like much of the work in this field, this article first appeared in an internal technical report. Fortunately, however, it was picked up by Eugene Jackson (1980) and included in his book *Special Librarianship, A New Reader*. However, the fact that it never appeared in this sort of venue, the journal literature, where one would expect to see important new findings, was a major missed opportunity.

The Exxon findings were new and dramatic. The study built on previous research in user studies, but was novel in its attempt to extrapolate and quantify the effect the services provided. The study participants (Exxon researchers) logged information-impact events on twenty randomly selected days. The participants reported that sixty-two percent of these events were beneficial, and in two percent of the cases they were able to estimate the value of the benefit quantitatively. Basing their analysis on only that two percent, assigning no value to the remaining sixty percent of the beneficial impacts, and subtracting the cost of the researcher's time spent in gathering information from the benefits, the authors concluded that the observable benefits were still eleven times greater than the cost of providing external literature information services to the Exxon research community. And that, one can conclude, is a lower bound for benefits, based as it is on only a small percentage of the beneficial outcomes.

A much larger study, using similar techniques was conducted in the late 1970s on NASA's information services (Mogavero, 1978). This study, however, was conducted on a much broader scale than the one at Exxon. A stratified sampling procedure was used to elucidate data about the use and impact of seven different NASA information products and services. Respondents were asked three basic questions: 1) What was the nature of the consequent utility (termed "application mode") of the use of the information source? (Responses to question 1 were classified as: 0—not relevant or no application; 1—information use only; 2—improved products or processes; 3—new products or processes.); 2) (If the response was application mode 2 or 3) What were the estimated benefits likely to be achieved or costs likely to be saved? 3) What was the probability of accomplishing those benefits or cost savings? For each of the seven services, the study reports: the probability for "application modes" 2 and 3; the unit cost (to NASA) for the information transaction; the cost to the user; and the expected net benefit (likely benefit x probability) per transaction.

Unfortunately, the study did not aggregate the data and failed to draw the salient conclusions that could and should have been drawn. Working from the published data, the aggregate can be extrapolated as follows: The cost to NASA for providing the information service over the five-year period 1971-1976 was $14.3 million ($2.9 million per year), and the expected benefit was $191 million ($28 million per year), while the time expended by the user was valued at $82 million ($16.5 million per year). The ratio between expected benefits and NASA costs is 13:1. The author, Mogavero, recommends that user cost be subtracted from the expected benefit in calculating a cost-benefit ratio (the same technique as that used in the Exxon study). Thus,

$$\text{Cost-benefit ratio} = \frac{\text{Gross estimated benefit-Gross user cost}}{\text{NASA production cost}}$$

Calculated this way, the cost-benefit ratio is 7.6 to 1. While not quite as dramatic as the Exxon results, this result is still very compelling. Note that the methodology that asks for both the anticipated benefit and the likelihood of achieving that benefit (in effect a deflator index) is a cautious and conservative one.

One can argue that the formula used is not the appropriate one, and that from the organization's perspective, the salient ratio is that between benefit and cost (benefit foregone). (See the article by Bickner (1983) for further discussion of this point.) Therefore, from the organization's perspective, the formula should be:

$$\text{Cost-benefit ratio} = \frac{\text{Gross estimated benefit}}{\text{NASA production cost} + \text{Gross user cost}}$$

which yields:

$$\frac{\$191 \text{ million}}{\$14.3 \text{ million} + \$82 \text{ million}}$$

or 1.98 as the ratio (effectively two to one) of benefit to cost. Note, however, the very dramatic internal ratio of the users' expended cost of accessing information versus the cost of providing information services, a ratio of almost six to one. This implies that there is substantial opportunity for systems or service enhancements that diminish user costs and, thereby, enhance the cost-benefit ratio. It also points out that the nominal cost of providing information services is only the tip of the iceberg. In this case, for every dollar expended in providing information services, the user in using those services spent another six dollars.

Using a related methodology, Mason and Sassone (1978) analyzed the operations of an information analysis center (IAC). In this technique, the investigators, while working with the users, tried to estimate only the employee's time saved, ignoring all other benefits achieved, and then assigned value by calculating the burdened salary cost of the employee's time. This technique was applied to an unidentified IAC, and the net present value of the time saved exceeded the net present value of the invested resources and operating cost by four percent. Mason and Sassone call this technique a "lower bound cost benefit" because the calculations are based solely on the user's time and costs, and no attempt is made to estimate either any larger benefits to the organization or any societal benefits.

A very important recent study is that done by Marshall (1993) on the impact of the special library on corporate decision making. The study involved is important not only for its findings, but also because it involved financial service firms, a sector for which there was previously very little research. Managers of financial service firms in Toronto, Canada, were the subjects of the study. The methodology was similar to that discussed below in Marshall's (1992) Rochester study. Eighty-four percent of the respondents agreed that the information led to better-informed decisions, and seventy-three percent said that it gave them greater confidence in their decision or recommendation. Ten percent said that they had definitely and forty-four percent said they had probably handled the situation differently as a result of the information received. Almost two-thirds, sixty-three percent, of the respondents said that the information contributed toward the ability to exploit a new business opportunity. Of these, seven percent reported that the information helped them to a "great extent" not merely some extent or a considerable extent. Comparable percentages for improving relations with a client were sixty-two percent and six percent, for improving a policy and procedure were thirty-nine percent and two percent, and for proceeding to the next step on a project or task were seventy-three percent and seven percent.

The most common constructive criticism made by the respondents was that librarians and information officers needed more industry-specific expertise, and needed to respond more successfully to open-ended questions that required analysis, as well as to straightforward factual questions.

Valuation methodologies of this general type have been most fully developed and most widely applied by King Research, Inc. For many years, their work either resided in obscure places such as technical reports or the proceedings of arcane conferences, or was proprietary and, therefore, generally unavailable. Much of it was only made available through Koenig's (1990A) ARIST chapter. Fortunately, Griffiths and King (1993) have recently compiled much of this work into one very useful volume.

The methodology first analyzes the value of the information services to the organization in terms of the value of the time (as measured by salary and overhead) that the users are willing to expend on those services (Griffiths and King, 1990; King and Griffiths, 1988; King & Roderer, 1979). This is taken as an indication of the organization's willingness to pay for the services. With this methodology, the cost to the user, as indicated by time the user spends in accessing information, is treated as an indicator of implicit value, rather than as a debit to savings or value achieved as in the three studies above. To be sure, such a measure is an indicator of the motivation to seek information, but as King points out, it seems to be fairly constant across organizations (King et al., 1981; Roderer et al., 1983) and, therefore, not likely to be very sensitive to the quality of service provided. In five different organizations studied, the following ratios were reported:

Ratios of Willingness to Pay (measured in terms of user professionals' time) to Nominal Cost of Providing Information Services (Koenig, 1990 A)	
Institution	Ratio
Air Products and Chemicals	2.5 to 1
Kodak	4.3 to 1
AT&T Bell Labs	4.4 to 1
PSE&G (Major Public Utility)	19 to 1
U.S. Department of Energy	26 to 1

The spread of ratios is very wide, an order of magnitude in fact, but in all cases the value of the service as measured by the time users were willing to spend using it was very substantial. If, as King (1988) points out, the time that information workers spend information seeking is relatively constant across different organizations, then the numbers above may also serve as an indicator of the intensity of the information services provided. Note that Poppel (1982), in his study of business organizations' managers, reports a very similar proportion of time spent (twenty-one percent as opposed to twenty-five percent) in information seeking. Note also the fascinating phenomenon that the more competitive the domain in which the organization competes, the more the organization invests in information services in proportion to simply relying on the employees' time and effort.

In a second phase, value is attached to the information services by calculating the additional cost that would be incurred if there was no in-house information service and the documents had to be obtained elsewhere. The values calculated for this approach were (Koenig, 1990A):

Ratios of Cost to Use Alternative Services to Nominal Cost of Providing Information Services	
Institution	Ratio
Air Products and Chemicals	2.6 to 1
Kodak	2.7 to 1
AT&T Bell Labs	3.6 to 1
PSE&G (Major Public Utility)	8 to 1

Again, the ratios are all highly favorable.

Based on the observations stating that professionals tend to spend a relatively fixed proportion of their time on information seeking and reading (a homeostatic function?), the methodology calculates the number of readings that would have to be foregone by the requirement to spend more time in information seeking if no in-house information service was available. From this figure one can derive a value of the savings (or research cost avoidance) that would be lost or incurred if the library or information center did not exist. Knowledge workers surveyed at each institution estimate the savings (or benefit) achieved by reading. However, these estimates are applied only to the transactions foregone, not to all transactions.

The intermediary results from a number of studies are summarized by Griffiths and King (1990) as:

Proportion of Readings at which Various Levels of Savings (Benefit) Are Reported to be Achieved	
Savings ($)	Proportion (%)
0	73.9
1-11	12.5
11-100	3.9
101-1,000	4.2
1,001-10,000	3.4
>10,000	2.1

The value calculated at specific institutions for this approach were:

Ratios of Research Cost Avoidance to the Nominal Cost of Providing Information Services (Koenig, 1990 A)	
Institution	Ratio
Air Products and Chemicals	4.8 to 1
Kodak	14 to 1
AT&T Bell Labs	16 to 1
PSE&G (Major Public Utility)	17 to 1
U.S. Department of Energy	25 to 1

Calculated over the various studies, Griffiths and King (1988) report the following data for the value of reading an item:

- $385 for reading a journal article
- $1,160 for reading a book

- $706 for reading an internal technical document

King Research, Inc. also examined the value of the energy database (EDB) of the U.S. Department of Energy (DOE) (King et al., 1982, 1984). The apparent value—the burdened salary cost of the time spent using the database—was approximately $500 million, out of a total research budget of $5.8 billion (including principal users of the database such as contractors, not just DOE). The estimated total savings attributed to those readings were approximately $13 billion. Thus,

Generation		Information	Future
of	+	Processing	Savings to DOE
Information		and Use	Scientists
$5.3 billion	+	$500 million	$13 billion

This can be interpreted as an investment of $5.8 billion, yielding a return on investment of approximately 2.2 to 1.

Using the research cost avoidance approach discussed above, and assuming that there were to be no energy databases, there would be a loss of over 300,000 searches and almost 2.5 million readings (a value equivalent to $3 billion). If the current research and development (R&D) budget is $5.8 billion, then without the EDB, an R&D budget of $8.8 billion would theoretically be required to maintain the same level of output. That is equivalent to saying that the EDB increases organizational productivity by fifty-two percent.

Griffiths and King estimate that, if one extrapolates these techniques broadly, the readings by all scientists and engineers in the United States resulted in savings of about $300 billion for the year 1984 alone (Griffiths and King, 1985). They admit that this figure sounds enormous, but they ask what could scientists and engineers accomplish without access to information? They calculate that the actual time value that scientists and engineers spend in reading exceeds $20 billion per year, based on an average burdened salary, which is in effect a ratio of fifteen to one for benefit to cost invested in reading.

The calculation of cost-benefit figures is a complex and disputatious exercise, of rather more subtlety than is often realized. The article by Bickner (1983) on "Concepts of Economic Cost" is an excellent analysis of the issues and of some of the fallacies to avoid. The calculation of cost-benefit figures where a principle commodity is information, a commodity particularly ill addressed by conventional economics, is even more fraught with peril.

The caveat above not withstanding, the magnitude of the effects reported in these studies is quite striking, but even more so is the very high degree of their consistency, both across different techniques and across different cases. This creates a high degree of confidence that the findings are not mere artifacts, but that they reflect a genuine phenomenon.

A possible criticism of the approach of that using the value of the time expended by users on information gathering and information services as a measure of the organization's perception of the value to the organization of information services may be a bit too simplistic. First, there is little evidence that organizations make any conscious decision about, or relating to, the amount of time their employees spend informing themselves, at least pre-knowledge management this was true. Second, the evidence seems to indicate that knowledge workers, whether administrators (Poppel, 1982) or researchers (King et al., 1981), seem to be very consistent in spending twenty to twenty-five percent of their time in information seeking. This phenomenon may very well be one over which management has very little control and may, therefore, only partially reflect management's values, perceptions, or desires. This consistency of time that professionals spend on information seeking is consistent with the notion that individuals don't necessarily persevere to the conclusion or to the correct information. Instead, they weigh benefits and opportunity costs, and cease information seeking when they expect the benefits of further pursuit of information begin to be outweighed by the opportunity costs of not diverting their attention to other aspects of their job. The typical intuitive perception of the threshold at which opportunity costs begin to outweigh further benefits is at twenty to twenty-five percent of one's time spent information seeking. The consistency of this percentage implies that in very few situations do professionals receive adequate information. If they did, we would find companies or industries where information seeking ceases because adequate results were achieved at some level below twenty to twenty-five percent. We don't see that phenomenon.

That observation can be turned around into an argument of some considerable appeal and strength. If knowledge workers are going to spend a significant proportion of their time on information seeking, whether management likes it or not, then it is administratively foolish not to provide the library and information services that will leverage and make more productive use of that time. If someone's employees were going to spend twenty to twenty-five percent of their work time growing corn or rice, regardless of company policy, it would be foolish not to provide the tools that would make their effort more productive. The same logic equally applies to employees' information-seeking habits. If employees are working with less than optimal information, as certainly seems to be the case, then there should be substantial leveraging efforts made to provide a more effective information environment. It is senseless for professionals to spend an even greater percentage of their time information seeking when the opportunity costs of their other functions are too high; the better alternative is to create the information and knowledge environment that increases the effectiveness of their efforts.

ECONOMETRIC CALCULATIONS

Some attempts have been made to calculate the overall effect of information as a factor (in the mathematical sense) in industrial productivity. Hayes and Erickson (1982) used the Cobb-Douglas production function to estimate the value added by information services. In the basic Cobb-Douglas formula, the value of goals and services sold is calculated to be the product of a constant multiplied by the values of the classic economic inputs, new materials, labor, and capital, each raised to a different power (exponent). The exponents are solved by seeing which best fit the aggregate of a number of separate cases. Hayes and Erickson added the value of information services and calculated the value added (V) in manufacturing industries as a function of labor (L), capital (K), purchase of information services (I), and purchase of other intermediate goods and services (X). Their equation takes the form:

$$V = AL^a K^b I^c X^d \text{, or}$$
$$\text{Log } V = \text{Log } A + a \text{ Log } L + b \log K + c \log I + d \log X$$

(where A, a, b, c, d are constants). Braunstein (1985) elaborated on this approach using the constant elasticity of substitution (CES) and the translog production functions, both of which make less rigid assumptions about the substitutability between factors other than one. In all cases, the marginal product of information was at least 2.34. That is, every unit of information service input yielded at least 2.34 units of output value. Not only is there striking consistency in these results, Braunstein argues, but they indicate substantial under-investment in the purchase of information. A marginal product of 2.34 or better is unusually high. Also striking is the similarity of these numbers to the 2.2 to 1 value for the return on information investment calculated by King Research, Inc. in their analysis of the value of the EDB, and the 1.98 to 1 reported by Mogavero (1978) in his analysis of NASA's information services, values that were derived in an entirely independent fashion.

INFORMATION PROVISION AND THE DELIVERY OF HEALTH CARE

A small but very important cluster of articles on the impact of information services on the delivery of health care has emerged in the last few years. There are three key papers in this cluster. The first was a study by King (1987) of health professionals, physicians, nurses, and allied health professionals at eight hospitals in the Chicago area. Each participant was asked to fill out a questionnaire relating to his or her next instance of using the library to seek information related to patient care. Nearly two-thirds of the respondents reported that the information provided by the library would definitely or probably result in their handling that case differently. Marshall (1992) conducted a more elaborate study among fifteen hospitals in the Rochester, New York, area. Of the 448 physicians randomly sampled, 208 responded with useable, completed questionnaires. Of those, eighty percent said that they probably or definitely handled some aspect of patient care differently than they would have if they had not used the library. In forty-five percent of the cases, that change involved drug therapy; in nineteen percent, it resulted in reduced hospital stay; in twelve percent, the avoidance of hospital admissions; in forty-nine percent, the avoidance of additional tests or procedures. In nineteen percent of the cases, the information had a possible effect on patient mortality. Another study by Klein et al. (1994) analyzed cases about which the physician had requested a MEDLINE search and compared them to other cases within the same diagnosis related group (DRG). Not surprisingly, the cases for which MEDLINE searches were requested were found to have a higher severity of illness. In addition, a significant relationship was found between doing a MEDLINE search early in the patient's hospital stay and a reduced length of stay and reduced hospital expense.

These studies are not only important in that the provision of library and information services results in better patient care, but also because, from an administrative and political point of view, there is strong evidence that it results in more cost-effective patient care (shorter hospital stays, avoidance of hospital admission, reduced diagnostic tests, etc.). There are many ways to improve patient care by spending more money—but the argument that information services, and the use thereof, improve patient care and reduce costs may be almost unique.

CHARACTERISTICS OF THE INFORMATION ENVIRONMENT IN PRODUCTIVE ORGANIZATIONS

There have been a number of studies regarding the characteristics of productive companies, studies that shed light on the relationships between information services and organizational productivity. A very consistent thread in these studies is the importance of information access and information services.

In one of the more rigorous studies Orpen (1985) examined productivity in R&D intensive electronics/instrumentation organizations. He analyzed the behavior of research managers as perceived by the research staff, and found that in the more productive organizations (as defined by rates of growth and return on assets), the managers were perceived to be significantly more characterized by the following three behaviors: 1) they routed literature and references to scientific and technical staff; 2) they directed their staff to use scientific and technical information (STI) and to purchase STI services; and 3) they encouraged publication of results and supported professional visits and continuing education. Equally striking was the finding that information-related management behavior tended strongly to discriminate between high-performance and low-performance companies, while non-information-related management behavior did not.

In reviewing the work on R&D innovation, Goldhar et al. (1976) concluded that there are six characteristics of environments that are conducive to technological innovations. Of the six, four are clearly related to the information environment, specifically: 1) easy access to information by individuals; 2) free flow of information both into and out of the organizations; 3) rewards for sharing, seeking, and using "new" externally developed information sources; and 4) encouragement of mobility and interpersonal contacts. The other two characteristics are rewards for taking risks and for accepting and adapting to change. These findings and their implicit prioritization (the top three of Goldhar's six factors are all information-related factors) are striking in that—except for the work of Allen (1977) who specifically looks at information flow within R&D organizations and who found that more productive teams and individuals had more diverse information contacts outside the project team than did the less productive teams and individuals—none of the work reviewed by Goldhar comes from the traditional areas of information science or communications. Instead, it comes almost entirely from the literature of economics and management. Interestingly and frustratingly, both Orpen (1985) and Goldhar et al. (1976) fail to note or comment upon the predominance of information-related factors.

A consistent macrotheme in this literature is that of the link between productivity and diversity of information contacts. Koenig (1982, 1983A & B, 1990B, 1992B) studied the relationship between research productivity and the information environment, using the pharmaceutical industry as the setting. The measure of productivity used was the number of approved new drugs per research dollar expended, refined further by weighting in regard to: 1) whether or not the FDA regarded the drug as an important therapeutic advance; 2) the drug's chemical novelty; and 3) the filing company's patent position with regard to the drug, an indication of where the bulk of the research was done. Research productivity, thus measured, differs among large pharmaceutical companies by more than an order of magnitude. The more-productive companies are characterized by:

- Greater openness to outside information
- Less concern with protecting proprietary information
- Greater information systems development effort
- Greater end-user use of information systems and more encouragement of browsing and serendipity
- Greater technical and subject sophistication of the information services staff
- Relative unobtrusiveness of managerial structure and status indicators in the R&D environment (Koenig, 1992B)

Subsequent events gave this work particular credibility. A classic problem in looking at correlates of excellent performance is that this year's apparent stars often look rather lackluster a short time later, and that in turn casts doubt on the influences drawn from those stars. An example was the fate of Peters and Waterman's *In Search of Excellence* (1982). In this case, the opposite is true. For example, Koenig's assignment of the number one rank to Pfizer seemed somewhat dubious at the time in comparison to apparently more glamorous companies like Merck or Syntex, but now given Viagra and Pfizer's rating on the street, it seems prescient if not brilliant. Similarly, when American Home Products merged their previously separate pharmaceutical divisions, Wyeth and Ayerst, many observers were surprised that the much smaller Ayerst emerged on top, but it is entirely consistent with their comparative R&D performance rank as calculated by

Koenig—(Ayerst number six, Wyeth number nineteen). The fate of Smith Kline, acquired by Beecham (unranked, as the study examined only companies doing the bulk of the R&D in the United States), who skillfully and tactfully called it a merger, is also entirely consistent with Smith Kline's rank, a lowly seventeen.

The findings above are part of a larger body of literature, which finds that contact with external information sources and diversity of information sources are key factors in successful innovation. Project Sappho (Scientific Activity Predictor from Patterns with Heuristic Origins) conducted by the University of Sussex (1972) paired successful and failed attempts at innovation in a similar industry segment to determine what led to success. One of the major conclusions was that "successful innovators make more effective use of outside technology and scientific advice, even though they perform more of the work in-house. They have better contacts with the scientific community, not necessarily in general, but in the specific areas concerned."

There are three particularly good review pieces in this area. Utterback (1971, 1974) reviewed a number of studies on innovation, principally from management literature, and concluded, "In general, it appears that the greater the degree of communications between the firm and its environment at each stage of the process of innovation, other factors being equal, the more effective the firm will be in generating, developing, and implementing new technology." Wolek and Griffith (1974) reviewed the sociologically oriented literature on this topic and came to substantially the same conclusion. McConnell (1985), writing on how to improve productivity from an operational standpoint, and reviewing the literature in a less formal fashion, remarks: "Information flow, through both formal and informal networks, should be full and free—up, down, and across the organization. This requires continuous effort and attention. The more open and free communication existing in the organization, the greater the productivity."

Kanter (1982, 1983) conducted an extensive survey of innovations initiated by middle managers. From her findings, she made six major recommendations for structuring organizations to support creativity. One recommendation was: "a free and somewhat random flow of information." She further reports that to accomplish productive changes, three things the manager needs are "information, resources, and support," in that order (Kanter, 1982).

When examining the literature about what characterizes productive organizations, it is clear that not only does a consistent theme emerge of greater openness toward and greater access to information, both internal and external, but that information access related factors emerge in positions of very high priority in comparison to other factors under management control. Also striking, and very corroboratory in its implications, is that these findings are consistent whether the investigator or the literature reviewed is from the areas of library and information science, management science and economics, or sociology.

CHARACTERISTICS OF PRODUCTIVE INFORMATION WORKERS

There is also a large, related body of literature on characteristics of productive information workers, and the findings are quite consistent with and supportive of those above. In a large-scale study of information use at Oak Ridge National Laboratories in the United States, King Research, Inc. (Griffiths and King, 1990) documented a significant and positive relationship between the productivity of professionals and the amount of time spent in reading. Several indicators were used to measure productivity, including: number of formal records (for example, of research, of project management); number of formal publications; number of proposals or research plans; number of formal oral presentations; and number of times the professionals were consulted for advice. All were found to be positively correlated with the amount of reading done.

Mondschein (1990) studied the productivity of researchers in several major corporations as measured by publishing activity, vis-à-vis their use of automated current-awareness services or selective dissemination of information (SDI). He found that scientists who use SDI frequently were more productive than their colleagues who either do not use such services or use them only infrequently. Further, the productive researchers were characterized by their use of a wider variety of information sources, particularly by the extent of their efforts to stay current and by their use of patent information sources.

Ginman (1988), in studying the information use of CEOs, observes a very different information style of CEOs in companies in the revival phase as compared with those in the stagnation phase. The former are more extroverted in their information use style, and have an information culture that is characterized by greater width and depth, with greater use of external information sources and greater ability to pinpoint and recall specific items of information input, such as specific authors and articles.

Chakrabarti and Rubenstein (1976), in studying NASA innovations adopted by industry, conclude that quality of information as perceived by the recipient is a major factor in the adoption of innovations. This is an extension to the high-tech environment of the classic work by Rogers (1983) on innovation and change agentry (use of agents who deliberately introduce beneficial change), most of which was done in relatively low-tech situations, and is consistent with Rogers' findings.

Johnston and Gibbons (1975) examined the characteristics of information that contributed to the resolution of technical problems with some thirty ongoing innovations in British industry. They found that: 1) information obtained from the literature contributed as much as information obtained from personal contact; 2) different sources were selectively used to acquire different types of information; and 3) a wide range of information sources is important.

The studies reported above are typical of the larger body of research findings. The consistent theme is that more productive individuals make greater access to and greater use of information services.

CONCLUSION

There is very scattered but remarkably consistent and very cohesive literature that documents that there is a clear relationships between the information environment of an organization and its productivity, particularly research productivity. Since a good operational definition of knowledge management is the deliberate introduction of an improved and more effective information environment, what we know about this relationship is clearly relevant to knowledge management.

What Conclusions Can We Draw from This Body of Work?

1. Information flow and openness to information, both internal and external, correlate positively with productivity in information intensive organizations.
2. Management and the scholars examining organizational effectiveness have, until recently, demonstrated an extraordinary obliviousness toward the importance of the information environment to organization productivity.
3. Most organizations substantially under-invest in improving their information environment.
4. Generally, investment in the information environment and information support services consistently has had a substantial leveraging effect.
5. Most professionals receive less than satisfactory information and information services, and are constrained by opportunity costs to accept that. The way to increase the productivity is not to spend more time on

information seeking, but rather to increase the effectiveness of their information and knowledge seeking, hence, better knowledge management.

6. Unduly emphasizing the proprietariness of information tends to be counterproductive, and the more information intensive the field, the more this is true.

7. The culture of the organization is important, and the more egalitarian the culture, the greater the sharing of information and knowledge.

8. End users use of information systems should be encouraged, as this correlates with organizational productivity.

9. Information professionals need to be industry and context savvy, and provide analysis (knowledge) as well as information.

In summary, the business community very much needs knowledge management.

References

* Allen, Thomas J. 1977. *Managing the Flow of Technology: Technology Transfer and the Dissemination of Technological Information within the R&D Organization.* Cambridge, MA: MIT Press, p. 320.

Bawden, David. 1986. "Information Systems and the Stimulation of Creativity." *Journal of Information Science.* 12(5): 203-216.

Bearman, Toni Carbo; Guynup, Polly; Milevski, Sandra N. 1985. "Information and Productivity." *Journal of the American Society for Information Science.* November; 36(6): 369-375.

* Bickner, Robert E. 1983. "Concepts of Economic Cost." In: King, Donald W.; Roderer, Nancy K.; Olsen, Harold A., eds. *Key Papers in the Economics of Information Systems.* White Plains, NY: Knowledge Industry Publications, Inc. for the American Society for Information Science, pp. 107-146.

Braunstein, Yale M. 1985. "Information as a Factor of Production: Substitutability and Productivity." *Information Society.* 3(3): 261-273.

Chakrabarti, Alok K.; Rubenstein, Albert H. 1976. "Interorganization Transfer of Technology: A Study of Adoption of NASA Innovations." *IEEE Transactions on Engineering Management.* February; EM-23 (1): 20-34.

Cronin, Blaise; Gudim, Mairi. 1986. "Information and Productivity: A Review of Research." *International Journal of Information Management.* June; 6(2): 85-101.

Drucker, Peter F. 1994. "The Age of Social Transformation." *The Atlantic Monthly.* November; 274(11): 53-80.

Ginman, Mariam. 1988. "Information Culture and Business Performance." *IATUL Quarterly.* 2(2): 93-106.

Goldhar, Joel D.; Bragaw, Louis K.; Schwartz, Jule J. 1976. "Information Flows, Management Styles, and Technological Innovation." *IEEE Transactions on Engineering Management.* February; EM-23(1): 51-61.

* Griffiths, Jose-Marie. 1982. "The Value of Information and Related Systems, Products and Services." In: Williams, Martha E., ed. *Annual Review of Information Science and Technology,* vol. 17. White Plains, NY: Knowledge Industry Publications, Inc. for the American Society for Information Science, pp. 269-284.

Griffiths, Jose-Marie; King, Donald W. 1985. *The Contribution Libraries Make to Organization Productivity.* Rockville, MD: King Research, Inc., p. 12 OCLC: 16389522. Available with permission from: King Research, Inc., P.O. Box 572, Oak Ridge, TN, 37831.

Griffiths, Jose-Marie; King, Donald W. 1988. *An Information Audit of Public Service Electric and Gas Company (N.J.) Libraries and Information Resources: Executive Summary and Conclusions.* Rockville, MD: King Research, Inc., Spring; p. 15.

Griffiths, Jose-Marie; King, Donald W. 1990. *A Manual on the Evaluation of Information Centers and Services.* Oak Ridge, TN: King Research, Inc., p. 370. (Submitted to the North Atlantic Treaty Organization, Advisory Group for Aerospace Research and Development). Available with permission from: King Research, Inc., P.O. Box 572, Oak Ridge, TN, 37831; and King, Donald W., Griffiths, Jose-Marie *An Information Audit of Eastman Kodak Company and InfoSource*, Rockville, MD: King Research, Inc., December 1989 (proprietary).

* Griffiths, Jose-Marie; King, Donald W. 1993. *Special Libraries: Increasing the Information Edge*, Washington, D.C., Special Libraries Association.

Hayes, Robert M.; Erickson, T. 1982. "Added Value as a Function of Purchases of Information Services." *Information Society.* 1(4): 307-338.

Johnston, Ron; Gibbons, Michael. 1975. "Characteristics of Information Usage in Technical Innovation." *IEEE Transactions on Engineering Management.* February; EM-22(1): 27-34.

Kanter, Rosabeth Moss. 1982. "The Middle Manager as Innovator." *Harvard Business Review.* July/August; 60(4): 95-105.

Kanter, Rosabeth Moss. 1983. *The Change Masters: Innovations for Productivity in the American Corporation.* New York, NY: Simon and Schuster, p. 432.

King, Donald W.; Roderer, Nancy K. 1979. "Information Transfer Cost/Benefit Analysis." In: *Information and Industry: Proceedings of the North Atlantic Treaty Organization, Advisory Group for Aerospace Research and Development (AGARD)*, Technical Information Panel's Specialists' Meeting; 1978 October 18-19; Paris, France. Neuilly-sure-Seine, France: AGARD, 1979 January; pp. 8:1-8:10. (AGARD CP-246).

King, Donald W.; McDonald, Dennis D.; Roderer, Nancy K. 1981. *Scientific Journals in the United States: Their Production, Use, and Economics.* Stroudsburg, PA: Hutchinson Ross Publishing Co., p. 319.

King, Donald W.; Griffiths, Jose-Marie; Roderer, Nancy K.; Wiederkehr, Robert R.V. 1982. *Value of the Energy Data Base.* Rockville, MD: King Research, Inc., October; p. 81. (Submitted to the U.S. Department of Energy, Technical Information Center.) NTIS: DE82014250; OCLC: 9004666; DOE: OR11232-1. Available with permission from King Research, Inc., P.O. Box 572, Oak Ridge, TN, 37831.

King, Donald W.; Griffiths, Jose-Marie; Sweet, Ellen A.; Wiederkehr, Robert R.V. 1984. *A Study of the Value of Information and the Effect on Value of Intermediary Organizations, Timeliness of Services and Products, and Comprehensiveness of the EDB*, 3 volumes in 1. Rockville, MD: King Research, Inc., (Submitted to the U.S. Department of Energy, Office of Scientific and Technical Information). NTIS: DE85003670; OCLC: 11712088; DOE: NBM-1078. Available with permission from King Research, Inc., P.O. Box 572, Oak Ridge, TN 37831.

* King, David N. 1987. "The Contribution of Hospital Library Services to Clinical Care: A Study in Eight Hospitals." *Bulletin of the Medical Library Association.* October; 75(4): 291-301.

King, Donald W.; Griffiths, Jose-Marie. 1988. "Evaluating the Effectiveness of Information Use." In: *Evaluating the Effectiveness of Information Centres and Services.* Material to support a lecture series presented under the sponsorship of the North Atlantic Treaty Organization, Advisory Group for Aerospace Research and Development (AGARD), Technical Information Panel and Research, and the Consultant and Exchange Programme. September 5-6, 8-9, 12-13; Luxembourg, France; Athens, Greece; Lisbon, Portugal. Neuilly-sur-Seine, France: AGARD, pp. 1:1-1:5.

* Klein, Michele S.; Ross, Faith V.; Adams, Deborah L.; Gilbert, Carole M. 1994. "Effect of Online Literature Searching on Length of Stay and Patient Care Costs." *Academic Medicine.* June; 69(6): 489-495.

Koenig, Michael E.D. 1982. "Determinants of Expert Judgement of Research Performance." *Scientometrics.* 4(5): 361-378.

Koenig, Michael E.D. 1983 A. "A Bibliometric Analysis of Pharmaceutical Research." *Research Policy.* February; 12(1): 15-36.

Koenig, Michael E.D. 1983B. "Bibliometric Indicators Versus Expert Opinion in Assessing Research Performance." *Journal of the American Society for Information Science.* March; 34(2): 136-145.

* Koenig, Michael E.D. 1990 A. "Information Services and Downstream Productivity." In: Williams, Martha E. ed. *Annual Review of Information Science and Technology,* vol. 25. New York, NY, Elsevier Science Publishers for the American Society for Information Science, pp. 55-86.

Koenig, Michael E.D. 1990 B. "The Information and Library Environment and the Productivity of Research." *Inspel.* 24(4): 157-167.

Koenig, Michael E.D. 1992 A. "The Importance of Information Services for Productivity Under-recognized and Under-invested." *Special Libraries.* Fall; 83(4): 199-210.

* Koenig, Michael E.D. 1992 B. "The Information Environment and the Productivity of Research." In Collier, H., ed. *Recent Advances in Chemical Information.* London, England: Royal Society of Chemistry, pp. 133-143.

* Marshall, Joanne G. 1993. *The Impact of the Special Library in Corporate Decision-Making.* Washington, D.C., Special Libraries Association.

* Marshall, Joanne G. 1992. "The Impact of the Hospital Library on Clinical Decision Making: The Rochester Study." *Bulletin of the Medical Library Association.* April; 80(2): 169-178.

Mason, Robert M.; Sassone, Peter G. 1978. "A Lower Bound Cost Benefit Model for Information Services." *Information Processing and Management.* 14(2): 71-83.

* McConnell, J. Douglas. 1985. "Productivity Improvements in Research and Development and Engineering in the United States." *Society of Research Administrators Journal.* Fall; 12(2): 5-14.

Mogavero, Louis N. 1978. "Transferring Technology to Industry through Information." In: *Information and Industry: Proceedings of the North Atlantic Treaty Organization, Advisory Group for Aerospace Research and Development (AGARD),* Technical Information Panel's Specialists' Meeting. 1978 October 18-19; Paris, France. Neiully-sur-Seine, France: AGARD, 1979 January; pp.14:1-14:6 (AGARD CP-246).

Mondschein, Lawrence G. 1990. "SDI Use and Productivity in the Corporate Research Environment." *Special Libraries.* Fall; 81(4): 265-279.

Orpen, Christopher. 1985. "The Effect of Managerial Distribution of Scientific and Technical Information on Company Performance." *R&D Management.* October; 15(40): 305-308.

Peters, Thomas J.; Waterman, Robert. 1982. *In Search of Excellence.* New York, NY: Harper & Row.

Poppel, Harvey L. 1982. "Who Needs the Office of the Future?" *Harvard Business Review.* November/December; 60(6): 146-155.

Roderer, Nancy K.; King, Donald W.; Brouard, Sandra E. 1983. *The Use and Value of Defense Technical Information Center Products and Services.* Rockville, MD: King Research, Inc., June; p. 115. (Submitted to the Defense Technical Information Center.) OCLC: 12987688, 11599947. Available with permission, from King Research, Inc., P.O. Box 572, Oak Ridge, TN, 37831.

Rogers, Everett M. 1983. *Diffusion of Innovations,* 3rd edition. New York, NY: Free Press, p. 453.

University of Sussex. Science Policy Research Unit. 1972. *Success and Failure in Industrial Innovation*. Report on Project Sappho. London, England: Center for the Study of Industrial Innovation, February; p. 37.

Utterback, James Milo. 1974. "Innovation in Industry and the Diffusion of Technology." *Science*. February 15; 183: 620-626.

Utterback, James Milo. 1971. "The Process of Technological Innovation within the Firm." *Academy of Management Journal*. March; 14: 75-88.

Weil, Ben H. 1980. "Benefits from Research Use of the Published Literature at the Exxon Research Center." In: Jackson, Eugene B., ed. *Special Librarianship: A New Reader*. Metuchen, N.J.: Scarecrow Press, pp. 586-594.

Wolek, Francis W.; Griffith, Belver C. 1974. "Policy and Informal Communications in Applied Science and Technology." *Science Studies*. July; 4 (4): 411-420.

*Key Papers

CHAPTER 7

Key Challenges Facing the Evolution of Knowledge Management

Mark Mazzie
Chief Knowledge Officer
Barrett International

INTRODUCTION

The recent emergence of knowledge management as a key component of the strategic planning process has forced senior executives across a wide variety of industries to develop methods of implementing knowledge sharing programs within their organizations. This chapter discusses issues that need to be addressed prior to introducing knowledge management (KM) and intellectual capital concepts within a corporation.

Increasingly, corporate strategists view KM as an organization's only long-term sustainable competitive advantage. Thus, as in any historical economic transformation, the market is witnessing an organized effort to identify and implement a standardized methodology that quantifies the value added via the management of a corporation's intellectual assets. The conversion from twentieth century emphasis on maximizing the benefits of an organization's fixed assets to ensuring that our human assets are fully utilized is causing a seismic shift in the way we manage.

The transformation from an industrial economy into the first half of the twenty-first century that will be dominated by the knowledge economy creates tremendous opportunities for those with enough foresight to comprehend the changes that must be instituted to exploit these new competitive strategies. Managers who fail to achieve maximum utility of their intellectual assets will find their organizations withered and increasingly irrelevant within the marketplace and the financial community.

The emergence of KM as a distinct management discipline has forced many who are active in the field to address challenges that are present with any newly defined and evolving method of assessing organizational and strategic effectiveness. These challenges include how to introduce employees to more productive methods of performing their day-to-day tasks, as well as how to measure the added value that KM brings to the bottom line.

As the world has evolved from an agrarian to an industrial society, the management of an organization's knowledge or the exploitation of employee expertise has played a key role in the development of creative and innovative industrial strategies. Further evolution from an industrial economy into what Lester Thurow calls the "knowledge economy" heightens the need for successful management of intellectual assets.

From the master-apprentice system of the sixteenth and seventeenth century to the current corporate university in which the transfer of employee knowledge is a primary driver in the development of competitive advantage, organizations have realized that their most important sustainable asset is the expertise and experience of their personnel. The recent emergence of KM as an identifiable initiative simply places a label on activity that has long been an informal part of every organization.

When a new management discipline or theory emerges, many executives who think the present way of doing things works quite well, run screaming for the exits in reaction to the prospect of once again living through reengineering, total quality management (TQM), or quality circles. Many of these movements, hawked by expensive consultants as the only way for senior management to keep their jobs, are simply the latest fad.

Industry leaders who developed KM programs that capture employee and customer knowledge have discovered that, far from being a fad, the latest developments in this field have placed a structure on previously scattered but highly useful efforts to improve a company's intellectual assets. One need only look at the market worth of companies like Microsoft and Coca-Cola to understand that the financial community is placing a significantly higher value on their intellectual assets than on fixed assets. This fact alone should make every corporate manager re-evaluate how he/she capitalizes on organizational assets.

If executives are not maximizing the value of their human capital much in the same manner they protect and exploit the value of fixed assets, the day will soon arrive when Wall Street regards their organizations as perennial corporate laggards. Try explaining to your shareholders that the reason your stock dropped is because senior management couldn't comprehend the value of its workforce and failed to fully exploit its most important asset.

ISSUES THAT NEED TO BE ADDRESSED

As with any newly defined corporate strategy, many of the senior managers that I've spoken with fully understand that although they need to address the issue of KM, there is no business plan or road map that can be followed. The most frequent comments I hear from CEOs regarding KM revolve around the following two issues:

- They've read enough about KM or intellectual capital to understand that their organization must begin to develop a plan to collect and disseminate employee knowledge. However, they have no idea where to begin. Questions abound regarding where the management of this function should be housed within a corporation, at what level it should operate, what the characteristics of a good knowledge manager are, etc.
- They realize that their more savvy competitors understand its value and have assigned personnel and budget to execute the process of collection and dissemination of knowledge. Some leading firms, like Monsanto, have made it a key driver of their strategic planning process. According to one of their KM executives, Monsanto budgeted over $11 million in one division alone for the purpose of collecting and capitalizing on employee knowledge. Again, place yourself in the shoes of a competing executive who can't understand or explain why Monsanto continues to sharply improve employee productivity while his/her productivity remains stagnant.

As the need to harness corporate brainpower for competitive advantage becomes an increasingly obvious strategy, firms around the world are quickly initiating plans to achieve maximum return on their intellectual capital. This requires that a firm assess its current knowledge sharing capabilities. This process, while complicated, can quickly be completed if management focuses on uncovering information that will assist them in addressing issues that inhibit the sharing of employee experience.

To begin the process of reviewing an organization's ability to compete in this area, the following issues must be addressed:

1. Does a knowledge sharing culture exist within the organization? If not, what steps need to be taken to change employee performance? In addition,

what methods can be used to obtain quick hits or initial success stories that will drive adoption of KM across the organization?

2. What is the core knowledge utilized by our employees that provides a sustainable competitive advantage?

3. What type of infrastructure exists that will allow for the easy access and transfer of knowledge worldwide?

4. Is the corporate environment conducive to knowledge sharing? Are the rewards and recognition programs sufficient to encourage employees to participate?

5. Does senior management fully support the concept of a knowledge sharing culture?

KM is unlike most new management disciplines in that, while attention to it has increased significantly over the past two years, in many organizations the collection and dissemination of corporate knowledge has become a natural function. Thus, today's executive is faced with the difficult task of either developing a KM system or risk being left behind by competitors who are exploiting their employee's intellectual assets as a routine operational strategy.

Korn/Ferry recently completed a study of the evolution of information technology and concluded, "Companies that can effectively manage the transition from the IT [information technology] function as one focused primarily on information processing to one that concentrates on knowledge management will have the competitive advantage. This ability to evolve the role from one that is very tactical, to one that contributes significantly to the strategic planning function of the business will mean all the difference in terms of future success."

The most difficult issue encountered by the majority of those who wish to develop a successful knowledge sharing organization, is the question of how to change the culture of a company. In most firms, the evolution of a knowledge hoarding culture has long been apparent. For decades, the employee who seemed to have the most knowledge was the employee who was recognized and/or promoted. Very often there were no incentives to share one's expertise and, in many cases, those that did ended up with no discernible enhancements to their careers. Therefore, the first question a manager must ask is: What can be done to encourage employees to share knowledge and how do we convince them that it is in their best benefit? The simple but often incorrect answer is: Our employees work as one big team and they know how important they are to the organization, therefore, sharing will come naturally. This is hardly true. Most organizations have absolutely no mechanism to encourage sharing and transfering internal knowledge.

GETTING STARTED

The thought of sharing one's experience and expertise is foreign to most employees. The first step necessary to develop an effective KM system is to review the way an organization operates and determine the easiest method of collecting and transferring the type of knowledge that will provide a strong competitive advantage. This task is often the most time consuming of the initial KM process. Having conducted several of these assessments, answers to the following questions should be gathered to determine the current state of knowledge sharing.

- Do our employees understand the value of sharing their expertise?
- Are there examples of sharing already apparent?
- What is the current state of the information technology infrastructure? Is there a system in place that can be used to share knowledge or does one have to be developed?
- Is there a formal system to reward and/or recognize those who share knowledge?
- What level of management understands and supports the concept of a knowledge-sharing organization (i.e., senior management, business unit management, mid-level management, etc.)?

Most of these issues can be addressed either in focus groups or one-on-one interviews. In my experience, the one-on-one interviews often are the most productive. Once this process is complete, a plan can be developed that will fit the requirements of the organization. Without this assessment model, organizations find that their personnel spend considerable time trying to frame a KM strategy without fully understanding the needs or present culture of the company.

IDENTIFYING KEY KNOWLEDGE DRIVERS

Most large global organizations believe they excel at a number of business deliverables. An important aspect in assuring success of any KM system is to identify the key strategy or business process that brings the most value to the organization. When there is more than one easily identifiable key strategy, an assessment of which process most quickly delivers value to your customers can act as the qualifier. The goal of developing a KM program around the most obvious strategy is to provide a clear example of how shared knowledge can provide immediate and highly visible returns to both individuals and the organization as a whole.

After this strategy has been identified, the individual assigned to collect and disseminate knowledge should, with the help of business unit management, target the employee or team of employees who have historically performed this function in the most efficient and cost-effective manner. Once that person(s) is identified, the process can proceed in numerous ways. Many organizations simply develop a narrative that describes the business process. Others with more sophisticated infrastructures use video clips or video streaming in order to capture the success and transfer it throughout the organization. Examples of several processes that I've witnessed that have provided significant value to their organizations are the following:

- A global pharmaceutical firm concentrated on capturing successful sales and marketing strategies. One of these practices was developed by a mid-level manager in a southwestern state. The structure of the practice consisted of a series of steps that ensured that the firm's products replaced those of a competitor's on a managed health care formulary. The practice, which resulted in a sharp increase in market share, was soon copied around the U.S. Prior to the development of this KM initiative, this firm had no method of sharing similar success stories.
- A major oil exploration firm was having a significant amount of trouble drilling at a site in a remote location. The drilling team was encountering significant problems getting past a certain depth and was ruining equipment while trying to drill through a type of sediment with which the rig manager was unfamiliar. The company set up a method by which rig managers around the world could videoconference with each other and discuss the successes and challenges faced on a daily basis. In this case, the video communication tool was used to show the damaged equipment and describe the problem to other more experienced personnel. Immediately, a rig manager located on the other side of the globe identified the issue and suggested a method to overcome the problem. The suggestion was adopted and the rig was back in full production.

This type of knowledge sharing or linking of "communities-of-practice" (e.g., those who perform similar functions but who are geographically dispersed) has evolved as a key component of any well-developed knowledge-sharing system. The obvious benefits obtained from a well developed and utilized community-of-practice result in the organization's use of one employee's expertise to maximize efficient product or service delivery. Additionally, the entire organization can witness the "quick hit" that KM delivered. In the case of the oil exploration company mentioned above, every rig manager who was online at the time the drilling solution was delivered immediately realized the value of knowledge sharing.

REWARDS AND RECOGNITION

A method commonly used to ensure implementation is the development of a system that rewards and recognizes individuals who understand, value, and participate in knowledge sharing. One of the quickest methods of developing a knowledge-sharing culture is to promote and reward the creative and innovative employees who are willing to share their expertise. The programs developed inside a number of organizations to meet this challenge are as diverse as the companies themselves. Certain organizations found that simple recognition from senior management is enough to drive the initiative. Others have discovered that the most effective way to ensure participation is to offer a variety of monetary and non-monetary incentives. The system that works best is usually predicated on the type of culture that exists within the organization. Often during the initial assessment process, the most effective type of reward system can be identified and developed.

SUPPORT OF SENIOR MANAGEMENT

With the explosion of KM initiatives over the past several years, one constant issue continually arises when reviewing programs that have failed. The one consistent barrier to a well-developed knowledge sharing effort is the failure of senior management to vocally and continuously support the efforts of the knowledge managers. The difficulty encountered in trying to change years of knowledge hoarding is multiplied when employees are not fully convinced that the highest levels of the organization support the change in behavior.

The continuous support of senior management sends the unequivocal message that the organization is committed to overhauling the way it operates. One of the best examples of senior management support driving the success of a KM system is the actions of Jack Welch at GE. Welch uses every opportunity to promote the sharing of experience and expertise at all levels of his organization. In numerous interviews and speeches, he discusses the importance in developing a collaborative atmosphere in which employees are free to contribute their knowledge. At the same time, employees who are facing workplace challenges are encouraged to seek the advice of their more experienced colleagues. His constant and vocal recognition of the advantages that knowledge sharing provides to GE leave no doubt in anyone's mind that the quickest way to be either recognized by senior management or promoted within the GE culture is to freely share what one has learned.

Placing a Value on Shared Knowledge

One of the great difficulties facing the emergence of any new management discipline is the paradox of how to value an activity that provides a benefit that cannot be directly placed on the balance sheet. Information services faced this issue several decades ago as the need for computing power grew in a time when executives couldn't quantify the value it added to an organization. In many cases, the determination of the dollar amount that is added to a company's assets via a well-developed information technology infrastructure still cannot be quantified. However, most executives stopped trying to place a dollar value on this type of investment, as everyone easily understands the downside of not having adequate computer technology. There isn't an executive alive who doesn't fully comprehend the disadvantages his/her organization would face if tomorrow morning all the desktops, laptops, printers, and mainframes disappeared.

Yet many of these executives can't seem to understand the value accumulated via the exchange of what is, in reality, their most important and valuable asset. Wall Street certainly has come to value the intellectual assets of a corporation much more than fixed assets. One need only look at the market capitalization of companies like Microsoft or Coca-Cola to understand that the vast majority of shareholder wealth lies in the minds of their employees and not in their brick and mortar.

Therefore, identification of the value that knowledge sharing provides to the bottom line is often a considered measurement by less enlightened executives. The enlightened executive that can conceptualize the additional advantages that a collaborative workforce provides and establish a structure to exploit this advantage is destined to control his/her markets. There are currently a number of complicated and thorough analyses being performed in an attempt to determine an identifiable measurement of the value added via KM. Several business, government, and academic institutions are hard at work to be the first to propose a valuation device that the financial community will find useful in assessing the worth of intellectual capital.

While I do not promise that any of the following tools will eventually be adopted, it is significant that so many diverse organizations are working to solve this perplexing equation. The following are summaries of several evaluation initiatives currently underway:

American Society for Training and Development

Purpose

"We provide leadership to individuals, organizations, and society to achieve work related competence, performance, and fulfillment."[1]

Background

Founded in 1944, ASTD represents more than 70,000 members in the field of workplace learning and performance, who come from every area of the growing industry and from more than 150 countries across the globe. Our leadership and members work in multinational corporations, small- and medium-sized businesses, government agencies, colleges, and universities...

ASTD leads the field by providing the statistics and reports through our research department and Benchmarking Forum, and by promoting public policies which support training and development to the U.S. Congress, Administration, and state governments...[2]

Involvement in Intellectual Capital/Intangible Assets
Research Effective Knowledge Management Working Group

The ASTD is working with several firms on a three-year project to develop an Intellectual Capital tool. The ASTD, in collaboration with these firms, will ultimately develop an assessment framework that identifies two things: 1) the core indicators of intellectual capital that are valid/reliable from company to company; and 2) the key enablers/processes that allow companies to leverage and manage their capital.[3]

Other

The 1998 ASTD State of the Industry Report, "Last Stop, The Practices": A solid relationship does exist between a company's performance and its workplace learning and development practices. Companies that use innovative training practices are likely to report improved performances over time and better performance than their competitors...[4]

Center for Business Innovation, Ernst & Young

Purpose

"We exist to discover and develop innovations in strategy, people, process, and technology that deliver high value to business."[5]

Background

Since 1992, the Center for Business Innovation has been at the forefront of this emerging topic [knowledge management]. Its inquiry into effective knowledge processes, tools, and organizational structures has been pursued in cooperation with progressive firms and other leading researchers, and has yielded numerous important insights and management solutions.[6]

Involvement in Intellectual Capital/Intangible Assets Research Center for Business Innovation

Our inquiry into knowledge management explores intellectual capital as the most important and under-leveraged source of competitive advantage...knowledge-based business[es]...use knowledge as their competitive asset, creating value through their ability to apply knowledge more effectively than their competitors.[7]

The CBI's [Center for Business Innovation] research currently focuses on the four ways that firms can leverage this valuable knowledge: 1) Knowledge-Based Process Improvement: Does more explicit management of knowledge directly related to a particular process improve the execution of that process continuously? 2) Knowledge-Based Offerings: What are the ways that firms create revenue by utilizing knowledge in products and services; what value is created for the company and its customers by these offerings? 3) Knowledge-Based Networks: In what ways do knowledge-based networks, both internal and external, create a powerful benefit and how do companies support these relationships? 4) Knowledge-Based Strategy: Do strategies based on leveraging knowledge lead to above average growth and how do they provide competitive advantage?[8]

Other

Researchers at the Center for Business Innovation have been exploring...performance measurement...Past research has focused on ways to diagnose dysfunctional performance measurement systems, effective ways of integrating financial and non-financial measures, appropriate sets of metrics to guide management, and the advisability of disclosing non-financial information to investors.

Performance measurement research at the Center involves a number of activities: 1) Surveys; 2) Collaboration/Partnering: through working relationships with other leading organizations such as the Brookings Institute, the Organization for Economic Co-operation and Development, and the New York University Stern School of Business, the Center is able to play a role in shaping important issues surrounding performance; 3) Research Clearinghouse: The Intangibles Research Center Web site—New York University Stern School of Business and the Center for Business Innovation, assists researchers in obtaining...data on corporate intangible investments; 4) PM2000:...a performance measurement dashboard for diagnosing the adequacy and quality of current systems of performance measurement and for identifying more effective, real-time feedback information, using financial as well as non-financial measures and information.[6]

Danish Ministry of Business and Industry

Purpose

"The Ministry of Business and Industry works to provide better conditions for the Danish trades and industries."[9]

Background

The Ministry of Business and Industry administers laws and regulations which are essential for trades and industries...The Ministry...performs in-depth analyses of the challenges of the future and carries on an open dialogue with enterprises, organizations, and other authorities....[10]

Involvement in Intellectual Capital/Intangible Assets Research

Business Environment 1997, chapter 1, Ministry of Business and Industry, version 1.0. 1997:

Together with the organizations, the government will spearhead an effort to put new organizational structures on the agenda. A number of initiatives which are the results of an inter-ministerial project under the heading Management, Organization and Competencies in the Knowledge-Based Society will be launched. The initiatives have been developed by three working groups, consisting of corporate managers, employee representatives, organizations and people from the educational sector...

...The government, therefore, wishes to enhance the collaboration between trade and industry on the one hand and research on the other. In the autumn of 1997, the government will select a number of innovative environments around universities or similar centers of knowledge and research. The intention is to establish environments in which research and industry together conceive new ideas and help them to grow. The government will contribute pre-project capital to entrepreneurs who develop new ideas. Subsidies to product development or innovation grants are another possibility. An annual sum of DKK 100 million has been allocated to the initiative for the period 1998-2000.[11]

Financial Accounting Standards Board (FASB)

Purpose

"The mission of the FASB is to establish and improve standards of financial accounting for the guidance and education of the public, including issuers, auditors, and users of financial information."[12]

Background

"Since 1973, the FASB has been the designated organization in the private sector for establishing standards of financial accounting and reporting. Those standards govern the preparation of financial reports. They are officially recognized as authoritative by the Securities and Exchange Commission and the AICPA."[12]

Involvement in Intellectual Capital/Intangible Assets Research
Business Reporting Research Project

In January 1998, the Board (FASB) decided to undertake a research project to consider the types of information (in addition to financial statements) that companies are providing investors and the means for delivering it. The plans for the project call for an important portion of the work to be done by the Board's constituents—preparers, users, and auditors...Possible activities for the working groups include: Identifying present practices in selected industries for disclosure of various types of information such as operating data and performance measures, forward-looking information, background about the company, and information about intangible assets that have not been recognized in financial statements...Paul Kolton is the chair of the steering committee on this project. Mr. Kolton was chairman of FASAC from 1978 to 1992, has held key executive positions at the New York and American Stock Exchanges, and has served on the boards of numerous major corporations. The other members of the steering committee are: Joseph V. Anania, FASB Board member...John W. Albert will be an observer from the SEC staff...It is expected that the steering committee's (and each working group's) work will be completed within 24 months following its first meeting.[13]

Skandia Insurance Company

Purpose

" ...to explore the driving forces of the business environment."[14]

Background

"Activities are currently being carried out at Skandia to develop a complementary accounting taxonomy and an overall view of operations...."[15]

Involvement in Intellectual Capital/Intangible Assets Research

General

At Skandia we have always maintained that our intellectual capital is at least as important as our financial capital in providing truly sustainable earnings. That is why we have made substantial efforts in recent years to visualize and more concretely describe those assets that are difficult to distinguish in the overwhelming mass of financial information.

...The process of developing indicators and intellectual capital ratios is now in progress in several units of the Skandia organization. Activities are currently oriented towards developing a complementary accounting taxonomy and way of managing based on awareness and insight into intellectual capital development.[16]

IC Index

...a compilation of various IC indicators' relevance, robustness and relative weight...This development work is leading into greater insight into what drives shareholder value in the new knowledge economy...By devising various ways of combining in [this]...future shareholder value can be realized...Skandia will continue its IC exploration....[17]

Skandia has thus far developed a range of methods of reporting its intellectual capital and its various components, through IC indicators. The next step is to consolidate the various IC indicators into one measurement that will dynamically describe the group's intellectual capital. This will facilitate the benchmarking units within Skandia and with other companies...Skandia is breaking new ground by applying this "IC-Index", which is a compilation of various IC indicators' relevance, robustness and relative weight.[18]

Skandia Navigator

"Skandia AFS (a subsidiary of Skandia insurance group) has chosen to make their measurement system for intangible assets a differentiation device."[19]

"The Skandia Navigator is a new business management model...[that] provides a more balanced, truer picture of operations...."[20]

Skandia's new reporting model, the Skandia Navigator, is designed to provide a balanced picture of the financial and intellectual capital. The focus on financial results, capital and monetary flows is complemented by a description on intellectual capital and its development... intellectual capital ratios are grouped into four major focus areas: the Customer focus, the Process focus, the Human focus, and the Renewal and Development focus...The specific ratios compiled from the measurements will then become leading indicators.[21]

Endnotes

1. ASTD, "Vision, Mission and Strategic Directions" http://www.astd.org/CMS/templates/template_1.html?articleid=10834 (accessed August 1998)

2. ASTD, Laura Liswood President and CEO. http://www.astd.org/virtual_community/about_astd/about_astd_main.html (accessed August 1998)

3. ASTD, Mark Van Buren, September 1, 1998, phone interview.

4. ASTD, Laurie J. Bassie and Mark E. Van Buren. "The 1998 ASTD State of the Industry Report, 1998" http://www.astd.org/virtual_community/comm_trends/state_of_industry_td0198_cms.htm (accessed August 1998)

5. Ernst & Young LLP, "About the Center" http://www.businessinnovation.ey.com/center/center.html (accessed August 1998)

6. Ernst & Young LLP, Rudy Ruggles. "Managing Organizational Knowledge" http://www.businessinnovation.ey.com/journal/issue1/features/whykno/loader.html (accessed August 1998)

7. Ernst & Young LLP, "Research Overview: Knowledge Management" http://www.businessinnovation.ey.com/research/overview.html (accessed August 1998)

8. Ernst & Young LLP, "Research Overview: Knowledge Management" http://www.businessinnovation.ey.com/research/knowle/overview.html (accessed August 1998)

9. The Danish Ministry of Business and Industry. http://www.em.dk/engorg/ide/tekst.htm (accessed August 1998)

10. The Danish Ministry of Business and Industry. http://www.em.dk/engorg/ide/tekst.htm (accessed August 1998)

11. The Danish Ministry of Business and Industry, "Investments in the Future—Industrial Policy in Focus" http://www.em.dk/engpol/erhverv/kap1.htm (accessed August 1998)

12. FASB, "The Mission of the Financial Accounting Standards Board" http://www.rutgers.edu/Accounting/raw/fasb/facts/fasfact1.html (accessed August 1998)

13. FASB, "Technical Research Activities" http://www.rutgers.edu/Accounting/raw/fasb/tech/techactv.htm (accessed August 1998)

14. Skandia Insurance Company, "Future Projects: Skandia Group" http://www.skandia.se/group/future/intellectual/unic_a.htm (accessed August 1998)

15. Skandia Insurance Company. http://www.skandia.se/group/future/svensk/cv_leife.htm (accessed August 1998)

16. Skandia Insurance Company, "Hidden Values in Skandia." http://www.skandia.se/group/search/frame_search.htm (accessed August 1998)

17. Skandia Insurance Company. http://203.32.10.69/CompaniestoLearnFrom.html (accessed August 1998)

18. Skandia Insurance Company, supplement to Skandia's 1996 annual report, "Value-Creating Relationships" http://www.skandia.se/group/search/frame_search.htm (accessed August 1998)

19. Skandia Insurance Company. http://203.32.10.69/CompaniestoLearnFrom.html (accessed August 1998)

20. Skandia Insurance Company. http://www.skandia.se/group/brief_facts/brief_intellectual_capital.htm (accessed August 1998)

21. Skandia Insurance Company, "Indicators for the Future" http://www.skandia.se/group/search/frame_search.htm (accessed August 1998)

CHAPTER 8

Ethics for Knowledge Management

David P. Schmidt
Associate Professor
Fairfield University

OVERVIEW

This chapter argues that ethics is first a matter of vision or discernment, not decision making about particular dilemmas. The implications of this position will be developed for the ethics of knowledge management by first reviewing the traditional approach to business ethics that uses normative theory to guide decisions. The chapter then develops the contrasting position of ethics as discernment, which is argued as more suited for illuminating the rapid changes in computer technologies that underlie knowledge management. At closure, examples are given of metaphors and images that shape our understanding of knowledge management and the ethical issues that arise in its practice. The chapter concludes with a call for an ongoing process of critical inquiry among knowledge managers, ethicists, consumers, and citizens to advance ethics in knowledge management.

INTRODUCTION

On a rugged, isolated planet in distant space, Captain Jean-Luc Picard of the Federation Starship *Enterprise* had a dramatic rendezvous with Dathan, captain of a Tamarian spaceship (Nemecek, 1995). Dathan belonged to an advanced but mysterious race, the Children of Tama, whose indecipherable language made them an enigma to the Federation. Their encounter on the planet ended tragically, with Dathan killed by a hostile creature who had attacked him and Picard. But Dathan's death was not in vain, for he had helped Picard deduce that Tamarians speak in narrative images from their rich folklore. Back on the *Enterprise*, reflecting upon his encounter with Dathan, Picard turned to his rare copy of ancient mythology for insight. Picard had learned from Dathan the crucial role of images and metaphors for cognition, interpretation, and communication, especially over issues of disputed values and ethical judgments. He knew that to converse better with the Tamarians, he needed to absorb the root metaphors and images of his own cultural tradition. And so, alone in his ready room on the *Enterprise*, Picard pondered metaphors handed down from ancient planet Earth.

What does this fictional story of a futuristic space explorer have to do with today's knowledge managers? There are some surface similarities. Both tackle complex issues. Both encounter difficulties of communication that impede achieving a goal. Both possess state-of-the-art technology. Both must make quick decisions that may have far-ranging consequences for others. But there is more to Picard's story than just making the right decision, a fact that is central to this chapter on ethics for knowledge management. Picard's retrieval of metaphor raises a more fundamental question for ethics: How can we discern what is really happening, especially in rapidly changing, challenging, complex situations?

While technology plays a key role in Star Trek stories, as it does in knowledge management issues today, this chapter makes the important assumption that technology alone cannot provide solutions to problems that call for a normative or ethical judgment. It is worth noting that at the end of the Star Trek episode, Picard turned to an ancient technology, a book, instead of accessing the *Enterprise's* computer or holodeck. What mattered to Picard was the content of certain ideas and images, not the technology that stored and communicated them. In our own time, there is a tendency to blame information technology for the failure of knowledge managers to deal effectively with tough issues. Knowledge managers who attempt to apply a solution before adequately defining the problem may actually cause the problems supposedly caused by technology. What these knowledge managers need is a better grasp of the purpose and meaning of their technological tools. They need a better vision of knowledge management, which is the main concern of this chapter.

Traditionally, professionals look to ethics for theories to help them make decisions about particular problems. Though decision making is important in business ethics, even more important is the capacity of managers to see the ethical dimensions of professional and business practices. In this chapter, I wish to show that ethics is first a matter of vision or discernment, not decision. Before knowledge managers can decide what to do about any particular issue, they must first have the imaginative capacity to interpret their circumstances in an illuminating way. Granted, knowledge managers must develop defensible judgments on particular issues, and they need to justify particular actions, or lack of action. But their judgments and actions will only be as sound as their initial perception of their circumstances, for it is their perception (or lack of it) that may decisively shape everything that follows in terms of judgment, decision, and action.

To develop the implications of ethics as discernment for knowledge managers, I will first review the traditional approach to business ethics that presents normative theory as a resource or tool for making decisions about tough cases. This brief review does not mean to disparage the use of normative theory for decisions. However, without acknowledging the priority of discernment, the dominant account of ethics as normative theory will remain mired in interminable disputes about seemingly incommensurable values. Second, I will develop the position that ethics is first of all a matter of discernment and vision, not decision and action. While I acknowledge that this emphasis on vision is still something of a minority view (albeit an ascendant view) in modern ethics, I believe it is particularly relevant to the ethical challenges facing knowledge managers. To help show why I think this to be so, I will conclude with some thoughts about how metaphors shape our understanding of knowledge management and the ethical issues we encounter in its practice.

Normative Ethical Theory as a Decision Tool

Most business ethics textbooks written from the humanistic perspective of normative philosophy share a similar structure. The first section of these books provides an overview of ethical theories. This is followed by "applied" sections that develop the implications of these theories for business topics. These following sections usually take the form of case studies on various contemporary business issues. The theories provide an analytical tool for sorting out different moral aspects of particular cases. They also provide a framework for making reasoned judgments about particular dilemmas.

Almost without fail, these business ethics texts compare and contrast two fundamental options in normative ethical theory: teleology (an ethic of ends or consequences) and deontology (an ethic of duties or rights). Many texts will also consider theories of justice as a separate topic in ethical theory, to emphasize issues of fairness and just distribution of resources. More recently, other topics like the development of moral character and the virtues (which can at least hint at the related subject of discernment) have begun to creep into business ethics textbooks. For my purposes, it is sufficient to consider only the uses of teleology and deontology in these texts.

Normative ethical theory helps us decide what to do when faced with an ethical choice or dilemma. (This kind of theory contrasts with metaethical theory, which addresses more abstract questions about the nature of the good itself, questions which are rarely mentioned in business ethics textbooks.) Teleological theories, one major type of normative ethical theory, answer this question with reference to the end results or consequences of our choices or decisions. Utilitarianism is one popular version of teleological theory that generally says we should choose the course of action that benefits the most people overall. Egoism is a less pretty version of teleology that says I should choose the course of action that benefits *me* the most. To illustrate with a classic business ethics case of the Ford Pinto, we decide whether to recall and fix allegedly faulty Pintos by calculating and comparing the financial consequences of recalling and fixing the cars, against the financial consequences of doing nothing and fighting accident victims in court.

Deontological theories answer the question of what we should do when faced with an ethical choice or dilemma with reference to duties or rights that are morally binding and independent of particular consequences. This theoretical alternative to teleology says that we should not consider the outcomes of our ethical decisions (especially when we may stand to benefit from those outcomes). Rather, we should do the "right thing" because it is our *duty* to do it. Kantian ethics typically provide the paradigm for this approach, with business ethics texts offering succinct formulations of this highly complex and original thought, as in the following: "We should never treat other persons as means to an end. We should treat them only as ends in themselves." Concerning the example of the Ford Pinto, a deontologist might argue that we have a duty to recall the Pinto regardless of the costs because of a more basic duty not to harm others.

Teleological and deontological theories are useful for managers because they provide different frameworks for making decisions. These theories help managers take into account a wide range of factors pertaining to a particular dilemma, thereby preventing a hasty reductionism to a narrow set of considerations. For example, a deontological orientation may help a manager remember to acknowledge basic duties and rights that might not easily fit into a teleological cost-benefit analysis. Also, business textbooks claim these theories are useful because they help the manager achieve an analytical clarity that common sense alone does not provide. These theories help managers make finer, more nuanced discriminations among various facts, and so enable the manager to make articulate, defensible positions.

However, there are also critics of the emphasis on normative theory as a useful tool for managerial ethical decision making. A very common objection is that theory is too abstract for the concrete situations and concerns facing people at work. Indeed, one challenge of most business ethics textbooks is to make a meaningful connection between the normative theories in the first section of the book with the cases that follow. Faculty who teach business ethics to undergraduates probably often encounter the problem of students wanting to get quickly past the "boring" theory so they can talk about the more "interesting" cases—often with scant reference to any of the earlier ethical theory! Whether we agree with that old saw, "It's great in theory but it won't work in practice," probably depends in part on how the theoretical material is presented and related to more practical concerns. It may be difficult to make connections between theory and the actual practices and concerns of managers, but the experiences of many faculty seem to indicate that it is not impossible.

There is a more important objection to the usefulness of normative theory for ethical decision making, related to a shortcoming inherent to normative theory as such. This objection, popularized by philosopher Alisdair MacIntyre (1981), says that ethical theories generally do not clarify issues in a way that leads to more effective decisions, if by "effective decisions" we mean an intellectual process that builds consensus or agreement among disputing parties. Ethical theories only help to clarify the points over which managers disagree; however, by themselves the theories do not show managers how to settle their more finely tuned disagreements.

This is especially true when the disagreements cause disputes between competing normative perspectives, such as teleological versus deontological. All the reasoning in the world will not reconcile opposing managers who use teleological and deontological arguments to get to clashing conclusions. Battling teleologists and deontologists lack something more fundamental that is necessary to compel agreement, namely, a shared vision of what morally is really at stake. For this reason, according to this objection, vision and discernment must be logically prior to decisions about particular cases.

To summarize, the dominant account of ethics in business ethics focuses on justifying decisions and actions. Normative theory is valued insofar as it helps us solve moral quandaries (Pincoffs, 1986). Implicit to this dominant account is a picture of the moral life as a series of specific, and quite possibly unconnected, problems each requiring its own efficient calculus so that we can make a decision, resolve the issue, and progress to more important business. Making decisions is important, even vital, for ethics. But an overemphasis on resolving particular issues can obscure the role of other important aspects of ethics and the moral life that are more concerned with vision, discernment, imagination, and feeling.

ETHICS AS DISCERNMENT

To characterize ethics as discernment is to put description before decision, vision before action. Of course, ethics issues require us to make decisions and to act, and to justify these decisions and actions with carefully argued reasons. But before we can decide what to do, we must give a description of what is happening that helpfully illumines what is at stake. It is a mistake to think that issues are simply "given" to us as an objective state of affairs, for we do not see objectively. Instead, we interpret what passes before us, and our interpretations are shaped by many factors, including who we are, our relationships to others, how we may be affected by outcomes of our interpretations, and so on. For example, different witnesses to a crisis or catastrophe might honestly provide contrasting eye-witness accounts of what happened, especially if they have a personal stake in a judgment of who is to blame for the crisis (Mermann, 1997).

Ethics as discernment places great emphasis on the qualities of the person who must describe and respond to an ethical issue. The modern approach to ethics, which would guide decision with normative theory, tends to discount the features of the person who needs to make the decision. The modern approach stipulates only that this person be rational and capable of maintaining an objective distance from the ethical issue. Against this highly abstract and overly rationalistic account of moral agency, ethics as discernment emphasizes the importance of all aspects of one's moral character.

According to philosopher Iris Murdoch (1985), the chief obstacles to ethical perception and action are character flaws like egoism, insecurity, and self-deception. These qualities tend to distort our vision of ourselves, of others, and of the issues we encounter. Murdoch argues that traditional ethical theory over-emphasizes the freedom and agency of the moral actor. In contrast to this, she would have us focus instead on the way quiet habits of action and virtue, especially humility, encourage appropriate action through perceptive discernment.

Metaphors are an important part of interpretation and discernment. Recent scholarship on metaphor has shown that the "metaphors we live by" play an implicit but crucial role in shaping our experience and judgment (Lakoff and Johnson, 1980). Metaphors are tools we use to portray and understand one thing in terms of another, typically using a familiar idea or experience to make intelligible an unfamiliar or complex concept or phenomenon. For instance, if I had bad luck with love, and so feel a need to get a firmer grip on just what is involved with this messy, complicated human experience, I might be inspired to say something like, "Well, what did I expect, after all? Love is war." Here I am using the graphic idea of war to help me acknowledge and cope with the conflictual and harmful possibilities of romantic attachments. The choice of metaphor is crucially important to my experience and understanding of love because any particular metaphor will focus my gaze on certain aspects of love and not others. (In an effort to boost my spirits, I might have said instead, "I shouldn't give up, for love is a fragrant rose.") By helping us comprehend partially what is difficult to understand totally, metaphors are indispensable tools for interpreting and evaluating complex issues that require good descriptions.

We rarely acknowledge the metaphors that shape our thinking and perception, an oversight that could lead to ethically misguided decisions. For one thing, if metaphors play an important—if tacit—role in shaping our decisions, then a complete justification of our decisions should include identifying and justifying those metaphors that guide our perception. If I am going to try to convince you to avoid love because of all the conflict and heartbreak it will bring, you might be interested to know why I place so much confidence on "love is war" in the first place. Our perception and thought are only as rich as the ideas that are available to us. By paying more attention to the metaphors that underlie most of our thinking, we are likely to develop a richer and more sophisticated understanding of complicated developments, like computer technologies.

Robert Solomon (1992) has argued for the impact of fundamental metaphors on the perceptions of business managers. He identifies several "macho myths and metaphors" that pervade contemporary business, including "It's a Jungle Out There," "The Brutal Battles of Business," "The Great Machines of Business," and "The Game of Business." Solomon argues that "How we look at what we do has a lot to do with how we do and I would argue that much of the infighting within corporations and many of the casualties of corporate competition can be laid at the feet of the malevolent images that we impose on business and on ourselves" (Solomon, 1992). Thus, in Solomon's judgment, metaphors that shape business perception and action have demonstrable bottom-line and *moral* consequences. He thinks that business executives will remain mired in perennial difficulties until they develop a critical awareness of the metaphors they tacitly use, which may lead to a discovery of better metaphors upon which to organize business activity. While there is room for disagreement about Solomon's particular judgments about specific metaphors, I think his general point about the function of metaphor is persuasive. For this reason, I think it very important to examine the metaphors that shape the perceptions and judgments of knowledge managers.

LEARNING TO SEE THE WEB

Because Lotus Notes or a Web Intranet is often the basis for a knowledge management technology infrastructure, this section will use the Web to illustrate the significance of metaphors for discernment. The examples that follow will show how people use metaphors to discern what is at stake with computers and the Web. They show us that we always need to test the adequacy of previous metaphors that describe computer innovations and, when necessary, we may need to invent new ones.

In his stimulating exploration of computer archetypes, myths, and metaphors, Mark Stefik (1996) recalls how mainframe computers were once described as brains. By that, nobody literally meant that computers are brains, but the metaphor of brains forcefully conveyed the aspect of computers that we think resembles human thinking. More recently, Stefik notes, many have characterized the Web as an information superhighway—a metaphor that leads us to think of distributed communication networks in terms of roads, and, thus, pointing us to certain kinds of policies. Just as real highways need speed limits and traffic cops, the reasoning goes, so perhaps the Web needs to be closely regulated and policed. However, metaphors other than information superhighway are not only possible but perhaps warranted by new directions in technology.

Allucquere Rosanne Stone (1995) urges us to move beyond utilitarian images (like superhighways) as well as prosthesis-based metaphors (like the artificial limb), which focus our attention on the instrumental, number-crunching character of computers. Instead of functional, computers-as-tools kinds of images, Stone advocates thinking of computers in terms of recreation and play, images that she thinks better capture the shift from corporate mainframes to mischievous kids innovating technology in their garages and bedrooms. Something other than "information superhighway" is needed to illumine what is going on in chat rooms, computer games, and virtual environments.

Stories are a rich source of metaphors, and literature uses metaphor (along with myth, legend, and parable), to teach us new ways to look at life. In this regard, it is instructive to note Phil Agre's argument (1997) that all technologies are based on a grand story or narrative. The rise of the Internet is in fact a collection of stories that gives us heroes and villains. Agre identifies in these stories the roles of the good hacker, the rebel hacker, and the cyber utopian—roles that provide images for imaginative concepts that lie outside ordinary experience. Importantly, Agre worries that the images of these Internet actors do not provide adequate normative guidance for the rapidly evolving Web. He asks whether we need to envision new roles and images, such as that of the public hacker, to adequately discern the important public issues posed by the Internet and the Web.

Different metaphorical renderings of technology open our eyes to particular ethical issues and close our eyes to others. For this reason, it is important to be aware of the basic metaphors and images that we use to make sense of our technology, especially in professional work like knowledge management that relies heavily on computers. Ethics issues in computer technology are not simply there for us to make judgments about. Rather, the ethics issues we encounter are in large measure a function of the metaphors we use to describe computers and related technologies.

Two related points are important for this discussion. First, our moral life is only as vibrant and fully dimensional as the images we possess for our descriptions. People who live in cold climates have a richer vocabulary for describing snow than do people from warmer regions. A fertile vocabulary for describing snow will allow finer discriminations among different kinds of snowy conditions, a linguistic achievement that may make a life-or-death difference for surviving the cold. Similarly, people who work closely with technology need to develop a robust vocabulary for describing the tools of their trade. In fact, professional expertise requires one to develop a sufficiently powerful vocabulary for doing work in a professional manner. People who work with knowledge management technology must have at their command the requisite vocabulary for dealing with the complexities of their discipline.

Of course, computer nerds *do* possess a more colorful jargon for describing computers than do people who avoid computers, which leads to the second related point: It is not sufficient merely to possess a rich metaphorical vocabulary; we also need to be aware of the images that shape our vision so that we can judge whether or not the images are fitting for the task at hand. Normally, the basic metaphors that shape our perceptions operate at an unconscious or unreflective level. These metaphors seem "natural" to us and so do not seem to require any special justification. To the contrary, precisely because our perception is shaped by tacitly held metaphors or images, it is vital that we explicitly recognize those metaphors and bring them to our critical attention.

To use Solomon's (1992) observation about popular images in business: Many people in business apparently operate on the basis of a tacit metaphor that "business is war"—a way of looking at business that legitimates highly aggressive, unconscionable behavior. Precisely because this metaphor is unreflectively accepted by many in business, and because it leads to such negative behaviors, Solomon argues that it is important to make people more aware of the way this popular metaphor widely shapes perception, judgment, and action. The same point is true for knowledge managers and their information technology counterparts: Both need to be self-consciously aware of the tacit metaphors and images that shape the way they discern issues in their field, especially issues of ethics and values.

Metaphors of Knowledge Management

Knowledge managers, like any business professional, tacitly rely upon basic metaphors or images. Since the methods of knowledge management are based upon rapidly changing technologies, knowledge management is a field that requires imaginative professionals to discern the significance of pertinent technological developments. To assist this imaginative discernment, this section will briefly discuss some metaphors from knowledge management. My purpose is not to provide a complete or thorough analysis of knowledge management metaphors—that would be a much larger task best undertaken by knowledge managers themselves, as they are the ones most deeply acquainted with the language of their work.

As an ethicist interested in computer technology, and as an outside observer of the field of knowledge management, my modest contribution is appropriately limited to pointing out several metaphors that I have picked up from a general reading of knowledge management literature. No doubt my observations will be challenged and corrected by persons more conversant with the details of the field, which is exactly as it should be. By trying to make more explicit some tacit metaphors or images from the practice of knowledge management, I intend to provide more support for my general thesis about the importance of metaphors for ethics as discernment in the case of knowledge management. I also hope to provoke a critical response to this subject by those in a position to speak more knowledgeably than I can about knowledge management and discernment.

This section will consider container metaphors, transfer metaphors, political metaphors, and community metaphors. There will be overlap across these metaphors, and clearly any serious analysis of ethics in knowledge management would draw upon multiple metaphors to illumine fully the complex dimensions of any particular case or issue. That kind of sophisticated analysis and that kind of detailed case study are beyond the limits of this chapter. Here I simply identify each metaphor, some images associated with it, and some implications that follow for the duties or responsibilities of knowledge managers.

Container Metaphors

These metaphors imply that there is knowledge to be captured and managed, an implication that suggests that knowledge is something that needs to be kept somewhere or contained in something. There are various images for this, including "bucket-o-knowledge," "repository of knowledge," or "treasure house of knowledge." Granted, there are different ways to put knowledge into some kind of structured form. It might be put in the form of static information, as in a paper document; it might be put in the form of evolving information, as in a discussion database where people contribute ideas and responses; or it might consist only of pointers to other places or persons where the knowledge resides. But, viewed from the perspective of container metaphors, these different ways of organizing knowledge are similar because they portray knowledge as something that is put somewhere, in this place rather than in that.

Metaphors or images that situate knowledge in this manner, as in a "bucket-o-knowledge," evoke a physical entity into which knowledge can be put. It gives us a vocabulary for manipulating knowledge that emphasizes words like "obtain," "organize," "restructure," "warehouse," and "distribute." In this way, container metaphors shape what we think we can do with knowledge and they suggest specific responsibilities for knowledge managers. For example, if knowledge is something to be kept in a place like a bucket, we should be concerned about what kind of knowledge is allowed to pour into the bucket, to guard against contamination and to prevent the bucket from overflowing. We will also carefully monitor who has access to the bucket and how much anyone can draw from its contents. Once the knowledge is out of the bucket, we may be concerned about where it goes and whether or not we can retrieve it. If the knowledge is spilled, we will want to have procedures for mopping up the mess, as well as for specifying consequences in case the spillage was due to negligence or wrongful intention. Thus, container metaphors tend to prompt ethical issues that have to do with access, control, regulation, and maintenance.

Transfer Metaphors

These metaphors help us visualize the movement of knowledge. Knowledge transfer presupposes knowledge containment, in the sense that knowledge moves from one place to another. But the metaphor of transfer emphasizes the dynamic quality of knowledge as it travels from place to place and as it is put to different uses. If we think of knowledge as something that we move in order to improve operations, we will use images that correspond to this metaphor, including "getting," "moving," "shipping," or "dumping" information. To accomplish this movement of information, we will use different conduits, from snail mail through advanced computer telecommunications. But whether we say "I'll shoot a memo over to you by tomorrow," or "The files will download immediately," we are using terms that portray knowledge as something that moves.

Metaphors or images for knowledge transfer suggest tasks and issues for knowledge managers that will be different from those suggested by container metaphors. Instead of acting as "keepers of information," transfer-oriented knowledge managers will be responsible for supporting communication, for collaborating and mediating among suppliers and demanders of knowledge, and for exploring or searching for elusive or hard-to-pin-down knowledge. Rather than functioning as architects of static repositories, knowledge workers will be more like cartographers mapping the passages through which knowledge can travel. They may serve less as keepers of knowledge and more as tour guides for knowledge routes.

Transfer metaphors may shape what we judge to be the appropriate policies for ethics and knowledge management. For example, if knowledge is viewed as something like the movement of traffic on roads, there will be a perceived need for reliable roadmaps, consistent rules of the road, and traffic regulations. Someone will have to take responsibility for managing and maintaining the roadways across which information travels. Someone will need to learn how to describe what counts as a traffic accident and how to conduct a traffic court to penalize risky drivers. Thus, transfer metaphors tend to prompt ethical issues that have to do with the dynamics of movement. They focus our attention on that which obstructs and facilitates interaction, on that which promotes cooperation and conflict in the movement of information.

The evolution of images for computer-based libraries suggests ways in which container metaphors and transfer metaphors may be related. As libraries first went online, they were initially referred to as "libraries without walls"—a way of still viewing them as containers, but with highly porous or permeable boundaries. The notion of boundary became less clear as we moved more to an understanding of "virtual libraries" or "digital libraries," which obliterated barriers imposed by hours of access and geographical location. A digital library seems to exist only in the communication or transfer of knowledge from a supplier to a demander. As our images of libraries continue to evolve, we may find it even more appropriate to describe them with transfer metaphors, not containment metaphors. Or perhaps we will need to develop a new set of metaphors that illumine better what is transpiring when information is neither "here nor there" nor "moving from one place to another." If information becomes universally present (in the sense of Bill Gate's vision of "information at everyone's fingertips"), what would this mean ethically for the duties and responsibilities of knowledge managers?

Political Metaphors

These metaphors call attention to the issues of power and control that inevitably accompany the management of knowledge. The metaphorical phrase, "knowledge is power," underscores the political ramifications of the technology that makes knowledge available to an organization. Traditionally, large businesses have been modeled upon systems of autocracy and bureaucracy. More recently, some qualified forms of participatory democracy have been introduced into the workplace. However, the pervasive and rapid growth of knowledge technologies in business may be challenging the conventional systems of organizational politics. Newer technocratic and libertarian systems are beginning to contest the older political models. With these new systems come new images and metaphors that challenge the conventional political outlooks. When the anarchistic hacker metaphor of "information wants to be free" collides with the bureaucratic "need to know" attitude, traditional boundaries of power within organizations are contested.

Metaphors like "knowledge is power" and "information wants to be free" suggest particular responsibilities and ethics issues for knowledge managers. This way of thinking attunes us to the political role and authority that the knowledge manager may exercise—both in terms of formal power (job title) and informal power (wheeling and dealing). Gareth Morgan (1986) has shown us ways that knowledge managers can influence outcomes of decision-making processes. By controlling important information sources, a knowledge manager can influence how organizational issues are defined. This is the gatekeeper function highlighted by the "knowledge transfer" metaphor, although when viewed politically the information gatekeeper is seen as advancing certain organizational interests over others, thus creating patterns of dependency. Even the simple process of slowing down or facilitating particular knowledge transfers has political consequences, as the gatekeeper can make information available in time or too late for the purposes of people who need to use it. Thus, political metaphors make us more aware of the ethical issues caused by conflicts of interest within organizations and the associated issues of power that arise when people use information to exercise control over others.

Community Metaphors

These metaphors alert us to the ways in which successful knowledge management is dependent upon a certain kind of environment or context. Some knowledge managers attest that having a knowledge-friendly culture is the most important factor for successful knowledge management initiatives. Others advocate a hospitable environment that nurtures the growth of knowledge management projects. A positive community would display traits of culture and workers such as intellectual curiosity, an enjoyment of discussing knowledge, pleasure in helping others, and even a sense of play at work. These benign features contrast sharply with the characteristics typically associated with "political" communities (in the pejorative sense of politics) that include mistrust; resentment; and a punitive, taskmaster work environment.

Images that focus our attention on the kind of community within which knowledge management is practiced suggest other kinds of responsibilities and ethics issues for knowledge managers. These images enlarge the relevant arena of action for knowledge managers by emphasizing that there is more at stake than particular knowledge management methods or tools. Also important is the organizational context, or broader community, that can make or break particular knowledge management initiatives. Taking this broader perspective, we would expect the knowledge manager to be involved with issues concerning support for knowledge management within an organization. This perspective will emphasize issues concerning the nature of leadership within an organization, specifically whether or not that leadership understands and supports knowledge management.

Community metaphors will also focus our attention on the kinds of incentives and rewards that are appropriate for knowledge management. Community metaphors for organizations, which were popularized in the 1980s with the corporate culture management literature, tend to take a long-term perspective on organizational dynamics. That which follows is one celebrated business ethics example that emphasizes corporate culture: Johnson & Johnson's Corporate Credo was regarded as indispensable for that company's adept handling of the Tylenol poisonings, precisely because the company's culture had encouraged serious managerial discussion of the Credo for forty years prior to the Tylenol incident! Business today is pressured to take a short-term perspective when assessing the bottom-line impact of any new project or initiative. New programs to implement knowledge management are compelled to demonstrate quick financial benefits. The perspective of community metaphors, which should remind us that "Rome wasn't built in a day," run contrary to the prevailing short-term financial perspective. This constant tension between short- and long-term perspectives will continue to generate many ethical issues for knowledge managers.

CONCLUSION

This chapter argued that discernment is prior to decision in ethics. While this point has general validity, it is especially apt for ethics in knowledge management, as such rapid innovation and change mark this field. Because of this continual flux, knowledge managers always need to ask what is happening. To do this well, it is important to acknowledge and assess the metaphors and images that shape discernment. I have provided some examples of metaphors from knowledge management to provoke further discussion and reflection.

The main purpose of this chapter was to stimulate an ongoing process of critical inquiry into the ethics of knowledge management. Several different participants can join this inquiry. First, ethicists should continue to develop the significance of metaphor and vision for professionals, including knowledge managers. One hopes that they will do this work in terms that are accessible to the pragmatic interests of practicing professionals. Second, knowledge managers should more closely investigate the metaphors that underlie their own literature, methods, and practices, to bring them out in the open for more careful articulation and assessment. To the extent that knowledge managers desire to be taken seriously by the public as professionals, they will embrace this process of critical inquiry because this will elevate their practice above the mundane mechanics of information technology. Third, consumers and citizens who are affected by the work of knowledge managers should also participate in this critical inquiry about the ethics of knowledge management. The metaphors of knowledge management should be assessed against metaphors drawn from broader cultural practices and institutions. There is no reason to assume that any particular professional practice, including knowledge management, possesses the final or most fruitful perspective from which to make ethical judgments. Professional images and norms ultimately must be justified against the values of wider society.

If they are like most professionals, knowledge managers may initially be reluctant to let others—ethicists, consumers, citizens—have a voice in a process of critical inquiry that they would like to call their own. Professionals prefer to think that they know best about matters of their own professions. But even Captain Picard of the *Enterprise* surrounded himself with smart and perceptive people whom he consulted regularly. Knowledge managers will most ably advance the state of their ethics by remembering to include the knowledge of those whom they serve.

References

Agre, Phil. (1997) The Next Internet Hero. *Technology Review*. November/December, p. 61.

Lakoff, George; Mark Johnson. (1980) *Metaphors We Live By*. Chicago: The University of Chicago Press.

MacIntyre, Alisdair. (1981) *After Virtue: A Study in Moral Theory*. Notre Dame, Indiana: University of Notre Dame Press.

Mermann, Alan C. (1997) *Some Chose to Stay: Faith and Ethics in a Time of Plague*. Atlantic Highlands, New Jersey: Humanities Press.

Morgan, Gareth. (1986) *Images of Organization*. Newbury Park, California: Sage Publications, pp. 141-198.

Murdoch, Iris. (1985) *The Sovereignty of Good*. London and New York: Ark Paperbacks.

Nemecek, Larry. (1995) *The Star Trek: The Next Generation Companion*. New York: Pocket Books, pp. 176-177.

Pincoffs, Edmund L. (1986) *Quandaries and Virtues*. Lawrence, Kansas: University Press of Kansas, pp. 13-36.

Solomon, Robert C. (1992) *Ethics and Excellence*. New York and Oxford: Oxford University Press, pp. 22-33.

Stefik, Mark. (1996) *Internet Dreams*. Cambridge and London: The MIT Press.

Stone, Allucquere Rosanne. (1995) *The War of Desire and Technology at the Close of the Mechanical Age*. Cambridge and London: The MIT Press.

Part III :

Knowledge Management—Creating the Culture of Learning & Knowledge Sharing in the Organization

Knowledge Management—
Creating the Culture of Learning &
Knowledge Sharing in the Organization
Introductory Notes

This section is perhaps the most important in the book. What most distinguishes knowledge management from previous related concerns, such as information resources management or managing the archipelago of information sciences, is the awareness that to successfully exploit and leverage knowledge resources requires the creation of an organizational culture that enables, facilitates, and encourages the creation and sharing of information and knowledge.

Addleson's "Organizing to Know and to Learn…" places knowledge management as an organic part of the transition from a modernist positivist organization as factory view of the organization to a post-modernist view of the organization, characterized as a series of interwoven projects, and characterized to a degree defined by the sense-making and learning of its participants. This process of evolution has ramifications for the managerial style, the management process (if indeed management is not already too narrow a term) of organizations in general, with knowledge management simply representing the vanguard of the new management style.

The observant reader will be struck by the congruence of Addleson's arguments about what is required to be successful in this newly evolving context. Gregory's "Knowledge Management and Building the Learning Organization" continues this theme and traces the development of the concepts surrounding the learning organization and its convergence with knowledge management. This analysis is grounded, however, in specific examples and concrete advice.

Sawyer, Eschenfelder, and Heckman ("Knowledge Markets: Cooperation Among Distributed Technical Specialists") examine the actual knowledge markets and knowledge exchange of geographically distributed information technology support specialists, the quintessential example of the knowledge worker in a rapidly changing environment in which the acquisition of new knowledge is essential to job performance. Their findings have important ramifications for the design of knowledge management systems.

Crowley ("Tacit Knowledge and Quality Assurance: Bridging the Theory-Practice Divide") examines tacit knowledge, not merely from the viewpoint of knowledge management, where it plays a crucial role, but also from a larger, even philosophical perspective of what constitutes tacit knowledge and how knowledge management's perception of tacit knowledge relates to that larger concept. More particularly, Crowley examines what corollaries relating to the handling of tacit knowledge in the knowledge management context can be derived from that more fundamental view.

Muralidhar ("Knowledge Management: A Research Scientist's Perspective") looks at knowledge management in the scientific arena and concludes by likening knowledge management to the human cell's self-regulatory process. This eye-opening metaphorical description can be viewed as another way of describing the post-modern management of an organization with which Addleson commenced this section.

CHAPTER 9

Organizing to Know and to Learn: Reflections on Organization and Knowledge Management

Mark Addleson

Director, Program on Social and Organizational Learning

George Mason University

INTRODUCTION

The idea of knowledge management has stimulated the imagination of many writers, consultants, and managers, but is it practical to manage knowledge? For a variety of reasons, the pairing of knowledge and management seems unlikely and ill suited. The main purpose of this chapter is to explore connections between knowledge and management, including the relationship between knowledge management and organizational learning, explaining how they can be seen to converge.

The proliferation of ideas on knowledge management reveals two distinctly different approaches to this topic. In one, knowledge is identified as something physical and is described as an asset. Organizations are urged to leverage their intellectual capital by applying to knowledge tried and tested principles of management, which have developed around the conception of organizations as factories. This approach of treating knowledge as a possession of organizations, affirms conventional management thinking. The object is to control and direct knowledge to serve the organization's goals. The approach, however, runs into difficulties in its implementation. Knowledge proves to be elusive, difficult to measure let alone to try to store, direct, and control.

The other approach is more radical in challenging conventional ideas. Knowledge management signals the demise of the hierarchical, bureaucratic, factory-type organization and reflects the need for more participatory, less authoritarian approaches to management. Knowledge, or more specifically knowing, happens when people interact. This view of knowledge emphasizes process and participation. Knowledge management, which I call "organizing to know," means facilitating interaction among people and groups because that is the source of both knowledge creation and knowledge sharing.

Organizing to know is based on the recognition that contemporary organizations draw their strength and direction from the interaction of people with diverse capabilities, different experiences, and varied perspectives. The focus is people, in the form of networks, teams, groups, or communities of practice. Organizing to know is an approach to managing that is compatible with organizational learning. In this chapter, I will discuss what it means to organize in order to know and to learn, including a view of the role of information technology in knowledge management.

In addition to its more conventional function, the World Wide Web serves as a barometer of popular opinion, taste, and interests. Judging by the number of Web sites that contain something on knowledge management, this is a very fashionable topic. But what are we and organizations to make of it? For many people, the World Wide Web exemplifies the role that technology can play in storing and communicating information. It is not easy, however, to think of the Web as a candidate for managing knowledge by applying particular principles. Is it possible to manage the abundance of information that is on the Web? How much of it is knowledge? How would one set about managing knowledge?

Managing has connotations of systematizing, providing structure, and contributing an overall sense of coherence to an organization. It is also generally associated with coordinating and controlling. The very dynamics of the Web, the constantly changing content contributed by thousands of people for different purposes, which in some ways mirrors the dynamics of business and other organizations, hardly inspires confidence that the information is capable of being managed. In the proliferation of knowledge management Web sites, for example, we find multiple definitions of knowledge management, innumerable attempts to classify knowledge, many different categories of knowledge, and a variety of different descriptions of how organizations are approaching knowledge management. The content evolves and changes. If two people set out on a hypertext journey to gather all the appropriate knowledge on knowledge management they might go in entirely different directions. Will they succeed? If fifty or 100 people do this and try to share their findings, will they be more effective? Will each have more and better knowledge of knowledge management? Can we lay down rules or principles governing what they should do to ensure that their searches are optimal and that they share knowledge properly? Are there means for assessing whether knowledge management is effective?

In the social circumstances of the Web, knowledge and management is an unlikely and uncomfortable pairing. The idea may even appear to be an oxymoron. Is it any different for organizations? Perhaps organizations are more structured and not as open to the variety of "information inputs." Allee (1997, 1998), however, refers to knowledge as "messy." Sparrow's (1998) attempt to define knowledge reveals that it is a perplexing notion, eluding efforts to identify, categorize, or capture it. I intend to argue that the apparent difficulties of managing knowledge are neither especially attributable to the newness of knowledge management nor to the novelty of the Web but are mirrored in organizations. Those difficulties are attributable to the way people see knowledge management and its purposes. If management is associated with giving something structure, coherence, and the integrity of a "whole" (as it usually is), knowledge and management don't belong together. If so, why are people talking about knowledge management (and clearly many are)? Is it possible to manage knowledge?

As a way of shedding some light on these fundamental questions, the main purpose of this chapter is to explain how knowledge and management can be seen to converge and why this depends on appropriate concepts of knowledge and management. In the process of describing what it takes to attain a knowing organization (Choo, 1998), I will show why making sense of knowledge management involves re-examining the meaning of knowledge and management as well as conventional conceptions of organization. My argument is that we should *expect* to find variety, diversity, and disorder when we talk about knowledge. Knowledge management is not so much about creating order or structure as it is about facilitating the ability of organizations to know or to use knowledge. In this context, I will explore how two of the current catch phrases in management circles, "organizational learning" and "knowledge management," are intimately connected.

Although there is anything but consensus about the meaning of knowledge management, the position I adopt and discuss is that the proliferation of ideas on knowledge management (see for example Choo, 1998; Nonaka and Takeuchi, 1995) reveal two distinctly different approaches to this topic. One treats knowledge as a thing that can be possessed, measured, stored, processed, and readily distributed to people who are designated as users of knowledge. The other focuses on knowing, a process involving the interaction or engagement of different people over particular issues.

According to the former, knowledge is like a physical asset and the principles of management are the same as those that apply to a machine. The object is to use it as productively as possible, to get the most out of it, making the organization effective in order to strengthen the bottom line. This way of regarding knowledge is a consequence of adopting a concept of knowledge compatible with an existing theory of organization and management. In line with the general tenor of that theory, knowledge is both capable of control and is a means of control, for example, to gain a competitive advantage. It turns out, however, that this concept of knowledge is unsatisfactory and we encounter serious problems in trying to apply it.

The other more promising, but also more radical, approach to knowledge management focuses on the act of knowing or making sense of events. The underlying premise is that knowledge is what happens in the process of peoples' interaction and that the way to facilitate the creation and use of knowledge is by encouraging people to interact, participate, and to generate and share ideas (Cook and Brown, 1996). This is something that mainstream management practices may discourage in the interests of efficiency and productivity.

At present, the knowledge-as-asset view of knowledge management is the more popular one. That concept of knowledge is compatible with a theory of organization and management that still bears the strong imprint of ideas put forward nearly a century ago, when the issues of what people know and how to use knowledge were not seen to be as important or controversial. Quite different views are being accepted today. In fact, my position is that the interest in knowledge management and organizational learning is evidence of changing views about the world and how it works. It is not the case that in the late twentieth century people in organizations suddenly possess knowledge. People have always had knowledge and have always used it. No doubt people are required to do different things over time and many jobs did not exist a century ago. Equally relevant to the current interest in knowledge management is that our conceptions of what knowledge is (how people know and also what they know), where it comes from, and how it matters in organizations are changing as post-modern views of the world take the place of modern ones. As people come to embrace post-modern ideas, knowledge is regarded as important and problematic in ways that were not appreciated before.

At the same time, there is acknowledgment and a growing awareness of how knowledge and its uses are intimately related to the social side of organization, i.e., to organizational practices that concern the relationships among people.

The social nature of organization comes to the fore when thinking about how to manage organizations to facilitate knowing, rather than about managing knowledge. A discussion of how to organize to know raises questions about exchanging knowledge and of what this means. It also provides the context for speaking about organizational learning in a practical and sensible way. Organizing to know, focusing on processes of interaction, supports learning in organizations; but, as we will see, it also requires a different role of managers than the conventional one that most organizations expect and reward. In the following sections, I examine each of the conceptions of knowledge management and explain the significance of approaches that focus on knowing rather than on knowledge. In the final section, I turn to the question of what it means to "organize to know and to learn."

Knowledge Management Version 1: Knowledge as a Possession

In recent years, various authors have appealed to managers to think of knowledge as an important resource, perhaps the most valuable resource that their organizations possess. These writers include Peter Drucker (1995), who coined the phrase "knowledge revolution." The idea that organizations have a responsibility to manage knowledge stems from a growing belief that knowledge matters in organizations. The prevailing view on how to manage knowledge has its roots in the conventional theory of organization.

Conventional organizational thinking, which has evolved over the past century, has two sources. One of these is the factory (Albrow, 1997). When a formal, scientific theory of management came to be formulated early in this century (e.g., Fayol, 1916; Taylor, 1916), practices associated with managing a factory had a marked impact on the content of the theory. The other source is the philosophy of positivism-empiricism, also known as modernism, that has dominated Western thought and science in this century. When organizational theory and management science was formulated, it was shaped by the particular conception of the world and how it works that is embedded in positivism (see Cooper and Burrell, 1988; Reed, 1993 on modernism in relation to organizations).

Both these elements, modernism and the organization as a factory, are responsible for the fact that, until recently, very little was said about knowledge and its use in organizations. As a philosophy of scientific enquiry, positivism and empiricism tends to obscure rather than to highlight questions about knowledge. In addition, in a machine-dominated organizational environment the management process and knowledge needs are very different, say, to a government welfare agency, a hospital, or an environmental monitoring and lobbying association. As a consequence, the conventional theory of organization is an inappropriate foundation for thinking about how to manage knowledge. In this section, I examine how the two elements constrain the view of knowledge in organizations. My objective is to set the stage for a more congenial approach for understanding how knowledge matters in organizations.

Prompted by the contributions of scholars like Kuhn (1970) and Feyerabend (1978) on the philosophy of science, from the 1970s onwards the foundations of Western science have come under close scrutiny and in the process much has been written about the theory of knowledge that underpins modernist intellectual thought (see for example, Rorty, 1980). Here, it is appropriate to describe briefly those issues that have a bearing on the view of knowledge as an asset or as a thing able to be possessed.

Modernism, which emphasizes the role of observation, measurement, and testing in science, depicts the whole world as a set of tangible, physical things (see Addleson, forthcoming). From a positivist standpoint, the world is analogous to a huge set of building blocks of different shapes, colors, and sizes. Each type of block represents some aspect of the world, from atoms to animals. Careful observation of the world will enable the researcher to gain knowledge of what is in the world. Knowledge is gained by observing the different elements as well as their interconnections to each other. The sort of knowledge that people want to acquire is knowledge about what the world consists of, what the different things are that exist in the world; and how the world works, how the different components are interrelated.

Once a person has acquired knowledge, he/she possesses a representation of part of the world, a sort of blueprint, which can then be passed on to others. That knowledge, which is depicted as an entity, can be stored (a stock of knowledge), expanded (the growth of knowledge), and distributed. It is a blueprint in the sense that it bears a one-on-one relationship with things in the world, which is why Rorty (1980) refers to scientific models as a "mirror of nature." Once people have knowledge they have an understanding of how the world works and can predict what will happen. People who possess knowledge have the power to control what will happen in the world and, therefore, to change the way the world works in order to attain goals that are identified as necessary or desirable or in order to correct problems or deficiencies in the way things work.

This is the world view reflected in Western management thinking. Managing means organizing part of the world—planning and structuring it—to achieve desired goals. There is a widely held belief that the purpose of organizational theory is to provide managers with knowledge, or blueprints, of how organizations work and of what they should do to achieve desired goals. In recent years, as knowledge came to be seen as an important part of what makes organizations work, it became necessary to find a place for knowledge in management thinking. The obvious question is how to represent knowledge. In consideration of the above arguments, it is not surprising that knowledge was equated with a physical asset and that people began to think and speak of managing knowledge in the same way that they spoke of managing assets. The argument that knowledge can be managed has much to do with the conception of an organization as a factory.

A factory is an organizational environment in which machines are prominent and the workplace takes on some of the characteristics of a machine: repetitiveness; a fixed structure; specific processes or sequences of events. I have described below three sets of attributes of factories that, when taken together, help to sustain a belief that managing knowledge is a practical goal and doing so involves collecting and distributing knowledge.

An Interrelated Organizational "System" or Integrated Structure

The physical layout of plant as well as a flow of materials, which are successively transformed as they proceed through the factory, both lend credence to the notion of an integrated system. Viewing a factory as a bounded system is also possible because manufacturing operations are described as a separate and distinct part of a "chain" consisting of suppliers, manufacturers, distributors, and customers.

The Repetitive, Piecemeal Nature of Work

In a factory, most of the people whose contributions are part of a clearly defined workflow do the same jobs over and over. This is the basis of the division of labor exemplified by Adam Smith's (1981) description of pin making. One implication is that people require only a limited range of readily identifiable skills to do a particular job and can be trained to perform them. Once trained for a specialized function there is not much they can learn that will be useful to them. Both the division of labor and the segmentation of the production process into discrete operations mean that people operate largely independently of each other and that there is little opportunity for cooperation. On the factory floor, human interaction generally revolves around the requirements of the plant rather than, say, out of a need to collaborate in order to arrive at a decision.

The Dominance of Machines in Organizational Life and Management Thinking

In many factories, machines are purposely made to perform particular operations in a production line geared towards a specific product. The big, strategic decisions are about whether or not to invest in these fixed assets and the embedded technology. Investment decisions are largely irreversible for, unless a factory can be sold as a going concern, purpose-made machines generally have a small resale value. Once these decisions are made, the question of how things will be done has been answered and the nature of the business is fixed. It will produce whatever the machines have been designed to produce and the task at hand is to achieve the greatest possible throughput and to contribute to the bottom line, covering overheads and then adding to profits. The important management decisions concern these issues. They are not made on the factory floor by the people working there; rather a few senior managers who strategize and coordinate the whole operation make them. Under the circumstances described, most of the knowledge required to run a factory can be, and is, centralized or concentrated at the top.

The senior managers, with engineering and accounting know-how, make the decisions. Production-engineering and accounting-financial knowledge is what is needed to run a factory, except for some additional marketing expertise about distribution and pricing. Efficiency and the basis for measuring the organization's performance is closely related to physical-engineering considerations and both the concept and the means of assessing performance are relatively clear cut. The same is true when it comes to assessing whether or not the organization is successful. Managing means focusing on inputs and outputs as well as costs and receipts. Once the factory is up and running the most important consideration on a day-to-day basis is producing and selling the greatest amount of output at the lowest possible cost.

Given that the workflow is largely determined by technological requirements and product specifications and is preprogrammed into the production process, it is realistic to suggest that those at the top have a more or less complete view as well as overall control. In the planning stages, the people at the top are able to treat the organization as an integrated whole and they have an understanding of how the whole system works. The design of the machines and factory determines what is produced and how it is done so most of the day-to-day activities involve carrying out plans that were originally made at the top. Many of the factory's activities are the result of decisions made some time ago.

Workers, identifiable as a distinct group, are literally appendages to machines, there to serve and service them. People's relationships are with machines, not each other. Most of the people in the factory can do little but work according to a predetermined schedule. Each needs definite skills to perform specific activities. Each is required to demonstrate a limited set of competencies to fulfill their responsibilities as a small part of an overall system. Because a job is a series of repetitive activities, people can be trained, rather like performing animals. Experience is relatively unimportant. A person's responsibilities are geared to the rate at which the machines are capable of processing materials and their performance is indexed on this rate.

Efficiency in production also demands that various activities are coordinated. This is the task of outsiders as opposed to people working on the line. The supervisors are responsible for observing a number of people at work and they have authority over them. Managers too are outsiders. They have a different education and know-how and constitute another distinct group, probably from a different socioeconomic class. They make operating decisions, translating the strategic plans into the requirement for operating the machines efficiently and keeping production lines running smoothly on a day-to-day basis. The process of coordination is reflected in a hierarchical chain of command that serves to link the various parts and to integrate the overall system.

This is a model for bureaucracy: an organization comprising many separate parts linked to an intrinsic structure that has an inherent rationality in the physical flow of materials as they are transformed. The ability to run a factory from the top, by the people who have a view of an integrated production process and possess the financial and engineering know-how, also explains the conception of managing as a "top-down" process. Because activities are geared to getting the most out of the investment in machines, the mass-production environment of a factory is also potentially authoritarian with ordinary people being subject to the dictates of machines and managers. That authoritarianism is often manifested in practice under the guise of efficient and profitable production. Because machines rule the process of physically transforming inputs into outputs, the organization described here is rigid, highly structured, somewhat determinate, and technical-know-how intensive.

These characteristics account for the type of assumptions that are associated with the favored approach to knowledge management: a belief that an identifiable, determinable, and attainable "set" of knowledge is required to organize efficiently; that knowledge can be managed, as if it is just another aspect of the material flow of production; and that knowledge is a source of control, a means to solve problems and to optimize. The emphasis on such characteristics as structure, determinism, and optimization identifies this as an archetypically modernist depiction of an organization. Since these are characteristics of a factory, it is perhaps not surprising that, without making the connection explicit, industrial organization served modernist writers as an archetype for all organizations and that, as Morgan (1986) explains, the machine is a dominant metaphor for organization.

The majority of people in industrial organizations need to know very little. As depicted so vividly in films like Charles Chaplin's *Modern Times* and Fritz Lang's *Metropolis*, employees are cogs in the machine. Their organizational lives are highly regimented and they are unable to influence or shape their circumstances. Whatever they learn beyond their initial training is largely irrelevant to what they can do in their jobs. The repetitive, somewhat determinate, circumstances of the mass-production factory, however, are far removed from those of most people in organizations today, even in manufacturing. Unfortunately, a concept of knowledge as technical know-how, which has relevance in managing production lines even though it is not the only sort of knowledge on which people draw, is still with us. Even more unfortunate, with the growing interest in knowledge management, possessable knowledge is being cast as the only knowledge that matters in organizations.

In the context of the modernist-factory theory of organization, the knowledge-as-possession approach to knowledge management is a paradoxical idea. The theory does not take into account knowledge or its uses in organizations, so asking managers to pay attention to knowledge, and to think about how to leverage it, is in some way an appeal to move beyond standard approaches to management. Referring to knowledge as a resource or asset, however, is an indication that they should remain within conventional theory. This begs the question of how to deal with knowledge within the ambit of standard approaches where managing is about efficiency and bottom-line performance. For example, what guidelines of performance are relevant in managing productive capabilities and in assessing whether or not value is being maximized? The conventional principles and measures of performance don't seem to be appropriate. What is the meaning of productive capacity in knowledge-based organizations? How is it measured? What is the unit of knowledge that organizations are supposed to value? Is it the person? Is it his/her learning? What determines the value of a knowledge asset? Is the value based on a person's age or experience? The arguments in the next section suggest that it is fruitless to try to find answers to these questions. The questions are misguided because the conception of knowledge that shapes them is problematic. In order to understand the nature of knowledge and its role in organizations we have to move well outside the box of conventional, organizational thinking.

Knowledge Management Version II: Knowing Through Participation

In the West, as Max Weber (1948) saw early on, one of the defining characteristics of this century was the attempt to make all organizations look like factories and to run them along bureaucratic lines. Yet at the close of the century, bureaucracy is clearly on the wane (Albrow, 1997) and the management principles associated with that style of organization are now becoming outmoded. Why is this so?

The answer rests on two considerations. One is that the modernist concept of knowledge, as a set of facts about the world that people can possess and distribute, is giving way to postmodern ideas that highlight social processes of knowing (see, for example, Bergquist, 1993; Eccles and Nohria, 1992 on post-modern views of managing and organization). The viability of bureaucracy involves dual assumptions—that people operate almost independently of each other guided only by rules and occasional advice from supervisors, and that all the important knowledge needed to run an organization is in the hands of a few people who pass it on to whomever needs it. Changing views of organization, on both what an organization is and how it works, which highlight the social interaction associated with organizing, discredit both assumptions. This is the second factor behind the demise of bureaucracy. The two sets of issues are inter-linked in that emphasis on the social nature of knowing leads to questions about organizations as social groups and about what organizations know and how people use knowledge. These questions as well as their answers are beyond the compass of modernism. Once posed, they require us to consider the notion of knowledge management much more thoughtfully than has been the case and also to be more circumspect in claims about what knowledge management might accomplish.

Scholars like Polanyi (1973), whose work provides important insights into questions about knowledge, including what it is and how it is used in everyday life, typically have drawn their ideas from a tradition of Western intellectual thought referred to as "interpretive understanding." That tradition, which includes phenomenology (Schütz, 1972) and hermeneutics (Gadamer, 1975), associates knowledge with the way people understand or see things; i.e., with the way they interpret their circumstances. Compared with the modernist view of knowledge as a thing that can be possessed in the form of "facts about the world," the interpretive tradition relates knowledge to people's understanding. Understanding is interpretation and interpretation is a social process in which people come to make sense of things in the context of their relationships with other people and against the background of the diverse meanings that are given to things by groups with different languages and varied cultures (Addleson, 1995). Because knowing, as interpretation, relies on meanings that people give to things, in particular social circumstances, this view of knowledge is also known as "social constructionism" (Berger and Luckmann, 1967; Mangan, 1987).

Social constructionism literally turns a modernist view of knowledge upside down. Instead of regarding knowledge as something derived from the world, the world is a reflection of how social groups have learned to see it. The world is the meaning that people give to things. Knowing is understanding those meanings and making sense of the world, or giving meaning to it, in order to make one's way in life. It is in the context of a paradigm embracing social constructionism that postmodern ideas about organization are intelligible (see Hassard, 1993, 1996; Boje, et al., 1996; Linstead, et al., 1996 on post-modern approaches to organization and management), that the idea of a learning organization is meaningful, and that it is practical to make connections between a learning organization, or organizing to learn, and knowledge management, or organizing to know.

In the preceding section, I identified how an industrial organizational setting influences the way people think about knowledge in organizations, and I showed that this has a bearing on how knowledge management is conceived. What is it about contemporary organizations that require us to think differently about "knowledge requirements" of people in these organizations? The answer is just about everything, starting with the matter of what an organization does, i.e., what its business is about. The business of a factory is nearly always clear. A factory produces something and organization takes place around the plant or physical assets, in order to put them to work. If the heart of an industrial organization is its assembly line, what is the heart of a biotechnology organization, a systems integration business, a group dedicated to the eradication of poverty, or a government regulatory agency? In the case of these examples, *what* is the organization and *where* is the organization? To what can one point and say, "This is what the organization is about"? Questions like these, I believe, illustrate the demise of modernism and the rise of post-modern approaches to knowledge because these are questions about knowledge, what we know about organization, and how we gain this knowledge. The answers reveal that the definition of an organization is not at all clear cut. At the same time, they help to direct us towards other conceptions of knowledge management.

In answering the question, "Where is the organization?" it does not help to look for something tangible, such as a building. The names that appear above doors and on letterheads also do not identify the activities through which things get done. Organization, rather, is found in something as intangible as a sense of shared purpose among one or more people or among a group, such as a community. Indeed, today it is increasingly common to hear organizations being referred to as "communities of practice" (Lave and Wenger, 1991; Brown and Duguid, 1991; Boland and Tenkasi, 1995), groups of people with similar interests doing things together to achieve some end. What makes an organization is people's mutual understanding of their own and others' interests and purposes, and the recognition that their interests are somehow bound up in doing something to which they all contribute. Organization has to do with participation.

It is not always clear to the people in an organization as to in what they are participating. One of the things that people do when they are together is continually clarify this matter. The business of many organizations can change as quickly as it takes people to identify and respond to emerging challenges or to pursue new opportunities. The organization may be in the field of systems integration, public relations, or consumer protection, but what the people actually do—how they see their purposes, understand priorities, identify opportunities, and who they regard as potential competitors—emerges in the process of organizing through the interaction of people as they participate in conversations with others. In a strict sense, organization is found in the interaction among people and organization is an emergent phenomenon. It is in the course of interaction that people's sense of purpose, and even their contributions, come to be defined. From this standpoint, the knowledge base as well as people's knowledge requirements are very different from the mainly technical and financial considerations associated with managing factories, so too is the nature of management. Compared with conventional metaphors of organization as system and structure, this view, which associates organization with discourse and stories, has profound implications for our conception of organizational life and what it means to manage or to organize (Addleson, 1998).

In answering the question "What do people do in organizations?" Weick (1995, 1996) adopts a similar post-modern, interpretive perspective to the one that I presented. He argues that much of what occurs daily in an organization is "sense-making." In almost every organizational setting and at all levels of the organization, in groups and teams, in meetings, around water coolers, and even in bathrooms, collective sense-making is the order of the day. People are usually engaged in a process of making meaning of their circumstances, coming to understand opportunities, clarifying tasks, and reflecting on progress, asking for others' advice and assistance. Sense-making is virtually continuous and, in the process, people come to know and learn about what they themselves and other people are doing and they establish or redefine priorities, objectives, and interests.

The idea that organizational life is about sense-making involves two underlying assertions. One is that, for practical purposes, it is useful to view organizations as comprising a wide variety of projects in which different people are engaged at different times. The other is that, for the most part, people do not have a fixed, well-defined sense of what they are doing, could be doing, or should be doing.

I use the term "project" to bring two aspects of organization to the fore. The first is in the contrast between projects and repetitive, routine activities that characterize a factory floor. In addition, I want to make the point that organizations are *not* tightly knit, integrated communities bound by a strong sense of common purpose or a common vision. Projects involve people coming together to work on something, then moving on when they have done the work. Projects may include producing a prototype, undertaking a contract for a client, drawing up a budget, writing a set of departmental regulations or a report, reviewing the lessons from a previous contract, and so on. Any of these projects in themselves might consist of other projects. A project involves people working together for a time. During any workday, a person will almost certainly be engaged in a variety of projects, each involving different groups of people and in different stages of completion. The participants may change during the course of the project and, when the work is done, they will already be involved in new projects, again most probably consisting of different groups of people.

The other implicit assertion involved in describing organizations as groups of sense-makers is that, even when projects are ostensibly well specified along such lines as "our goal is to complete the installation of a new operating system by June 30" and the details of the project are laid out in both a proposal and a plan of action, people still identify and clarify their purposes and priorities, make decisions, and take action as they proceed. That is what sense-making concerns. If an organization consists of a series of projects and the parameters and activities of projects are established and clarified while the projects are in progress, then the organization itself may be considered as emerging or evolving over time.

These points help to underscore that sense-making is a social process. Weick (1995) says of sense-making that "It is never solitary because what a person does internally is contingent on others. Even monologues…presume an audience. And the monologue changes as the audience changes." In a formal organizational setting, the social nature of sense-making is even more apparent. People engage one another in the course of their day-to-day activities. They meet as a planning group, call on subcontractors, report to their departmental colleagues, present reports to clients. Those interactions are the context of sense-making—in face-to-face conversation, in the boardroom or the mail room, on the telephone, by e-mail, and so on. If we think of the organizations as multiple narratives all going on simultaneously, those narratives where the sense-making occurs are the heart of organization (see Czarniawska, 1997 on narrative approaches to organizations). The narratives actually represent our sense of organization, of people doing things together for a purpose; they are the organization. In meetings and on the telephone, people establish direction, clarify purpose, identify opportunities, examine concerns, make plans, make decisions, delegate responsibilities, and so on.

Conventional organizational theory treats organizations as monolithic, well-integrated systems all under the authority of a chief executive, and controlled by the managers to whom the CEO delegates authority. One popular image of organization, which this description brings to mind, is of a ship. The arguments set out above, however, present an entirely different view of organization; one where groups of different people with diverse agendas interact, make sense of their circumstances, and get things done. Even when detailed directives are handed down from "above," the people for whom they are intended interpret them in the context in which they are received, in the light of their own perspectives and priorities on organizational matters. They may act on the directives or put them aside. Perspectives differ for a variety of reasons. People's circumstances are different. The interests of people in the boardroom and mailroom generally cannot be compared and the boardroom's view of the mailroom no doubt is very different from that of the people who actually work there. The working groups that represent organization manifest a variety of cultures. People in the marketing department generally have a different outlook and way of doing things than people in software engineering. When people are working within their groups, they make sense of the organization differently. They develop different approaches to doing things, have different concerns, and pursue different agendas. In other project contexts, people from marketing, software engineering, and training may be working side-by-side. Once again interaction among them provides the ground for sense-making and decision making.

Far from the image of an organization being coordinated by specifically designated managers whose activities supposedly produce a tightly-knit, smoothly functioning system, in the organizational context, I am describing such coordination as takes place as being largely the result of people participating in overlapping conversations. As they do so, they take their views, for example, about the decisions made and the problems identified in the course of one project, to another project and another group of people. This description gives practical meaning to the idea of a "learning organization," where people are continuously finding out, making sense, and learning; taking their insights and experience to social contexts in which others learn and act. The creative energy behind organization, which shapes what the organization is and what it does, stems from the diverse views of a range of people who, through their participation in a range of activities or projects, bring their individual experiences, different skills, varied ideas, and different levels of enthusiasm and commitment to bear. Participation is the basis of learning, sense-making, and action.

ORGANIZING TO KNOW, ORGANIZING TO LEARN

The idea behind "knowledge management version II" is that, with a good grasp of the social, discursive nature of organization, it is both possible and desirable to facilitate or manage the interactions that shape the course of the organization and, in the process, to make more effective use of what people learn and know. In this section, my objecive is to examine briefly what it means to organize to know and to learn.

Open Organization

A central point in the discussion above is that both knowing—as sense-making—and learning, as well as being closely related, are a consequence of social interaction. The most important element of organizing to learn and to know, therefore, is an organizational culture where people are able to interact effectively, to share ideas, relate their experiences, give their points of view, and also to be heard in the process of doing so. I call this an open organization. It is helpful to think of the organization as both a physical and virtual space where people interact. One role of managers is to encourage the effective use of that space, nurturing a climate where people interact easily, are open to the ideas and suggestions of others, and are exposed to what different groups are doing.

Unfortunately, the management practices of many organizations do just the reverse, they fragment and segment, emphasizing division (and authority over separate divisions) rather than integration. Hierarchy and rank, rather than interests and experience, influence who has a voice and whose voices are heard. The disaster that killed the crew of the space shuttle *Challenger* offers a sobering reminder of a situation where people had both the expertise and the experience to give a view on possible consequences of the engineering defects of the solid rocket boosters and knew from experience that problems were looming. Although they tried to express their concerns they were ignored. Organizations also encourage adversarial conduct, looking approvingly upon competition as a means to maintain and enhance efficiency but remaining silent about collaboration. Even the physical layout of the workspace in many organizations speaks volumes about the lack of opportunity for people to interact and possibly even about the desire of managers to prevent them from doing so. *Dilbert* effectively lampoons a widespread corporate culture that places people behind cubicles and expects them to remain there.

Diversity and Participation

In discussing learning, in much the same way that I have explained the context of sense-making, Lave and Wenger (1991) argue that people are involved in a variety of communities of practice. Their main point is an important one in the context of organizing to know and to learn. Participation, they say, is always peripheral. Communities do not have a center. Because the interactions of people are complex and the conversations of communities shift among different topics, no matter how much experience people have in a particular area or how much of an expert they may regard themselves as being, they, like everyone else, participate on the periphery of communities and their conversations.

One lesson to be drawn is that when it comes to participation in the sense-making processes, which influences decisions and shapes the direction of organizations, everyone potentially has something to contribute and everyone's voice is potentially important. Conventional organizational thinking sees organizations as problems waiting to be solved and concludes that the way to do this is to put experts, who have the answers, in charge. The result is an authoritarian approach to organizing that is reinforced by hierarchy. The social constructionist foundations of sense-making hold that human action rests on being able to make meaning of situations rather than on finding answers. Meaning-making is not the exclusive domain of formally trained experts or of designated leaders. Practical experience and insight counts and all sorts of people have a contribution to make.

A learning organization, which encourages people to apply constructively what they know, is an open organization where the peripheral nature of participation is appreciated and people value, and look for, diversity in the contributions of their colleagues. In organizing to know, what is relevant is the people's willingness and ability to engage each other. Another task of managers is to facilitate engagement, providing opportunities for people to ask questions and to provide their points of view, while having a perspective on what seems to be important, when it is useful to open discussion and reflection, and who may have the insights or experience to guide the group. An open organization means recognizing the creativity of sense-making, in terms of identifying opportunities and objectives, a point that Malhotra (1997) makes in describing measures for facilitating knowledge management. His statement stresses the need to avoid the pitfall of trying to direct people's decisions and conduct by predetermined plans and goals. "Instead of the traditional emphasis on controlling the people and their behaviors by setting up pre-defined goals and procedures ...[we] need to view the organization as a human community capable of providing diverse meanings to information...generated by...technological systems" (Malhotra, 1997).

Information Technology

The knowledge-as-possessable-facts approach to knowledge management focuses very heavily on information technology. Technology, which is useful in storing, retrieving, and routing data (in the form of bits and bytes), is heralded as the key to managing knowledge and, thus, as a potential savior of organizations in what is described as a knowledge-intensive world. A more considered view of knowledge and knowing suggests that technology is not and cannot be the heart of knowledge management, but only plays a supporting role. In organizing to know, the main emphasis always has to fall on people and their ways of knowing. I will explain why.

Because Western society is generally enamored of technology, information technology is sometimes regarded as an end in itself. For example, one hears people saying, "This technology will enable us to do the following." But technology is always a *possible* means of doing things and whether or not it serves the intended purposes depends in part on users' attitudes towards it. Although the issue is seldom considered, the question of whether or not people feel comfortable with technology is very important in an organizational setting, especially with GroupWare. If it is to be useful as a means of sharing ideas and of collaborative sense-making, a relatively large number of people have to participate in using it. If one or more people fail to participate, the groups using GroupWare are effectively restructured by their lack of participation and communities become divided into insiders and outsiders, users and non-users.

Like all tools, the usefulness of information technology depends on whether or not people can "connect" with it. Connecting is the same sort of appreciative, interpretive process associated with making sense of a book or a work of art (Gadamer, 1975) although, in the case of information technology, developing an affinity probably requires more practice, a much greater effort, and is time-consuming. Like the beauty of a painting, however, the value of information technology stems from a relationship between the technology and the people who appreciate and use it. In organizations, this often means a large number of people with different interests, expectations, and capabilities. Unless they make that connection, appreciate its contribution to their everyday activities and their ways of doing things, and make the effort to *cooperate* in using it, it won't serve much purpose at all (Orlikowski, 1993; Schrage, 1995).

When assessing the role of information technology in the context of knowledge management, another consideration is that the technology does not provide knowledge, although it can play a useful part in the social process of sense-making. Well-designed information systems can help people who are willing to use them to find information. Finding information, however, is an interpretive process not a technological one. Whether or not something is information and whether or not the information is appropriate or relevant is always established when people give meaning to things in the context of the narratives and their interests pertaining to the particular projects with which they are involved. The process of making sense of information is both social and personal. For example, the narrative of a particular group influences individuals' views about how to do some aspect of a project. As a result they look for certain information, although various people may look for very different information. What they make of the information that they come up with depends on what it means to them, or how they interpret it, which is a personal process (Polanyi, 1973). What one person regards as potentially useful another completely overlooks because she/he does not appreciate it now or simply does not understand it.

Action and decisions follow *understanding*—the way people see, interpret, and know—rather than information. Information technology only partially affects understanding and it is only one of many factors that do. A large investment in information technology cannot guarantee that people have the right information. In fact, an irony is that people make sense of their circumstances and take action in light of whatever information they have. There is also no denying that intuition may prove to be just as important as the word of an expert. Databases are only one of a large number of possible sources from which decisive information may come. These include trusted confidants, for trust is an important consideration when people make sense of others' views or interpret information. They may be more willing to listen to trusted colleagues or friends than to search for information on the Web or in a library. Social networks, based on relationships, are always central in organizing to know. "Managing to know" means focusing first on social processes of sense-making and only then on how information technology may help people to make sense of organizational matters.

What Is a Manager?

As I noted earlier, conventional approaches to management depict the manager as an outsider who has little direct or ongoing involvement with the people he/she manages and whose role in organizing subordinates is vested in a position with a title. Some people are designated as managers while others are not, and the position supposedly gives the manager control over the others. In order to organize to know and learn, it is necessary to cast the manager in an entirely different role as a participant among peers or a collaborator with colleagues. There are two interrelated reasons for this, one that explains the importance of collaboration and participation and one that concerns the nature of people's relationships.

With a view of the contemporary organization as a large number of projects, or of various groups simultaneously engaged in a variety of activities, it is difficult to make good sense of what a group of people are doing or why they are doing it unless one participates in the narratives of that group. Bear in mind that each group is making sense of what it is doing as it progresses. Knowing what the group is doing—for example, who is involved, how they are contributing, and who is at loggerheads with whom—comes from understanding the context of activities and that understanding involves participating in the interactions of the group. Someone who does not participate, but is an outsider engaged in other activities and pursing other interests, has a different perspective. His/her knowledge of what he/she is doing is different. On occasion, it is useful to have an outsider's view, recognizing that it is a different perspective. However, since groups make their own meanings and forge their own directions based on these in order to organize groups effectively, participation rather than outside control is important.

The other related reason why managing involves participating is because effective collaboration revolves around people's relationships with each other (Schrage, 1995). Relationships involve commitments and responsibilities towards others, which is the basis of self-management. Through close working relationships people get a sense of each other's capabilities and interests, come to appreciate their contributions, and develop the trust that is an essential ingredient in creating an open organization where people are able to speak and to be heard. In turn, this influences what people contribute and how they do so, for example, whether or not others are able to make use of their experience and points of view. People's sense of self and self-worth is affected by the extent of their participation while their views of others' commitments and credibility are similarly influenced by their assessment of others' involvement.

Organizations, like the social relationships and communities that underpin them, are complex. Organizing to know, where "making use of knowledge" is understood as a social process of sense-making, involves an understanding of the complexities of social relationships. When boundaries between groups come into play, people either cannot or will not see what others are saying or recognize their capabilities and contributions. Organizing to know means working to bridge these boundaries. Because the strength of organization lies in drawing people to work together, organizing to know involves doing just that—fostering new communities of practice, helping to develop relationships and networks, and helping to find common points of interest.

When viewed in the context of peripheral participation in loosely-defined communities or groups, the ability to organize is not a permanent quality that one person possesses. It depends on people's experience, capabilities, and interests within the group and on others' recognition and appreciation of those qualities. Management is not a position. Managing to know and learn is the *process* of organizing and leading rather than the *role* of controlling. The former is undertaken by a variety of people and is best done by different people at different times. In this and other ways, organizing to know and to learn highlights the paramount position of community. Getting anything done is a collaborative effort not least because the social nature of sense-making means that gaining knowledge and using knowledge is a reciprocal process requiring the commitment and involvement of a variety of people. Organizing to know ultimately means recognizing and rewarding people's *joint* contributions as a community, a consideration that indicates that organizing to know and to learn from one another actually constitutes a major departure from conventional principles of management.

References

Addleson, M. (forthcoming) "Stories about Firms: Boundaries, Structures, Strategies and Processes," *Managerial and Decision Economics*, special issue on Strategy and the Market Process.

Addleson, M. (1998) "Languages of Possession and Participation: Traps, Tropes, and Trapezes of Organizational Discourse," paper delivered at the 3rd International Conference on Organizational Discourse, Kings College Management Centre, London, 29-31 July.

Addleson, M. (1995) *Equilibrium Versus Understanding: Towards the Restoration of Economics as Social Theory*, London and New York, Routledge.

Albrow, M. (1997) *Do Organizations Have Feelings?*, London and New York, Routledge.

Allee, V. (1997) "12 Principles of Knowledge Management," *Training and Development*, November, pp. 71-74.

Allee, V. (1998) *The Knowledge Evolution: Expanding Organizational Intelligence*, Boston, Butterworth-Heineman.

Berger, P.; Luckmann, T. (1967) *The Social Construction of Reality*, London, Allen Lane.

Bergquist, W. (1993) *The Postmodern Organization: Mastering the Art of Irreversible Change*, San Francisco, Jossey-Bass Publishers.

Boje, D.M.; Gephardt, R.P.; Thatchenkery, T.J. (eds) (1996) *Postmodern Management and Organization Theory*, Thousand Oaks, CA, SAGE Publications.

Boland, R.J. Jr.; Tenkasi, R.V. (1995) "Perspective Making and Perspective Taking in Communities of Knowing," *Organization Science*, vol. 6, no. 3, pp. 350-372.

Brown, J.S.; Duguid, P. (1991) "Organizational Learning and Communities-of-Practice: Toward a Unified View of Working, Learning, and Innovation," *Organization Science*, vol. 2, no. 1, pp. 40-57.

Choo, C.W. (1998) *The Knowing Organization: How Organizations Use Information to Construct Meaning, Create Knowledge, and Make Decisions*, New York, Oxford University Press.

Cook, S.D.N.; Brown, J.S. (1996) "Bridging Epistemologies: The Generative Dance Between Organizational Knowledge and Organizational Knowing," *Mimeo*.

Cooper, R.; Burrell, G. (1988) "Modernism, Postmodernism and Organizational Analysis: An Introduction," *Organizational Studies*, vol. 9, no. 1, pp. 91-112.

Czarniawska, B. (1997) *Narrating the Organization: Dramas of Institutional Identity*, Chicago and London, University of Chicago Press.

Drucker, P. (1995) *Managing in a Time of Great Change*, New York, Truman Talley Books.

Eccles, R.G.; Nohria, N. (1992) *Beyond the Hype: Rediscovering the Essence of Management*, Boston, Harvard Business School Press.

Fayol, H. (1949) *General and Industrial Management*, Storrs, C. (trans), London, Pitman Publishing Ltd.

Feyerabend, P.K. (1978) *Against Method: Outline of an Anarchistic Theory of Knowledge*, London, Verso.

Gadamer, H.-G. (1975) *Truth and Method*, Barden, G.; Cumming, J. (eds and trans), New York, Seabury Press.

Hassard, J. (1993) "Postmodernism and Organizational Analysis: An Overview," In Hassard, J.; Parker, M. (eds), *Postmodernism and Organizations*, London, SAGE Publications.

—— (1996) "Exploring the Terrain of Modernism and Postmodernism in Organization Theory," In Boje, D.M.; Gephardt, R.P.; Thatchenkery, T.J. (eds), *Postmodern Management and Organization Theory*, Thousand Oaks, CA, SAGE Publications.

Hassard, J.; Parker, M. (eds) (1993) *Postmodernism and Organizations*, London, SAGE Publications.

Kuhn, T.S. (1970) *The Structure of Scientific Revolutions*, 2nd ed., Chicago, University of Chicago Press.

Lave, J.; Wenger, E. (1991) *Situated Learning: Legitimate Peripheral Participation*, New York, Cambridge University Press.

Linstead, S.; Small, R.G.; Jeffcutt, P. (eds) (1996) *Understanding Management*, London, SAGE Publications.

Malhotra, Y. (1997) "Knowledge Management for the New World of Business," University of Pittsburgh, Katz School of Business, article available at: http://www.brint.com/km/whatis.htm.

Mangan, I.L. (ed) (1987) *Organizational Analysis and Development: A Social Construction of Organizational Behaviour*, Chichester, John Wiley and Sons.

Morgan, G. (1986) *Images of Organization*, Newbury Park, CA, SAGE Publications.

Nonaka, I.; Takeuchi, H. (1995) *The Knowledge-Creating Company: How Japanese Companies Create the Dynamics of Innovation*, New York, Oxford University Press.

Orlikowski, W. J. (1993) "Learning from Notes: Organizational Issues in Groupware Implementation," *The Information Society*, vol. 9, no. 3, pp. 237-250.

Polanyi, M. (1973) *Personal Knowledge: Towards a Post-Critical Philosophy*, London, Routledge and Kegan Paul.

Reed, M. (1993) "Organizations and Modernity: Continuity and Discontinuity in Organization Theory," In Hassard, J.; Parker, M. (eds), *Postmodernism and Organizations*, London, SAGE Publications.

Rorty, R. (1980) Philosophy and the Mirror of Nature, Oxford, Basil Blackwell.

Schrage, M. (1995) *No More Teams!: Mastering the Dynamics of Creative Collaboration*, New York, Currency/Doubleday.

Schütz, A. (1972) *The Phenomenology of the Social World*, Walsh, G.; Lehnert, F. (trans) with intro. by Walsh, G., London, Heinemann Educational Books.

Shafritz, J.M.; Ott, J.S. (1996) *Classics of Organization Theory*, 4th ed., Belmont, CA, Wadsworth Publishing Company.

Smith, A. (1981) *An Inquiry into the Nature and Causes of the Wealth of Nations*, vol. 1, Todd, W.B. (ed) Indianapolis, Liberty Classics.

Sparrow, J. (1998) *Knowledge in Organizations: Access to Thinking at Work*, London, SAGE Publications.

Taylor, F. W. (1916) "The Principles of Scientific Management," Bulletin of the Taylor Society, December. Reprinted in Shafritz, J.M.; Ott, J.S. (1996) *Classics of Organization Theory*, 4th ed., Belmont, CA, Wadsworth Publishing Company.

Weber, M. (1948) "Bureaucracy," In Gerth, H.; Mills, C.W. (eds), *From Max Weber*, London, Routledge and Kegan Paul.

Weick, K (1995) *Sensemaking in Organizations*, Thousand Oaks, CA, SAGE Publications.

—— (1996) "Prepare Your Organization to Fight Fires," *Harvard Business Review*, vol. 74, no. 3, pp. 143-148.

CHAPTER 10

Knowledge Management and Building the Learning Organization

Vicki L. Gregory
Associate Professor
University of South Florida

INTRODUCTION

Ubiquitous change makes rapid responses and adaptation critical to the continued viability of organizations today. The learning organization is an ideal way to meet this challenge. In order to build a learning organization, steps must be taken at all levels to ensure that the organization's members receive appropriate knowledge when, where, and as needed to facilitate adaptation to changing environments and circumstances, which is the essence of a learning organization.

Organizations of all types must become more knowledge intensive in order to experiment with new approaches and to learn from past experience and from others, thereby discerning how best to reshape themselves and to change in order to survive and prosper. The application of knowledge management techniques by information specialists is integral to the successful creation of a learning organization.

In a very real sense, the practice of the art of knowledge management is the raison d'être of the information science profession. Perhaps at one time this art functioned in something of an academic vacuum. However, with the worldwide explosion of information resources occurring in the last third of the twentieth century, interactive application of knowledge resources in the conduct and management of organizations of all types, whether business, governmental, or otherwise, has become more widespread as it has become more necessary. Those entities that have institutionally adjusted to this new paradigm have often come to be called "learning organizations," and as such organizations become more commonplace, the role of the information specialist will become even more important in building those organizations. In this chapter, I will endeavor to examine what it is that constitutes a learning organization, why the paradigm model of a learning organization is needed, on which learning and pedagogical theories a learning organization is based, what the key elements of a learning organization are, and how information specialists and their work as managers of knowledge can fit into the overall model and help to build the learning organization.

What Is a Learning Organization?

Peter Senge (1990) initially popularized the concept of the "learning organization" in his seminal work *The Fifth Discipline: The Art and Practice of the Learning Organization*. Senge et al. (1994) later listed and further amplified upon the five "learning disciplines" that he describes as being at the core of the learning organization: personal mastery; mental models; shared vision; team learning; and systems thinking, concepts that may be briefly described as follows as they relate to the learning organization concept. Personal mastery has to do with individual learning, and can be seen as the basic building block through the actualization of which the learning organization is typically constructed. Mental models are about how individuals reflect on their own knowledge, using such models to improve the internal understanding of a process, an organization's functions, etc. Shared vision implies a sense of group commitment to a matrix of organizational goals, while team learning describes a sharing and utilization of knowledge involving collective thinking skills. The purpose of systems thinking is to understand relationships and interrelationships (rather than seeing merely the static "snapshots" of organizational patterns or events), as well as the context and the forces that affect the behavior of a system or organization.

Garvin (1993) describes learning organizations as follows:

> ...skilled at five main activities: systematic problem solving, experimentation with new approaches, learning from past experiences, learning from the best practices of others, and transferring knowledge quickly and efficiently throughout the organization. And since you can't manage something if you can't measure it, a complete learning audit is a must. That includes measuring cognitive and behavioral

changes as well as tangible improvements in results...*A learning organization is an organization skilled at creating, acquiring, and transferring knowledge, and at modifying its behavior to reflect new knowledge and insights.* (emphasis original)

Ikujiro Nonaka (1991) defined knowledge-creating companies as places where "inventing new knowledge is not a specialized activity...it is a way of behaving, indeed, a way of being, in which everyone is a knowledge worker."

On his Web site, Rasmussen (1997) indicates the increasing importance of learning organizations in today's world:

> The Learning Organization is perhaps the dominant management buzz-word for the last half of the 1990s. Some suggest that it is merely the reincarnation of earlier ideologies, such as organization development, quality management, and the like. Others suggest that the particular combination of paradigm shift and practical tools make it stand out from earlier change/transformation theories focused on how organizations might be reshaped to meet the challenges of today's world.

As more entities adopt the practices underlying the learning organization, it appears that the learning organization is passing from buzzword status to a meaningful expression of best organizational practices. Benson (1997) notes in the results of a survey of managers that high percentages of his respondents report familiarity with the learning organization concept and that it is becoming more common, if not yet prevalent in the workplace. But most authors in the management field agree that the learning organization is best viewed as an ideal, a model toward which an organization should strive, and that certainly no existing organization perfectly fits the model. Even Senge et al. (1994) state that "the learning organization exists primarily as a vision in our collective experience and imagination." Jashapara (1993), when discussing the literature of learning organizations, expresses the opinion that:

> This rather simplistic portrayal of a complex process can be viewed metaphorically as a firm's continual quest for the "Holy Grail." A competitive learning organization is seen as an ideal rather than a steady-state condition. It is unlikely that many firms will be able to maintain a position of continual strategic change and continual competitive analysis in response to the changing environment. Instead, firms are

more likely to go through phases such as "competitive learning," "teaching" or "static organizations."

An organization that goes through a competitive learning phase and subsequently moves into a teaching or static mode may not necessarily exhibit continual learning, but learning is still likely to exist sporadically when organizational conditions favor it, and teaching is often said to be the best learning device. Assign someone to teach a workshop and you can be sure that, at the very least, the teacher will learn the desired lesson! A learning organization in practical reality is one best seen as an organization that effectively balances these phases or modes at any particular time.

On the other hand, many organizations that are engaged in constantly revamping and retooling themselves may be seen as reaching for that ideal goal and from time to time are referred to in the literature as learning organizations. Karash (1996) states that "A 'Learning Organization' is one in which people at all levels, individually and collectively, are continually increasing their capacity to produce results they really care about."

In fact, in this modern age of information technology and swift change, learning has frequently become an integral and necessary part of the employee's task itself. Without it, the capabilities of an enterprise's employee cannot fully benefit the organization of which he/she is a part. One might suggest that learning and work have today become nearly synonymous terms and that employees in almost all fields of endeavor now need to "learn" their way through the work that they perform, in much the same way as persons engaged in those specialized, "cerebral" fields such as law and medicine have been traditionally said to "practice" their respective "learned" professions. Performance of simple work on a rote/repetitive basis is no longer the norm and certainly not the ideal it might have been seen to be, from a management point of view, in the early days of mass production and the development of the factory assembly line. To some, learning has become the new form of labor, not just something that merely requires the allocation of sufficient time to attend formalized conferences or training sessions; in effect, learning has become an integral part of the work of an organization (Willard, 1994).

It is certainly more than just a sort of glorified on-the-job training regimen. William H. Starbuck (1992) uses the term "knowledge intensive" in describing an entity built or run along principles intended to encourage constant reshaping and change rather than the term learning organization, but the basic concept he is discussing is essentially the same. Starbuck explains his use of the knowledge-intensive concept thusly:

> The term *knowledge intensive* imitates economists' labeling of firms as capital-intensive or labour-intensive. These labels describe the relative importance of capital and labour as production inputs. In a capital-intensive firm, capital has more importance than labour; in a labour-intensive firm, labour has the greater importance. By analogy, labeling a firm as knowledge-intensive implies that knowledge has more importance than other inputs.

This emphasis on knowledge implies more than just the collection of information or data. Indeed, an organization may process data as its main business, but still not necessarily be an entity that may be said to deal in knowledge. Knowledge in the learning organization context implies a use of information; it is the connecting of the various bits and pieces of information to show their relationships and then being able to apply the product of these connections that constitutes knowledge.

Argyris et al. (1994) state that:

> I believe that learning, which we can define as the detection and correction of any kind of error, is going to become increasingly important rather than decreasingly important. That will happen not only for the usual reasons of competitiveness and so on, but because information technology makes what we do or don't do more transparent to our managers, to our boards of directors, and to our society.

Library technical services departments experienced (some would have said suffered) this "sea change" to the environment of their work when they began cataloging online in the 1970s through the utilization of electronic bibliographical networks. Suddenly, the kind of sloppy, even if locally quite usable, bibliographical work that had been tolerated in-house was no longer permissible in a networked environment, where mistakes were so easily seen by everyone and institutional responsibility for errors became so easy to trace.

Why the Need for the Learning Organization?

As implied by Senge et al. (1994), technological changes and the rapid growth and pervasiveness of modern technology in the last decade of the twentieth century, especially with regard to communications technology as represented in the rise of the Internet and the World Wide Web as essential elements in business organizations, have made rapid responses and quick adaptations to change critical in today's markets. For example, it is becoming not just desirable but increasingly necessary for an organization of almost any type to have not only a Web presence, but a dynamic and changing one, in order to meet the expanding and rising expectations of that organization's customers, patrons, or constituency. For the balance of the 1990s, and for the foreseeable future, individual, collective, and organizational learning will be critical to an organization's continued survival and viability in the marketplace. The concept of the learning organization is now an ideal paradigm, for it is rooted in adapting to change, in learning and transitioning in order to avoid past mistakes, and in retaining critical information in the collective memory of the organization.

But while the learning organization concept may be seen as among the best ways to meet today's challenges of quick and constant change, it is important to recognize that the full realization of this concept dictates that the knowledge and learning processes characteristic of learning organizations must extend to all the levels of an organization, and not be permitted to reside just in the hands of the privileged few or of only the upper levels of the organization's management. On the importance of learning to an organization, Peter Drucker (1993) aptly states:

> [I]ncreased productivity needs continuous learning. It is not enough to redesign the job and then to train the worker in the new way of doing it—which is what [Frederic Winslow] Taylor did and taught. That's when learning begins, and it never ends. Indeed, as the Japanese can teach us—it came out of their ancient tradition of Zen learning—the greatest benefit of training is not in learning the new. It is to do better what we already do well.

But if change and learning are not necessarily synonymous, nevertheless their close linkage must be recognized in order to ensure that people in an organization will embrace change with the enthusiasm necessary to react appropriately and effectively to a quickly changing environment.

Rochelle Turoff (1998) stresses the importance of knowledge to the modern business organization:

> Knowledge has become the business of every business. "Knowledge work" is no longer the province of an elite few, but the requirement

of many. Knowledge is the esteemed core competency, the competitive advantage for the present and the future. Today knowledge is power, and organizations will succeed or fail based on their ability to learn and adapt.

According to Michele Darling (1996), many management theorists are today properly viewing "intellectual capital" as a form of an "economic operating system," which may turn out to be an organization's most valuable asset. By contrast, most management experts have traditionally confined themselves to examination of the questions and issues surrounding the management and control of the physical and financial assets of an organization. But, as organizations become much more attuned to the needs of an information-driven economy, it is clear that competitive advantage is much more likely to rest with those possessing the greatest intellectual capital as opposed to the more traditional physical or strictly financial assets. Darling (1996) notes that:

> The primary challenge in managing knowledge is recognizing that knowledge is an asset that is just as intangible for the corporation as social capital is for the nation state. So how do you organize something you can't see? Can you turn it into an important strategic and competitive tool?

The answer seems to be to build a learning organization. In the learning organization, knowledge or intellectual assets must be accumulated, stored, organized for retrieval, and then intensively and coherently applied by all members of the organization. Thus, the real challenge in building a learning organization will be determining how to simply and cogently organize the collective knowledge of organizational members because inevitably much of the organization's institutional knowledge will currently reside only in the minds of its members. Actualizing power will exist, of course, not in the mere collection of data or even of ideas, but rather in the efficient sharing of information among the members of the organization. This has always been the trick.

Traditionally, it has been far too difficult to move information across the various internal borders of an organization. In the past, in the library and information science field, we have seen this barrier most clearly manifested in respect to the sharing of information between public and technical services departments in libraries. It was only with the widespread institution of integrated automation systems that we have begun to see the collapse of the old "baize door" barrier between the public and technical sides of the library house. Other types of organizations are also feeling the same pressure, rightly discerning that, to ensure their continued institutional survival, it will be necessary to destroy any existing barriers to the free flow of information throughout the organization in question, an event that will usually have to be accompanied by a significant and concomitant leveling of bureaucratic layers within the organization.

Chris Argyris (1991) sums up the situation neatly:

> The fact is, more and more jobs—no matter what the title—are taking on the contours of "knowledge work." People at all levels of the organization must combine the mastery of some highly specialized technical expertise with the ability to work effectively in teams, form productive relationships with clients and customers, and critically reflect on and then change their organizational practices.

LEARNING THEORY BEHIND THE LEARNING ORGANIZATION

While the understanding of individual learning presents a complex question that defies a simplistic answer, a full understanding of organizational learning is an even more difficult, and generally to some, an enigmatic task. Obviously, an organization learns only through its individual members and is thus directly or indirectly affected, for good or ill, by the individual learning styles of those members. Argyris and Schon (1978) posed this primary dilemma in understanding organizational learning:

> There is something paradoxical here. Organizations are not merely collections of individuals, yet there are no organizations without such collections. Similarly, organizational learning is not merely individual learning, yet organizations learn only through the experiences and actions of individuals. What, then, are we to make of organizational learning? What is an organization that it may learn?

Argyris and Schon (1978) propose a theory of organizational learning based on the conceptualization that organizational learning takes place through those individuals in the organization in question whose actions are based upon what Argyris and Schon describe as a set of shared models. Their theory assumes that, in most established organizations, individual members exhibit common assumptions that tend to be protective of the status quo and thereby effectively prevent individuals, whether working from within or being brought in to the organization from the outside, from easily or effectively challenging existing troublesome procedures or the problematic characteristics in the behavior of others in the organization. Such common assumptions may actually provide for the silent approval, in the case of individuals, of their behavior, or, in the case of procedures, the continuation of the old or traditional ways of doing things, even if someone can clearly demonstrate the advantages of the proverbial "better mousetrap."

For example, if a manager of an organization does not want to hear any opposition to his/her position or any "helpful comments" from his/her employees, many of those employees may just accept this situation as "that's the way X operates," and transmit this organizational culture to all new employees, thereby virtually assuring that there will likely be evinced a paucity of learning within this organization, perhaps not even over the long term. Therefore, for an organization to learn (i.e., to become a learning organization) its organizational culture must ensure that learning is the mode of operation that is deemed the most valuable and the best rewarded by management, and the importance of the learning concept must be fully and clearly transmitted all the way down the organizational ladder.

Argyris (1980, 1991) stresses organizational learning, especially in regard to risky or potentially threatening organizational situations, in terms of what he calls "single-looped" or "double-looped" learning. He defines single-loop learning as "whenever a match between intentions and results is produced or whenever a mismatch is corrected without having to question or change organizational assumptions or policies" (1980). By contrast, double-loop learning is "whenever a match is produced or a mismatch is detected and corrected and changes are made in the basic assumptions and policies of the unit" (1980). Argyris (1991) provides the following analogy to help differentiate single-loop learning from double-loop learning:

> [A] thermostat that automatically turns on the heat whenever the temperature in a room drops below 68 degrees is a good example of single-loop learning. A thermostat that could ask, "Why am I set on 68 degrees?" and then explore whether or not some other temperature might more economically achieve the goal of heating the room would be engaging in double-loop learning.

Argyris (1991) also posits that many professionals often excel at single-loop learning but perform quite badly when it comes to double-loop learning because they do not know how to learn from their failures since they have rarely failed throughout their educational and professional backgrounds and careers. When single-loop strategies do not perform as expected, these persons often become defensive and may seek out a "scapegoat." Such behavior, if widespread within an entity, can never auger well for the development of a true learning organization since "defensive reasoning can block learning even when the individual commitment to it is high, just as a computer program with hidden bugs can produce results exactly the opposite of what its designers intended" (Argyris, 1991).

Argyris considers double-loop learning to be much the more important of the two types of learning and indeed crucial to the long-run health of any organization. However, he does recognize the basic problem usually faced by managers intent upon developing a learning organization:

> All administrators, therefore, face a dilemma. Organizations cannot be managed effectively without routinizing activities. Yet, the very managerial technology invented to make sure routines work may inhibit double-loop learning that is crucial to the long-run effectiveness and survival of the organization.

In Argyris's writings, there is a constant theme: in order to create a learning organization, the top management must become genuinely innovative and clearly exhibit a willingness to take risks. It is only at this point that it can become possible for a sea change in organizational behavior, such as that involved in instituting a learning organization to spread down through the layers of an established, traditionally hierarchical organization. Old-style management control mechanisms, particularly those dealing with budget and communication channels, must be changed to fit within the paradigms of new organizational development theories.

But innovation must be recognized as having its own special pitfalls. In a more recent article, Kim (1993) acknowledges that:

> There is little agreement on what constitutes "appropriate" learning, those actions or lessons that should be incorporated into an organization's memory. Organizational routines, such as standard operating procedures (SOPs) are generally viewed as an important part of an organization's memory and a repository of its past learning. However, some argue that SOPs are dangerous because they become so institutionalized that they delay the search for new procedures when the environment changes radically. These theorists advocate minimal levels of consensus, contentment, affluence, faith, consistency and rationality.

In much the same vein, Starbuck (1992) makes the further point that:

> Routinization helps to make knowledge intensity unstable. As with physical capital, converting expertise to routines is risky. Routines may become targets of imitation, spread, and gradually lose the character of being esoteric and advantageous. A routine used by many firms confers small comparative advantages on its users.

Of course, the opposite side is that overly wild and free-range thinking and behavior may lead to insufficient caution and care in overthrowing customs and traditions and may result in the establishment of systems prone to countless trial-and-error mistakes (Levitt and Marsh, 1988). There can, of course, be no greater inhibition to a new employee's initiative and creativity than hearing from the old hands in the shop the words, "But we've *always* done it this way!" but at the same time some restraints will need to remain in place if the learning and knowledge of the past is to be passed on to others. The wheel doubtless needs to be re-engineered from time to time, but not necessarily reinvented.

So how can this necessary balance be best achieved? Herbert Simon (1981), in writing about organizations as behavioral systems, proposed the following general hypothesis that has relevance to this question: "A man, viewed as a behaving system, is quite simple. The apparent complexity of his behavior over time is largely a reflection of the complexity of the environment in which he finds himself."

Thus, instead of worrying about how to "keep it simple," we need to recognize that what we are dealing with here is, at base, a simple matter—applying and creating knowledge are really best viewed as twin aspects of the same concept. Starbuck (1992) aptly states that:

> Creating, applying and preserving [knowledge] intertwine and compliment each other. At least over long periods, merely storing knowledge does not preserve it. For old knowledge to have meaning, people must relate it to their current problems and activities. They have to translate it into contemporary language and frame it within current issues. Effective preserving looks much like applying. As time passes and social and technological changes add up, the needed translations grow larger, and applying knowledge comes to look more like creating knowledge. For new knowledge to have meaning, people must fit it into their current beliefs and perspectives; and familiarity with existing knowledge signals expertise.

Argote, Beckman, and Epple (1990) found that, at least in production settings (they looked particularly at the data resulting from the building of the Liberty Ships during World War II), organizational learning tends to depreciate rapidly. In terms of the transfer of knowledge, they found that once full-scale production began, there was little transfer of knowledge from one organization to another. It would be interesting to conduct such an empirical study with data from a knowledge-intensive organization to see if similar patterns occur in very different settings.

Key Characteristics of a Learning Organization

Those engaged in attempting to build learning organizations are involved in the risky business of creating a new organizational culture. To create an entirely new organizational culture requires effort and commitment on the part of everyone involved, as well as a good imagination in the mind of the person charged with directing its implementation. The organization's members need to thoroughly know their organization as it currently exists, as well as have a vision of what its members desire for it to become in the future. Simply imitating another organization's culture is unlikely to succeed in the long run because each organization is different, with different traditions, employing different people with different abilities and skills, and having different prevailing attitudes. There is no structural "quick fix" applicable across the board to every type of organization; simply ordering from on-high the process desired to be implemented will not do the trick. As Senge et al. (1994) note, "hierarchical authority is much more effective at securing compliance than it is in fostering genuine commitment." However, a learning organization requires changes in basic corporate values. "There is no substitute for commitment in bringing about deep changes. No one can force another person to learn, especially if the learning involves deep changes in beliefs and attitudes or fundamentally new ways of thinking and acting" (Senge et al., 1994).

However, a number of management theorists have nevertheless compiled lists of so-called essential elements that an organization striving to become a learning organization should demonstrate. Taking these theoretical aspects and views into account, King (1996) describes the following attributes as those that an organization wishing to become a learning organization would necessarily exhibit or strive to implement:

- Facilitation of effective communication throughout the organization in order to diffuse needed information quickly and effectively, coupled with a willingness on the part of the organization's members both to accept and put that information to use

- Retention of organizational memory; it is essential that access to information be assured whenever it is needed and at whatever level of the organization it may be needed
- Establishment of information systems/software that will allow new information to be related to other information and to existing knowledge in order to create new knowledge and know-how
- Implementation and installation of information systems that facilitate the managerial decision-making processes

In other words, a learning organization requires the creation of a knowledge infrastructure that can serve both as a repository of knowledge and as a facilitator for the creation of knowledge in a form that is usable and suited to individual needs, while simultaneously allowing for the distribution of that knowledge to the members of the organization when and where the information is needed and when the members of the organization are ready to accept and to put the provided information to work.

King (1996) also states that an administrator's or manager's role in facilitating a learning organization requires direct and extensive participation in the development and creation of the organization's knowledge infrastructure to support people in their work. Administrators and managers are responsible for ensuring that the knowledge infrastructure being created contains, as a minimum, the following key elements:

- A communications infrastructure that facilitates teamwork
- A knowledge-based infrastructure that fosters the creation of knowledge, and allows that knowledge to be easily shared, thereby further facilitating the diffusion of knowledge throughout all levels of the organization
- A strategic capabilities infrastructure that can be used to identify, develop, and nurture the core capabilities of the organization
- A human assets infrastructure that can be used to identify the people and their special skills that are available within the organization
- A partner infrastructure that encompasses information about the external people and organizations that can be utilized to form strategic alliances and joint ventures or that may be potential providers of out-sourced operations
- A negotiation system that encourages and facilitates the establishment of such partners and outsourcing providers as mentioned above

- A tasking infrastructure that encourages the organization and coordination between projects and teams
- A resource allocation infrastructure to accommodate all of the above

Slocum et al. (1994) identify three new practices essential for a learning organization: a strategic intent to learn new capabilities; a commitment to continuous experimentation; and the ability to learn from both past successes and failures.

Toby Tetenbaum (1998) describes how one small, privately owned company developed a "knowledge transfer network," which makes a steady flow of information accessible to everyone in the company worldwide. Answers to problems or questions can come from anyone anywhere in the world, including the CEO of the company. The company's reward structure offers incentives and rewards for sharing knowledge in an attempt to ensure that everyone benefits from the institutional memory and data and does not try to hoard information for the benefit of a particular unit within the company. Another company attempts to create an atmosphere of tolerance even for the opinions and ideas of company "mavericks" by hanging whiteboards in the hallways to encourage anonymous criticisms and by providing bulletin boards at meetings, so that people unwilling to speak up in a group can post their comments. These are all ways to try to ensure that all information/opinions are shared among all members of the organization and that top management can be better assured of getting that input from the lower levels of the organization that may be closer to the production or customer sides of the business and, therefore, perhaps more knowledgeable concerning what product improvements may need to be made.

Darling (1996) states that when the management of the Canadian Imperial Bank of Commerce (CIBC) determined that the CIBC would become a learning organization, the necessity to create a "knowledge culture" was recognized, i.e., an organization that necessarily and as a matter of course institutes the following:

1. *Values knowledge and puts that knowledge where needed*. Knowledge is placed directly at the customer's service and into the hands of the people who deal with the customer.
2. *Democratizes knowledge*. It is delinked from the individual holder, transferred to others, and valued according to its effectiveness in dealing with problems and meeting customer needs.
3. *Values diversity*. It recognizes that new ideas and insights are not the preserve of age, experience, race, or gender.
4. *Has a subversive effect on traditional management hierarchies*. Instead of operating in command-and-control mode, managers must become coaches,

advisers, and cheerleaders for their teams, and facilitators, brokers, and networkers to link their teams with others in the organization.

5. *Always watches what academics call the "knowledge grid."* Succinctly, the knowledge grid examines what we know, what we know we don't know, what we don't know we know and what we don't know we don't know.

CIBC has found the knowledge grid to be an important tool and the don't-know elements to be the most important elements of the grid. This is quite sensible when one thinks about it, in that, for an organization that is dependent upon knowledge, the greatest institutional effort must be exerted in those areas where organizational learning most needs to take place, and the areas that an organization does not itself know enough about are the obvious prime targets.

To build a learning organization requires systematic problem-solving based on hard data, not managerial assumptions. Statistical tools and other scientific methods, including benchmarking, are a necessity in order to provide the accurate information needed by a learning organization. This is an area where information specialists can provide their skills to further the goals of the organization. Garvin (1993) takes this further to suggest that managers and employees of a learning organization need to be "trained in the skills required to perform and evaluate experiments." For some organizations, this would include benchmarking activities.

WHERE DO LIBRARY AND INFORMATION SCIENCE PROFESSIONALS FIT INTO AND FURTHER THE BUILDING OF A LEARNING ORGANIZATION?

The application of knowledge management on many fronts is essential in the day-to-day activities of an organization striving to become a learning organization. It is perhaps axiomatic that a learning organization can only be effective to the extent that the information that feeds it (i.e., the data acquired from the conduct of those activities from which the organization learns) is indeed accurate and relevant. Even more to the point, that information must, in addition to being accurate, timely, and made available at the right time to those persons in the organization who require the information, be presented in a format that will facilitate the effective use of the information provided by those persons who need to have it. In line with this approach, McGill and Slocum (1993) have expressed the opinion that a learning organization will necessarily put its information and information systems to the test with the following two questions: How does the information aid in decision making? And how does the information get filtered down to the people who need it?

Correctly responding to these questions implies the necessity for a source of knowledge that is capable of fast and effective dissemination of its information resources. Rory L. Chase (1998) states that:

> Most of the formal knowledge communities have their own databases—or "silos"—of expert knowledge. Many of the informal knowledge communities also have created databases, mainly in the form of discussion bulletin boards and newsgroups. A key goal of any knowledge-based organization is to encourage the active participation of these formal and informal knowledge communities—through the integration of experts into knowledge teams and linking the knowledge databases into the organizational knowledge warehouse.

These are all areas in which information specialists are ideally educated to manage and effectuate. Obviously, a well-run and well-organized internal information system is critical to a learning organization. Information specialists trained in the traditional library skills of bibliographic control and information services, when coupled with additional education in such areas as database management and the management and organization of Intranets, can help to ensure that employees of a learning organization have the necessary access to required information in a form that is useful for their decision-making processes. Further, the education and background of information specialists should make them excellent candidates for proactively bringing the required information to the attention of the "right" individuals, not just sitting back and waiting for information queries to come to them. Experience with the selective dissemination of information from outside sources can be adapted to organizational information as well as to external information.

The new digital information environment may tempt some managers to attempt to deny the continued need for an information specialist as a key part of their organizations. They may feel that information in superabundance is today always only a "click away"; however, we all know the difficulty of locating information on the Web without some kind of in-house organization, coupled with searching expertise. Managers and other employees of a learning organization, just as any other, are typically subject-based experts, not knowledge experts. They will continue to need the help or guidance of an information collector, cataloger, and analyst so that they can spend their time doing what it is that they do best—using the information provided and not looking for it. For this to be the case, they will always need the help of an information specialist.

Chase (1998) notes that "The challenge facing librarians and information professionals is how to package knowledge to make it usable by individual knowledge workers and communities of practice." However, he goes on to assert that librarians tend to overlook the need to custom-package the information they provide, noting that all too many librarians tend to assume that most knowledge is an objective and neutral "thing" that can necessarily and intuitively be understood by all. Chase further points out that knowledge is thus idiosyncratic to individuals in two specific ways:

1. Personality plays a critical role in the way people acquire, understand, value, and use knowledge; and
2. The creation of knowledge is affected by the worldview of the individual.

With this in mind, information specialists, in helping to manage knowledge in those ways that will better facilitate the building of learning organizations, will need to concentrate their efforts more fully on delivering information to those individuals in their organizations requiring it in ways that match the approaches of those particular individuals to their anticipated use of the knowledge in question.

CONCLUSION

In order to become a valued member of the team in tomorrow's learning organization, an information specialist must proactively work with the organization's members in order to discern what they need in the way of information, when it is that they need it, and in what form the required information needs to take, whether it be information derived from external sources or from in-house files and databases or other organizationally specific compilations of knowledge. Information specialists must be creators of a virtual organizational library to assist in building a learning organization. Needed information may no longer come just from printed sources, but also from computer databases, in-house reports, the World Wide Web, and other Internet resources. Therefore, within many true learning organizations, at least the smaller ones, the same type of physical library presence now enjoyed by many organizations will probably not continue to exist, as indeed the learning organization environment dictates decentralization of information resources as opposed to the traditional concentration of resources in what we have always been pleased to call a "library." However, effective learning organizations will always need information to create the new knowledge or to further the know-how on which those organizations are based. Information specialists must prepare themselves both by education and by mental outlook to work effectively in this brave new knowledge-based world of building the learning organization.

References

Argote, L., Beckman, S. L., and Epple, D. (1990, February) The persistence and transfer of learning in industrial settings. *Management Science* 36 (2): pp. 140-154.

Argyris, C. (1980, May/June) Making the undiscussable and its undiscussability discussable. *Public Administration Review* 40: pp. 206-207.

Argyris, C. (1991, May/June) Teaching smart people how to learn. *Harvard Business Review* 70 (3) pp. 327-340.

Argyris, C. & Schon, D. (1978) *Organizational Learning: A Theory of Action Perspective.* Reading, MA: Addison-Wesley.

Argyris, C. et al. (1994, May) The future of workplace learning and performance. *Training and Development* [Online] 48: pp. s36-s47. Available: Lexis-Nexis Academic Universe, 1998, August 6.

Benson, G. (1997, July) Battle of the buzzwords. *Training and Development* [Online] 51: pp. 51-52. Available: Lexis-Nexis Academic Universe, 1998, August 6.

Chase, R. L. (1998, September) Knowledge Navigators. *Information Outlook* 2 (9): pp. 17-26.

Darling, M. S. (1996, Winter) Building the knowledge organization. *Business Quarterly* 61 (2): pp. 61-66.

Drucker, P. F. (1993) *Managing for the Future: The 1990s and Beyond.* NY: Truman Tally Books.

Garvin, D. A. (1993, July/August) Building a learning organization. *Harvard Business Review* [Online] 72 (4): pp. 78-86. Available: Lexis-Nexis Academic Universe, 1998, August 6.

Jashapara, A. (1993) The competitive learning organization: A quest for the Holy Grail. *Management Decision* [Online] 31 (8): pp. 52-62. Available: ABI/Inform, 1998, August 13.

Karash, R. (1996) Learning-Org dialog on learning organizations. [Online] Available: http://www.world.std.com/~lo/, 1998, July 22.

Kim, D. H. (1993, Sept. 22) The link between individual and organizational learning. *Sloan Management Review* [Online] 35 (1). Available: Lexis-Nexis Academic Universe, 1998, August 7.

King, W. R. (1996, Summer) IS and the learning organization. *Information Systems Management* 13 (3): pp. 78-80.

Levitt, B. and Marsh, J. G. (1988) Organizational learning. *Annual Review of Sociology* 14: pp. 319-340.

Nonaka, I. (1991, November/December) The knowledge-creating company. *Harvard Business Review* 70 (6): pp. 96-99.

McGill, M. E. and Slocum, J. W. Jr. (1993, Sept. 22) Unlearning the organization. *Organizational Dynamics* 22 (2) [Online] Available: Lexis-Nexis Academic Universe, 1998, August 7.

Rasmussen, R. V. (1997) Learning organization links [Online] Available: http://courses.bus.ualberta.ca/org-a652/learninglinks.htm, 1998, August 13.

Senge, P. M. (1990) *The Fifth Discipline: The Art and Practice of the Learning Organization.* NY: Doubleday/Currency.

Senge, P. M. (1996) Rethinking leadership in the learning organization. *The Systems Thinker* [Online] 7 (1). Available: http://www.pegasus.com/article1.html, 1998, August 25.

Senge, P. M.; Roberts, C.; Ross, R. B.; Smith, B. J.; and Kleiner, A. (1994) *The Fifth Discipline Fieldbook: Strategies and Tools for Building a Learning Organization.* NY: Doubleday/Currency.

Simon, H. A. (1981) *Sciences of the Artificial.* Cambridge, MA: MIT Press.

Slocum, J. W., Jr.; McGill, M.; and Lei, D. T. (1994) The new learning strategy: Anytime, anything, anywhere. *Organizational Dynamics* [Online] 23 (2): pp. 33-47. Available: Lexis-Nexis Academic Universe, 1998, August 7.

Starbuck, W. H. (1992, November) Learning by knowledge-intensive firms. *Journal of Management Studies* 29 (6).

Tetenbaum, T. J. (1998) Shifting paradigms: From Newton to chaos. *Organizational Dynamics* [Online] 26 (4): pp. 21-32. Available: WilsonSelect, 1998, August 7.

Turoff, R. (1998, March) An arranged marriage: Knowledge management and organizational development. *American Programmer* 11 (3): pp. 30-33.

Willard, B. (1994) Ideas on the 'Learning Organization' [Online] Available: http://www.oise.on.ca/~bwillard/ideaslo.htm.

CHAPTER 11

Knowledge Markets: Cooperation Among Distributed Technical Specialists

Steve Sawyer
Senior Research Fellow

Kristin Eschenfelder
Doctoral Candidate

and

Robert Heckman
Faculty
Syracuse University

INTRODUCTION

Knowledge management issues are highlighted when organizational functions are decentralized. For example, distributed computing environments place more computer power in the hands of the end user, and often demand increased technical support. In response, organizations may choose to move technical support personnel close to end users. This can isolate them from each other, and may limit their ability to share knowledge. Thus, the growth of distributed computing calls for an increased ability to share knowledge across organizational boundaries. In that context, this chapter presents the results of a case study investigating the roles of knowledge markets among distributed technologists. Our perspective is that knowledge markets are cultural entities shaped by the underlying work culture of their participants, and that the cultural forces that define knowledge markets are powerful, deeply held, and difficult to change. Thus, improving the effectiveness of any given knowledge market will have less to do with the installation of information technology than with the ability to create a facilitating work culture. This study's identification of clique knowledge markets, operating efficiently in parallel to the public knowledge market, may provide a hint of the type of work culture that will foster knowledge trading.

Organizational decentralization often leads to the distribution (or dispersion) of competence. This, in turn, encourages managerial interest in techniques for sharing important job-related knowledge among (potentially dispersed) organizational members. A second factor that encourages sharing of knowledge among organizational members reflects an interest in better using the knowledge that their workers have accumulated. These forces, coupled with the increasing power and flexibility of information technologies, help give rise to the "knowledge management" movement. For us, knowledge management means an organized and planned approach to gathering, storing, and distributing knowledge within an organization (Davenport, 1997).

One contemporary approach to managing knowledge encourages diffusion of existing expertise through naturally occurring "knowledge markets" (Davenport and Prusak, 1998; Ernst and Young CBI, 1997). Knowledge markets draw their participants from groups connected via what some call radial personal networks (Rogers and Agarwala-Rogers, 1976); communities of practice (Orr, 1990; Seeley-Brown and Duguid, 1991) or communities of interaction (Nonaka and Takeuchi, 1995). In this chapter, we use the term "informal social networks" as a broad descriptor that encompasses these concepts. Sharing knowledge through informal social networks allows members to reap the benefits from that learned by the most expert. Furthermore, knowledge transfer via both formal and informal social networks takes advantage of the richness embedded in the social realm. The knowledge market approach, however, assumes that no "trade barriers" exist, and that knowledge flows relatively freely through the marketplace.

One example of organizational decentralization is the movement to distributed computing, exemplified by client-server systems. This distribution of computing leads to impacts that extend beyond changes to the technological infrastructure (Kling, 1980, 1987; Kling and Scacchi, 1982; Sawyer and Southwick, 1996). Distributed computing environments place more computer power in the hands of the end user. This, in combination with commensurate end-user computing sophistication, demands increased technical support. As organizations move to distribute their computing into discrete business units, they may also move computer support personnel, referred to in this chapter as distributed technical support staff (DTS), to these units.

Moving DTS close to their end users may, however, inadvertently isolate them from each other. This isolation may limit their ability to share knowledge and can waste organizational resources if several individuals simultaneously work to solve similar problems. Thus, the growth of distributed computing in organizations calls for increased sharing of knowledge among DTS across organizational boundaries (Heckman, 1998).

The DTS exist, in part, because of the temperamental technical complexity of most organizations' computing infrastructures and the rapid pace of technological change. These forces require DTS to constantly "learn through work" (Seeley-Brown and Duguid, 1991). That is, DTS are similar to Orr's (1990) technicians in that their work requires frequent non-canonical practice. A need for constant learning from others' experiences makes it imperative that DTS develop strong social networks, for these are the mechanisms they use to share information. The physical dispersal of DTS into functional units, however, isolates DTS from one another and may impede their ability to share knowledge in this manner. Furthermore, culturally based trade barriers may stymie the flow of knowledge in knowledge markets.

To highlight the structure and value of knowledge markets, we report a case study investigating how distributed technologists share knowledge through knowledge markets. Following the discussion of the importance of knowledge markets in distributed computing environments, the chapter continues with a summary of pertinent literature. This includes a review of current knowledge management work and the connection between this work and social exchange theory. Schein's (1997) model of organizational (or work) cultures is presented as the basis for describing the DTS knowledge market culture. Following that, the third section includes a description of the research approach, data collection and analysis, and the findings. The final section includes a discussion of the findings—drawing conclusions based on both previous research and the current data—and suggests directions for future research.

THE IMPORTANCE OF KNOWLEDGE MARKETS IN A DISTRIBUTED ENVIRONMENT

Knowledge markets, an example of natural cooperation or discretionary collaboration, rely upon behavioral factors such as reciprocity, repute, altruism, and trust to govern exchanges (Smith, Carrol and Ashford, 1995; Heckman, 1998;

Davenport and Prusak, 1998). Knowledge markets are composed of repeated patterns of behavior—they arise from a group of people sharing knowledge over time. In this case, this suggests that knowledge markets are aspects of the work culture that is created among the DTS who share knowledge using their informal and formal social networks. This perspective leads us to using a cultural perspective to understand the DTS knowledge market.

The fundamental premise of this chapter is that knowledge markets are a primary vehicle for knowledge sharing in organizations. Thus, understanding how they work should improve organizational efficiency, effectiveness, and performance. Independent of the broader issues regarding a better understanding of the roles of knowledge markets, understanding, in detail, the role of knowledge markets in the distribution of knowledge among DTS is helpful to organizations for two reasons. First, improving knowledge sharing among DTS may help attract and retain high-quality personnel. Second, consideration of the social context of knowledge management impacts the development of reward systems.

A thorough understanding of the social context of a knowledge market in any given organization should underlie the development of both the administrative mechanisms (such as reward structures and guidelines of practice) and information systems to gather, store, and disseminate knowledge. The use of incorrect reward systems limits the value of a knowledge management system. For example, Orlikowski (1993) found that the individually oriented reward structure of the large consulting firm she studied doomed the use of Lotus Notes as a means to manage knowledge among the consulting staff.

At a pragmatic level, increased knowledge sharing among DTS will help reduce their work stress and increase their retention. This is an important organizational consideration, given the current shortage of trained information technology (IT) personnel. More than one IT job in ten is currently unfilled (Information Technology Association of America, 1997). For areas such as DTS, this shortage is exacerbated by the need to have both cutting-edge technical skills and excellent people and management skills. For example, in the course of this study we found that DTS jobs at the studied site turn over every thirty months, and about fifteen percent of the positions are constantly vacant.

Improving knowledge sharing among DTS will improve their ability to support the organization's computing infrastructure. Although the computing infrastructure of each functional unit may vary greatly, DTS often find themselves facing the same kinds of technical and non-technical problems (e.g., "What is the easiest way to keep records of the work I do for my users?"). By sharing expertise and knowledge, DTS can avoid duplicating efforts and wasting organizational resources.

KNOWLEDGE MANAGEMENT, EXCHANGE THEORY, AND WORK CULTURE

Knowledge markets are implicitly grounded on assumptions that are central to social exchange theory (Homans, 1950). And, these knowledge markets arise from within the cultural context of the members of that market—in this case the DTS's work culture. The following sub-sections provide a brief overview of knowledge management, the underlying precepts of social exchange theory, and Schein's (1997) model of work cultures in organizations. This model provides a framework for our data analysis and illuminates the underlying cultural assumptions that guide behavior in the knowledge market.

Knowledge Management

The contemporary knowledge management literature is largely normative, suggesting strategies for improving the management of knowledge and information in large organizations (Davenport and Prusak, 1998; Davenport, 1997; Stuart, 1997; Brethenoux, 1997; Blair, 1997; Demarest, 1997; Nonaka and Takeuchi, 1995). Knowledge includes values, insights, and contextual information and knowledge distinguished from information by characterizing knowledge as an outcome of information (Davenport and Prusak, 1998; Stuart, 1997).

Davenport and Prusak (1998) provide a concept for understanding knowledge sharing called a "knowledge market." A knowledge market depicts organizational actors as knowledge buyers or sellers within a marketplace. The knowledge market draws on the idea of a community's information markets—a concept well defined within the information science literature (Kingma, 1996; Schwuchow, 1995; Foldi, 1986). Davenport and Prusak (1998), however, focus specifically on information markets within organizations. The knowledge market concept defines knowledge buyers as "people trying to solve an issue whose complexity or uncertainty precludes an easy answer." It further defines "knowledge sellers" as "people in an organization with an internal market reputation for having substantial knowledge about a process or subject" (Davenport and Prusak, 1998).

Social Exchange Theory

The knowledge market concept contains the precepts of social exchange theory. That is, the existence of a knowledge market assumes that knowledge sellers, as rational actors, will evaluate the potential costs and rewards of sharing their knowledge with a particular knowledge buyer. The decision to share knowledge with another results from the seller's conclusion that the buyer can offer some reward—either extrinsic (e.g., help with another problem in the future) or intrinsic (gratitude, friendship).

Exchange theory depicts people as rational profit seekers choosing between alternative actions in order to obtain the greatest value at the lowest possible costs. As Blau (1964) explains "human beings choose between alternative potential associates or courses of action by evaluating the experiences or expected experiences with each other in terms of a preference ranking and then selecting the best alternative." Social exchange theory provides a useful theoretical backdrop for explaining why individuals choose to exchange knowledge with others (Mohr, 1982; Blau, 1964; Emerson, 1962; Ritzer, 1996). Social exchange theory draws on both economics' rational choice theory and psychology's behaviorism to study dyads and group relationships, or "exchanges," in terms of the costs and rewards to their participants. Rewards for exchanges may be extrinsic, such as material goods, or intrinsic, such as social approval or friendship.

Work Cultures in Organizations

An organization's culture shapes how its members work and the knowledge markets in which these members participate. These workers' behaviors, influenced by the behaviors of their peers, are repeated over time and this repetition leads to the formation of cultural norms and culturally accepted forms of action. One of these actions is the formation of the work culture's knowledge market(s). Schein's (1997) model is a useful way to describe an organization's work cultures. Table 11.1 presents the three interacting levels of Schein's (1992) model of culture. Schein (1997) defines culture as:

> ...a pattern of basic assumptions that the group learned as it solved its problems...that has worked well enough to be considered valid and, therefore, to be taught to new members as the correct way to perceive, think, and feel in relation to those problems.

We selected this model for two reasons. First, the model arose from studies of the work cultures of organizations and the DTS work culture is one such example. Second, the model is well known in the broad research community that is interested in the issues of work in organizations.

Table 11.1 Schein's Cultural Model	
Artifacts and Creations	Schein describes artifacts as "the visible behavior of the group and the organizational processes into which such behavior is made routine, written and spoken language, artistic production and the overt behavior of its members" (Schein, 1997).
Espoused Values	"Derived beliefs and morals [which] remain conscious and are explicitly articulated because they serve the normative function of guiding members of the group in how to deal with certain key situations and in training new members how to behave...What people will say in a variety of situations...[but not what] they will actually do in situations where those values should, in fact, be operating" (Schein, 1997).
Basic Assumptions	"[Beliefs which] have become so taken for granted that one finds little variation in the cultural unit... [defines] what to pay attention to, what things mean, how to react emotionally to what is going on, and what actions to take in various situations" (Schein, 1997).

This categorization provides a relatively accessible means to understand the cultural forces at work. For instance, in an organization promoting the importance and use of cross-functional teams, both the teams' weekly status meeting and the individual reward structures are examples of "artifacts." The teamwork slogans on the walls of the meeting room are an example of the work culture's espoused values. However, each individual's quest for personal glory reflects an underlying basic assumption that individual recognition is the best means to earn rewards (and is reinforced by individual performance-based reward structure artifact) helps to both explain why espoused values are not always enacted and how artifacts reflect deeply held assumptions of that work culture.

CONDUCTING THE RESEARCH

Data collection employed a multi-method approach including electronic collection of listserv messages, open-ended interviews, and participant observation of meetings. This multi-method approach allows the research team to triangulate data from multiple sources in order to both increase validity and gain deeper understanding of the collected data (Jick, 1979; Brewer and Hunter, 1989; Gallivan, 1997). The rest of this section presents information about the site, our data collection efforts, and our data analysis.

The Site

This study focused on a group of thirty DTS at a medium-sized, research-oriented university. In the early 1990s, the site began a transition away from a mainframe-based computing environment toward a client/server architecture. In the mainframe environment, all computer support services came from a centralized technology support unit (Central IT). In 1991, several business units requested financial assistance from Central IT in order to hire their own computer support personnel to support the growth in desktop computing. In response to these requests, Central IT began a formal program to subsidize the salaries of the distributed computer support personnel for the business units. By establishing the subsidy program, Central IT leaders hoped to shift some of the costs of the planned desktop-centric client/server change to the business units.

Presently, each DTS reports directly to a supervisor in the business unit, and maintains a "dotted line" relationship with the DTS program coordinator (an employee of Central IT). In exchange for the salary subsidy, Central IT asks that the DTS participate in two monthly meetings with their peers. These meetings are organized and moderated by the DTS coordinator. In addition, this coordinator maintains a DTS listserv, to which all the DTS (and many central IT employees) belong. According to the DTS coordinator, both the meetings and the listserv are intended to create an atmosphere that will "foster cooperation" between the DTS. Still, the coordinator is unwilling to penalize individual DTS for choosing not to participate in the meetings and the listserv because of the heavy time demands placed on the DTS by their business units, and a "hands-off" policy regarding the DTS program administration promoted by the site's CIO.

The site had several revelatory aspects. First, it lacked any official knowledge management efforts. Absence of any sponsored knowledge management program allowed the researchers to observe the knowledge market in a natural state. Second, the site's commitment to a complete transition to client-server technology means increased responsibility, influence, and power for the DTS.

A third revelatory aspect is the "federal" IT architecture of the site (Brown, 1994; King, 1983). Fourth, DTS comprise a virtual community of practice (Orr, 1990, Seeley-Brown and Duguid, 1991). They meet infrequently physically, but use electronic mail, voice mail, and phone calls to communicate with each other. Lessons learned from this study are applicable to many other scenarios involving teams of physically separated technical specialists sharing knowledge through knowledge markets. Given the exploratory nature of the research and the revelatory nature of this site, the case study method is the appropriate research method (Yin, 1990).

Data Collection

The research team used three data collection techniques: electronic collection of postings on the group's listserv; semi-structured interviews with the DTS; and participant observations of bimonthly staff meetings. Site observations and documentation analysis began in March 1996. Listserv data collection ended in January 1997. Observation of meetings and follow up interviews continued until August 1997. The use of different data collection techniques has allowed for the triangulation of findings (Jick, 1979; Brewer and Hunter, 1989).

Data include 248 listserv messages posted to the DTS listserv, 26 formal interviews ranging from forty-five to ninety minutes in length, eight informal follow-up interviews, and observations of twenty-four bimonthly meetings. One researcher conducted all interviews, using the active interview method (Holstein and Gubrium, 1995).

Data Analysis

We analyzed the interview, observation, and listserv data using the analytic inductive technique (Shelly and Silbert, 1992, Dewey, 1938; Znaniecki, 1934). Analytic inductive analysis begins by grouping together like data into preliminary categories. Observing commonalties among the grouped data leads to the creation of a definition of these categories and identification of their attributes.

We tested working hypotheses by examining interview, observation, and listserv data in the code categories in matrix form (Miles and Huberman, 1994). From this, we created a smaller list of eight to ten prevalent themes expressed by the data. Higher level analysis made use of the theme lists created for each code category. Table 11.2 provides an example of the theme lists for a sampling of code categories.

Table 11.2 Theme Lists from a Sampling of Code Categories

DTS Meetings	Interaction with Others	Stress Patterns
Can't get to know others personally	Can't show your deficiencies	Time versus overtime
Good way to evaluate others	Group feeling, share ideas, isolation, time together to network	Burnout!
Broadcast-oriented style, manager chooses what to talk about	Frustration, annoyance, jobs so diverse that interaction is difficult	Learning curves
Good way to gather new information, get diverse points of view	Interaction takes up too much time	Driven/Drive technology changes
Home unit demands preclude attendance	Social time, friends mostly inadequate time	Freedom in job

THE KNOWLEDGE MARKET CULTURE OF THE DTS

Table 11.3 summarizes the findings, and provides a framework for the discussion that follows. The findings section is organized so that each sub-section of text corresponds to a level of Schein's three cultural models, reflecting the artifacts, espoused values, and assumptions of the DTS work culture relative to their knowledge market.

Table 11.3 Cultural Model of the DTS Knowledge Market

Artifacts and Creations	The Physical Distribution of the DTS Personnel Listserv Meetings
Espoused Values	Cooperation Is Important We Are a Group
Underlying Assumptions	I Am Alone in the World I Can Only Count on My Friends to Help Me Technical Knowledge Brings Social Power

Artifacts

The artifact level includes physical manifestations, language, stories, technology, and visible traditions (Schein, 1997; Schultz, 1994). In studying the knowledge market culture of the DTS, three important artifacts emerged: the physically distributed environment in which the DTS work; the lack of listserv-based knowledge exchange; and the lack of meeting-based knowledge exchange. The following paragraphs discuss each of these points in more detail.

Physical Distribution

Most DTS did not see other DTS very often apart from the monthly meetings. Day-to-day life involved interaction with business unit coworkers, not chatting with other DTS. Most DTS had stronger personal relationships with users in their business units than with other DTS. For the most part, DTS did not think of each other as coworkers. For example, one DTS explained that he never forwarded jokes to the DTS listserv. He would only forward them to the coworkers he worked with on a daily basis in his business unit.

The DTS' offices were scattered around the campus, and a few had offices quite distant from the others. One of the most physically isolated DTS reported feeling like "Moses coming out of the hills" when he left his office. Several DTS who had previously worked together with other information technology workers reminisced about how much co-location facilitated knowledge sharing, stating how one can find someone at the coffee machine and ask a question, or one can learn a new skill just by watching over someone's shoulder.

The Listserv

To understand the use of the listserv, the listserv messages were analyzed by first dividing them into messages from Central IT, messages from the DTS coordinator (DC), and messages from the distributed technical staff group members (DTS). Following this division, the divided messages were sub-coded into three main message types: offers, help requests, and answers.

First, listserv members can post information offers, which assumes a need for information and attempts to fulfill that need by forwarding useful information. Second, members can solicit answers to questions through a help request posting. Finally, members can post answers to help requests posted by others. Table 11.4 presents a detailed summary of listserv message traffic during the six-month observation period.

In general, the DTS did not make heavy use of the listserv to exchange knowledge or information. During the study period, forty-three percent of the DTS did not use the listserv at all. Of the fifty-seven percent that used the listserv, only four people posted more than two messages, and three DTS accounted for twenty-five out of the total thirty-four DTS messages.

Table 11.4 Overview of Listserv Message Traffic

Total Messages		248	Percentage
Messages from Central IT	CIT Total	161	65%
	CIT Offers	147	59%
	CIT Help Requests	14	6%
	CIT Answers		
Messages from Distributed Technician Group Coordinator	DC Total	53	21 %
	DC Offers	50	20%
	DC Help Requests	1	‹1%
	DC Answers	2	‹1%
Messages from Distributed Technician Group Members	DTS Total	34	14%
	DTS Offers	16	6%
	DTS Help Requests	16	6%
	DTS Answers	2	‹1%

Further, the DTS almost exclusively posted questions in which they did not admit to any lack of technical skill or understanding. Table 11.4 shows that only sixteen questions (six percent of the total postings) constituted help requests. Of these, thirteen questions requested alternative solutions or the location of a resource. In these two types of questions, the questioner always implied that he/she already had at least one possible solution to his/her problem; or the questioner asked about the location of a particular resource, not how to use it. In a "stuck" question, however, the questioner admitted that he/she did not have the ability to solve a problem. Of all the posted questions, only three fell in the "stuck" category.

Finally, the DTS posted only two answers to the sixteen posted questions. Follow-up, email-based interviews revealed that DTS sent another twenty-two answers directly to the querier, completely bypassing the listserv. This suggests that the DTS prefer alternative media, including phone calls and private email, to the listserv for exchanging knowledge.

Findings from current literature show that introducing computer mediated communications (CMC) technology into an environment will not guarantee cooperative behavior. For example, fear of breaking traditional organizational hierarchy protocols, distaste for aggressive communications styles, reluctance to share certain kinds of expertise, and inability to control others' perceptions of their postings may preclude people's usage of CMC tools like listservs (Orlikowski and Hofman, 1993; Crowston and Kammerer, 1996; Finholt, 1993; Weisband et al., 1995). The listserv data from this study suggest that cultural/behavioral factors inhibit optimal DTS use of their CMC device.

Meetings

Meetings took place twice a month. Most DTS attended either sporadically or not at all. A small group frequently attended. Typically, a small number of assertive, frequently attending members dominated the meetings by asking questions during the question and answer period or making other short comments during the DTS coordinator's announcements. The group's coordinator was also an active contributor to the meeting's dialog. Frequently, this bordered on monopolization as he tried to stimulate conversation by asking questions. Many of the other DTS never said anything during meetings. Most DTS seem so used to not talking that when the coordinator directly solicited opinions on a subject during a meeting, they would refuse to answer publicly, suggesting instead that the coordinator solicit opinions via email.

The period directly before and after the meetings, however, served as a prime opportunity for knowledge exchange among DTS. During this post-meeting period, DTS congregated informally and talked in small groups from two to ten minutes. "When you go to the meetings, you end up doing business with people. Someone stops you on the way out and says 'Are you doing this?' and that kind of stuff. It just happens," one DTS explained.

Espoused Values

Schultz (1994), writing about Schein's (1997) cultural model, explains that espoused values consist of "what the organization's members say during and about situations, and not necessarily what they do in situations where these values ought to be in operation. We derived the following two espoused values based on the content analysis of the listserv, observations of the meetings, and the interviews: cooperation is important and we are a group. The following sub-sections describe these espoused values in more detail.

Cooperation Is Important

While all DTS would agree with the statement "knowledge sharing is important," they would want to attach qualifiers. The DTS realize that constant technical change and the continual need for new technical skills make it impossible to have all the knowledge they need to do their jobs. "DTS are set up to fail," one explained. "Without someone to turn to for help, you are screwed." With a few exceptions, the DTS' attitudes about cooperation varied with their level of experience. Less experienced DTS complained about the need for more cooperation. "If I knew people better," one explained "I would have a better understanding of available resources." More experienced DTS were ambivalent. These interviewees often stressed that they didn't have enough time to fulfill their job duties and help solve someone else's problems. One experienced DTS explained:

> There are people who have this kind of job, and what they do is never answer their phone, they don't return phone calls, and its a way of filtering...I can see why some people don't want to get involved, it's like opening Pandora's box, and it's going to be another drain on you.

Most DTS agreed that one should be able to ask others for help, but stressed that one shouldn't ask for *too much* help: "You have to make the person do it on their own. Offer help—but you can't commit your life." "When you ask someone for help, you must be respectful, you have to do your homework first and be up to speed on things." They acknowledged cooperation and knowledge sharing as important principles, but didn't think anyone should do anything to encourage more of it. One DTS said, "...it happens when it's called for. I wouldn't overhaul everything..."

We Are a Group

The DTS' group status does not equate to automatic knowledge sharing between its members. Participation in the salary subsidy program, the fact that most work directly with end users, and their representation of their business units' interests in the broader organizational community distinguish the DTS from other IT workers on campus. On a daily basis, however, the group status means little for most DTS. The DTS group members are not obligated to share knowledge with other group members. The DTS' work culture does not particularly encourage knowledge sharing among its members. "If I was a new employee, I would get the feeling that cooperation is not an issue in terms of what we do...we don't talk about cooperation. If I just walked in, I would probably get the feeling that after we meet, we just go by ourselves and do whatever we need to do and that's it."

Underlying Assumptions

Schein (1997) explains that groups form cultural assumptions from actions or attitudes that help to successfully solve problems. As these actions or attitudes solve problems over and over again they come to be taken for granted. Soon actors see them as the only right way to do things. Based on analysis of the interview, listserv, and observational data, we believe the DTS group holds the following knowledge market related assumptions: I am alone in the world; I can only count on my friends to help me; and technical knowledge brings social power. The following paragraphs discuss each of these in more detail.

I Am Alone in the World

This assumption recognizes a basic rule of the knowledge market. A knowledge exchange depends upon perceived potential for reciprocation in the future. DTS should not assume that others will share knowledge with them. No DTS is obliged to assist any other DTS.

Although the DTS espouse a "group" identification, they readily admit that the heterogeneity of their interests, responsibilities, and technologies limits what they have in common. Furthermore, they also admit that they cannot expect other members of the group to assist them with their problems. In a high-stress, time-pressed environment, some DTS must refuse to help others in order to ensure that they can finish their primary work tasks. To manage this time pressure, several culture-based knowledge exchange principles emerged.

This assumption is reflected in knowledge-exchange criteria that we state as: "You should only ask a question of another if you have tried really hard to answer the question yourself, using readily available reference sources." Some DTS refer to questions that do not meet this criterion as "dumb questions." Another principle asserted that you should only ask questions that can be answered in a short amount of time. For example, DTS should not ask, "How do I set up a server?" However, they might ask, "Which server file is the virus update on? Virstop 2.1 or

Virstop 2.3?" Pentland (1992) reports a similar phenomenon, where help desk operators could only ask for a technician's assistance under certain culturally established circumstances.

Some DTS had very little interest in getting to better know other members. Many had already established strong relationships that fulfilled their knowledge needs. This attitude manifested itself in the group's resistance to participate in social events that would encourage social networking. Some admitted that their lack of interest in the events resulted directly from a general lack of interest in meeting other DTS.

I Can Only Count on My Friends to Help Me

The knowledge exchange criteria described above do not apply to all interactions. Many DTS reported reserving knowledge requests—which violate the principles—for specific people. "I would never post that question to the listserv," one DTS explained. "I save all my dumb questions for my friends." Another DTS noted, "I don't feel bad calling Joe with my PC questions because when I call, he usually has a couple of Mac questions for me." The unwritten rules that you should only ask a question if you have tried really hard to answer it yourself, or that you should only ask easily answerable questions, did not seem to apply in these special relationships. One DTS admitted that he always called his friend when he had a Mac question because this was much easier than spending time flipping through a manual.

This assumption reveals that the previously mentioned assumption is not universally true. In some instances, DTS can assume that others will help them. In these instances, which we call "clique markets," DTS can ask questions without concern for their reputation (see Rogers and Agarwala-Rogers, 1976). Clique market members have such high inter-group credibility that the group knowledge exchange principles are altered. Table 11.5 provides a matrix showing how social exchange helps to highlight the differences in costs and rewards for knowledge exchanges in public and clique knowledge markets.

Table 11.5 presents two types of markets. Clique markets are private markets in which all parties have such credibility that all exchanges occur without hesitation. The seller automatically assumes that the buyer will reciprocate at some point in the future. The broader knowledge market encompasses all the members of the community—the entire group of DTS in this case.

Table 11.5 Outcome Matrix Use of Social Networks in Knowledge Markets

	Costs		Rewards	
	Question	Answer	Question	Answer
Open Knowledge Market	Fear of refusal; discomfort at making initial social contact. Asking an inappropriate question may hurt your knowledge market reputation.	Providing an incorrect or misleading answer may hurt knowledge market reputation.	Get the information you need; expand social network.	Providing correct answer increases your reputation as a good knowledge seller.
Clique Knowledge Market	You owe your friend a favor in the future.	Low–friend will not penalize you for giving incorrect information.	Get the information you need; reinforce social relationship.	Reinforce social network.

Technical Knowledge Brings Social Power

The DTS see technology as a means to both learn new skills and gain status among their peers. This glorification of technical knowledge encourages them to customize their business units' systems away from Central IT standards to a format that optimally fulfills their business units' needs and highlights their technical skills. This cultural assumption, however, may lead to a situation where, in increasingly customized environments, DTS may become less able to help each other because of the lack of similarity of their technology.

The appearance of "knowing what you are doing" technically is important for gaining status within the group. All the group's members recognize their need to stay current with technology and all show respect for group members with high levels of technical expertise. As one DTS explained, "In your job (in the business unit) interpersonal skills are as important, or more important, than technical skills. But in a (DTS) meeting—technical knowledge is king!"

The appearance of technical expertise is also important for maintaining relationships with specialists in the Central IT group. One DTS told us of how he worked very hard to post "impressive" answers to questions posted to the listserv to which the Central IT specialists subscribed. He explained that the goal was to increase the amount of respect the Central IT specialists had for him so that they would be more attentive to his help requests in the future.

DTS preferred not to reveal their technical inadequacies to anyone. "Some people would rather crash and burn than say 'I don't know' and try to get some help," one explained. "I always respond directly to the individual because I'm not confident of the way I have gotten stuff to work. I tend to just hack through it," another noted in explaining his decision not to respond publicly to a posted question. "I don't want any criticism of my answer," another confided. The lack of stuck questions shown in Table IV also supports the explanation that DTS try not to reveal technical inadequacies. Stuck questions required the poster to specifically admit to a lack of knowledge in a specific area.

DISCUSSION

The following questions guide our discussion: How can we shed light on the work lives of DTS personnel? How can we describe the DTS knowledge market/work culture at this site? How can we provide a useful interpretation of that described culture? Schein's (1997) model of organizational cultures guided us to think of our data in terms of artifacts, espoused values, and assumptions. We have already described the findings related to each of these parts of the framework. We will briefly review each of them in providing an exchange-theory-based interpretation of the DTS knowledge market culture.

Physical Distance Between Each DTS

The artifact of the physical distribution of DTS affects their knowledge market in at least three ways. First, it makes it difficult for them to meet and socialize with each other. They do not accidentally run into each other at the water cooler or the coffee machine. In particular, newly hired DTS have a difficult time meeting other DTS. Therefore, new DTS must enter the knowledge market without really knowing who the knowledge sellers are. Second, their physical distribution makes it inconvenient for DTS to easily share knowledge. Most DTS must walk some distance to physically meet with another DTS. This makes the physical collaboration, which is often needed in a complicated technical environment, inconvenient. Third, the DTS' physical distribution makes it difficult for them to assess each other's levels of expertise. This means that DTS must form opinions about each other from sources other than personal contact, including broadcast listserv postings, observed behavior during meetings, and rumor.

Knowledge Sharing Behavior on the Listserv and During Meetings

The artifacts of the observed listserv and meeting knowledge sharing behavior impacts the DTS knowledge market in several ways. Social exchange theory posits that the DTS will resist posting to the listserv and speaking during meetings because their publicly broadcast questions may reflect dubiously on them and may damage their reputation as a knowledge seller within the knowledge market. This is similar to findings reported by Crowston and Kammerer (1996). The broadcast nature of both the listserv and the meetings heightens the risk. A message sent to the listserv is forwarded to all members of the knowledge market. Many members of the knowledge market hear words spoken at a meeting. Therefore, the costs of posting both questions and answers are quite high. Table 11.6 depicts the costs and benefits for question asking and answering on the listserv and during meetings.

Table 11.6 Outcome Matrix Use of Listserv for Question Asking/Answering on the Listserv or During Meetings		
	Costs	Rewards
Posting/Asking a Question	Posting a question others perceive as "dumb" may damage knowledge market reputation.	Getting the correct answer. Others may perceive your question as insightful, positively affecting your knowledge market reputation.
Posting/Announcing an Answer	Posting an answer that others perceive as incorrect or misleading may damage knowledge market reputation.	Posting an answer that others perceive as correct or insightful may positively affect knowledge market reputation.

If others interpret a DTS' broadcasted question and answer as incorrect, or revealing a lack of knowledge, that DTS' perceived value as a knowledge seller within the knowledge market will decrease. Oppositely, if others interpret the DTS' questions or answers as intelligent and insightful, that DTS' perceived value as a knowledge seller within the knowledge market will increase. Others will sell their knowledge to the DTS more easily, assuming the DTS will have useful knowledge for them at some time in the future.

Cooperation Is Important and We Are a Group

Both of these espoused values depict an idealistic world in which information flows freely between members of the DTS program. In this ideal world, a knowledge market would not exist. DTS would have the time, resources, and interest to share their knowledge and expertise with anyone who needed it. The DTS, however, do not exist in an ideal world. The real world constraints require them to make decisions about with whom they will share knowledge and what kinds of knowledge they will share.

Some DTS however, do make special efforts to assist others as much as they can. One can still interpret this apparent selflessness within a social exchange theory framework. Blau (1964) argues that, "beneath this seeming selflessness an underlying 'egoism' can be discovered; the tendency to help others is frequently motivated by the expectation that doing so will bring social rewards (e.g., gratitude, social approval)." Davenport and Prusak (1998) explain that helping others inflates the value of your knowledge on the knowledge market as others learn through the "grapevine" that you are a good source of help. Thus, even selflessness has value in a knowledge market.

Social exchange theory perspective also helps to explain why DTS cannot always enact espoused values. The group's underlying assumptions provide a means to more accurately reflect the true nature of the knowledge market among DTS. That is, the three assumptions regarding the DTS' knowledge markets—I am alone in the world, I can only count on my friends to help me, and truth comes from those with greater expertise or experience—help shape how the DTS' knowledge market functions, often contradicting the espoused values. However, these assumptions are reflected in the DTS' artifacts.

Truth Comes from Those with Greater Expertise or Experience

The final assumption acknowledges the major currency within the knowledge markets—technical expertise. Davenport and Prusak (1998) list reciprocity, repute, altruism, and trust as the currencies of the knowledge market. The assumption that a person has quality knowledge to sell or give away, however, underlies each of their four price factors. McAllister (1995) defines this as cognition-based trust, or trust in the goodness or correctness of someone's information. The high value of perceived technical expertise within the market helps to explain the lack of listserv- and meeting-based knowledge exchange. Participants are unwilling to risk damage to their reputations by publicly asking or answering a question.

The Knowledge Markets of the DTS

The combination of Schein's (1997) cultural model and social exchange theory provides both a rich description and a useful explanation of the DTS work culture, which gives rise to the DTS knowledge market culture. Analysis using both revealed three main practices that inadvertently block the flow of knowledge within the DTS knowledge market. First, the challenging workload of the typical DTS does not allow much time for sharing knowledge. Second, people base their opinions of others primarily on actions observed through meetings and listserv postings. Third, new DTS, whether knowledge buyers or sellers, have a difficult time entering the knowledge market.

Increasing the amount of slack time in a DTS schedule might increase knowledge sharing. Davenport and Prusak (1998) argue that slack time is one of the best metrics of a firm's real commitment to knowledge management. Employees cannot share knowledge with others, or learn new knowledge, if they don't have time. DTS frequently complain about their busy schedules, the unpredictable "fire-fighting" aspects of IT management, and lack of time to do long-term planning. Furthermore, the lack of slack time prohibits them from forming, joining, or strengthening existing, clique networks. Forming or joining a clique network requires developing close relationships with other DTS. The current workload does not easily accommodate socially oriented activities that encourage such relationships.

As long as people's opinions of one another are based primarily on public signals such as meeting behavior and listserv postings, DTS will hesitate to speak out in these media. Given that the primary knowledge market currency is perceived technical expertise, the risks of speaking out are often just too great. Reducing these risks would encourage DTS to ask more questions and offer more answers, greatly facilitating the flow of information in the market.

A newly hired DTS has little or no knowledge of any other IT personnel at the site. Confronted with a question, he/she has no idea who to call for help and must rely on the references of the DTS coordinator. Similarly, if a very expert DTS is newly hired, no one will know of, or be able to take advantage of, his/her expertise for some period of time. Gaining entrance to the knowledge market takes time because one must figure out who the key players are.

CONCLUSION

These factors inhibit the free flow of knowledge in the open, public knowledge market described in this study. Yet they inhibit knowledge flow to a lesser degree in the clique sub-markets that also exist. Thus, it would probably be naive to think that removal of these "trade barriers" (even if that were possible) would automatically lead to unencumbered public knowledge movement in this organization. People will still view knowledge sharing as a social exchange and, therefore, make their decisions to contribute based on perceived costs and benefits. We have argued that, to a significant extent, perceived costs and benefits are a function of deeply held underlying cultural assumptions.

We have highlighted the cultural basis of knowledge markets and how these markets are shaped by the underlying work culture of their participants. The cultural forces that define knowledge markets are powerful, deeply held, and difficult to change. Improving the effectiveness of any given knowledge market will have little to do with the installation of formal information technology mechanisms (such as listservs and GroupWare) and more to do with a thorough understanding of its underlying work culture. Increasing the effectiveness of knowledge markets requires a series of difficult changes, including changes to basic assumptions and changes to organizational reward structures to promote and support the new underlying assumptions. Only after an organization has accomplished this will members fully utilize enabling technology mechanisms.

This study's identification of clique knowledge markets, operating efficiently in parallel to the public knowledge market, may provide a hint of the type of culture that will create fewer knowledge trade barriers. Clique knowledge markets operate efficiently because rewards are higher than costs. Perhaps this is because the basis for the clique relationship lies (at least partially) outside of the performance mission of the organization. Table 11.6 suggests that much of the reward obtained through questioning and answering in clique markets is simple reinforcement of the social network—another instance of the power of weak ties (Granovetter, 1980).

Finally, research in other settings suggests that one of the strongest antecedents of discretionary collaboration is the existence of strong relational bonds that lie outside an organization's performance mission (e.g., Heckman and Guskey, 1998). Future efforts to better understand the kind of work cultures that facilitate effective knowledge management might well focus on those factors and deep assumptions that create commitment, trust, and openness in the cultures of discretionary social groups. Perhaps such groups can help us learn how to reduce the costs associated with public knowledge sharing.

References

Alavi, M.; Keen, P. (1991) "Business Teams in an Information Age" *The Information Society* 6, 179-195.

Bandura, A. (1971) *Social Learning Theory*. New York: General Learning Press.

Brewer, J.; Hunter, A. (1989) *Multimethod Research: A Synthesis of Styles*. Newbury Park: Sage.

Blair, J. (1997) "Key Issues for Knowledge Management" *Gartner Group Research Note/Key Issues* K-KMGT-1650.

Blau, P. (1964) *Exchange and Power in Social Life*. New York: Wiley.

Brethenoux, E. (1997) "Knowledge Management: Myths and Challenges" *Gartner Group Research Note/Strategic Planning Assumptions SPA-ATS 437*.

Brown, C.; Magill, S. (1994) "Alignment of the IS Functions with the Enterprise: Toward a Model of Antecedents" *Management Information Science Quarterly* 18(4) 371-403.

Brown, J.; Duguid, P. (1991) "Organizational Learning and Communities of Practice" *Organizational Science* 2(1).

Crowston, K.; Kammerer, E. (1996) "Communicative Style and Gender Differences in Computer-Mediated Communication" Presentation at the Organizational Communication and Information Systems Division of the Academy of Management Meeting, Cincinnati, OH, August 11-14.

Davenport, T. (1997) *Information Ecology*. Oxford: Oxford University Press.

Davenport, T.; Prusak, L. (1998) *Working Knowledge: How Organizations Manage What They Know*. Cambridge: Harvard Business School Press.

Demarest, M. (1997) "Understanding Knowledge Management" *Long Range Planning* 30(3), 374-384.

Dewey, J. (1938) *Logic, The Theory of Inquiry*. New York: Henry Holt and Company.

Emerson, R. (1962) "Power—Dependence Relations" *American Sociological Review* 27: 31-41.

Ernst & Young CBI (1997) *Executives Perspectives on Knowledge in the Organization*. Boston: Ernst & Young Center for Business Innovation and Intelligence.

Finholt, T. (1993) *Outsiders on the Inside: Sharing Information Through a Computer Archive*. Unpublished dissertation, Department of Social and Decision Science, Carnegie Mellon University.

Foldi, T. (1986) "A Sketchy Introduction to the Problems of the Information Market" *International Forum on Information and Documentation* 11(1), 3.

Gallivan, M. (1997) "Value in Triangulation: A Comparison of Two Approaches for Combining Quantitative and Qualitative Methods" In Lee, A.; Liebenau, J.; and De Gross, J. (eds.) *Qualitative Method in Information Systems* (83-107). New York: Chapman & Hall.

Heckman, R. (1998) "Planning to Solve the 'Skills Problem' in the Virtual Information Management Organization" *International Journal of Information Management*, vol. 18.

Heckman, R.; Guskey, A. (1998) "The Relationship Between Alumni and University: Toward a Theory of Discretionary Collaborative Behavior" *Journal of Marketing Theory and Practice*, forthcoming.

Holstein, J. A.; Gubrium, J. F. (1995) *The Active Interview*. Thousand Oaks, CA: Sage.

Homans, G. (1950) *The Human Group*. New York: Harcourt Brace.

Information Technology Association of America (1997) "Help Wanted: The IT Workforce Gap at the Dawn of a New Century" Available at: URL: http://www.itaa.org

Jick, T. (1979) "Mixing Qualitative and Quantitative Methods: Triangulation in Action" *Administrative Science Quarterly* 24, 602-611.

King, J. (1983) "Centralized versus Decentralized Computing: Organizational Considerations and Management Options" *Computing Surveys* 15(4), 320-349.

Kingma, B. (1996) *The Economics of Information: A Guide to Economic and Cost-Benefit Analysis*. Englewood, Colorado: Libraries Unlimited.

Kling, R., (1987) "Defining Boundaries of Computing Across Complex Organizations" In Boland, R.; Hirschheim, R. (eds.) *Critical Issues in Information Systems*. New York: John Wiley & Sons.

Kling, R.; Scacchi, W. (1982) "The Web of Computing: Computing Technology as Social Organization" *Advances in Computers* vol. 21.

Kling, R., (1980) "Social Analyses of Computing, Theoretical Perspectives in Recent Empirical Research" *Computing Surveys* 12(1), 61-110.

McAllister, D. J. (1995) "Affect- and Cognition-Based Trust as Foundations for Interpersonal Cooperation in Organizations" *Academy of Management Journal* 38(1) 24-59.

Miles, M. B.; Huberman, M. A. (1994) *Qualitative Data Analysis, An Expanded Sourcebook*. Beverly Hills, CA: Sage.

Mohr, L. B. (1982) *Explaining Organizational Behavior*. San Francisco: Jossey-Bass.

Nonaka, I.; Takeuchi, H. (1995) *The Knowledge Creating Company*, New York: Oxford University Press.

Orlikowski, W. (1993) "Learning from Notes: Organizational Issues in Groupware Implementation" *The Information Society* 9, 237-250.

Orr, J. (1990) "Sharing Knowledge, Celebrating Identity: Community Memory in a Service Culture" In Middleton, D.; Edwards, D. (eds.) *Collective Remembering* (169-189). Newbury Park: Sage.

Pentland, B. T. (1992) "Organizing Moves in Software Support Hot Lines" *Administrative Science Quarterly* 37: 527-548.

Ritzer, G. (1996) *Modern Sociological Theory*. New York: McGraw Hill.

Rogers, E. M.; Agarwala-Rogers, R. (1976) *Communications in Organizations*. New York: The Free Press.

Sawyer, S.; Southwick, R. (1996) "Implementing Client-Server: Issues from the Field" In Glasson, B.; Vogel, D.; Bots, P.; Nunamaker, J. (eds.) *The International Office of the Future*. New York: Chapman-Hall.

Schein, E. (1997) *Organizational Culture and Leadership*, 2nd edition. New York: Jossey-Bass.

Schultz, M. (1994) *On Studying Organizational Cultures*. Berlin, Germany: Walter de Gruyters.

Seeley-Brown, J.; Duguid, P. (1991) "Organizational Learning and Communities of Practice" *Organizational Science* 2 (1).

Shelly, A.; Silbert, E. (1992) "Qualitative Analysis, A Cyclical Process Assisted by Computer" In Hueber, G. (ed.), *Qualitative Analyses*, Computereinstaz inder Socioalforshung. (71-114). Munich, Vienna, Germany: R. Oldenbourg Verlag,

Smith, K.; Carrol, S. J.; Ashford S. J. (1995) "Intra and Interorganizational Cooperation, Toward a Research Agenda" *Academy of Management Journal* 38(1) 7-23.

Stuart, T. (1997) *Intellectual Capital*. New Jersey: Doubleday.

Schwuchow, W. (1995) "Measuring the Information Market(s): A Personal Experience" *Journal of Information Science* 21(2), 123-132.

Weisband, S. P.; Schneider, S. K.; Connolly, T. (1995) "Computer-Mediated Communication and Social Information, Status Salience and Status Differences" *Academy of Management Journal* 38(4) 1124-1151.

Yin, R. (1990) *Case Study Research: Design and Methods*. Newbury Park: Sage.

Znaniecki, F. (1934) *The Method of Sociology*. New York: Farrar and Rinehart, Inc.

CHAPTER 12

Tacit Knowledge and Quality Assurance: Bridging the Theory-Practice Divide

Bill Crowley

Assistant Professor

Dominican University

INTRODUCTION

This chapter explores the new understandings emerging in the area of *tacit knowledge*, the practical wisdom possessed by experts that is difficult to capture yet repeatedly demonstrated in contexts as varied as factory floors, research laboratories, army bases, and corporate boardrooms. The philosophical basis for tacit knowledge will be identified and explained as found in the writings of the philosophers Gilbert Ryle and Michael Polanyi. In the pages that follow, findings of tacit knowledge are presented that are published in the literatures of such diverse areas as business, human resource management, information science, library science, law, military science, philosophy, psychology, public administration, and sociology.

The possession of "expert" tacit knowledge seems to be characteristic of achievers in every occupation and discipline. Drawing on a broad range of disciplinary perspectives has both positive and negative aspects. There is undoubted value for the generalist reader in works that integrate prior research involving a) multiple disciplines and b) varying approaches to understanding effectiveness in a variety of practitioners. However, the process of summarizing findings across disciplinary lines tends to minimize the valuable nuance and perspective found in the original studies.

No field or discipline has established control over the study of tacit knowledge. Nor is any likely to do so. There is thus little possibility of "an official agenda" guiding future researchers. The complexities of intellectual diversity existing in the research community are likely to be mirrored in the every-day realities of working practitioners. Arguably, even effects to minimize uncertainty and maximize effectiveness through development of "best" and "benchmarking" practices databases are likely to be ineffective (Nonaka and Takeuchi). At a minimum, since tacit knowledge is constantly being created, such databases will need to be updated almost as often in order to retain their usefulness.

After examining how neglect of the relevance of tacit knowledge and context has limited the usefulness of academic studies in addressing "real world" issues, the effective use of tacit knowledge understandings in business and library case studies will be examined. I will then explain how enhancing researcher effectiveness in identifying and addressing practitioner needs will involve the abandonment of the concept of a *priori knowledge* (knowledge not based on experience, biology, chemistry, etc.) and the embrace of Gilbert Ryle's assertion that even Aristotle himself found inspiration for theory in actual practice.

Indeed, given the appeal of tacit knowledge to both practitioners and researchers, this present overview is undoubtedly outdated even as it goes to press.

THE KNOWLEDGE BEYOND CINCINNATI

Several years ago, Patrick B. Drotos, founder of the Market Information Services component of Arthur D. Little International, Inc., warned that even database expertise is becoming insufficient to compete for information leadership in the emerging corporate future. In an *Online* article entitled "From Online Specialist to Research Manager—Changing with the Times," Drotos (1994) built on the work of management sage Peter Drucker to advise his readers that real effectiveness means looking beyond databases—in some cases far beyond—for information vital to meeting client needs. For both Drotos and Drucker, only information professionals willing to do anything or go anywhere to secure vital knowledge—even to spend the equivalent of two days as assistant service managers in Cincinnati—were likely to be perceived as resources vital to the organization (Drotos, 1994). In describing how his operation at Arthur D. Little International, Inc. functioned, Drotos (1994) stressed that computer searches are but one source of intelligence since, "for our clients, it is irrelevant whether their information needs are satisfied online or by rumor."

Throughout his article, Drotos (1994) repeatedly underscored the obstacles to information effectiveness faced by practitioners lacking effective teaching, analysis, and presentation abilities. He also argued for familiarity with "well-documented methods for documenting the undocumented," including competitive intelligence observation approaches, journalistic interviewing techniques, and market research procedures, all of which are useful in a variety of contexts. Among the other professional sins of information professionals cataloged by Drotos (1994) was a lack of "the requisite analytical skills to integrate this heterogeneous information into a strategic briefing." For him, such professionals have only limited value to their employers since computer dependency equals inability to exploit "a universe of information that is never documented, never printed, and never touched by the document-oriented information specialist" (1994).

To "onliners" still chained to their terminals Drotos (1994) counsels:

> Beyond online is a great mass of statistical information and printed information that must be researched through conventional channels. Beyond the conventional publications lie a quantity of gray literature published by institutes, conference organizations, market research companies and corporations. This gray literature is often not accessible through bibliographic searching. Even beyond the gray literature there exists the uncharted seas of undocumented, unprinted primary information that can be extracted from experts and the public only through interviews and questionnaires.

Increasingly, librarians, information specialists, and MIS personnel are becoming aware that "beyond the gray literature" is a source of knowledge, expertise, and (often) wisdom that resides in the minds of an organization's employees and customers, as well as in the staff of its current and future partners and/or competitors. In addressing the necessity for information professionals to develop competence in utilizing the wealth of resources found, not in databases but in human beings, Drotos brought his readers to the edge of the emerging and imperfectly understood world of *tacit knowledge*.

As will become clear in this chapter, it is impossible to divorce the concept of tacit knowledge—and its opposite *explicit knowledge*—from the myriad contexts in which people and organizations operate. Tacit or "private" knowledge—as opposed to explicit or "public" knowledge (fuller definitions follow)—represents an under-researched resource connecting with—and offering value for—the programs of libraries, information centers, corporations, governments, and a wide spectrum of other organizations. Arguably, research into understanding tacit knowledge represents a unique opportunity for practitioners and scholars to cooperate in devising procedures and theories to identify, capture, refine, and utilize a

potentially unlimited information resource. The key to such collaboration, however, will be the willingness of researchers to avoid utilizing "canned" or preexisting theories that might hamper understanding practitioners as they describe
their work.

A Bit of Philosophy

Although it is theoretically possible to link tacit knowledge with Plato (Polanyi,
1966/1967), the key to establishing a realistic account of the development of tacit
knowledge is to identify when the idea was "formulated definitely enough and
emphatically enough that it cannot be overlooked by contemporaries" (Merton,
1968). On any chart tracing the development of tacit knowledge, a central location
must be allocated to Michael Polanyi, scientist, philosopher, and author of the influential *The Tacit Dimension*. Since Polanyi's early work, writers on tacit knowledge
have cited him as the concept's originator or popularizer (Reber, 1993; Wagner and
Sternberg, 1985). Even so, Polanyi admitted, albeit in passing, his own intellectual
debt to Gilbert Ryle, "Waynflete Professor of Metaphysical Philosophy in the
University of Oxford" (Ryle, 1949/1958). Polanyi credited Ryle for a distinction
useful to the concept of tacit knowledge, i.e., the difference between "knowing that"
and "knowing how" (Polanyi, 1966/1967).

As a fellow philosopher, Polanyi may have had minimal difficulty reading
Ryle's classic *The Concept of Mind*. Others are likely to have more of a problem
since Ryle does not offer concise definitions, a shortcoming common to many in
his discipline. In consequence, readers of *The Concept of Mind* must puzzle out a
number of significant concepts from discussions scattered throughout the work.
Such examination will reveal variations on defining *knowing how* as knowledge
possessed by the professional or craftsperson, learned in the process of doing and,
therefore, difficult to describe.

On occasion Ryle (1949/1958) could be more specific:

> In ordinary life...as well as in the special business of teaching, we are
> much more concerned with people's competencies than with their cog-
> nitive repertoires, with the operations than with the truths that they
> learn. Indeed even when we are concerned with their intellectual excel-
> lences and deficiencies, we are interested less in the stocks of truths
> that they acquire and retain than in their capacities to find out truths for

themselves and their ability to organise [British] and exploit them, when discovered.

Ryle designated the "stocks of truths" people "acquire and retain" as the *knowing that* form of knowledge. As suggested above, *knowing that* can include the facts and theories learned in a university classroom. It can also include what is heard in a corporate training center or in a session at a professional conference. More recently, this sort of knowledge has been discussed in the literature under such term variations as *knowing what* or *knowing why*. Although *knowing that/knowing what/knowing why* describes the knowledge prized throughout institutions of higher education, and is particularly prized in Western culture, Ryle saw such knowledge as ultimately derivative. For him, *knowing that* came after *knowing how* since "efficient practice precedes the theory of it" and "methodologies presuppose the application of the methods" (Ryle, 1949/1958). He stressed that critical figures in areas as seemingly diverse as philosophy and fishing have been dependent on practice for their theories since:

> It was because Aristotle found himself and others reasoning now intelligently and now stupidly and it was because Izaak Walton [*The Compleat Angler*] found himself and others angling sometimes effectively and sometimes ineffectively that both were able to give to their pupils the maxims and prescriptions of their arts (Ryle, 1949/1958).

Michael Polanyi was much less concerned than Ryle to distinguish between *knowing how* and *knowing that* types of knowledge. Rather than so differentiate, he developed the active concept of tacit knowing in order to "cover both practical and theoretical knowledge" (Polanyi, 1966/1967). Polanyi's thought is both challenging and worth an extended treatment. However, the aspect most relevant to this review lies in an assertion stated throughout his *The Tacit Dimension* and repeated in print by authors who drew on his thought for inspiration: "We can know more than we can tell" (Polanyi, 1966/1967). Arguably, this phrase represents a fundamental understanding of *tacit knowledge*. Or, as Polanyi would no doubt prefer, *tacit knowing*.

DEFINITIONS AND DEFINITIONAL ISSUES

In addition to Polanyi's (1966/1967) maxim that "we can know more than we can tell," examination of a number of proposed definitions is useful to discern the capabilities of tacit knowledge as an intellectual tool. The use of the plural "definitions" is deliberate. The literatures reveal a growing number of professional and more theoretical fields where the concept of tacit knowledge has relevance. Yet, to borrow and extend terminology from Glaser and Strauss (1967), tacit knowledge inquiry falls short of the point where definitions developed at the *substantive* or empirical level of inquiry can be reconstructed and combined to create *formal* theory and a standard definition with explanatory power that might apply across the fields and disciplines.[1] Given a vibrant condition of emerging understandings, constructing such a definition *at this point* threatens to result in "a forcing of data, as well as a neglect of relevant concepts and hypotheses" (Glaser and Strauss, 1967). However, I have provided a compilation of "significant definitional characteristics" below.

Before reviewing the useful definitions of tacit knowledge and its counterpoint, explicit knowledge, it must be stressed that the concept is of the "natural kind" (Harper, 1995). A *natural concept* such as "furniture" does not spell out the "necessary and sufficient conditions" for items or individuals described by the term. Rather:

> Because tacit knowledge is a natural concept, we should not expect that judgments about what is and is not tacit knowledge would be "all or none." Rather, judgments should depend on an item's strength or resemblance to the concept. Thus, some knowledge will seem to be a particularly clear example of tacit knowledge and other knowledge will seem marginal. For marginal items, individuals may disagree about whether or not the item is a valid instance of the tacit knowledge (just as individuals may differ over whether or not a hammock is a piece of furniture). Given acceptable levels of agreement among judges, however, the "tacitness" of knowledge can be determined with some confidence (Horvath et al., 1994).

Definition # 1

The first definition places *tacit knowledge (implicit knowledge)* in the larger sociological traditions of *practice guidance* and *consensual sociology*.[2] It asserts the concept's cross-disciplinary nature since "Implicit knowledge (tacit knowing) and practice guidance are appropriate subjects for sociological attention, and have great relevance for a fruitful understanding of the common law tradition" (Swartz, 1997).

They [implicit knowledge/tacit knowing and practice guidance] seem to belong within the portion of the sociological tradition which Shils called *consensual sociology*. We must be aware, however, that treatment of these subjects cannot be achieved within the restrictions laid down by positivism. *Practice guidance* is knowledge, much of it implicit knowledge, and much of it handed down by tradition, which guides practitioners in the proper or fruitful conduct of their activities. Implicit knowledge [tacit knowledge] is knowledge not presently made explicit in words or mathematical symbols and the like. Some of that knowledge we are aware of, and some not. Some can be readily articulated in words or mathematical symbols, and so on; other parts of it cannot. Valuable contributions to our understanding of implicit knowledge and practice guidance have been made in several fields, including science, cognitive psychology, and law (Swartz, 1997).

Definition # 2

In the context of examining the cross-national transfer of technology, Ashish Arora (1996) offered the following business/technological definition: "Tacit knowledge represents those components of technology that are not codified into blueprints, manuals, patents, and the like. In other words, tacit is intangible knowledge, such as rules of thumb, heuristics, and other 'tricks of the trade'."

Definition # 3

Another definition from the business literature asserts that "Tacit knowledge refers to knowledge that is gained only experientially and therefore cannot be articulated to inexperienced parties" (Levitas et al., 1997).

Definition # 4

The most complicated definition of tacit knowledge derives, not unexpectedly, from an extensive study of the concept as it relates to factors making for success in military leadership.

> First, and most importantly, tacit knowledge is knowledge that is generally acquired on one's own—through personal experience rather than through instruction. Second, tacit knowledge is knowledge that people may not know they possess and/or may find it difficult to articulate. Like much expert knowledge, it is knowledge that guides behavior without being readily available to conscious introspection. Obviously, the hidden or opaque quality of tacit knowledge is the feature that gives

the construct its name. Finally, tacit knowledge is action-oriented knowledge with practical value to the individual. Unlike much disciplinary knowledge, it is knowledge that helps people pursue goals that they personally value (Horvath et al., 1996).

Definition #5

Succinct definitions of tacit knowledge and explicit knowledge, by authors with business and public policy/communications backgrounds, were offered in 1996: "Tacit knowledge is personal, context-specific, and, therefore, hard to formalize and communicate. Explicit knowledge or codified knowledge, on the other hand, refers to knowledge that is transmittable in formal, systematic language" (Nonaka et al., 1996).

Significant Definitional Characteristics

Suggested by some but not all of the preceding definitions, as well as the fuller accounts from which the definitions were drawn, are assumptions that tacit knowledge is:

- Personal in origin
- Valuable to the possessor
- Job specific
- Related to context
- Difficult to fully articulate
- Both known in part and unknown in part to the possessor
- Transmitted, where transmission is possible, through interpersonal contact
- Operative on an organizational level
- Applied, in part, through "if-then" rules. "*If* certain conditions exist, *then* apply the following."
- Capable of becoming explicit knowledge and vice versa
- Intertwined with explicit knowledge along unstable knowledge borders
- Poorly reflected in contemporary knowledge literature

Researcher Knowledge and Practitioner Realities

In discussing the applicability of researcher theories to the real work of practitioners, it is important to keep in mind Ryle's (1949/1958) critique that:

"Theorists have been so preoccupied with the task of investigating the nature, the source and the credentials of the theories that we adopt that they have for the most part ignored the question what it is for someone to know how to perform tasks." As will be discussed, emphasis on the finer points of theory construction tends to overshadow the question of whether or not a given theory actually makes intelligible what it claims to explain.

A critical point missing from much of the knowledge literature is the fact that researchers—including researchers into tacit knowledge—also operate utilizing tacit knowledge. Tacit knowledge understandings constituting models of what a researcher does can be derived from:

- Interactions with mentors and other faculty during doctoral education socialization into fields and disciplines
- Discernments of unspoken university/college/school/department standards
- Perceptions of the preferences of university promotion and tenure committees
- Concepts held by colleagues and other significant academic players, assumed if not articulated, regarding the overall nature of good scholarship, endorsed methods of inquiry, limits of permissible generalization, etc.

There is significant potential for communication misunderstanding when a researcher operating with both formal theory (explicit knowledge) and contextual understandings (tacit knowledge) interrogates a practitioner who may share the same explicit knowledge but interprets it with a tacit knowledge developed in a dissimilar context. The results can and do have negative real-world effects.

The publication *Research Policies for the Social and Behavioral Sciences* (1986), prepared by the Library of Congress Congressional Research Service for the Task Force on Science Policy of the Committee on Science and Technology of the U.S. House of Representatives, offered an extended review of why social science research is seldom used by policy makers. It must be noted, however, that the term tacit knowledge could not be discerned in the report. Nevertheless, I am of the opinion that awareness of the differences in tacit knowledge understandings between researchers and policy makers constitutes a useful lens for viewing the researcher and decision maker disconnection identified in *Research Policies for the Social and Behavioral Sciences* (1986). In consequence, discussion of the factors identified by the Congressional Research Service staff (below) will include tentative explanations supplied by this writer of how such factors may be related to differences in researcher and practitioner tacit knowledge.

According to the House Committee on Science and Technology (1986), the "factors which impede the utilization of behavioral and social science research findings in decision making" include:

1. *Political Naivete*: Researchers may have a tacit understanding of the political contexts of universities and departments but do not understand the comparable contexts of clients/decision makers. Thus handicapped, researchers cannot provide what the decision makers need.

2. *Counterintuitive Findings*: Irrational and illogical factors often predominate in decision-making contexts. Government and corporate policies are not made solely on the basis of "objective" or academically prized criteria. Such criteria often reflect a "local" tacit knowledge (individual or group) which is not easily accessed by "outside" researchers and which serves to discount any "objective" facts that do not reinforce existing policies or power allocations.

3. *Irrelevance*: Social science research does not meet the needs of decision makers since it is not "holistic" (as defined by decision makers), does not factor in the "purposeful nature of human behavior" (as defined by decision makers). Issues of relevance are often subjective and determined at the tacit, not explicit, level.

4. *Difference in Reward System May Generate Research Which Is Too Late, Overly Quantified, and Inappropriate as a Guide to Policy*: Inquirers utilize their own explicit and tacit understandings when they research and publish a) for promotion and tenure and b) to impress other academics. However, this approach does not necessarily meet the needs of policy makers who want research oriented to their needs as determined, in part, by their own tacit knowledge.

5. *Deception and Fraud*: Social scientists frequently engage in deceptive practices to gather information. Researchers and decision makers view issues of deception and fraud from different tacit knowledge contexts.

Arguably, research approaches that 1) recognize that researchers are influenced by their own tacit knowledge in addition to theories, and 2) include procedures for drawing on the tacit knowledge of researchers, those who make policy, and those who are affected by policy are most likely to produce recommendations with a potential for implementation. In a related but not less crucial area, academic "self studies" which examine both the explicit/formal objectives and the tacit/unarticulated aims of university scholars represent a potentially fruitful area for inquiry. Another useful approach for exploring the explanatory power of tacit knowledge is to apply the concept to existing, in-print accounts of library and information center activities to determine if tacit knowledge understandings can provide new insights.

"Insourcing" the "Sun Library"

Cynthia Hill's article "Insourcing the Outsourced Library: The Sun Story" was published in the March 1, 1998 issue of *Library Journal*. It is an account of how Library Manager Hill and her staff demonstrated that the library ranked as a "core competency" of Sun Microsystems, Inc., "a Fortune 500 company [which] designs and sells network computers in 150 countries" (1998). This recognition was important since Sun employees are responsible for core competencies. Non-core activities, deemed less vital, are outsourced to other firms.

In describing the library history of Sun Microsystems, Inc., Hill (1998) noted that the company had started in 1982 without a library, but in 1991 added an out-sourced library component to meet the demands of "a critical mass within Sun—including engineering, research and development, and market research groups." However, the outsourced operation encountered barriers to utilizing significant Sun resources, did not have complete access to proprietary information, was unable to participate fully in company activities, and, in short, was not "part of the team" (Hill, 1998). These negative circumstances formed a catalytic context in which Hill and her staff were able to make the case that Sun and its employees would be better served if the library became a core competency, staffed by librarians who were part of the team.

As stressed by Hill (1998):

Our concerns had been heard, and Sun's management recognized that our status as contractors prevented us from adding full value. Also, they recognized that outsourced staff would be more likely lured away by other offers and Sun would lose some corporate history.

Arguably, what Hill described in her article as "part of the team," "adding full value," and "corporate history" can be seen as shorthand references to the critical tacit knowledge that effective professionals, in this case librarians, bring to the analysis and solving of significant corporate issues.

BRIDGING THE THEORY-PRACTICE DIVIDE

In examining the emerging recognition of the value of tacit knowledge, this summary has sought to provide an awareness of the concept as it is being utilized in the "real world" and across and within a variety of fields and disciplines. Throughout this approach, an effort has been made to avoid dwelling on the details of the research, which helped establish the validity of the tacit knowledge concept (Fischbein, 1994; Horvath et al., 1996; Reber, 1993; Sternberg et al., 1993), or to concentrate overmuch on a disciplinary literature, such as that of business, where tacit knowledge has become a "hot" area (Alic, 1997; Grant and Gregory, 1997; Jordan and Jones, 1997; Nonaka et al., 1996). In addition, a decision was made by this writer to completely avoid the morass of artificial language discussions.

Given the thrust of this chapter and the preceding limitations, the question yet remains: How may a greater awareness of the value of tacit knowledge bridge the theory-practice divide?

The first step in intermingling the now distinct interests of practitioners and researchers is to highlight the fact that tacit knowledge is already contributing to the effectiveness of libraries, information centers, corporations, and government entities on a daily basis. It is an administrative truism, for example, that the formal process of revising "official" policies or procedures in any office or department is often a means of capturing and formally endorsing the improved "ways of doing things," which have been unofficially implemented by experienced staff since the last time the policies or procedures were revised.

The irreplaceable value of tacit knowledge is demonstrated every time an inexperienced staff member is assigned to an "old timer" who can "show him/her the ropes." It is also in play when a new director is advised not to make radical changes during the first six months, the minimum amount of time seen as necessary for grasping how things actually work within a given organization. Tacit knowledge is also invoked when an experienced researcher casually mentions to a new assistant professor that a certain journal "may be peer-reviewed but nobody who counts in this department would ever accept an invitation to join its editorial board."

The preceding instances of the use of tacit knowledge are most likely to be encountered on the individual and institutional levels. However, what may be the longest-running effort within the library and information world to transform tacit knowledge into its explicit counterpart is regularly 1) taking place throughout an entire state, and 2) being publicized and replicated on the national level.

IMPROVING REFERENCE EFFECTIVENESS IN MARYLAND

Since 1983, the Division of Library Development and Services of the Maryland Department of Education has been conducting statewide reference/information studies in public libraries throughout the state. Over the years, the objectives of these studies have become progressively more ambitious, with the 1994 study seeking to:

- Determine to what degree a customer is likely to receive a complete and correct answer to his/her question
- Investigate which environment or behavioral factors influence the performance
- Explore which activities support the continued use of behaviors that contribute to a complete and correct answer
- Analyze how perceptions about the model reference behaviors affect the actual use of the behaviors (*1994 Maryland Statewide Reference Survey: Statewide Objective, Objectives, Facts and Figures*)

A total of twenty-one Maryland public library systems participated during the 1994 version of the statewide reference survey. Librarians were asked forty questions in each of the eighty-three outlets, for a total of 3,320 questions asked statewide. Questions were divided on the basis of twenty telephone questions and twenty walk-in questions per outlet (*1994 Maryland Statewide Reference Survey: Statewide Objective, Objectives, Facts and Figures*). The survey revealed that the statewide percentage of reference questions that were answered correctly rose from fifty-five percent in 1983 to seventy-five percent in 1994. In addition, the "Model Reference Behaviors" exhibited by librarians that contributed to correctly answering questions remained the same.

The librarian:

- Clarifies or paraphrases [the question]
- Uses open probe [question] to initiate
- Uses open probe after initial probe
- Verifies the specific question
- Asks a follow-up question (*1994 State-Wide Reference Survey: Overall Conclusions*)

Since the start, accounts of the sequential efforts of the Maryland Division of Library Development and the state's public libraries to upgrade reference effectiveness have appeared in print (Dyson, 1992; Gers and Seward, 1985; Stephan et al., 1988). Although the term was not used, the key to Maryland's success in raising the statewide average of correctly answered questions in the state's public libraries from fifty-five percent to seventy-five percent—in my opinion—is directly attributable to a multi-year, multi-format approach *to transform tacit into explicit knowledge.* The tacit knowledge involved included that of experienced reference librarians, reference supervisors, and reference effectiveness trainers.

Arguably, the Maryland Division of Library Development can be analyzed by academic researchers and used as a possible model for bridging the current theory-practice divide.

Conclusions and Recommendations

For the more philosophically minded, this effort to define tacit knowledge, to explore its value in raising the quality of practitioner work and the relevance of researcher studies to meeting practitioner needs, may be summarized quite succinctly. A *priori knowledge,* knowledge that comes to a theorist independent of biology, chemistry, or experience, simply does not exist. To return to the thought of Gilbert Ryle, both Aristotle the philosopher-scientist and Walton the gentle fisherman found inspiration for theory in actual practice. In analyzing practice and formalizing theory upon it, they gave "to their pupils the maxims and prescriptions of their arts" (Ryle, 1949/1958). They also provided a lasting precedent for others to follow with profit to theory and enhancement for practice.

It can be argued that numerous private and public entities are accepting the fact that expert practitioners possess knowledge of a type that is transmitted with difficulty yet is of inestimable value for individuals and organizations alike. The differences that do exist tend to cluster over how such expertise is best transmitted and retained (Nonaka and Takeuchi, 1995). If academic and other researchers accept the fact a) that practitioners (directly or indirectly) are the best source of theory; and b) that tacit knowledge offers the best possibilities for developing useable theory, then the long-existing theory-practice divide can, at last, be bridged.

Endnotes

1. "By *substantive theory,* we mean that developed for a substantive, or empirical area of sociological inquiry, such as patient care, race relations, professional education, delinquency, or research organizations. By *formal theory,* we mean that developed for a formal, or conceptual, area of sociological inquiry, such as stigma, deviant behavior, formal organization, socialization, status congruency, authority and power, reward systems, or social mobility. Both types of theory may be

considered as 'middle-range.' That is, they fall between the 'minor working hypotheses' of everyday life and the 'all-inclusive' grand theories. Substantive and formal theories exist on distinguishable levels of generality, which differ only in terms of degree. Therefore, in any one study, each type can shade at points into the other" [italics added for emphasis] (Glaser and Strauss, 1967).

2. "A *consensual sociology* seeks to speak to ordinary people about matters important in their lives, in language they can readily understand without extensive orientation in a strange vocabulary" [italics added for emphasis] (Swartz, 1997).

References

Alic, J. A. (1997) Knowledge, skill, and education in the new global economy. *Futures* 29, (1) 5-16.

Arora, A. (1996) Contracting for tacit knowledge: The provision of technical services in technology licensing contracts. *Journal of Development Economics* 50, (2) 233-256.

Drotos, P. V. (1994) From online specialist to research manager—Changing with the times. *Online* 18, (1) 54-58.

Dyson L. J. (1992) Improving reference services: A Maryland training program brings positive results. *Public Libraries* 31, (5) 284-289.

Fischbein, E. (1994) Tacit models. In Tirosh, D. (ed.) *Implicit and Explicit Knowledge: An Educational Approach* (96-110). Norwood, NJ: Ablex.

Gers, R.; Seward, L. J. (1985 November 1) Improving reference performance: Results of a statewide study. *Library Journal* 110, 32-35.

Glaser, B. G.; Strauss, A. L. (1967) *The Discovery of Grounded Theory: Strategies for Qualitative Research*. New York: Aldine de Gruyter.

Grant, E. B.; Gregory, J. J. (1997) Tacit knowledge, the life cycle and international manufacturing transfer. *Technology Analysis & Strategic Management* 9, (2) 149-161.

Harper, W. (1995) Natural kind. In Audi, R. (general ed.), *Cambridge Dictionary of Philosophy* (519-520). Cambridge: Cambridge University Press.

Hill, Cynthia. (1998, March 1) Insourcing the outsourced library: The Sun story. *Library Journal* 123, (4) 46-48.

Horvath, J. A.; Forsythe, G. B.; Sweeney, P, J.; McNally, J. A.; Wattendorf, J.; Williams, W. M.; Sternberg, R. J. (1994 October) *Tacit Knowledge in Military Leadership: Evidence from Officer Interviews* (Technical Report 1018). Alexandria, VA: U.S. Army Research Institute for the Behavioral and Social Sciences.

Horvath, J. A.; Sternberg, R. J.; Forsythe, G. B.; Sweeney, P.J.; Bullis, R. C.; Williams, W. M.; Dennis, M. (1996 May) *Tacit Knowledge in Military Leadership: Supporting Instrument Development* (Technical Report 1042). Alexandria, VA: U.S. Army Research Institute for the Behavioral and Social Sciences.

House Committee on Science and Technology, Task Force on Science Policy (1986) *Research Policies for the Social and Behavioral Sciences*, (Science Policy Study Background Report No. 6, prepared by the Library of Congress Congressional Research Service, 99th Congress, 2nd session).

Jordan, J.; Jones, P. (1997) Assessing your company's knowledge management style. *Long Range Planning* 30, (3) 392-398.

Levitas, E.; Hitt, M. A.; Dacin, M. T. (1997) Competitive intelligence and tacit knowledge development in strategic alliances. *Competitive Intelligence Review* 8, (2) 20-27.

Merton, R. K. (1968) *Social Theory and Social Structure* (English ed.). New York: Free Press.

1994 Maryland Statewide Reference Survey: Statewide Objective, Objectives, Facts and Figures (1995) [Leaflet]. (Available from the Maryland State Department of Education, Division of Library Development and Services, 200 West Baltimore Street, Baltimore, Maryland 21201).

1994 State-Wide Reference Survey: Overall Conclusions (undated). [Leaflet]. (Available from the Maryland State Department of Education, Division of Library Development and Services, 200 West Baltimore Street, Baltimore, Maryland 21201).

Nonaka, I.; Takeuchi, H. (1995) *The Knowledge-Creating Company*. New York: Oxford University Press.

Nonaka, I.; Takeuchi, H.; Umemoto, K. (1996) A theory of organizational knowledge creation. *International Journal of Technology Management* 11, (7/8) 833-845.

Polanyi, M. (1966/1967) *The Tacit Dimension*. Garden City, New York: Doubleday Anchor.

Reber, A. S. (1993) *Implicit Learning and Tacit Knowledge: An Essay on the Cognitive Unconscious*. New York: Oxford University Press.

Ryle, G. (1949/1958) *The Concept of Mind*. London: Hutchinson.

Stephan, S.; Gers, R.; Seward, L.; Bolin, N.; Partridge, J. (1988) Reference breakthrough in Maryland. *Public Libraries* 27, (4) 202-203.

Sternberg, R. J.; Wagner, R. K.; Okagaki, L. (1993) Practical intelligence: The nature and role of tacit knowledge in work and at school. In Puckett, J. M.; Reese, H. W. (eds.) *Mechanisms of Everyday Cognition* (205-227). Hillsdale, NJ: Lawrence Erlbaum Associates.

Swartz, L. H. (1997, April 11) *Implicit Knowledge Tacit Knowing, Connoisseurship, and the Common Law Tradition*. Paper presented at the faculty workshop of the University at Buffalo School of Law, Buffalo, NY.

Wagner, R. K.; Sternberg, R. J. (1985) Practical intelligence in real-world pursuits: The role of tacit knowledge. *Journal of Personality and Social Psychology* 49, (2) 436-458.

CHAPTER 13

Knowledge Management: A Research Scientist's Perspective

Sumitra Muralidhar

Research Assistant Professor

Georgetown University Medical Center

INTRODUCTION

The phenomenon of knowledge management could not have arrived at a better time. With global changes in economy, science and technology, information technology, and telecommunications, managing our growing knowledge in the interest of sustainable and environmentally appropriate development will be crucial for protecting our natural foundation of life. Progress in science depends largely on harnessing the tacit knowledge of scientists and, as such, scientific research organizations can be considered as "learning organizations." This chapter examines the National Institutes of Health (NIH), one of the largest medical institutions in the world, as a case study. A look at the organization of the smallest unit of life, i.e., a living cell, reveals a number of lessons that can be drawn into the world of knowledge management and learning organizations.

With the new millennium just around the corner, human civilization finds itself at the peak of scientific and technological revolution. Biotechnology has facilitated radical advances in the fields of medical diagnosis and treatment, in energy saving, and in solving food problems of the world. The Human Genome project is well on its way to cracking the genetic code of every one of the approximately 100,000 genes in the human DNA. The explosion in information technology and telecommunications has influenced every aspect of human life and brought the world literally at our fingertips. What then is our challenge as we journey into the 21st century?

Global change is creating the biggest challenge yet for humanity. The world's population is expected to grow from nearly six billion today to about eight billion by the year 2025. With this comes a rise in global energy and food requirements. It is estimated that about a billion people still live in poverty without sufficient food and adequate educational opportunities. Increased economic growth and modernization in larger areas of the globe are wreaking havoc with the environment. At the turn of the century, as we move from an industrial society to a knowledge-based society, it is vital that we use and manage our growing knowledge in the interest of an environmentally appropriate and sustainable development, to protect the natural foundation of life. The most important challenge for scientists, economists, and politicians alike will be the optimization of interactions between nature, society, and the economy in seeking strategic solutions. Incorporating the principles of value-based knowledge management into the scientific research process not only at the micro-level (within a scientific organization) but at the macro-level (across scientific disciplines) as well as at the global level (across scientific, economic, and social disciplines) will become essential for the survival of the human species.

Is Knowledge Management a Redundant Terminology in Science?

Before we address this question, let us very briefly review the phenomenon of knowledge management. Today, global economy is driven by knowledge and the currency of this knowledge-based economy is "intellectual capital." Organizations worldwide are striving to become learning organizations by relying more and more on their intellectual capital—their knowledge, experience, expertise, and related intangible assets. To quote Denis Waitley (1995): "Yesterday, natural sources defined power. Today knowledge is power. Yesterday hierarchy was the model. Today synergy is the mandate. Yesterday, leaders commanded and controlled. Today leaders empower and coach." The key strategic questions are 1) What sorts of knowledge and competence assets are worth developing, and 2) How is value to be derived from those assets?

Knowledge can be tacit, explicit, or implicit. Tacit knowledge is what people carry around with them, what they observe and learn from experience, and what is internalized and, therefore, not readily available for transfer to another. This tacit knowledge forms the basis for intellectual capital. Explicit knowledge on the other hand is that which has been formalized in our heads, or documented in books and papers. Therefore, it can be easily disseminated. Knowledge can also be implicit, where it is hidden within procedures, management practices, or even in the corporate culture. Knowledge management practices aim at maximizing the explicit knowledge by drawing the tacit and implicit knowledge and converting them into an explicit form so that it can be disseminated.

Annie Brooking (1996) describes the first steps in managing knowledge as follows:

- Identify knowledge (including the levels of knowledge and critical knowledge functions)
- Audit knowledge (identify optimal knowledge required to perform the optimal job)
- Document knowledge (using knowledge-based systems and tools)
- Disseminate knowledge

These processes are schematically represented in Figure 13.1.

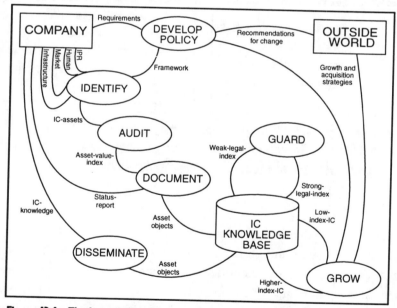

Figure 13.1 The knowledge management process. From Annie Brooking, "Knowledge Management and Corporate Memory" In Brooking, A. (ed.) *Intellectual Capital-Core Asset for the Third Millennium Enterprise*, International Thomson Business Press, 1996.

The above steps are comparable to that proposed by Boynton (1996), as shown in Figure 13.2. They include:

- Making knowledge visible
- Building knowledge intensity
- Developing a knowledge culture
- Building a knowledge infrastructure

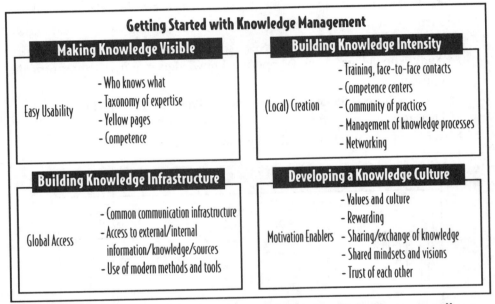

Figure 13.2   From A. Boynton, "'Exploring Opportunities in Knowledge Management: How to Get Started " Knowledge Management Symposium: Leveraging Knowledge for Business Impact, IBM Consulting Group, Sydney, 1996.

Now let us turn to the field of scientific research. Science rests on the premise of curiosity and is by definition the pursuit of knowledge through a continuous process of learning. The pure scientific method consists of five steps: establishing a hypothesis; designing and conducting effective experiments to test the hypothesis; making observations and gathering data from the experiments; analyzing the data and drawing relevant conclusions; and applying those conclusions to the real world issues. A fundamental step in scientific research is the development of an idea, an insight, asking a critical question. This then lays the foundation for establishing a hypothesis. This fundamental process relies entirely on tapping the tacit knowledge of a scientist. As such, scientific organizations, especially research organizations have recognized and exploited tacit knowledge from times immemorial. Is knowledge management then a redundant terminology in the field of scientific research? Isn't every scientific organization a learning organization? To quote Annie Brooking (1996), "Knowledge management, like other parts of intellectual capital management, is a topic in its own right. However, it is emerging as an area of interest to corporate strategists who are turning to the research community for answers to some complex questions."

Before we look at a case study, let us examine the culture of a scientific research organization. At the outset, we can distinguish three subcultures: 1) industrial research organizations such as biotech companies; 2) academic research institutions such as universities; and 3) federal research institutions such as the world renowned NIH, NASA, FDA, etc. Of these, the industrial sector has caught up with the whirlwind phenomenon of knowledge management and many of them have formally incorporated knowledge management tools into their culture. Organizations in this sector are driven by specific goals such as development of a product/range of products or a service/range of services. Consequently, they can be grouped with the rest of the business enterprises. Academic institutions are different. Universities have to balance their emphasis on research with that on education. Research at a university is primarily dependent on federal and private sources of funding. This then becomes a limiting factor and to some extent dictates the culture of the institution. Federal research institutions have yet another culture. With a handsome research budget granted to them annually, research scientists are free to challenge their inquisitive minds to the limit. Let us now examine the NIH as a prototype.

The NIH—A Case Study

Today, fifty years since its conception, the NIH is undoubtedly the world's greatest medical organization with an annual budget of about $13.5 billion. The Senate Appropriations Committee recently approved a bill that will increase the 1999 budget by about two billion, to $15.6 billion. The NIH is made up of twenty-four Institutes and Centers, each with a separate annual budget and commitment to a specific domain of medical research (e.g., cancer, heart disease, mental health, etc.). To comprehend how NIH emerged to be what it is today, we have to understand how science works. The aim of science is to move from the realm of unknown to the realm of known things and then, with a greater knowledge base, begin again, as if advancing a frontier.

This basic truth about science makes it different from other enterprises. Unlike many industries that manage their resources, labor, and money to produce the same or similar products over and over, science deploys its resources and talents to continuously explore new areas and produce new results that in turn pave the way for future explorations. Science requires both creativity and precision and since it deals with the unknown, results are often unpredictable. The uncertainty of where the most valuable discovery lies makes it extremely difficult to set priorities in science. But it is this uncertainty that has fostered creative and collaborative tension within the scientific community, which in turn has imposed the discipline of evaluation, competition, and productivity. The following are some of the guiding principles of the NIH that have generated science of the highest quality.

Global Approach to Medical Research

The overall objective of the organization is to foster high-quality medical research to fight disease and improve human health. NIH's mission and history have demonstrated that no one thing—no one single disease, no single investigator, no single institute, and no single method of funding research comes first or claims priority over others. As such, the following criteria continue to shape NIH's scientific policy:

- An obligation to respond to public health needs and scientific opportunities.
- Applying stringent review for scientific quality on all research proposals.
- Having a large and diverse portfolio. Since discoveries and opportunities cannot be predicted, NIH must support research along a broad, expanding frontier.
- NIH must continue to support the human capital and material assets of science.

Setting Research Priorities— Every Voice Counts

Determining the requirements of basic and clinical research, identifying the best means of funding a particular area of research (e.g., a contract, a grant, or a center), and responding to the emergence of new medical problems and new patient advocacies—is a constant challenge that the NIH faces.

While constantly assessing the public health needs and scientific opportunities, the NIH seeks advice from several diverse yet pertinent sources. These include:

- Scientist groups
- Scientific review committees
- Boards of scientific counselors
- Industry scientists
- Professional societies
- Industry managers
- President and administration

- Patients and their advocates
- Physicians and other health professionals
- General public
- Voluntary organizations
- Institute staff
- Ad hoc advisors
- Congress

This redeeming feature of NIH to interact and gain input from all the sources that are affected in one way or another by scientific progress has proved to be invaluable in determining its success.

Collaborative Success Story

Most of the NIH's budget supports the individual research projects conceived of and conducted either by government scientists working on the NIH campus or scientists based elsewhere—i.e., at universities; medical, dental, nursing, and pharmacy schools; schools of public health; nonprofit research foundations; and private research laboratories. Only about eleven percent of NIH's annual budget supports research on the NIH campus. Roughly over fifty percent is awarded to extramural research. NIH also funds research and development contracts to non-profit and commercial organizations for work requested and overseen by NIH staff. For example, the development of the drug Taxol for treating breast and ovarian cancer was the result of such collaboration. NIH also fosters extensive collaboration between its institutes as well as between basic and clinical researchers through frequent workshops, symposia, and an annual research festival.

Flexibility and Concentrated Enterprise

There are limits to planning science. Unforeseen crises and opportunities may require scientists to abandon their plans or change the direction and focus of their research. When the AIDS epidemic emerged as a public health threat in the early 1980s, NIH had the flexibility to redirect resources and expertise in a timely manner. In addition, a concentrated expertise that focussed exclusively on research and an atmosphere that encouraged discussions and collaborations across disciplines within NIH, and an informal series of patient conferences led to the following advances in the field of AIDS research at the very beginning of the epidemic: 1) understanding the unique biology of HIV; 2) effects of HIV on the immune system; 3) early policies to screen blood donors to prevent further spread of AIDS; 4) development of a blood test for HIV; 5) formulation of hospital guidelines for working safely with AIDS patients; and 6) early studies of the first treatment for AIDS, the drug AZT. Today, the NIH is at the cutting edge of AIDS research.

Communication Is the Key

The NIH has made a persistent effort to keep all channels of communication open between researchers, clinicians, patient populations, and the general public. As an example, let us look at the National Cancer Institute (NCI), which is one of the largest institutes at NIH. The NCI conducts three classes of research: laboratory; clinic; and population. In the laboratory, research is mainly focussed on the biology of cancer, properties of cancer-causing agents and their mechanisms, and the body's defense against cancer. In the clinic, research is focussed on cancer prevention, detection, diagnosis, treatment, and rehabilitation. In the population, research is carried out on the causes, risks, predispositions, incidence, and behavioral aspects of cancer. These three settings influence one another and, therefore, it is important to keep constant communication between them all the time. The primary avenues used by the NCI to achieve this as well as communicate with the public and the health care community are as follows:

World Wide Web

NCI's Web site at http://www.nci/nih.gov is designed for its optimal usefulness as a communication tool. It is organized so that clinicians, researchers, and the public can quickly and easily locate up-to-the-minute information relevant to their needs. Several of NCI's offices and labs maintain their own Web sites. In addition, there is an NCI Intranet that is accessible only to the NCI staff in order to allow information sharing among scientists at the institute without jeopardizing the confidentiality of their work.

The Cancer Information Service (CIS)

This service provides accurate up-to-date cancer information to patients and their families, and the public and health care professionals in every state, through offices located at NCI-funded cancer centers. One call to 1-800-4-CANCER connects callers, free of charge, to the office serving their region.

The International Cancer Information Center (ICIC)

The ICIC develops and maintains PDQ, the NCI's comprehensive cancer information database, as well as the bibliographic CANCERLIT database. It also maintains the CancerNet Web site (http://cancernet.nci.nih.gov), a repository of current cancer related information.

NCI's effort in building this Web of communication to complement its concentrated research program has paid off finally. For the first time since the 1930s, the nation witnessed a 2.7% decrease per year in the overall cancer incidence and death rates from 1992 to 1995.

Embracing Information Technology

A diverse range of scientific material is currently available online, often freely, including Web home pages of scientists, universities, and projects, preprints, technical reports, databases such as gene sequences, molecular structures, image libraries, and teaching resources. In addition, several full-text articles copyrighted by authors or publishers of major journals are available online through fee-based systems. The number of (citable) scientific articles on the publicly indexable Web is growing.

Scientists at the NIH have access not only to all the above, but also to an extensively developed, updated, comprehensive Intranet for every institute and center so that unpublished, confidential information can be exchanged. This knowledge infrastructure allows the scientists to access both external and internal information and knowledge sources instantly. Every institute has built into its budget a percentage to develop informatics and information flow. For example, NCI has allotted twenty million out of its proposed $3.1 billion budget for 1999, to develop informatics and information flow. Building a knowledge infrastructure is one of the essential steps in knowledge management.

Scientific Research and Then Some More

In the words of Goery Delacote, scientist and educator, " The noblesse of being a scientist brings obligations to stay open and alert to dialogue in the public domain, among educators and in the media, and to develop communication channels between the world of science and the larger world." In the recent years, NIH has embarked on several missions along these lines. These include educating and empowering the public in the area of biomedical research through the Medicine and the Public program; providing high school students and teachers a hands-on training in the various labs at NIH through an interactive program with the local and national high schools through the Science and Education program; and establishing a cordial relationship with the media in order to disseminate scientifically accurate information to the public in a timely manner through the Science and the Media program.

The NIH is not without its share of problems. With extensive collaborations and federally funded research being carried out at universities, nonprofit and private research institutions, and industries, the question of intellectual property ownership has become a subject of debate. Lack of sufficient incentives to sustain the human capital and federal restrictions on certain kinds of research have led to a recent exodus of talented scientists from the NIH into the industrial and academic sectors. In conclusion, the NIH represents a prototype of a learning organization in the present context of knowledge management. But as we embrace new frontiers and face new challenges in the next century, there will always be room for improvement.

A Lesson from Life: The Living Cell as a Model for Knowledge Management

Skimming the surface of the exhaustive literature on knowledge management, I was repeatedly struck by the relevance of a living cell—the smallest unit of life—as a model for knowledge management. I must emphasize that this section does not intend to test the reader's knowledge or understanding of biology, but merely to draw attention to certain key terms that reveal the analogy. A cell is the smallest unit of life that can grow and self-perpetuate. Cells are a complex system in and of themselves. Add to a cell its environment and you get a complex web of interactions. Consider the human body. Every cell in the body contains the same genetic material, yet, there are over 200 types of cells, which are of different sizes and shapes, and carry out very different functions (e.g., brain cell versus a muscle cell). How does a cell know its identity? How does it know when to grow and divide? A cell has to grow and divide but at the same time uncontrolled division can lead to diseases like cancer. How does it respond to changes in its environment? How does it deal with adverse conditions in the environment? The cell, one might say, is a supreme organization. What follows is a highly simplified version of how a cell responds to its environment.

A cell's knowledge base is the genetic material, the DNA that resides in the nucleus (center of a cell). The knowledge contained in the genes is decoded with the help of certain factors, which in turn have cofactors to assist them. Every decoding event requires the cooperation of several factors and their cofactors. The decoded message is transported to another cellular compartment, the cytoplasm, where it is translated into an effector molecule, the protein. The effector may be directly involved in a function (for example, when cells in the pancreas make the protein insulin, it is secreted into the blood and functions in controlling the blood sugar level). Alternatively, the effector may trigger a chain reaction by interacting with other effector molecules in a cascade, ultimately resulting in a function. Having such a cascade allows the cell to have several checkpoints for control. Sometimes the final effector molecule may be released from the cell and act at a remote site. At several steps in such a cascade there are auto-regulatory feedback loops. This way the knowledge base is constantly kept aware of the progress so that it may continue to function or shut off depending on the need of the cell.

How do cells sense their environment? They have on their surfaces molecules called receptors that constantly act as a surveillance mechanism. They pick up specific signals from the environment and transmit them via a chain of messengers to the DNA or the knowledge base. Specific messages are then decoded from the DNA to elicit an appropriate response. For example, if the signal is a growth factor, the cell would make effectors required for growth. If the signal is a danger signal like a virus, cells of the immune system would make effectors to combat them. There is a certain amount of redundancy built into the knowledge base. If the primary knowledge base (gene) is inactive or defective, there are standby secondary genes that can take over and get the job done. One has to remember that a cell performs hundreds of such reactions at any given time. This gives an idea of the complexity and the efficiency with which the knowledge has to be managed at every step of the way. Mistakes do occur and mistakes are allowed. Cells have repair systems built into them. When key surveillance mechanisms fail or when repair systems or checkpoints fail, it usually results in disease or cell death.

The organizational flatness, flexibility, cooperation, and sensitivity to the environment and interconnectedness in a cell are all designed to maximize its responsiveness to complexity inside and outside the organization. Some of these ideas may prove to be invaluable in developing knowledge management strategies.

In conclusion, although certain principles of knowledge management are ingrained in the scientific research process, it will be useful to formalize them and make a conscious effort to incorporate them into the workings of a scientific culture. With information technology and communications advancing rapidly, we are now in an advantageous position to combine these advances with knowledge management principles and maximize the conversion of tacit knowledge to explicit knowledge. To end with the beginning, knowledge management processes will have to be applied not only at the organizational level but also at the global level in order to maximize the communication channels between science, economics, society, and the larger world.

References

Boynton, A. (1996) "How to Get Started with Knowledge Management" extracted from Exploring Opportunities in Knowledge Management, Knowledge Management Symposium: Leveraging Knowledge for Business Impact, IBM Consulting Group, Sydney, Australia.

Brooking, Annie (1996) Knowledge Management and Corporate Memory. In Brooking, A. (ed.) *Intellectual Capital—Core Asset for the Third Millennium Enterprise*, International Thomson Business Press, London, U.K.

Waitley, Denis (1995) Self-Leadership and Change. In Waitley, D. (ed.) *Empires of the Mind— Lessons to Lead and Succeed in a Knowledge-Based World.* William Morrow and Company, Inc., New York, NY, U.S.A.

Part IV :

Knowledge Management– The Tools

Knowledge Management—The Tools
Introductory Notes

No matter how much we emphasize that knowledge management (KM) is essentially the recognition of a technology enabled change in the culture and operation of an organization, and that cultural and organizational change is fundamentally what KM is all about, there remains the fact that KM has been and still is information technology (IT) enabled and that IT issues are of extreme importance. In the introduction and in the chapter "The Evolution of Knowledge Management" (section two), KM is described as the Intranet out of intellectual capital. This is an acknowledgement of the centrality of IT to the development of KM. Sahasrabudhe's "Information Technology in Support of Knowledge Management" provides a quick general overview of various technologies, such as e-mail, videoconferencing, and data mining, and how they are used in the context of KM. White's "Telecommunications and Networks in Knowledge Management" describes the technological advances in networks and telecommunications that have enabled KM to develop into what it is today. He also draws conclusions about how further advances in network and telecommunication technology are likely to drive KM.

Despite KM's focus on the organization and its tacit knowledge, the phenomenon remains that access to external information, both formal access and informal access (see "Information Services and Productivity: A Background"), is essential to a fully developed KM program, and increasingly the Internet is the channel for that access. Black, in his chapter, "Internet Search Engines and Knowledge Management" examines Internet search engines and the role they play and are likely to play in KM.

Ideally, tacit knowledge must not only be shared, but in many cases it must be captured and organized. This is an extension of traditional indexing and abstracting, but the context of KM introduces new complexities and constraints. Fiddler's "Knowledge Management and Vocabulary Control" develops this issue from her professional experience.

Ideally, traditional information retrieval should be extended, and a more browsable interface should be provided, one that maps information space and allows navigation over it. A number of commercial packages are available that attempt to do this with varying levels of success. Tsai's "Infomapping in Information Retrieval" presents one such graphical approach, which illustrates the general technique and presents in a concrete fashion some of the promises and some of the limitations of such methodology as it exists today. The state of affairs might best be described as frustratingly tantalizing and inadequate, but evolving at an encouraging rate. As organizations become more international, the transmission of data on a widely geographically dispersed Intranet becomes more important to KM, and data coding and compression become more important. Bookstein reviews this topic, which a KM manager will have to become increasingly comfortable with, in "Information Coding in the Internet Environment."

Finally, Agada in "Repackaging Information" reviews the packaging and repackaging of information. How successfully information is communicated and received is, to a large extent, a function of how it is packaged. In most cases, the information professional will routinely make decisions about the packaging of information and will also make decisions about which tools and capabilities to provide to the users for their utilization in packaging and communicating information.

CHAPTER 14

Telecommunications and Networks in Knowledge Management

Curt M. White

Associate Professor

DePaul University

INTRODUCTION

In the previous chapters, we closely examined many facets of knowledge management systems, including the history, the basic principles, knowledge representation, and the role of the search engine as a means for accessing the knowledge in the knowledge base. But what do we know of the actual technology that drives and supports a knowledge management system? In this chapter, we will examine more closely the communications technology behind the system. More precisely, we will examine the computer networks and telecommunication systems that allow users to access the knowledge.

Knowledge management systems can reside on a variety of computer platforms. It is possible to access a knowledge management system via a workstation/terminal and a mainframe computer, from a personal computer/workstation connected to a network server, or from a personal computer/workstation connected to the Internet or a corporate-wide Intranet. Since many readers of this work will be interested in the creation of their own knowledge management system, and since the majority of knowledge management systems will be accessible through network servers and the Internet, we will concentrate more on those systems and less on the mainframe technology. In that regard, we will first turn our attentions to the Internet and a discussion of many of its parts, including the World Wide Web, HTML (hypertext markup language), dynamic HTML, XML (extensible markup language), the file transfer protocol, and TCP/IP (transmission control protocol/Internet protocol).

In order to support the Internet and its many protocols, we need to then discuss the differences between local area networks (LANs) and wide area networks (WANs). In dealing with LANs, we will examine the different network topologies, their access methods, and the operating systems that support those networks. With WANs, we will discuss the differences between circuit-switched networks, such as the telephone system, and packet-switched networks, such as the Internet.

Finally, we will examine the various technologies that are in place that support the communications between computers on WANs. In particular, we will examine modems and dial-up access, the faster communication technologies such as Integrated Services Digital Network (ISDN) and frame relay, and the latest technologies such as digital subscriber line (DSL), cable modems, and multi-channel multi-port distribution service (MMDS).

THE INTERNET

During the late 1960s, a branch of the U.S. government titled the Advance Research Projects Agency (ARPA) created one of the country's first wide area packet-switched networks, the ARPANET. Select research universities, military bases, and government labs were allowed access to the ARPANET for services such as electronic mail, file transfers, and remote logins.

In 1983, the Department of Defense broke the ARPANET into two basically similar networks: the original ARPANET and MILNET for military use. While the MILNET remained essentially the same, the ARPANET was phased out and replaced with new technology. It was primarily the work of the National Science Foundation that funded the creation of a new high-speed, cross-country backbone called the NSFNET. It was to this backbone that regional or midlevel networks connected. A set of access or "campus" networks then connected to these midlevel networks.

Within the last several years, the government essentially has withdrawn all direct support of the Internet and has turned it over to private industries and universities. Thus, there is no longer a single backbone but multiple backbones supported by different businesses, each in competition with one another. At the present moment, there are estimates that there are more than 29,670,000 hosts connected to the Internet (Network Wizards) with more than 65 million people accessing the Internet (TABNet).

World Wide Web

While the Internet still offers the old tried and true services such as file transfer protocol, email, and remote login, there is a relatively newer service that has grown dramatically in the last few years: the World Wide Web (WWW). Using a Web browser such as Netscape's Navigator or Microsoft's Internet Explorer, one can download and view Web pages on a personal computer. All the personal computer needs is a connection to the Internet, which we will examine shortly.

These Web pages consist of text, graphics, links to other Web pages, and sometimes even music and video. While the WWW can provide information on essentially any topic, some of the more promising areas include the humanities, government, medicine, law, commerce and retail, and entertainment. Despite the wide range of topics found, it is relatively easy for a knowledge manager to create a series of Web pages that can be used for accessing a knowledge base. These Web pages can be created using the HTML computer language, or by using a Web page authoring tool. (In a later section, we will see one or two simple examples of HTML.)

Based upon this widespread growth of the WWW and the relative ease at creating and accessing Web pages, the Web will clearly be the best way to reach the largest base of knowledge users. The WWW browser can be used to:

- Allow external public users to access a public knowledge center
- Allow external private users to access a corporate-wide knowledge center using a password
- Allow only internal users to access a corporate-wide knowledge center

File Transfer Protocol

The file transfer protocol (FTP) was one of the first services offered on the Internet. Its primary function is to allow a user to download a file from a remote site to the user's computer. These files could be data sets or executable computer programs. While the WWW has had a major impact on the retrieval of text- and image-based documents, many people still find it essential to create a repository of data files or program files. Using specialized FTP software or even a Web browser, one can easily access an FTP site. Furthermore, these FTP sites can be designed such that an ID and password are required for entry.

To access an FTP site via a Web browser and download a file, at least three pieces of information are necessary. First, a user must know the address, or uniform resource locator (URL) of the FTP site. Second, the user must know the directory/subdirectory in which to look for the file. Third, the user must know the name of the file that they are trying to download. Thus, downloading FTP files is not a "browsing" activity. That is, one must have a good idea of what one is looking for and where it is located. However, with a properly designed interface, a knowledge manager could create an environment in which the searching for and the downloading of files could be a useful and pleasant experience. Software is available that allows a person to easily create an FTP site.

Electronic Mail

While most computer users consider email to be such a basic staple of conducting business (and leisure for some), one might ask how a knowledge manager could use email other than for basic operations. Two possible uses are email distribution lists and email listservs. The email distribution list is simply a table of participants' email addresses. Since it is possible to have multiple distribution lists, each list is identified with a unique name. When someone wishes to send an email to all the participants on a particular list, the email is sent to the name of the desired distribution list. The email software then sends a copy of the email to all the email addresses in that list. This could be a simple but effective way to disseminate information to a group of users.

The second technique, the email listserv, is a variation on the distribution list theme. With a listserv, members "subscribe" to a particular listserv by sending an email to the listserv's administration software. The administration software removes the sender's email address from the email message and inserts it into the listserv's table of member addresses. Then, if a user wishes to "broadcast" an email to all the members of the listserv, that member sends an email to a unique email address that is recognized by the listserv software. When the email arrives, the listserv software copies the email and sends it to each member in the listserv. In this way, every member of the listserv can broadcast an email message to all the other members of the listserv.

To keep the volume of email messages to a reasonable level, or to avoid inflammatory or irrelevant email messages, many listservs are moderated by someone who is willing to read each incoming email message before it is forwarded to all members. If the moderator deems the message inappropriate, the email message can be discarded. Thus, the listserv is another way that knowledge can be disseminated to a select group of knowledge users.

Directories and Search Engines

Someone once compared finding something on the Internet to shopping in a store the size of Texas where everything is arranged randomly on the shelves. There are too many Web sites offering too much information and there is no single site that indexes all the information. There are, however, many sites (directories) that offer some form of indexing on unique subjects. The following list provides some sample directories on the Internet.

Yahoo: *www.yahoo.com*—an extremely popular directory with information on many subjects

A2Z : *a2z.lycos.com*—yellow pages for businesses

Yellow Pages: *theyellowpages.com* and *www.switchboard.com* and *www.bigbook.com*

USA City Link: *usacitylink.com*—links to lots of city pages

Lycos People Finder: *www.lycos.com/pplfndr.html/*—white pages of the phone book

BigBook: *www.bigbook.com*—more white pages

Liszt: *www.liszt.com*—searchable directory of email discussion groups

ClNet Shareware.com: *www.shareware.com*—listings of free software

Merriam-Webster: *www.m-w.com/netdict.htm*—online dictionary

Quotations: *www.columbia.edu/acis/bartleby/bartlett* and *www.starlingtech.com/quotes*

Thesaurus: *www.thesaurus.com*

Almanac: *www.almanac.com*

Ask an expert: *www.askanexpert.com/askanexpert/* and *www.findout.com*

Dates: *www.calendarzone.com*—celestial, cultural, religious, and historical calendars

General reference: *www.refdesk.com*

Often, it is valuable to have links to sites such as those listed above. In this way, the users will have a convenient access to one or more directory services. As a precaution, however, if you are going to include a link in your Web page to another site, you should check with that site for any possible copyright violations.

A second service that is extremely useful in locating information on the Web is the search engine. While humans usually create the contents of directories, computers create search engine indexes. Thus, a search on a subject may yield results that sometimes have nothing to do with the subject desired. Nonetheless, a search engine can be an extremely valuable tool for finding information on many subjects. Some of the more common search engines are:

Alta Vista: *www.altavista.digital.com*—advanced query supports and, or, not, near, and results ranking criteria

Lycos: *www.lycos.com*—supports and, or, multiple terms, (loose, fair, good, close, strong) match

InfoSeek: *www.infoseek.com*—no Boolean operators but supports + - and searches for strings of words

OpenText: *index.opentext.net*—supports and, or, but not, near, followed by, within (anywhere, summary, title, first heading, URL)

Excite: *www.excite.com*—supports +, -, and, or, and not, ( ) grouping

Webcrawler: *www.webcrawler.com*—supports and, or, not, near, adjacent

Newriders: *www.mcp.com/newriders/wwwyp/index.html*—no Booleans

Magellan: *www.mckinley.com*—supports +, -, and, or, and, not, ( )

Worm: *wwww.cs.colorado.edu/home/mcbryan/wwww.html*—supports and, or

Aliweb: *web.nexor.co.uk/public/aliweb/aliweb.html*

CUI's W3: *cuiwww.unige.ch/w3catalog*

HotBot: *www.hotbot.com*—very powerful, >36 million indexed pages, simple or advanced searches

DejaNews: *www.dejanews.com*

Inktomi: *inktomi.cs.berkeley.edu:1234/*

JumpCity: *www.jumpcity.com*

Northern Light: *www.nlsearch.com*

Look Smart: *www.looksmart.com*

Planet Search: *www.planetsearch.com*

Search.com: *www.search.com*

Many of the popular search engines can be incorporated directly into a Web page of your creation. This search engine can then be directed to search through your Web pages looking for a key word or words. Knowledge managers interested in incorporating this feature into a Web page should contact the creator of the search engine for more specific details.

HTML, Dynamic HTML, and XML

HTML is the language one can use to create a Web page. Actually, it is not a programming language like COBOL, FORTRAN, or C, but is a scripting language. A scripting language is a computer language that is very English-like and is very easy to use. For example, the following is a small HTML file. The line numbers added at the end of each line are placed there for comments and are not part of an HTML document.

```
<HTML>                                              1.
<HEAD>                                              2.
<TITLE> DePaul University Home Page   </TITLE>      3.
</HEAD>                                             4.
<BODY>                                              5.
This is the first line. <BR>                        6.
This is the second line. <BR>                       7.
<P>Start a new paragraph.</P>                        8.
<H1> First Header </H1>                              9.
<H2> Another Header </H2>                           10.
<H2> Same size as last </H2>                        11.
<H3> Smaller yet </H3>                              12.
<HR>                                                13.
<B> Bold this line. </B> <BR>                       14.
<I> And italicize this one. </I><BR>                15.
<IMG SRC="c:\images\skyline.gif">                   16.
<A HREF="http://www.cs.depaul.edu">DePaul CS Page</A>  17.
</BODY>                                             18.
</HTML>                                             19.
```

Line 1 starts the beginning of every HTML document. Documents are broken into a HEAD and a BODY. Line 2 starts the HEAD section. Line 3 is the title that will appear on the title bar of the browser. Line 4 denotes the end of the HEAD and line 5 denotes the beginning of the BODY. Lines 6 and 7 are simply text lines with break commands at the end. If a break command is not inserted, the browser will wrap the text to the end of the screen. Line 8 skips a line and begins a new paragraph. Lines 9, 10, 11, and 12 are Headers. A header is similar to a bolded title one places at the beginning of a paragraph. Headers come in different sizes, with the size H1 being the largest, H2 the next smaller size, etc. Line 13 is an example of a horizontal rule, which is a graphic dividing line that reaches across the page. Lines 14 and 15 are examples of bolding and italicizing text, respectively. Line 16 is the command that will place an image at this point on the Web page. The image in this example is apparently on the C: drive in directory "images" and has the file name "skyline.gif." All images must be either .gif or .jpg format. Line 17 is an example of a hyperlink. The text "DePaul CS Page" will appear in blue (usually) and be underlined. When a cursor is moved over this text, the cursor will turn into the "clickable hand" cursor. If the user then clicks on this text, the browser will try to load the next Web page from http://www. cs.depaul.edu. Lines 18 and 19 denote the end of the BODY and the end of the HTML document respectively.

HTML pages are simple static text documents that browsers read, interpret, then display. Dynamic HTML (DHTML) pages are documents that take on a structure of their own. When a browser reads a dynamic Web page, the browser places each element from the page on a stack with similar elements. Essentially, the browser creates a database each time a page is loaded, and each dynamic HTML tag becomes a record into this database. Then, the browser uses script languages such as JavaScript or VBScript to manipulate the tags.

Stated another way, DHTML can grab any element on a page and change its appearance, content, or location on the page. While DHTML is not yet one standard, and its approach differs between Microsoft and Netscape, it is possible to incorporate DHTML into your documents using a combination of HTML, style sheets, and scripts.

Some examples of DHTML follow. The standard for Dynamic HTML continues to be developed at this time. HTML version 4.0 contains many of these dynamic elements.

Changing tags and contents—by clicking on some text (such as a heading), additional text appears on the page (with no help from the server).

Live positioning of elements—one can position text or images anywhere on the page, even on top of other elements. Each "layer" can be moved or hidden independently of the others. These layers can overlap, let other layers show through, or hide everything underneath.

Dynamic fonts—Netscape browsers can download highly compressed font formats with a Web page. This font information is then used to assemble the current page.

Data binding—Microsoft browsers enable page elements such as table cells to "attach" themselves to database records. This will greatly simplify the chore of sending and retrieving records to and from a server database.

The final "version" of HTML is eXtensible Markup Language (XML). Actually, XML is not a version of HTML at all. One could think of XML as being the parent and HTML as being one of the parent's children. The syntax of XML is fairly similar to HTML, however, there are a number of very important differences. First, XML is "extensible," which means a user can define his/her own "tags" (the <B> <IMG ...> things). These tags can be created to define entire data structures, such as an auto parts catalog that requires tags such as <PARTNAME>, <DESCRIPTION>, and <PARTCOST>. Second, XML is much less forgiving than HTML. Unlike HTML, a document created in XML will not display if there is a mistake in the coding. The browser usually ignores a mistake in the HTML coding and the rest of the document is displayed. The third big difference is that XML documents require many more syntactic rules. For example, all tags must be properly nested, all attribute values must have quotation marks around them, and all tags with empty content must end in "/>".

Knowledge managers desiring to create one or more Web pages to allow users access to a knowledge management system will have to become versed with HTML, dynamic HTML, and XML. At the least, they will need to be expert users of the tools that create HTML, dynamic HTML, and XML documents. Just like we all use word processors to create word-processed documents, more and more Web page designers are using Web page editors to create Web pages. As dynamic HTML and XML become better known by Web page creators, more software tools will emerge that can more easily create HTML, dynamic HTML, and XML Web pages.

TCP/IP
(Transmission Control Protocol / Internet Protocol)

To allow the interconnection of so many types of computers and networks, the Internet depends on a set of protocol standards that allow someone to connect a computer to the Internet. These two standards, TCP and IP, together provide a reliable system for interconnecting to and transferring information over the Internet. While most would agree that a knowledge manager does not need to know the inner workings of TCP and IP, one should understand that for any computer to "talk" to the Internet, TCP and IP, or one of their other "forms" is necessary. These other forms come with names such as SLIP (Serial Line Internet Protocol), PPP (Point-to-Point Protocol), and WinSock, which is found on older versions of Microsoft Windows.

INTRANET

An Intranet is a TCP/IP network *inside* a company that links the company's people and information in a way that makes people more productive, corporate and non-corporate information more accessible, and navigation through all the resources and applications of the company's computing environment more seamless than ever before. An Intranet is a perfect vehicle for providing a corporate-wide knowledge center. It is very easy to create an Intranet such that only employees in-house will have access to the Intranet knowledge center.

For example, to access the corporate knowledge center, a user would sit down at a personal computer and run the browser of his/her choice. The browser could be set up such that it defaults to the corporate knowledge center's home Web page. When the home page appears on the screen, the user will be presented with a page that looks like thousands of other Web pages. There will be a menu with a selection of topics, each being a hyperlink to another internal Web page or perhaps to an external Web page that someone else has created. These links could execute local search engines, take the user to a "bulletin-board" type service that allows a user to read or post questions on a particular subject, or execute any number of online database catalogs. Since an Intranet can be designed only for internal users, these online catalogs could be established without requiring passwords. The following are a few examples of companies that have created Intranets:

- Company A maintains a *parts* database. It shows what the part looks like, its dimensions, bill of materials, assembly instructions, and assembly timings. Vendors, people on the shop floor, and engineers can view this information online.
- Company B uses an Intranet to create a *virtual laboratory*. Research labs abroad can share information, debate research topics, and share experiences and project results with their colleagues.
- Company C publishes multimedia files saving thousands of dollars previously incurred for printing, duplication of videocassettes, and distribution among its 200-300 sales representatives.

- Company D distributes graphic and textual sales information to over 300 salespeople worldwide.
- Company E uses an Intranet to provide employees with information on research seminars, company announcements, building facilities, the employee directory, commuting options, benefits, child care, how to place purchase orders, how to get business cards, safety equipment, and more.

Thus, the Intranet is clearly a fascinating and relatively simple way to allow users access to a company-wide knowledge center.

One step beyond the Intranet is the extranet. An extranet is an interconnection of corporate Intranets in a business that finds itself spread over a wide geographic area.

NETWORK SUPPORT STRUCTURES

In order to support the Internet, Intranets, and extranets, and to better understand how these types of networks work, the knowledge manager should have a very basic understanding of the underlying LAN and WAN support structures. These support structures include the topologies, access methods, and operating systems of LANs, and the basic design differences between packet-switched WANs and circuit-switched WANs. We'll begin our discussion with LANs, then move on to WANs.

LANs

A LAN is an interconnection of computers and peripherals involving high-speed data transfers over a small geographic area (such as a room, a building, or several adjacent buildings). A knowledge manager should know the advantages and disadvantages of LANs, their physical layouts (topologies), how a workstation places its data onto the network (access methods), and the operating system that controls the functions of the network (network operating system).

LANs have the following advantages:

- Ability to share software and peripherals, such as a laser printer.
- Individual workstations can survive a network failure, as long as that workstation does not require the services of the network, and it should be possible to upgrade the workstations or peripherals without replacing the network.
- Likewise, it should be possible to upgrade the network without replacing the workstations or peripherals.

- Most LANs provide some form of connection to the Internet or to other WANs.
- The LAN can be privately owned.

Unfortunately, LANs also have disadvantages:

- They can be expensive, including the hardware, software, and personnel to support the network.
- Despite the appearance that any hardware or software will work on a particular LAN, this is not always the case.
- Management and control of a LAN requires many hours of dedication and service.
- A LAN is only as strong as its weakest link. Since there are so many links within a LAN, there is great potential for weakness.

Once a knowledge manager understands the basic advantages and disadvantages of LANs, one should next learn the three basic topologies, or layouts, of the networks: bus; ring; and star. The earliest topology designed was the bus. It is basically a long section of wire to which workstations and peripherals are connected. The wire is usually coaxial cable (like the cable that delivers cable television into the house). When one workstation transmits data on the bus, all the other workstations receive that data. Of course, only the workstation for which the data is intended will pay attention to the data, while the others will simply ignore it.

A newer topology is the ring. Essentially, all workstations are connected in a big loop, or ring. Data on the ring travels in one direction only, thus, if a workstation wishes to send data to the workstation that is immediately "upstream," the data must travel all the way around the ring. One immediate advantage of the ring over the bus is making connections. The designers of the ring made it relatively simple to add or remove a workstation to or from the ring by creating a "box" into which all workstations plug. A second advantage of the ring will be apparent when we later discuss the access methods. The wiring often used with the ring is twisted pair, similar to the wiring connecting telephones within a house, but much thicker.

The third LAN topology is the star. With the star, there is a central device called the hub. All workstations within a small geographic area, such as a room or rooms, plug into this hub. The wiring used to connect workstations to a hub is also twisted pair. But this form of twisted pair is very similar to the wiring used to connect telephone lines within the house. When a workstation transmits data to the hub, the hub repeats the data and sends it out to every other workstation connected to the hub.

Because of the simplicity of the wiring and plugging into the hub (plus other factors that we will see shortly), the star is the most popular form of LAN.

Now that there is an understanding of the basic topologies, one asks, "How does a workstation get its data 'inserted' onto the network?" Another way of saying that is: "How does a workstation get access to the network?" To accomplish this, there are three basic access techniques. The oldest and most popular technique is carrier sense multiple access with collision detection (CSMA/CD), or Ethernet. A station wishing to transmit listens to the network. If there is no one else transmitting, it transmits. If there is someone else transmitting, it waits. A problem occurs if two or more stations transmit at the same time, causing a collision. In that case, both stations back off and wait a random amount of time before trying again.

The beauty of CSMA/CD is its simplicity. The software is relatively simple and the hardware is the least expensive of all the access techniques. Unfortunately, the collision problem can escalate to serious levels on networks with many simultaneous users. Fortunately, faster versions of CSMA/CD are being developed all the time. CSMA/CD can be found on bus and star topologies.

A second popular access technique found on ring networks is the token ring access method. For any station to transmit onto the network, the station must possess the token. Once a station has completed its transmission, the station passes the token onto the downstream neighbor. If a station does not have anything to transmit, the token is passed on once again. The primary advantage of the token ring access method is that there are no collisions. You can only talk if you possess the token, and there is only one token. With no collisions, there is no uncertainty as to when a station will get a chance to transmit data. One can fairly closely calculate when the token will arrive at each station. Unfortunately, token ring has never achieved the widespread success of CSMA/CD. Three of its biggest drawbacks are the complexity of the software, the cost of the hardware, and its relatively slower transmission speeds.

A network needs a network operating system to control access to its resources and to allow users to login and perform numerous network operations. Some of the more popular LAN operating systems include Novell's NetWare, Microsoft's Windows NT, IBM's OS/2, UNIX, Linux, and Banyan Vines. The choice of a network operating system may influence issues such as the user interface, security, network maintenance and administration, and overall costs.

WANs

WANs are also interconnections of computers and peripherals and may also transmit data at high speeds, but typically over larger geographic areas such as cities, states, and countries. The Internet is probably the best known example of a WAN designed to transmit data. The U.S. telephone system is the best known example of a WAN designed to carry voice. However, as we shall see, telephone networks are becoming suitable for both voice and data with different varieties appearing almost daily.

What should a knowledge manager know about WANs? A knowledge manager should know the differences, advantages, and disadvantages of WANs designed for voice and those designed for data. Once this information is known, the knowledge manager can better understand the underlying communication lines necessary to access and to support a WAN.

One way of categorizing WANs is by the basic design of a network's underlying subnet (the physical interconnections of computer nodes and communication links). If the subnet is designed to transfer *packets* (relatively small packages) of data, then the network is a packet-switched network. If a user in Chicago wishes to transmit fifty packets of data to a user in Spokane, a packet-switched network will get those fifty packets delivered over whatever route the network feels is the most efficient at the given moment. A good analogy to a packet-switched network is an overnight delivery service such as UPS or Federal Express. A good example of a packet-switched network is the Internet. It is very good at transmitting computer data, but not yet very good at transmitting a voice conversation.

The opposite of a packet-switched network is a circuit-switched network. With this form of network, a physical connection is temporarily created from source to destination. All traffic then flows over this connection. When there is no more traffic, the connection is dissolved. A good example of a circuit-switched network is the U.S. telephone system. When you call someone across the city/state/country, you have a dedicated connection that will last until you hang up the telephone. Circuit-switched networks are great for voice connections, and can also be used for transmitting computer data. Unfortunately, if a large amount of computer data has to be transmitted, a switched circuit can become very expensive. That is where a packet-switched network might be more economical.

A second way to categorize WANs is by looking at the software connection that is established. A network can be classified as either *connection oriented* or *connectionless*. Connection-oriented networks are ones in which a connection or dialog is established before any data is transferred. This connection creation would create a more secure connection since both sender and receiver have agreed upon the parameters of a connection and both understand that they will be receiving data from the other. A connectionless network is the opposite: No connection is established before data transfer. The data is simply transmitted.

As an example of a connection-oriented network, consider a banking system. Before transferring money from one account to another, the network wants to make sure that both sides are ready to communicate and that certain transfer protocols have been established. An email system is typically a connectionless network. If a user wants to send an email, the email is sent. There is no need to establish a connection since the destination email server will hold the email until the destination user is ready to read his/her mail.

WAN Communication Lines

Now that the basic differences between packet-switched networks and circuit-switched networks are understood, we will examine the infrastructures that support these networks. In other words, we will examine which type of communication lines is available to gain access to WANs and to support the internal workings of WANs. As the internal workings of WANs are not directly the concern of the knowledge manager, we will concentrate solely on the types of communication lines available that allow a user to gain access to WANs.

Ten years ago there were essentially two ways for a user to connect himself/herself to a WAN: using a dial-up or leased phone line with a modem or using a communication service such as T-1 that was offered by the local phone company. Today, there are dozens of ways a user can connect his/her computer to a computer network. The following examines eight of the more common forms of communication lines.

The first is the old tried-and-true technology of a dial-up phone line and a modem. Dial-up lines can offer speeds of up to 56 Kbps (actually that is the theoretical limit while the actual speed is much less than that). This technology is the most common and well proven, and the hardware is very reasonably priced. The disadvantages include slow transmission speeds and potentially high telephone connection charges.

A second technology, which is offered by the local phone companies, is an ISDN. ISDN can obtain data transfer speeds up to 128Kbps and can transfer the data using a digital format. A computer wishing to transmit data over an ISDN line will need an ISDN modem (a little more costly than a dial-up modem) and an ISDN contract with a telephone company. ISDN costs roughly $40-$50 per month and is available in most locations around the country.

A third technology, and one of the newest, is a DSL. DSL transfers data digitally at speeds up to several million bps. DSL comes in many varieties and at many different costs. As a rough estimate, you can expect to spend around $200 per month for a 128 Kbps and faster line. However, contact your local phone company to find out if they even offer DSL service and then ask them how much it costs.

A fourth technology is the cable modem. This service is offered by your local cable television operator and is not yet available in most areas. More than likely, this service will be slow to expand due to the very large start-up costs required of the local cable operators. It is likely that you will see DSL services expanded before you see cable modem service offered. Nonetheless, cable modems are capable of speeds up to 2 Mbps and cost roughly $40-$50 per month.

The fifth form of technology has been around for quite some time. T-1 lines are digital phone lines that transmit data at 1.544 Mbps. The local phone company can offer a T-1 line, but expect to pay several hundred dollars per month for such a service.

Frame relay is the sixth form and is a relatively new entrant in the communications arena and is also a service that is offered by the local telephone company. A high-speed packet-switching protocol used in WANs, it has also become popular for LAN-to-LAN connections across remote distances. Frame relay is faster than traditional packet-switched networks because it was designed for today's reliable circuits and performs less rigorous error detection.

Some sample transmission rates and prices as of the writing of this chapter are:

128 Kbps for $400 per month

1,536 Kbps for $1,980 per month.

The seventh form, ATM, has been around for a number of years but has been gaining wider acceptance within the last few years. ATM is a network technology for both LANs and WANs that supports real-time voice, video, and data. The technology uses switches that establish a circuit from input to output port and maintain that connection for the duration of the transmission. One of the powers of ATM is its ability to grow in speed, if necessary (scalability). Presently, it can support transmission speeds of 25, 100, 155, 622, and 2,488 Mbps.

ATM works by breaking all data into 53-byte packets, or cells. This fixed-length unit allows very fast switches to be built, thus allowing for the very high transfer speeds. The small ATM cell also ensures that voice and video can be inserted into the stream often enough for real-time applications. Finally, the ability to specify a quality of service is one of ATM's most important features, allowing voice and video to be transmitted smoothly. Unfortunately, ATM is also quite expensive, on the same level as frame relay, if not more expensive.

Finally, there is MMDS. MMDS is a very new technology that allows one-way wireless digital data and cable television transfers from a service provider to a user at speeds up to 800 Kbps. While this service is only one way, it may prove to be an attractive alternative to DSL and is currently much less expensive.

CONCLUSION

Clearly the knowledge manager has a large amount of technical information to absorb and apply. While many might argue that the knowledge manager does not need to be so well versed in technical matters, it is the strong opinion of this author that the knowledge manager must learn all he/she can with respect to computer and telecommunications technology, if for no other reason than to be able to engage in an intelligent conversation with a technical expert. Simply stated, the knowledge manager will be creating a system that will exist on computer hardware and be transmitted over telecommunication lines. It is to the vast benefit of the knowledge manager that he/she be in the best position possible to make well-informed decisions.

This problem is further compounded by the incredible growth in the networking and telecommunications industries. The only way a person can attempt to stay current with new developments is to set aside time each week to scan and read the trade journals, newsletters, and magazines devoted to the computer and knowledge management arenas. Only then will a knowledge manager keep abreast of this exciting and rapidly changing field of study.

CHAPTER 15

Internet Search Engines and Knowledge Management

Ken Black
Director of Teaching and Learning Technology
Dominican University

INTRODUCTION

Tapping the World Wide Web in the most efficient manner is a necessity in today's information society. Used properly, Internet search engines can be a valuable asset to a knowledge manager. It is incumbent upon the knowledge manager, however, to learn as much about these engines as possible and to convey this information to his/her clients, many of whom may still not be aware of the proper use of these engines.

The terms "knowledge management" and "Internet" together in any sentence would seemingly be mutually exclusive. After all, how could one reasonably expect to use any sort of knowledge management in a worldwide network that is all but unmanageable in size? The most recent estimate of the size of the Internet comes courtesy of a study of search engines from two computer scientists at NEC Research Institute, who estimated that the "indexable" Web contained 320 million pages as of December 1997 (Lawrence and Giles, 1998). Two scientists from Digital's Systems Research Center immediately countered shortly after the Lawrence and Giles article appeared that the number was closer to 275 million "distinct, static pages on the Web" as of March 1998 (Bharat and Broder, 1998). Not surprisingly, the *Digital* scientists' paper also concluded that *Digital's* AltaVista engine indexed 110 million pages, thereby indexing forty percent of the distinct pages on the Web, compared to HotBot's 100 million with thirty-six percent of the Web; Lawrence and Giles (1998) placed HotBot higher in coverage of the Web at thirty-four percent compared to AltaVista's twenty-eight percent.

Regardless of the "real" size of the Web, attempting to find anything on it with any degree of accuracy is seemingly impossible. To actually rely on the Internet to any degree to find pertinent documents or information would appear downright foolhardy.

THE USE OF SEARCH ENGINES

The first search engine to use a "spider" to roam the Web searching for pages that actually indexed the full text of a page was WebCrawler in 1994. Several search engines followed, including Lycos, Infoseek, and AltaVista (Sonnenreich and Macinta, 1998). Lawrence and Giles (1998) evaluated six major search engines for their article, and the six they selected are agreed upon by almost every writer on search engines to be the major players in the business of indexing the Web. The six chosen are: AltaVista; Excite; HotBot; Infoseek; Lycos; and Northern Light. The introduction of the latter in 1997 helped to only further blur the distinction between finding free Internet resources and fee-based resources since, in addition to indexing the Web, Northern Light also sells copyrighted articles from various sources for fees ranging from one to four dollars. However, it did serve to inform the less informed of a basic premise that most librarians have known for some time: Information is not free, and "everything" is not available on the Internet.

While trying to counter the misinformed argument that "everything is on the Web" when attempting to convince his/her CEO that a value-added service, such as The Dialog Corporation or Reed Elsevier's LEXIS-NEXIS, is necessary for a corporate library, a librarian is also faced with the task of deciding when, indeed, a Web search is appropriate for a query. By the time a question reaches the librarian, it is very likely that the questioner has already given a search engine or two a try. And who could blame them? Thanks to shrewd marketing agreements with both Microsoft and Netscape, searching the Web is as easy as clicking a search button on one's favorite browser. Even without that temptation, the average user is likely to already know about search engines just based on advertising. Most of the major engines now advertise either in print or on commercial television, and thanks to Yahoo!'s incorporation of the AltaVista engine into its site, a user could start a search of the entire Web (or, at least, AltaVista's index of the Web) without leaving the Yahoo! site (Sonnenreich and Macinta, 1998). (As of the writing of this article, Yahoo! later shifted to using the Inktomi engine, which is the backbone of the HotBot service.) Considering that Media Metrix, The PC Meter Company, placed Yahoo! on top of its listings as the most visited search-related site while at work (1998), even users who go nowhere except for Yahoo! in order to start an Internet search will likely stumble into a major engine like AltaVista sooner or later.

Public awareness of search engines is likely to grow. A spring 1997 research study by CommerceNet/Nielsen Media shows that among "frequent Web users, seventy-one percent most often use search engines to find Web sites," according to a press release posted on the Web (CommerceNet Research Center, 1997). Therefore, since the question is not if but when a corporation's employees start using the search engines to find information on the Web, how can a knowledge manager hope to properly harness use among workers? The key is communicating the proper usage of search engines to all likely users, which is easier said than done.

If anything, the sheer amount of articles on using search engines creates more chaos than assistance. Review any popular computing magazine and you will likely find that within the past year at least one article appeared in each magazine on using search engines. The problem with such articles, not to mention books on the topic, is that they are quickly dated since the search engines change at dramatically fast rates in their constant attempts to outdo the others. Even during preparation of this chapter (May 1998), the two largest search engines have undergone some changes, albeit cosmetic rather than functional. AltaVista changed the look of its opening page entirely in early June 1998. Also, after steadfastly refraining from having any subject directory on its site, AltaVista finally succumbed to the competition in early 1998 by adding one using the LookSmart service. HotBot introduced a new look in May 1998, finally jettisoning the familiar green screen for a somewhat more subdued look. Although material in books will certainly be helpful for a general understanding of search engine technology and basic techniques common to all of them (such as putting a + before a term to guarantee the engine will include the term in its results), it is unlikely you will convince any of your casual users to read a book on searching the Internet.

Some Helpful Sites

Fortunately, there are several sites on the Internet itself that do an admirable job of differentiating the search engines and give proper strategies to use. Among them are Greg Notess's "Search Engine Showdown" site at **http://imt.net/~notess/search/index.html** and the "Internet Search Engines" page at the Hekman Library of Calvin College at **http://www.calvin.edu/library/ghsearch.htm**. Both use tables to compare the search engines, including their use of Boolean operators, field searching capabilities, and other factors. More importantly, both sites have, so far, have remained updated. (I prepared two similar comparison charts for the Dominican University library beginning in 1996 while teaching an online searching class. The latest versions appear as an appendix to this chapter and also on the Web at **http://207.56.177.198/library/engines.htm**.)

Larger sites have not been blind to the importance of searching the Web, either. The popular About.com (formerly the Mining Company) site has a frequently updated "Web Search" site devoted to engines and other Internet searching tools at **http://websearch.about.com**, as does the Ziff-Davis "Web SearchUser" site at **http://www.zdnet.com/products/searchuser.html**. Although your users may not be interested in the site, every knowledge manager who wants to remain abreast of the ever-changing world of search engines should be required to check the very valuable information at Danny Sullivan's "Search Engine Watch" page at **http://www.searchenginewatch.com**, which is affiliated with Mecklermedia.

Advice for Knowledge Managers

Knowledge managers owe it to their constituency to help them become as accurate as possible using search engines. Let them know about the difference between AltaVista's simple search mode and advanced search mode. For broad searches where a few good hits will do just fine, the built-in relevancy ranking in the simple search may work, but using the advanced search page for field searching and Boolean operators is important, too. Do they realize using Boolean operators will turn off Excite's concept-based relevancy? The "More Search Options" button in HotBot (formerly labeled SuperSearch until the recent revamping) should be a required click of the mouse before inputting any terms to open a myriad of options. Do the people researching events overseas realize that HotBot and Infoseek have the ability to restrict searches to specific domains? Are people doing competitive intelligence? Rather than going to a competitor's Web site and aimlessly clicking away, do they know AltaVista and HotBot can have searches limited to a specific company's Web site using the "host:" or "domain:" search in AltaVista and the "domain:" search in HotBot? (This won't reveal any trade secrets, of course, but can still save some time wandering around a site that doesn't have its own search engine.) All of these techniques can be found on help screens, and the old Internet axiom of RTFM applies to these search engines, but how many users really check the help screens?

If nothing else, valuable time is saved when doing an accurate search, but there may be other dividends, too. Many of the same techniques learned on the major engines will work when searching a corporate Intranet that has a search engine. AltaVista, Excite, and Infoseek all market their search engines for Intranets, and there are many others on the market. Furthermore, once knowledge of how a search engine operates is known, the ability to use HTML to its greatest advantage is revealed. It is necessary, for example, to realize the importance of the <TITLE> field in HTML coding. For one thing, search engines tend to rank the title field higher in relevance but, even more importantly, nothing stands out more than a misspelled title (assuming one is able to retrieve it), since it is also the line that displays most prominently in search engine results. Try a search on AltaVista for **title:management** or **title:university** and see how many hits you get. (For that matter, try a search on **title: "knowlege managment"** in AltaVista.)

Posting company documents on your Intranet? Give them accurate titles with no typos.

If your site is open for all to see and search, such tips are even more important. Learning to "massage" the engines has become an industry in itself; a look at **http://www.webposition.com** will show one company trying to make a business of it with the Web Position Analyzer software package. A similar package is Position Agent offered at **http://www.positionagent.com**.

Based on my own experience of conducting workshops on effectively using search engines, the following aspects of what to teach or not to teach are prominent. The use of the + and - for including/excluding terms, as well as double quotation marks for a phrase, is so common today that most semi-experienced searchers know of their use. Less likely is the knowledge that there is a NEAR operator in AltaVista that searches within ten words of the two terms entered. The most valuable time-saver, however, is eliminating the .COM sites in those engines (such as AltaVista and HotBot) that allow it, or limiting to a site such as .ORG or .EDU in engines such as Infoseek or Lycos Pro. To eliminate a .COM site may very well eliminate some perfectly valid hits, but it will also eliminate a number of irrelevant hits for scholarly topics. Working in an academic environment, I remember a student trying to study a psychology-related topic of whether men or women make greater use of imagination. A Web search on WOMEN IMAGINATION unfortunately led to some pretty racy hits. ("More women here than in your wildest imagination!") Getting rid of the .COM sites helped considerably. Field searching in general is probably the best advice any knowledge manager can give to a client. It has been my experience that field searching in those databases that have the most options (AltaVista, HotBot) changes little once the basics are learned, and that other engines (Lycos Pro, Infoseek) are adding the capabilities, particularly for domain searching. Ran Hock (1998) gave the most recent detailed overview of field searching, and this was another case where constant checking of the help screens was in order.

I recommend checking the help screens on your favorite search engines at least once a month. Although any major changes will probably be publicized by the engine itself on its home page, they will be unlikely to advertise items that were removed. For example, I lament Lycos' abandoning its use of truncation (wildcards). At one time, Lycos offered perhaps the best user-definable use of wildcards available, allowing the increase or decrease of the engine's built-in truncation parameters by use of the dollar sign ($) and period (.) at the end of terms, respectively. Now AltaVista is the only major engine that allows the use of an asterisk for truncation, while the others either automatically pluralize or do not offer it at all.

Most users know that search engines use an automated process to index the pages. The sheer number of seemingly irrelevant hits convinces users that no human could have possibly generated all of them. After becoming aware of how often an engine is updated (the **Searchenginewatch.com** page is of enormous help with this), it is advantageous for a knowledge manager to know how to tweak each engine's effectiveness through common sense and taking advantage of any option each engine has to offer. Using an engine's built-in relevancy parameters is the easy part. Fine tuning it is the challenge. After all, the Internet is not getting any smaller.

APPENDIX 15

World Wide Web Search Engines

For more precise searching, it is recommended that you try an engine's advanced search mode, if one exists. All search strategies given here are, of course, subject to change at virtually any time!

	ALTA VISTA	EXCITE	HOTBOT
URL	http://www.altavista.digital.com	http://www.excite.com	http://www.hotbot.com
Method of Getting to Advanced Searching Mode (If Applicable)	Click **Advanced** search link from main URL.	Click **Power Search** link for pull-down menu mode of searching.	Users may perform more advanced searches directly from the main search window after selecting **Boolean phrase** from menu or by clicking on the **More Search Options** link to open more menus.
Boolean Searching?	*In Basic Mode:* + before term to specify term must be present – before term to exclude it	**AND** **OR** **AND NOT** (All Boolean operators must be in capitals.) + before term to specify term must be present – before term to exclude it	Through pull-down menus, select either: **All the words** OR **Any of the words.** Additionally, click the **More Search Options** button and specify **MUST, SHOULD,** or **MUST NOT** contain specific words or phrases.
	In Advanced Mode: **AND** **OR** **AND NOT**	*Note:* Use of Boolean operators in Excite will automatically search for the exact words used, whereas use of pluses and minuses will use *Exite's* Intelligent Concept Extraction (ICE), which may pick up related terms.	For more advanced searching, select the pull-down menu option **Boolean Phrase** under main search menu, and use: **AND OR NOT** May also use: + before term to specify term must be present – before term to exclude it
Nested (Parenthetical) Boolean	Yes.	Yes.	Yes, within main search box.

	ALTA VISTA *con't.*	**EXCITE** *con't.*	**HOTBOT** *con't.*
URL	http://www.altavista.digital.com	http://www.excite.com	http://www.hotbot.com
Bound Phrase Searching?	Double-quotation marks around phrase in either basic mode or advanced mode. Note that anything with punctuation marks within it is considered two or more words and should be searched as a phrase.	Double-quotation marks around phrase.	Through pull-down menus, select: **The exact phrase.** If doing more advanced searches, within the main search box place double-quotation marks around phrase.
Proximity Searching?	**NEAR** (retrieves within 10 words of each other) in advanced mode only.	No.	No.
Case-Sensitive?	Yes, use of any capital letters will cause system to look for the exact case. Otherwise, always use lowercase.	No.	Generally, no. HotBot will, however, make an exception for what they call an "interesting case." EXAMPLE: NeXT
Truncation?	In either basic or advanced mode, an asterisk at end of term retrieves up to 5 characters past term. The root word must be at least 3 characters long. Asterisk may also be used internally: **colo*r.**	No.	No.
If Truncation Is Automatic, Can It Be Shut Off?	Does not apply, as truncation is not automatic.	Does not apply.	Does not apply.
Field Searching?	In either basic or advanced mode: **anchor:** **applet:** **domain:** **host:** **image:** **link:** **text:** **title:** **url:**	No.	In **More Search Options** mode can click domain button, where up to 3 levels of a domain name may be specified (such as STATS.BLS.GOV). Domain names may be *excluded* within this box by placing a minus sign in front of them.

	ALTA VISTA *con't.*	EXCITE *con't.*	HOTBOT *con't.*
URL	http://www.altavista.digital.com	http://www.excite.com	http://www.hotbot.com
			Can click in the **PAGES. MUST INCLUDE** section to specify an image, audio, etc. with even more options available after clicking **More Search Options.**
			In main search box for more advanced searches, the following may be used: **depth:** (use a number to restrict depth of pages retrieved) **domain:** **feature:** (EXAMPLES: image, video, etc.) **linkdomain:** **linkext:** (for pages with specific embedded file type) **newsgroup:** (for Usenet article searches) **scriptlanguage:** **title:** Consult help screens for complete examples.
Other Special Features/ Comments	Can limit by specific dates by filling in **From:** and/or **To:** boxes (in advanced mode only). Automatic relevancy ranking in basic mode. In advanced mode, there is no relevancy ranking unless words are typed in above the "Boolean expression box." The *only* search engine that allows one to specify several different languages, or that will perform on-the-fly translations for some languages. **Refine** button on results page will help you narrow down results via clickable category boxes to include/exclude specific terms to further refine your search.	Will find similar Web pages through a **MORE LIKE THIS** link. Selecting **Web Guide** from main search screen will lead to a directory-type listing with reviews of Web sites. **Search Wizard** will suggest additions to search with each search result.	It is easiest to search date ranges using the **DATE** panel button. One may also use the main search box (after selecting **Boolean phrase**) and use the following: **after:** (day/month/year) EXAMPLE: **after: 15/01/97** **before:** (day/month/year) **within:** EXAMPLE: **within: 6/months** Will search Usenet newsgroups via separate option.

	ALTA VISTA *con't.*	EXCITE *con't.*	HOTBOT *con't.*
URL	http://www.altavista.digital.com	http://www.excite.com	http://www.hotbot.com
Sample Searches Using Advanced Search Methods (When Available)	"state of the union address" and url:gov From: 01/Jan/98 To: 01/Mar/98 censor* and (internet or "world wide web") and domain:org Ranking: blocking From: 15/Jan/98	"parental control" AND (internet or "world wide web") In POWER SEARCH mode with pull-down menus: Results CAN contain the word: blocking Results MUST contain the phrase: parental control Results CAN contain the word: internet	"state of the union" and clinton and domain:whitehouse.gov "parental control" and (internet or "world wide web") not domain:gov not domain:com and within:7/months

	INFOSEEK	LYCOS	NORTHERN LIGHT
URL	http://www.infoseek.com	http://www.lycos.com	http://www.nlsearch.com or http://www.northernlight.com
Method of Getting to Advanced Searching Mode (If Applicable)	Click **Advanced Search** link.	http://lycospro.lycos.com	http://www.nlsearch.com/power.html
Boolean Searching?	+ before term to specify term must be present - before term to exclude it, though not necessarily eliminate it entirely In **Lycos Pro** only: **AND OR NOT**	+ before term to specify term must be present - before term to exclude it, though not necessarily eliminate it entirely	+ before term to specify term must be present - before term to exclude it **AND OR NOT**
Nested (Parenthetical) Boolean Searching?	No.	Yes.	Yes.
Bound Phrase Searching?	Double-quotation marks around phrase.	Double-quotation marks around phrase or use of **OADJ** operator, which specifies words must be adjacent but in order specific in search. EXAMPLE: **car oadj race** is the same as **"car race"**. Alternatively, may specify **Exact Phrase** in pull-down menu within **Lycos Pro.**	Double-quotation marks around phrase.

	INFOSEEK *con't.*	**LYCOS** *con't.*	**NORTHERN LIGHT** *con't.*
URL	http://www.infoseek.com	http://www.lycos.com	http://www.nlsearch.com or http://www.northernlight.com
Proximity Searching?	No.	**ADJ** [Next to each other, in any order] **ADJ/[#]** [Within *x* number of words of each other, any order] EXAMPLE: **cars adj/4 race** **NEAR** [Default is 25 words] **NEAR/[#]** **FAR** [Same options as for NEAR] **BEFORE** [One term must appear before another anywhere in document]	No.
Case-Sensitive?	Yes.	No.	Capitalized terms ranked higher.
Truncation?	Automatic. Will also automatically search variants of a word: **wolf/ wolves, mouse/mice.**	Automatic.	Automatic "stemming" for common plurals and singulars (**cat** will retrieve plural version, **cats** will retrieve singular). Otherwise, use asterisk for multiple characters, percent symbol for one character, as long as the root word has at least four characters. EXAMPLES: **psych*y councilm%n**
If Truncation Is Automatic, Can It Be Shut Off?	No.	Does not apply.	No.
Field Searching?	From main search box, the following will work: **link:** **site:** **title:** **url:** Note that a minus sign (-) in front of **site:** or **url:** may *not necessarily* eliminate all hits from very common domains such as **gov** or **edu.**	Can select **Pictures** or **Sounds** from pull-down menu in main search box. Both are concept searches rather than exact words. **Lycos Pro** allows one to limit by title, URL, or site.	In basic or advanced search mode, can specify: **url:** **title:** **text:** The following will retrieve hits from their "Special Collection" documents that will cost money to retrieve: **pub:** [specific publication] **company:** **ticker:**

	INFOSEEK *con't.*	**LYCOS** *con't.*	**NORTHERN LIGHT** *con't.*
URL	http://www.infoseek.com	http://www.lycos.com	http://www.nlsearch.com or http://www.northernlight.com
Other Special Features/Comments	**Stock/Companies** option on main page will link to Hoover's directory and to SEC Web site. Retrieval page will allow one to select option to search for **Related Topics.** Allows one to **Search within** the pages retrieved to further narrow down a search.	Selecting **Top 5%** from pull-down menu on main search page retrieves reviewed Web sites. Results page will provide links to subject search page, pictures, and other links. Results list **Related Topics.** **Lycos Pro with Java Power Panel** enables one to rank importance of such items as appearance in titles, appearance early in text, etc.	Date, language, and domain level searching possible on Power Search page through clickable boxes or pull-down menus. (Languages searchable are English , French, German Italian, and Spanish) **Industry Search** link from main page allows one to focus on an industry, with date-range capability. **Search Folders** appear on left side of screen after every search, providing on-the-fly narrowing of topic. **Special Collection** library sells full-text documents for a fee that are not ordinarily available over the Web.
Sample Searches Using Advanced Search Methods (When Available)	+title:"state of the union"+title:1998 In *ADVANCED SEARCH* mode with pull-down menus: Document MUST contain the phrase: *parental control* Document SHOULD contain the word: *internet* Document SHOULD contain the phrase: *world wide web* Search by location: *.org*	"state of the union" near/10 1998 "parental control" near/20 "world wide web" and children	+"state of the union" +1998 +clinton text:"parental control" and child* and url:org In *POWER SEARCH* mode: Words Anywhere: television and censorship Start Date: 4/15/98 Limit to non-profit Web sites

DOMAINS

Since several search engines support use of domains, remember that they are: **COM** (commercial); **EDU** (education); **GOV** (government); **INT** (international); **NATO** (NATO); **NET** (network infrastructure); **ORG** (nonprofit organization); and **MIL** (U.S. military). A complete listing of these, plus all two-letter country codes used in domain names, is available in a HotBot FAQ located at: **http://help.hotbot.com/faq/domains.html**

Other Searching Destinations

Subject Directories

Search engines may give you too many hits for your topic. If so, try the subject directory approach instead. Subject directories group topics under broad headings and subheadings. The major subject directory is at Yahoo!: **http://www.yahoo. com**, which is divided into 14 major subjects. If you can't find the correct subject heading, however, the entire Yahoo! directory is searchable, and accepts phrases (within quotation marks) as well as use of the + and − keys to include/exclude terms. If Yahoo! finds no match for your search, it will automatically be sent to Inktomi (makers of HotBot). Be aware that all major search engines—with the exception of Northern Light—now have their own subject directories available, too.

For an extremely selective, and somewhat scholarly, alternative Britannica Corporation has launched its *Encyclopaedia Britannica Internet Guide*, featuring about 75,000 sites selected by editors at Britannica. Unlike the publisher's encyclopedia, it is completely free of charge. It is available at: **http://www.ebig.com**

Usenet News

Although many search engines have Usenet news searchable, several point towards a separate service: DejaNews. DejaNews is available at: **http://www. dejanews.com** and covers all newsgroups. Another service is Reference.Com at: **http://www.reference.com**

Meta-Search Engines

Meta-Search engines search several different Web search engines simultaneously. This is typically not recommended except for relatively simply searches or for searches that cover very obscure topics. Two popular engines are:

http://www.dogpile.com

Searches AltaVista, Excite, GoTo.Com, Infoseek, Magellan, Planetsearch, and others.

http://www.metacrawler.com

Searches AltaVista, Excite, Infoseek, Lycos, WebCrawler, and Yahoo! simultaneously.

NATURAL LANGUAGE SEARCHING

Tired of figuring out search strategies? Try typing in a natural language search, such as *Why is the sky blue?* at AskJeeves, available at: **http://www.AJ.com** or at **http://www.askjeeves.com**. AltaVista also accepts natural language searching at its basic search page, and Lycos has a similar capability at its Lycos Pro site (**http://lycospro.lycos.com**) if you select **Natural Language Query** from the pull-down menu.

References

Bharat, Krishna; Broder, Andrei (1998) Measuring the Web. Available at: http://www.research. digital.com/SRC/whatsnew/sem.html [30 May 1998].

CommerceNet Research Center (1997) Search Engines Most Popular Method of Surfing the Web. Available at: http://www.commercenet.com/research/stats/4-8-97.html [2 June 1998].

Hock, Ran (1998) How to Do Field Searching in Web Search Engines. *Online* 22(3): 18-22.

Media Metrix, The PC Meter Company (1998) Media Metrix Reports Top 25 Web Site and Web Property Rankings for April 1998. Available at: http://www.mediametrix.com/corp/press/ press_mm60.htm [1 June 1998].

Lawrence, Steve; Giles, C. Lee (1998) Searching the World Wide Web. *Science* 280 (April 3, 1998): 98-100.

Sonnenreich, Wes; Macinta, Tim (1998) *Web Developer.Com® Guide to Search Engines*. New York: John Wiley & Sons, Inc.

CHAPTER 16

Information Technology in Support of Knowledge Management

Vikas Sahasrabudhe
Principal Training Officer
World Bank

INTRODUCTION

The objective of knowledge management is to make appropriate knowledge available from provider(s) to receivers when and where needed. Knowledge providers and receivers could be internal or external to an organization. The providers could be individuals or other forms of sources of knowledge, e.g., stored knowledge. In the "Global Village" environment, the providers and receivers could be spread across the world. Indeed, the receivers ought to be able to tap into the worldwide knowledge pool. The traditional modes of sharing knowledge, such as face-to-face meetings, conferences, and printed reports and books continue to be useful, but in today's environment, knowledge must be accessible when needed and where needed. And that is where information technology can provide effective and efficient tools to enable all the facets of knowledge management, from capturing knowledge, to sharing it, to applying it.

Knowledge can be broadly divided into two categories. *Explicit knowledge*, such as that about economies of countries, can be "codified" and, therefore, can be stored and shared with receivers. *Tacit knowledge* is usually stored in someone's head and cannot be codified. Sharing tacit knowledge can only occur through networking among those people in possession of tacit knowledge, referred to as communities of practice. Information technology provides tools to support management of explicit knowledge, and also to support communities of practice. Since most practical situations involve a combination of explicit and tacit knowledge, only an integrated set of information technology tools can provide effective and efficient support to knowledge management.

At the very outset, it should be made clear that information technology is a powerful and necessary enabler for effective knowledge management, but it is not sufficient. Other factors, (as described in the other chapters of this book) include top-executive support, appropriate business strategy, behavioral/cultural adjustment, etc. Detailed below are the most common technologies that could be used in support of managing explicit knowledge and tacit knowledge. Only in some instances are specific products mentioned. The rate of new developments in information technology is so high that new products are introduced in quick succession and become obsolete equally fast, and new technologies get developed spawning yet more products. The reader is strongly advised to refer to professional and trade publications and Web sites to keep up with the latest developments.

INFORMATION TECHNOLOGY SUPPORT FOR MANAGING EXPLICIT KNOWLEDGE

Managing explicit knowledge generally involves generation, creation, or acquisition of that knowledge; codification and organization of that knowledge for easy access; publishing or communicating the availability of that knowledge; searching for and accessing that knowledge; and using or applying that knowledge for problem solving, decision support, performance support, coaching, and analysis in support of business activities. Information technology provides tools to support each of these steps in managing explicit knowledge.

IT for Codification and Organization of Explicit Knowledge

Depending on the characteristics of the form in which knowledge is codified, one of the most commonly used tools is a relational database management system (RDBMS) for knowledge that can be codified as a set of discrete entities. Another tool would be a document management system for knowledge that is in the form of documents.

RDBMSs

A database that is organized and accessed according to relationships between data items is called a relational database. It consists of tables, rows, and columns.

In its simplest conception, a relational database is a collection of data files that relate to each other through at least one common field. Account numbers and names are examples of such common fields. Software that enables creation, maintenance, and access to relational databases is called relational database management systems. For example, relational databases could be used to obtain knowledge of country economies, worldwide weather and weather patterns, international trades, directories of expertise on given topics, etc. Examples of commonly used RDBMSs are Oracle, Sybase, and Informix.

Document Management Systems

In many organizations, knowledge is embedded in documents. Most of these documents have, in the past, contained knowledge in text form, as in reports, books, or working papers. Hence, document management has meant production of such text documents using word processors, keeping an electronic copy of the documents for search and access, and then printing and distributing as required. But now a document may consist of knowledge in different media, such as text, graphics, audio, and video. Document management systems can support production, storage, search of, and retrieval of these mixed-media documents. The new document management systems can be integrated with other technologies, such as workflow, to direct the documents to different individuals as defined by their workflow.

Information Technology for Accessing Explicit Knowledge

With the vast amount of knowledge that exists, which continues to increase rapidly, providers face the challenge of making the knowledge available to others and receivers constantly look for tools to use to search for and access useful knowledge. Information technology provides a number of tools for just that.

Internet

With its simplicity and ubiquitous presence, the Internet provides extensive pathways with worldwide coverage to share knowledge. Knowledge providers are setting up Web sites accessible either gratis or for a fee (subscription or per use). HTML or other tools are used to design and set up such Web sites. Those looking for knowledge can access the Web sites over the Internet using appropriate browser software on their computer and a connection to an Internet service provider. Netscape and Internet Explorer are examples of browser software.

Search Engines

Search engines are software programs and services that accept a set of key words, or other forms of query, search various sites for information that matches the query, and return the results to the requester. Since new sites come up frequently and information in existing sites gets updated continuously, using the search engines becomes an extremely useful tool to keep up with the latest knowledge. Yahoo!, Alta Vista, and Lycos are examples of useful search engines. Searching for useful knowledge can also be accomplished by individuals specifying their interests to a software "agent" that makes that knowledge available by scanning the knowledge-horizon continuously. Some publications use such agents to provide that as a service to its customers.

Intranets

Internet technology used within an organization, with restricted access from outside, is called an Intranet. Those within an organization can access sites outside the Intranet, but access from outside an organization to an Intranet is usually restricted. If the knowledge within an Intranet is proprietary, the appropriate security measures must be implemented, e.g., firewalls.

Workflow Tools

These information-technology-based tools allow documents and other forms of information to be routed among individuals and applications according to predefined processes. This may include routing a new document to various members of a work team or sending a draft document to individuals for review and approval. These tools enable provision of information required to support each step of the business processes. These processes may be predefined and never varying, or they may vary depending on specified rules. The information-technology-based workflow tools allow setting up the workflow environment in terms of users, types of information, processes, timing constraints, alternatives, etc. These tools also include mechanisms for alerting predesignated individuals about problems for appropriate resolution of those problems.

IT for Using or Applying Knowledge

Often the available data or information is so enormous that finding useful knowledge from it is a monumental task. Performance support systems, decision support systems, and online analysis tools provide some of the necessary support to using or applying the knowledge accessed. New tools are also becoming more widely available, often called data mining or data warehousing tools, which enable extracting useful information from a vast amount of data.

Performance Support System

Performance support systems are software products aimed at assisting individuals or groups in carrying out specific tasks. These are intended for quick assistance without requiring special training on how to use them. Examples of such performance support systems would be assistance in income tax returns or creation of an entry for a financial transaction into an organization's financial system. These systems may incorporate multimedia delivery and use techniques such as expert systems and natural language recognition.

Decision Support Systems

Decision support systems are software products that transform data into useful information such as statistical models and trend analysis, which are used by management in making business decisions. Generally, these systems can access data stored in large databases and can analyze the data to produce graphs, charts, and simple reports, which management can access from desktop computers. These systems may retrieve data from internal and external sources. Such systems are also referred to as executive information systems.

Data Mining

Data mining refers to using sophisticated data search capabilities that use statistical algorithms to discover patterns and correlation in vast amounts of data.

Data Warehousing

Most organizations have vast amounts of data spread across different databases. Trying to get useful information out of those databases is almost impossible. New information-technology-based tools are available, which consolidate data from many sources and enable easy search and online analysis to present the results in specified formats. These data warehousing tools can assist in extracting from a mass of data the nugget of knowledge that may be crucial to the business objectives of an organization.

Information Technology Support for Management of Tacit Knowledge

At present, the most prominent use of information technology is to enable effective working of communities of practice. The choice of technology tools will depend upon the desired characteristics of the networking. Meeting face-to-face continues to be an effective means to share knowledge, but that requires both parties to be present in one place at the same time. Communicating using paper-mail also continues to be used extensively, mainly between two parties in different places asynchronously; however, it is often too slow for today's needs. Use of fax has increased the speed of paper communications, but it remains a means solely for communicating between two parties. Talking on the telephone also is an effective means of sharing knowledge but both the parties have to be available at the same time (i.e., synchronously) although they need not be in the same place. Information technology provides other tools to support communities of practice that may be dispersed geographically and in time.

Email

Email enables a community of practice to share knowledge asynchronously. One individual from a community can share knowledge with the rest of the community by sending a message to all of them. Use of distribution lists eliminates the need for everyone to remember the names of all those in the community and ensures that everyone gets the message. Maintaining the distribution list is quite easy. With the increasing access to email via the Internet, a community of practice can be spread across the world. Of course, everyone sending a message has to use the distribution list. Every member of that community gets all the messages, whether or not one is interested in all the messages. Email can be very effective, but may become too impersonal if there are no occasions for the individuals of the community to get to know each other. Also, it can be difficult to link messages that refer to a specific topic or issue.

Video-Conferencing

Video-conferencing enables a community of practice to share knowledge and have visual contact with each other. The conferencing may be between two or more nodes. Each node may be a conference room or a studio with equipment, e.g., from PictureTel, to allow a group of people to participate in the videoconference, or it may consist of one individual sitting in front of a personal computer equipped with a small camera and appropriate software. These may be nodes in different parts of the world that have to be connected with sufficiently high-speed, otherwise the video portion of the communications can be too jerky to be effective. Many individuals can participate in sharing knowledge through video-conferencing and they can be located across the world; however, they have to be present at the same time. The effectiveness of communications depends upon the bandwidth of the network, which needs to be sufficiently high.

Electronic Workplace for Collaborative Work

Collaborative work is an essential element of communities of practice, and information technology tools provide electronic workspace to enable such collaboration. Calendering/scheduling tools, such as LotusNotes, enable members of a community to synchronize their activities more effectively. Setting up discussion groups, bulletin boards, and news groups allows members of a community to share substantive knowledge with each other. These tools allow such sharing to be either open or moderated by designated individuals. GroupWare tools allow two or more individuals to have brainstorming sessions electronically. These tools also permit anonymous participation, if desired. Such electronic workplaces can be set up on the Internet, on local area networks, and on other communication networks.

CHALLENGES FOR PLANNING INFORMATION TECHNOLOGY IN SUPPORT OF KNOWLEDGE MANAGEMENT

There are many information technology products available to support knowledge management and, in fact, different products may be the most effective for different facets of knowledge management. Knowledge management, however, always involves some combination of tacit and explicit knowledge. Therefore, these information technology tools must be properly integrated so as to support all aspects of knowledge management. An organization's information technology strategy and architecture must support knowledge management strategy and architecture. Since planning for information technology came before the concept of it as a means to support knowledge management, in practice, knowledge management applications in most organizations are built on existing information technology architecture. Nevertheless, common information technology standards throughout an organization are essential to facilitate knowledge management.

Ongoing support and maintenance of information technology and knowledge management applications have to be in place, similar to any other system. Appropriate security measures must be built into the information technology infrastructure (e.g., firewalls), particularly if external access is allowed. Since communities of practice generally include knowledgeable individuals and sources within and outside of an organization for business reasons, appropriate security measures should be in place.

As stated above, although information technology alone is not sufficient for effective knowledge management, it can support knowledge management very well. The challenge is to develop innovative applications of information technology to support knowledge management so as to enable getting the nugget of knowledge in a timely fashion when and where needed, including when new knowledge becomes available.

References

Allee, Verna. *The Knowledge Evolution: Expanding Organizational Intelligence*, Boston, Mass., Butterworth-Heinemann, 1997.

Leonard-Barton, Dorothy. *Wellsprings of Knowledge: Building and Sustaining the Sources of Innovation*, Boston, Mass., Harvard Business School Press, 1995.

van Krogh, George; Roos, Johan (eds). *Managing Knowledge: Perspectives on Cooperation and Competition*, London, U.K., Sage Publications, 1996.

Wiig, Karl M. *Knowledge Management Methods: Practical Approaches to Managing Knowledge*, Arlington, Texas, Shema Press, 1995.

American Productivity & Quality Center. "Using Information Technology to Support Knowledge Management," final report, 1997.

The Computer Desktop Encyclopedia.

Newton's Telecom Dictionary.

Marshall, Edward M. *Transforming the Way We Work: The Power of the Collaborative Workplace*, 1995.

Simon, Alan R.; Marion, William. *Workgroup Computing*, 1996.

Gartner Group Report. "Electronic Document Management: Making the Leap from Paper to Digital Document," report 5214, 1996.

Komorowski, Jan; Zytkow, Jan (eds). "Principles of Data Mining and Knowledge Discovery," First European symposium, 1997.

Lloyd, Peter; Whiteheads, Roger (eds). *Transforming Organizations Through Groupware: LotusNotes in Action*, New York, IBM, 1996.

Ciborra, Claudio U. *Groupware and Teamwork: Invisible Aid or Technical Hindrance*, 1996.

CHAPTER 17

Knowledge Management and Vocabulary Control

Ileen Fiddler
Knowledge Specialist
Comdisco, Inc.

INTRODUCTION

Comprised of more than half a million words, the English language offers a seemingly infinite array of possible terms that convey similar concepts (*Oxford English Dictionary*, 1998). For example, some people may refer to knowledge as information, insight, wisdom, experience, enlightenment, intelligence, expertise, or intuition. While this richness allows for a wonderfully expressive language, it can also present semantic complications and ambiguities in locating information and retrieving documents. Because of the broad spectrum of word choices, using uncontrolled terms, sets of words, or phrases to search for documents or works may limit a search's success and result in wasted time.

CONTROLLED VOCABULARY

Basically an authority list, a controlled vocabulary, is a consistent set of index terms used to represent a document or work and assist searchers in locating it. These index terms are usually a subset of a master list previously compiled by a professional indexer. Frequently referred to as descriptors, these index terms are assigned to the content and concepts of, or embodied in, documents for which each descriptor has a high degree of relevance. Descriptors are used to index subject matter of documents of all types—books, articles, media, art, films, etc.—and to retrieve items on that subject matter from a collection.

A controlled vocabulary serves as a powerful searching aid for information scientists and end users that, in many instances, can effectively navigate the English language. Once the searcher establishes the correct term or terms for a concept, all similar items, whether or not they are used within a document, should be collocated. In contrast to natural language searching, a controlled vocabulary greatly reduces the number of search terms that are needed to locate materials on a given subject. An additional benefit of a controlled vocabulary is the reduced time spent retrieving those items that are most relevant for the research query.

The significance of a thoughtfully constructed controlled vocabulary and useful thesaurus may be seen in the growing arena of knowledge management. There is very little in the literature about indexing the evolving and expanding vocabulary of knowledge management. However, several companies, most notably the consulting firms, employ full-time indexers to index their internal (and external) documents. Applying the general theories and rules of indexing in creating an indexing system, a controlled vocabulary and thesaurus with terms specific to a company's knowledge management needs, has proven to be of much greater value in the precise retrieval of relevant information than using preexisting generic thesauri.

When assigning terms to documents for information retrieval, an indexer can only select from those descriptors that appear in the controlled vocabulary list that is utilized by the organization for which she/he is employed. A controlled vocabulary is an indexing language, however, that goes far beyond being a mere list of terms. Representing a conceptual structure of a subject area that presents the user with a guide to the index, a controlled vocabulary embodies a semantic structure that controls synonyms to increase consistency, distinguishes among homographs, defines ambiguous terms and brings together terms that are closely related. Cross-references reveal the horizontal and vertical relationships among the terms (Cleveland and Cleveland, 1990).

Formats for Controlled Vocabulary

The three major formats for controlled vocabularies consist of bibliographic classification schemes, such as the Dewey Decimal Classification, subject headings lists, and thesauri. All three devices provide authority by controlling synonyms, distinguishing between homonyms, grouping closely related terms, and presenting terms both alphabetically and systematically. The methods they use to accomplish these goals, however, differ.

Bibliographic classifications generally employ a primary arrangement that is hierarchical, within which the alphabetical arrangement of the index is secondary. Subject headings, standardized terms used to describe a particular topic, are similar to the thesaurus in that they are both alphabetically based; however, the traditional list of subject headings, unlike the thesaurus, does not clearly distinguish between the hierarchical and the associative term relationships. And unlike a thesaurus, in which the descriptors are frequently dependent on other terms, subject headings normally can stand by themselves.

The Thesaurus

Descriptors in a thesaurus are frequently combined with other terms to create a taxonomy in order to express more specific concepts. Additionally, the thesaurus normally employs a primary arrangement that is alphabetical, within which a secondary hierarchical structure is incorporated by the use of cross-references. The thesaurus generally utilizes a number of pre-coordinated phrases—descriptors that are combined prior to searching and that are not under the control of the user —in order to reduce the number of false drops. Additionally, some thesauri allow for the permutation of individual words in a concept phrase.

Initially, thesauri were simple alphabetical term lists showing exact relationships among the words to be used in post-coordinated indexing systems—terms that are combined at the time of searching by the user—and classification systems were to be used with pre-coordinated indexing systems. Stemming from continued attempts by librarians at vocabulary control, the contemporary thesaurus has evolved into a much more complex tool and is used in pre-coordinated systems, while classification schemes are used in post-coordinate systems (Cleveland and Cleveland, 1990). A thesaurus can be used at either the indexing or searching stages. Professional indexers use a thesaurus to select the exact term or terms they need to represent document concepts. Users consult the thesaurus to locate the correct descriptor to gain entry to the index.

An indispensable tool for indexers and searchers, the taxonomy of a thesaurus is an elaborate hierarchical structure of authorized terms and phrases, including term variants and synonyms, within which the specific relationship between the terms is displayed. It is almost always developed to serve the needs of a particular audience, subject, and/or database (American Society of Indexers, 1998). As such, the thesaurus functions as a powerful information storage and retrieval system for that specific topic and its particular audience. The thesaurus also controls the vocabulary by providing specificity of the language and by distinguishing between terms that are valid and those that are invalid to use, resulting in a reduction in vocabulary size.

Some fields seem to benefit from thesauri more than others do. For example, far more thesauri are available in the areas of science and technology than in the humanities. Similarly, some forms of documents lend themselves better to a thesaurus than others. For example, monographs usually do not require a separate thesaurus as the index in the back of book, along with the cross-references, serve as the "thesaurus" for that entity. An already existing thesaurus may be useful, though, in determining terminology for an index. A thesaurus can be valuable, however, for large ongoing indexes, or when several indexers are involved, as a way to maintain consistency.

Thesaurus Construction

Constructing a thesaurus is a complex and challenging undertaking that requires numerous decisions. Building a thesaurus can be approached in two ways. The top-down method centers on gathering a group of subject experts who determine the scope and broad categories and term relationships to be included in the thesaurus. This method is not document based; it relies on the knowledge of the subject specialists to supply all the terms they believe are necessary to retrieve items about the subject for which the thesaurus is being constructed. Already existing thesauri and dictionaries aid in this process. After a preliminary set of terms is reviewed and organized, selecting preferred terms narrows the vocabulary. Use references are constructed from the variants and synonyms and the hierarchical and associative relations among the preferred terms are constructed. A draft thesaurus is then tested and revised.

In the second approach, the bottom-up method, a group of subject experts is convened to serve as advisors; indexers work with the team of experts to determine the scope of the thesaurus. Unlike the top-down method, this method is document based. If an existing set of representative documents has already been indexed, the index terms from this set act as the preliminary term list. If this is not the case, indexers assign natural language terms to the document set and use the index terms from this set as the preliminary list of terms. Reviewing and organizing the terms further develops the thesaurus. Existing dictionaries and thesauri are used as aids in the same manner as in the top-down method. The group of subject experts is consulted on those terms with unclear meanings or usage, as well as for variant or synonym preference. A draft thesaurus is then tested and revised.

Regardless of which approach is used, constructing and maintaining a thesaurus involves a major investment of intellectual effort, time, and money. An effective thesaurus is not a static tool, but rather an ongoing process for however long it is being used for indexing and/or its database is being updated. Constructing a high-quality thesaurus is a costly project, involving salaries for professional indexers and clerical staff, as well as materials, equipment, and space. And the maintenance of a thesaurus is a continuing expense. To remain an effective, essential tool for information retrieval, it is imperative that a thesaurus is maintained and allows for the addition of current terminology. Updating involves more than including new terms; it also necessitates replacement of some terms and changes in the structural hierarchy of older terms. Several thesaurus management software programs aimed toward the needs of professional indexers are available to automate the clerical tasks of maintenance.

Traditionally, thesauri have been available in print and, in the past few decades, in some commercial online databases. More recently, however, a wide range of thesauri with varying search and browse features is available on the Internet and World Wide Web. Conventional thesauri, such as *Medical Subject Headings* (MESH) and *Educational Resources Information Center (ERIC)*, as well as such innovative and wonderfully inventive thesauri as the *Plum Design Visual Thesaurus*, which displays three-dimensional clusters of synonyms in varying degrees of brightness when the user enters a word or words, reside on the Internet (*Plum Design Visual Thesaurus*, 1998).

A Model for a Knowledge Management Thesaurus

Constructing a mini-thesaurus provided me with a window into the challenges, complexities, intellectual efforts, and time investment involved in thesaurus construction. *The Thesaurus of ERIC Descriptors*, 13th edition served as the structural model on which the mini-thesaurus, *Thesaurus of Knowledge Management Descriptors*, 1st edition was based (Houston, 1995).

The development process itself entailed numerous intellectual decisions, revisions and refinements, attention to detail, a great deal of patience, and considerable time. In order to keep the effort manageable, not all entries from the initial list of candidate terms appear as entries in the mini-thesaurus reproduced for this chapter. An asterisk indicates terms selected from the candidate list that appear as full entries in the mini-thesaurus. Reflections on the preparation of the mini-thesaurus for knowledge management resulted in a general method that should be applicable to most, if not all, thesauri constructions for emerging areas of knowledge management.

Step 1: Compile a Candidate List

I chose to designate the specialized topic of knowledge management around which the mini-thesaurus is built and envisioned the needs of an audience whose organization practices knowledge management principles and concepts. The approach began with the compilation of an initial list of eighty candidate terms taken from natural language words. In selecting candidate terms, a broad base of literature on the topic was consulted. Because this area is continuously evolving, several decisions regarding synonyms and preferred terms had to be made.

Step 2: Determine the Hierarchical Relationship Between Terms

After the initial candidate list was formulated, the design of the *Thesaurus of ERIC Descriptors*, 13th edition was studied to gain an understanding of the terminology used and the taxonomic relationships among the terms. Subsequent steps involved selecting the preferred descriptor for all synonyms, assigning "use" and "use for" to invalid terms, identifying the broad terms, determining the narrower terms and related terms, and arranging the hierarchical structure. This was a reiterative process that continued until an internal consistency emerged.

Scope notes were used extensively in the mini-thesaurus to define the context in which the terms are used. The determination of the hierarchy and the relationship among terms underwent numerous revisions and refinements.

Step 3: Formatting and Typing

The formatting and typing of the mini-thesaurus was time consuming. It is in this aspect of building a thesaurus that thesaurus management software is of most benefit and draws on automation to support the process rather than lead it.

A segment of the *Thesaurus of Knowledge Management Descriptors*, 1st edition, follows. It contains an alphabetical, word-by-word listing of terms used for indexing and searching in the knowledge management system. Modeled after the *Thesaurus of ERIC Descriptors*, 13th edition—which extensively covers the areas of education, information science, and library science—this partial thesaurus consists of a listing of terms primarily constructed from the initial candidate list of eighty terms that centered on knowledge management. Knowledge management is defined in this thesaurus as the systematic creation, capture, exchange, use, distribution, and leverage of an organization's intellectual capital (Remeikis, 1995). This relatively new arena of thought necessitated the use of several new descriptors, as well as the frequent assignment of narrower terms to more than one broader term. As the partial thesaurus began to evolve, incorporated terms expanded well beyond the initial candidate list.

Due to increasing implementation of knowledge management initiatives within organizations, scope notes (SN)—brief statements of the intended usage of descriptors—are used for every term to define usage with the context of knowledge management. In some instances, the scope notes for particular terms were derived directly from *ERIC*, while others were modified to best reflect the nuances of the context within which they are used. With respect to the scope notes for specific knowledge management terminology in the mini-thesaurus, definitions were derived from (concepts and descriptions in) current literature.

The used for (UF) reference is frequently employed to solve problems of synonymy occurring in natural language. UF references required several decisions regarding descriptor terms as the emergence of knowledge management terminology is rapidly evolving. Within this framework, the USE reference, the mandatory reciprocal of the UF, refers the user from a non-usable, less current or prevalent term to the preferred indexable, current or prevalent term or terms.

The broader term (BT) and narrower term (NT) notations are used to indicate the existence of a hierarchical relationship between a class and its subclasses. Narrower terms are included in the broader class represented by the main entry. The BT is the mandatory reciprocal of the NT. Broader terms include, as a subclass, the concept represented by the NT. A term may have more than one BT.

The related term (RT) has a close conceptual relationship to the main term, but not the direct class/subclass relationship described by BTs/NTs. Part-whole relationships, near-synonyms, and other conceptually related terms, which might be helpful to the user, appear as RTs.

Because this is a first edition, as well as only a partial thesaurus, the entries do not contain add dates, former descriptor dates, posting notes, etc. As a thesaurus develops from edition to edition, these notations should be included as well.

While the hierarchical thesaurus arrangement requires an entry for each BT, NT, and RT, some of these were deleted to limit the length here. Selected descriptors from the original candidate list appear as full entries and are denoted with an asterisk following the term. Every UF term, however, appears as an entry. These relationships and structures are illustrated in the following excerpts from the *Thesaurus of Knowledge Management Descriptors*.

BEHAVIOR

SN	The aggregate of observable responses of a human being to internal and external stimuli
UF	Conduct
	Deportment
NT	Behavior Change*
	Collaboration
	Competition
	Group Behavior
	Group Dynamics*
	Leadership
	Resistance to Change
RT	Attitudes
	Coaches*
	Development
	Informal Networks
	Information Politics
	Knowledge Politics
	Networks
	Spontaneous Behavior
	Teamwork

* = Term that appears as an entry

BEHAVIOR CHANGE

SN	Complete or partial alteration in the observable activities or responses of a human being
NT	Behavior Modification
BT	Behavior*
	Change*
RT	Attitude Change
	Behavior*
	Change Strategies*
	Compensation
	Incentives
	Performance Evaluation
	Professional Development
	Resistance to Change

Brainpower

USE	INTELLECTUAL CAPITAL

BRAINSTORMING

SN	Activity or technique to encourage the creative generation of ideas—usually a group process, in which group members contribute suggestions in a spontaneous, non-critical manner
BT	Creative Activities
RT	Divergent Thinking
	Group Discussion
	Group Dynamics*
	Innovation
	Spontaneous Behavior

CHANGE

SN	The process of altering, modifying, transforming, substituting, or making or becoming different (Note: Do not confuse with "development," which refers to sequential, progressive changes. Use a more specific term if possible.)
UF	Transformation
NT	Attitude Change
	Behavior Change*
	Change Agents
	Change Strategies*
	Organizational Change
RT	Change Management
	Development
	Professional Development
	Innovation
	Resistance to Change

CHANGE STRATEGIES

SN	Methods used by those who would alter the practice of an organization, institution, or other group to incorporate knowledge, products, procedures, or values toward improved service or results
BT	Change*
	Methods
RT	Attitude Change
	Behavior Change*
	Change*
	Change Agents
	Change Management
	Knowledge Management*
	Compensation
	Incentives
	Organizational Change
	Resistance to Change
	Strategic Planning

Chief Knowledge Officers

SN	Senior management who advocates for, designs, implements, and oversees an organization's knowledge infrastructure, knowledge culture, knowledge processes, and strategic approaches
BT	Roles
RT	Anecdote Management
	Chief Information Officers
	Chief Learning Officers
	Information Politics
	Knowledge Culture
	Knowledge Management*
	Knowledge Managers
	Knowledge Politics
	Knowledge Workers
	Leadership
	Organizational Culture*
	Professional Development
	Strategic Planning

Coaches

SN	Experienced and trusted knowledge workers who have direct and personal interest in the professional development and/or education of less experienced individuals within an organization
UF	Mentors
BT	Role Models
RT	Behavior Change*
	Change Agents
	Incentives
	Development
	Knowledge Transfer*
	Professional Development

Conduct

USE	BEHAVIOR

Deportment

USE   BEHAVIOR

ECONOMY

SN   The management of the resources, revenue, expenditures, and
          investments of a household, organization, private business, com-
          munity, or government

NT   Knowledge-Based Economy
          New Economy

RT   Intangible Assets
          Intellectual Capital*
          Knowledge Workers
          Return on Assets
          Return on Investment
          Tangible Assets

GROUP DYNAMICS

SN   Formation and functioning of human groups—includes both the
          interaction both within and among groups

UF   Group Interaction
          Group Processes

BT   Behavior
          Interaction

RT   Brainstorming*
          Collaboration
          Group Behavior
          Groups
          Interpersonal Communication
          Organizational Communication
          Spontaneous Behavior
          Teamwork

Group Interaction

USE   GROUP DYNAMICS

Group Processes

USE   GROUP DYNAMICS

Human Capital

USE   INTELLECTUAL CAPITAL

Insight

USE   KNOWLEDGE

Information Professionals

USE   INFORMATION SCIENTISTS

Intellectual Assets

USE   INTELLECTUAL CAPITAL

INTELLECTUAL CAPITAL

SN   Intellectual material that has been formalized in some useful
             order, captured in a way that allows it to be described, shared, dis-
             tributed, and leveraged to produce a higher valued asset; pack-
             aged, useful knowledge (Stewart, 1997)

UF   Brainpower
             Human Capital
             Intellectual Assets
             Knowledge Assets

BT   Assets
             Knowledge*

RT   Corporate Knowledge
             Innovation
             Intangible Assets
             Knowledge-Based Economy
             Knowledge Culture
             Knowledge Management*
             Knowledge Management Systems
             Knowledge Management Technology*
             Knowledge Workers

KNOWLEDGE

SN	The fluid mix of framed experience, values, contextual information, and expert insight that provides a framework for evaluating and incorporating new experiences and information—often embedded not only in documents or repositories but also in organizational routines, processes, practices, and norms
UF	Insight
	Wisdom
NT	Corporate Knowledge
	External Knowledge
	Individual Knowledge
	Intellectual Capital*
	Internal Knowledge
	Knowledge Culture
	Knowledge Repositories
	Knowledge Transfer*
	Knowledge Workers
	Organizational Knowledge
	Soft Knowledge
RT	Data
	Information
	Knowledge-Based Economy
	Knowledge Management*
	Knowledge Management Technology*

Knowledge Assets

USE	INTELLECTUAL CAPITAL

Knowledge Exchange

USE	KNOWLEDGE TRANSFER

KNOWLEDGE MANAGEMENT

SN	The systematic creation, capture, exchange, use, dissemination, and leverage of an organization's intellectual capital
BT	Administration

RT   Anecdote Management
        Chief Knowledge Officers*
        Competitive Intelligence
        Information Scientists
        Intellectual Capital*
        Knowledge Access
        Knowledge Codification
        Knowledge Culture
        Knowledge Generation
        Knowledge Management Systems
        Knowledge Management Technology*
        Knowledge Mapping
        Knowledge Repositories
        Knowledge Roles*
        Knowledge Transfer*
        Knowledge Workers

KNOWLEDGE MANAGEMENT TECHNOLOGY

SN   The application of modern communication and computing tech-
        nologies to the creation, exchange, dissemination, management,
        and use of knowledge
BT   Technology
RT   Communications
        Computer Software
        Computers
        Corporate Intranets
        Downloading
        Electronic Text
        GroupWare
        Knowledge Access
        Knowledge Codification
        Knowledge Dissemination
        Knowledge Generation
        Knowledge Management*
        Knowledge Repositories

Knowledge Management Software
Knowledge Management Systems
Knowledge Transfer*
Telecommunications
Vendors
Web-Based Intranets

KNOWLEDGE POLITICS

SN	The engagement in practices by an individual or individuals who advocate for, or, more often, impede knowledge access, capture, generation, exchange, distribution, and/or leverage, across an organization
NT	Knowledge Fifedoms
BT	Politics
RT	Knowledge Access
	Behavior*
	Behavior Change*
	Change*
	Chief Knowledge Officers*
	Competition
	Corporate Culture
	Incentives
	Individual Power
	Information Policy
	Information Politics
	Intellectual Capital*
	Knowledge Culture
	Knowledge Mapping
	Organizational Culture*
	Organizational Knowledge
	Individual Power
	Power Structure
	Professional Development

Resistance to Change
Work Environment

Knowledge Roles

SN	Professional positions within an organization designed to generate, capture, exchange, distribute, use, and leverage knowledge
NT	Chief Knowledge Officers*
	Knowledge Managers
BT	Roles
RT	Abstractors
	Chief Information Officers
	Chief Learning Officers
	Coaches*
	Corporate Librarians
	Indexers
	Information Scientists
	Knowledge Culture
	Knowledge Gatekeepers
	Knowledge Workers
	Professional Development

Knowledge Sharing

USE	KNOWLEDGE TRANSFER

Knowledge Transfer

SN	The process of both formalized and spontaneous unstructured knowledge exchange (Note: Do not confuse with "knowledge dissemination," which refers to the distribution of knowledge.)
UF	Knowledge Exchange
	Knowledge Sharing
BT	Knowledge*
RT	Coaches*
	Chat Rooms
	Communications

> Compensation
> Incentives
> Informal Conversations
> Informal Networks
> Interpersonal Communications
> Knowledge Culture
> Knowledge Dissemination
> Knowledge Repositories
> Networks

Mentors

USE   COACHES

Organizational Climate

USE   ORGANIZATIONAL CULTURE

Organizational Culture

SN	Properties, procedures, conditions, etc. of an organization that influence or interact with its members
UF	Organizational Climate
NT	Corporate Culture
	Knowledge Culture
BT	Environment
RT	Collaboration
	Behavior*
	Behavior Change*
	Group Behavior
	Compensation
	Competition
	Creative Activities
	Incentives
	Information Politics
	Innovation
	Knowledge Politics*
	Morale

Organizations
Organizational Knowledge
Professional Development
Power Structure
Work Environment

Transformation

USE   CHANGE

Wisdom

USE   INTELLECTUAL CAPITAL

References

American Society of Indexers. "Thesaurus Information." Internet. Available at: http://www.well.com/user/asi/thesonet.htm. 25 February 1998.

Cleveland, Donald B.; Cleveland, Ana D. *Introduction to Indexing and Abstracting*, 2d ed. Englewood, CO: Libraries Unlimited, Inc., 1990.

Houston, James E. (ed.) *Thesaurus of ERIC Descriptors*, 13th ed. Phoenix: Oryx Press, 1995.

Oxford English Dictionary, 2d ed. Online version; Internet. Available at: http://hplus.harvard.edu/descriptions.oed.html. 4 April 1998.

Plum Design Visual Thesaurus. Internet. Available at: http://www.plumbdesign.com/thesaurus. 13 March 1998.

Remeikis, Lois A. "Knowledge Management—Roles for Information Professionals." *Business & Finance Bulletin*, no. 100, Fall 1995.

Stewart, Thomas A. *Intellectual Capital: The New Wealth of Organizations*. New York: Doubleday/Currency, 1997.

CHAPTER 18

Infomapping in Information Retrieval

Bor-sheng Tsai

Associate Professor

Pratt Institute–Information Science Center

INTRODUCTION

The capability and capacity in handling the topology of a special subject information field have made infomapping techniques and systems instrumental in information searching, monitoring, and navigation. The revelation of the communication networks can show intellectual interrelationships among senior and junior researchers in the field. It can also show the continuing popularity of a particular researcher's citation record within a period.

This chapter reports the use of Java in making a cartoon series of chronological maps based on citation analysis on a special subject field. The map-making methods, Java programming, and statistical analysis on map data will be presented. Also, the advantage and significance of constructing Java maps in enhancing information retrieval will be discussed.

Information retrieval is considered to be the center of information business. It mainly includes searching printed reference sources, online, CD-ROM, hypermedia, and Internet databases. To maintain high-quality control in information production and services in the highly competitive information business world, the speed of retrieval, the accuracy of retrieved information, and the cost in searching a very large scale of information field must be strategically planned and tactically coordinated. These concerns are the focus of "information economics" and "knowledge discovery."

Information economics can be defined as the study of scarce information resources that enables managers and policy makers "to quantify the benefits and costs for each stakeholder (people or groups with an interest in the decision) and make economically efficient decisions" (Kingma, 1996). It is "a collection of research methods and topics dealing with how individuals produce, transmit, and use knowledge and ideas" (Noll, 1993). Both research areas study the efficiency and the effectiveness of the information retrieval process. The researchers in studying information economics may include people from computer science, business administration, communication science, and library and information science. Information science research that focuses on the application of informetrics in developing techniques and systems for promoting efficiency and effectiveness of information retrieval operation is called infomapping.

As an important component in visual programming and graphical representation of knowledge, infomapping has become a significant searching, monitoring, and navigation instrument for its capability and capacity in handling the topology of a special subject information field (Murray and McDaid, 1993). Vigil suggested to use graphics to represent "the dynamics of the algebra of sets involved in information retrieval" and to provide spatial interpretation and search dialog (Vigil, 1986). Infomapping involves scholarly communications and mainly applies citation analysis on data collected from the Science Citation Index. While arranging constructed citation maps in chronological order (time series), it was found that an animated map series can be automatically formed. By applying the virtual reality technology, any map in the series can be transformed into 3-D citation data blocks. With the arrival of the Java language and the virtual reality modeling language (VRML), the infomapping techniques can be further developed to help advanced subject researchers in reviewing the historical development of a subject field.

As applied in making dynamic Web pages for institutions, companies, and the public, Java can enhance the outlook of graphics and provide animated cartoon series on Web pages. More companies' commercial logos are adopting animation to provide a dynamic and attractive presentation format. This technique should be and can be applied in the academic activities, particularly in the searching, monitoring, and navigation of a special subject information field. The time for Web-based subject infomapping has arrived.

MAKING JAVA-ANIMATED CITATION MAPS

A set of ninety-nine significant contributors in the field of nutrition and dietetics was chosen for infomapping. This set was used as the guidebook for collecting citation data from the Science Citation Index, 1961-1993. Thirty bitmap-based annual citation maps were constructed (Appendix 18.A).

The mapping operation applies animation techniques for compiling and displaying chronological electronic citation maps into a continuous series. The electronic format of citation maps was originally two-dimensional. Aided by Sun's new technology, the Java programming language, the static 2-D electronic slide shows (map series) can be converted into a dynamic continued cartoon series. Applets can be inserted for translating the animated map series into Web pages that allow researchers to view through the network browsers such as Netscape, Virtus Voyager, and Microsoft Internet Explorer (Appendix 18.B). The animation can be used to show the changing organization (appearance and disappearance) and growth (cumulative recurrence), and migration and oscillation of points, lines, strings, and clumps (Dorling and Openshaw, 1992; Dorling, 1992). More importantly, the animation series allows a researcher to immediately visualize the cumulative strengths and easily identify groups of frequently/highly cited leading (senior) contributors with their collaborators and (junior) followers.

The dynamic displaying of these visual data series has become a highly significant instrument for statistical analysis. The operation requires a control of the speed of representation in animation and the threshold value—the filtration of the frequency of citation. The frequency of citation can be decided by counting the number of times that a document is cited within a specified period. For example, if a document was cited five times in a particular year such as 1993, its frequency of citation in 1993 would be five. The filtering device is a number-checker used as a threshold to select qualified items (e.g., contributors or documents). A user or a research agent arbitrarily determines the threshold value. For instance, a user or a research agent can set a threshold value to fifteen, which means that the research requests for retrieving those items were cited at least fifteen times within the desired time frame such as 1993. The filtration of citation frequency can be conducted from the lowest to the highest number usually ranging from zero to ten for recent publications or from fifteen to ninety for older ones. A user or a research agent can freely choose a desirable threshold value, view its display, and determine which accessing point(s) to take—as well as determine what other telepaths one could take.

Although the determination of a threshold value seems arbitrary, an objective choice of a number may be derived from scanning and compromising the values of citation frequencies that appeared in the neighborhood. By raising/lowering the threshold value, a set of qualified items can be captured to suit a user or a research agent's need. The speed control of animation presentation and the frequency filtering of qualified items yield a smooth display with a proper (human-readable) density of maps on the computer screen. In other words, the duration of time (allowing each slide image in an animation series to stay in the vision/mind of a viewer) and the amount of information (shown on the computer screen) greatly affect the viewer's attention and appreciation. They, in return, strengthen the viewer's cognitive ability and help the viewer stay focused on the subject.

The filtering device equips a set of threshold values for dissecting each annual map into several topological layers. The images of map layers can be captured starting from the lowest citation frequency, which will include and display all citers (citing contributors/documents) and citees (cited contributors/documents). The overpopulated items that appeared on the monitor screen might cause viewers some difficulty in visualizing overcrowded citation data, as well as some difficulties in relocating cross lines on maps. To avoid jamming and to improve visualization, the threshold value T might be gradually increased. As the results showed in various threshold levels (e.g., $T > 15$, 55, or 90), the maps with a higher threshold value excluded non-qualified citers and citees and displayed less complicated citation relationships that were much clearer and easier to read (Appendix 18.A). When the threshold value reached its optimal number (i.e., ninety times of citations), a most concise map with highly qualified (ninety or more citations) items (usually less than twenty-five in this case) was generated. The flexible selectivity of concise layers of the maps enables flows of citation data to be easily visualized in a dynamic cartoon series and in chronological order. Appendix 18.A shows a long-term (more than three decades) animation map series (1961-1993). A slice of its short-term, Java-supported animated map series focusing on the 1990-1993 citation relations can be viewed through the Netscape or other network browsers (Appendix 18.B).

From this animation map series, a cumulative leadership in this subject field from 1961-1993 was easily recognized. Using citation counting, the academic leadership and contribution of a subject information field can be weighed. The higher the frequency of occurrence of an element (a contributor or a document) on the map series, the greater its academic leadership and contribution scored.

The viewing of this long series (1961-1993) of animated citation maps enables a researcher to visualize the historical development of the academic leadership and contribution of this special field. This chronological map series can help an experienced subject researcher in efficiently identifying the academic leadership and contribution relations within the field in a particular time frame. Apparently the 2-D animation map series is a less cumbersome approach than its 3-D counterpart. Although the 2-D animation mapping approach may not provide the spatial impact that the one in a 3-D virtual environment does, it is obviously more process-efficient, cost-effective, and informationally economical.

STATISTICAL ANALYSIS OF THE JAVA-ANIMATED CITATION MAP SERIES

As aforementioned, the Java-aided animation series of citation maps shows the continuum of citees' contributions to the subject field. Besides visualizing the animated maps, a researcher can use the statistical data derived from reading the maps. Table 18.1 (see page 304) can help researchers quickly identify significant contributors (continuously and heavily cited authors such as B4, B9, B11, D1, F2, G6, G7, H5, H7, J1, K2, K3, M3, P2, P5, S2, S4, S6, S8, T2, W2). The checking of the authority file immediately reveals the list of the names of the above significant contributors with information on their research interests, and linkages to their collaborators' information file.

Furthermore, an analysis based on the change of numbers of citing and cited contributors can also allow researchers to see the dynamic shift in 1961-1979, and 1980-1993 (Table 18.2 and Figure 18.1 on page 305 and 306). The most significant parts of this analysis are that the commonality (denoted as & representing informational overlapping or continuum of the population of contributors) and the frequency of co-occurrence of the original ninety-nine contributors (denoted as X which is the sum of IN and &) remain in steady proportion (columns X and &— see also Figure 18.1 on page 306).

DISCUSSION

The infomapping approach takes the advantages of subject concentration, expert grouping, scholarly communication networking, topological filtration, and animation series. These advantages allow us to form a critical mass for observation and quality control in information retrieval process, and to perform informational genetic factor analysis on a population composed of special subject experts. The special features of this approach may include: 1) the completeness of the coverage of citation data enables and affects the determination of threshold values during the process of topological filtration; 2) the maps provide a many-to-many correspondence (i.e., the historical overview on scholarly communication networks focusing on a special subject field) that saves researchers' time to easily hit the quality targets; 3) both electronic (stand alone or networked) and printed versions of maps are available and accessible; 4) the animation maps can be continuously added and easily updated; and 5) the maps inform researchers of the dynamic changes in the time series (see Figure 18.1).

One of the greatest potentials in infomapping in information retrieval is the construction of a Web-based electronic document depository. This depository can be easily linked to a 3-D map that is composed of data blocks. For instance, a researcher can click on R. A. Brown's data block on the VRML-based 3-D map and be immediately linked to Brown's Web site that displays a collection of Brown's bibliographic information. For example, "Key Publications of BROWN RA, 1990-1993, BROWN RA (1990): 1. "Effect of Acetaldehyde on Membrane-Potentials of Sinus Node Pace Maker Fibers" ALCOHOL 7(1):33-36; 2. "High Dose Etoposide and Cyclophosphamide without Bone-Marrow Transplantation for Resistant Hematologic Malignancy" BLOOD 76(3):473-479, to name a couple. By clicking on the title line, the document can be instantly recalled for review (Appendix 18.C).

CONCLUSIONS

Infomapping is an alternate searching, monitoring, and navigating instrument used to support information retrieval. As discussed above, it benefits researchers by providing a set of histograms in time series revealing the scholarly communications of a special subject information field. The application of Java in animating the map series creates a possibility of connecting the maps with the electronic document depository represented by Web pages (Appendix 18.C).

This approach also empowers us to extend and link the database usage to multimedia and virtual reality technologies, e.g., the application of Multimedia Toolbook, and the building of a VRML-based spatial indexing system connecting with 2-D maps and Web pages (Appendix 18.C). The continuous application and development of a VRML-based spatial indexing system will transform the 2-D map series into 3-D data blocks. As recognized that "when using an integrated media system, [the system] behavior tends to become entropic, goal-lost, impulsive, and distracted by the many opportunities to browse offered by the system" (Hasselbring et al., 1993). Continuous effort will focus on the improvement of the interactive capability among 2-D maps, 3-D data blocks, and the Web-page-based electronic document depository and delivery.

References

Dorling, D.; Openshaw, S. (1992). Using computer animation to visualize space-time patterns. Environment and Planning B: *Planning and Design*, 19, 639-650.

Dorling, D. (1992). Stretching space and slicing time: From cartographic animation to interactive visualization. *Cartography and Geographic Information Systems*, 19(4), 215-227.

Hasselbring, T; Bransford, J.; Goin, L. (1993). Examining the cognitive challenges and pedagogical opportunities of integrated media systems: Toward a research agenda. *Journal of Special Education Technology*, 12(2), 118-124.

Kingma, B. R. (1996). *The Economics of Information: A Guide to Economic and Cost-Benefit Analysis for Information Professionals*. Englewood, CO: Libraries Unlimited.

Murray, B. S.; McDaid, E. (1993). Visualizing and representing knowledge for the end user: A review. *International Journal of Man-Machine Studies*, 38, 23-49.

Noll, R. G. (1993). The economics of information: A user's guide. In *The Knowledge Economy: The Nature of Information in the 21st Century, Annual Review of the Institute for Information Studies*, 1993-1994 (pp. 25-52). Nashville, TN: Northern Telecom, & Queenstown, MD: Institute for Information Studies.

Vigil, P. J. (1986). The software interface. *Annual Review of Information Science and Technology*, 21, 63-86.

Table 18.1   Continuum of Frequently and Heavily Cited Authors (1980-1993)

AU	80	81	82	83	84	85	86	87	88	89	90	91	92	93
B4	94	79	95	81	51	69	64	63	55		63	60		
B9	34	44	25	47			42	53		13	46		29	
B11	199	186	258	240	156	222	293	203	229	174		253	223	197
D1	63	87	110	90	89	105	107	83	93	72	90	96	115	90
F2	467	378	327	209	277	295	266	272	224	202	213	199	181	80
G6	100	121	83	106	110	109	109	72	68	80	106	88	100	82
G7	131	126	136	132	111	99	126	115	82	77	71	90	80	66
H5	73	63	69	55	63	74	76	58		41	70	59	49	
H7	127	126	135	132	135	138	119	112	165	166	187	223	273	213
J1	236	211	174	224	200	220	242	178	177	167	206	203	306	217
K2	126	176	144	135	112	94	87	82	64	67	65		60	
K3	274	282	268	230	185	316	174	208	158	191	250	232	297	239
M3	314	282	58	260	229	271	294	286	316	303	266	303	352	244
P2	1209	1193	1150	1032	945	1053	1039	1130	1238	929	1071	1096	1167	940
P5		48			63	70	66	87	73	73		60		55
S2	153	145	125	163	125	116	151	178	194	204	182	207	230	124
S4	104	65	97	146	98	126	107	111	139	143	203	242	183	226
S6	99	118	87	128	124	167	141	133	147	131		188	235	172
S8	321	364	269	388	298	319	248	255	269	214	207	214	261	165
T2		84	61	66	60	76	67	78	76	70	66	73	82	73
W2	157	151	146	152	128	133	118	113	82	83	97	72	91	79

Table 18.2   Dynamics of Author Citation Network (1980-1993)

Year	IN	OUT	dX	X	AU_{cd}	AU_{cg}	Y	&
1980	30	9	21	37	37	4835	4866	7
1981	10	12	-2	35	35	4983	4977	25
1982	7	12	-5	30	30	4111	4138	23
1983	19	7	12	42	41	4417	4454	23
1984	3	22	-19	23	23	3704	3724	20
1985	9	2	7	30	30	4311	4338	21
1986	13	9	4	34	34	4327	4356	21
1987	4	11	-7	27	27	4165	4190	23
1988	1	7	-6	21	21	3913	3933	20
1989	11	2	9	30	30	3460	3488	19
1990	5	11	-6	24	24	3716	3737	19
1991	4	6	-2	22	22	4078	4098	18
1992	4	5	-1	21	21	4201	4219	17
1993	3	5	-2	19	18	3323	3339	16

AU	author	AU_{cg}	citing author
AU_{cd}	cited author	**IN**	number of incoming original authors
OUT	number of outgoing original authors	**dX**	change of number of original authors
X	number of original authors	**Y**	number of citing and cited authors
&	number of original authors appeared in two consecutive years		

Note: Original authors refer to those ninety-nine significant contributors who were chosen for observation.

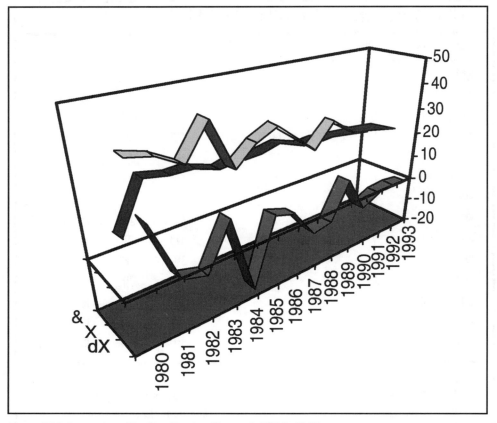

Figure 18.1 Dynamics of Author Citation Network (1980-1993)

Appendix 18.A
Animated Citation Map Series (1961–1993)

YEAR = 1961
T > 1

⟶ G7

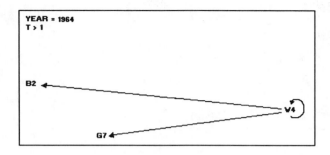

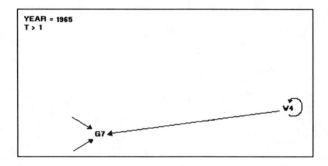

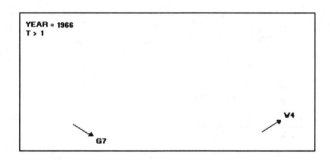

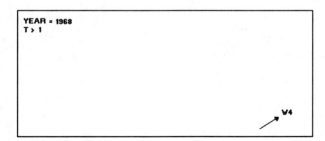

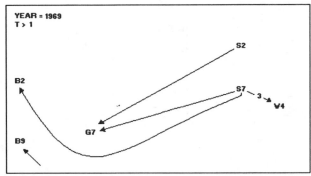

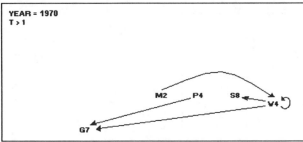

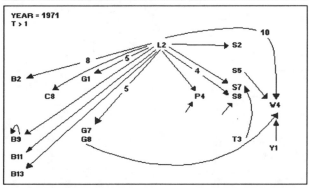

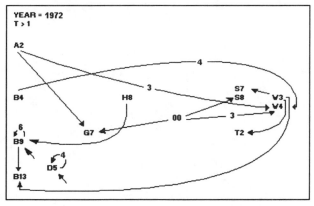

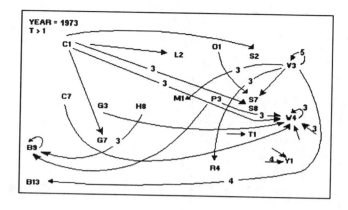

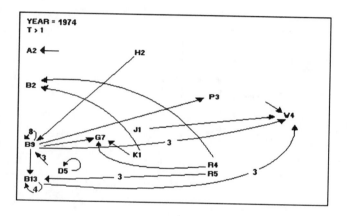

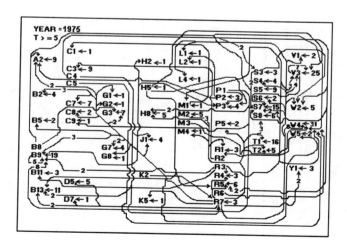

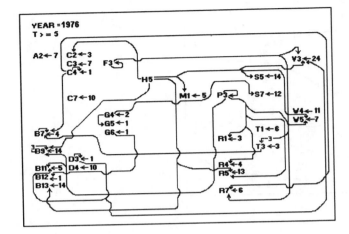

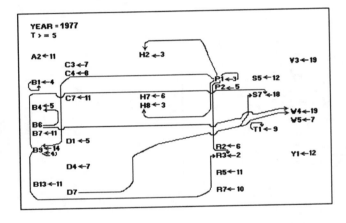

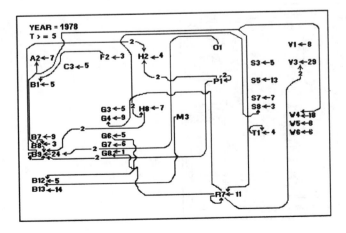

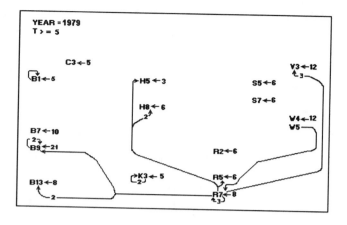

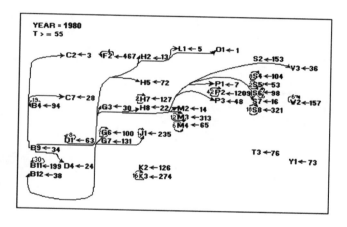

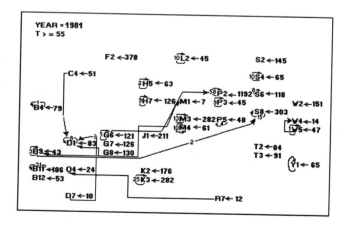

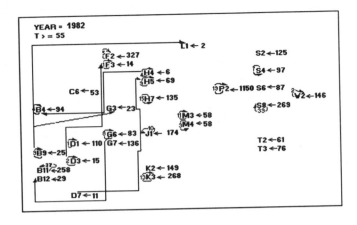

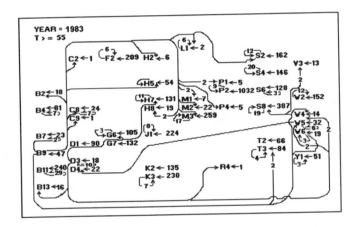

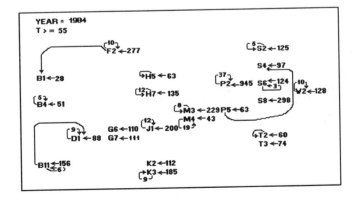

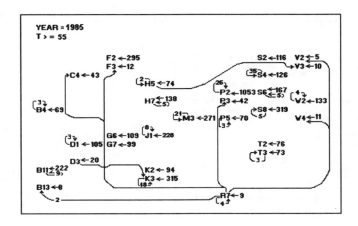

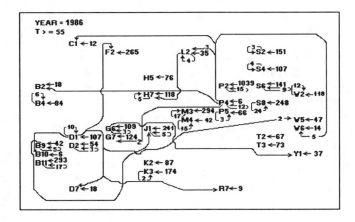

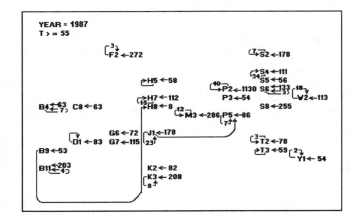

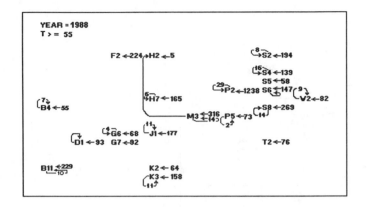

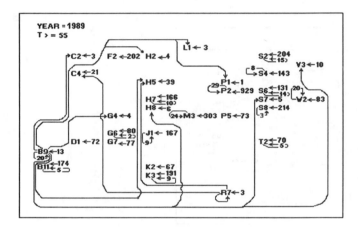

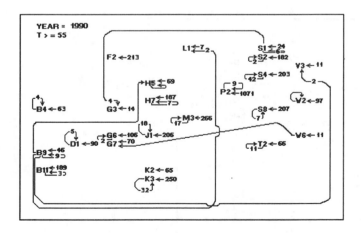

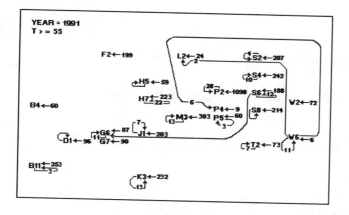

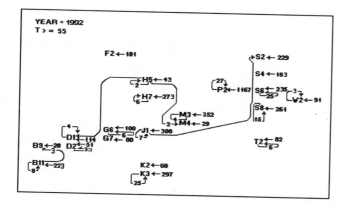

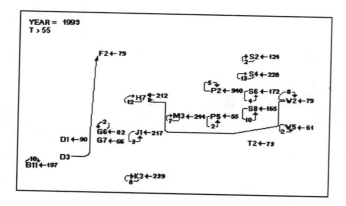

APPENDIX 18.B

Source Code of a Java-Supported Animated Map Series (1990–1993)

```
<html>
<head><title>1990—1993 Animated 2-D Maps</title></head>
<body>
<center>
<font size=6>1990-1993 Animated 2-D Maps</font>
<br><br>
<table border=5>
<tr><td align=center>
<applet code="AnimateMap.class" width=402 height=277>
</applet>
</table>
</center>
</body>
<address>
<a href="mailto:btsai@pratt.edu">Programmed and copyrighted by: Bor-
sheng Tsai</a>
</address>
</html>

import java.awt.*;
import java.applet.*;

public class AnimateMap extends Applet {
 Image map[] = new Image[5];
 public void init() {
  for (int i = 0; i < 4; i++) {
   map[i] = getImage(getDocumentBase(), (i+1) + ".jpg");
  }
 }

 public void paint (Graphics g) {
  while (true) {
   for (int i = 0; i < 4; i++) {
    g.drawImage(map[i], 0, 0, 402, 277, this);
    for (int j = 0; j < 50000; j++);
   }
  }
 }
}
```

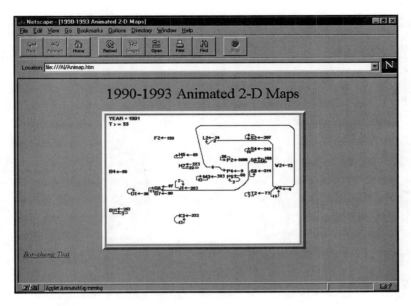

Figure 18.B1

APPENDIX 18.C
External Linkage Between a VRML Data Block and an HTML file

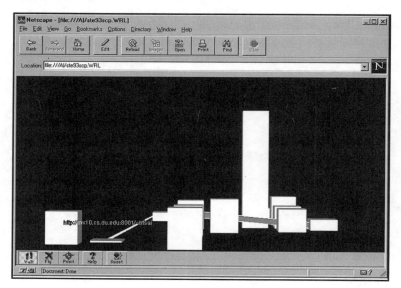

Figure 18.C1   (Click on the http://address to connect to the Electronic
Document Depository.)

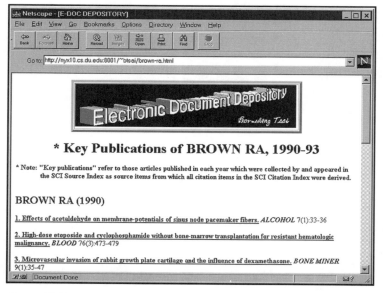

Figure 18.C2

CHAPTER 19

Information Coding in the Internet Environment

Abraham Bookstein

Professor

University of Chicago

INTRODUCTION

Most of us are interested in data for some function it has for us, whether as information, as images, as programs. But before information can be stored, manipulated, or used, it must be encoded. Most familiar is the ASCII code for representing textual information, consisting of alphanumeric data and control information. But modern times increase the demands made on information systems, and codes for information must adapt to these. In particular, codes must be defined for a broader range of information types, such as images and audio. These codes must represent these data in a useful way, but the modern computer environment also puts enormous pressure on system designers to develop formats that meet a wide variety of requirements. In spite of tremendous technological progress, storage resources remain limited, so storage efficiency is a consideration. Increasingly, computers are able, and required, to communicate with one another over noisy and insecure channels, introducing the issues of privacy and data integrity.

Although how information is represented plays a key role in our ability to control it, much of the details of how information is stored are ignored by information systems managers. When implemented well, they act at lower levels of the protocol hierarchy and are invisible to the user. But an understanding of their function and importance is essential for a complete command of the data management process.

Much of coding technology consists of specialized mechanisms designed to solve particular problems (consider, by way of illustration of the diversity of existing codes, the bar codes on retail merchandise, the ISBN in publishing, or the Gray codes used to sense the position of rotors in machines). But several problems recur, and three bodies of codes that deal with these now exist and are based on highly developed theory and experience. The purpose of a code is to represent information in a way that solves a problem. The problems that the three bodies of code that I have in mind to respond to are: 1) efficient use of resources (data compression); 2) privacy and data-integrity (encryption); and 3) reliability of stored and transmitted data (error correction).

Each of these problem areas has an extensive body of literature associated with it, and is based on highly developed and often mathematically rigorous theory. It is rare, and satisfying, to find a body of technique that is at the same time both so elegant and useful. Interestingly, the theoretical foundations for each were laid in a pair of extraordinary articles by Shannon (1949a and 1949b). On reading them, one is struck by how much of what is of concern today was already broached in these articles, now half a century old!

To treat any of these bodies of codes in any depth is outside the scope of a chapter this size. Rather, the purpose of this chapter is to emphasize to the reader the easily overlooked significance of the problems they treat, to give an overview of some of the techniques that are currently getting most attention, and to point to literature through which these techniques can be studied in greater depth.

Data Compression

Data Compression subsumes the body of techniques by which a stream of bits (or bytes, for textual data) is transformed into a stream of bits reduced in size. It might appear curious that such techniques should be getting attention at a time when computer memory and storage devices are increasing so dramatically in capacity. But, as much else in life, our appetite for data grows at a far greater rate than our ability to satisfy it. For example, earlier in the history of information systems, the databases associated with information retrieval systems were made up of records allowing access to printed information (Salton, 1975); today we demand online access to the full text itself (Lesk, 1997; Witten et al., 1994).

Another voracious consumer of storage resources is image-based data. Consider, for example, the resources that would be required to store a simple image if no space conserving mechanism were adopted. We may think of an image as consisting of a rectangular block of picture elements, or pixels, each of which must be represented in the file storing the image. (A good general reference on digital image processing is Netravali and Haskell, 1988.)

For example, this chapter was composed on an antiquated Sun workstation, whose monitor has a usable resolution of 900 lines, with 1,152 pixels per line. To represent a black and white image (for example an engineering drawing, or the scanned image of a book page), each pixel need store only the values zero or one. Thus, we need allocate only one bit per pixel, but 1,035,800 bits all told. If the image is expressed in shades of gray, then a full representation might need eight bits to represent the gray scale value of each pixel, or 8,294,400 bits for the image. Finally, if color is introduced, each pixel might be represented by a vector of three bytes each, to indicate the values of the three primary colors for each element. This now requires 24,883,200 bits, or about three megabytes of storage for a single color image in standard resolution.

It is easy to see how multimedia databases, including images, can greatly expand our requirements for storage. Medical databases, including multiple X-rays per patient; geophysical or weather-oriented satellite databases; and motion pictures— each involve large numbers of images, each of which, naively stored, is expensive.

Similar considerations apply to audio information. For example, the standard music CD could hold as much as eighty minutes of music: the music is represented by 40,000 samples of audio level per second, each in turn requiring sixteen bits of storage. The CD requires about three gigabits of data for the program information alone (with additional data needed for error-correction and formatting information). However, in a large database, we must store not only the target data, but also the data structures that allow us to access the data. This can be considered: for a full text database, the concordance to the database can equal the database in size (Bookstein et al., 1989).

Compression is valuable not only for data storage, but also for data transmission. Whether our concern is the flow of data over the Internet, the broadcasting of high-definition TV programming, or the transmission of satellite information to earth, the magnitude of information being moved is stressing the capacity of available channels. Of course, much costly attention is being given to improving the quality of the channels (for example, replacing copper wires with fiber optics), but we must realize that reducing a file to ten percent of its original size is equivalent to developing a data channel with capacity increased by a factor of ten! It is the existence of such compression techniques that has made even old technology, such as fax transmission of pages from a book, practical.

How effectively can information be compressed? Here we must recognize the existence of two classes of techniques: 1) lossless compression; and 2) lossy compression. The former, which requires that it be possible to accurately reconstitute the original database, is used most heavily for text and number-based data, such as might appear in business files.

Huffman coding is typical of the techniques used for lossless compression, as well as often appearing as a component in lossy techniques. Huffman-coding-based techniques logically divide into two stages: first some mechanism (or model) is created to estimate the probability, within a given context, of the next unit to be encoded assuming a particular value. Then, given these probabilities, the Huffman algorithm is invoked to derive the code words that may be used next.

Considerable compression can be achieved. A Huffman code is a variable length code, with frequently occurring units receiving short code words and rarely occurring units receiving longer code words. Thus, whenever the entities being encoded have widely differing occurrence frequencies, savings are possible. In its simplest form, a single character of text may be encoded, assuming a global, context-independent, frequency distribution for characters. For example, we would exploit the fact that the character "e" occurs frequently, while characters such as "q" or "x" are rare in standard English text.

With more complex models, sensitive to context, and by using larger encoding units (e.g., diagrams or even words), compression could be improved. Huffman codes can be proven to be optimal among the class of codes to which they belong. The Huffman algorithm is described in almost all good books on data-structures, for example Cormen et al. (1990). It is put more directly into a data management context in Witten et al. (1994), which too discusses an alternative, also probably optimal, technique, arithmetic encoding. A discussion of the advantages and disadvantages of Huffman coding relative to arithmetic encoding appears in Bookstein and Klein (1993).

One must note the distinction between statistical and adaptive methods (Witten et al., 1994). In statistical methods, a detailed analysis is carried out of the file and a code is derived on the basis of the analysis. For example, the encoding method may be based on Huffman or arithmetic encoding. Such a strategy requires two passes, and if global statistics are used, assumes a relatively static file. In addition, there is a cost associated with storing the code itself, and this could be expensive if a complex model is used.

It is often convenient to circumvent the two-pass requirement. An adaptive technique, of which the Lempel-Ziv (L-Z) methods predominate, is appropriate here. These, in effect, collect statistics on-the-fly, in such a manner that the encoder and decoder are able to construct and update consistent versions of an encoding dictionary, and use this dictionary to encode the next unit. Thus, when the next unit is scanned, it is encoded, and the dictionary itself updated. Such a method is especially valuable when only a single pass is permitted—for example, when transmitting satellite data in real time over a very expensive channel. It is also effective when the statistics of the file are changing, and when storing the dictionary that defines the code is expensive or awkward. However, L-Z methods tend to run slowly. In static files, where the file can be encoded once at the convenience of the producer, but must be decoded frequently and quickly, a Huffman encoding based on prior analysis can be highly advantageous.

The requirement that the file be exactly reconstructable limits the compression effectiveness. But, for image and audio data, it is often tolerable to encode the data in a manner that permits us to reconstruct a good approximation of the original file. In some situations in which lossy compression is used, the loss is mostly noise and the decompressed image may actually be improved.

The importance of the distinction between lossy and lossless compression is that lossy compression permits much more effective file reduction. Of course the precise compression effectiveness will depend on the nature of the original file and the details of the implementation. But as a rough order of magnitude, techniques for the lossless compression of text typically will reduce the file to somewhere between fifty percent and thirty percent of its original size. If lossy compression is tolerable, as is often true for images, compression techniques allow reduction from about ten percent to five percent of its original size, with little observable impact on the original image.

To some extent, data compression is inherent in most graphics file formats. For example, while it is possible to store sequences of pixel values at three bytes per pixel, it is very common to first create a colormap that gives a precise representation of, for example, 256 colors, and then represents the image itself by a sequence of pointers into the map. Although this requires the additional burden of storing the colormap itself (not inconsequential if a large number of colors must be represented), if only 256 colors need be stored, representing the image itself requires only one byte per pixel.

A variety of popular formats for storing and transmitting images exist that incorporate compression techniques (Murray and vanRyper, 1994). In the GIFF format, for example, a colormap or palette, is defined, and the image itself is expressed as a sequence of indices to the colormap, it is then compressed using a form of L-Z encoding.

The JPEG protocol is among the most highly developed and complex of the standard image compression methods (Pennebaker and Mitchell, 1993). It is a suite of methods incorporating a wide variety of options. Central is the possibility of throwing away Fourrier components of the image to which the eye isn't sensitive, and applying a variety of compression encoding methods (e.g., Huffman or arithmetic coding) for the rest.

Other image compression methods, going under the rubric of "vector quantization" (Gersho and Gray, 1992), rely on creating a relatively small dictionary of "vectors" representing common blocks of pixel values, and encoding actual pixels by an index to a good approximating value within the dictionary. (The use of colormaps noted above is a simple example of this approach). Since an index to an entry in the dictionary requires fewer bits than the precise representation of a block of pixel values, considerable compression is possible. These methods are sensitive to the manner in which the dictionary is constructed, and how well actual pixel blocks are mapped into the dictionary.

Some protocols rely heavily on ad hoc prediction methods; if on the basis of already encoded information, we can reasonably predict the value taken by the next item, it is often more efficient to encode the deviation from the prediction than the true value directly. Fax transmission is an example. Much of the material sent by fax, such as text or line-based diagrams, is white space, and the black values tend to form linear patterns. Thus, adjacent scan-lines are often similar, and differ in a very regular manner. Group 4 fax encoding, which actually combines a variety of techniques, takes advantage of these regularities by anticipating one scan-line on the basis of the line previously encoded.

Fax, along with many other image encoding formats, also depends on run length coding, in which long strings of repeated values are succinctly encoded by indicating the repeated value and the number of repetitions. Continuing with the fax example, long strings of white space (0-bits) are frequently encountered. These can be represented by indicating the number of 0 bits, rather than by transmitting the detailed string of 0 bits. For example, to represent explicitly a string of 256 zero bits, we need 32 bytes of storage. But the value 256 itself can be represented in just one byte (plus perhaps an additional bit of structural information). Fax encoding uses a variant of this approach, and achieves further savings by using a variable length Huffman code to represent the run sizes.

The MPEG standard for storing motion pictures also depends on predictive coding: It allows for representing one frame of a series by changes from the preceding frame—in effect, predicting the frames will be identical, and recording the differences. Since, in motion pictures, much of the scene is invariant, and the movements tend to be regular, this can result in great savings.

CRYPTOGRAPHY

Cryptography, the methods for transforming a message to make it unreadable by anyone but the intended target, has long been the concern of the military and diplomatic corps of government (Kahn, 1967). Examples go back to classical times. (A cryptographical technique still widely discussed is known as the "Caesar cipher.")

The advent of computers and the networks connecting them have radically changed the situation. Most conspicuously, they have greatly transformed the consumer base of cryptographic technology. Increasingly, encryption is being demanded for private and commercial use, as personal and business files become vulnerable to invasion via the Internet, or must be transmitted over insecure communication channels. The shift of interest from highly secret agencies within government to the more open commercial and academic environment has not occurred without conflict.

An interesting example is the potential for encrypting digitalized telephone communications. With highly public cellular telephony becoming increasingly popular, the interest in encrypting conversations is obvious. But this has created a tension with government law enforcement, which demands a right to intercept telephone conversation as part of its crime detection operations. Recommendations that keys be escrowed for possible access by law enforcement agencies have been highly controversial (for example, see the discussion of the Clipper chip in Schneier, 1996). Another contentious issue involves the sale of cryptographic technology, which includes floppy disks storing programs for cryptographic algorithms outside of the

United States. Although Schneier focuses on one popular cryptographic system, Garfinkel (1995) gives an excellent overview of the history of the conflict between researchers and entrepreneurs in cryptography and the federal government.

The existence of computers also raises some fascinating issues of principle. For example, computers make it possible to break codes that were previously believed secure, while offering the computational power to implement new forms of code that may, in principle, be stronger. This possibility has brought to the fore the theoretical question of what it means for a cryptographic system to be strong. The cryptographic algorithms in common use are understood not to be intrinsically unbreakable. Rather, the effort in cryptography is to design algorithms for which the cost of unauthorized decryption is thought to be too expensive to be practical—that is, to be "computationally secure." But the history of cryptography consists of cases illustrating how codes thought to be secure were broken.

The increased computational power of computers has forced more attention to the theoretical problem of how to design algorithms that can, in some sense, prove to be computationally secure. Although this task is still unsolved, it has caused a shift of focus in cryptography from techniques that appear hard to break because they are made up of a complex combination of intuitively hard operations, to developing algorithms that depend on simple mathematical operations that can potentially be proven difficult to break. These predominantly arithmetical methods are easily implemented by computer. Excellent texts discussing in detail the current spectrum of ideas in this rapidly changing field now exist (Schneier, 1996; Stinson, 1995).

Traditionally, discussions of cryptographic security have focused on the algorithms by which messages are transformed. It is now becoming clear that the security of a system depends not only on the cryptographic algorithm at the heart of the system, but also on the protocols into which these are embedded, and which control of the flow of information between source and target as a communication channel is established. This flow is vulnerable to a variety of attacks, and research is increasingly directed to understanding the totality of the message interchange process. Concern ranges from the possibility of an intruder simply intercepting messages passing between source and target (i.e., "passive attacks") to situations in which an intruder can initiate an exchange by impersonating another party, change messages, or steal messages, perhaps storing them for future use (i.e., "active attacks").

An interesting example of the need for secure protocols is the need for key exchange. Modern cryptographic systems are based on shared, widely understood, methods; their security is based not on the secrecy of the method, but rather on the secrecy of keys or passwords. Within traditional approaches, each pair of communicating parties must somehow securely transmit a single secret key before secure communication over an insecure channel can occur. The means by which this is done is part of the cryptographic system, and attention must be given to make this phase secure, if the total message exchange system is to be secure.

The problem is especially acute in a large network, where vast numbers of potential communication pairs must be accommodated. The best known modern example of the traditional approach is the "DES encryption algorithm," adopted by the National Bureau of Standards in 1976, and still much in use. This is a highly efficient method, especially when implemented in hardware, and likely to be secure in standard usage. Though controversial from its birth, no efficient method of breaking it is known to exist. But the challenge of such procedures is that the number of keys required for N parties to communicate with each other is approximately $N^2/2$. For example, a network of 10,000 computers could require as many as 100,000,000 keys to be determined.

Mechanisms have been suggested, using a key-server, that respond to the problem. But increasingly prominent today is the use of "public key" methods (Diffie and Hellman, 1976). This genre of cryptographic methodology is based on the recognition that, if huge numbers of parties must be able to communicate over highly insecure channels, then much of their interactions, including key determination, will in effect be public. Thus, the question raised by public key cryptography is: "How can such fully public transactions be made securely?" Phrased in terms of the key-exchange problem: "How can two parties, in full view of a hostile onlooker, determine a key that can be used for further message exchange in such a manner that the onlooker can't read the messages?"

A typical public key system in effect requires each participant to derive a pair of complementary keys, one that is kept private, the other that is distributed as widely as possible. Techniques are developed that make it relatively easy to construct such a pair, though given only one member of the pair, it is believed to be very difficult to construct the other. The difficulty is based on the existence of "hard" problems. For example, the popular RSA cryptosystem is based on the problem of factoring a number that is the product of two large primes (a problem believed, but not rigorously proven, to be hard).

A user looks up the public key of the target and uses it to encrypt the message. While it is, or should be, easy to locate a target's key (it is publicly available) and easy to encode the message, it is very difficult to decrypt the message without knowledge of the private key. For example, if private information, such as a credit card number, must be sent over a publicly accessible channel, the intended recipient can send a "certificate" indicating his public key, and that key can be used to encrypt the private information. An intruder may very well intercept both the certificate, revealing the public key, and the encrypted message, but, without knowing the private key, will be unable to recover the original message. (In fact, the public key methods tend to be slow, since they involve relatively expensive arithmetic operations. For this reason, typically they are used to confidentially send a secret key to be used subsequently with a faster private key method.)

The advent of computer networks raises other fascinating demands that, while not directly related to privacy, can exploit cryptographic technique. A particularly important example is that of authentication. In the paper and ink world, user authentication is provided by means of a signature. Imperfect as this is, it has served commerce since the invention of contracts. But how does one prove to an impartial third party, or judge, that a message (for example, a check or contract) sent over the Internet was sent by the person believed to have sent it? Similarly, how can one prove that the recipient hasn't modified the document presented to a judge?

Cryptographic methods serve us well here. Recall that public key methods involve the creation of two keys, one kept secret, the other made as public as possible. In the most commonly used public key system (the RSA cryptographic system), the existence of the secret key can be exploited for person and message authentication. Typically, one first creates a reduced, fixed-size version of the document by means of a public "message digest" algorithm. These should have the property that it is extremely difficult to modify a message in such a way that the original and modified message reduces to identical digests (by no means a trivial problem). Then, the "private" key is used to encrypt the digest. The messages, accompanied by the encrypted digest, are sent to the recipient, the encrypted digest serving as a digital signature.

To verify the signature, the recipient, or a judge, first applies the digest algorithm to the claimed received message and then applies the public key of the alleged sender of the message to the signature. For RSA, applying the public key undoes the effect of the private key, and the two digests should be identical. We know that the message could not have been modified, otherwise the digests would differ. And we know the alleged sender indeed sent the message, since only he/she could have applied his/her private key to the digest.

A wide range of applications is now possible because of the ability to use the private key to "sign" messages. An interesting example is the possibility of "digital money," where certificates representing cash are authenticated by a bank's signature. For details, see Schneier (1996).

Many problems remain within the public key domain. Paradoxically, relying solely on the computational difficulty of solving a simple mathematical problem makes such systems especially vulnerable, should the problem be shown not to be difficult after all. For example, driven by the public key cryptography challenge, great progress has been made in techniques for speeding up the factoring of large numbers (though it is still generally believed that the RSA technique, with keys derived from large primes, is secure).

Also paradoxical, given that the development of public key systems was driven by the desire to avoid the need of third-party responsibility for key distribution, is that many implementations depend on precisely such a third party to ensure the authenticity of public keys. That is, a user of a public key system must have confidence that the public key of an intended communicant in fact belongs to the communicant, and has not been altered or replaced by a mischievous opponent. Here again, careful attention has been given to develop protocols by means of which a trusted third party can become involved in the exchange of public keys, and which are resilient to known possible attacks by a fiendishly clever and remarkably industrious opponent.

Error Correction

It is commonly observed that computers don't make mistakes. But data storage and transmission channels do. Magnetic materials deteriorate and, occasionally, have bad patches. Lightning, nearby electrical equipment, faulty switches, and the like introduce errors in data being transmitted. Stamping machines, producing large numbers of copies of a CD-ROM database, are imperfect. Data needs to be encoded in a way that neutralizes the damage these can do.

The earliest and most heavily used error-control technique is the well-known introduction of a parity bit—adding an eighth bit to each seven bit ASCII character, forcing the number of one-bits within the eight bit byte to be even. This technique permits single (or odd numbers) of errors to be detected, but not corrected. For example, it can be used with protocols that allow the receiver to require a data packet to be retransmitted.

More advanced error management codes permit more complex errors to be detected, and may allow actual correction of the errors, provided the size and nature of the error observes certain constraints. These extend the idea of a parity bit to appending multiple parity bits. Suppose we extend an n-bit message to create, for transmission, a bit-string that has N bits (the n information bits and the added N-n parity bits). A useful conceptualization of these resulting Code words is to think of them as points in an N-dimensional vector space, where each dimension can take only the values of zero or one.

The mechanism for generating the parity bits from the initial message is designed so that, of all the possible N-dimensional vectors, only a subset is acceptable as the encodings of legitimate messages, for example, of a character. Such was the case with the traditional single-parity bit. But, in terms of the geometry interpretation, the use of a single-parity bit, which may allow us to detect the existence of an error, leaves the space too crowded to correct the error: Given an invalid bit string, too many legitimate code words are near it to permit an unambiguous correction. By increasing the number of parity bits, the space can be made more sparse, so it becomes meaningful when an error is detected to ask to which legitimate code word the corrupted bit string is most close. Here, the distance between two bit strings (the "Hamming distance") is the minimum number of bits that must be changed to convert one string into the other.

An example illustrates the approach. For simplicity, let us use a word with only two bits. Suppose we wish to transmit the following information bits, represented in bold face: **10**. If we insist on even parity, we would append the bit 1 (represented, for emphasis, in a contrasting typeface), to get the code word **10** 1. If the received message is: **00** 1, **11** 1 or **10** 0, it is easily determined that an error was made. But if, for example, the message **00** 1 was received, several possible legitimate (i.e., even parity) messages are equally close to the one received, e.g., **10** 1 and **01** 1—both being close in the sense of requiring only a single-bit-change to transform it to a legitimate message.

It is easy to extend the parity concept to permit error correction. For symmetry purposes, now consider a four-bit message: **1000** represented for illustration in a square:

10

00

Suppose we now append five parity bits to end of the message, to obtain the code word: **1000** 10101. To understand the role these additional bits play, it is useful to rearrange the bits as a square as follows:

101

000

101

Displayed in this form, we see that the additional bits make each row have even parity, and also each column has even parity. Such an arrangement not only can detect a single error, but can actually correct it. For example, suppose that (after rearrangement) the following is received:

001

000

Conclusion

How data is coded is invisible to most of us, other than via the mysterious extensions often added to file names, such as .zip or .giv, to indicate that the file is compressed or is an image, encoded in a manner consistent with some protocol. However, to fully understand how data is stored or transmitted in a way that satisfies the demands we make of the system, an awareness of the types of codes used is important. A manager of information has to ascertain that the various criteria for secure and efficient storage/transmission are met, and should be aware of the mechanisms available for doing this. This should not be done in an ad hoc manner. To be most effective, lower levels of the operating system should do the coding in a systematic way so that the various, sometimes apparently contradictory, steps are well coordinated. For example, compression removes redundant bits for storage efficiency, while an error correction stage adds redundant bits. If done properly, the system costs are minimized, consistent with all requirements being met to a predetermined degree. It is the purpose of this chapter to introduce both the requirements and offer an overview of what is available—that is, to provide a range of concepts and vocabulary to permit an information manager to engage in discussions in which these issues are involved.

References

Bookstein, A.; Klein, T.; Deerwester, S. (1989) Storing Text Retrieval Systems on CD-ROM: Compression and Encryption Considerations. *ACM Transactions on Information Systems.* 7(3), 230-245.

Bookstein, A.; Klein, T. (1994) Is Huffman Coding Dead? *Computing.* 50(4), 279-296.

Cormen, T.H.; Leiserson, C.E.; Rivest, R.L. (1990) *Introduction to Algorithms.* New York: McGraw-Hill.

Diffie, W.; Hellman, M.E. (1976) New Directions in Cryptography. *IEEE Trans. Inform. Theory.* IT-22, 644-654.

Garfinkel, S. (1995) *PGP: Pretty Good Privacy.* Sebastopol, CA: O'Reilly.

Gersho, A.; Gray, R.M. (1992) *Vector Quantization and Signal Compression.* Boston: Kluwer.

Kahn, D. (1967) *The Codebreakers.* New York: Macmillan.

Lesk, M. (1997) *Practical Digital Libraries.* San Francisco: Morgan Kaufmann.

Murray, J.D.; vanRyper, W. (1994) *Encyclopedia of Graphics File Formats.* Sebastopol, CA: O'Reilly.

Netravali, A.N.; Haskell, B.G. (1988) *Digital Pictures.* New York: Plenum.

Pennebaker, W.B.; Mitchell, J.L. (1993) *JPEG Still Image Data Compression Standard.* New York: Van Nostrand Reinhold.

Roman, S. (1992) *Coding and Information Theory.* New York: Springer Verlag.

Salton, G. (1975) *Dynamic Information and Library Processing.* Englewood Cliffs, NJ: Prentice Hall.

Schneier, Bruce. (1996) *Applied Cryptography*, 2nd ed. New York: Wiley.

Shannon, C.E. (1949a) A Mathematical Theory of Communications. *Bell System Technical Journal.* 28(4), 379-423, and 623-656.

Shannon, C.E. (1949b) Communication Theory of Secrecy Systems. *Bell System Technical Journal* 28, 656-715.

Stinson, D.R. (1995) *Cryptography.* Boca Raton, Florida: CRC Press.

Wicker, S.B. (1995) *Error Control Systems for Digital Communication and Storage.* Englewood Cliffs, NJ: Prentice Hall.

Witten, I.H.; Moffat, A.; Bell, T.C. (1994) *Managing Gigabytes.* New York: Van Nostrand Reinhold.

CHAPTER 20

Repackaging Information

John Agada

Associate Professor

University of Wisconsin at Milwaukee

INTRODUCTION

In the competitive corporate environment, managers need fast and easy access to information for decision making. Knowledge management systems have, therefore, evolved specifically to support the information needs of their organizations. Such systems, however, cannot anticipate the circumstances, information needs, and use characteristics of individual managers in the organization. For instance, most managers lack the time, relevant knowledge, and skills to efficiently search for, evaluate, interpret, synthesize, and adapt information for their tasks. A service that provides them information already processed and tailored to fit their decision plans would boost work efficiency and productivity.

Information repackaging is such a service. Repackaging combines the concepts of information counseling (Dosa, 1997) and consolidation (Saracevic and Wood, 1981). It consists of the knowledge management processes of adding value to information to facilitate physical and conceptual access to information. The physical level of repackaging includes restructuring the symbol, code, channel, and media systems of information sources, while the conceptual level entails analysis, editing, interpreting, translating, and synthesizing information from several sources to create a new document. Unlike traditional information services that are evaluated largely by the provision of relevant sources, repackaging services are evaluated by the degree to which the client's need is satisfactorily resolved.

For example, an information professional manager assisting a manager in preparing a budget proposal for his/her department does not stop at providing access to relevant documents, but customizes information from documentary (e.g., professional and government literature) and non-documentary (e.g., organizational archives, lore, and "stories") internal and external sources into a persuasive package. Repackaging might entail creating graphs from these sources to illustrate trends, relationships, and projections. Primary data from diverse sources would be analyzed and checked for accuracy, comprehensiveness, and timeliness. It is then synthesized and edited into a single document pertinent to the manager's needs and circumstances. Repackaging services may entail a series of interactions between the manager and the information professional and may lead to development of several documents. This chapter describes the principles and processes by which information professionals diagnose client's needs and reconstruct information packages to meet those needs.

PURPOSE AND GOALS OF REPACKAGING

The need for repackaging information derives from the phenomenon that Richard Wurman (1989) described as "information anxiety": a situation "produced by the ever-widening gap between what we understand and what we think we should understand...when information doesn't tell us what we want or need to know."

This phenomenon, which has been attributed to the information explosion, has created a number of information problems. Some of these problems are:

- The volume of information sources relevant to a client's needs might mitigate against efficient use.
- The sources might not be written or recorded in the language or at the comprehension level of the client.
- The sources might not address the information need from the point-of-view of the task, objectives, and context of the client.
- Available information might be coded in symbols, channels, or media that are unfamiliar or inconvenient for the client to process.
- Available information might be inappropriate in detail or complexity relative to the client's prior knowledge, experience, role, or other information use characteristics.

Whereas traditional information services focus on providing access to relevant information sources, repackaging services customize information so that it is not only relevant but also pertinent and usable by the client. The ultimate goal of repackaging is to effectively resolve the manager's need to his/her satisfaction. To attain this goal, the information professional monitors, evaluates, and advises on the use of information until the task is successfully executed. The repackager might employ human support networks, create new documents, or recreate existing ones, representing and leveraging them to enhance their utility in the decision and problem solving plans of the manager.

REPACKAGING: PRELIMINARY PROCESSES

Information Needs Diagnosis

The diagnosis of needs is a precursor to the design and provision of repackaging services. Diagnosis is the first of the systematic cycle of services consisting of diagnosis, prescription, implementation, and evaluation (Greer et al., 1994). The information professional designs a new information service based on knowledge of the manager's environment and the roles he/she plays in that environment. In order to customize information services for the manager, the information professional focuses on the manager's role responsibilities and activities. Fine tuning an existing delivery system, on the other hand, requires shifting the main focus to the manager's information use characteristics (Hale, 1986).

The manager's information use characteristics may be determined through a combination of the following:

- Interviews and observations of the client
- Examinations of patterns of information use (human resource networks and documents used and judged useful)
- Client's feedback on potential usefulness of information sources or repackaged products
- Drawing on previous experiences with similar clients and situations

The information use characteristics that may emerge from the diagnosis include level of subject knowledge in area of need, language, perceptions of task complexity, and context; role and stage in information use or task execution; and cognitive or learning style (see Figure 20.1). The information professional now uses these characteristics as parameters or criteria for assessing appropriateness of information sources and recommendations for repackaging. No single document could address all the specifications implied by any client's characteristics. Therefore, after assembling all information sources relevant to the task and information need of the manager, the features of the documents need to be juxta-posed with the client's information use characteristics.

Client characteristics (Skills and perceptions)	Document characteristics (Content and style)
1. Domain knowledge	A. Subject coverage
2. Comprehension level	B. Level of subject treatment
3. Language	C. Language
4. Context of problem	D. Context of problem
5. Task complexity	E. Task complexity
6. Role and stage of information use	F. Perspective to problem
7. Learning and cognitive style	G. Focus and explication style
8. Communication style	H. Presentation format: style and illustrations

Figure 20.1 Client/Document Characteristics Model

For example, if a document matches the manager's knowledge base, task context, and complexity but is written in inappropriate language and at an inappropriate comprehension level, the information professional would need to translate the document into the language understood by the manager and rewrite the content at the manager's comprehension level. Furthermore, the documents may hold information in symbols, channels, and media (defined below) that may be unfamiliar or unsuitable to the client or his/her circumstances. The information professional might undertake to encode the information using new sets of symbols, channels, and media systems to facilitate use. For instance, audio recording a report to be audited by the manager as he/she commutes to and from work represents conversion of text on paper to audio symbols on cassette (celluloid) medium.

The information professional may use conceptual models to categorize some of the manager's characteristics. Some process models enable diagnosis of the manager's stage in information use or task execution (e.g., Rogers' innovation diffusion model (1983); and Kuhlthau information search process model (1993). Others, such as the Myers-Briggs Type Indicator (Briggs-Myers and McCaulley, 1985) and the learning style inventory (Kolb, 1984) assess cognitive and learning styles. Although there is considerable overlap between different models, a model may be used to analyze more than one characteristic. Rogers' innovation diffusion model is used to illustrate the use of models in diagnosis.

Rogers' innovation diffusion model may be used to analyze the process of adapting an innovation, such as new technology. The information professional may use the model to monitor the immediate and projected needs of the manager as he/she interacts with information about the technology so as to provide information sources that are not only timely but proactive with regards to the client's circumstances. The stages of the model are delineated as:

- Awareness—when the client learns of the existence of an innovation
- Interest generation and knowledge acquisition—when the client seeks further information about the innovation
- Attitude formation—when the client evaluates the innovation and decides whether he/she likes or does not like it
- Trial decision—when the client tries to apply the innovation on a small scale
- Adoption or rejection—when the client rejects the innovation or embarks on continuous and full-scale use

An information professional supporting a manager's bid to introduce an innovation in a corporate setting could facilitate awareness of the innovation by providing promotional brochures and newsletters. Subsequently, the interest and quest for additional knowledge about the project would be supported through state-of-the-art reviews and synthesized reports of research and critical data, resources, and economic analysis. Evaluative studies with comparative, competitive, and impact analysis would be more appropriate at the attitude formation stage. Data presented in graphical, film, or video formats, depicting familiar contexts and experiences and credible sources (e.g., respected authorities, opinion leaders) are effective tools at this stage to aid the decision to adopt or otherwise. Establishing contact with individuals or groups who have experience with the respective technology should also be explored.

Technical and training manuals, handbooks, and synthesis of comparative experiences would be invaluable at the trial decision stage. Graphical materials, films, video, pictures, and tables are invaluable as both staff and management learn to apply new knowledge to their routines. The final stage of adoption requires more manuals (operational), handbooks, market reports, trends and evaluations, results, and impact analysis.

Some process models, such as Kuhlthau's, delineate the client's emotional states as he/she progresses through the stages of information use. Such knowledge enables the information professional to anticipate and respond appropriately.

Since information needs are dynamic, the information professional continually monitors shifts in the manager's needs and evaluates his/her use of information. The interactions between the manager and information professional are, therefore, underscored by cyclical and systematic processes of diagnosis, prescription, implementation (repackaging and use of product), and evaluation.

Repackaging at the Conceptual Level

Information Analysis and Synthesis

Documents deemed relevant to the manager's needs are now analyzed and synthesized. Information analysis is the identification of units within a document and their structural relationships. Information synthesis is the editing, re-purposing, merging, and restructuring of document units to convey new focus, purpose, or perspective. Information contained in these sources needs to be evaluated to ascertain its validity, reliability, and intrinsic merit. Evaluation at this stage is based largely on intrinsic qualities of the content. For critical data, such as health information, emphasis is placed on accuracy, timeliness, and utility values. Some disciplines, particularly in the hard sciences have standardized data that enhance technical communication. The Committee on Data for Science and Technology (CODATA) of the International Council of Scientific Unions (ICSU) produces the CODATA Bulletin where data evaluation and critical tables are published (Saracevic and Wood, 1981).

Less hard data (such as statistical and observational data), however, are less suitable for standardization by disciplinary and professional bodies. Interpretations of such data may be more subjective. Analysis and evaluation of such data are, therefore, more oriented to interpretations of user goals in the context of the problem situation in question. Where non-document sources are used (e.g., resource persons, and real-life activity), their information would need to be verified and the credibility of the sources ascertained.

Information Analysis

Information analysis may be defined as the process of breaking down a body of information into its component units on the basis of their relevance to the task or problem of the client. The process consists of the following steps:

- Reading/viewing/auditing the relevant documents and ensuring that their contents are pertinent to the client's needs by way of his/her goals
- Categorizing the sources on the basis of selection and evaluative criteria relevant to the task, i.e., their language and subject/topic subdivisions (see information diagnostic model above)
- Extracting the most relevant pieces and aspects from the documents; comparing redundancies and selecting for extraction only those features that best reflect the client's needs
- Where no documents exists on an aspect of the client's needs, the information professional may fill the gap by creating the information (e.g., locating and interpreting relevant data) or recording it (interviewing resource persons or videotaping a live process) as the case may be
- Verification of the contents or data in individual extracts by checking their accuracy, timeliness, and credibility of sources
- Arranging the extracted information into categories according to a helpful table of contents, classification scheme, or typology as dictated by the client's goals (Saracevic and Wood, 1981)

Information Synthesis

Information synthesis is the process of integrating and consolidating the information culled from the selected sources into a new structure. The synthesis process may involve changing the symbol, code, channel, and media systems of the documents. The process entails:

- Merging the extracted pieces of information that belong to the same categories.
- Comparing and evaluating the different pieces, checking for coherence or consistencies, and contradictions. Validating their relative accuracies, e.g., inconsistencies may be accounted for by differences in publication dates of sources, units of analyses, or projections.
- Choosing which pieces, perspectives, and data to present. Here again decisions have to be made between redundancies and contradictions. There may be a need to present conflicting data so as to appraise the client of his/her respective contexts and rationales. In presenting options for decision making, this approach may enable the client to appreciate the scenarios of the different options before committing to one.

- Integrating the information in an appropriate package(s) for presentation to the client. The client should have the opportunity to preview or audit the package so as to provide feedback on fine-tuning the package.

Ideally, the processes of analysis and synthesis should be undertaken in conjunction with the client. The client's feedback at strategic points are crucial to ensuring that the final product is not only pertinent to the client's need but applicable to executing the task.

REPACKAGING AT THE PHYSICAL LEVEL

Repackaging may be undertaken at symbol, channel, and media system (defined below) levels of documents to enhance physical and conceptual access.

Symbols, Channels, and Media

- Symbols are signs that represent something other than themselves, e.g., words, pictures, and graphs. Their use is governed by systems of rules and conventions known as codes, e.g., grammar for language and aesthetics for art or graphic works. The meanings of symbols may be obvious (denotative), or implied through cultural use and norms (connotative).
- Channel is used here to denote the physical means by which signs may be transmitted or perceived such as light, sound, and radio waves.

The relationships between symbols, channels, and codes may be illustrated using human speech. Speech uses verbal language as a primary code. Words can, however, be re-encoded into secondary codes such as paralanguage forms (e.g., intonation, stress, volume) and other codes: deaf-and-dumb sign language; Morse; Braille; printing; etc. The codes of camera angle and movement (e.g., close-ups, long and medium shots, frontal or side views, panning, and zooms), lighting, color, speed, framing, and editing are examples of TV medium-specific codes.

- Medium is the physical or technical means of converting the symbols into formats capable of being transmitted along the chosen channel. For examples, our voices are the media for transmitting word symbols as sound waves (channel). Text on paper constitutes the print medium: Letters, pictures, and graphs symbols are perceived by the aid of light waves (channel) on the paper medium. TV and radio broadcast media use the channels of light and radio (electromagnetic) waves for transmission. Again, the words and pictures on TV are the symbols that bear information.

Some symbols and channels are best coded and transmitted via particular media, e.g., radio for sound symbols and TV for moving images with sound. The effectiveness of different media in transmitting information is a function of the symbol and channel systems they carry and the human cognitive processes necessary to decode them.

Repackaging Symbol, Channel, and Media Systems

Documents may be repackaged without changing the symbol system as in preparing a textual executive summary from reports in text format. When the text is converted to charts, graphs, and pictures, however, the symbol system has been altered. A change in the symbol system may entail a change in the code as well. If the executive summary were documented in diagrams and charts on paper, for instance, codes for textual grammar and vocabulary would have been switched for graphic codes. For example, with pie charts, the codes would consist of the rules for translating percentages to slices of a pie in relative sizes and the use of color to enhance contrasts and aesthetics. Codes for transferring text on paper to electronic text, on the other hand, entail word-processing codes, e.g., WordPerfect protocols. The channel for the symbol systems (i.e., light waves) however, remains the same.

If the executive summary was recorded on audiotape, the channel in which symbols are transmitted would have been changed from light waves to sound waves. Consequently, the new channel requires a new medium for transmission. Audio tape or CD-ROM media now replaces the paper medium. When a novel is made into a movie, the symbol system of text is substituted by those of moving images, color, and sound (i.e., dialogue, music). The channel changes consist of the addition of sound waves to light waves. Celluloid film and video media replace the paper and book media. Choices made at each level of repackaging are informed by properties of the symbol, code, and channel and media systems with respect to their appropriateness to the manager's information use characteristics.

PROPERTIES OF SYMBOL, CHANNEL, AND MEDIA SYSTEMS

Decisions in the use of different symbols, channels, and media in repackaging should be shaped by the information needs and use characteristics of the client manager. Guidelines for appropriate combinations of symbols, channels, and media abound in the literature of instructional technology. A few illustrative examples will be discussed here.

When deciding to code information in print or electronic text, for instance, one needs to take into consideration the reading skills (skilled or unskilled) and subject knowledge (expert or novice) of the client. For the unskilled reader and subject novice, the stability of text on paper enables: variable pacing in reading and rereading of unfamiliar or technical information; and sufficient time to recall appropriate meanings of the context being read from long-term memory. For more skilled readers who have some relevant subject knowledge, text stability facilitates: scanning for selective reading of large quantities of text; and using single words to scan vast amounts of information (drawing on their extensive knowledge base to fill in for areas of text being glossed over).

To facilitate reading, comprehension, and retention, the information professional might:

- Restructure the text using verbal and visual cues, chunking, and page layout for poor readers and subject novices.
- Build internal connections among different concepts in the text.
- Focus attention on aspects of the topic relevant to the client's needs (repurposing and restructuring).
- Place visuals (e.g., pictures, graphs) next to relevant text so novices can go back and forth between text and pictures. For skilled readers who have some prior knowledge, visuals may be located early in the text. These readers want to examine closely, commit the visual to memory, and proceed to the text.
- Provide executive summaries and overviews at the beginning of the report for skilled readers and subject experts. Also including frequent reviews in the text enhances retention, especially for novices.
- Use pointers to identify critical attributes to facilitate subsequent identification.

Knowledge of interactions between characteristics of clients and other symbol, channel, and media combinations such as visuals (e.g., still images); audio-visual (e.g., moving images with sound); and interactive, hypertext, and multimedia environments, suggest different strategies for repackaging.

TYPES OF REPACKAGING SERVICES

Repackaging services may be categorized into three types. The categories differ along a continuum by degree of the value added to original information sources. At one end of the continuum are locational and access tools; at the other end are repackaged documents and services tailored to facilitate resolution of the client's information need. The three categories are:

- Locational and access tools
- Representation (analysis and synthesis) sources
- Interpretation and evaluation services

A discussion of these categories and their constituents follow below.

Locational and Access Tools

Some repackaging services entail the design and provision of guides that facilitate the identification and retrieval of primary documents that are of interest to clients. Clients who are initiating research on a problem may need to scan the literature broadly to better define their problem. Information professionals supporting this

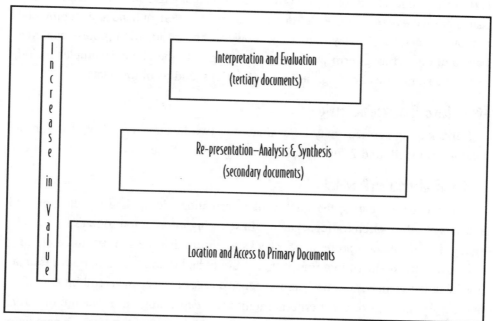

Figure 20.2   Value-Added Model of Repackaging Services

information-gathering quest need to construct guides to assist their clients. These guides, unlike those provided commercially or by libraries, need to be tailored to the client's unique needs. Some examples of guides are pathfinders, source lists, bibliographies, indexes, abstracts, and customized databases.

Representational (Analysis and Synthesis) Sources

Unlike the locational and access tools that identify and assist in the selection and location of sources, representational tools are reformulations of primary documents into secondary and tertiary documents. The primary documents are merged and re-presented in a variety of new formats. The merging and re-creation of new document formats are based on analysis of the primary document contents and their synthesis as dictated by the needs of potential clients. Examples include translations, reviews, state-of-the-art reports, handbooks, and manuals.

Interpretation and Evaluation Sources

These are customized documents or services to help the client resolve his/her information need. Information is interpreted within the perspectives, goals, and context of the client. The information professional who engages in evaluation briefs the manager on the options available for resolving the problem at hand and recommends appropriate actions. To play such a role, however, the information professional must have a close and long-term working relationship with the client. Examples include executive summaries/briefings, analysis of options, and recommendations.

Evaluation of Repackaging Services

Repackaging services may be evaluated at two levels: 1) quality of the information provided; and 2) usefulness or utility value of the service for the client.

Quality of Information Provided

Criteria for evaluating the quality of information are applied in selection and analysis of information for repackaging. In selecting information sources for repackaging, the information professional checks to ensure that the sources and their content have intrinsic merit in terms of their validity and reliability. Criteria for evaluation include accuracy, currency, comprehensiveness, balance, and credibility of information. Application of these criteria might vary, depending on the nature of information and the manager's needs. For research-based services, the research paradigm or orientation of the sources must be in accord with those of the client. Other criteria for research and non-research works include the following:

- Authority of the source—author(s), publisher, sponsoring and funding institution, reviews, citation indexes, etc.
- Comparison and correlation of the information units with other sources of repute. Comparisons and correlation may confirm or reveal discrepancies.

This is especially useful for critical data meant for planning experiments and projects, verifying information to establish conditions for different variables, and comparing descriptions of such variables within and between records. For instance, if one description of a phenomenon is correct, by implication, other measures found in other sources should meet calculated estimates, e.g., by normal distributions, historical facts, etc.

• Common sense, intuition, and impressions based on one's knowledge and experience, matched with those of the client as well as reputable and impartial third parties.

Usefulness of Service to Clients

Whereas the criteria for evaluating the quality of information may be deemed "objective," those for assessing its usefulness are subjective because they are largely dependent on the task, goals, and information use characteristics of the client.

Task, Goals, and Information Use Characteristics of the Client

The information diagnostic model (mentioned previously) may be used to assess the compatibility of the client's characteristics (knowledge, skills, perspective) and the demands of the task (context, complexity) with the repackaged product. When there are good matches between the two sets of characteristics, the repackaged product should be easy to understand and apply. Other factors that affect ease of use differ from media to media. For textual symbols, for example, such factors include legibility (e.g., visual clarity and aesthetic appeal) and the use of comprehension aids (e.g., use of identifiers that highlight key elements of content).

The ultimate goal of repackaging is that the manager's information needs are satisfactorily resolved. Since the client's "satisfaction" is a subjective criterion, it should be complemented with use of more objective measures, such as improvement in the problem situation that necessitated the quest for information and an increase in the manager's productivity. The overall evaluation must also include the extent to which the client learned and was empowered in the course of the repackaging service, for example, by becoming more self-reflective of his/her information use characteristics and more knowledgeable about information sources. As a result, a higher level of service building on the experience gained by both the client and the professional from the previous service would mark interactions between the information professional and the manager on subsequent projects. If these ends are attained, repackaging will have saved the time of the manager, as well as enhanced his/her information literacy skills and productivity.

Conclusion

The competition in the corporate environment calls for services that go beyond traditional information management activities. The explosion in knowledge creation and management makes it imperative that information intermediaries who understand their (manager's) environment, roles, and individual characteristics work closely with corporate managers. Such professionals could retrieve, interpret, synthesize information, and advise on its use until the manager's task is successfully executed. Information repackaging is defined as a systematic process of adding value to information to enhance its use by a target client. By offering repackaging services to support the work of the manager, the information professional will enhance the work efficiency and productivity in the organization.

References

Briggs-Myers, I.; McCaulley, M. H. (1985) Manual: A guide to the development and use of Myers-Briggs Type Indicator. Palo Alto, CA: Consulting Psychologists Press, Inc.

Dosa, M. (1997) From informal gatekeeper to information counselor: Emergence of a new professional role. In *Across All Borders: International Information Flows and Applications*, collected papers. Lanham, MD: The Scarecrow Press.

Greer, R.; Agada, J.; Grover, R. (1994) An analytic model for library staffing patterns. *Library Administration and Management.* 8 (1), 35-42.

Hale, M. L. (1986) Administrators and information: A review of methodologies used for diagnosing information use. *Advances in Librarianship.* 14, 75-99.

Kolb, D. (1984) *Experiential Learning: Experience as the Source of Learning and Development.* Englewood Cliffs, NJ: Prentice-Hall.

Kuhlthau, C. C. (1993) *Seeking Meaning: A Process Approach to Library and Information Services.* Norwood, NJ: Ablex.

Rogers, E. M. (1983) *Diffusion of Innovations*, 3rd edition. NY: The Free Press.

Saracevic, T.; Wood, J. (1981) *Consolidation of information: A handbook on evaluation, restructuring, and repackaging of scientific and technical information.* Paris, France: UNESCO (PGI-83/CONF. 609/ COL.1).

Wurman, R. S. (1989) *Information Anxiety.* NY: Doubleday/Bantam.

Part V :
Knowledge Management—
Application

Knowledge Management—Application
Introductory Notes

The final section of this book covers strategies for and examples of the actual implementation of knowledge management in practice. Thomas Short begins the section by defining generic strategy and a framework for developing a knowledge management implementation in his chapter, "Components of a Knowledge Strategy: Keys to Successful Knowledge Management." The approach is perhaps best described as a development of the enterprise-wide information analysis planning methodology developed by IBM in the 1980s. This methodology is extended and generalized, incorporating intellectual capital and the information audit, with the goal of identifying "information levers"—the ways in which a firm can leverage its knowledge resources. Short's chapter is also more than that, it is an excellent portrayal of what knowledge management is and what it means.

Ryske and Sebastian in "From Library to Knowledge Center—The Evolution of a Technology Infocenter" describe the evolution of an already forward-thinking corporate library into something more, a proactive participant in knowledge management. Their chapter is full of lessons learned, and though it is fashionable to disparage so-called pieces of the "how we did it good in our shop" genre, this is one such piece that should not be missed.

Dalrymple in "Knowledge Management in the Health Sciences" traces the inter-linked evolution of knowledge management and evidence-based practice in clinical medicine. Both are based upon the sharing and utilization of information and knowledge, but with an important difference. Knowledge management is usually defined in the business context where it is typically imagined to support one firm or organization to be more effective and more competitive, whereas evidence-based practice ideally transcends organizational boundaries and encompasses the entirety of medical practice.

Platt's chapter, "Knowledge Management: Can It Exist in a Law Office?" examines both what constitutes or should constitute knowledge management in a law office, and the problems of implementation. She provides a number of specific examples and from them derives a number of precepts.

Shelfer in her chapter, "The Intersection of Knowledge Management and Competitive Intelligence: Smartcards and Electronic Commerce," examines the interrelationship of knowledge management and competitive intelligence in the specific context of the current introduction of the smartcard in North America and its role in the evolving context of electronic commerce. This situation is one of rapid flux, driven by technical, political, and commercial considerations; one where assessment of the context, including the technological capability, the needs and desires of the marketplace, and the likely regulatory climate is crucial. This is a classic situation where success is likely to attend better knowledge management and better competitive intelligence, a fascinating arena in which to demonstrate the interrelationship between the two.

Srikantaiah's chapter "Knowledge Management in Developing Countries" describes the potential for knowledge management not, as it is typically done, in the context of the information-intensive firm in the developed world, but rather in the developing world. While knowledge management can be viewed as a problem or an opportunity in developing countries, Srikantaiah analyzes knowledge management development with the background of demographics such as GNP, literacy rate, health, and other such issues. This chapter also argues that knowledge management is important not only in its own right, but also because it plays an important role in catalyzing and supporting economic and political policies in developing countries that are supportive of and contribute to economic growth and poverty reduction.

Debons et al., in "Knowledge Counseling: The Concept, The Process, and Its Application," examine the role of knowledge counseling and report on several case studies. Knowledge counseling, a concept that predates the enthusiasm for knowledge management, nonetheless serves as a model for what should be and ideally will prove to be an important component of the information professional's role in knowledge management.

Nelke's chapter, "Knowledge Management in Swedish Corporations—The Value of Information and Information Services," analyzes the information and knowledge management environments in a number of Swedish corporations. The analysis examines the situations as they exist, concludes that the organizations under-invest in library and information services, and speculates on the future of information and knowledge management and the library's role therein.

CHAPTER 21

Components of a Knowledge Strategy: Keys to Successful Knowledge Management

Thomas Short
Senior Consultant
IBM Global Services

INTRODUCTION

Knowledge management is a hot topic in business. Intranets, global connectivity, distributed expertise, and rapid change in products and processes are all driving companies to search for ways of working smarter. In his book, *Post-Capitalist Society*, management guru Peter Drucker stated that knowledge would become the only source of sustainable competitive advantage as we move into the next century. How do the principles of knowledge management relate to the firm's business objectives? Which business issues present the richest opportunities for leverage?

To explore these issues, I will review a knowledge strategy framework. This framework combines a general, issues-based approach to defining operational strategy and objectives with specialized knowledge management principles and approaches. The result is a way of identifying how the firm may best leverage its knowledge resources. Once this fundamental knowledge strategy is defined, baselining and technology options may be explored.

Knowledge management may be defined as the set of practices, tools, interventions, and infrastructure, aimed at improving a firm's ability to leverage its knowledge resources to achieve business objectives. Using this definition, a broad spectrum of information- and behavior-based approaches is subsumed under the knowledge management rubric. Culture change, best practices, benchmarking, learning organization, business intelligence, competitive intelligence, data mining, workflow, communities of practice, collaborative filtering, and document management are only a sampling of the tools, practices, and infrastructure-based approaches that firms have embraced in an effort to better leverage knowledge and information.

Each of these approaches (and many others not listed above) may well have efficacy in many of today's larger firms at a given time. In addition to the vast troves of data and information now accessed, collected, and stored on a firm's networked computer system, larger firms also tend to be more dispersed and complex than smaller firms, and they tend to compete against competitors of various sizes and locales. The resulting information overload, collaboration issues, performance variance and innovation needs are some of the issues firms seek to address using knowledge management approaches. But which approach, or set of approaches, will bring the most value to the firm? How is a firm to prioritize alternatives when any one or several of the alternatives are appealing and resources are limited?

This is one issue a well-crafted knowledge strategy addresses. Simply put, a knowledge strategy identifies the knowledge resources that should be leveraged against knowledge-based business issues that arise from the firm's overall business strategy. Once the knowledge strategy is defined, the firm has a map that can be used to identify and prioritize knowledge management tools and approaches in a way that supports achievement of long-term strategic business objectives.

Given the above definition of a knowledge strategy, it becomes clear that a knowledge strategy comprises several discrete components:

- An articulated business strategy and objectives
- A description of knowledge-based business issues
- An inventory of available knowledge resources
- An analysis of recommended knowledge levers

How is a knowledge strategy created? How can each of the components be described? The remainder of this chapter describes each of these components in more detail, and discusses how each of these may be created.

ARTICULATED BUSINESS STRATEGY AND OBJECTIVES

The way firms develop and use business strategies and objectives are as varied as the firms themselves. Strategic planning as a formal staff function has waxed and waned in popularity over the years, as management writers continue to refine and revise their view of the role of this rather lofty-sounding pursuit. Regardless of how a firm's strategy is developed and later used, one could conclude that much of the value in creating a strategy and supporting business objectives is gained from the creation process itself. Once the creation activity is completed, management has learned much about the current competitive, regulatory, and marketplace landscape, and can then go about prioritizing operational and tactical projects and reacting to change.

Framing a knowledge strategy generally begins with gaining an understanding of the firm's business strategy and strategic objectives, regardless of the degree to which these concepts have been formalized. To the extent they have been codified, they can generally be taken as given. However, if they have not been formally defined, then it may be worthwhile to create them as a precursory exercise to defining the knowledge strategy. Based on our client experience, the non-existence of a current strategy is more frequent than one might imagine.

At a minimum, the business strategy should set out the following:

- The product or service
- The target customers
- The preferred distribution or delivery channel
- The chief competitors, including other firms and products
- The positioning of the firm's product or service in the market (e.g., the lowest priced alternative)
- The forecasted trajectory of the above

In undertaking the development of a knowledge strategy, the above information should be gleaned from the firm's chosen business strategy. The knowledge strategy does not intend to change or define any of the above items. Over time, however, the implementation of an effective knowledge strategy may well provide the firm with the ability to compete in new or different ways. In this respect, a knowledge strategy can be thought of as having a recursive relationship with the firm's business strategy.

BUSINESS ISSUES

Once the firm's business strategy is defined and understood, it is then possible to inductively identify the business issues with which the firm is faced. Based on a sampling of issues that clients raise as they inquire about knowledge management, we have identified four basic business issues that may be thought of as knowledge-based business issues or needs:

- Need for collaboration
- Need to level performance variance
- Need for innovation
- Need to address information overload

Only two of these issues, performance leveling and innovation, add value directly when they have been successfully addressed. The other two, collaboration and information overload, may be considered as a means to an end—successfully addressing collaboration does not directly drive business value, although it may well enable or support improving productivity (performance leveling) or innovation. This point is nicely summarized by Peter Drucker, who stated [emphasis added]: "Knowledge is becoming the one critical factor of production. It has two incarnations: Knowledge applied to the new is *innovation*; and knowledge applied to the existing processes, services, and products is *productivity*." Still, firms need to recognize the intermediate issues of collaboration and information overload as well as the two "end" issues, productivity and innovation, if they are to create a knowledge strategy that supports business objectives and takes account of the current operating state.

KNOWLEDGE RESOURCES

Once key business issues are identified and linked to the firm's business strategy and objectives, the current state of managing knowledge is assessed. The primary questions to be addressed at this stage are: *Which* knowledge resource is the firm leveraging against the identified business issues; and *how* is it leveraging those resources?

Knowledge resources may be identified in any of three categories: knowledge capital; social capital; and infrastructure capital.

Knowledge Capital

Knowledge capital includes all the firm's tacit and explicit knowledge. In a sense, it is the "content" of the firm, from a knowledge and information perspective. Knowledge capital exists in several forms, including *embodied*, *embedded*, and *represented*. Knowledge is embodied in the minds of knowers, as well as in communities or networks of knowers. This type of knowledge, sometimes referred to as "know how," is based on the collective experience, insights, and contexts of individuals and groups of knowers. Thus, it is highly tacit and generally difficult or impossible to codify, represent, or transfer.

Knowledge capital may also be embedded in work routines, processes and procedures, job roles and responsibilities, and organization structures. Knowledge embedded in these systems is used regularly to perform tasks or work process steps at a consistently high level of quality, often by actors lacking in the expertise or knowledge to perform these tasks absent these systems.

Finally, we can identify knowledge represented in artifacts. Artifacts may include virtually anything deliberately created to serve a purpose. Therefore, paperclips, telephones, buildings, automobiles, and research reports may all be collected under the rubric, artifact. Knowledge is represented in these items in the same way it is embedded in systems (as per above). The difference is that artifacts are discrete entities, rather than processes or systems.

It is difficult, if not impossible, to draw clear, unambiguous lines in classifying knowledge as either embodied, embedded, or represented. Inevitably there is overlap. As we shall see later, this overlap is not limited to distinctions within knowledge capital—it extends to overlap among and between the three types of knowledge resource as well. Fortunately, these ambiguities do not hinder our ability to identify knowledge resources. Whether we classify a given resource as knowledge capital or social capital, embedded knowledge or represented knowledge, the important point is to identify the resource. Perhaps it is useful to consider the above categorizations as a means of prompting us to look in various places for the firm's knowledge resources, so as to identify these resources as completely as possible, rather than concern ourselves with absolute accuracy in categorizing what we find.

Social Capital

In their latest article on social capital, Nahapiet and Ghoshal (1998) provide an excellent overview of the topic as it relates to knowledge management:

> Social capital is defined as the sum of the actual and potential resources embedded within, available through, and derived from the network of relationships possessed by an individual or social unit....The central proposition of social capital theory is that networks of relationships constitute a valuable resource for the conduct of social affairs, providing their members with the collectively-owned capital, a credential which entitles them to credit, in the various senses of the word.

Social capital is multidimensional and includes some familiar attributes such as culture, trust, anticipated reciprocity, context, and informal networks. As a construct, social capital can be found in sociology literature at least as far back as 1965 [Jacobs, 1965, as cited in Nahapiet and Ghoshal (1998) et al.]. However, lately social capital has begun to receive attention from economists, including Robert Putnam (1993; 1995) and sociologists, such as Cornelia Butler Flora (1995).

As economists begin to develop new frameworks for measuring and valuing social capital, firms may well be able to do the same and incorporate this intangible dimension into balance sheets and asset measures. Certainly investors are beginning to evaluate the worth of firms on measures other than the traditional ones. For instance, Microsoft Corporation, in the third quarter of 1998, became the largest listed company in the world, based on stock market capitalization (General Electric was previously largest). Yet what are Microsoft's assets? Are the copyrights on its software products really what investors are betting on, or does it have more to do with Microsoft's knowledge resources, such as its *knowledge capital* (i.e., its whiz kids, with leader Bill Gates regarded as among the best) and its *social capital* (culture of innovation and collaborative exploration; willingness to experiment, and to fail, without fear of repercussion).

Social capital is important as a knowledge resource for the firm because it is what facilitates the creation and transfer of knowledge. Understanding the dimensions of social capital is easier due to the work of Nahapiet and Ghoshal (1998). Their framework for social capital includes three dimensions: structural; relational; and cognitive.

The structural dimension of social capital includes explication of the social networks in which employees participate. Tools such as network analysis are useful in building maps of these informal networks, based on surveys of the people who participate in them. The relational dimension is described by the level of trust among actors in the network, as well as behavioral norms, obligations, and identification with a particular group. These attributes can be assessed via surveys and qualitative interview data. The cognitive dimension explicates the shared context existing among actors in a network. This shared context can be described using qualitative interview data to detect in-group language, corporate myths, and dominant mental models in use by the actors in a network.

The above dimensions of social capital can be assessed using various tools and surveys. An understanding of these dimensions is important to the implementation of projects aimed at improving the way a firm leverages its knowledge resources, since success often hinges on the degree to which the projects are consistent and compatible with the existing culture of the firm. A closer look at each of these dimensions follows.

Infrastructure Capital

Infrastructure capital includes the firm's physical knowledge resources—LAN/WAN networks, file servers, Notes networks, Intranets, personal computer infrastructure, and applications. In short, the entire information technology infrastructure could be considered part of a firm's infrastructure capital. But it doesn't stop there. Infrastructure capital also includes the organization structure, codified (and filled) roles and responsibilities, and geographic office locations that provide physical presence in various markets. These resources are routinely leveraged by the firm to perform daily tasks, both administrative and operational.

Taken together, the three knowledge resource types—knowledge capital, social capital, and infrastructure capital—comprise nearly the entirety of what constitutes a given firm. The only things left out are financial-related elements, such as accounts receivable, owner's equity and the like, and brand capital. In some aspects, brand capital could also be considered a knowledge resource, since it exists in the minds of knowers. The difference is that these knowers (i.e., people in the market place) happen to be external to the firm's traditional boundaries.

KNOWLEDGE LEVERS

Knowledge levers describe the ways in which a firm can leverage its knowledge resources. These levers, each of which consists of an action mode and an intent (see Figure 21.1), may describe everything firms do in the name of knowledge management.

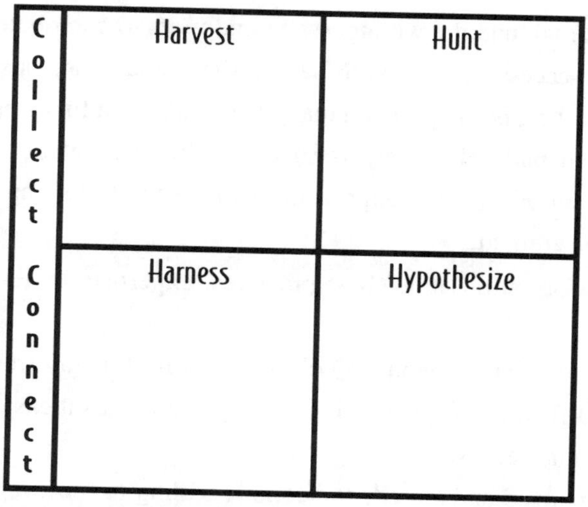

Collect	Harvest	Hunt
Connect	Harness	Hypothesize

Figure 21.1   Knowledge Levers

The action modes describe what can be done with knowledge or knowledge artifacts. Artifacts may be collected, while knowledge, being tacit, may only be connected. Firms undertake various projects aimed at deliberately collecting artifacts, or connecting knowers. These projects are undertaken with intent. When the intent is convergent, aimed at solving a particular problem or issue, we describe it as an intent to exploit. Conversely, when the aim is divergent, we describe it as an intent to explore.

The action modes crossed with the intents yield four varieties of knowledge management approaches: harvesting, hunting, harnessing, and hypothesizing. For each of these there exist archetypal examples. It should be noted, however, that in many cases the actual outcomes for any of these approaches resembles more of a hybrid approach, rather than one that may be neatly categorized in one of the above four quadrants.

Harvesting

Harvesting approaches are perhaps the most recognizable approaches to knowledge management. "Best practices" databases and "lessons learned" databases are the most obvious examples of attempts to collect artifacts with an aim to exploit them against a specific issue in the future. Online article collections are another example of the harvesting approach to knowledge management. These approaches work or do not work in varying degrees, depending upon factors such as the way in which the repositories are constructed; the ability to identify best practices as such, and then codify those practices in a meaningful way; the ease with which end users can navigate and find targeted material; and the willingness of end users to contribute information or artifacts, and then access and exploit those artifacts in addressing business issues.

In short, harvesting is an approach many firms take as a first step on the knowledge management path. However, its successful implementation and use is not necessarily a given. Harvesting approaches assume the following, none of which may be taken for granted:

- Useful information about best practices, expertise, or lessons learned is codifiable
- Once discovered, someone is willing to codify this information
- Once codified, it is organizable in a way that makes it easy for an end user to locate and retrieve
- Once organized and stored, someone is willing to retrieve it
- Once retrieved, an end user is willing to trust it and, thus, use it

Hunting

Firms sometimes collect and store data, information, or other knowledge artifacts in a database or other repository for future use. Data warehouses and competitive intelligence gathering are two examples of collections of data or information that is gathered without a specific issue or problem in mind. The value of these collections comes from further exploration of the content, in order to "see what's in there." We describe this approach as hunting, since benefit derived from these repositories relies more on serendipity than on the focused harvesting approach one might use in a best practices database.

One of the uses of data mining on large data sets is to identify trends in the data. It is not always clear which analysis will produce the most meaningful result, or even whether or not any meaningful result will be obtained. Likewise, a scan of competitive intelligence information gleaned from a software agent's foray onto the World Wide Web (or news feeds) may or may not yield additional insights into a given competitor's strategy, products, activities, etc.

Nevertheless, since data capture is now often a byproduct of many types of transaction processing, and data storage and processing costs are relatively insignificant, hunting approaches may make sense. These approaches assume that:

- Significant business value may be derived from the serendipitous discovery of meaningful trends or other information contained in a large data set.
- Large data sets may be created in a cost-effective manner (i.e., the cost of creating and analyzing the data set is more than offset by the expected benefit of doing so).
- Appropriate data mining or text mining tools and expertise are available.

Harvesting and hunting approaches both rely on collecting data, information, and knowledge artifacts, with an aim to storing them in an organized fashion that will yield future business value. Both approaches tend to rely heavily on accessible and inexpensive computing power, hence, their current popularity. Yet effective knowledge management encompasses another dimension of deliberate activities of which many firms are perhaps only beginning to take advantage. We are entering the age of *connection*.

Harnessing

Consider this example involving British Petroleum, taken from the book, *Working Knowledge* (Davenport and Prusak, 1998):

British Petroleum's [BP] Virtual Teamwork project involved nothing other than providing a desktop videoconferencing infrastructure to help people exchange knowledge across vast distances. BP experts in Italy and Alaska, for example, fixed a problem with a drill rig compressor in Latin America in a videoconference. Instead of the days it would have taken experts to fly in and solve the problem—days when oil wasn't coming out of the ground—the defect was corrected in hours.

No databases, no collections, no repositories. Here is an example of a solution that relied on connecting knowers to each other and to a problem, with an aim to exploit what the knowers know. This is an example of the power of harnessing knowledge.

Firms that undertake harnessing strategies realize that the firm has access to all the expertise needed to address many if not all of the problems and issues that arise for the firm, if only this expertise could be appropriately connected. Consider the often-cited quote from Hewlett-Packard, "If HP knew what HP knows we would be four times more profitable." This quote highlights what many other firms are now coming to realize—exploiting the knowledge of the firm's people resources is a pathway to great returns. Quality circles and other attempts to increase shop-floor employee involvement in problem solving and production improvement are other examples of harnessing (connecting to exploit) what knowers know. Effective harnessing approaches assume that:

- Significant knowledge and expertise exists among employees (or outsiders with access to the firm).
- This knowledge and expertise is highly tacit, and not readily reducible or codifiable for capture and storage in a database.
- Issues and challenges arise that, if addressed in a significantly better way, could drive meaningful business value.
- Significant improvement in the way these issues and challenges are addressed would be likely if a greater proportion of the firm's tacit expertise was brought to bear on them.
- A cultural willingness to collaboratively solve problems exists.
- There exists a means of mapping "who knows what;" and wide access to such a map is possible.

Hypothesizing

As the pace of business accelerates and the complexity of decision making increases, some firms are developing approaches to manage uncertainty and increase the richness of the decisions that are made. An example of a deliberate approach to managing uncertainty is a technique called "scenario planning." First introduced into Royal-Dutch Shell in the late 1960s, this technique is not aimed at predicting the future as most strategic planning approaches attempt to do. Rather, scenario planning aims to develop alternative scenarios of the future, based on the identified known and unknown data points at a given time. By asking a series of "what-if" questions, and then developing a course of action in the event that any one of the three or four most probable scenarios was to eventuate, Shell was able to define its operational strategy in the event of an (at that time) unprecedented oil price shock. This planning approach turned out to be invaluable.

When the oil embargo of the early 1970s produced a sixfold jump in oil prices within a year (Kleiner, 1996), Shell had already identified the early warning indicators of such a shock from a set of scenarios it created months earlier. Having detected the correctly identified, early warning signal, Shell quickly revised its refining and shipping investment and operations plans to accommodate reduced volume and different source countries, while its competitors continued to build shipping capacity that would lie idle for the next few years. This deferral of capital expenditure was worth millions to Shell, and earned them newfound status among the "big oil players."

So, how did the planners at Royal-Dutch Shell construct these prescient scenarios with their early warning indicators? Led by Ted Newland and Pierre Wack, the Shell planners introduced the technique of scenario planning. A key aspect of scenario planning is that it relies on connecting knowers with an intent to explore alternative futures. We use the term hypothesizing to describe connecting-to-explore approaches to knowledge management.

Examples of other hypothesizing approaches are perhaps more common in firms. Brainstorming is often used in meetings to generate a large quantity of ideas. The best brainstorming sessions are often those that involve participants with diverse backgrounds and some knowledge of the topic or issue being brainstormed. This notion, referred to as *requisite variety*, is a central principle of scenario planning.

A simple example of hypothesizing is also a common experience: the so-called "water cooler conversation." Here we find two or more people who happen to engage in a conversation with no predefined agenda, meeting time, or list of attendees. Since they provide for a cross-pollination of ideas and information that doesn't arise from routine transactions and meetings, these chance conversations are being encouraged by some firms, as evidenced by the presence of comfortable chairs or couches on stairwell landings and the presence of flipcharts in cafeterias.

Hypothesizing can produce new insights and breakthrough visions of value to the firm. Firms seeking to leverage knowledge resources by connecting people with the intention to explore issues or future possibilities can maximize the benefit derived from these approaches by ensuring that the following are present:

- Requisite variety—a diversity of expertise, experience, or point-of-view
- Brownian motion—increased probability of chance meetings
- Slack time—enough employee free time during the workday so that chance meetings can be used to explore ideas
- Culture—acceptance of diversity; openness to new or outlandish ideas

The Knowledge Strategy

The above sections present the various components that comprise a knowledge strategy. These components include business issues, knowledge resources, and knowledge levers.

A knowledge strategy identifies the ways in which a firm's knowledge resources may be leveraged against business issues in support of the firm's overall business strategy and objectives. A knowledge strategy is created by reviewing the firm's articulated business strategy and objectives, identifying business issues that arise from the business strategy, assessing the knowledge resources available to the firm, and defining the way in which those resources should be leveraged against the business issues to support the business strategy.

The knowledge strategy is used to define a plan of action by undertaking a gap analysis. The gap analysis involves establishing the current and desired status of the firm's knowledge resources and knowledge levers. Once the current and desired state of these is defined, approaches to bridge the difference between the two may be explored and defined as specific projects.

References

Davenport, Thomas; Prusak, Laurence (1998) *Working Knowledge*. Harvard Business School Press, Cambridge, MA.

Flora, Cornelia Butler (1995) Social capital and sustainability: Agriculture and communities in the Great Plains and Corn Belt. *Sustainable Agriculture Newsletter*, 7: 4, University of California—Davis.

Kleiner, Art (1996) *The Age of Heretics*. Currency Doubleday, New York.

Nahapiet, J.; Ghoshal, S. (1998) Social capital, intellectual capital, and the organizational advantage. *Academy of Management Review* 23 (2): 242-266.

Putnam, Robert D. (1993) *Making Democracy Work: Civic Traditions in Modern Italy*. Princeton University Press, Princeton, NJ.

————. (1995) Bowling along: America's declining social capital. *Journal of Democracy* 6:1.

CHAPTER 22

From Library to Knowledge Center: The Evolution of a Technology InfoCenter

Ellen J. Ryske
Senior Manager

and

Theresa B. Sebastian
Research Specialist

Andersen Consulting

INTRODUCTION

How does a special library adapt when the business organization it serves is virtualized; when departments "outsource" to each other under service-level agreements; and when those who need information are working at home or at customer locations? How does a physical library then best serve its customers?

Two years ago, the Technology InfoCenter, a specialized library and information service department, started a journey to evolve from a physical library to a virtual research organization with ever-increasing, value-added services. Using purchased industry information as well as the World Wide Web, the InfoCenter teamed with the organization's knowledge management initiatives, and now provides secondary research, analysis, synthesis, current awareness, and other knowledge services using both internal and external knowledge sources effectively. The InfoCenter has aligned with the associated communities of practice of the organization it serves. The research team can then build deeper knowledge of the subject area and establish a relationship with specific InfoCenter customers in order to build added awareness of its services.

This evolution has provided value both to the business organization and to the information professionals of the InfoCenter. The first step in the evolution was the subtle, but important, shift from information provider to value-added partner. This chapter illustrates a successful evolution away from a physical corporate library, and the mutual benefit when a special library teams with knowledge management initiatives in an organization.

A Case Study Defined

Although the organization was buzzing about knowledge management (KM) and a major KM initiative was under way, Technology InfoCenter was not a part of it. In this large, global consulting organization, the KM effort was initially developed and launched independently of the organization's libraries. KM focused on internal knowledge capital, and the libraries continued to focus on knowledge content external to the organization.

The organization's libraries were dispersed, largely based in major metropolitan areas. Each was funded independently and operated autonomously. Staff size and resources varied, ranging from solo professionals limited to fee-based online sources to multi-staff centers offering both electronic resources and a traditional physical collection. A few libraries specialized in subject areas that required deep expertise.

The Technology InfoCenter ("InfoCenter"), the subject of this case study, is one of these specialty libraries. Because of the fast-moving changes in information technology (IT), the InfoCenter was established to provide vital timely information services to the organization's technology specialists. Its continuing focus is the market, application, and use of IT. The InfoCenter's customers are the business integration consultants working for clients in many different industries who are located primarily in the United States, Canada, and Latin America. Similar groups are in place for Europe and Asia Pacific that provide secondary research as well as other knowledge, including electronic newsletters.

Those consultants posed many types of requests/questions. For example:

- Please provide a high-level overview of UNIX security issues.
- I need information on NT/SQL Server 6.5. Who within the organization has experience with this product?
- Find information on the market and competitors for remote software distribution tools over dial-up connections.

- Can I get a copy of ANSI Standard X.12.N and an example of #837 message format and #997 acknowledgment and response to that message?
- I have a meeting with the CEO of this company next week. I'm familiar with the company's strategic direction, but has the CEO been quoted in the press in the past six months? What do others say about him?

From its original home in an office high-rise, the InfoCenter relocated to one of the organization's Technology Parks, north of Chicago. Here, the InfoCenter occupied a large remote corner of the facility where, in a traditional library setting, it maintained a physical collection of journals and magazines, conference proceedings, books, IT-related CD-ROMs, and Internet workstations. Although the InfoCenter's primary customers were consultants specializing in IT, any employee was welcome to visit and use the collection. The InfoCenter staff would coach consultants who preferred to conduct their own research.

The majority of the InfoCenter's customers were not located at this Technology Park. The services provided to these remote clients, who communicated their requests via email or telephone, largely involved the specialty IT resources which the research staff accessed electronically. Results were delivered to the requester by email supplemented by facsimile transmission and package delivery. The cost of these specialty electronic resources prevented open access to all employees. Researchers occasionally needed the physical collection to handle an inquiry but its use was being replaced rapidly by electronic sources.

The InfoCenter was divided into three functional areas: 1) the administrative team, consisting of a manager and an administrator, who managed the business and financial aspects of the InfoCenter; 2) the librarians—the degreed information professionals, who responded to customer inquiries that required content from external information resources; 3) the help desk team who handled customer inquiries for organization-related documentation and contacts. A twelve-year employee led the help desk with significant tacit knowledge of the organization.

The help desk and research teams worked independently in separate areas of the InfoCenter. Interaction between the two groups was generally limited to redirecting customer requests that had been routed incorrectly. When a customer's request required both external and internal information, the individual receiving the call would walk over to physically hand-off the second part of the request. The teams worked cooperatively but not collaboratively, and neither handled both internal and external components of any request. Team meetings, led by the manager, were used to balance the daily workload. Allocating work across the teams was never an option. The dichotomy extended to the fees charged back for service. Research involving external content was priced at a different hourly rate than the rate charged for internal content.

The InfoCenter was, in many ways, organizationally segregated as well as physically segregated from its customers. Technology InfoCenter's customers are scattered over the Americas—and even around the world. Its physical location separated the InfoCenter staff from other residents at the Technology Park. There was little opportunity to casually interact with the other employees on site. There was no library, research, or help desk professional community within the organization with which they could affiliate. All of these factors imbued a sense of isolation and exclusion.

As far as professional advancement within the organization, there was no formal career model established for secondary researchers. This meant there was no guarantee of consistency with other libraries or research groups for positions, skill requirements, compensation, or professional education. The fledgling KM organization was pursuing a career model for KM professionals, but the librarian and researcher skill domains were only just being considered for inclusion.

The IT specialty community served by the InfoCenter had sprouted an enthusiastic and successful KM initiative. This KM team collected and catalogued internal knowledge capital, launched communities of practice, and networked with other KM groups across the organization. Two years ago, Technology InfoCenter became a part of the KM team for IT, bringing together both the external and internal knowledge infrastructure and expertise for the IT specialty area. The link between InfoCenters and KM, while embryonic two years ago, has evolved into a standard operating procedure today as other specialty groups are organized similarly, and a network of all the organization's libraries is forming under the leadership of the overall KM sponsor.

For Technology InfoCenter, integration with KM triggered a strategic shift from "library" to "virtual research center." This shift provided increased value to the IT consulting organization as well as benefits to the InfoCenter team itself. A powerful way to communicate the InfoCenter's strategic—yet in many ways subtle—change is to describe the shifts that resulted:

from *cost center*   to *value-added center*
from *offering a service*   to *meeting the needs of customers*
from *information provider*   to *knowledge partner*

The evolution began with these modifications in mindset, attitude, and perspective, and resulted in actions to partner better with the customer to add value. Figure 22.1 summarizes the qualities that transitioned the InfoCenter from library to knowledge center.

InfoCenter as Library	InfoCenter as Knowledge Center
Library/Librarian	Virtual Service/ Project Chief Knowledge Officer (CKO) and Knowledge Partner
Provide External or Internal Information	Best Information (External and Internal) with Perspective and Analysis Knowledge Projects Current Awareness Other Knowledge Services
Charge-by-Information Type	Measure Value
Segregated	Integrated with Other Knowledge Managers and Experts
Externally-Directed Group	Self-Directed Group
No Career Development Model within Organization	Career Development Model Defined within Organization

Figure 22.1 Transitional Qualities

LIBRARY/LIBRARIAN → VIRTUAL SERVICE/ PROJECT CKO AND KNOWLEDGE PARTNER

Part of the InfoCenter's self-defined role was to provide a place—a library—that offered traditional services such as ordering and routing materials, a collection of periodicals, a reference and circulating book collection, and workstations enabling access to CD-ROM resources and the Internet. Included in the InfoCenter's services were quick reference, research services, and the help desk. With a renewed focus on the customer, the InfoCenter began a critical reevaluation of each service.

The InfoCenter's customers use email, voice mail, and the organization Intranet extensively. Project teams are typically located at client sites, not the consulting offices. Since most of the IT consultants are spread over a wide geographic area, most customers never visited the InfoCenter. Even those consultants based at the same facility as the InfoCenter work at client sites most of the time. Visitors to the InfoCenter mainly seemed to be new employees who needed temporary access to a computer.

In terms of its primary collection, the InfoCenter concentrated on selected IT industry and market analysts. Whenever possible, electronic access for researchers was obtained for these materials. With physical representations of knowledge, physical access is needed, but a physical library is not a factor in the successful use of these electronic materials. In short, the physical space was costly, and not used by the majority of InfoCenter's customers. As Davenport and Prusak (1993) point out, the value of the physical corporate library has waned with changes in work style—few workers have time to browse library shelves, even on their lunch hour since they work through lunch, and today more and more workers are telecommuting.

Any question about Technology InfoCenter's physical library vanished after a quick survey of a few members of the senior management group. Supportive comments on secondary research and current awareness activities were balanced with this one-word comment about the physical library itself: *anachronism*.

It took almost one year to relocate the InfoCenter and change the cost structure for its space. In the interim, a project team needing a work area rented out half the InfoCenter's space for four months. The resulting funds were used to purchase additional IT information sources. The InfoCenter group now works in the same open office environment, using the same cubicle layout, as consulting professionals and everyone else at the Technology Park. A small storage room contains a collection of periodicals and the InfoCenter's scanner, facsimile machine, and a workstation with a CD-ROM tower for accessing historical materials and IT reference discs. The InfoCenter's new location is much closer to the KM group, consultants, and project teams who are working in the office.

The shift away from a traditional library also impacted staffing at the InfoCenter. For example, one administrator was dedicated to routing periodicals, delivering documents, and purchasing books. The position contributed clerical cost-savings, but gave the InfoCenter a clerical image and did not take advantage of the InfoCenter's unique competencies. The administrative position was eliminated and the tasks transferred to the organization's executive assistants. Individual subscriptions eliminated the need for routing and new Web-based solutions, such as CARL Uncover and

Amazon.com, facilitated document delivery and book ordering. The funds created by the position's elimination were used to add more IT information sources, which improved the overall value of the InfoCenter to its customers.

Another example of the effects on staffing is how the Help Desk function had grown from two to three full-time personnel but requests for distributing internal documents were down, probably because of the increasingly successful electronic delivery provided by the new KM infrastructure. Decreased demand suggested that this particular service had lost its value to customers who now had self-service channels to obtain this material. The Help Desk as a separate function was discontinued. The roles were converted to research positions that provided a value to customers that exceeded the incremental cost, and eliminated the InfoCenter's problematic dichotomy in providing internal and external information to a customer.

One member of the Help Desk team opted to remain with the InfoCenter in a research role and increased her skills in using external resources since she had previously focused on internal information. Correspondingly, the other researchers increased their proficiency with internal knowledge repositories. Customers now receive a complete response that integrates both internal knowledge capital and external information, and researchers have the satisfaction of handling a request completely. Coincidentally, in the year since many of these changes were effected, the InfoCenter's turnover rate was zero, except for one new hire who wanted a more traditional library setting.

Along with eliminating the lower value activities inherent in maintaining a conventional lending library, Technology InfoCenter reassessed its high value-added services. What were its core competencies and unique capabilities that enabled it to provide value to its customers and—more broadly—the entire organization?

Again, an important clue was discovered in feedback received from senior management. These high-profile leaders were enthusiastic about the InfoCenter's ability to effectively identify information; choose high-quality information sources; analyze and evaluate material; synthesize and summarize key points; and distribute new information about topics of interest on a regular basis. At times, consultants also wanted the InfoCenter to help them take the next steps beyond simply obtaining information; they wanted the InfoCenter to use their extensive network of contacts to help them save time.

Unsolicited comments during this time offered additional insight. One customer, working on a project about the role of the Chief Information Officer (CIO) in Fortune 500 companies, said to his researcher: "You are our CIO." In another instance, a researcher was told: "It was just like you were part of our project team." Consultants valued researchers as virtual members of their teams in the role of knowledge experts.

The details of the InfoCenter's value proposition and marketing messages are described in the next section. Some of these ideas have roots in KM literature, but all were customized for this particular organization. The services demanded by the InfoCenter's customers require the most complex and sophisticated skills of information professionals—and happily match the type of work that the information professionals thrive on!

Provide External *or* Internal Information → Best Information (External *and* Internal) with Perspective

The mission of KM for an IT group is "to provide the right information, in the right way, at the right time, to consultants needing IT knowledge around the world." Clearly, the InfoCenter could contribute key components to that vision and that of the organization to have the best people with knowledge capital.

The organization's CEO was quoted in the press last year as saying, "...our objective is to arm every man and woman in this organization with as much information as we can practically gather...I'm going to measure success by, did we pull that off? Did we get it in their fingertips?"

The InfoCenter aligned perfectly with this objective since it was in the business of putting information at the consultants' fingertips everyday. To articulate that into a specific value proposition required in-depth discussions with KM professionals who did not have library backgrounds. This process helped spotlight the InfoCenter's unique competencies and articulate clearly, for the first time, the group's activities in terms of value-added, rather than services provided. The new value proposition formed the nucleus of a new InfoCenter marketing and communications plan.

Technology InfoCenter's Value Proposition and Key Marketing Messages

Professional researchers provide better results because they have knowledge of more information sources, better skills in using a variety of information tools, access to additional information sources, are networked with content experts, networked with other researchers within and outside the organization, and use

professional experience and perspective to analyze the results. The InfoCenter has access to multiple services from several leading IT industry analysts. These are costly services whose access is subscription based. The vendors' pricing model is such that organization-wide open access is often impossible, and there is no public domain, free access to these materials. The InfoCenter's subscription allows selected use of material on consulting and internal projects. An information professional understands the available sources and how they can be distributed and used. This provides a practical, viable option for consultants who need this information occasionally.

Professional researchers are more efficient in obtaining results because they have ready access to information sources, deep skills from extensive daily use of similar tools, and the benefit of some unique tools designed for specialty-advanced information searches. The Technology InfoCenter has invested in specialized tools for information searching. Researchers have in-depth skill in searching from experience, professional education, and specialized training.

Professional researchers enable the project team to offload information projects to those who can do it better and more efficiently, so the project team can focus its resources on serving the client doing what they do best. The Technology InfoCenter increased staffing in order to handle longer-term projects related to IT issues and knowledge activities. Since requests do not arrive at a predictable or consistent rate, this added capacity helps improve customer service during peak times. During slower periods this extra capacity allows researchers to tackle long-term projects, which not only helps the customer but also deepens the researcher's knowledge of that subject area.

VALUE PROPOSITION EXAMPLES

To bring the value proposition to life, these everyday examples are offered:

Example 1: Better Results

A project team was developing a proposal based on a particular service—and so was a major competitor. The project team contacted the InfoCenter for information about the competitor's strategy. Using the World Wide Web, a researcher easily found the competitor's Web site that would help the project team understand how the competitor positioned this service, and their experience, in a very positive light. The researcher also checked several IT analyst services and identified a report from a well-respected source that presented a more balanced review of the competitor's service, highlighting both positive aspects and drawbacks. Although the project team could have searched the World Wide Web, the more leveling viewpoint would have been unavailable to them without the InfoCenter's involvement.

Example 2: Better Results

For a presentation, an InfoCenter researcher was asked to find the camera model preferred by a renowned photographer. After searching the World Wide Web for this information without success, the researcher executed a single, complex search algorithm in a sophisticated online database service. The answer appeared in a one-year-old Sunday feature article from an Oregon city newspaper. In this case, an experienced and skilled information professional was able to construct an efficient search strategy and to choose the most cost-effective service in which to run that search. Most consultants would be unaware of the various online services available, uncomfortable composing such a query, and would probably require multiple attempts at significantly greater cost and without getting the same result.

Example 3: More Efficient

In response to a request, a researcher identified an excellent report with solid material. Only a portion of the $5,000 report was relevant, however. The InfoCenter had invested in a specialized information access tool that allowed the researcher to provide only a section of this report at a prorated cost of $300.

In another example, a caller wanted more information about a cryptic slide that had come from an unknown internal presentation. The researcher tried a couple of likely internal databases without success. Stumped, the researcher tried the speed search tool that was built by the KM for the IT group's technical team. This tool allows an advanced search capability intended only for "power" users, and it enables the researchers to search a collection of over thirty of the organization's Intranet databases simultaneously instead of one-by-one. With this tool, researchers can scan databases faster and more comprehensively than consultants can on the self-service Intranet. In this case, the researcher keyed in a few unusual phrases from the slide and did find the presentation. Admittedly, some luck was involved, since the item had not yet moved into the larger electronic storage repositories that are not directly accessible or indexed.

Example 4: Offload Projects

The InfoCenter fielded a request for information about project management software. The researcher identified the leading software packages and, after conferring with the customer, contacted five vendors for more specific and detailed information about fitting the software into a specific environment and set of requirements. This illustrates the value of timesavings achievable by outsourcing information projects.

Aware of the importance of tacit knowledge, to bring even more value, the InfoCenter began developing relationships with the technology communities of practice. These communities, another linkage with the KM group, provide a structure for the organization's experts in all technology areas. In tapping these communities, the InfoCenter uses the organization's expertise, builds stronger relationships with these experts, and becomes better integrated with KM and the business. The value proposition of the Technology InfoCenter aligns with the six characteristics that give information economic value: "... accuracy, timeliness, accessibility, engagement, applicability, and rarity" (Davenport, 1997).

Looking at value from that perspective, additional examples come to mind:

Accuracy

Researchers have learned to distinguish the respected IT industry analysts from those without the same track record. In some cases, the researcher probes multiple sources as data sometimes varies significantly between sources—for example, the size and demographics of the electronic commerce marketplace.

A very detailed example resonates with Davenport's statement that "information staff should also consider other things that affect accuracy, such as resolution of measurements (1997)." While looking for the market size of an IT product line, a researcher found data from a reliable source, but for the Canadian market stated in Canadian dollars. Using a currency conversion site on the World Wide Web, she converted to United States dollars using the rate in effect at the time of the report. She also noted the markets were not interchangeable, of course, but this was the best (only) information available.

Timeliness

Recognizing that an acceptably "timely" response depends on the customer's context and requirement, a question about responsiveness is part of the feedback requested by the InfoCenter. In a fast-paced consulting business, customers can't always provide lead-time, but sometimes the deadline can be negotiated. Therefore, timeliness depends on how well the InfoCenter has met the negotiated deadline, and how responsively the request was addressed initially. The ten-month average for timeliness: 4.7 on a scale of 5.0, an outstanding result.

Accessibility

Accessibility is what the InfoCenter is all about, providing information that may not be accessible to all consultants for cost reasons, and that may not be accessible at all for some consultants who are temporarily offline.

Engagement

Per Davenport's description, engagement deals with presenting and formatting information. Aside from basics such as choosing email versus fax delivery, each researcher is adept at formatting, fonts, colors, collapsible sections of text, and hyperlinks to present results to the customer's best advantage. Summarization is also a key part of how the researcher delivers information to the customer effectively. As one customer said, "Beautifully compiled and summarized. It's great to see an actual answer instead of a pile of articles. Keep up the good work."

Applicability

Applicability is being able to apply information to the problem at hand. The InfoCenter scores high in this category since it provides custom answers to specific questions. Therefore, information is gathered and customized to be applicable to each particular situation. This characteristic is enhanced by the InfoCenter's standard practice of insisting upon interviewing the requestor to understand the context, and setting the parameters of the transactions before starting work.

Rarity

Aside from its access to uncommon information sources, as part of some vendor contracts, the InfoCenter has access to industry analysts at several respected organizations. The ability to speak directly with industry analysts is a unique capability, highly valued by consultants who are dedicated to top-quality client service. Just recently, an InfoCenter researcher scheduled a conference call between a leader in the organization and an industry analyst to gain additional perspective in interpreting the IT industry's history with a particular operating system.

A colleague from KM summarized Technology InfoCenter's value proposition this way in a memo:

> Access to the best and most current technology information allows us to deliver consistently greater value to our clients. It is also an important aspect in creating new technology knowledge.
>
> Without the benefit of the Technology InfoCenter, individual consultants must conduct research on their own. There are many disadvantages to this approach. Individuals cannot be given access, in any practical manner, to expensive and complex resources such as online services, analyst reports, and subscription-based materials. Individuals are less efficient than professional researchers at retrieving the information they desire. Individuals are less effective, due to lack of experience, at understanding the viewpoint of specific sources of external information.

The InfoCenter stated its message of value. But how would it determine that it had delivered as promised? Were customers satisfied? If so, how satisfied? Was value delivered? If so, how much value?

CHARGE BY INFORMATION TYPE → MEASURE VALUE

Prior to the shift from "provider of information" to "provider of value," the InfoCenter measured success by the quality and quantity of its external and internal knowledge resources and its volume of calls. These measures are a good start, but seem to fall into the category of "what can we measure" instead of "what do we want to measure." The desired type of measure—value added—aligns with the KM literature that suggests KM measures are really business measures, such as cycle time improvement, quality, business growth, and proposal success rates. However, if the InfoCenter claimed credit for some of these business measures, that rationale would not be credible to senior management or other groups, since the InfoCenter's contributions are but one of many factors influencing these outcomes. So the InfoCenter kept thinking.

In the free market, price helps to set value and balance supply with demand. The InfoCenter had a multi-tiered pricing model that complicated value measurement. Two groups used the InfoCenter heavily and both sponsored the InfoCenter on an annual basis. Customers from these two sponsoring groups were not charged per request, so customers viewed services as free. Therefore, at that time, price as a measure of value was limited. The lack of a consistent financial measure diminished the value of the InfoCenter in the minds of senior management—the level of revenue charged back to customers was a small percentage of costs.

In discussing KM value, O'Dell and Grayson (1998) use the analogy of early quantum mechanics theorists—these physics pioneers knew the atom was there, even if they could not see it. Similarly, the value provided by the InfoCenter is there, even if it cannot be seen or measured directly. The usual challenges of measurement are further complicated because, for the InfoCenter, any measurements had to be practical and simple to survive the realities of a very busy, sometimes frantic, workload for both the InfoCenter and its customers.

Once More, How Could the InfoCenter Measure Value?

The InfoCenter decided to simply ask each customer for feedback on its services at the time of delivery. Just as "beauty is in the eye of the beholder," likewise, the value of knowledge is in its user. The complexity of measuring knowledge value is that it can never be evaluated independently of the context in which it is used (Davenport, 1997). Instead of trying to analyze the context of each request, the InfoCenter finessed this issue by letting the customer declare the value received, automatically including the customer's entire context in the value assessment. The call tracking system was modified by the KM for the IT technical team. A short email survey is sent when a researcher completes a research call.

Knowing how busy its customers are, the InfoCenter's design principles for the feedback message were that the survey would be quick and easy to complete, yet still provide enough information to understand the level of value delivered. In the first ten months, with over 2,000 calls logged, 500+ feedback requests were returned by customers. At approximately twenty-five percent, this was a much better return rate than was initially expected. In contrast, a similar feedback survey for materials delivered by the KM self-service infrastructure, like other surveys, received less than a five-percent response rate.

A rating is requested on four accounts: quality; timeliness; value; and an overall rating. Each question has a "radio button" format so the customer only needs one click per measure. The customer can elaborate in a comment area, and many customers do.

An interesting point was discussed in the design of the survey. The only question that is under the direct control of a researcher is timeliness—that is, responsiveness. The measure for quality of response depends not just upon the researcher's skills, knowledge, and tools, but upon the extent of information sources at hand. Sometimes, information is simply not available, or the question may be unanswerable, or a seemingly simple question can be amazingly time-consuming—all facts that are quite familiar to any information professional, but that may not be obvious to the customer. The quality question is, therefore, carefully worded to ask if the customer was confident all sources were checked, rather than asking about the quality of the answer, but it's likely some customers still respond based upon the answer itself.

This systematic feedback provides insight into the actual value delivered in the words and perspective of the InfoCenter's customers, and is an excellent way to communicate to senior management why the InfoCenter is important to business every single day. It helps researchers gain insight into how customers perceive their service and ideas on how, if necessary, to modify their approach. Each researcher views only his/her own feedback as it arrives. Customer comments are used plentifully in performance appraisals to illustrate how individual's goals of customer service and satisfaction have been achieved.

While the feedback has been overwhelmingly positive, the InfoCenter staff was absolutely and courageously prepared for any and all feedback. In the first year of tracking, the question that asks, "Would you use the InfoCenter again?" produced a rating of 4.6 on a 5-point scale, another excellent result.

A second measure of value required a change in the group's pricing model. Pricing was streamlined so that all callers were charged one hourly rate. Previously, six different rates were used depending upon the type of information delivered, and other factors. As mentioned previously, some callers were not charged at all. This new model better matches costs with the services provided to projects, and everyone involved gained a deeper understanding of the value provided since most projects have proven to be willing to pay.

In one year, revenue increased 300% as a result of this collection of charges!

Note that while the hourly rate helps illustrate the InfoCenter's value, in some instances customers, especially new customers, are not familiar with the value proposition and balk at being charged by an internal group. This is counterproductive to the organization overall, so the pricing approach may be changed again in the future. Other value measurements are being considered, including the percentage of repeat customers.

To summarize, discussing the InfoCenter's benefits in terms of customer value—in the customers' words—has proven to be a powerful method of assessing and communicating about Technology InfoCenter.

Segregated → Integrated with Other Knowledge Managers and Experts

In addition to being physically separated in a library setting, organizationally the InfoCenter was not linked with the consultants or the other knowledge groups in the IT specialty area. In joining KM, this started to change.

A good example of synergy is how the InfoCenter teamed with the Americas customer support group within KM. This group had provided financial sponsorship and now stepped up to help market and communicate the InfoCenter's services. Together, KM and the InfoCenter collaborated to create a marketing plan, hone the value proposition and resulting marketing messages, and arrange for a message from the top operational executive for IT in the Americas that explained the InfoCenter's mission and value. This message was delivered to 5,000 of the InfoCenter's current and potential customers. During the year, KM published two success stories in monthly newsletters to remind this audience again and again about the Technology InfoCenter.

Another benefit of joining KM for IT was that this group had a solid programming unit. Technical support was turned over to these professional system developers. This resulted in straightening out the networking and security of a news-feed database that was causing problems, implementing a daily profiling feature for that news-feed, creating a special speed search tool just for the InfoCenter, and numerous major and minor changes to the call tracking system. More importantly, relying on these developers allowed the InfoCenter to outsource these functions and not worry about them, since the InfoCenter did not have the skills or mission to grow these technical specialties.

Being visible within the KM group created new opportunities for the InfoCenter staff. One researcher was asked to participate in a six-month, organization-wide task force to refine internal searching tools. Another researcher served on the advisory group for a second task force reviewing all information sources purchased by the organization. Two groups asked the InfoCenter to handle their research operations. The InfoCenter was asked by the leading internal community of practice to participate in two important projects. The InfoCenter's participation in these initiatives not only provided direct value towards specific project goals and deliverables, but helped the InfoCenter get out and team with other groups, provided a practical research perspective, and developed a deeper understanding of the organization and how it works.

In other examples, two other internal InfoCenters specializing in IT are located in France and Australia. The three locations have to date operated independently but, as part of the KM for IT group, have now started to network with each other and exchange best practices. The InfoCenter will soon start to take advantage of the same subject matter experts that the KM group has cultivated in seventeen internal communities of practice.

Davenport and Prusak (1998) provide this insight:

> If there is no system in place to locate the most appropriate knowledge resources, employees make do with what is most easily available. That knowledge may be reasonably good, but in today's competitive environment reasonably good is not good enough.

The KM for IT group's vision to "provide the right information, in the right way, at the right time" to consultants can only be achieved with the InfoCenter. The other KM functions focus on the self-service knowledge infrastructure, high-quality internal knowledge capital, and orchestrating internal experts. Technology InfoCenter has a unique depth of understanding of the IT market analysts as well as other external information sources, and is organized to assist consultants with all kinds of knowledge resources using human guidance and expertise that is personalized to each customer.

EXTERNALLY-DIRECTED GROUP → SELF-DIRECTED GROUP

The InfoCenter became increasingly self-managed, and now operates as a self-directed work team. This shift was due, in part, to the shift to a customer focus and, in part, to the style of the KM group. Several of the comparisons Fisher (Fisher and Fisher, 1998) makes between self-directed work teams and traditional organizations provide a good summary of the characteristics of the new InfoCenter: customer-driven versus management-driven; whole business focus versus function focus; purpose—and achievement—emphasis versus problem-solving emphasis; continuous improvements versus incremental improvements; self-controlled versus management-controlled; values/principle-based versus policy/procedure-based.

Here are some of the changes that achieved this shift in operations. First, a process change was made to define objective- and customer-based goals at the beginning of a researcher's performance appraisal period. Instead of wondering what the manager's assessment would be at the end of the period, these well-defined expectations helped each information professional target effective day-to-day operating performance and helped schedule professional development (training) activities.

Performance goals also include quality of service. To start, the quality measures were admittedly rough; the measures consisted of a goal for "unsolicited" spontaneous thanks from pleased customers, plus results from an ad hoc survey. As the feedback system was established, quality was redefined in terms of customer feedback. Goals are now aligned with pleasing and delighting the customer, not just pleasing the InfoCenter's manager.

The researchers divided into small teams, and selected IT specialty areas of focus that were consistent with the internal IT communities of practice. For example, one team chose to focus upon electronic commerce and advanced IT research, and another team selected networking. Each experienced researcher was encouraged to work with the KM professionals in his/her community of practice to learn more about internal knowledge capital and IT experts, to build professional relationships with consulting practitioners, and by taking advantage of advanced training to deepen skills in the specific IT subject areas. Researchers deepened their understanding of the business organization's processes and approaches via these ongoing relationships.

These specialty areas were incorporated into the InfoCenter's research assignment process. Calls are classified based on the community of practice and routed to the appropriate research team automatically. While the realities of a small team and high demand still require manual re-balancing, when possible, work is assigned with these specialties in mind.

Researchers have internalized the InfoCenter's major operating principles of outstanding customer service, productivity, unique information sources and tools, and reasonable prices. Each researcher uses his/her own professional judgment in applying these principles. For example, while the InfoCenter's policy is to charge for all time spent in fulfilling a request, researchers apply these operating principles and use judgment to determine exactly how much to charge each customer. If a researcher did not feel "up to speed" on the subject and required extra time to complete the request, he/she may only charge part of the time spent. In practice, most researchers decided not to charge for most calls less than fifteen minutes to develop positive relationships with customers for future business. ("I'm supposed to charge you for this, but it didn't take long….I'll catch up with you next time…") These decisions are guided not only by operating principles, but also by individual's performance and quality goals. The researchers as a group have "ownership" of key operating practices as well—they prioritize which information sources to purchase, and establish the pricing policies for document delivery requests.

A key success factor in becoming self-directed was building the researcher's confidence that their services were indeed highly valued. The KM group helped indicate that what an information professional might consider straightforward or even "easy" cannot be done by most people – and certainly not within a tight time-frame or budget. Customer feedback helped the researchers see the value provided, and reinforced this point time and time again. Here are some examples taken from several feedback surveys:

> *Last week we were scrambling, pulling together and designing the presentation. We'd never have found such good stuff so quickly. The client has agreed to begin the pre-implementation steps of our recommendation. Again, my sincere thanks for a job well done. I'll keep you in mind for future research.*

> *You were able to compile in a matter of days, the data I have been researching for several weeks. I'm impressed and pleased with the results.*

> *I am extremely impressed with the amount and quality [of the] information you found on my research topic...Again, I am extremely impressed with your professionalism and the quality of information that you provided.*

> *Great response and service. The data was a compelling component of the presentation.*

> *I was amazed at how quickly you got the information and that you found the exact article that I had referenced. I was impressed.*

> *I'm sorry it has taken me this long to get back with you, but I just wanted to say thanks. The information you sent is just what I was looking for and it has been tremendously helpful in getting me up to speed...*

Thanks a lot for all your help...I apologize for not getting back to you on Friday, but the information you provided was perfect!

You are awesome!! You make us look like heroes when this stuff is found. Great job.

As in the past, I had great success for this particular request...you ask the right questions up front to narrow down the search criteria.

...very knowledgeable on the subject. There was an extremely quick response on what I would call "a needle in a haystack mission." Thanks!

...courteous and professional...able to ask me some questions and with the limited feedback I was able to give, you were still able to handle my request and find what I needed. I will definitely use the InfoCenter again and also reference the InfoCenter to others.

Thanks for the great service! It makes my job so much easier!

The InfoCenter put me in touch with a key contact that led to finding the firm resource I was looking for. It was a great help.

The information provided was exactly what I was looking for. The analysis and additional help added to the presentation we made to the Management Committee.

InfoCenter is a cost effective research resource that I will continue to use to leverage work for my projects.

Excellent response, no matter how ridiculous the question. Always willing to go the extra step or 10 if required.

The result? In two years, the group has become increasingly self-managed and self-confident. Recently, the group initiated, negotiated, and mutually agreed to redesign their call management process—and implemented a two-week pilot period to test their ideas. The change was explained in terms of benefits for both researchers and customers. It's hard work, but fun and rewarding, to be part of a customer-driven, continuously improving, motivated, and self-managed team!

No Career Development Model within Organization → A Career Development Model Defined within Organization

While the organization had library professionals and researchers for many years, as a support service, information professionals did not have a formal career track as the consultants did. Networking of information professionals across geographic locations was strong and effective, and occasionally transfers occurred, but no articulated or consistent job role, pay structure, training curriculum, or career path was offered officially.

To compound the problem, library and research professionals had no natural fit in the organization, and worked for any number of various internal roles. Unlike finance with a CFO, or human resources with a human resources executive, research had no senior executive to provide leadership or organization. Almost universally, library and research professionals reported to groups who did not understand or fully appreciate the services provided and skills required.

Aligning with KM, the library and research professionals participated in defining a new set of KM and KM-research skill tracks for information professionals. These tracks followed the same structure for skill definitions, skill sets, and career tracks as the rest of the organization. So, for the KM and KM-research skill tracks, the human resources terminology, tools, and framework are the same as for consultant skill tracks.

The KM-research skill track uses many skills that were defined for the consultants. For example, professional qualities such as writing, initiative, confidence, negotiation, and teamwork are also critical for researchers, as well as success factors such as confidence, integrity, and self-starter. As a side note, a meaningful milestone in this process was adding an entirely new professional quality for everyone in the organization: knowledge sharing.

Technology InfoCenter customized the career track and selected key skill areas, such as business operations, knowledge of the IT industry, and secondary research. Proficiency in the professional qualities of knowledge sharing, negotiation, oral communications, professional relationships, and teamwork/collaboration are also high priorities. Each researcher is assessed annually on proficiency in these skills and offered the chance for professional development through training, self-study, professional associations, conferences, and job experience.

The KM-research skill track was sponsored by the senior executive in charge of KM and is another important advantage of aligning with the KM initiative.

Establishment of the skill track was a major accomplishment and brought consistency and opportunity with others in similar functions across the entire organization. The rollout of this skill track formally acknowledged research as a valued function, and the researchers as professionals in their own right.

To support the skill track, a specific training curriculum was established with recommended training, workshops, conferences, and self-studies, providing a road map as an individual progresses and gains experience. The InfoCenter customized this curriculum by experience level, and used these skill dimensions: secondary research; IT; IT specialty areas; KM; and professional skills. This matrix was created to ensure that each area was considered in developing a solid training plan. Each year, the training plans of the individuals in the InfoCenter are balanced to ensure representation at key IT, research, and KM events while furthering the skill development of each individual researcher.

Like everyone else in the organization, each researcher prepares a "professional development plan" outlining each job experience, course, and self-study needed to develop knowledge and skill. After review with his/her career counselor, the researcher is then responsible for enrolling and making it happen! Time and expenses are paid by a training budget. In the last year, individuals have attended KM workshops, electronic commerce workshops, external conferences by Gartner Group and Giga (leading IT industry analysts), networking self-studies, plus current awareness reading, not to mention professional association conferences such as the Special Libraries Association, Society for Competitive Intelligence, and Digital Libraries.

One more advantage of the transition to KM has been the opportunity to pursue training programs outside the traditional library scope. While it is important to continually update search skills and attend information vendor training to keep current with ways to navigate the data in a cost-effective way, the added choices that are now available are amazing and offer a rare opportunity for a researcher to be sponsored for training as diverse as Lotus Notes Development, project management, and effective presentations.

The career track has also given visibility and added understanding to the rest of the organization about the research role, resulting in added career opportunities. For example, one researcher transferred from the InfoCenter to another group to investigate and report on new technology applications. Another moved into an organization-wide role, directing the acquisition of all globally sponsored information sources.

In addition, the KM group understands the role of the InfoCenter, the education and experience needed to do the job, and appreciates the results! With a common customer and complementary services, KM and research have aligned in the IT area, and also throughout the organization, to mutual benefit and improved customer service.

CONCLUSION

An organization's information requirements in the new knowledge economy are not limited to that contained in well-known external sources. While external content expertise is a valuable component of KM, it is not the whole story. Organizations thrive on "living" knowledge capital—tacit knowledge in the heads of its employees and the explicit internal knowledge capital produced as an outcome of knowledge sharing. Indeed, some cognoscenti (Davenport and Prusak, 1998; Stewart, 1997) contend that an organization's knowledge is the only true competitive advantage in the knowledge age.

The InfoCenter's mission requires partnering with the global knowledge management community—subject matter experts, knowledge integrators, knowledge base administrators, systems developers, knowledge champions, and the comprehensive global knowledge center network of the organization. It's the inter-relationships in this complex network of KM functions that provide the context and framework to enable the InfoCenter to contribute its greatest value.

The transition from library to knowledge center is not yet complete. The first part of the change journey, as described here, was to become customer-driven and to integrate into the rest of the organization. We abandoned traditional library services that were of lower value to this customer base, in favor of strengthening our virtual research capabilities—a highly valued service. We reallocated the budget from physical space and facilities to additional information sources and tools to help us better serve the needs of our (internal) technology clients around the globe. We asked for customer feedback and took action. We are valued and respected, and manage ourselves to best serve our customers.

There are three key points from this case study. The evolution from library to knowledge center provided value both to the InfoCenter's internal customers and to the information professionals of the InfoCenter. The first step in the evolution is the subtle, but important, shift in the InfoCenter's definition of its role—the shift from information provider to value-added partner. A corporate library can benefit by teaming with other knowledge management initiatives in the organization, and those initiatives can benefit by teaming with the library.

References

Davenport, T. H. (1997) *Information Ecology: Mastering the Information and Knowledge Environment.* New York: Oxford University Press.

Davenport, T. H.; Prusak, L. (1993) Blow Up the Corporate Library. *International Journal of Information Management.* 13(6), 405-412.

Davenport, T. H.; Prusak, L. (1998) *Working Knowledge: How Organizations Manage What They Know.* Boston: Harvard Business School Press.

Fisher, K.; Fisher, M. D. (1998) *The Distributed Mind: Achieving High Performance Through the Collective Intelligence of Knowledge Work Teams.* New York: Amacom.

O'Dell, C.; Grayson, C. J., Jr. (1998) *If Only We Knew What We Know.* New York: The Free Press.

Stewart, T. A. (1997) *Intellectual Capital: The New Wealth of Organizations.* New York: Doubleday.

CHAPTER 23

Knowledge Management in the Health Sciences

Prudence W. Dalrymple

Dean, GSLIS

Dominican University

INTRODUCTION

This chapter describes the evolution of knowledge management techniques within the health science environment. It describes and examines tools developed to analyze and disseminate the findings of medical research. In particular, I will examine the growth and influence of evidence-based medicine as a specific instance of the management of knowledge in a scientific and professional field, as distinct from the corporate sector. The field of health sciences encompass medicine as well as allied health and health administration. My primary emphasis here is on clinical medicine, which includes both researches in clinical medicine and the application of research findings to patient care.

DEFINING KNOWLEDGE MANAGEMENT IN THE CORPORATE SETTING

Knowledge management in corporate settings focuses on eliciting the knowledge possessed by various workers within the corporate environment, and on identifying and capturing data that can be used for competitive intelligence, data that are not even written down, let alone published through traditional channels. As Broadbent (1998) states: knowledge management is "the purposeful management processes which capture often personal and contextual information that can be used for the organization's benefit." Knowledge management is about enhancing the use of organizational knowledge through sound practices of information management, and organizational learning. Its purpose is to deliver value to the business.

> It rests on two foundations: utilizing and exploiting the organization's information (which needs to be managed for this to occur); and second, the application of peoples' competencies, skills, talents, thoughts, ideas, intuitions, commitments, motivations, and imaginations (Harari, 1994).

In corporate settings, the goal of knowledge management is an improvement in the bottom line, the creation of a new line of products and services, or an increase in competitive advantage.

DEFINING KNOWLEDGE MANAGEMENT IN THE HEALTH SCIENCES

The term knowledge management has been used throughout the health science literature where it is often linked with the notion of knowledge work. Knowledge work uses professional intellect in activities, harnessing individual and external knowledge to produce outputs characterized by information content (Davis, 1991). Knowledge management, particularly in the academic medical setting, can transform the scientific communication process, potentially placing ownership and control back into the hands of the scientific community. It may also close the gap between research faculty and students and integrate the library into research and education programs in a significant way. Knowledge work is clearly about the acquisition, creation, packaging, application, or reuse of knowledge. In clinical medicine, the goal of knowledge management is improved patient care (Lucier, 1992).

The Welch Medical Library at the Johns Hopkins Medical Center has defined knowledge management this way:

> ...knowledge management represents a collaborative enterprise in which scientists and the library work together to develop and maintain knowledge bases and derivative information products. It encompasses the entire information life cycle and moves the library and librarians to a point closer to the creation of knowledge through collaboration (Lucier, 1992).

Knowledge management is part of knowledge work, linking libraries and librarians in the creation of knowledge *products*, not just provision of information *services*.

> To build effective tools for scientific communication, libraries need to be deeply involved in the creation and management of new knowledge

developed at their institutions. Helping researchers locate published knowledge does not provide sufficient insight into the functional requirements of tools for knowledge work....the library must be charged with the responsibility for finding and/or building tools for managing knowledge. Librarians must be constantly evaluating new products in light of their clients' information needs, making office calls, providing consultation services, offering themselves as contractors, gathering feedback, and measuring product effectiveness (Florance and Matheson, 1993).

EVOLUTION OF THE HEALTH SCIENCES LIBRARY

As Lucier (1992) points out, the knowledge management environment places the library at the beginning of the information transfer cycle rather than at the end and it focuses on information capture rather than access and use. Knowledge management applications for clinical medicine originated in the 1980s when two important reports were released that proposed a new approach to the teaching and learning of clinical medicine, and to the role of the library in these processes. These two reports, along with the strong presence of the National Library of Medicine, have exerted a profound influence on the development of medical libraries over the past twenty years. "Physicians for the 21st Century," known as the GPEP report, called for medical students to learn medical information retrieval skills in the context of a problem-based approach to medical education (Association of American Medical Colleges, 1990). This provided an opportunity and incentive for medical librarians to act as instructors, although most of the instruction was done in the library and was not fully integrated into the medical education curriculum.

"Academic Information in the Academic Health Sciences Center," known as the Matheson-Cooper report, proposed integrated academic information management systems (IAIMS) (Matheson and Cooper, 1988). In the IAIMS environment, the library sits at the center of the campus information network, serving as an integrating force and a central access point for the medical center's disparate scientific, administrative, and scholarly databases. The creation, organization, and dissemination of information are coordinated, and librarians are members of integrated institutional information programs (Anderson and Fuller, 1992). Although models such as IAIMS give increased importance to the library, the library must restructure itself significantly in order to take on this expanded role successfully.

In hospitals and clinics, as well as in academic medical settings, the last twenty years have witnessed a steady evolution. Most clinicians have traditionally accessed the medical literature primarily through mediated searches performed by trained medical librarians. Gradually, however, the National Library of Medicine (NLM) has placed greater emphasis on clinicians' ability to access the medical literature directly through a specially designed end-user system known as Grateful Med. Even though they were concerned initially that they were being asked to operate as a "field force for the distribution of products developed by NLM," most librarians quickly realized that there was an important role for them as instructors and coaches, even in non-academic, primarily clinical settings. Many librarians also expressed serious reservations about the quality of the information being consulted by health care practitioners when they were not provided with adequate consultation and support, or when the search retrieved information that was incomplete or unfocused.

At the same time, librarians introduced programs such as clinical librarianship and literature attached to charts (LATCH) to increase the likelihood that high-quality medical literature would be incorporated into clinical decision making. Clinical librarianship (Cimpl, 1985) and LATCH (Brenner, 1976) were programs welcomed in hospitals and clinics, but in the managed care environment of the 1980s, parent institutions downsized or merged and individual institutional libraries were closed. Limited material resources and personnel meant that such customized services could no longer be sustained.

Meanwhile, the size of the medical literature continued to grow and the changes in medical practice brought about by new diseases and therapies continued to encrease. The need to transfer the latest findings from basic and clinical research to the repertoire of the clinical health care team reached a crisis point. In an effort to ensure that busy practitioners had the latest and best information at their fingertips, the National Institutes of Health, along with other groups, undertook projects to sift, winnow, consolidate, and otherwise make more accessible the findings of ongoing research. Private insurers in the form of health maintenance organizations (HMOs) have been keenly interested in this topic because of pressure to increase the efficiency and efficacy of health care, and to reduce exposure to malpractice suits based on physicians failure to update their practice of medicine.

KNOWLEDGE MANAGEMENT TOOLS IN MEDICINE

Collaborative teams of librarians, scientists, clinicians, and computer scientists have developed many varied knowledge management tools. They illustrate the ways in which improved tools can transform traditional librarianship from its focus on non-evaluative retrieval of published information to a practice in which librarians and information specialists form an essential part of the team providing expert consultation to medical researchers and clinicians.

At the NLM at the National Institutes of Health, interdisciplinary teams have produced several important knowledge management tools to facilitate and improve retrieval from its databases. For example, Grateful Med provides an intelligent interface for searching MEDLINE, and PubMED offers sophisticated searching capabilities, including citation links, as well as the full text of 100 biomedical journals. PubMED links to molecular biology databases containing DNA/protein structures and three-dimensional structured data. NLM has also undertaken a major project, the Universal Medical Language System (UMLS) to support coordinated retrieval across disparate databases by linking controlled vocabulary terms. Because health information encompasses such varied fields as health administration, psychology, sociology, economics, medicine, and biology, creating a universal approach to retrieve from multiple databases is not trivial. The UMLS will provide a much needed platform for the solution of information management problems (Squires, 1993).

The NLM is not the sole producer of innovative products in health information. The Online Mendelian Inheritance in Man database (OMIM) and the Human Genome Data Base (GDB) are produced by Johns Hopkins University. Both databases provide information about the human body, through citations to the literature and basic genetic data. Librarians participated in the teams that created both products.

The preceding examples fall chiefly into the creation stage of the information transfer cycle. Other projects focus more on dissemination and use. The Welch Medical Library at Johns Hopkins University created WELCH (Welch electronic library and center for health knowledge), a workstation that integrates both human and knowledge resources. In addition to providing access to traditional databases, including those developed locally, it provides an expertise menu that supports the knowledge organization and management needs of the library's clients. It describes products and services available via individual consultations with library staff in the areas of database design, curriculum support, and question answering. A tools menu makes available tools that are useful to clients who are engaged in creating and manipulating new knowledge, often as researchers. Examples are acquisition tools, which capture data such as snapshots and images for use in scientific work; organizational tools; and quality-control tools such as reference managers, spell-checkers, and evaluation tools (Florance and Matheson, 1993). A publishing menu provides tools to support writing and publishing—the creation and dissemination of knowledge. These tools include SGML, text analysis, and indexing products. These tools have been selected and evaluated by librarians.

In these examples, the librarian acts as partner or member of a product development team; the products are used to facilitate the retrieval and application of information. In contrast, LATCH and CML are services that are delivered to a health care professional at the bedside, but the librarian does not actively participate in health care delivery outside the library and does not extend services beyond those usually associated with the library. The librarian delivers information, but does not actively manage it, evaluate it, or provide guidance in its application.

Enhancements to MEDLARS/MEDLINE

Readers unfamiliar with medical literature may benefit from a brief overview of the way the NLM has structured its indexing and retrieval system to take advantage of the innate structure of the literature and how recent enhancements reflect specific knowledge management concerns.

The MEDLARS family of databases, the most familiar of which is MEDLINE, consists of bibliographic citations from the published biomedical literature (MEDLINE indexes only published materials). These are indexed using a structured vocabulary known as MeSH (medical subject headings). The searcher develops a strategy to optimize retrieval of only the most relevant items. In the typical MEDLINE search, the extent to which the skills of the searcher and the indexer "match" will determine the results. Rudimentary filtering is accomplished by the NLM's decision to include the journal on its list of titles indexed.

Recently, NLM indexers have been able to assign terms that characterize the kind of research the article reports. This is a departure from the traditional review article, which consists of items selected, read, and referenced by the author. Additional terms now available for assignment are, for example, "systematic overview," "practice guideline," and "metaanalysis." These terms allows the enormous MEDLINE database to be partitioned into those articles that report a particular kind of research or that meet a specified criterion, such as randomized controlled trial. Several of these types are described below.

Review Articles

A review article consists of items selected and read by the author after completing a literature search. It may also include items known to the author but not included in MEDLINE. Articles are grouped by concept and/or by the perspective (point-of-view) of the author who also determines what is included and excluded from the review. Review articles may be critical or evaluative, which adds a kind of quality filter, or they may be a non-evaluative compilation.

Academic Reviews

An academic review is a comprehensive, critical or analytical review. It uses explicit and rigorous methods to identify, critically appraise, and synthesize relevant studies from medical research.

Practice Guidelines

A practice guideline provides bottom line messages that are clinically applicable and scientifically valid (McKibbon, 1995). They are systematically developed statements to assist practitioner and patient decisions about appropriate health care for specific clinical circumstances. They represent an attempt to distill a large body of medical knowledge into a convenient, readily useable format. They gather and combine evidence, but they go further by attempting to address all the issues relevant to decisions and all the values that might sway a clinical recommendation, such as socioeconomic or psychosocial factors.

Metaanalysis

A metaanalysis is a review that uses both quantitative and qualitative methods to summarize the results of clinical research, preferably randomized controlled trials. It begins with a comprehensive MEDLINE search, selecting articles for inclusion according to pre-established criteria and subjecting them to rigorous analyses to consolidate findings. Metaanalysis can be useful when only small studies have been done and there are no large sets of randomized controlled trials. A metaanalysis is also appropriate when several treatment options exist, when literature results in conflict, or when there is a need for a generalized, population-based set of recommendations.

EVIDENCE-BASED MEDICINE (EBM)

Evidence-based medicine is the systematic examination of scientific evidence underlying a proposed therapeutic approach (Sackett et al., 1997; Health Information Research Unit, 1997). The practice of EBM distinguishes itself from "current practice" in that it is based upon the careful analysis of scientific studies that have been selected from the medical literature according to strict criteria for rigorous design and scientific validity. It distinguishes itself from "current practice" or consensus because it does not presume to reflect how clinicians practice medicine, but rather, what the scientific evidence indicates should be done—not always one and the same.

> EBM is notably characterized by its beginning and ending points: the patient. It is a patient's problem, which prompts the need for appraisal of the current best evidence. And it is the patient's needs, values, willingness to accept risk that ultimately must weight heavily in the decision whether or not to apply the relevant, valid findings from the best available evidence to the specific patient's case (Mrtek, 1998).

EBM focuses on clinical medicine, but it is also relevant to researchers because it can identify gaps in scientific knowledge where further research is needed, and identify areas where the research has become repetitive to the point where no further investigation needs to be done. The latter is important because it has implications for the allocation of scarce research resources.

EBM goes beyond traditional library service, and even extends beyond innovative services such as LATCH and CML. EBM draws upon librarians' experience in quality filtering of the literature, and requires a more comprehensive understanding of research design and critical evaluation. Multidisciplinary teams undertake most EBM projects because the breadth and depth of knowledge required extends beyond a single discipline. These teams usually include librarians who identify, select, filter, evaluate, and aggregate the literature. EBM utilizes tools and products designed by librarians and aimed at retrieving and analyzing the literature in response to actual clinical problems. Librarians and information specialists may deliver services and products directly to the health professional, or provide them as part of an instructional or consultative program.

Clinicians who practice EBM are aware of the evidence that supports clinical practice, and can assess the strength of that evidence. EBM requires the ability to access, summarize, and apply information from the literature to day-to-day clinical problems. This requires an understanding of the structure of medical literature and the use of clinical filters in searching medical databases (Dorsch, http://www.uic.edu/depts/lib/health/ebm.html).

Effective practice of EBM is a life-long enterprise because the practice of clinical medicine is constantly changing. It is essentially problem-based since the impetus comes from a patient care problem. Practitioners must be able to convert an information need into a focused question, and then do a search to find the best evidence with which to answer the question, critically appraising the evidence for validity and clinical usefulness and applying the results in clinical practice. The final step is to evaluate the evidence as it is applied to the clinical problem (Dorsch, http://www.uic.edu/depts/lib/health/ebm.html).

Products Exemplifying EBM

While knowledge management encompasses both published and non-published materials, aggregation, evaluation, and analysis can be usefully applied to published materials, and the results themselves made available to practitioners (McKibbon, 1995). A useful survey of these tools is available at http://hiru.mcmaster.ca/hiru/medline/mdl-ebc.htm. The series *Users' Guides to the Medical Literature* is produced by Evidence Based Medicine Working Group at the Institute for Clinical Evaluative Sciences at the University of Toronto and has been published periodically in JAMA since 1993. The full text of the articles may be viewed at the McMaster University Web site: **http://hiru.hirunet.mcmaster.ca/ebm/userguid/default.htm.**

The American College of Physicians (ACP) also publishes a series of EBM articles as a supplement to its journal *Annals of Internal Medicine*. Known as the *ACP Journal Club* series, the series is aimed at the individual practicing internist who is a subscriber to the journal. The series selects published articles according to strict criteria and abstracts those studies and reviews that warrant immediate attention by physicians who are attempting to keep pace with important advances in treatment, prevention, diagnosis, cause, prognosis, and economics of the disorders managed by internists. The emphasis is on selecting articles whose quality of evidence might justify changes in clinical practice. One of the beneficial effects of the *ACP Journal Club* is that it substantially reduces the number of articles that a busy clinician must view in order to stay current (McKibbon, 1995). More information is available at: **http://acponline.org/journals/ebm/pubinfo.htm.**

HSTAT Health Services Technology Assessment Texts provides access to the full text of documents useful in health care decision making. It includes clinical practice guidelines, quick-reference guides for clinicians, consumer brochures, and evidence reports sponsored by the Agency for Health Care Policy and Research, National Institutes of Heath Consensus Development Conference and research protocols. It also links to the Centers for Disease Control (CDC) Prevention Guidelines database. This amalgam of information is not true EBM since it includes a variety of types of materials, although it is an example of aggregating and repackaging information. It is important to distinguish between consensus reports and EBM. The former reflects what a group of experts agree to be the case; EBM attempts to at least be scientific and objective about its work.

Guyatt and Rennie's (1993) introduction to JAMA's *Users Guide to the Medical Literature* series includes a cogent and compelling argument for reliance on EBM rather than consensus. It also serves to differentiate the EBM scientific movement from the purely knowledge management movement, which has its origins in the corporate environment where perception and intuition enjoy greater respect than in the scientific community. They emphasize the importance of a systematic *search* for appropriate answers in the literature, rather than relying on what comes across the desk or in the mail, followed by a systematic evaluation of the articles. Physicians will find themselves more clearly differentiating between clinical practices based on sound evidence from studies in human beings and those that are based on physiological rationale or standard practice. As a result of conscientiously consulting evidence-based medicine, physicians may find themselves relying less on sources of information like trade journals, word of mouth, and conferences, which may be proprietary or commercially sponsored. Clearly, objective appraisal of the information sources must be done in any practicing environment—whether clinical or corporate. Because of their training and their ability to see the broad picture, librarians are often in a prime position to perform that critical appraisal.

Most EBM projects are collaborative in nature, reflecting the interdisciplinary environment in which librarians, researchers, and clinicians of many varieties can pool their expertise to improve patient care. One of the most ambitious projects is the Cochrane Collaboration, which produces the *Cochrane Database of Systematic Reviews*. This quarterly electronic journal is produced by an international network of individuals and institutions committed to preparing, maintaining, and disseminating systematic reviews of the effects of health care. It also provides a bibliography of systematic reviews done outside the collaboration.

The Cochrane Collaboration began at a meeting of about eighty people at Oxford University in 1993. The goals of the collaboration are: "to produce high quality systematic reviews (where possible, metaanalysis) of trials of every sort of health care intervention, to ensure that these are subjected to rigorous peer review and, when necessary, updating and to disseminate these systematic reviews electronically both on CD-ROM and via the Internet" (Bero and Rennie, 1995).

The Cochrane Collaboration is largely a volunteer effort of the members of the collaborative review groups, although for many of them, this work is an accepted and integral element of their salaried positions. The spirit of collaboration is exemplified in the fact that the NLM enhanced its indexing by tagging some 30,000 controlled trials that had not been previously tagged in MEDLINE. Such indexing assists in the initial search to identify relevant research. The copyright remains in almost all cases with the authors, not the publishers, a decision that enables the widest possible dissemination of the results. This is a value system that is more compatible with the scientific community than with the corporate environment. While only the most naive would assume that all scientists are altruistic and all corporate workers are self-serving, the ethos of the environment in which information is managed has a profound effect on practice (Bero and Rennie, 1995).

Librarian's Role in EBM/Knowledge Management

In order for EBM to be effective, the librarian must be fully integrated into the culture of the clinical team. These requirements—aggregation, selection and application of evidence, and full integration into the clinical team—suggest that the practice of EBM is a form of knowledge management. Knowledge managers—or knowledge workers as they are usually referred to in the health information arena—select facts or information and apply them in a particular context to solve a problem. Effective knowledge managers must be sensitive to the contextual setting in which they are working and, thus, must be integrated into the management team. The responsibility for applying tacit knowledge, which is so important in a corporate setting, rests primarily with the health care practitioner who is educated and licensed to perform a particular task. Physicians, nurses, and other health care personnel who also have been trained in information management techniques can be expected to apply the tacit knowledge necessary to make assessments, diagnoses, and prognoses. Such individuals are relatively scarce today, and so the health information community has made a concerted effort to establish education and training programs whose objective is to produce practitioners who are skilled in both traditional health care as well as in health informatics (Giuse et al., 1997; Braude, 1994).

The impact of applying the findings of medical literature to clinical situations has already been demonstrated (Marshall, 1992; Urquhart and Hepworth, 1996); the question remains whether and how librarians will contribute to effective application of research findings to patient care. The answer to that question may well depend upon how librarians interact with the medical care team. "Will they interact as equals and in the same way; will they step in front of the group and present what they discovered through their research?" asks Giuse (1997), who holds both MD and MLS degrees. She points out that "librarians' verbal interaction with the team is a vital step in establishing *trust*—the most important element in a clinical culture" (Giuse, 1997).

A second factor involves shifting from the library culture to the clinical culture.

> ....the movement from the library to clinical rounds is a movement between cultures, each with a different hierarchy, organizational structure and language. Effectiveness in the culture requires an initial period of study followed by an ongoing, lifelong expansion of skills and knowledge in medical specialty areas (Giuse, 1997).

The literature of knowledge management frequently refers to the importance of establishing trust in order to collect, organize, and manage all kinds of knowledge (Ellis, 1996). It is often this factor—trust—that makes librarians effective knowledge managers because they bring to this task a long history of integrity, trustworthiness, and discretion.

CONCLUSION

There are some significant differences between EBM and KM. These derive partly from the different circumstances and environments in which they exist. For example, in the clinical arena, practitioners are faced with a series of apparently random problems, particularly primary care physicians. One effort has been directed at encouraging clinicians to approach the literature directly through MEDLINE (GRATEFUL MED) as an alternative to the person-to-person collegial consultation that is known to have existed for decades. In the corporate environment, KM encourages the tapping of personal bodies of knowledge in addition to external, published knowledge. In the clinical environment, the librarian is primarily a knowledge worker, a tool maker who can design and develop tools that will assist the practitioner's direct access to the research findings. In the corporate environment, the librarian is seen as capturing and managing both external knowledge and internal tacit expertise and creating tools to assist the corporation in achieving its goals. Despite these differences in both environments, the librarian must be viewed as a trusted colleague. Her/his expertise must be understood and valued, or her/his contribution will be ignored and, therefore, ineffective.

In both the corporate and the health science settings, libraries and librarians must change in fundamental ways, redefining their mission, re-educating their staff, and re-engineering their programs (Florance and Matheson, 1993). Davenport and Prusak (1997) suggest that corporate librarians should get themselves "out of the routine of 'fetching' information that users knew existed but couldn't find" and concentrate instead on "creating navigational tools—knowledge maps...to acquaint their customers with available knowledge resources and on advising them on how best to use internal and external knowledge resources [emphasis added].

Differences in environments must be understood and acknowledged. The characteristics of the social setting where work takes place must be understood and accepted. It is not only librarians who find that they must adapt to new settings. One non-physician, non-librarian involved in evidence-based medicine stated:

> While I view my role in Morning Report as a guest in a traditional and highly ritualized setting, with growing frequency now some clinicians and some residents will look to me and our librarian colleagues as on-the-spot resource consultants....I am delighted when there is something unique we can add from our own bases of specialized knowledge about the use of evidence in the medical decision process, but we don't view ourselves as central to any part of the Morning Report. (Indeed the process would be nearly as valuable a learning experience for us if we were able to be present but totally invisible.) Much more likely to occur is the encounter initiated by resident or faculty before/after the session to provide assistance in finding materials, organizing efficient (10 minute) presentations for the group, refining questions as searchable formats, or acting as a mirror and sounding board for the interpretation of the literature findings/study design/statistics.
>
> Probably the real value of our "being there" is to serve as a continual, subtle reminder to everyone (resident and faculty alike) that an important

new foundation for the medical care of patients is to base decisions whenever possible on the critical assessment of the best available evidence—including high quality valued evidence in the published and unpublished domains (Mrtek, 1998).

The clinician's ability to use that scientific information in clinical practice may well depend on multidisciplinary health care teams in which librarians are key members. Indeed, the librarian's presence in this transaction links the scientific approach to the knowledge management approach where the tacit and expert knowledge of trusted individuals is harnessed to achieve a goal. It is the librarian's acceptance as trusted member of the health care team that will make the link between EBM and knowledge management in the health sciences.

References

Anderson, R.K.; Fuller, S.S. (1992) Libraries as members of integrated institutional information programs: Management and organizational issues. *Library Trends*, 41:198-213.

Association of American Medical Colleges. (1990) Physicians for the 21st century. *Journal of Medical Education*, 59 (11), part 2: 125-134.

Bero, L.; Rennie, D. (1995) The Cochrane Collaboration: Preparing, maintaining, and disseminating systematic reviews of the effects of health care. *Journal of the American Medical Association*, 274 (24): 1935-1941.

Braude, R.M. (1994) Medical librarianship and medical informatics: A call for the disciplines to join hands to train tomorrow's leaders. Editorial Comments. *Journal of the American Medical Informatics Association*, 1: 467-468.

Broadbent, M. (1998) The phenomenon of knowledge management: What does it mean to the information profession? *Information Outlook*, 2 (5): 23-36.

Cimpl, K. (1985) Clinical medical librarianship: A review of the literature. *Bulletin of the Medical Library Association*, 73: 21-28.

Davenport, T.H.; Prusak, L. (1997) *Working Knowledge: How Organizations Manage What They Know*. Boston: Harvard Business School Press.

Davis, G. et al. (1991) *Conceptual Modes for Research on Knowledge Management*. Minneapolis: University of Minnesota. MIS-RC Working Paper MISRC-WP-91-10, 1991. Quote from Davenport; Jarvenpaa; Beers, quoted by Broadbent, M. (1998) The phenomenon of knowledge management: What does it mean to the information profession? *Information Outlook*, 2 (5): 30.

Dorsch, J. http://www.uic.edu/depts/lib/health/ebm.html.

Ellis, C. (1996) Making strategic alliances succeed: The importance of trust. Briefings from the editor. *Harvard Business Review*, 74 (4): 8-9.

Florance, V.; Matheson, N.W. (1993) The health sciences librarian as knowledge worker. *Library Trends*, 42:196-219.

Giuse, N.B. (1997) Advancing the practice of clinical medical librarianship. Editorial. *Bulletin of the Medical Library Association*, 85 (4): 437-438.

Giuse, N.B.; Huber, L.T.; Katantans, S.R.; Giuse D.A.; Miller, M.D.; Giles, D.E.; Miller, R.A.; Stead, W.W. (1997) Preparing libraries to meet the challenges of today's health care environment. *Journal of the American Informatics Association*, 4:57-67.

Guyatt, G.H.; Rennie, D. (1993) Users' guide to the medical literature. Editorials. *Journal of American Medical Association*, 270 (17): 2096-2097.

Health Information Research Unit. (1997) *Evidence-Based Medicine Informatics Project.* McMaster University.

Harari, O. (1994) The brain based organization. *Management Review*, 83 (6): 57-60. Quoted in Broadbent, M. (1998) The phenomenon of knowledge management: What does it mean to the information profession? *Information Outlook*, 2 (5): 24.

Lucier, R.E. (1992) Towards a knowledge management environment: A strategic framework. *EDUCOM Review*, 27: 24-31.

Marshall, J.G. (1992) The impact of the hospital library on clinical decision making: The Rochester study. *Bulletin of the Medical Library Association*, 80: 169-178.

Matheson, N.W. (1995) Things to come: Postmodern digital knowledge management and medical informatics. The practice of informatics. *Journal of the American Medical Informatics Association*, 2 (2): 73-78.

Matheson, N.W.; Cooper, J.A.D. (1988) Academic information in the academic health sciences center. *Journal of Medical Education*, 57 (10):

McKibbon, A.K. (1995) The medical literature as a resource for evidence based care. Available at: URL<http://hiru.mcmaster.ca/hiru/medline/mdl-elsc.htm>

Michaud, G.C. et al. (1996) The introduction of evidence-based medicine as a component of daily practice. *Bulletin of the Medical Library Association*, 84: 478-481.

Mrtek, R.G. (1998) Personal correspondence: Dr. Prudence Dalrymple with Robert G. Mrtek, PhD, Professor of Medical Education, University of Illinois at Chicago, College of Medicine. Used with permission.

Oxman, A.D.; Sacket, D.L.; Guyatt, G.H. (1993) How to get started. Users' guides to the medical literature. Part 1. *Journal of the American Medical Association*, 270 (17): 2093-2095.

Sackett, D.L.; Richardson, W.S.; Rosenberg, W.; Haynes R.B. (1997) Evidence-based medicine. How to practice and teach EBM. New York: Churchill Livingstone.

Squires, S.J. (1993) Access to biomedical information: The unified medical language system. *Library Trends*, 42: 127-151.

Urquhart, C.J.; Hepworth, J.B. (1996) Comparing and using assessment of the value of information to clinical decision-making. *Bulletin of the Medical Library Association*, 84 (4): 482-489.

CHAPTER 24

Knowledge Management: Can It Exist in a Law Office?

Nina Platt

Director of Library Services

Faegre & Benson LLP

INTRODUCTION

Being a bit of a pessimist myself, I hope that the optimists among us are right. If they are, we are heading into a very interesting time where the early adopters of the idea of knowledge management will see their dream of storing and retrieving their firm's collective knowledge (to improve the delivery of legal services) realized. The technology is available for us to move forward with the implementation of such systems. Now the challenge is left to the partners and administrators to implement fee structures and compensation plans that make sharing and reusing knowledge effective. Once that barrier has been removed (or at least lowered), they will need to take the next step towards creating an environment where shared knowledge is valued by supporting the creation of the types of systems mentioned above. Is it a huge task? Yes. Let's hope we're up to it.

I attended Online World this fall where knowledge management and Intranets were the buzzwords. Session after session, one speaker after another described his/her involvement in knowledge management and Intranet development. As I sat in the meetings, I could not help but wonder how knowledge management could be applied in law offices, how some librarians are already involved in the management of knowledge, and what needs to happen for knowledge management to occur.

WHAT IS KNOWLEDGE MANAGEMENT?

Upon returning from the conference, I was eager to solidify my understanding of knowledge management and to learn how such a concept could be (or is being) implemented in law offices. I quickly discovered that there is no easy definition. A recent article in *Library Journal* defines it as "accessing, evaluating, managing, organizing, filtering, and distributing information in a manner that is useful to end users....knowledge management involves blending a company's internal and external information and turning it into actionable knowledge via a technology platform" (DiMattia and Oder, 1997). Another article, this time in *Information Week*, quotes Gordon Petrash of Dow Chemical Company who says it is "getting the right knowledge to the right people at the right time" (Hibbard, 1997).

Other writers on the subject define it more broadly. Verna Allee in *The Knowledge Evolution: Expanding Organizational Intelligence* states "Real knowledge management is much more than managing the flow of information. It means nothing less than setting knowledge free to find its own paths. It means fueling the creative fire of self-questioning in organizations. This means thinking less about knowledge management and more about knowledge partnering" (Allee, 1997). Her book describes how the organizational structure of a business can create a collaborative environment where knowledge is shared.

After listening to the speakers, reading several articles, and browsing through a few books, I began to understand knowledge management as the creation of systems or processes in a learning environment that allow all employees to have access to the information resources they need to develop the knowledge necessary to do their jobs. Those resources may be data that has been collected and stored in a database or knowledge that a coworker or manager developed and stored in memory. The vital component in knowledge management is that the resources are shared.

This definition is based on the following bits of knowledge I picked up while reading:

- Knowledge itself cannot be managed. Only the processes or systems through which we share knowledge can be managed.
- A collaborative learning environment that promotes and rewards sharing of resources must exist in order for knowledge management to succeed.

Despite these two complex requirements, knowledge management is a thriving concept being implemented in businesses throughout the world. Many companies are rushing to purchase and implement a variety of knowledge management tools (databases, GroupWare, Web technologies, etc.) in an effort to reap the benefits of knowledge management.

A Concept by Any Other Name

Knowledge management, it is reported, had its start in the Big Six Consulting firms and is now being embraced by other industries because of "the explosive growth of information resources such as the Internet, and the accelerating pace of technological change" (Hibbard, 1997) that is leaving workers "both overwhelmed by information and fearful that they're missing important details" (Hibbard, 1997).

It would seem that those of us in law offices must have been overwhelmed long ago since law librarians have been engaged in knowledge management for years. Examples of the work we have been doing are many. On the traditional end, law librarians have been working within their organizations to develop what the MBA types are now calling Best Practices collections. We have given them such titles as Brief Banks, Research Memo Collections, Attorney Work Product Systems, and Pleadings/Forms Banks.

Less Traditional Examples

Conflict Management

Depending on the size of the firm, conflict management can be an integral part of the services the library provides. In smaller firms, the librarian may be called upon to run conflict checks and maintain a database of clients detailing corporate relationships between parents, subsidiaries, and spin-offs. In larger firms, a conflict management department will process these same checks. Some of the larger firms have this department reporting to the director of the library. Others have the conflict group as its own entity but have hired a librarian to manage the group. Becky Brass, a veteran librarian in special libraries, is the manager of the conflict management group at Dorsey & Whitney in Minneapolis. Her responsibilities include the management of a staff who performs such tasks as maintaining a conflicts database and running searches through online services for corporate relationships.

Records Management

Some law librarians have shunned the possibility of adding this responsibility to the services provided by their libraries because they think others view it as a thankless job. Others have viewed it as their responsibility to manage information from both external and internal sources. Those who work with records management are responsible for the creation and maintenance of a records management database that allows them to track documents and data from cases, transactions, and such.

Marketing Information Management

Increasingly, law librarians are taking on the role of tracking and maintaining marketing information. For Ann Roberts, director of Client and Information Services at McQuire Woods Battle & Boothe, it means managing the entire marketing process. Managing the information needed for the marketing process may include creation of databases to track work referred in and out, tracking client contacts and the client relationship, maintaining competitive intelligence, and tracking news about existing clients and/or prospective clients. The information that could be maintained to support the marketing process seems endless. Moreover, it is not only necessary that this type of information be maintained—the right people have to be able to have access to it.

Document Management

While the document management process seems like a secretarial responsibility, setting up and maintaining such a system requires many of the skills possessed by librarians. With document management, we are making it easier to save and retrieve work in progress. The manager of a system like DOCS Open (one of the document management systems used by many law offices today) must be familiar with database management and full-text retrieval. Part of setting up the system is working with various parts of the organization to determine how they want to access the documents they are creating. A system like this (properly set up) allows departments, teams, and individuals to maintain different information about a document depending on the type of document, the client, matter numbers, and so forth. Library Director, Deb Muntean of Briggs and Morgan in St. Paul, Minnesota, took on the responsibility of implementing an upgrade of DOCS Open when the MIS director left at the onset of the project.

Contact Management and Other Databases

Prior to the use of office-wide contact managers that are being implemented in many offices, librarians in those same firms were developing databases that tracked contact information (and other bits of data) for expert witnesses, litigation support services, judges' biographies, CLE conferences, and such. All of these databases have one thing in common—they provide lawyers and staff with information that makes their jobs easier.

Case Management

New to most law offices, case management (also called practice management by some vendors) seems as difficult to define as knowledge management, depending on who is defining the concept. At the Minnesota Attorney General's Office, where we are currently working on the selection of case management software and implementation of the same within the next year, we are looking for a system that will provide attorneys and staff with information on the cases on which they are working. The case management system will be integrated with our time, billing, and calendar systems and will provide contact management, matter management, transaction management, docketing, access to documents generated, time and billing reports, and many other benefits.

Build It and They Will Come?

When I was first asked to participate in the case management project, I had a difficult time seeing what skills I could bring to it. Since then, I discovered that I had a lot to contribute. Besides the usual skill of gathering information on case management and its vendors, I also contributed project management and database development skills. The other librarians described in the above examples are also using both traditional and non-traditional skills to manage information produced both internally and externally. But does this make us knowledge managers? Well, yes and no.

Yes, we are doing knowledge management work if we are working to create systems or processes that are intended to assist attorneys and staff in the creation or transfer of knowledge from one entity to another. No, we are not, if those systems are not being used or if the systems exist but the people who need the information do not have access.

Anyone who has worked on the creation of a Brief Bank or Attorney Work Product System has experienced the challenges that come about as the result of trying to manage knowledge. Thomas Davenport (1998) echoes what we know in his book, *Some Principles of Knowledge Management*:

1. Knowledge management is expensive (but so is stupidity!)
2. Effective management of knowledge requires hybrid solutions of people and technology
3. Knowledge management is highly political

    4. Knowledge management requires knowledge managers

    5. Knowledge management benefits more from maps than models, more from markets than from hierarchies

    6. Sharing and using knowledge are often unnatural acts

    7. Knowledge management means improving knowledge work processes

    8. Knowledge access is only the beginning

    9. Knowledge management never ends

    10. Knowledge management requires a knowledge contract

While the creation and maintenance of a knowledge management system is an expensive endeavor, the advantages it gives by creating more knowledgeable attorneys and staff who in turn are able to provide better service to clients make it worth developing. Because knowledge is intangible and, therefore, hard to measure, many managing committees of law offices will not allow the expenditures necessary to be successful.

Besides the failure that can happen because the necessary resources are not available, many Brief Banks, Work Product systems, etc. are not successful because the environment does not allow it. If knowledge is seen as power and sharing knowledge is not placed high among skills that all attorneys and staff must possess, it is very likely that the implementation of such a system will fail. A learning environment where knowledge is not a commodity but instead a shared resource is required for success.

That seems to pound the last nail in the coffin of knowledge management in law offices. After all, law is an adversarial sport (I mean profession). One question (that I don't have the answer to at this time) must be answered before we can move ahead in knowledge management. "How can we create a collaborative learning environment in a law office?" The two, collaboration and the practice of law, seem mutually exclusive. The Big Six firms' answer to this challenge is to tie the success of such a system to compensation. Collaboration and sharing is a requirement of each employee's job. Performance evaluations include a review of how well the employee is doing in participating in the knowledge management process. Can that begin to happen in law offices?

Pretend We Solved the Problem

So, we have a collaborative learning environment, what's next? What does a knowledge management system look like in a law office? As is seen in many implementations, it is probably Web based. An Intranet exists that provides access to the various systems that were put in place to make the transfer of knowledge flow easily. Through the Intranet, attorneys and staff (with security in place so only those who have a need to see the information) have access to:

- Best Practices—An attorney work product system that includes briefs, research memos, pleadings, transactional documents, forms, etc.
- Resumes—A system where resumes for attorneys and staff are maintained that allow others to identify expertise that would otherwise not be known.
- Office Directory—Staff telephone numbers, email addresses, etc.
- Client Information—Access to articles/news about the client, information on cases/transactions (contacts, matters, docket, etc.), information on marketing efforts involving the client, time and billing information, etc. The articles/news could be purchased through a wire service and delivered via the Internet to the law office where it is filtered and added to a database accessible via the Intranet.
- Variety of systems depending on need—Expert witness database, litigation support services directory, judges' biographies, and many other databases that are created and maintained in-house or purchased from vendors and accessed via the Internet.
- Conflict and records management information.

The list of what could be included in such a system will depend on the law office's needs and the policies in the office that permit the exchange of information. Looking at this short list, it is evident that the benefits of such a system are many. Now if we could only figure out how to share.

In the Beginning (Or At Least a Few Years Ago)

In 1986, Ann Carter, library director at Dorsey & Whitney in Minneapolis Minnesota, with the support of then managing partner Robert Johnson, developed a plan to improve how the firm managed its work product. Four information specialists (I was lucky to be one of them) were hired to take on the responsibility of developing a system to collect, maintain, and make available any and all work product that the office decided was examples of best practices. We were each given responsibility for different practice groups divided up between transaction and litigation. Each practice group assigned an attorney as liaison to work with us in determining what the group needed and wanted in the way of work product retrieval.

Using a database management software called SEEK (originally developed for the U.S. government for defense purposes), we created intricate indices to paper files of research memos, opinion letters, briefs, pleadings, forms, and so forth. We were intermediaries. Collecting, indexing, abstracting, and retrieving the documents whenever they were needed. While the technology used may seem a bit archaic now, it was pretty forward thinking for a time when word processing was still being done on Wang dumb terminals. Even though the system itself was not full text, the indexed records with abstracts could be queried and documents retrieved in ways not possible with paper index systems.

A couple years later, across town at Oppenheimer, Wolff & Donnelly, attorney LaVern Pritchard was working on determining how to "implement a system that would more reflect how lawyers actually would want to manipulate information in an adversary setting." In 1989, he discovered Maxthink [http://www.maxthink.com] (a software company owned by "hypertext visionary" Neil Larson) and went on to develop what may very well have been one of the first hypertext knowledge management systems in the legal community. The hypertext system was built primarily on a suite of DOS hypertext products from Maxthink, using Hyplus, later Hynet_LAN (the hypertext engine), Transtext (hypertext word processor), and Houdini (the matrix outliner). In a 1990 *Minnesota Lawyer* article, he referred to the system as an "integrated litigation knowledge system."

Oppenheimer librarian, Barb Minor, worked with Pritchard to develop a variety of uses for the system including witness information, document information, pleadings, research, discovery, and the like. MIS director Mark Thuston was also supportive in the duo's efforts to network the system. Their work served as a prototype for other applications, including multiple case management system, legal research browsing system, and general legal Intranet. Pritchard's description of the system follows:

> The system was hypertext delivered and ASCII text based but structures were built with a combination of handcrafted ASCII menu files, outliner generated hierarchical structures, database generated structures and occasional hybrid structures like experimenting with flow charting that required proof over a series of hyperlinked pages...It held witness information for about 100 witnesses, 16,000 pages of deposition testimony, about 4500 "executive level" analytical document abstracts, 6000 pages of trial transcript, 14,750 files in total, 58,000+ total links, average file size 5K, greatest "depth" in links from opening screen to the most remote buried file: 8 levels. The magic of the

system was the ability to deliver browsing capability to litigation case-specific knowledge.

Fast Forwarding to Today

Today there appears to be new opportunities in managing shared knowledge. Many of the individuals I talked to as I prepared this chapter are very optimistic about the near future. They are quick to indicate that the technologies needed to create systems that work are becoming commonplace. At the same time, the economic atmosphere in which law is practiced is such that law firm and law office administrators are looking for ways to improve the cost effectiveness of the product their organizations deliver to their clients. Many clients are looking to their lawyers to provide them with new fee structures that don't rely as heavily on hourly billing and are shopping around for law firms that are willing to be creative. This means developing systems that reduce the time spent "reinventing the wheel." It also means making the best use of the knowledge held (and hopefully shared) by the partners, associates, librarians, legal assistants, secretaries, and other administrative staff.

Jones, Day, Reavis, & Pogue know what it means to create an environment that makes knowledge sharing a reality. Kingsley Martin, director of Legal Technology Planning at Jones, Day, points to his firm's use of Lotus Notes in making information accessible throughout the firm. The firm's office Intranet provides access to 300+ Lotus Notes databases that include forms files, directories, office bulletins, information feeds, work product, and discussion groups. Besides specific subject areas and resources, users can also navigate information that is organized by practice group, individual offices, and administrative and legal work groups. When asked about skills needed to effectively manage knowledge, Martin places high value on the skills possessed by librarians including understanding the practice of law and knowing how to organize information. It's not enough to know how to put technology in place, you need to know how to put people together with technology and make that technology work to produce the desired results.

John Hokkanen, Legal Technologist at Alston & Bird (A&B) [http://www.alston.com/firminfo/technology.htm], has played a central role in developing the knowledge-based systems/Intranet at his firm. A&B made a large commitment to technology evidenced by the slogan on the firm's Web site: "Maximizing Technology to Serve Our Clients Better. Better Tools. Better Job. Better Representation."

Hokkanen's development platform has been a combination of application development tools including Cold Fusion, Access, Fulcrum, and Verity.

Using these tools Hokkanen developed a core Intranet backbone application called Pure Oxygen that has been deployed within his organization to provide access to work product, case tracking, subject databases, and other resources. Go to "The Law Practice Technology Center," available at http://www.lptc.com/WELCOME.CFM to see pure oxygen in use in a collaborative environment. (The Law Practice Technology Center is a Web site dedicated to the sharing of information in law practice technology.)

Gail F. Schultz at Mobil Business Resources Corporation also played a part in developing her company's knowledge system (The Mobil Intellectual Capital Bank) that makes legal documents including precedent documents, model forms and clauses, legal memorandums, litigation materials, and checklists available. Her account of the development and use of this worldwide system was published in the November 1997 issue of *Law Technology Product News* [http://www.ljx.com/ltpn/november97/mobil_p37.html].

Intranets and knowledge management systems aren't just for the large firm or corporate law office. Richard Granat, director of the Center for Law Practice Technology, is involved with research and development for the virtual law office, multi-office law firms, and other complex legal organizations like the fifteen legal service offices in Maryland, the Maryland Legal Services Corporation [http://www.mlsc.org]. He is currently investigating the possibility of deploying an all-Java based knowledge management system called the Chakra Knowledge System developed by a company called Huskylabs [http://www.huskylabs.com] at this site and others.

Developed for large law firms and legal organizations, the Chakra application is "a complete software system for providing privileged, perpetual access to a wide range of information stores located throughout corporate networks and the Internet." Chakra For Law "allows legal teams to manage cases in secure collaborative workspaces." Using such an application in an extranet deployment will allow pro bono attorneys and other legal service providers to access document archives that include forms, pleadings, legal memos, appellate briefs, and other shared work products that will make the job of bringing legal services to low-income families in Maryland more efficient and effective.

The Equal Justice Network [http://www.equaljustice.org] is another project Granat is working on that will use the same technology. Sponsored by the National Legal Aid and Defender Association and the Center for Law and Social

Policy, The Equal Justice Network, which recently became operational, later this year, is a Web site developed for lawyers serving low-income clients. It will allow them to participate in discussion groups, access libraries of work product, conduct private conferences with clients and colleagues, and communicate with their peers. It will also provide training on using the Internet for legal research.

Challenging Sacred Cows

Creating a learning environment (where none exists) is a complex task that involves changes in corporate culture and changes in individual behavior, and is perhaps too large a topic for this chapter. Instead, I would like to discuss the processes that need to be in place in order to make a learning environment a reality (should the human factors be resolved). Verna Allee in her book, *The Knowledge Evolution: Expanding Organizational Intelligence*, assists knowledge managers in assessing their own organizations through a series of assessment questions that deal with a number of areas. They are too numerous to be listed in complete form in this chapter and will make more sense to you when read in context with the rest of the book. (At $17.95, the book is a great buy.) Here is a subset of the questions that have been extracted from various chapters and thrown together to illustrate the resource:

1. Do people have ready access to databases, trade journals, and library resources relevant to their work?
2. Do you have processes and technologies to distribute and access data throughout the organization?
3. Do people get basic skill training in using equipment, software, and work tools?
4. For new employees, is there a formal orientation to policies, procedures, and standards?
5. Is there an open, collaborative, ongoing process for creating, updating, and retiring procedures, regulations, policies, and standards?
6. Are databases and information interfaces organized in a way that is consistent with how the organization actually functions?
7. Do people understand the key performance and productivity measures for their work?
8. Do people work together as teams to seek improvements and redesign their work as needed?

9. Do you experiment with knowledge building technologies, such as GroupWare and internal Web sites?

10. Are there company-wide processes for openly questioning assumptions and challenging "sacred cows"?

CHIEF KNOWLEDGE OFFICER— HELP WANTED: WHO SHOULD APPLY

How do we move forward in answering the questions listed above and making the necessary changes to develop a learning environment? The trend in many corporations throughout the country is to employ a chief knowledge officer whose job it is to work with the corporations to develop the processes and systems that will support knowledge management. An article by Mary Corcoran and Rebecca Jones in the June 1997 issue of *Information Outlook* entitled "Chief Knowledge Officers? Perceptions, Pitfall, and Potential" discusses the competencies needed by knowledge managers. They include:

- Knowledge and understanding of the business rules and processes of the organization
- Entrepreneurial skills (communication, salesmanship, product development)
- Information technology skills (ability to understand current and envision tomorrow's technology)
- Leadership skills (inspire people, create alliances)
- Financial management skills

To this list, I would like to add: a thorough understanding of how people learn and how knowledge is developed, shared, renewed, and so forth.

MORE ON KNOWLEDGE MANAGEMENT

This chapter barely touches on what knowledge management is and how it is being used. To learn more visit the following sites:

- *CIO Magazine* [http://www.cio.com/CIO/]
- The Knowledge Management Forum [http://revolution.3-cities.com/~bonewman/]
- Knowledge Associates International—includes links to *Knowledge Management Journal* [http://www.knowledge.stjohns.co.uk/]

- KM *Knowledge Management Server*—The University of Texas at Austin's contribution to Knowledge Management literature. Many of Davenport's writings can be found here. [http://www.bus.utexas.edu/kman/]
- SLA's *Selected References on Knowledge Management*—includes a bibliography of books, journal articles, and Web sites. [http://www.sla.org/membership/irc/knowledg.html]
- *World Wide Web Virtual Library on Knowledge Management.* [http://www.brint.com/km/]
- Originally published in two parts in Law Library Resource Xchange [<http://www.llrx.com>]

References

Allee, Verna. *The Knowledge Evolution: Expanding Organizational Intelligence.* Butterworth-Heinemann, 1997, 231.

Davenport, Thomas H. Some Principles of Knowledge Management. Available at: http://www.bus.utexas.edu/kman/kmprin.htm.

DiMattia, Susan; Oder, Norman. "Knowledge Management: Hope, Hype, or Harbinger?" *Library Journal*, September 15, 1997, 33-35.

Hibbard, Justin. "Knowing What We Know." *Information Week*, October 20, 1997. Available at: http://techweb.cmp.com/iw/653/53iukno.htm.

CHAPTER 25

The Intersection of Knowledge Management and Competitive Intelligence: Smartcards and Electronic Commerce

Katherine Shelfer

Assistant Professor

Drexel University

INTRODUCTION

The knowledge management and competitive intelligence (KMCI) strategy combines effective knowledge management (KM) and appropriate competitive intelligence (CI) to provide the right mix of the right information to the right decision maker at the right time. The right decision still rests with the decision maker, but this integrated approach makes beneficial outcomes more likely than the use of either KM or CI alone. An integrated approach to KMCI is crucial for the success of firms engaged in electronic commerce. KMCI supports the process of continuous improvement needed for the successful new product development that is so vital to electronic commerce (e-commerce). A study of the needs and concerns of stakeholders involved in implementing chipcards on colleges' campuses provides a vehicle to better understanding KMCI and underscores the need for an integrated KMCI approach in e-commerce.

As shown in the model in Figure 25.1 (see page 420), KM and CI functions support each other. Information obtained through the CI process is integrated into the KM process and the firm identifies its CI priorities through its KM efforts.

There is considerable value gained by developing an integrated approach since only the combination of KM and CI can provide all of the information needed by the

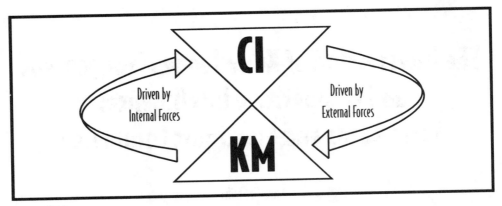

Figure 25.1

decision makers, and neither KM nor CI operates "in a vacuum." This KMCI model clearly demonstrates this relationship. In Spitzer's[1] 1998 keynote address to the Society of Competitive Intelligence Professionals, he pointed out six key factors that impede effective competitive intelligence: 1) lag between the decision and its implementation (decision drag); 2) data overload; 3) outsourcing the "thinking"; 4) teams that do not understand the critical thinking process; 5) lack of context (organizational values); and 6) lack of creativity and innovation. Adding KM components to the CI process can help to resolve many of these problems.

The purpose of KM is to add value to information already held by the firm, resulting in knowledge that will be of strategic use to the firm. Although specifics vary, KM generally deals with 1) expertise or human capital; 2) general and financial management; 3) customers, operations, marketing and sales; and 4) intellectual property, technical processes, and products. Another important aspect of knowledge is the integration of the firm's existing CI into the knowledge base. CI, on the other hand, has an external focus. CI is defined as the legal collection and analysis of information regarding the capabilities, vulnerabilities, and intentions of competitors by using "open sources and ethical inquiry."[2] Where KM attempts to lever internal information and expertise, CI works to filter information, develop an understanding of the multidimensional nature of the competitive arena, spot trends, and articulate changes in advance of the market. According to Bensoussan (1998),[3] "the keys to a company's future are not found in forecasts, predictions or media gurus, but through patiently, carefully and strategically turning a company's knowledge into competitive intelligence." She identifies the components of CI as available data and expert judgment, and calls for intelligence to be "future-oriented, accurate, objective, relevant, useful, and timely" (Bensoussan, 1998). In other words, each drives the other.

As shown below in Figure 25.2, there are significant differences in the focus and activities of KM and CI, but the results of both processes must reach the desktops of those who are charged with making strategic decisions that change the course of corporate and economic history. This is the point at which KM and CI intersect—the fulcrum. The actual point of intersection will vary depending on the type of decision to be made and the action/reaction that results. Regarding the importance of KMCI, Kirk Tyson writes:

> ...the transition of the economy...to the Intelligence Age should compel companies to create a knowledge base about their competitive environment and develop a perpetual strategy process for the constant renewal of this knowledge base. This competitive knowledge base should consist of information regarding competitors, customers, suppliers, strategic alliances, potential opportunities and threats.

Knowledge Management	Competitive Intelligence
- Internal	- External
- Reactive	- Proactive
- Technology-based	- Source-based
- Dependent on employee willingness to contribute	- Environment-driven

Figure 25.2   A Comparison of Knowledge Management and Competitive Intelligence

THE SIGNIFICANCE OF KMCI FOR E-COMMERCE

E-commerce is the obvious next evolutionary step toward a currency-free (or cash-less) society. It has already altered the information industry and much of our national economy, and it has begun to completely change the way the world does business. In a speech given in Ireland, Ira Magaziner, President Clinton's Special Advisor on the Internet, stated that the potential impact of e-commerce could equal the Industrial Revolution. He projected over a trillion United States dollars of annual online transactions by the year 2010. Magaziner believes that the key to understanding the impact of e-commerce lies in the fact that e-commerce allows businesses to improve service levels while slashing costs. Magaziner reported that transaction costs for a typical business can be reduced by up to 500%[4] (Jupp, 1998). In fact, the explosive growth of e-commerce has only been restrained by lack of sufficient computing and telecommunications resources. As more resources are put into place, e-commerce increases exponentially. Since even the smallest player's actions can have global consequences, small players become global (or die) very quickly. The dynamic nature of e-commerce has clearly created numerous challenges for companies and individuals who are engaged in it, wishing to engage in it, or who merely want to track it. This makes effective KMCI activity a critical success factor for e-commerce firms.

E-commerce is one visible area in which organizations must transform in order to cope with an increasingly turbulent environment. It is also an environment in which the direction is unclear. For example, there is widespread disagreement in online banking about whether "one-stop shopping" or Web portal design (e.g., Hotbot, Lycos, Yahoo!, etc.) will be the most lucrative direction to take. Jupiter Communications, a research firm that monitors financial services, believes that the array of products loses importance as consumers use the Internet for comparison shopping. At the same time, Citicorp and Travelers made the combined development of an online financial services supermarket a priority. According to the Jupiter study, discount brokerages are "the only institutions that have understood the needs of the on-line consumer" while Yahoo's chief operating officer, Jeff Mallett, believes that the best portal, or gateway, to financial services will win. He projects that the winner will be a "lifestyle company where people from all walks of life can come and pay bills or make purchases"[5] (Clark, 1998).

With so much at stake, e-commerce firms must not only find the right course, they must do it quickly. As a result, KMCI for e-commerce is focused, inclusive, and streamlined, and it provides the firm with numerous benefits. Through KMCI, there is continuous improvement, innovation, and on-going creation of useful new intellectual property, reducing the pressure of short lifecycles for the firm's intellectual property. It is axiomatic that the use of knowledge-based systems generates more knowledge and can make existing knowledge more useful. In other words, such systems gain utility and flexibility the more they are used. Integrating KM and CI encourages their use, improves their quality, and allows the firm to respond more rapidly to changing business conditions[6] (Davis and Botkin, 1998; Senge et al., 1994).

According to the law of requisite variety in cybernetics, in order for any system to preserve its integrity and survive, its rate of learning must at least match the rate of change in its environment[7] (Boisot, 1996 and 1998). Any company active in e-commerce, particularly a solution provider (SP) who installs chipcard systems, epitomizes the concept of *a learning company* and a *knowledge-intensive company*, terms that are widely used to emphasize the intellectual property and human expertise on which the e-commerce firm's viability depends. The characteristics of such companies are a fundamental part of e-commerce[8] (Alverson, 1995). By analyzing both the information flow and the information needs of smartcard systems integrators, or SPs who supply chipcard systems to college campuses, we can develop an increased awareness of the general benefits inherent in an integrated KMCI approach.

The strategic importance of the intersection of KM and CI is clearly visible in the arena of e-commerce. E-commerce—already used by Sony, Gateway, and others—helps retailers to avoid the high costs associated with staffing, managing, and maintaining inventory in individual stores. It also provides a new form of shopping experience for consumers. One example of this is the interactive e-commerce Web site *(http://www.fatface.co.uk)* created for Fat Face using Blueberry New Media for creative design, Intershop's e-commerce software, and Hewlett Packard's Open Pix imaging technology. The company's aim was to produce a Web site that combined a lifestyle experience and a powerful selling tool. Jules Leaver (1998), joint managing director of Fat Face, believes that:

> We are providing our customers with more than an online shop; the site embraces the outdoor lifestyle and reflects "high octane" living. The Internet is rapidly becoming a part of everyone's lives, and through our Web site we're making sure we're at the forefront of this evolving technology. Another great strength of the site is that due to the "real time" nature of the Internet, unlike traditional mail order, we have complete control over the retail environment.[9]

The processes and priorities of KMCI in e-commerce are vitally important because an e-commerce firm's success depends upon its ability to develop strategies for continuous real-time problem solving and ongoing information-gathering techniques, both of which are critical to the drive for continuous improvement.[10] (Morrison et al., 1998) KMCI also provides crucial support for new product development[11] (Caffyn, 1997). The rate of change in e-commerce is so fast that even the industry leaders experience varying degrees of uneasiness to the point of fear. If the right business strategies can be identified and implemented, then that fear (especially the fear of change) can be harnessed and controlled[12] (Shearer, 1996). Integrating and streamlining the KMCI process can contribute significantly to directing the firm's activities into the most productive channels.

The centers of expertise in e-commerce firms are not related to the management structure. In fact, the viability of an entire e-commerce company may actually hinge on the expertise of a single programmer. For this reason, KMCI seeks to involve as many employees as possible in the process. Implementation of an integrated KMCI strategy has very visible benefits to the firm. First, KMCI protects the e-commerce firm's control of its own intellectual assets by capturing the knowledge of key individuals. Second, it provides insights into the firm's operating environment that encourage all of the firm's employees to continually refocus their efforts in order to increase the firm's competitive advantage. Engaging in the KMCI process both empowers employees and provides insights to management about strengths and weaknesses of the firm. KMCI serves to boost morale while improving operating results, supporting the goal of total quality management.

One major innovation that demonstrates the value of KMCI for e-commerce is the smartcard. The smartcard's latest evolution, the chipcard, is the most advanced, most integrated, most secure, and most flexible contribution to e-commerce transactions. Chipcards with biometric functionality will provide even more security, of course, but these are not yet common. Chipcards provide authenticated access to a matrix of distinct services that extend far beyond the capabilities of basic magnetic stripe cards used in banking and other financial services. It is this integration of commercial transactions, data warehousing, and data mining that has the most complexity and the most potential social and economic impact. It is also this less visible arena where there is the most potential for change—the development, implementation, and integration of products and processes both distinct from and related to e-commerce transactions.

Such innovations enable organizations to obtain (and better utilize) more of their own information. The chipcard also allows organizations to integrate their internal information with the technologies of telephony, the Internet, all forms of e-commerce including an array of banking and other financial services, plus a host of services yet to be conceived. This desire to integrate internal information and separate services has seen the emergence of a new business opportunity—the smartcard system SP. The SP integrates a wide variety of hardware and software products, data management services, and distinct e-commerce merchant services that meet an identified set of client needs. A look at the chipcard-based integration of management and e-commerce functionalities on college campuses helps us gain insights useful for understanding the complexity of KMCI for many aspects of e-commerce, and for knowledge-based organizations in general.

THE EVOLUTION OF SMART CHIPCARDS

The first smartcards were developed and patented in Japan. They were first tested in France, but were not initially successful for a number of reasons: 1) the high cost and poor quality of the chipcard itself; 2) the lack of technology that could utilize the chip; and 3) the lack of client-readiness.

Table 25.1 Smartcard History	
1970	Arimura invents and patents in Japan
1974	Moreno invents and patents in France
1976	French DGT initiative, Bull (FR) 1st licensees
1980	First trials in 3 French cities
1982	First US trials in North Dakota, New Jersey
1996	First campus deployment of chipcards

In migrating from basic laminated identification cards, college campuses went first to cards that used magnet stripes with some form of proprietary coding, although the standards developed by the American Bankers Association have since been widely adopted.

Some campus cards have two stripes—the ABA-standard stripe and a separate impersonal junkstripe used mainly for vending. The junkstripe uses low level cryptography and is not suited to large purchases due to the potential for fraud. It generally works well for vending and copying services that are small value transactions, and cardholders generally have little stored value in the junkstripe. The introduction of single-function memory (junk) chipcard to the card was basically a replacement for the magnetic junkstripe.

One of the earliest campus chipcard systems was installed for The Florida State University (FSU) in 1996. FSU migrated from its initial use of the private label bank interface in 1988 to electronic financial aid distribution in 1995, and was the first campus to implement the smartcard in 1996. Although FSU is a large campus system, institutional size is not a factor, as similar functionality (meal plans, library, financial aid distribution) are common across all institutions. In addition to the chip and the magnetic stripe(s), the cards generally have the university name/logo as well as the individual's name, identification number, library number, photograph, signature, and the date the card was issued. The logo provides cardholders a linkage with their campus identity superimposed between the cardholder and the services that operate through the card, although the verso of the card may include bank logos, long distance trademarks, and customer support numbers.

The basic chipcard is now an increasingly important aspect of e-commerce. Sales of 1.3 billion chipcards in 1997 are expected to increase 23.1% in 1998 to 1.6 billion chipcards.[13] Growth is further projected to result in 2.8 billion cards issued by 2010.[14] During this year alone, Germany, The Netherlands, Belgium, Switzerland, and Spain are expected to issue nearly 100 million electronic purse chipcards. One firm, Proton, has 35 million chipcards worldwide. The flexibility of the chipcard changes dramatically when multiple electronic "purses," or programmable stored-value accounts, are added to the chips used on chipcards.[15] The campus chipcard market is a very complex part of the chipcard market.

The Campus Chipcard System

The structure of a chipcard system implementation on college campuses is represented in Figure 25.3. Although the use of campus identification cards to authenticate users seems to have been around forever, the integration of back office database management systems and campus identification cards is relatively new, as is the technology that drives it.

The laminated photo identification card that uses stickers as a validation method is still used in higher education. With such a system, there is no functional integration of services and systems because there is no electricity involved. A technological evolution of the campus identification card did begin with the addition of a machine-readable functionality to the card—optical character recognition—first with a barcode and then with a magnetic stripe. The impetus for this may have been the campus library's need to match patrons with books—most of which are already

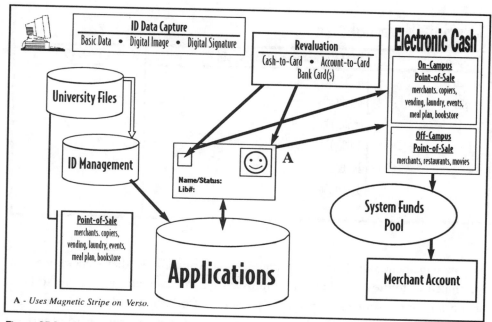

Figure 25.3   Campus Chipcard Systems

Table 25.2   Chipcard Sales

Company	Cards Sold 1997 (millions)	% Change 1996-1997	% Market Share 1997
Schlumberger	450.00	21.3	34.6
Gemplus	424.55	21.3	32.7
GPT	140.00	25.0	10.7
Group Bull	35,000,000	52.2	2.7
ODS Landis & Gyr GmbH & Company	30,000,000	53.3	–

in an electronic database, and many of which are already barcoded. Until recently, few college campuses had extensive automated systems or expanded service requirements that would make upgrading to the chipcard beneficial, nor have they had sufficient telecommunications infrastructure. The rapid wiring of campuses for Internet connectivity changed this situation. As campuses improve their internal

Table 25.3   Chipcard Market Leaders

Company	1997 Microprocessor Cards Sold	Market Share (%)
Schlumberger	81,250,000	25.0
Gemplus	81,250,000	25.0
Giesecke & Devrient	58,500,000	18.0
Bull	35,000,000	10.8
Orga	30,000,000	9.2
Other	39,000,000	12.0

data management and their telecommunications capabilities, they generally reach for chipcards to provide additional improvements in data management and to later obtain additional sources of revenue. It should also be noted that most financial institutions were involved in the expansion of their own magnetic card programs and were not ready or willing to work with the campus market. It is no surprise, then, that many of the major chipcard programs to date have a campus credit union as their first financial service provider.

Campuses that do elect to use a smart chipcard are concerned with many issues: identification; data security; physical security; service enhancement/expansions; revenue enhancement; and reduction of overhead. They see the chipcard as a means of integrating financial transactions, merchant services, and institutional records for students, faculty, staff, and other affiliated users of campus services. Campuses that invest in chipcard systems expect the increased functionality of the chipcard to go far beyond the simple ID card. They expect the chipcard to improve their access to crucial information on which they base their strategic and operational decisions. The successful implementation of smartcards can also be managed in stages.

College campuses function as closed-systems, but interact with a number of external systems, meaning that there is a blend of e-commerce and traditional database management. As a result, there are numerous stakeholders who generally have different priorities. In short, the chipcard technology adds layers of complexity to already complex campus services. Campus clients must protect the privacy of student records and financial institutions need access to personal data on cardholders who use their services. These are two sides of a previously impenetrable barrier.

Legislative and regulatory issues, including questions of escheat (in this case, the cash value remaining in abandoned cardholder accounts), are of great concern, as is data security. There are only a handful of solutions available to providers capable of providing card-based integration of systems and services on college campuses, even though the number of campus clients is now increasing rapidly. The campus chipcard business is full of risk, and the reasons for this are clear. In the face of a rapidly evolving technology, the chipcard SP must maintain transaction and user privacy, and guarantee the absolute accuracy of the records of individual and institutional financial transactions. The system must meet existing technical and industry standards while positioning itself to meet future ones. It must offer a continually expanding array of services, and watch for the emergence of competitors and competing technologies. Yet the solutions supplier does not actually control any of the technology or the software.

At the same time, the client must not be bothered by the chipcard. The system must be easy and quick to implement; appear seamless; integrate generally incompatible hardware, software, and database management systems; and protect against unauthorized access. This is no small task. It requires insider knowledge of campus business operations, as well as awareness of cardholder demographics, legal and regulatory matters, finance, and many other operating constraints. The firm must have technologists who can manage the implementation process and generate supporting marketing materials for their campus clients.

KMCI FOR THE SP

The campus client needs its SP to monitor and filter information related to: hardware, software, systems, and human expertise involved in the collection, maintenance, and analysis of pure information (such as student records); security and flexibility of financial transactions (such as financial aid or meal plans); regulatory concerns from both a local and a global perspective (such as privacy and escheat); and market concerns (such as competitors, systems, cardholder demographics, consumer behavior, and the protection of intellectual property). The SP must begin its KMCI effort by structuring a needs assessment, developing priorities, and implementing a strategy. The following examples indicate the scope of the effort.

1. What is the current and potential legal and regulatory operating environment facing the SP and the client? How can the SP support the client's changing data management objectives?

Example: Escheat. What happens to abandoned stored value? (Assume parents have funded long distance (LD) services using an electronic purse on the chip.)

KM: Identify staff who understand industry and client positions on the issue.

CI: Research appropriate federal, state, and local laws/regulations. Find out about relevant pending legislation/committee hearings.

KMCI: Prep experts and have them meet key lawmakers and arrange for them to testify at significant hearings.

2. What services are most useful to the client's client (the actual cardholder) that also meet the client's demands for increased revenue from non-traditional sources? What are cardholder demographics and psychographics, including card usage and buying behaviors?

Example: How can cardholder usage for long distance telephone service be increased?

KM: Generate a report on cardholder usage patterns for long distance. (Assume LD is part of the service mix.)

CI: Find secondary data on consumer response to various LD brands. (Assume negative for current carrier.)

KMCI: Given consumer response is negative to current LD carrier, drop symbol from card, market generic LD service, and compare usage data pre/post.

3. What components of the e-commerce process in which the SP is engaged are (or might become) important? How can we identify and obtain expertise or establish alliances that would improve existing client services and/or implement new ones?

Example: Would revenue increase by adding card-activated cell phone accounts (if the cellular account was activated by the card not the physical phone)?

KM: Identify current revenue figures and growth rates for existing LD accounts. (Assume positive.) Plan marketing campaign.

CI: Identify cell phone companies that are compatible with the card. Run a trial. (Assume positive.)

KMCI: Identify the service, project the growth, find the technology, test, and market.

4. Who are the emerging players from various industries that have the technology and/or the ability to structure alliances that could enhance or threaten the SP's market position?

> **Example:** Will Internet connectivity go through cable companies or telephone companies?

> **KM:** Identify telecommunications sources and capacity currently used. Develop a position map for SP's existing, potential services.

> **CI:** Research cable and telephone company penetration into SP's services. Map all known alliances and monitor news sources for rumors, reports.

> **KMCI:** Identify market leaders with most potential to ally or threaten SP.

Based on these examples, the SP is able to identify a KMCI priority that includes monitoring current cardholder use of LD carrier service as well as activity in the telecommunications industry. Through KMCI, the SP finds that Regional Bell operating companies and cable companies are locked in mortal combat over provision of related telecommunications services. The SP realizes that it must participate in the establishment of telecommunications standards, monitor and choose between new developments in telecommunications hardware/software, and participate in the legislative process that affects future revenue. Through the KMCI process, the SP is able to identify and monitor key players who might ally with or undercut the SP's market position.

Since chipcards can be used in a variety of unrelated industries—from the campus to the airports, the SP must evaluate every industry's development of an e-commerce service for its potential to enhance what it provides its campus clients. In one case, Peter Harrop, a technology consultant, believes that "paperwork will be eliminated from cargo handling by 2020, and that most baggage, freight, people, and vehicles will be automatically located, via electronic tags and contactless smartcards by 2010. This development is analogous to campus needs for property records management and inventory control. In another case, e-commerce is forecast to account for sixty percent of bank, airline, and travel agency transactions by 2007, and intelligent ticketing is forecast to become the norm by 2005." Since nearly every cardholder will fly somewhere at some point in time, and airlines offer educator discounts and special programs for college students, it takes very little effort to identify loyalty points programs that could benefit cardholders and enhance revenue for campus clients. The potential for integration of services is endless, so there is a need to prioritize those services that will solidify the SP's market, increase revenue for the SP and the client campus, and manage increases in system traffic.

It should also be noted that extending such services to alumni means that eventually business and companies would be forced to choose between corporate and campus-based chipcard programs. The SP must forecast such competition and prepare for it. With so many challenges, the best business model to date has been the use of strategic alliances. Chipcard card SPs operate through strategic alliances that allow them to integrate a variety of products and services to meet the needs of their clients. These alliances are dynamic, and must be structured in such a way that the SP remains allied with reliable leading edge technologies most suited to the college market. This, in turn, means the SP must monitor cardholder usage and articulate changes in general college demographics and psychographics in every country in which it operates (or hopes to operate). Assigning priorities and relative weights to the degree of effort becomes a critical success factor for KMCI.

There are many ways to identify critical success factors in the KMCI process. The previous set of examples started with categories of information needs. However, it is also important to analyze the KMCI initiative from the technology standpoint. For example, chipcards provide certain basic services:

- User authentication that allows validated users to have access to the library and other services restricted by user validation requirements
- Financial services such as debit (or stored value), credit, and general banking
- Secured access to the virtual and real world—both the Internet and physical facilities, such as computer labs
- Merchant services ranging from long distance to local fast food, with optional loyalty programs

In this chipcard example, the SP can easily identify technology-based KMCI initiatives, for example, the identification of potential alliances with companies that:

- Make and sell unattended point-of-sale, data collection, card dispensing, and revalue equipment
- Manufacturer the plastic, the chip, and the chipcard platform
- Provide turnkey, secure, financial transaction software systems
- Make and sell card read/write devices able to handle debit, credit, and smartcard point-of-sale transactions in person, over the Internet, and other payment technologies as they develop
- Provide authentication, encryption, and access control for secure communications network traffic over open networks (e.g., the Internet)

- Provide software for multi-application card design and ongoing card management

The campus card market is business-to-business. Its success relies on establishment and maintenance of good working relationships between technology and telecommunications companies, financial institutions, government agencies, and merchants. Card services such as direct delivery of financial aid streamline operations and improve turnaround time. The benefits of smartcards to the campuses that implement them include:

- Reductions in paper and cash-handling, with attendant reductions in theft/fraud
- Reduced risk of robbery by reducing the amount of cash physically transported
- Reduced overhead through automation and integration of service delivery
- Reduced costs through redeployment of campus services, such as transportation routes
- Revenue enhancement through the ability to implement, monitor, and modify a mix of merchant services and loyalty programs

Despite the fact that the campus card provides students, faculty, and staff with a single vehicle for identification, library privileges, data and even building security, these are not sources of revenue to the client system, and would be required regardless of which card system the client used. Therefore, the SP's KMCI initiatives must provide client campuses with data that reflects improvements in overhead costs, such as those listed above. This requires KM processes such as data warehousing, report generation, and data mining using appropriate statistical analysis techniques. The CI function would help the SP acquire appropriate data on overhead costs for alternative systems.

Although the SP provides the chipcard system to the campus, in regard to the e-commerce functions, the chooser is not the user. The actual success of the campus chipcard program rests on cardholders—the customers' customers—and their willingness to choose the chipcard over alternative methods. Therefore, services should be based on demographic analysis (CI) and knowledge of current and trend data on cardholder usage. When the SP shares this type of market information with its client systems and relevant partners, it can benefit all the stakeholders and solidify the working relationships.

Both the campus and the chipcard provider must clearly understand the complexities inherent in this environment, however, and have the requisite skills to integrate and manage such systems. Once the card system is in place, there is a "hometown syndrome"—an unwillingness by the campus to change card systems. This makes market penetration by new e-commerce SPs very tough. It also means that they must identify and market to the most visible priorities of the campus client, which, as indicated above, may not be cardholders' priorities, or the area that produces the most revenue for the SP. Since usage of the chipcard may be from services that do not generate revenue for either the SP or the campus, the SP will have to able to manage high-volume transactions that generate low/no revenue. This makes it important to identify current costs (KM) and industry benchmarks (CI). Through use of KMCI, the client system and the SP can both avoid costly failures, for example, offering e-commerce merchant services that cardholders ignore or merchants find too expensive to implement.

Despite the complexities of chipcard systems, there are other incentives to migrate to advanced card systems. For example, as Figure 25.4 indicates, the use of smartcards allows campuses to identify different service levels for many additional categories of cardholders, such as alumni association employees or summer enrichment students. In the matrix, the establishment of different types of privileges (represented by the letters A-G) may have philosophical and/or economic impact on the campus, but provision of select services might generate revenue in other areas. Integrating these records becomes a KM issue for the campus and a CI issue for the chipcard SP, but the two must work together using the same data in order to accomplish the goal. Once the data is integrated, it becomes a KM issue for both the SP and the campus client, with CI implications for both. Both mine the data to identify patterns of use of existing services, and both try to identify potential sources for reducing overhead and/or generating new revenue, for example, through the addition of new merchant services. Both use the same data to increase market exposure and revenue.

Status	Privileges						
	A	B	C	D	E	F	G
undergraduate	Y	Y	Y	Y	Y	Y	Y
faculty/staff spouse	Y	Y	Y	N	F	F	Y
visitor	Y	N	N	N	N	N	N
Y= eligible			N= ineligible			F= eligible with fee	

Figure 25.4   Cardholder Privilege Matrix

Benefits of KMCI: The Parking Problem Example

The most basic function of an identification card is identification. However, most cards are limited in who they can identify and which services they can authenticate. Most identification cards are merely a snapshot of the affiliation of a specific user at some point in time. Campus administrators cannot improve services if they do not know when categories of cardholders use services such as transportation and vending. Campuses could improve services, generate additional revenue, and increase alumni connections if databases could be integrated and transaction tracked.

E-commerce and Campus Parking: New Solutions

The matrix in Table 25.4 (see page 436) shows how a single basic service, such as parking, has KM and CI significance for both the campus client and the chipcard SP. In this example, parking on the campus has become a problem. It is easy to see that the information needed by the campus decision-maker and the chipcard SP could be either internal or external at varying points in time. The KMCI model allows the stakeholders to share information, streamline the overall process, reduce the cost of the solution, and improve the level of service for cardholders.

Use of campus chipcards provides a number of futuristic-sounding free and e-commerce solutions to the campus parking problem.

FREE: Access to parking can easily become a variable of day/time, capacity, and event. The chipcard validates authorized users and opens the gates of authorized lots at authorized times of the day/night. In this scenario, traffic can be monitored and the planning process improved.

FEE:

1. The *debit/credit* functionality allows cardholders to be automatically surcharged/credited during periods of heavy/light use, and for specific lots.

2. The *loyalty points* function lets cardholders be rewarded for

    (a) not parking on campus during specific times

    (b) taking alternative transportation, such as city busses in free fare zones

    (c) The merchant services functionality could allow adjacent commercial lots to charge cardholders (debit/credit), simultaneously providing key data on usage to campus planners.

The e-commerce functionality of chipcards provides campus administrators with incentives and information not previously possible. In fact, chipcards have been implemented in the parking lots of two California campuses, The University

Table 25.4   The KMCI Parking Example

Parking Problem	Campus	Chipcard SP
Needed	• day/time gate counts by user category • user choice behaviors, current and future • transportation options, current and future • current and projected available funding	• hardware/software for gate counts • access to database–sample(s) • expertise to integrate use/users • cost-benefit analysis for solution
Options	• restrict permits, locations, times • allocate resources to transit alternatives • just throw money at it–add spaces, security staff	• use own technology/expertise • acquire technology/expertise of others • avoid or accept challenge
KM Strategy	*Find:* match use with campus activities 　　• look at use of current transit *Plan:* integrate use/user records with activities, available transit options *Do:*　implement and monitor changes	• identify, develop report functions • identify existing clients with need • mine available data for a fee
CI Strategy	• monitor hardware/software options • identify solutions of other campuses • price parking and transit options • forecast available revenue • obtain community, legislative, regulatory information, attitudes	• monitor hardware/software options • use this to attract new clients • identify similar needs outside campus market
KMCI	• monitor current, future use/user demographics • monitor current, future transit options • analyze failure/success of own/other campuses • monitor/respond to external stakeholder concerns	• monitor current, future technology/expertise • monitor situation on this and other campuses • evaluate cost-benefit of providing solution • find analogous situations that need solution

of California at Berkeley and San Francisco State University.[16] It takes very little imagination to identify numerous other e-commerce possibilities for a campus that implements the chipcard, and each of these has a KMCI component.

The same individuals who oversaw implementation of FSU's card program now provide card systems for client campuses in several countries through CyberMark, a joint venture of Sallie Mae, Huntington Bancshares, and the Batelle Institute. In fall 1998, First USA and CyberMark jointly issued a credit-stored value card for FSU alumni and supporters, called the Seminole Seal. With this card:

alumni and supporters can put up to $100 in stored value, using either cash or their FSU MasterCard USA for concessions at Florida State's football stadium. There will be no fee for reloading the chip from the credit card. The card has a 3.9% introductory annual percentage rate followed by a 9.99 APR, and no annual fee. New cardholders will receive $25 in electronic cash to encourage use of the chip portion of the card. First USA says about 10,000 existing FSU Visa cardholders, starting with those in the Tallahassee area, will receive the new cards soon. FSU students have been using smart-cards since 1996, but they cannot yet use their cards at the stadium. This appears to be the first time in the United States that a MasterCard has carried a non-Mondex stored-value application. MasterCard, which is the majority owner of Mondex International, did not return calls.[17]

Clearly, the chipcard company must monitor potential services such as stadium concessions that the cardholders and potential cardholders might want. At the same time, the chipcard SP must also monitor changing market conditions, legal and regulatory conditions, and realignment of strategic alliances that face the financial institutions with which they are (or might become) affiliated (e.g., Visa, MasterCard, and American Express). Moreover, the global nature of the industry means that it must watch the situation on a global front. Companies involved in the initial development and testing of smartcards (e.g., Schlumberger and Bull) have also identified campus cards as a major market initiative.

To date, the major campus installations are shown in Table 25.5.

Table 25.5 Major Campus Installations: Source "More U.S. Universities Traveling The Smart Card Payment Route" Debit Card News, 3.19 (March 30, 1998)

School	Cards	Financial Institution
University of Michigan	125,000	First of America Bank
University of Pennsylvania	100,000	PNC Bank
Penn State University	85,000	Penn State Federal C.U.
University of Toronto	60,000	None
University of Arizona	50,000	Suguaro Credit Union
Florida State University	40,000	SunTrust
University of Kansas	35,000	Commerce Bank
Memorial University of Newfoundland	35,000	None
Robert Morris College	20,000	PNC Bank
Eastern Illinois University	15,000	None

Use of chipcards that integrate campus information and financial transactions is more expensive than other forms of identification cards, but chipcards are attractive to campus business officials for many reasons: reduction of the need to carry cash; streamlined paperwork; automation of numerous operations; and inclusion of new services that enhance revenue. The SP's college campus client offers a complex environment, but the actual KMCI process for the SP is simple, cyclical, and iterative—find out, plan, do. The first step is for the SP to identify, analyze, and monitor the information needs and the changing interests of the various external stakeholders—the campus client, the cardholders, e-commerce merchant and financial services, and any other stakeholders that can be identified. The SP then identifies which technological, legal, social, and cultural events to monitor for each stakeholder. There are both internal and external components of this needs analysis process. In other words, different bits of information must be directed through the SP's internal information pipelines in order to be useful, so the optimal internal channels and cross channels must be identified.

In step two, the results of the needs analysis are used to identify and establish the relative importance and time constraints of the information needs. This framework is then used to develop a system to filter and extract value from the most relevant information sources to meet the highest priority needs—those that will provide competitive advantage. Other data—in effect, the waste—is shunted to a storage facility (data warehouse) or discarded. Establishing an efficient system requires the involvement of internal stakeholders, such as the marketing and information systems staff.

In step three, the KMCI specialist implements the system and integrates and streamlines the communication of relevant information to the relevant parties. Once this system is in place, it reduces the time that the decision makers must spend to integrate internal and external information. It also reduces the cost of uncertainty and improves the decision process. In other words, the KMCI specialist delivers the right information at the right time to the right decision maker. In the rapidly evolving world of e-commerce, reducing the decision maker's stress levels related to the decision process is a significant added benefit.

Although the process itself is simple, the implementation of KMCI for an SP does present a few challenges: 1) the rapid pace of development and implementation of e-commerce functionalities; 2) the mix of global companies, joint ventures; and 3) confusion surrounding reporting practices. The two tables following illustrate the second problem. In the original table from which Table 25.6 was extracted (Rigney, 1998),[18] Group Bull and ODS Landis & Gyr GmbH & Company show Bull with less than three percent market share and ODS Landis & Gyr not reporting. But notice the different perspective shown for Group Bull in Table 25.7.[19] (Rigney, 1998) Where Group Bull was reported to have fewer than three percent of 1997 sales, it has nearly an eleven percent share in the second table taken from the same news article. What we really know is that Group Bull is very much a player in this market. The growth rate found in Table 25.6 is one indicator that this is a dynamic market, but review of the article's full text and comparison of all the tables is required to obtain a true picture of where the company is positioned and who else needs close scrutiny. This process must extend far beyond the single article referenced here, of course.

Table 25.6   Chipcard Sales

Company	Cards Sold 1997 (millions)	% Change 1996-1997	% Market Share 1997
Schlumberger	450.00	21.3	34.6
Gemplus	424.55	21.3	32.7
GPT	140.00	25.0	10.7
Group Bull	35,000,000	52.2	2.7
ODS Landis & Gyr GmbH & Company	30,000,000	53.3	–

Table 25.7   Chipcard Market Leaders

Company	1997 Microprocessor Cards Sold	Market Share (%)
Schlumberger	81,250,000	25.0
Gemplus	81,250,000	25.0
Giesecke & Devrient	58,500,000	18.0
Bull	35,000,000	10.8
Orga	30,000,000	9.2
Other	39,000,000	12.0

KMCI for Smart Chipcard Technology

Smartcards are integrated chip circuit cards with a small on-board micro-processor chip. In other words, like a PC, they have input and output, storage, memory, an operating system, and a microprocessor. They use a limited set of instructions, are secured with a personal identification number (PIN), and a single chip can support multiple applications. The failure rate of magnetic cards is two percent, but only .3% for smartcards[20] (France Telecom, 1998). Magnetic card readers need one technician per twenty readers on average, but only one for 100 smartcard readers. This is because smartcard readers have fewer moving parts, better resistance to the environment and physical abuse, and more sophisticated levels of security.

Smartcards use ABA-standard encoding that determines what, where, and how data is encoded. There are generally three tracks available:

- Track 1 - International Air Transportation Association (IATA), 79 optical characters

- Track 2 - American Bankers Association (ABA), 40 numeric characters

- Track 3 - Thrift industry (read-write), 107 numeric characters

The expansion of the smartcard market has been facilitated by three major standards, as shown in Table 25.8.

Table 25.8 Standard Use in Chipcard Production	
International Standards Organization (ISO)	16-digit ISO number and basic smartcard standards, e.g. 7816 /1 dimensions 7816/2 contact positions 7816/3 exchange protocol 7816/4 file structure and command subset
American National Standards Institute (ANSI)	Assignment of ISO number/Batch ID number (BIN)
American Bankers Association (ABA)	Encoding standard (what goes where) on Track 2 of the magnetic stripe

This small amount of technical information creates high-priority KMCI activities. The SP must monitor physical standards; new developments in chip, plastics, and die technology; and chip and hardware/software reliability, in addition to the changing nature of its clients' and cardholders' requirements.

Conclusion

As demonstrated above, the integration of KM and CI processes provide the appropriate model for identifying and prioritizing the information needs of e-commerce companies, particularly the SP, because it is able to recognize and reflect changes in usage, client needs, technologies, and working relationships between suppliers and clients. Since challenges extend in every direction, only effective integrated KMCI strategies can tame the savage beast.

References

1. Dysart, Jane I. "The SCIP Conference for CI Professionals." *Information Today*, May 1998.
2. Bergsman, Steve. "Corporate Spying Goes Mainstream." CFO, *The Magazine for Senior Financial Executives*, 13 (12) December 1994: 24.
3. Bensoussan, Babette. "Why Spy?" *Management* (Aukland), 45 (7) August 1998: 56.
4. Jupp, Vivienne. "Managing for the Millennium: An Online Government Business and Finance." *World Reporter* 8/13/98. In Dow Jones Interactive. 10/8/98.
5. Clark, Drew. "On-line Banking: One-Stop Shopping Not Seen as Answer to Client Need." *American Banker*. 163(186) (October 1, 1998): 14.
6. Davis, Stan; Jim Botkin. "The Coming of Knowledge-Based Business." In Dale Neef (Ed.) *The Knowledge Economy*. Boston: Butterworth-Heinemann, 1998; and Peter Senge, et al., *The Fifth Discipline Fieldbook: Strategies and Tools for Building a Learning Organization*, NY: Doubleday, 1994: 10.
7. Boisot, M. "The Context of Strategic Thinking." In B. Garratt (Ed.) *Developing Strategic Thought*, New York: Harpercollins, 1996. Also in Kostas N. Dervitsiotis, "The Challenge of Managing Organizational Change: Exploring the Relationship of Re-Engineering, Developing Learning Organizations and Total Quality Management." *Total Quality Management* 9 (1) February 1998: 109-122. In Proquest Direct, ABI Global 10/8/1998.
8. Alverson, Mats. *Management of Knowledge-Intensive Companies*. NY. Walter de Gruyter, 1995: 6.
9. "Blueberry New Media Introduces Fat Face to the Ultimate Ecommerce Solution." M2 Presswire, 8/12/98. In Dow Jones Interactive, October 6, 1998.
10. Morrison, Eileen; Debbie Mobley; Barbara Farley. "Research and Continuous Improvement: The Merging of Two Entities?" *Hospital & Health Services Administration* 41 (3) (Fall 1998): 359.
11. Caffyn, Sarah. "Extending Continuous Improvement to the New Product Development Process." *R&D Management* 27(3) (July 1997): 253
12. Shearer, Clive. "TQM Requires the Harnessing of Fear." *Quality Progress* 29(4) (April 1996): 97.

13. "Worldwide Chip Card Sales Could Reach 1.6 Billion Units This Year." *Smart Card Alert*: 3+; May 1998.

14. "Smart Card Market Growth to Continue." *Card Technology* (June 1998): 25

15. "Visa Wins One, Loses One in Europay Decisions." *American Banker*. 163(175) (September 14, 1998): 1.

16. "A Lot Smarter." *Card Fax*. 191(September 18, 1998): 2.

17. "Seminole Seal." *Card Fax*. 192 (September 18, 1998): 1.

18. Rigney, Melanie. "Smart Card Market Growth to Continue." *Card Technology*. (June 1998): 25. Online at Business & Industry, 10/8/98.

19. Ibid.

20. France Telecom. In Cybermark Seminar documentation, 1998.

CHAPTER 26

Knowledge Management in Developing Countries

T. Kanti Srikantaiah

Director, Center for Knowledge Management

Dominican University

INTRODUCTION

This chapter is presented in two parts. The first part discusses knowledge management (KM) from the perspective of developing countries. KM can be viewed as a problem or an opportunity in developing countries. I will analyze KM in developing countries with discussion of GNP, literacy rate, health, and demographics. An analysis of book, media, and electronic information is also provided, along with proposed "business cases."

The chapter's second part will focus on the funding perspective—how these countries are to be assisted, the viewpoint of the aid organization, and the supporting country.

THE COUNTRY VIEWPOINT

The need for knowledge is no less in a developing country than in a developed country. The difference is the absorptive capacity to generate, acquire, deliver, and utilize knowledge. The developing world is short of the infrastructure, the human resource base, and the institutional organization needed to exploit and manage knowledge to its fullest.

Most developed countries have made significant economic advances through managing their vast array of knowledge resources. These countries have demonstrated the importance of the knowledge sector as essential, impacting nearly all other economic activities including major sectors such as agriculture, industry, energy, and private sector development. The contribution of those sectors for economic and social development through managing knowledge has enhanced goods, works, and services in all walks of life.

As the economies are becoming knowledge-based, the success of any KM program depends on knowledge sharing, with as much speed as possible through utilization of modern technology. The new knowledge climate driven by technology has transformed the way we perform daily business and also has influenced our values and enhanced our productivity.

As we progress towards the twenty-first century, it is perhaps not over the top to say that KM will become the core of all human activities.

KNOWLEDGE MANAGEMENT AND DEVELOPING COUNTRIES

KM means different things to different practitioners, although everyone agrees that effective KM is a requirement to embrace their ability to work. The traditional thinking of modern KM has, especially in the western world, always been around explicit knowledge: creating information; documenting information; accessing information; selecting information sources; acquiring information; synthesizing information; packaging information; and disseminating information. Essentially, the knowledge climate has focused information packages, selection, collection, and management of those resources for institutions.

With respect to explicit knowledge, the increase of information in various formats, particularly in electronic formats, has changed knowledge behavior in developed countries and is influencing the developing countries as well. Today, developing countries are no longer treating libraries/information centers and other information providers as only suppliers, but as dynamic providers meeting the information demands of government and the private sector. Developing countries are re-evaluating their roles in meeting their countries' knowledge needs, as the majority of the population in many developing countries is illiterate.

However, an important dimension of KM is tacit knowledge. Knowledge resides with individuals and when this knowledge is properly tapped and shared it creates a better environment not only to increase productivity but also to improve social capital in the institutional climate. As of now, developed countries are making significant advances in economic development by applying new methodologies to capture and manage tacit knowledge to effectively increase productivity.

Recent technological advances make it possible to move information on a global basis at a speed, which was not only impossible, but also barely imaginable in previous decades. However, this movement of information has resulted in a dramatic transformation of knowledge work—client needs assessment, manufacturing, marketing, services, jobs, or processes and products. On the other hand, it has also created a gulf between the information-rich and information-poor economies. The developed economies are adapting to the new knowledge culture more readily than the developing countries. As the main knowledge culture in the developing world is evolving from a purely oral, community-centered, and informal system to one that combines the written, the visual, and the audiovisual and the oral in a variety of ways, the KM systems have grown larger and become more complex to fit into the environment. To address the issues arising from this growth and complexity, modern KM techniques are required.

What KM emphasizes, which previous generations of information technology applications have not, is tacit knowledge, the knowledge unrecorded in formal documents. This tacit knowledge is precisely what is available and largely under utilized in developing countries. In principle, the fit between KM and the context of developing countries, and the opportunity thereby provided is of immense potential; however, as of yet, with KM still in its nascent stages, our knowledge of how to capitalize on that fit is still very limited.

DEVELOPMENT CRISIS

There is a definite correlation between KM and economic growth, as evidenced by a significant contrast in the social and economic indicators between the developed and developing countries. The World Bank has provided some startling statistics on the differences between the advanced and less developed countries. It lists (all in United States dollars) 200+ countries as: low income economies (GNP $785 or less); lower-middle income (GNP $785-$3,125); upper-middle income economies (GNP $3,126-$9,655); and high-income economies (GNP $9,655 or more).[1] An analysis of selected developed countries and developing countries reveals considerable disparities not simply in wealth, but also in education, population, GNP per capita, adult illiteracy rate, infant mortality rate, and poverty indicators health services, which is shown in Table 26.1.

- GNP: The GNP is a well-known measure of economic development and forms the basis to measure other indicators, including information services. The 1997

Table 26.1 Selected Economic Indicators to Reflect Knowledge Management

	Population (1997) Millions	GNP Per Capita (1997)	Adult Literacy Rate (%)(1995)		Infant Mortality Rate per 1,000 Live Births (1996)	Poverty		Foreign Direct Investment (1996) (Millions in US$)
			Male	Female		Rural	Urban	
G-7 Countries								
USA	268	28,740	—	—	—	—	—	—
Japan	126	37,850	—	—	—	—	—	—
Germany	82	28,260	—	—	—	—	—	—
France	59	26,050	—	—	—	—	—	—
Canada	30	19,290	—	—	—	—	—	—
UK	59	20,710	—	—	—	—	—	—
Italy	57	20,120	—	—	—	—	—	—
Developing Countries								
Bangladesh	124	270	51	74	77	46.0	23.3	15
Brazil	164	4,720	17	17	36	32.6	13.1	9,889
Chad	7	240	38	65	115	N/A	N/A	18
China	1,227	860	10	27	33	11.8	22.0	40,180
Colombia	38	2,280	9	9	25	29.0	7.8	3,322
Ethiopia	60	110	55	75	109	14.7	6.8	5
India	961	390	35	62	65	43.5	33.7	2,587
Kenya	28	330	14	30	57	46.4	29.3	13
Korea, Rep.	46	10,550	1	3	9	N/A	N/A	2,325
Malaysia	21	4,680	11	22	11	N/A	N/A	4,500
Mexico	95	3,680	8	13	32	N/A	N/A	7,619
Niger	10	200	79	93	118	76.1	31.9	-
Nigeria	118	260	33	53	78	49.5	31.7	1,391
Pakistan	137	490	50	76	88	36.9	28.0	690
Sri Lanka	18	800	7	13	15	45.5	26.8	120

GNP (all in United States dollars) for G-7 countries includes: USA 28,740; Japan 37,850; Germany 28,260; France 26,050; Canada 19,290; United Kingdom 20,710; and Italy 20,120. On the contrary, the GNP for selected developing countries reveals the following (all in United States dollars): Bangladesh 270; Brazil 4,720; Chad 240; China 860; Colombia 2,280; Ethiopia 110; India 390; Kenya 330; Mexico 3,680; Nigeria 260; Pakistan 490; Sri Lanka 800.

• Literacy Rate: Many developing countries have adult illiteracy rates of more than fifty percent. This situation is much worse when illiteracy rates for women in those countries is considered.

• Health Services: In low-income countries, there was an average of one physician for a population of nearly 40,000-70,000, whereas in high-income countries there was a physician for every 400 people. Similarly, the infant mortality rate for every 1,000 births in developing countries is around five to twenty-five percent, whereas in developed countries the rate is almost zero.

Yet, in terms of lives, these developing countries have more than two-thirds of the world's population. India and China alone, the world's most populous countries, had in 1997 a population of 961 and 1,277 million, respectively, and are expected to increase significantly in the twenty-first century. Roughly one-fifth of the world's population still lives in acute poverty on less than one United States dollar a day—all living in developing countries.

What do these stark contrasts imply? The low-income countries are in a state that calls for immediate, strong, and multi-prolonged efforts to raise their standard of living. There has been a widening gap and disparity in knowledge between low-income and high-income countries during the last thirty to forty years and the gulf is widening with each decade, proving that the large number of the world's poor and disadvantaged are living in ignorance.

KNOWLEDGE ECONOMY

In the knowledge economy, the developing countries need to do a lot of work defining strategies and creating conditions to acquire and manage knowledge as quickly as possible. A conducive knowledge environment in those countries should encompass regulations protecting investment, intellectual property, and individual privacy, with regulated communication networks and sound education policies, creating conditions for the knowledge to grow—both through the acquisition of external information and stimulating the creation of indigenous information. An economic analysis of certain knowledge packages from the 1997 UNESCO Statistical Yearbook reveals the following in the area of explicit knowledge.

Book Environment

Western industrialized countries are predominantly "book" cultures (a product of formal education). Western civilizations during the twentieth century have developed newer and more extensive ways of creating, organizing, and disseminating knowledge. In contrast, developing countries are far behind in this area. These countries experience a severe shortage of raw materials that makes even extension of their publishing efforts difficult. The number of books (and availability per person) in developing countries is meager. Even dated books have immense value as evidenced by the library collections and the items in secondhand bookstores. The ratio between the developed and developing countries in terms of titles available per million inhabitants is about 9:1. Similarly, in newsprint production and consumption the ratio is 41.4:1.5.[3]

Media

The non-print media culture in developing countries covers radio, audio, video, and television systems. Radio provides a strong support to "oral" culture, giving prominence to voice with a lower unit cost per listener. Today, with government broadcasting policies in place and with the assistance from the international financial institutions and from donor agencies, most developing countries enjoy radio reaching out to the masses, even where electricity is low or lacking.

Television is another medium that could have a high impact in disseminating knowledge. Television appeals to a broad public and adds a wide range of possible ways in conveying knowledge. It is a powerful visual medium with capacity to capture the attention of a wide range of viewers. The video camera and video tape, both relatively cheap, extend the possibilities of inexpensive production and of viewing the products on television. Similarly, audiocassettes can and do go a long way in disseminating knowledge at a cheap cost.

The ratio of radio receivers between the developed and developing countries per 1,000 people is 6:1 and for television sets is 11:1.[4]

Computers and Electronic Information

Computers and telecommunication technologies have revolutionized the world of KM. They have penetrated every sphere, influencing the working lifestyle and even the social lifestyle, significantly impacting economic and social development. Computers and telecommunication technologies have become more valuable as their costs have plummeted in recent years and their processing powers and related capabilities, including portability, are increasing. However, their role in developing countries is still at the beginning stages and with only limited applications in government, academic, and private sectors. With further developments in computer and telecommunications technology, their expanded and important role in KM for developing countries is inevitable. A comparison summary of some knowledge indicators is found in Table 26.2 for ready reference.

KM in Context

KM in developing countries, just like in developed countries, covers all areas. To name several: MIS support systems; finance and accounting functions; data

Table 26.2 Some Knowledge Indicators

*Compiled from: UNESCO Statistical Yearbook, 1997.
**The data available only for 1994 is indicated in parentheses.

	Book Population (#of titles) (1995)	Newspapers and Periodicals		TV Licenses Issued (1995)	Radio Receivers (1995)	Libraries	
		Daily (1995)	Non-daily (1995)			Public Library	Service Points
G-7 Countries							
USA	62,039	1,611	9,728 (94)	215,000	559,000	Not Reported	Not Reported
Japan	Not Reported	121	Not Reported	85,500	114,500	1,475	1,950
Germany	74,174	406	38	46,000	77,000	13,032	13,032
France	34,765	80	227	34,250	52,000	2,315	3,366
Canada	17,931	107	1,650	21,000	309,950	1,045	3,672
UK	101,764	103	Not Reported	26,000	83,200	167	24,869
Italy	34,470	76	274	25,500	47,000	106	2,366
Developing Countries							
Bangladesh	Not Reported	51	Not Reported	525	5,600	Not Reported	Not Reported
Brazil	21,574(94)*	320	1,400	35,000	63,500	2,739	Not Reported
Chad	Not Reported	1	2	9	1,570	Not Reported	Not Reported
China	100,951	Not Reported	875	250,000	225,500	Not Reported	Not Reported
Colombia	Not Reported	34	Not Reported	4,200	20,200	1,378	Not Reported
Ethiopia	Not Reported	4	15	250	10,900	Not Reported	Not Reported
India	11,643	Not Reported	Not Reported	47,000	75,500	Not Reported	Not Reported
Kenya	300	5	Not Reported	500	2,600	1	21
Korea, Rep.	35,864	62	Not Reported	Not Reported	45,000	329	329
Malaysia	6,465	44	Not Reported	3,300	8,700	14	471
Mexico	Not Reported	310	45 (94)	20,000	24,000	5,630	Not Reported
Niger	Not Reported	2	5	105	620	Not Reported	Not Reported
Nigeria	1,314	27	Not Reported	6,100	18,700	12	76
Pakistan	124	223	719	2,680	12,500	4	10
Sri Lanka	3,933	9	Not Reported	915	3,700	Not Reported	Not Reported

management systems; demographics on education, health, labor, agriculture, environment, household surveys, and industry.

Anecdotal evidence, analyses of planning documents (sample), and a review of available World Bank project documents from India, China, and Brazil, indicate that in developing countries, information technology related work and projects undertaken by their governments, non-government organizations (NGOs), and the private sector, seldom support KM.[5] At best, they are heavily weighted towards technology rather than information or knowledge and in most developing countries there is a tendency to create "heavy" system models disassociated from the economic/social reality as evidenced from the analysis.

In developing countries, government plans and projects loosely in the realm of KM or with KM components display the following characteristics:

- Project designs and programs do not conceptualize and include the "KM sector."
- Project components are heavily weighed towards technology, particularly information technology.
- There are no action plans, in general, to fund training KM specialists and to manage explicit or tacit knowledge.
- Technical and human resource expertise does not exist to develop, maintain, and market KM considering the socioeconomic conditions in developing countries.
- Information specialists are not consulted in the development of national information policies and in designing KM systems.
- Information and knowledge acquisition and dissemination are supply-driven and system-driven, rather than market-driven to meet "real needs" of clients.
- There is a near total absence of marketing strategies.
- A "not invented here" syndrome that militates against the policies and implementation of projects to support KM exists in most developing countries.
- There is a general public perception that explicit, knowledge-based information systems do not really promote knowledge sharing.
- There is a tendency to create "heavy" information system models disassociated from the socioeconomic reality.
- There is an absence or lack of "sustainability plans" (i.e., budgeting for and the provision of indigenous resources for ongoing support) in national plans and in project implementations.
- An understanding of the role and importance of KM as an important tool in building a strategic national asset is necessary.
- Obtaining even basic day-to-day information is a constant source of frustration in most countries, and the application of basic KM technologies to resolve those issues are seldom considered.
- Tacit knowledge, an important ingredient in oral society in developing countries, remains strong, but strategies to capture and share "best practices" have not been articulated.

KNOWLEDGE MANAGEMENT BUSINESS CASES

Design and implementation of any business case depends very much on factors like country, region, type of political system, economic viability, and the available infrastructure. Here are some key elements to consider in implementing KM systems in developing countries:

- Formulate sound policies at the central, state, and local government level; library and information professionals should identify KM components for inclusion in policy documents.

- Create KM designs involving public and private sector partnerships contributing to the economic/national development; support the appropriate infrastructure to provide daily information needs to the public both in urban and rural areas.

- Address issues related to literacy and adult education, and make them an integral part of development, both in urban and rural areas. As the majority of the population in developing countries lives in rural areas, it is all the more important to promote reading habits and emphasize the importance of the basic three "Rs" to meet their needs.

- Configure the book industry and publishing sector to meet local needs (i.e., text, illustrations, and supporting material drawn from local environments); encourage local publishers to publish indigenously.

- Train information professionals to manage knowledge properly; they should have expertise in all knowledge activities such as identifying, collecting, organizing, indexing, storing, retrieving, preserving, and weeding.[6] Also, train librarians and information specialists to solve KM issues in communities.

- Tap into knowledge that is already available and develop systems to provide information in the areas of basic needs: health; prevention of disease; environmental protection; family planning; livestock and husbandry; food and agriculture; appropriate technology; education and literacy; rural development; child care; and the like.

- Utilize distance learning. Radios are as cost-effective as they are inexpensive, readily accessible, and profitable; wherever possible extend to other media, such as audio and videocassettes. Develop modules and make them available in libraries and community centers. Plan for the use of computer technology and telecommunications technology in the near future.

- Tap external funding. Utilize funding available from United Nations' agencies, regional agencies, and other aid agencies including multinational corporations. However, while external assistance can stimulate the economy and meet immediate needs, long-term solutions must be addressed in a fashion that allows self-support and self-reliance.

- Tap NGOs resources. They can be extremely influential in meeting continuing education goals, mobilizing communities, and mobilizing funding from other sources.

- Address women's issues. Many NGOs have done substantial work on these.

- Developing countries need to keep up with developed countries in accessing knowledge and filling the knowledge gap. The approach should emphasize two aspects:
    - Building and developing the capacity to apply, discover, analyze, and interpret data
    - Importing knowledge to meet daily information needs

The two aspects are almost inseparable and, in a sense, have a symbiotic relationship. In developing countries, youth and adults both in urban and rural areas are in need of both.

There is no simple solution that can be uniformly applied to all situations in developing countries. Developing countries share a large amount of information in the form tacit knowledge and, therefore, KM business cases also emphasize oral tradition to capture, acquire, organize, and develop appropriate systems. Each business case needs to be evaluated and customized to meet the individual needs of a country: priorities are to be sorted out depending on the available resources. Indigenous resources are to be tapped and, where necessary, resources from the outside are to be imported. The government should provide action plans through the help of educators, trainers, and KM planners. Action plans should be embedded in formal documents such as five-year plans and should be communicated to all concerned parties.

DEVELOPING COUNTRIES IN SUMMARY

Over the last decade (1987-1997) many developing countries have demonstrated enthusiasm for the information/knowledge sector, but unfortunately, in most cases, only focusing on "technology." Investing in "technology" has not been accompanied by other investments to trigger information and economic growth. Many developing countries are also constantly confronted with pressures from bilateral and multilateral agencies, global vendors and consultants, foreign as well as domestic, pushing specific areas and products irrespective of local and environmental conditions.

In most situations, the technology side of KM has high visibility in market terms of supply and demand, and policies relating to them become embedded in the various official documents of ministries, such as industry and energy. Several measures are required to prepare the developing countries for the twenty-first century in a KM setting. First, developing countries should place greater emphasize upon and should allocate more realistic budgets to KM and they should work collaboratively with donor communities to supplement their resources. Second, the governments in developing countries should prepare a sound national information policy into which various KM policies and projects can be fitted. Third, library and information work should not stay as marginalized services, given the new information culture and technology. Instead, information professionals should be trained properly so as to proactively take the center stage in managing knowledge and in providing services to the public at large and to specialists in the field.

The Funder's Perspective on Knowledge Management in Developing Countries

There is, however, another very interesting dimension to the role of KM in developing countries. A recent World Bank study (Dollar and Pritchett, 1998) has demonstrated in a rigorous fashion what economists have increasingly come to suspect—that foreign aid stimulates growth and reduces poverty only in countries with a supportive climate, and that in countries where policies and practices are not supportive, foreign aid, at least in terms of infusion of cash, is not only non-productive, it appears to be counter-productive.

A good climate is comprised of elements such as low inflation and concomitant monetary policies, small budget deficits, openness to trade, a strong rule of law, and a competent bureaucracy. Bad policies and practices are the obvious opposites. Inflationary monetary policies; substantial budget deficits; restrictive and protectionistic trade practices; weak and unpredictable rules of law; and bureaucracies that are inefficient, either because of corruption or because of the view that bureaucracies exist for their own sake or to create jobs within themselves, rather than to expedite someone to get the job done. If one views this phenomenon from an infocentric perspective, then in comparing the supportive and effective policies and practices with the counter-productive policies and practices, one will see the emergence of an important dimension that distinguishes the good from the bad—an environment where *information* is accessible, predictable, and reliable.

Granted, KM or any other information system cannot directly affect the quality and, to a degree, the predictability and reliability of information. The basic quality of the information—e.g., which permits does one need to accomplish something and how does one go about arguing for them—is basically a consequence of political decisions. Still, the recognition of the information dimensions of development and economic growth is a very important factor.

From this recognition derives two very important corollaries. The first corollary is rather straightforward; the second corollary is not so obvious. The first corollary is that information has an impact if it is accessed and used, the classic invention versus innovative distinctions. An invention that does not become an innovation has no impact, nor does information that is not accessed and used. From this derives the conclusion that a key target of a developing country should be KM, information systems that make relevant information accessible. The second corollary is somewhat more subtle, which is that good KM, good information systems, are important not just for providing access to information, but because they drive the very quality of the information itself.

It is more difficult for a bureaucrat to be whimsical or arbitrary if information is accessible about how similar situations have been handled in the past. The provision of precedent drives consistency and predictability. The ability to see how previous transactions or applications were handled gives the bureaucrat information with which to make a decision and a degree of comfort in the fact that he/she is not exposing him/herself.[7] It also gives greater comfort and confidence to the investor, and provides a tool with which to resist or appeal arbitrary rulings.

Even in an honest environment, as assumed above, the effect is important. It becomes even more so if the environment is not so honest. Corruption can, of course, be hidden behind lies, but it requires even more work; corruption becomes worth it only for larger and non-routine transactions, and when it does occur it is easier to trace later. Clearly, a corrupt administration has little to gain from making precedent public and from thereby making consistent and predictable information accessible. It limits their freedom of expedient action. KM systems will be put in place only if there is something in it for them.

The perception of information access as a key discriminator between good and bad climates does offer a tool to affect change. The World Bank report points out that development aid should be channeled preferentially to countries that are poor and have a supportive economic climate. Countries that are poor but do not have a supportive climate, it is agreed, should not be given monetary aid because in such institutions it neither promotes growth nor ameliorates poverty. Nevertheless, it is indicated that these countries should not be ignored. Rather, creative ways should be found to work with them. "Aid agencies need to find alternative approaches to helping highly distended, since traditional methods have failed in these cases" (World Bank, "Assessing Aid Overview," 1998).

How does one approach the delivery of aid in these cases? The World Bank report points out that "...even in the most difficult environments, there will be pockets of reform. Donors need to be patient and flexible, and look for windows of opportunity" (World Bank, "Assessing Aid Overview," 1998). The hypothesis here is that the promotion of KM and information systems is a way of attacking not just small pockets of opportunity, but that it is a means of enhancing and improving the "economic institutions and policies in the developing world, which are the key to a quantum leap in poverty reduction" (World Bank, "Assessing Aid Overview," 1998).

That reform can be made a target. Aid can be offered to develop a KM system. The rationale is that what facilitates investment and development is an environment where information is accessible, predictable, and reliable. The goal would be changing policies and institutions; however, that goal need not be addressed directly. An essential part of building a KM system is gathering the information. The process of gathering information illuminates inconsistencies and exposes malfeasance. Needless to say, the potential for exposure is likely to result in non-cooperation and counter-implementations, where malfeasance is the issue. Like any major systems implementation effort, the entire system need not be built at one time. The system can be built in pieces, and the least threatening pieces can be built first. Also, there is a very persuasive element—if no cooperation, then no aid.

The proposal is difficult to resist. No one, at least initially, is asking the target country to change its institutions and policies, or at least these need not be directly linked to building a KM system. The KM system can be justified and promoted in its own right. The target country needs to make good information consistently and easily accessible if you want to get either aid or investment—that is not a requirement that is insisted upon, it is simply a truism of the sort that "if you want to keep the rain out of your house, the house needs a roof." It is difficult (not impossible) to argue against support for building better information systems, for KM, as a quasi-imperialistic imposition of alien cultural values.

Aid for KM has another advantage. As the World Bank report states: "It is crucial to have objective and rigorous evaluation of outcomes and dissemination of new information" (World Bank, "Assessing Aid—Overview," 1998). With many forms of aid, particularly monetary aid, it is very difficult to monitor where that aid goes and whether it had any effect. With a KM system, the aid offered can be training and expertise, as opposed to monetary aid that may go astray and be pocketed. Furthermore, one can monitor whether or not the system is built and the information is there. Progress can be monitored remotely.

If nothing else, resistance to such aid is a clear litmus test of whether or not any aid is likely to be of utility, a clear signal of malfeasance and the desire to keep operations and procedures apart from any possible scrutiny. Total resistance is a clear signal to wait until the environment changes. Partial resistance is a signal to proceed cautiously and offer to provide KM in areas of commercial utility, but lower resistance. Another way of restating the hypothesis is as follows. First, to the degree that KM systems illuminate or are allowed to illuminate, the more congenial and hospitable to economic development and poverty reduction (and the more transparent) those institutions and policies become. Second, each area illuminated by KM makes it more difficult to keep a veil over adjoining areas.

Conclusion

The way to change institutions and policies to support economic development and poverty reduction is to build KM systems that illuminate their operation.

Endnotes

1. Compiled from: (1999) "World Development Report 1998/99." The World Bank: Washington, D.C.

2. Compiled from: (1999) "World Development Report 1998/99." The World Bank: Washington D.C.

3. Interpreted from: (1997) "UNESCO Statistical Report." UNESCO: Paris.

4. Ibid.

5. Presentation at the IFLA Conference, Ankara, Turkey, 1995.

6. Information repositories depend on commercially available, world output information published abroad. (The annual output of the number of monographs in the English language alone exceeds 100,000 titles.) In this background, we can look at the global extent of information as evidenced by famous libraries like the Library of Congress, which has more than 16 million items in its collection; online bibliographic databases like DIALOG, which holds several tetrabytes of information; and the Internet, which has been with us for about ten years and already holds hundreds of tetrabytes of information entered every month. Therefore, in the knowledge context, with more than 1,000 online services and more than 10,000 publishers all over the world, information purveyors have to deal with several gigabytes of information worldwide, yet many developing countries have access to less than five to ten percent of this global information.

7. Bureaucratic delay and apparent inefficiency is not very often a consequence of bloody mindedness or lack of vision, but rather is often a consequence of the bureaucrat's fear that the wrong decision will expose him/her to unpleasant consequences.

References

Altbach, Philip G. (1987) *The Knowledge Context: Comparative Perspectives on the Distribution of Knowledge.* State University of New York Press: Albany, New York.

Bender, David R.; Kadec, Sarah; Morton-Schwab, Sady (1991) *National Information Policies: Strategies for the Future.* Special Libraries Association: Washington D.C.

Bhatnagar, Subhash C.; Odedra, Mayuri (eds) (1992) *Social Implications of Computers in Developing Countries.* Tata McGraw-Hill: New Delhi.

Davis, Donald G. Jr.; Taher, Mohamed (1993) "Library History in India: Historiographical Assessment and Current Trends." *Third World Libraries* 3(2): 40-44.

Dollar, David; Pritchett, Lant (1998) *Assessing Aid, What Works, What Doesn't and Why*, published for the World Bank Oxford University Press: Oxford.

Duces, Brigette (1990) "World Bank Activities in Library and Documentation Services Provision in Developing Countries." *Government Information Quarterly* 8 (4): 381-386.

FIDD/CAO General Assembly and Congress (1990) *National Information Policies for the Asia Oceania Region: Proceedings of the Eleventh General Assembly & Congress of the International Federation for Information and Documentation Commission for Asia & Oceania.* FID/CAO Secretariat: Vic., Australia.

Gassol de Horowitz, Rosario (1988) *Librarianship: A Third World Perspective.* New York, Greenwood Press.

Gray, John (1988) *Information Policies: Problems and Progress.* Mansell: London, New York.

Hanna, Nagy (1994) "The Information Technology Revolution and Economic Development" (World Bank Discussion Paper 246). The World Bank: Washington D.C.

Hawkins, D.T. et al. (1992) "Forces Shaping the Electronic Publishing Industry of the 1990s." *Electronic Networking* 2 (4): 38-60.

Hernon, P.; Relyea (1968) "Information Policy." In Kent A.; Lancour, H. (eds) *Encyclopedia of Library and Information Science*, vol. 48, supplement II. Dekkar: New York.

Karni, R. (1983) "A Methodological Framework for Formulating Information Policy" *Information and Management* 6(5): 269-280.

Koskiala, Sinikka; Launo, Ritva (eds) (1989) *Information, Knowledge, Evolution.* (Proceedings of the 44th FID Congress held in Helsinki, Finland, August 28-Sept. 1, 1988. (FID Publication 675) Amsterdam, North Holland, p. 456.

Menou, M.J. (ed) (1993) *Measuring the Impact of Information on Development.* Informational Development Research Center: Ottawa.

Montviloff, Victor (1990) *National Information Policies: A Handbook on the Formulation, Approval, Implementation and Operation of a National Policy on Information.* UNESCO: Paris.

Moore, N. "Information Policy and Strategic Development: A Framework for the Analysis of Policy Objectives." *Aslib Proceedings* 45 (11/12) 1193: 281-285.

Patridge, W.G. (1988) *Low Budget Librarianship: Managing Information in Developing Countries.* Library Association: London.

Rowlands, Ian (1996) "Understanding Information Policy: Concepts, Frameworks and Research Tools." *Journal of Information Science* 22 (1): 13-25.

Salim Agh, Syed (1992) *Sustainability of Information Systems in Developing Countries: An Appraisal and Suggested Courses of Action.* International Development Research Center: Ottawa.

Talero, Edwardo and Gaudette, P. (1995) *Harnessing Information for Development: World Bank Vision and Strategy.* The World Bank: Washington D.C., p. 59.

World Bank (1996-1998) "Annual Reports." Washington, D.C.

World Bank Atlas (1998) Washington D.C.

World Bank (1993) *Turkey: Information and Economic Modernization* (A World Bank Country Study). The World Bank: Washington, D.C.

Wellenius, Bjorn et al. (1993) "Telecommunications: World Bank Experience and Strategy" (World Bank Discussion Paper 192). The World Bank: Washington D.C.

Gale Directory of Databases (January 1996) Online Databases, vol. 1.

Ross, Philip E.; Huthessing, Nilchil (October 23, 1995) "Along Came the Spiders." Forbes.

UNESCO (1997) Statistical Yearbook. UNESCO Publishing & Berman Press: Paris, France.

World Bank (1998) "Assessing Aid—Overview." Available at: www.worldbank.org/research/aid/ overview.htm.

(1998) "Making Aid Work." *The Economist* 349 (8094): 88.

CHAPTER 27

Knowledge Counseling:
The Concept, the Process, and Its Application

Anthony Debons
University of Pittsburgh

Jorge Encarnacion, Consuelo Figueras, Susan J. Freiband,
Mariano A. Maura, Annie F. Thompson
Graduate School of Library and Information Science

and

Edwin Reyes
Office of Management and Budget Information Center
University of Puerto Rico
Rio Piedras

INTRODUCTION

"Knowledge counseling" can be defined as a professional service, the aim of which is to aid individuals in dealing with the information and knowledge resources that are essential to their life's tasks and objectives. Knowledge counseling involves three primary functions: the identification of the client's or user's information and knowledge need(s)—the *diagnostic function*; the identification, acquisition, and organization of the information/knowledge products (i.e., books, reports, AV materials, consultants) necessary for the client's tasks—the *prescriptive function*; the determination as to whether or not the client's need was met satisfactorily, the efficiency and effectiveness of the counseling procedures and practices—the *evaluative function*. This concept is related to three others: life-long learning, tutoring, and library reference service. Each acknowledges the importance of an interactive process provided to meet an individual's need for information and knowledge.

The development of this concept can be traced back to Hershfield (1972), a librarian who recognized the increasing demands for information by the scientific community, brought about by the Soviet's launching of Sputnik. He reflected that clients often bring inadequate understanding and skills to deal with the resources available in the library. He stressed the need to bring the library patron closer to the resources of the library. To this end, he recommended an intermediary, an "information counselor."

Havelock (1971), a social psychologist, was interested in exploring ways by which the creativity and productivity of scholars could be improved. He proposed reshaping the service environment that provided the resources demanded in their work. Applying the medical clinic as a metaphor, Havelock proposed a model of an "information clinic," whereby the needs of scientists could be diagnosed, and information obtained and sorted according to the established needs of the client. Havelock envisaged the individual's need for information as similar, in many ways, to physiological states (hunger, thirst), the satisfaction of which led to pleasure; deprivation of which to pain. Based on this premise, Havelock emphasized psychological factors that influenced the individual's ability to deal with information needs. These psychological factors would be the basis upon which the diagnosis of the information need could be established. Havelock's information clinic would augment the services provided by other existing institutions, such as libraries and information analysis centers (Weinberg, 1983). Like Hershfield, Havelock did not differentiate between information and knowledge.

Debons, an information scientist and psychologist, integrated the Hershfield and Havelock concepts in the development of an academic program for the training of information counselors at the Graduate School of Library and Information Science, University of Pittsburgh. The basic theoretical framework for this program was centered on two concepts (Debons, 1983). The first concept is the differentiation of information as process and information as product or thing. Although interrelated, the difference is considered essential and fundamental to the service provided to meet the information needs of individuals. Process is a matter of cognition. Product is the result of cognitive processes. Dealing with products, in the acquisition, storage, retrieval, and dissemination of content contained in such records as books, documents, reports, and media is a matter of logistics, or the procurement, maintenance, and transportation of goods and people. The information counselor requires skill to deal with both process and product.

The second concept defines the proposals advanced by Havelock concerning the idiosyncratic attributes that the client brings to the information task. Each client has his/her own perception and expression of an information need. Consequently, the information counselor's role is to establish the perceptual, personality and learning dimensions that influence the individual's ability to use the resources that are demanded by the task.

At the early stages in the application of the theory, information and knowledge were not differentiated. However, interaction with clients soon revealed that most clients' needs often extended beyond the level of information, that is, awareness, which responds to such questions as "what," "where," " when," and "who." Their needs were at the knowledge level, which corresponds to questions of "how" and "why." An expanded notion of cognition that includes an identification of these different levels of need, broadened the concept from "information counseling" to "knowledge counseling."

In addition, the realization that individual needs for information and knowledge approximated the processes involved in teaching, extended the counseling concept from that focused on the individual's need for information to the need for knowledge. It is at this point that the work of Benjamin Bloom (1958), an educator, provided an important conceptual base for defining knowledge counseling as a service concept. Bloom's hierarchical taxonomy of cognitive functions is a structured framework for identifying information and knowledge needs of individuals. These needs include knowledge, comprehension, application, analysis, synthesis, and evaluation (Hershfield, 1972). Bloom's inclusion and description of "knowledge" is at the lowest level of the taxonomy, and is equivalent to what Debons considers "awareness" or "information." The role of the knowledge counselor is to establish or diagnose the cognitive level demanded by the client's task, to organize the products and the contents therein, and to prescribe a program for usage of such products, so as to enable the client to effectively accomplish his/her task or solve his/her problem.

HISTORICAL BACKGROUND

Information counseling was first introduced in the graduate curriculum of the School of Library and Information Science, University of Pittsburgh in 1976 (Debons, 1975). The program was included as a track of the Master's degree in information science. Approximately eighty-seven students completed the program, some now occupying positions in public and special libraries, industry, and government.

In 1988, Debons, as a visiting professor at the Graduate School of Library Science, University of Puerto Rico, studied the University of Pittsburgh information counseling program to determine its relevance to the needs of the Commonwealth of Puerto Rico. The University of Puerto Rico, Rio Piedras campus, as the major educational institution of the Commonwealth, serves the needs of a complex diversity of public and private interests. Puerto Rico benefits from advanced telecommunications and data information processing technologies. While these technological resources enjoy acceptance by both public and private constituents of the island, decision makers and problem solvers often express frustration in responding to the pace in the advances made in data processing technologies and the rapid growth of knowledge. They express the need for human intermediaries that could work with them daily, or on call, to assist them in synthesizing and organizing much of the data, information, and knowledge that comes to their attention (Dosa et al., 1989; Correia, 1988).

On the basis of this recognized need, the Graduate School of Library and Information Science, University of Puerto Rico, decided to explore the possibility of establishing a knowledge counseling program. In 1990, several members of the faculty (referred to as knowledge counselor interns or KCIs) were identified to undertake an intensive, year-long course on the theory and practice of knowledge counseling. The librarian from the information center at the government's office of budget and management also participated in the course. The course included the study of the principles of three major functions: 1) diagnosis of human needs for data, information, and knowledge (DIK); 2) formulation of a step-by-step procedure for the use of human, technological, and custodial resources to meet such needs (prescription); and 3) methods for evaluating the effectiveness of the professional service rendered. The theoretical portion of the course included a review and study of the principles governing human behavior, specifically, perception, cognition (learning, thinking, memory), and personality. These principles were directly applied to the practice of knowledge counseling. Each KCI was required to complete an exercise in the application of the theories they learned. This exercise involved the identification of clients from the private/public sector; the determination of the client's data, information, and knowledge needs; the organization of the physical, human, and institutional resources customized to the cognitive level demanded by the client's task; and the evaluation of the client's use of these resources.

KNOWLEDGE COUNSELING: THE PROCESS
The Questionnaire

The knowledge counseling process includes developing and designing a questionnaire to be completed by the client (see Appendix I). Following the submission of the completed questionnaire, interviews are scheduled with the client. The purpose of these interviews is to determine the cognitive level demanded of the client's task (diagnosis), to facilitate organization of the resources identified to satisfy the client's need (prescription), and to verify and validate the efficiency and effectiveness of the knowledge counseling process (evaluation). Some understanding of the client and the task (or problem) for which the knowledge counseling is sought should be obtained prior to the actual contact of the knowledge counselor and client by means of the questionnaire. It establishes the framework for the diagnostic, prescriptive, and evaluative functions that are fundamental to knowledge counseling. The data obtained from the client through the questionnaire enables the KCI to formulate alternative approaches and strategies by which the client's data, information, and knowledge needs can be best served. The questionnaire, in addition, guides the interview process, and is an essential aspect of the documentation requirement, which is an important part of this service. The reason for the individual development and design of the questionnaire is that the case in question may require the inclusion (or exclusion) of particular items more suited to clients from a particular culture and language, which may not be suitable to other clients from different cultures that express needs in a different language. Questionnaires need to be tailored to these differences. In any case, the questionnaire should be pre-tested to establish the validity of its format, clarity of language, and other factors that impact on its effectiveness. The questionnaire should include items on the client's background, technical and other expertise, time and other limitations, whether resources were acquired or were in the client's possession, and level of expertise in the use of resources.

The Diagnostic Phase: The First Interview

The purpose of the first interview is to establish the KCI's rapport with the client; to verify questionnaire entrees for accuracy; to establish an initial understanding of the client's task or problem; to identify the required physical and human data, information and knowledge resources; then to provide a tentative judgement or diagnosis of the cognitive level demanded by the client's task. During the interview, every effort is made by the KCI to identify and document the full breadth of personal and organizational factors that could impinge on the client's use of the resources. These are fully aired, accounted, and documented. This is particularly important with respect to the development of a program for the client's use of the resources in a manner consistent with the identified cognitive need. After this initial interview, continued contact with the client (by telephone or other means) is important to more clearly identify the task or problem, as well as to more definitively ascertain the cognitive level demanded by the task.

The Prescriptive Phase: Second and Third Interviews

The second interview aims to obtain feedback from the client on the diagnosis made during the first interview and subsequent communication. In addition, the KCI and the client engage in a person-to-person "brain storming" session that explores the details of the client's task. During this engagement, each idea, proposition, thesis, speculation, and idle reference relative to the task is randomly placed on a sketchpad by the KCI. The result is a mapping of the relationship of each of the recorded concepts to each other. This practice is very similar to that used by public and private institutions as an approach to problem resolution (Debons, 1983). The data from this exchange result in a clustering of the recorded concepts (Bloom, 1958). Mapping represents an extremely important part of the knowledge counseling process because it is the first step in the organization of the products of information and knowledge in a manner that can ease the cognitive burdens of the client. After the mapping process, each idea, speculation, sentiment, and reference included on the map is given a code (two or three letter symbol). These symbols or codes are then positioned in relation to each other. Coding is similar, in many respects, to classification. The creation of the code is the first step in developing the framework for organizing the data, information, and knowledge relevant to the task.

Based on the results of mapping and coding, library resources required to satisfy the client's task or solve his/her problem are identified. In addition, an order is established for the use of the physical, technological, and human resources to be used by the client. Physical resources (books, journals, news accounts, documents) are examined for duplication and deleted, if necessary. The characteristics of specific materials (statistical, graphic, prose) are carefully assessed with the client's expressed predilections for certain kinds of resources. The extensiveness of the subject content (level of detail) contained in the physical resources are carefully weighed for germaneness. Second order, supplemental materials are examined for overlap, given the possible impact on an overburdened client. All exclusions are documented and noted. A step-by-step program that details to the client when and how the resources are to be used and the rationale for their use is developed. Extensive reference to the KCI's case documentation is important in this process, including review of the questionnaire and notes from the first two interviews. Gaining a thorough understanding of the client, the task, and the socio-organizational context in which the client functions and the underlying behavioral factors are essential for successfully accomplishing this process.

During the third interview, the KCI presents the results of the mapping, coding, and concept organization process. The resources identified and the manner in which they are to be used are prescribed. The rationale for the ordering or organization of the resources is carefully explained. All exclusions of resources are noted to the client, along with the reasons for their exclusion. In the event that the client expresses an interest to include them, his/her reasons for these inclusions are documented.

The Evaluative Phase: Fourth Interview

The objective of the fourth interview is to establish the extent in which the KCI aided the client in meeting the DIK demands of the task or problem. In particular, the KCI aims to determine through an interchange with the client the extent to which the prescription effectively lessened the cognitive demands imposed by the task, how it lessened it, when it lessened it (initially or during the process of following the prescription), whether or not the resources identified for the task achieved a sense of completeness and integrity, whether or not certain resources were better than others, and whether or not some resources were missing. Feedback concerning the entire knowledge counseling service is also part of the fourth interview, including the client's degree of satisfaction with the service and his/her desire to use the service again in the future.

AN EXERCISE IN THE APPLICATION OF THE KNOWLEDGE COUNSELING CONCEPT

The exercise in knowledge counseling was conducted by the six KCIs at the Graduate School of Library and Information Science, University of Puerto Rico,

Rio Piedras, as part of the practical aspect of their intensive training program. The knowledge counseling service was provided by work teams of two KCIs, each with an identified client. The KCIs carefully documented the background and data on the three clients that participated in the experience, as well as the documentation related to each interview encounter with the client. This information is included in the "Knowledge Counselor Client Report" (see Appendix 27.B).

A summary of the three case profiles follows.

Case 1

The client was a management specialist in the office of budget and management, office of the governor, San Juan, Puerto Rico. He had good command of the English language. He needed information about licensing of social service institutions, including requirements, financing, organization, and evaluation of licensing programs. He was interested in locating models to use for comparison and contrast, in order to improve the licensing of Puerto Rican agencies and institutions. Nursing homes were of particular interest. The knowledge need based on these considerations was determined to be "evaluation."

The client did not have access to resources or materials, their identification or location. Time was critical.

The KCIs, using the DIALOG Information Retrieval System, conducted online searches. Databases were also searched on CD-ROM. The KCIs also searched ABI/INFORM, MEDLINE, PAIS, and ERIC. Manual searches were done using the *Monthly Catalog*. Several relevant government documents were identified and located, including pamphlets and guides to standards and reports on committee hearings. Journal articles were also identified. In addition to these print sources, names and phone numbers of two experts in the field of geriatrics and licensing of social service agencies at the University of Puerto Rico were identified through contacts with the medical school of this university.

The client followed the KCI's prescription, and found the sequencing of the resources presented useful. He reported that information on the organization and functioning of models was missing. He also mentioned the lack of information on the application of models to the private sector, and the privatization of licensing and its concurrent responsibilities. However, even given these limitations, the client expressed satisfaction with the KCI's service. He claimed that the materials identified were useful, and expanded his perspective and point-of-view about several issues involved in licensing. This feedback supported the claim that the service did meet the cognitive need of the client, according to the task described and detailed by him. The KCI's service saved the client time and effort. He was enthusiastic about the service and willing to continue to use it in the future.

Case 2

This client was a management analyst for the office of budget and management of the Commonwealth of Puerto Rico. She had a Bachelor's degree in Business Administration and, at the time of the exercise, was working on her Master's degree in Public Administration. The client had been working in her current position for three years. Her command of the English language was good. She was verbose and, at times, difficult to follow due to poor articulation. She spoke rapidly, in a low volume voice.

The client wanted to identify models for staff training in governmental agencies. At this level, her need was for information, or awareness, the lowest knowledge need level. The client, however, needed to present to the government a model and a plan of action for staff training. At this level her knowledge need was "application."

The concepts identified from the interviews with the client involved three main areas: training; product model; and cost benefit. The resources identified included six books, one dissertation, two technical articles, and one film. With the exception of the film, the resources were either checked out from libraries or photocopied. The film was recorded with its citation. The client stated that, due to time constraints, she asked her supervisor to ask her colleagues to read the articles identified in the prescription. Thus, the order or sequence in the use of the resources was not followed. The film was not viewed. As a matter of fact, the KCI discovered that the client did not actually understand the sequence at the time it was presented to her, although she was asked at the time whether she did or not. The client stated that she was satisfied with the service. She mentioned another information request during the final interview. However, the resources that were given to her contained information on this topic. Based on this fact, it is evident that without the client's careful review of all the materials supplied, the knowledge counseling service was much less effective.

Case 3

This client acted as the treasurer of a family business comprised of several corporations but he actually functioned as the chief executive officer. His major objective was to understand how to implement management changes in a company that consists of older, sensitive family members who resist change. He also required an awareness of principles and practices concerning management of small family corporations. The KCI determined that the client had a problem in exercising authority over older siblings. He wished to introduce change without causing instability in his personal relationships with family and colleagues. The knowledge need of this client was judged to be "application."

The KCI searched the business library and pertinent online databases for data on: 1) family corporation management; 2) personnel management; 3) human relations; and 4) human resistance to change. In the organization of the resources identified, each of these areas were placed in relationship to each other, representing what could be called a 4 x 4 matrix. The reading material was ordered sequentially, from the general to the specific, for each of the squares that were represented in the matrix. References to books, which were not readily available, were also included in the prescription. The client was advised of the rationale for this organization. The client was pleased with the service. He suggested that more flexibility be allowed for following the prescription. To the extent that the client's need was application, his assertions of pleasure with the service supported the fact that the knowledge need in this case was satisfied.

CASE ASSESSMENT

It should be emphasized that the assessment and conclusions are based on the outcome of an exercise conducted by individuals as part of a learning experience in library school. The process and procedures reported were affected by such constraints as time, client accessibility, and group evaluation pressures. These would not necessarily be part of a knowledge counseling service offered in "the real world."

Each case presented different problems, but certain aspects are sufficiently general to provide a framework for understanding the outcomes from the exercise. Most of the problems that were encountered in applying the knowledge counseling concept were related to the completeness of the data obtained from the client during the first and second interviews. More efficient probing of the client's problem after the first interview would have aided the diagnostic and prescriptive processes.

Even though positive communication and cooperation were evident in the interviews with the clients, this did not ensure that all relevant, important information needed to understand and diagnose the client's knowledge needs, and develop an effective mapping coding and prescription, was obtained. Practice in developing interviewing skills is absolutely essential for a high level of success in the knowledge counseling process.

The time constraints that governed the exercise created an artificial situation that served to mitigate the basic purpose of the exercise. Field conditions would suggest that, although time is of the essence and is normally a constraint, regulation of time as part of the knowledge counseling practice is often a matter of adjustment and compromise, given the circumstances at hand. Nevertheless, the time factor is critical in affecting the level of satisfaction of both the client and the knowledge counselor in relation to the prescription presented. When there is not enough time for the client to digest completely the materials presented, the entire experience is less successful as a result. Correspondingly, when there is not enough time for the knowledge counselor to locate and evaluate the relevant materials to satisfy the knowledge need of the client, the prescription is unlikely to be perceived as effective by either the client or the knowledge counselor. From the variety of types of resources used to identify relevant items for the prescription, and the different types of items identified by the KCI, it is evident that the level of ability to handle library searching, both manually and online, is a vital part of the service. Bibliographic and physical access to materials plays a critical role. Because the clients did not have either the searching skills or the access to materials, these efforts on the part of the KCI were essential to the success of the service. The use of paraprofessionals to handle the access aspect becomes an important consideration.

From the point-of-view of the knowledge counselor, the different steps involved in providing the service interconnect with and support each other. It is essential that the specific knowledge and skills needed to carry out each step be effectively included as part of the knowledge counselor's education and training. This exercise clearly demonstrated the importance of the links in this chain of knowledge and skills that ultimately determine the effectiveness and success of the knowledge counseling service.

IMPLICATIONS FOR THE FIELD

Knowledge counseling as a technique extends the practice of reference work beyond the traditional approach of answering reference questions, providing materials, and helping locate information. It represents a partnership between the work of the reference librarian dedicated to the identification, location, and delivery of information and knowledge resources, and the more personalistic, analytical dimensions of achieving intellectual or cognitive command of the resources required by the work or task at hand. Spaulding (1988), in presenting a future perspective for special librarianship, uses the concept of knowledge counseling as a goal to work toward, in an evolving process of going beyond traditional special library services. Using Spaulding's (1988) own words, what end users want "are not more documents or data, but the analysis of what is available, an analysis that enables them to decide if what they are getting contains anything germane to the solution of their present problem." Spaulding suggests that special librarians should move from the status quo to "knowledge counseling," which implies performing more intellectual work focussed on selection, analysis, and synthesis of information. Spaulding's point-of-view emphasizes the potential impact and importance of the knowledge counseling concept, process, and application as discussed in this chapter, to the field of special librarianship, as well as its implications for library education. It is clear from the University of Pittsburgh experience, that knowledge counseling represents an interdisciplinary service which library and information science graduates can be trained to successfully offer. Using as a basis their MLS preparation, they can build upon what they have learned, and in an advanced certificate program acquire the theory, knowledge, skills, techniques, and attitudes needed to become effective knowledge counselors. This offers them options for work outside a traditional library setting. It expands the possibilities for librarians interested in starting their own businesses, in becoming information entrepreneurs or information consultants. It also broadens the options available to library schools for advanced certificate programs in areas that reflect newer technological advances in the field and interdisciplinary orientations. At the same time, it broadens the Master's degree curriculum since other students may elect to study advanced database searching, for example, a field important for knowledge counseling, as one of their elective courses. Aspects of knowledge counseling skills and techniques can be integrated into reference, adult services, and advanced bibliography courses, enriching the curriculum from this perspective. The theoretical or conceptual basis of knowledge counseling, as well as its practical applications, represents an important fertile area for research.

Moreover, the effective application of knowledge counseling in a number of different field settings will help promote a more positive image of library and information science as a profession involved in a complex, sophisticated use of new technology, as well as drawing upon more traditional library skills. In this perspective, the Graduate School of Library and Information Science, University of Puerto Rico, Rio Piedras, has submitted a proposal for an advanced certificate program in knowledge counseling which it expects to implement in August, 1993. This program will begin to train library and information science professionals to provide knowledge counseling to users or clients, and in this way improve the quality of library and information service and, thereby, impact positively the development of the field.

Although many questions and issues remain to be considered and resolved concerning the conceptual and theoretical basis of knowledge counseling, the process, and its application in the practice of librarianship and information science, both within and outside of an institutional context, an important beginning and initiative has been taken by the library schools at the University of Pittsburgh and the University of Puerto Rico to develop and implement knowledge counseling as a new and innovative area of the field. It remains to be seen what future developments will affect knowledge counseling as it is further incorporated into the theory and practice of librarianship and information science.

References

Bloom, B.S. et al. (1958) *Taxonomy of Educational Objectives: The Classification of Educational Goals*. Handbook 1: *The Cognitive Domain*. New York: David McKay.

Celovani, V.A. (1984) An interactive modeling system as a tool of analyzing complex socio-economic problems (brain storming). In Richardson, J. (ed), *Models of Reality* (p. 79). Mt. Airy, MD: Lamond Books.

Correia, Ana Maria Ramalho (1988) The information intermediary in the information system for industry in Portugal. *Outlook on Research Libraries*, 10 (9): 4-9.

Debons, A. (1975) An educational program for information counselor. *In American Society for Information Science: Proceedings of the 38th ASIS Annual Meeting*, vol. 12. White Plains, NY: Knowledge Industry Publications.

Debons, A. (1983) Information counselors: Human aid for executive management. In Buckland, M.K.; Boehm, E.H. (eds), *Education for Information Management: Directions for the Future* (pp. 55 - 61). Santa Barbara, CA: The Information Institute.

Dosa, Marta; Farid, Mona; Vasarhelyi, Paul (1989) *From Informal Gatekeeper to Information Counselor: Emergence of a New Professional Role*. The Hague: International Federation for Information and Documentation. FID Occasional Papers, no. 1; FID Publication 677, pp. 1-54.

Havelock, R.G. (1971) *Planning for Innovation: Through Dissemination and Use of Knowledge*. Ann Arbor, Michigan: Center for Research and Utilization of Scientific Knowledge, University of Michigan.

Hershfield A. (1972) Information Counselors: A New Profession? In Atherton, Pauline (ed), *Humanizing of Knowledge in the Social Sciences* (pp. 29-34). Syracuse University: School of Library Science.

Katz, William A. (1987) *Introduction to Reference Work*, vol. 1 & 2. New York: McGraw Hill Publishing Company.

Penland, Patrick (1969) *Advisory Counseling for Librarians*. University of Pittsburgh, Pennsylvania: Bookstore.

Sherratt, C.S.; Schlabach, M.L. (1990) The Applications of Concept Mapping in Reference and Information Services. *RQ* 30: 60-69.

Spaulding, F.H. (1988) Special librarian to knowledge counselor in the year 2006. *Special Libraries* 79: 83-91.

Stone, Elizabeth W. (1985) Growth of continuing education. *Library Trends*, winter, 1986: 489-511.

Weinberg, A.M. (1983) Science, government and information: The responsibilities of the technical community and government in the transfer of information. *Report of the Presidents's Science Advisory Committee*, 10 January, 1983. Washington, D.C.: The U.S. Government Printing Office.

About the Authors of Chapter 27

Anthony Debons is an emeritus professor at the School of Library and Information Science, University of Pittsburgh, Pennsylvania.

Jorge Encarnacion is a professor at the Graduate School of Library and Information Science, University of Puerto Rico in Rio Piedras, Puerto Rico.

Consuelo Figueras is an assistant professor at the Graduate School of Library and Information Science, University of Puerto Rico in Rio Piedras, Puerto Rico.

Susan J. Freiband is an associate professor at the Graduate School of Library and Information Science, University of Puerto Rico in Rio Piedras, Puerto Rico.

Mariano A. Maura is an associate professor at the Graduate School of Library and Information Science, University of Puerto Rico in Rio Piedras, Puerto Rico.

Edwin Reyes was a librarian at the Office of Management and Budget Information Center in San Juan, Puerto Rico.

Annie F. Thompson is director and professor at the Graduate School of Library and Information Science, University of Puerto Rico in Rio Piedras, Puerto Rico.

APPENDIX 27.A

Knowledge Counseling Phase I Questionnaire

The purpose of this questionnaire is to obtain some basic background information that will serve as a basis for our knowledge counseling service.

Name: _____

Business: _____

Office Telephone No.: _____

1. What is your present position? _____

2. How long have you been in this position? _____

3. What are the major responsibilities of your present job? _____

_____

4. What other positions have you held in the same agency/corporation/business?

_____

_____

5. What other work experience have you had? (list most recent first) _____

_____

6. Educational background: _____

Degree Institution: _____

Year: _____   Field of Study: _____

7. What other special courses or training have you had? _____

_____

8. How aware are you of the library resources that are available to facilitate your work?

_____

9. How frequently do you use these resources? _____

_____

10. How do you keep up to date with new developments in your field? _____

_____

11. How comfortable are you in reading material in English? _____

_____

12. How comfortable are you in using the following material: (Rank according to preference with 1, most preferable)

__ Films   __ Video   __ Slides   __ Audiocassettes
__ Microfilms   __ Filmstrips   __ Microforms

13. Which of the following are you most comfortable in using: (Rank according to preference with 1, most preferable)

__ Tables   __ Graphs   __ Statistics   __ Charts

14. How familiar are you with using the computer for getting information? _____

_____

15. When doing a job, do you feel more comfortable when you take breaks or work non-stop until the task is done? _____

_____

16. Do you feel more comfortable working alone or with other people? _____

_____

17. What do you like to do in your spare time? _____

_____

Thank you for completing this questionnaire

APPENDIX 27.B

Knowledge Counselor Client Report

Name of KC Case I: _____

Date: _____

Part A: Client Description (sex, education, position)

Description of task requirements: Information about licensing social service institutions; requirements for financing; organizing an evaluation of licensing programs—especially nursing homes.

Part B: Diagnostic

Estimated knowledge (cognitive) need level (KNL)

Circle one: Awareness   Comprehension Application
            Analysis   Synthesis   Evaluation

Basis: Emphasis is on assessment; critically understand and apply the information obtained.

DIK resource requirements (book, records, experts, films, databases, etc.):
manual online resource; dialogue information retrieval system; ABI/lnform, medline, monthly catalog, PAIS and ERIC; journals; experts

Part C: Client Constraints: Time: Immediate Urgent

Resource access: No resource use

No problems expressed

Other: _____

Part D: Client's Response to Prescriptions

Cooperative; articulate; materials provided considered useful; personally read all items provided; information on organizational and functioning models missing—particularly as to private sector. Client satisfied with sequencing—saved time and effort.

Part E: Assessment of the KC Process

Level of effectiveness

	Low	Moderate	High	Uncertain	
Interview	XX				Client verbosity
Diagnostic				XX	
Prescription	XX				Not followed
Mapping			XX		
Coding		XX			
Organization				XX	

Part F: Remarks and Recommendations

Time constraints mitigated service; insufficient contact with client; more emphasis on first interview and maintaining (telephone) contact with client.

Part G: Follow-Up

KC signature: _____

Date: _____

Knowledge Counselor Client Report

Name of KC Case II: _____

Date: _____

Part A: Client Description (sex, education, position): Female; BA in Business Administration/pre-MS; Three years in current position as management analyst

Description of task requirements: Identify models for staff training in government agencies from any country—private and public agencies.

Part B: Diagnostic

Estimated knowledge (cognitive) need level (KNL)

Circle one: Awareness   Comprehension Application
              Analysis   Synthesis   Evaluation

Basis: DIK resource requirements (book, records, experts, films, databases, etc.): six books; dissertations; two articles; one film from library

Part C: Client Constraints: Time: YES

Resource access: KC

Resource use: Asked colleagues

Other: Agency need instead of client need

Part D: Client's Response to Prescription: Moderate to inefficient; Cooperative; Lacked perspective about the service

Part E: Assessment of the KC Process

Level of effectiveness

Part F: Remarks and Recommendations

Because of the client's personality and other factors, the KC service did not achieve optimum value.

It is questionable whether her need (evaluation) was satisfied.

Part G: Follow-Up

KC signature: _____

Date: _____

Knowledge Counselor Client Report

Name of KC Case III: _____

Date: _____

Part A: Client Description (sex, education, position)

Description of task requirements: Client needs information on small family corporations, specifically as to procedures for affecting management change in well-established, traditional environments.

Part B: Diagnostic

Estimated knowledge (cognitive) need level

Circle one: Awareness   Comprehension Application
                 Analysis   Synthesis   Evaluation

Basis: Client is CEO of family business. He searches for ways to 1) improve management of family corporation; and 2) implement changes in the organization without disturbing inter-personal relationships.

DIK resource requirements (book, records, experts, films, databases, etc.):
online databases on management; human psychology on change; ERIC

Part C: Client Constraints: Time: None specified

Resource access: Inter-library loans

Resource use: Need time to read

Other: _____

_____

Part D: Client's Response to Prescription

Needs more time to read articles. Feels prescription should be more flexible.

Part E: Assessment of the KC Process

Level of effectiveness (see table on page 481)

Part F: Remarks and Recommendations

The client was pleased with service but the effectiveness potential of the service was compromised by the time constraints of the exercise. The exercise revealed also the need for criteria upon which the effectiveness of the mapping/coding contributed to the overall satisfaction of the client.

	Low	Moderate	High	Uncertain	
Interview			XX		Client cooperative
					Receptive of service
Diagnostic			XX		
Prescription					Positive client response
Mapping				XX	
Coding				XX	
Organization			XX		

Part G: Follow-Up

KC signature: _____

Date: _____

Chapter 28

Knowledge Management in Swedish Corporations: The Value of Information and Information Services

Margareta Nelke

Library Manager

Tetra Pak Research & Development AB

Introduction

Information from external sources is of considerable value to corporations. It is of value to:

- Obviate one's own experiments and development work
- Discover and prevent patent infringements
- Facilitate investigations into the business environment, markets, competitors, and customers
- Develop new product ideas
- Open up new markets

A cost-benefit analysis shows that the benefits from using external information exceed the costs considerably, thus concluding that investments in accurate external information are very profitable to the corporation. One heavy cost is the time spent on reading external information, which is about nineteen percent of a year's working time. However, professionals, knowing the value of information to them in their work, took the time needed, even if it meant working during leisure time or when travelling.

The information supply into the corporation is very much dependent on each individual. Few of the companies have information strategies or other more "formal" methods to secure that the corporation gets the information it requires.

The persons interviewed strongly emphasized the need for selected relevant information available at their desktops, to decrease the amount of information and especially the amount of paper. They are looking for methods and means to retrieve and absorb relevant information and, at the same time, to be sure of not missing anything important.

All but two of the respondents considered a corporate library to be of benefit to the company. The advantages of having a library are the money savings by avoiding duplicating work due to lack of information, making otherwise distributed data structured and retrievable, and the offering of help to access relevant information. Information retrieval and the selection of relevant information were regarded as one of the most important activities of a corporate library.

The corporate libraries in this investigation emphasize their role as "knowledge managers," information consultants, providers of user education and customer support as well as of strategic, timely, relevant, and accurate information directly to the desktops. The Intranet has made the virtual library feasible. Gradually the libraries can minimize their activities of keeping collections of, purchasing, and circulating printed documents. However, the libraries should be given resources to invest in the future, especially now when new activities are emerging and while old ones must still be continued until satisfactory alternatives are found.

The trends for the near future are an accelerated growth in information and information published, an increase in the importance of information, and a greater demand on the individual to find, assimilate, and react quickly on strategic information. The corporate library can be decisive in the success of this process.

THE SURVEY

Nine Swedish corporations were investigated with a survey to professionals within research and development (R&D) and marketing departments. The survey was followed up with interviews with R&D, marketing, and library managers. Five of the corporations had a corporate library and four had not at the time of the investigation. The companies were Gambro (medical technology), Karlshamns (edible oils and fats), Perstorp (chemicals), Scania (trucks and buses), Swedish

Match (tobacco), Sydkraft (electricity), Trelleborg (mines and metals, rubber products), Vattenfall (electricity), and Volvo (cars, trucks, and buses).

In the survey, the respondents were asked to estimate the use they had of the information in electronic documents, journal articles, books, patents, and reports (internal and external). This is the kind of information normally managed by a corporate library. The respondents were asked to estimate, for five recently read documents, the time and money they had saved (if any) and the eventual direct revenues coming from the use of the information. The survey also held questions about the cost of the information and the time and money devoted to getting knowledge of, acquiring, and assimilating (reading) the information. The respondents were asked to state how they received the information and what other use they had besides the "economic" benefits. One hundred and eight out of 239 people answered the questions in the survey and the respondents evaluated a total of 477 documents in this way.

Electronic documents are defined as the documents published electronically and acquired through the Internet or commercial databases. External reports are marketing, technical, or other reports. Internal reports contain extensive documentation on marketing or R&D activities, which are written and published within the corporation.

The number of documents estimated per document type is shown in Table 28.1 below.

The interviews concentrated on the way the information was managed in the corporations and the role of a corporate library. More information about the corporate library now, and in the future, was collected through the interviews with

Table 28.1 Documents Estimated per Document Type

	The Companies with a Library	The Companies without a Library	All Companies
Electronic documents	49	26	75
Journal articles	67	47	114
Books	40	36	76
External reports	61	41	102
Patents	25	6	31
Internal reports	47	32	79
All documents	**289**	**188**	**477**

the library managers. A total of five R&D managers, five marketing managers, five library managers, and two information managers were interviewed.

The Value and Management of Information

All time estimations as to the cost and benefit of the information were translated to Swedish kronor (SEK) at the rate of 500 SEK an hour—the average internal standard hourly charge for this category of employees. At the time of the investigation (August 1997) the exchange rate was 7.8 SEK for one United States dollar (USD).

The Costs

In the survey, the respondents were asked to estimate how much time had been devoted to handle the documents (trace, access, and obtain them). In addition, they were asked to estimate their own reading time for each document. The purchase price is the cost that varies most depending on the item. The price of books and external reports ranges between a couple of hundred and several thousand SEK.

The total cost per item—price, handling, and reading costs—is in average for each type of document, shown in USD in Table 28.2.

Table 28.2 Average Total Cost per Item, Shown in USD

	Price	Reading	Handling	Total
Electronic documents	–	66	87	153
Journal article	114	66	50	130
Book	46	660	75	781
External report	641	404	117	1,162
Patent	13	205	83	301

The Internet Documents

I took a closer look at the Internet documents to see if the handling time for them differed from the handling time of the other electronic documents. Not unexpectedly, it turned out that the Internet documents took more time to trace and to obtain than the other electronic documents. The Internet documents took in average 92.5 minutes to find and to acquire, which is over ten minutes more time than for all electronic documents. Translated to money, it means an extra cost of thirteen USD per Internet document. There is a great need for training in searching the Internet for information in order to decrease the time spent on the Internet. The awareness of the need for training is growing in the corporations, but some of them prefer to do the reverse and restrict access to the Internet for their employees.

The Benefits

The benefits from using the information manifested as direct revenues, savings in time and money, and other gains not possible to measure in economic terms. The estimation of the benefits in monetary terms are, of course, quite uncertain as a considerable time lapse usually occurs from the time the information was used to the moment when the benefits were seen. It is very difficult to say that a certain benefit arose from the use of a certain piece of information. Despite these difficulties, I obtained estimations that were possible to translate into economic terms for 277 of the 477 documents. Forty of the total number of documents were considered to have saved neither time nor money. For 185 documents, it was stated that they saved resources, but the amounts could not be given. Only four percent of the documents were said to have been of no use at all.

The Revenues

The direct revenues the company had gained from external information were estimated for only twenty-eight documents. The amounts varied between 130 USD and more than ten million for a document. These values are not considered in the cost-benefit analysis due to the low number of documents and large amounts. However, it is important to consider the role of the external publications to get information on new markets, ideas to generate new products, take orders, and to make patent applications.

The Time and Money Savings

Slightly easier, although still difficult, to estimate than the direct revenues were the savings in time and money that were gained from using the information. Savings in time were translated to money. The average savings for one item is shown in Table 28.3.

Table 28.3   The Average Savings for One Item, Shown in USD

	Total Savings
Electronic documents	4,681
Journal article	2,856
Book	7,223
External report	10,600
Patent	15,730
Internal report	8,676

The Cost-Benefit Ratio

Considering the costs and the benefits expressed in monetary terms, the cost-benefit ratio appears in Table 28.4. (The cost is set to one.)

As shown from these figures, it is profitable for the corporation to invest in information. The benefits in economic terms by far exceed the costs; a fact that should be taken as a starting point for discussions concerning the way that information is managed.

The Other Benefits

Other benefits beyond the time or money savings are shown in Table 28.5.

Patents contributed most to the savings. Avoiding patent infringements was the most important resource saving for the patents, followed by avoiding doing one's

Table 28.4   Cost-Benefit Ratio

	Cost-Benefit Ratio
Electronic documents	1:30.6
Journal article	1:22
Book	1:9.2
External report	1:9.1
Patent	1:52.2
Internal report	1:68.2

Table 28.5   Additional Benefits

	% of the Documents that Contributed
To keep myself updated	72
To increase my basic knowledge	64
To give new ideas	47
To give a basis for decisions	46
To solve a specific problem	41
Increase the quality of my work	37
To write reports or give lectures	35
To confirm methods or results	24
To contribute to the allocation of resources to my project	12

own experiences and development work. However, when asked to rank the documents in order of importance, patents were ranked by forty-one percent as "not important," by twenty-two percent as "rather important," and by only thirteen percent as "highly important." The importance of the information in patents is probably underestimated, maybe because of the difficulties in reading and understanding the special patent language. Quite a large number of the respondents stated that they didn't use patents at all (eighteen percent).

Internal reports were ranked as "highly important" by fifty-six percent of the respondents and as "rather important" by thirty-four percent. Only six percent of the respondents thought internal reports were "not important." The internal reports also gave the highest cost-benefit ratio (the cost to write them is not included). Internal reports contributed in that they offered solutions to specific problems and/or made the decision process go faster. As many as seventy-four percent of the respondents in companies with a library and fifty percent in companies without a library got the internal reports without needing to ask for them. This means that the reports were sent to the professional, rather than him/her needing look for them. There were several comments from the respondents on the difficulties in retrieving internal reports if you did not know who had written them or in which organization. An improvement in the management of internal reports would be to make them retrievable over department boundaries, regardless of whether or not you know who has written them.

The information in external reports was especially useful when investigating markets and competitors. External reports were considered as "highly important" by forty-one percent of the respondents, as "rather important" by forty-two percent, and "not important" by eleven percent.

Journal articles were used for market and competitor investigations and in the development work. They were also used more often than the other types of documents to confirm previously achieved technical results or market data. Journal articles were quite popular: Half the number of respondents found them "highly important" and forty percent as "rather important." Only four percent thought that journal articles were "not important."

Assimilating the Information

Some factors facilitating or hindering access to external information were outlined during the interviews. Examples given of facilitating access to external information were:

- The corporation allowed access to the Internet.
- There was a corporate library.
- The employees were highly educated.
- There was a good network for exchanging information with the outside world.

Examples of obstructing access to external information were:

- A too decentralized organization
- Lack of routines for obtaining and disseminating information, which made it difficult to assure that persons needing the information actually received it
- A rigid information culture
- The fact that the personnel are not very educated and trained in using information
- A heavy work load
- No access to important information sources, such as public databases
- No common policy, it was up to each individual to handle these matters as best he/she could.

Assimilating, that is reading, the information is a heavy entry on the debit side. The professionals were quite aware of the need for reading information and devoted a lot of time to it. The average time spent on reading external information was

355 hours per year. This corresponds to about nineteen percent of a year's working hours in Sweden. It was, however, not totally approved to spend working hours reading. The R&D professionals found it more natural to read in working hours than the marketing professionals did, but many of the very busy individuals thought it was difficult to find the undisturbed time to read when at work. Instead, much of the reading was done during leisure time and travel. One interviewee pointed out the contradiction in that it was not accepted to read journals or books during office hours, while it was permissible to sit in front of the computer screen and read what was there.

The implications for information management are to confirm that the information read is of good quality, relevant, accurate, and reliable. If the corporation has access to good and relevant information sources, much of the time wasted on unneeded information is avoided. It is, of course, necessary to scan much information in the hope of finding something interesting as well. For example, this is the situation for the R&D professionals who are looking for new ideas without being able to specify beforehand exactly what those ideas may be. However, when they find it, they know that it is what they were looking for!

An Information Strategy

The value of external information is highly estimated in the corporations investigated. In fact, all corporations are quite aware that they are very dependent on information from the surrounding world in order to survive in today's difficult business atmosphere. This awareness did not, however, lead to the conclusion that information should be gathered, analyzed, and distributed in a systematic and carefully prepared way. It was very much the individual professional's responsibility to make certain that the company had access to the right information, was distributing it to the right people on time, and to confirm that important information was not missing. Only two of the persons interviewed saw the benefit of a strategy and a plan for the management of external information. Certain categories were taken care of, such as information connected to legal issues or rules the corporation had to follow. Often there was a department responsible both for the collecting of the information and implementing it in the corporation.

The greatest problems in the information management were the abundance of information and, at the same time, the uncertainty of whether or not the important information was there. Much of the information (about twenty-five percent) came to the professional without having to ask for it. The information user was a victim of information overload, trying to keep up with the ever-growing piles of paper while he/she, at the same time, had a strong feeling that he/she was missing essential facts. This is a situation that causes information stress. The respondents were adherent to have information available at their desktops, for example through the Intranet, and to know where to fetch it and only access it when the demand arose.

An information strategy should contain the following parts:

- The areas of interest to be monitored
- Who is responsible to monitor each area
- Which information sources should be used (this part has to be currently revised)
- The ways to access the information sources and the routines for doing it
- Who are the receivers of the collected information within each area
- The form in which the information should be distributed (raw/unprepared, compiled, or analyzed)
- The distribution medium (Intranet, email, databases, etc.)
- The eventual archiving of the collected information for future use, in what form, and in which medium. Whether or not it should be retrievable and, if so, how.

The Role of a Corporate Library

Five of the companies surveyed had a corporate library. However, questions regarding the role or eventual benefit of a corporate library were also put to the companies not having a library. One of the companies previously had a library but decided to close it. Of the persons interviewed at that company, one thought it was a good decision to close the library, but the other person missed the services. One of the companies had no library at the time of the survey, but soon afterwards they employed a special librarian to build up a complete library service.

The Benefits of a Corporate Library

All but two of the interviewees in all the investigated corporations considered a corporate library to be of benefit to the company. In their opinion, the following are some of the benefits:

- To save money for the company by eliminating double work
- To be a source of knowledge
- To support R&D activities with information

- To be a link between the internal and external information
- To make the current dispersed information accessible on the desktop
- To monitor the external world
- To save money by establishing a central handling of journals and books

(The list is not ranked.)

The library managers were not asked the question of whether or not a corporate library was of benefit, only how it could be of benefit. Their view of how a company could benefit from a corporate library was:

- To provide "early warnings"—signals from important changes in the environment
- "To be a big ear towards the external world"
- To save money by avoiding double work
- To provide a fast and cost-effective way of retrieving information
- To find the information that can contribute to a prosperous business, such as generating new ideas
- To contribute with information of good quality, for example, by evaluating the information sources and giving access to good information sources
- To contribute to creating contacts between different parts of the company

(The list is not ranked.)

A Corporate Library's Priorities

A common term for the advantages a company library can bring is "knowledge management," an expression not often used in Swedish corporations at the time of the survey. When the respondents were asked to state on which services the library should focus, the professionals in the companies without a library emphasized the knowledge management role of a corporate library more than the respondents from companies with a corporate library did. The latter group emphasized more concrete services, without really seeing them in a holistic perspective. The library managers, on the other hand, saw their libraries as part of the knowledge management process.

According to those interviewed who worked in companies without a library, the following lists the functions a corporate library should fulfill:

- To keep collections (a central archive function)
- To structure the information, and make the information retrievable
- See to it that the scattered information can be reached through the desktop
- To monitor and scan the surrounding world for news

- To provide answers to specific questions (to be a research function)
- To disseminate information in a proactive way
- To be an information technology center

According to those interviewed who work in companies with a library, the following lists the functions a corporate should fulfill:

- To provide selected information
- To swiftly find qualitative information within different areas
- To be a virtual library (One should not be forced to visit the library. The information should be at one's desktop.)
- To instruct clients in information retrieval
- To make sure clients have access to the information they need
- To provide alerts
- To handle journals

The library managers' opinions of which activities should be given priority were:

- To be information consultants and to contribute to larger information solutions
- To provide selected information
- To be a virtual library, to make information easily available on the user's desktops
- To train the clients in information retrieval
- To contribute to business intelligence
- To structure information and present it in a comprehensible way
- To scan the surrounding world for business news
- To evaluate information sources
- To handle journals

Most of the library managers were striving to turn the corporate library into a "knowledge management center." All but one library used the company's Intranet to disseminate information in order to provide their worldwide customers with useful information. They wanted to work with information solutions and to train their customers to access and search for information. All but one library also accessed general business information (copyright cleared) and distributed it on the Intranet.

However, there are problems in trying to develop the new activities and use the new information technology while simultaneously keeping the traditional services. The library managers tended to add more and more services without eliminating any former ones. This was because the library users wanted the services provided. One of the libraries did a survey on the services the library clients wanted from the library. The results showed that all departments put a high priority on subscribing and circulating journals. As the professional librarians, at least in Sweden, are trained to be service-oriented, they quite naturally do these kinds of surveys and follow the wishes of the clients.

Librarians should look at their services in a holistic perspective instead of asking the clients which services they want and asking management to what benefit the library should be for the company. Librarians also pose that question to themselves. To have a speaking partner among the management group is very important for a corporate library, although that could be difficult to accomplish. The information specialists/special librarians should not hesitate to think of themselves as the most competent people in the organization in regards to information management. They also should show this competence to management. They must be confident that they probably have the best insight as to what a corporate library can do and how it will be the most benefit to the corporation. To proactively plan for the library's role and discuss these plans with management is one of the best ways to assure that the library is in agreement with the corporation and will contribute in an efficient way to the improvement of the information management in the corporation.

Some of the libraries charged for their services. In that case, they had to keep the services that they could charge for, in most cases internal loans of books and journals, subscribing to and circulating journals, doing information retrievals on requests, and doing consultancy. It is difficult to charge for services like making information available on the Intranet, combining external and internal information, getting people to share knowledge and to contribute to common databases with internal information, and the like. To charge for information on the Intranet always means a user administration that is time consuming and troublesome. (Some of the business information providers are requiring a user administration— something that professional librarians should strongly resist!)

The fixed costs to run a library are rather high. If you have large collections the rent is a heavy expense, and it is time consuming to keep the collections in order. A library's success very much depends on personnel's skills and competence. Personnel cost is, therefore, expensive. This cost must, for the libraries charging for their services, be most often covered by selling large numbers of small pieces. This is not very easy to combine with the rather big investments to be done in developing new knowledge management services.

If no extra resources are added, the libraries must eliminate some of their traditional services. Purchasing books and circulating journals are examples of services that can be managed by other departments (for example, the purchasing departments and the internal mail departments), instead of the library. The collections keeping of books and journals must also be strongly questioned. Maybe the collections can be radically diminished in volume as a first step.

The development of knowledge management services requires extra resources in themselves. Information that is disseminated through the Intranet is, for example, much more expensive due to the need for copyright clearance. Extra information technology resources might be needed, e.g., intelligent agents or categorizing programs. Moreover, the time to develop and maintain these services is considerable. There is a lot of work done behind the scene to fulfill the vision that the information user is only to "press the button" to reach the information he/she needs.

Promoting the Library

The library clients and the library managers were asked if the library was visible enough in the organization. Both groups thought that the library should be more visible than it was (a very common remark to this question). One question was how much the library contributed to the external information coming to the company. The estimations from both the library managers and the others varied between ten and thirty percent. When I compared this opinion with the actual contribution from the library, expressed as the number of external documents the library had been involved in (tracing, accessing, or acquiring), a different picture appeared.

The library's contribution to the external information in the corporation was for

Journal articles	69%
Patents	60%
Books	55%
Electronic documents	39%
External reports	23%
Internal reports	2%

An interesting question is why the library's contributions are underestimated. The library is certainly not visible enough, but why? The answer to these questions was that the library had not been promoted enough and the solution to the problem mentioned both by the interviewed persons and the library managers was found in promotional activities. The library managers expressed a feeling of insufficiency there. They felt like they had spent much time on promoting the library without very much result. The respondents, on the other hand, would have liked to see more promotional activities from the library.

Neither of the groups questioned the implicit fact that it is not the library alone that is responsible for promoting its services. It is also the responsibility of the managers for the different departments to "promote" the use of the library. If the corporation decided to invest in a corporate library, it means that they consider the services useful. It also means that they want the employees to use the library as an efficient tool to reach the information needed. It is the responsibility of the managers to make certain that their employees use the different tools available in the corporation to facilitate their work and to make it more efficient. Therefore, it should be their responsibility to "promote" the library, to tell their staff to use it.

Is promotion the solution? Yes, it is one of the solutions, if the promotion activities go to the right group. I think that the libraries have spent much time promoting the library to the direct clients—the users of the library services. Instead, the promotion activities should be directed towards the managers (often more indirect than direct users of the library). Instead of only "campaign" activities, surveys or promotional material distributed to a lot of people, the library managers should work to develop natural contacts with the upper management. (Easy to say, not so easy to do!) To have the library's activities as a natural part of the normal activities in the corporation is the best method to make the library visible.

THE FUTURE OF INFORMATION MANAGEMENT AND THE ROLE OF THE CORPORATE LIBRARY

Some trends for the coming years can be discerned as follows:
- The rate of information growth and "publishing" is quickening.
- The increasing importance of reacting fast to "early warnings."
- In order to react fast, each individual would like the information needed at his/her desktop.
- The need for selected information is growing.
- The increasing need for training in finding and selecting relevant information, assimilating, and summarizing the information and communicating it, written or orally, in a concise but understandable way.
- A great deal of work is concentrated on the development and refinement of the tools for finding and disseminating information.

Since information growth will not diminish in the future, on the contrary, and the dependency of external information will not diminish, we must assure through efforts to manage information in a professional way, that the information will not be a burden instead of a help and that too much time will not be spent looking for and trying to manage information. The starting point is, however, to realize that information management is a profession that, like other professions, needs special education and competence.

In the coming days, there will be an even greater need to manage information and knowledge in a systematic and efficient way. It will be necessary to ensure that the business, market, competitor, technical and legal information that gives competitive advantages and, in some cases, is directly indispensable to the corporation also will be traced, accessed, and disseminated promptly to professionals. It will also be necessary to assure that knowledge and information already existing in the corporation can be efficiently used and reused. A knowledge management system is needed, reaching far behind the present business intelligence systems and connecting the external information and knowledge with the internal one.

When building knowledge management systems, one should take advantage of the competence and knowledge in the corporate library. The library can take an active part in strategizing, act as a speaking partner to the information technology department when the computer support is developed, and be an active contributor to the external information in the system. The competence available in the library, which is useful for building information systems, is:

- To organize information in computerized collections
- To make a fast selection of relevant information
- To have a full, and not a fragmentary, picture of the information needs of the company
- To have a knowledge of the information sources
- To have a contact network with suppliers of information and colleagues at other libraries
- To know a lot of the search behavior and the pitfalls when retrieving information
- To have a knowledge of new tools for retrieving and disseminating information

The implication for the corporate library is that its main task in the coming years will be to lead and support this process of information management. The corporate library will have to take on a new role and proactively engage in the development, instead of only reactively doing what their direct customers want them to do.

The dying corporate library is reactive and using most of its resources on keeping huge collections of books and journals, buying books, and circulating journals. The living and flourishing corporate library is proactive and using most of its resources on:

- Knowledge management systems using Intranets as the main tool
- Selection and evaluation of information sources
- Agreement and negotiations with information suppliers
- Information solutions to individuals or groups
- Training the clients to trace and access external information

The role of the information specialist as an intermediate in the searching for information will diminish in volume, but will still be an essential part of the work. The vision is that the information user should search for information him/herself, but some of the searches are still so complicated that an information specialist will be needed. It is, however, beyond reach that even a large group of information specialists could supply a large company with all the external information it will need today and in the future. The professionals must do the main part themselves, but must be supported in this process by an information specialist function and/or a library.

Crucial for the library's success is the degree to which they take an active part in knowledge management and also their ability to handle the elimination of some of its traditional services while simultaneously developing the new ones. We are in a period of turbulent changes, but the competence of an information specialist/special librarian is needed and maybe also be appreciated like never before!

Quotes

The following are some comments from the respondents of the investigated companies on examples of good or bad information, regarding the Internet, the corporate library, and other information issues.

"We found a method of analysis by doing a database search. The method worked exactly as described."

"In a journal article, I found a reference to another article. By reading this, I found out how another professional made an experiment. By using his results, I was able to develop our own method for the same kind of experiments."

"At a technical symposium, a lecturer presented technical data in a visual and pedagogic way. Since then I have been able to use it in my own work to spread important technical information in the company."

"Descriptions regarding methods of manufacturing from patents should be read with a certain caution. The essential information is often missing."

"Market forecasts are sometimes based on insufficient data and may contain errors."

"A competitor got articles published with only the purpose to spread misinformation."

"The new information systems increase the risk for the same information going round in circles. It has happened that the information I have given out myself has come back to me in another form some time later."

"The Internet has become an important information source for me in my work. It is a fast way to find the information by myself."

"The Internet is too unstructured. You know that there is important information somewhere, but it takes too long to find it."

"A three-hour Internet session yielded information on a competitor, which everybody was talking about but nobody knew anything about."

"The information retrieval in databases made by our corporate library has been of great use, especially the continuous scanning of technical news. I have also had good experience with the information from databases concerning technical cases that are directly applicable to our reality. Why re-invent the wheel when somebody else might have the solution already? However, it is very important to have access to professional information searchers."

"Information specialists could be auditors of information. Information audits could be done in the same manner as the company does audits of quality systems and annual accounts."

"People are tired of too much information; it can create 'decision cramp'."

"The future role of a corporate library is to become the information pilot and life belt in the flood of information, which threatens to drown us all—to become a link between the external and internal information and to make it available through the computer networks. The librarian should be the person who cares for the information users and the content of the databases when the computer technician is stuck in the technical opportunities."

Please note that the cost to write an internal report is not included.

Only one of the libraries had the pronounced responsibility to manage internal reports.

Part VI :
Appendices

A Course Syllabus for Knowledge Management

(Business, Records Management, Library and Information Science Disciplines)

A copy of the spring 1999 course syllabus for a graduate
course in the School of Library and Information Science
and in the Graduate School of Business.

LIS 880 and GSB 542: Knowledge Management
Dr. T. Kanti Srikantaiah

COURSE DESCRIPTION

Provides an awareness of current theories and foundation of knowledge management (KM) with an emphasis on profit and not-for-profit organizations. Discusses knowledge assets and their value to organizations in terms of products, processes, market, and services. Examines analytical tools and techniques for knowledge acquisition, assessment, evaluation, management, organization, and dissemination. Provides an analysis of commercially available documents, databases, and applications packages, reviews best practices and experiences, and addresses the design and execution of KM projects.

Prerequisites: Four core courses or permission of the instructor (GSLIS 1998-2000 Bulletin, p. 59).

COURSE OBJECTIVES

The goal of the course is to prepare students to become familiar with the current theories, practices, tools, and techniques in KM, and to assist students in pursuing a career in the information sector for profit and not-for-profit organizations. In addition, students will learn to determine the infrastructure requirements to manage the intellectual capital in organizations. Specifically, at the end of the course students will:

• Define clearly KM, learning organizations, intellectual capital, and related terminologies and understand the role of knowledge management in organizations

• Demonstrate an understanding of the history, concepts, and the antecedents of management of knowledge and describe several successful KM systems

• Identify and select tools and techniques of KM for the stages of creation, acquisition, transfer, and management of knowledge

• Analyze and evaluate tangible and intangible knowledge assets and understand current KM issues and initiatives

• Evaluate the impact of technology including telecommunications, networks, internet/intranet role in managing knowledge

• Identify KM in specific environments: managerial and decision making communities; finance and economic sectors; legal information systems; health information systems; and others

• Demonstrate an understanding of the importance of intellectual capital to benefit the competitive advantage in organizations

• Specify application packages in KM and the issues in designing and developing knowledge databases (including Intranets and GroupWare).

• Develop a working knowledge in the area through focused projects

• Articulate various career options in the field

COURSE APPROACH

The course will be conducted in a seminar style to develop students' analytical abilities in the area of KM and knowledge systems. The contents of the course are divided into various segments as indicated on the schedule to provide a balanced approach to the field. Each segment will serve as a link to the following segment. Readings will be provided for each segment and students are expected to participate in classroom discussions. Students will complete a KM project that includes an oral class presentation and a written report that will be presented and submitted toward the end of the course.

KNOWLEDGE MANAGEMENT PROJECT

Students will undertake and successfully complete an individual project or a group project in the area of KM. The project will serve as a practical learning experience in understanding various issues in KM. Students should submit their project proposals at the third class meeting, as per class discussion. The terms of reference for the project will cover:

• Title of the project
• Clearly stated objectives

- Scope and limitations

- Methods of data collection

- Analysis of data

- Specific costs and benefits

- Evaluation

- Presentation of findings and recommendations

Projects are to be generated through points of contact in the professional community. Students are encouraged to pursue projects suggested by local professionals. Initially, the responsibility of the point of contact is to assist the student, to fill them in on background and context, to provide entry where appropriate, or to coordinate where appropriate. Then, the responsibility of the student is to accomplish the project by carrying it out through the outlined terms of reference. The student is not to lean on the contact person for any other support, nor to burden him or her. Students are free, indeed encouraged, to provide points of contact in other organizations, either for their own use or for the use of other students. Project guidance, review discussions, midpoint corrections, and related support will be provided by the professor.

If a full-blown project is not feasible at the site for various reasons (such as confidentiality), students are encouraged to produce a case study, writing the KM status of the organization. The details of the case study will be agreed upon with the point of contact, along with student and professor. Students will agree to comply with the confidentiality/disclosure/publication rules of the organization where the KM study is undertaken, and they will submit their findings to the point of contact before submitting the report to the instructor. Naturally, students will delete and keep confidential a portion so indicated by point of contact.

A Gantt chart with schedules, milestones, and product deliverables should accompany the project terms and reference. Progress on the project should be reported at the eighth class meeting where, if necessary, midpoint adjustments will be made. An oral presentation of the findings and recommendations is due on the thirteenth meeting. A written report is also due at that meeting. (Please turn in two copies of the written report, one which will be put on reserve for all students to view.)

Course Requirements

Both regular attendance and active participation are expected. All assignments are to be submitted in complete form and on time. Any delay in submission of assignments will affect the grading. Since the course is taught in seminar style, student participation is mandatory. Students will be asked to make oral presentations as required in the course.

Grading

Grades are based upon the following:

a) Class participation	10 points
b) Assignments and oral presentations	40 points
c) KM Project	50 points

  • Proposal 10 points
    (properly formatted on agreed terms of reference)

  • Progress report 10 points (mid-term)

  • Oral presentation 10 points (13th class meeting)

  • Written report 20 points

Total	100 points

Required Text

Working Knowledge: How Corporations Manage What They Know, by Thomas Davenport and Laurence Prusak. Boston: Harvard Business School Press, 1998.

Supplementary Readings

Selected chapters from the forthcoming book *Knowledge Management for the Information Professional* will be assigned periodically during the semester to facilitate discussion under topics mentioned in the attached course schedule.

Supplementary readings will be recommended at the beginning of each segment from the attached comprehensive KM bibliography.

Course Schedule

Class Meeting	Date	Topics
1	January 12	**Overview** • Introduction: history; concepts; definitions; and the antecedents of KM • Information management to KM • KM: What it is and what it is not?
2	January 19	**Background and Issues** • The evolution of KM • Explicit knowledge, tacit knowledge, and the infrastructure • KM and ethics • **Selection of KM projects**
3	January 26	**KM for the Information Professional** • Information services and productivity • Learning organizations • Knowledge markets and quality assurance
4	February 2	**KM Domains** • Industrial/manufacturing sectors • Health and legal sectors • Business and finance sectors • Not-for-profit sectors • Professional organizations and consulting firms • Bibliographic information systems • **Discussion of Project Proposal**
5	February 9	**Organizational Concerns: Trends and Impact** • Information driven management: A thematic model • Trends in organizations: JIT, TQM, BIP, MIS, DSS, SDI, Data Warehousing and Data Mining, Enterprise Systems
6	February 16	**KM Tools** • Telecommunications and networks • Application packages • User needs assessment • Measuring knowledge behavior • Repackaging information

Class Meeting	Date	Topics
7	February 23	**KM—Application** • Corporate information centers • Information technology: Intranets • Best practices • Others
	March 2	**Mid-Semester Break**
8	March 9	**Progress Report on Projects: Oral Presentation and Submission of Written Reports (Mid-Term)**
9	March 16	**Knowledge Ecology** • Information policies • Information architecture • Institutional information strategies • Information professionals
10	March 23	**Systems Approach to KM** • Systems engineering techniques • System cycle • Design and evaluation of KM systems • Costs and benefits
11	March 30	**Systems Approach to KM** (continued)
12	April 6	**Case Studies** • Published works
13	April 13	**Student Presentation of Projects** • Oral presentation • Submission of written projects
14	April 20	**Review of the Semester Work** • Professional opportunities • The future of KM • Course evaluations • Return of evaluated project reports

A Comprehensive Bibliography on Knowledge Management

Prepared by Morgen MacIntosh

and

T. Kanti Srikantaiah

Director, Center for Knowledge Management

Dominican University

Contents

Number of Citations

Books   92
Articles   457
Knowledge Management Chapters in Conference Proceedings   21
Web Sites   36
Videos   5
Total   611

Books

Addleson, M. *Equilibrium versus Understanding: Towards the Restoration of Economics as Social Theory*. New York: Routledge, 1995.

Albert, Steven, and Keith Bradley. *Managing Knowledge: Experts, Agencies and Organizations*. Cambridge, Eng.; New York: Cambridge University Press, 1997.

Albrow, Martin. *Do Organizations Have Feelings?* New York: Routledge, 1997.

Allee, Verna. *The Knowledge Evolution: Expanding Organizational Intelligence*. Boston, Mass.: Butterworth-Heinemann, 1997.

Alverson, Mats. *Management of Knowledge-Intensive Companies*. De Gruyter *Studies in Organization*, 61. Berlin; New York: Walter de Gruyter, 1995.

American Productivity and Quality Center. *Knowledge Management Consortium Benchmarking Study: Best Practice Report*. Houston, Texas, 1996.

American Productivity and Quality Center. *Using Information Technology to Support Knowledge Management, Consortium Benchmarking Study: Best Practice Report*. Houston, Texas, 1997.

American Productivity and Quality Center. *Knowledge Management and the Learning Organization: A European Perspective*. Houston, Texas, 1996.

Amidon, Debra M. *Innovation Strategy for the Knowledge Economy: The Ken Awakening*. Boston, Mass.: Butterworth-Heinemann, 1997.

Argyris, Chris. *Knowledge for Action: A Guide to Overcoming Barriers to Organizational Change. The Jossey-Bass Management Series*. San Francisco, CA: Jossey-Bass Publishers, 1993.

Argyris, C., and D. Schon. *Organizational Learning: A Theory of Action Perspective*. Reading, Mass.: Addison-Wesley, 1978.

Badaracco, Joseph L., Jr. *The Knowledge Link: How Firms Compete Through Strategic Alliances*. Boston, Mass.: Harvard Business School Press, 1991.

Bassi, Laurie, J., and Brian Hackett. *Leveraging Intellectual Capital. HR Executive Review*, 5(3). New York: Conference Board, 1997.

Boisot, Max H. *Knowledge Assets: Securing Competitive Advantage in the Information Economy*. New York: Oxford University Press, 1998.

Brooking, Annie. *Intellectual Capital*. London, New York: International Thomson Business Press, 1997.

Bud-Frierman, Lisa, ed. *Information Acumen: The Understanding and Use of Knowledge in Modern Business. The Comparative and International Business: Modern Histories Series*. New York: Routledge, 1994.

Choo, C.W. *The Knowing Organization: How Organizations Use Information to Construct Meaning, Create Knowledge, and Make Decisions*. New York: Oxford University Press, 1998.

Czarniawska, B. *Narrating the Organization: Dramas of Institutional Identity*. Chicago: University of Chicago Press, 1997.

Davenport, Thomas H., and Laurence Prusak. *Information Ecology: Mastering the Information and Knowledge Environment*. New York: Oxford University Press, 1997.

Davenport, Thomas H., and Laurence Prusak. *Working Knowledge: How Organizations Manage What They Know*. Boston, Mass.: Harvard Business School Press, 1998.

De Geus, Arie. *The Living Company*. Boston, Mass.: Harvard Business School Press, 1997.

DiBella, Anthony J., and Edwin C. Nevis. *How Organizations Learn: An Integrated Strategy for Building Learning Capability. The Jossey-Bass Business & Management Series*. San Francisco, CA: Jossey-Bass Publishers, 1998.

Dillion, Patrick M. *The Quest for Knowledge Management: A New Service Organization to Address the Challenges & Opportunities*. Technology Management Report, T-303. Atlanta, GA.: Information Management Forum, 1997.

Drucker, Peter F. *Managing for the Future: The 1990s and Beyond*. New York: Truman Tally Books, 1992.

Drucker, Peter F. *Managing in a Time of Great Change*. New York: Truman Tally Books, 1995.

Edvinsson, Leif, and Michael S. Malone. *Intellectual Capital: Realizing Your Company's True Value by Finding Its Hidden Roots*. New York: Harper Business, 1997.

Enos, John. *The Creation of Technological Capability in Developing Countries*. London: Pinter, 1991.

Ernst & Young CBI. *Executives Perspectives on Knowledge in the Organization*. Boston, Mass.: Ernst & Young Center for Business Innovation and Intelligence, 1997.

Fisher, Kimball, and Maureen Duncan Fisher. *The Distributed Mind: Achieving High Performance Through the Collective Intelligence of Knowledge Work Teams*. New York: AMACOM, 1998.

Fruin, W. Mark. *Knowledge Works: Managing Intellectual Capital at Toshiba. Japan Business & Economics Series*. New York: Oxford University Press, 1997.

Gibson, Cyrus F., and Barbara B. Jackson. *The Information Imperative: Managing the Impact of Information Technology on Business and People*. Lexington, Mass.: D.C. Henth, 1987.

Glewwe, Paul, Michael Kremer, and Sylvie Moulin. *Textbooks and Test Scores: Evidence from a Prospective Evaluation in Kenya*. Washington, D.C.: Development Research Group, World Bank, 1997.

Gray, H.M. *Warfighting: The US Marine Corps Book of Strategy*. New York: Doubleday, 1989.

Hackett, Brian. *The Value of Training in the Era of Intellectual Capital: A Research Report*. Conference Board Report, no. 1199-97-RR. New York: Conference Board, 1997.

Halal, William E., ed., with Raymond W. Smith. *The Infinite Resource: Creating and Managing the Knowledge Enterprise. The Jossey-Bass Business & Management Series*. San Francisco, CA: Jossey-Bass Publishers, 1998.

Hudson, William J. *Intellectual Capital: How to Build It, Enhance It, Use It*. New York: J. Wiley, 1993.

Kafai, Yasmin and Mitchel Resnick, eds. *Constructionism in Practice: Designing, Thinking and Learning in a Digital World*. Hillsdale, NJ: Lawrence Erlbaum Associates, 1996.

Kingma, B. *The Economics of Information: A Guide to Economic and Cost-Benefit Analysis*. Englewood, Colorado: Libraries Unlimited, 1996.

Klein, David A., ed. *The Strategic Management of Intellectual Capital*. Resources for the Knowledge-Based Economy. Boston, Mass.: Butterworth-Heinemann, 1998.

Krogh, Georg von, and Johan Roos. *Managing Knowledge: Perspectives on Cooperation and Competition*. London: Sage Publications, 1996.

Latour, Bruno. *Aramis or, The Love of Technology*. Cambridge, Mass.: Harvard University Press, 1996.

Leonard-Barton, *Wellsprings of Knowledge: Building and Sustaining the Sources of Innovation*. Boston, Mass.: Harvard Business School Press, 1995.

Lesk, M. *Practical Digital Libraries*. San Francisco: Morgan Kaufmann, 1997.

Liebowitz, Jay and Lyle C. Wilcox, eds. *Knowledge Management and Its Integrative Elements*. Boca Raton, FL: CRC Press, 1997.

Malone, Samuel A. *How to Set Up and Manage a Corporate Learning Centre*. Aldershot, Hampshire, Eng.; Brookfield, VT, USA.: Gower, 1997.

Mansell, Robin, and Uta Wehn. *Knowledge Societies: Information Technology for Sustainable Development*. New York: Oxford University Press, 1998.

Marshall, Alfred. *Principles of Economics*. London: Macmillan, 1961.

McGee James V., and Laurence Prusak, with Philip J. Pyburn. *Managing Information Strategically. Ernst & Young Information Management Series*. New York: J. Wiley, 1993.

McGregor, Eugene B. *Strategic Management of Human Knowledge, Skills, and Abilities: Workforce Decision Making in the Post-Industrial Era. The Jossey-Bass Management Series*. San Francisco, CA: Jossey-Bass Publishers, 1991.

McKinnon, Sharon M., and William J. Bruns. *The Information Mosaic. Harvard Business School Series in Accounting and Control*. Boston, Mass.: Harvard Business School Press, 1992.

McWhinney, Will. *Paths of Change: Strategic Choices for Organizations and Society*. Thousand Oaks, CA: Sage Publications, 1997.

Miles, M.B., and M.A. Huberman. *Qualitative Data Analysis, An Expanded Sourcebook*. Beverly Hills, CA: Sage, 1994.

Mohr, L.B. *Explaining Organizational Behavior*. San Francisco, CA: Jossey-Bass, 1982.

Moingeon, Bertrand, and Amy C. Edmondson, eds. *Organizational Learning and Competitive Advantage*. Thousand Oaks, CA: Sage Publications, 1996.

Myers, Paul S., ed. *Knowledge Management and Organizational Design*. Resources for the Knowledge-Based Economy. Boston, Mass.: Butterworth-Heinemann, 1996.

Neef, Dale, ed. The Knowledge Economy: Resources for the Knowledge-Based Economy. Boston, MA: Butterworth-Heinemann, 1998.

Nonaka, Ikujiro, and Hirotaka Takeuchi. *The Knowledge-Creating Company: How Japanese Companies Create the Dynamics of Innovation*. New York: Oxford University Press, 1995.

Nordhaug, Odd. *Human Capital in Organizations: Competence, Training, and Learning*. Scandinavian University Press, 1994.

Polanyi, Michael. *The Tacit Dimension*. Garden City, New York: Doubleday Anchor, 1966/1967.

Polanyi, Michael. *Tacit Knowledge*. New York: Doubleday, 1966.

Polanyi, Michael. *Personal Knowledge: Towards a Post-Critical Philosophy*. London: Routledge, 1973.

Prusak, Laurence, ed. *Knowledge in Organizations. Resources for the Knowledge-Based Economy*. Boston, MA: Butterworth-Heinemann, 1997.

Quinn, James Brian. *Intelligent Enterprise: A Knowledge and Service Based Paradigm for Industry*. New York: Free Press, 1992.

Quinn, James Brian, Karen Anne Zien, and Jordan J. Baruch. *Innovation Explosion: Using Intellect and Software to Revolutionize Growth Strategies*. New York: Free Press, 1997.

Reber, A.S. *Implicit Learning and Tacit Knowledge: An Essay on the Cognitive Unconscious*. New York: Oxford University Press, 1993.

Roos, Johan, ed. *Intellectual Capital: Navigating in the New Business Landscape*. New York: New York University Press, 1998.

Roos, Johan and Georg von Krogh, eds. *Organizational Epistemology*. New York: Macmillan, 1995.

Rowe, Alan J., and Sue Anne Davis. *Intelligent Information Systems: Meeting the Challenge of the Knowledge Era*. Westport, CT: Quorum Books, 1996.

Ruggles, Rudy L., ed. *Knowledge Management Tools. Resources of the Knowledge-Based Economy*. Boston, MA: Butterworth-Heinemann, 1997.

Sanchez, Ron, and Aimae Heene, eds. *Strategic Learning and Knowledge Management. The Strategic Management Series*. Chichester, West Sussex, England; New York: J.Wiley, 1997.

Savage, Charles M. *Fifth Generation Management: Co-creating through Virtual Enterprising, Dynamic Teaming, and Knowledge Networking*. Boston, MA: Butterworth-Heinemann, 1996.

Savage, Charles M. *Fifth Generation Management: Integrating Enterprises Through Human Networking*. Bedford, MA: Digital Press, 1990.

Schneier, Bruce. *Applied Cryptography*. 2nd Edition. New York: Wiley, 1996.

Schrage, M. *No More Teams!: Mastering the Dynamics of Creative Collaboration*. New York: Currency/Doubleday, 1995.

Senge, Peter M. *The Fifth Discipline: The Art and Practice of the Learning Organization*. New York: Doubleday/Currency, 1990.

Senge, Peter M. *The Fifth Discipline Fieldbook: Strategies and Tools for Building a Learning Organization*. New York: Doubleday/Currency, 1994.

Shukla, Madhukar. *Competing Through Knowledge: Building a Learning Organization*. Thousand Oaks, CA: Sage India Private, 1997.

Skyrme, David. *Knowledge Networking: Creating the Collaborative Company*. Boston, MA: Butterworth-Heinemann, 1998.

Sonnenreich, Wes, and Tim Macinta. *Web Developer.Com® Guide to Search Engines*. New York: J. Wiley & Sons, 1998.

Sparrow, J. *Knowledge in Organizations: Access to Thinking at Work*. London: Sage Publications, 1998.

Spitzer, Quinn, and Ron Evans. *Heads You Win! How the Best Companies Think*. New York: Simon and Schuster, 1997.

Starkey, Ken, ed. *How Organizations Learn*. London; Boston, MA: International Thomson Business Press, 1996.

Sternberg, Robert, and Joseph Horvath, eds. *Tacit Knowledge in Professional Practice*. Hillsdale, N.J.: Lawrence Erlbaum Associates, 1998.

Stewart, Thomas A. *Intellectual Capital: The New Wealth of Organizations*. New York: Doubleday/Currency, 1997.

Sveiby, Karl Erik. *The New Organizational Wealth: Mangaging & Measuring Knowledge-Based Assets*. San Francisco, CA: Berrett-Koehler Publishers, 1997.

Talero, Eduardo, and Philip Gaudette. *Harnessing Information for Development: World Bank Group Vision and Strategy*, Draft Document. Washington, D.C.: The World Bank, July 1995.

Thomas, Vinod, Nalin M. Kishor, and Tamera C. Belt. *Embracing the Power of Knowledge for a Sustainable Environment*. Washington, D.C.: World Bank, 1997.

Tobin, Daniel R. *The Knowledge-Enabled Organization: Moving From "Training" to "Learning" to Meet Business Goals*. New York: AMACOM, 1998.

Wiig, Karl M. *Knowledge Management Foundations: Thinking About Thinking—How People and Organizations Represent, Create and Use Knowledge*. Arlington, Tex.: Schema Press, 1993.

Wiig, Karl M. *Knowledge Management Methods: Practical Approaches to Managing Knowledge*. Arlington, TX: Schema Press, 1995.

Wiig, Karl M. *Knowledge Management: The Central Focus for Intelligent-Acting Organizations*. Arlington, TX: Schema Press, 1994.

Winslow, Charles D., and William L. Bramer. *Futurework: Putting Knowledge to Work in the Knowledge Economy*. New York: Free Press, 1994.

ARTICLES
Knowledge Management–Background and Development

Abell, Angela, and Nigel Oxbrow. "Knowledge as a Corporate Resource: Moving Information to Center Stage." *IntraNet Professional* 1, no.1 (May 1998): 1, 7-8.

Allee, Verna. "12 Principles of Knowledge Management." *Training & Development* 51, no. 11 (November 1997): 71-74.

Alic, J.A. "Knowledge, Skill, and Education in the New Global Economy." *Futures* 29, no. 1 (1997): 5-16.

Anderson, Gary. "A Needle in a Haystack." *Industry Week* 243, no. 13 (4 July 1994): 41.

Anonymous. "Five Steps to Better Knowledge Management." *Computerworld* 29, no. 25 (19 June 1995): ss 3.

Anonymous. "Mr. Knowledge." *Economist* 343, no. 8019 (31 May 1997): 63.

Anonymous. "Tapping Corporate Knowledge." *Internal Auditor* 55, no. 4 (August 1998): 15 16.

Anonymous. "Tips for Know-How." *Computerworld* 32, no. 4 (26 January 1998): s6.

Arora, A. "Contracting for Tacit Knowledge: The Provision of Technical Services in Technology Licensing Contracts." *Journal of Developmental Economics* 50 (1996): 233-256.

Arthur, W.B. "Increasing Returns and the New World of Business." *Harvard Business Review* 74, no. 4 (July-August 1998): 100-109.

Birkett, Bill. "Knowledge Management." *Chartered Accountants Journal of New Zealand* 74, no. 1 (February 1995): 14-18.

Birkett, W.P. "Management Accounting and Knowledge Management." *Management Accounting* 77, no. 5 (November 1995): 44-48.

Blake, Paul. "The Knowledge Management Expansion." *Information Today* 15, no. 1 (January 1998): 12-14.

Bresnick, Peggy. "The Virtual Roundtable." *Insurance and Technology* 23, no. 6 (June 1998): 76.

Brethenoux, E. "Knowledge Management: Myths and Challenges." *Gartner Group Research Note/Key Issues K-KMGT-1650*. 1997.

"CAM-i Focuses on Knowledge Management." *Management-Accounting* 79 (November 1997): 66-67.

Coombs, Rod, and Richard Hall. "Knowledge Management Practices' and Path-Dependency in Innovation." *Research Policy* 27, no. 3 (July 1998): 237-253.

Cottrill, Ken. "Networking for Innovation." *Chemical Week* 160 (25 February 1998): 39-43

Davenport, Tom. "Some Principles of Knowledge Management." *Strategy and Business* (First Quarter, 1997) posted at http://www.bus.utexas.edu/kman/kmprin.htm.

"Defining Knowledge Management." *Public Relations Strategist* 4, no. 2 (Summer 1998): 34-35.

Demarest, Marc. "Understanding Knowledge Management." *Long Range Planning* 30, no. 3 (June 1997): 374-384.

Dove, Rick. "A Knowledge Management Framework." *Automotive Manufacturing and Production* 110, no. 1 (January 1998): 18-20.

Dragoon, A. "Knowledge Management: Rx for Success." *CIO* 8, no. 18 (July 1995): 48-56.

Drucker, Peter F. "The Information Executives Truly Need." *Harvard Business Review* (January-February 1995): 54.

Duhon, Bryant. "It's All in Our Heads." *Inform* 12, no. 8 (September 1998): 9-13.

Dykeman, John B. "Knowledge Management Moves from Theory Toward Practice." *Managing Office Technology* 43, no. 4 (May 1998): 12-14.

Evans, Philip B., and Thomas S. Wurster. "Strategy and the New Economics of Information." *Harvard Business Review* 75 (September-October 1997): 70-82.

Emery, Priscilla. "Knowledge Management." *Inform* 11, no. 10 (November 1997): 2.

Fischbein, E. "Tacit Models." In D. Tirosh, ed., *Implicit and Explicit Knowledge: An Educational Approach*. Norwood, NJ: Ablex, 1994.

Frappaolo, Carl. "Defining Knowledge Management: Four Basic Functions." *Computerworld* 32 (23 February 1998): 80.

Fuld, Leonard M. "Knowledge Profiteering." *CIO* 11, no. 17 (15 June 1998): 28-32.

Gopal, Christopher, and Joseph Gagnon. "Knowledge, Information, Learning and the IS Manager." *Computerworld* 29, no 25 (19 June 1995): ss1-ss7.

Grant, E.B., and J.J. Gregory. "Tacit Knowledge, the Life-Cycle and International Manufacturing Transfer." *Technology Analysis & Strategic Management* 9, no. 2 (1997): 159-161.

Grayson, C. Jackson, Jr., and Carla S. O'Dell. "Mining Your Hidden Resources." *Across the Board* 35, no. 4 (April 1998): 23-28.

Hannabuss, Stuart. "Knowledge Management." *Library Management* 8, no. 5 (1987): 1-50.

Hibbard, Justin. "Knowing What We Know." *Information Week* (20 October 1997): 46-64.

Hovath, J.A., G. B. Forsythe, P.J. McNally, J.A., J. Wattendorf, W.M. Williams, and R.J. Sternburg. *Tacit Knowledge in Military Leadership: Evidence from Officer Interviews*, Technical Report 1018. Alexandria, VA: U.S. Army Research Institute for the Behavioral and Social Sciences, October 1994.

Hovath, J.A., R.J. Sternberg, G.B. Forsythe, P.J. Sweeney, R.C. Bullis, W.M. Williams, M. Dennis. *Tacit Knowledge in Military Leadership: Supporting Instrument Development*, Technical Report 1042. Alexandria, VA: U.S. Army Research Institute for the Behavioral and Social Sciences, May 1996.

Infield, Neil. "Capitalising on Knowledge." *Information World Review*, no. 130 (November 1997): 22.

Inkpen, Andrew C. "Creating Knowledge Through Collaboration." *California Management Review* 39, no. 1 (Fall 1996): 123-140.

"Knowledge Management: A Basic Q & A." *Information Advisor Knowledge Management Supplement* 1, no. 1 (March 1997).

"Knowledge Management Consulting Gives CPAs a Competitive Edge." *CPA Journal* 68, no. 8 (August 1998): 72.

"Knowledge Management: Managing Intellectual Capital Within an Organization, Industry Trend or Event." *PC Week* 14, no. 35 (18 August 1997): 87.

Koeing, Michael. "The 1998 Conference Board Conference." *Information Today* 15, no.7 (July/August 1998): 13, 51.

Lloyd, Bruce. "Knowledge Management: The Key to Long-Term Organizational Success." *Long Range Planning* 29, no. 4 (August 1996): 576-580.

Maglitta, Joseph. "Know-How, Inc." *Computerworld* 30, no. 1 (15 January 1996): 73-75.

Maglitta, Joseph. "Smarten Up!." *Computerworld* 29, no. 23 (5 June 1995): 84-86.

Malhotra, Yogesh. "Knowledge Management for the New World of Business." University of Pittsburgh, Katz School of Business, posted at http://www.brint.com/km/whatis.htm., 1997. Manville, B., and N. Foote. "Harvest Your Workers' Knowledge." *Datamation* 42, no. 13 (July 1996): 78-80.

Marchand, Donald A. "Information Management: Strategies and Tools in Transition?." *Information Management Review* 1, no. 1 (1985): 27-34.

Mayo, Andrew. "Memory Bankers." *People Management* 4 (22 January 1998): 34-38.

Meyer, Christopher. "What Makes Workers Tick?" *Inc.* 19 (December 1997): 74-75.

McWilliams, Gary, and Marcia Stepanek. "Knowledge Management: Taming the Info Monster." *Business Week*, no. 3583 (22 June 1998): 170-172.

Murray, Philip. "New Language for New Leverage: The Terminology of Knowledge Management." http://www.ktic.com/topic6/13_TERM1.HTM.

Newman, Brian. "Knowledge Management vs. Knowledge Engineering." (Posted 5 January 1996) http://revolution.3-cities.com/~bonewman/kmvske.htm.

O'Leary, D.E. "Enterprise Knowledge Management." *Computer* 31, no. 3 (March 1998): 54-61.

Oxbrow, N., and A. Abell. "Knowledge Management: Competitive Advantage for the 21st Century." *Records Management Bulletin*, no. 83 (December 1997): 5-10.

Pascarella, Perry. "Harnessing Knowledge." *Management Review* 86, no. 9 (October 1997): 37-40.

Pastore, Richard. "The Importance of Getting Smart." *CIO* 8, no. 11 (15 March 1995): 62-66.

Pigott, Sylvia E.A. "Internet Commerce and Knowledge Management— The Next Megatrends." *Business Information Review* 14, no. 4 (December 1997): 169-172.

Rogers, Debra M. Amidon. "Knowledge Management Gains Momentum in Industry." *Research-Technology Management* 39, no. 3 (May-June 1996): 5-7.

Rowland, Hillary. "Doctor Know." *People Management* 4, no. 5 (5 March 1998): 50-52.

Sanderson, S.M. "New Approaches to Strategy: New Ways of Thinking for the Millennium." *Management Decision Conference* 36, no. 1. (United Kingdom: MCB University Press 1998). Managing in the New Millennium Conference, 12-14 June 1997.

Schrage, Michael. "Why Stop at Knowledge Management?" *Computerworld* 30, no. 46 (11 November 1996): 37.

Smith, Rebecca A. "Knowledge: Researching the Power Base of the Organization." *Information Outlook* 2, no. 6 (June 1998): 12-14.

Special Issue: Knowledge Management. *Harvard Business Review* (July-August 1997).

Spender, J. "Competitive Advantage from Tacit Knowledge? Unpacking the Concept and Its Strategic Implications." In *Organizational Learning and Competitive Advantage*, 56-73, Bertrand Moingeon and Amy Edmondson, eds., Thousand Oaks, CA: Sage Publications, 1996.

Sternberg, R.J., R.K. Wagner, and L. Okagaki. "Practical Intelligence: The Nature and Role of Tacit Knowledge in Work and at School." In J.M. Puckett, and H.W. Reese, eds. *Mechanisms of Everyday Cognition*. Hillsdale, NJ: Lawrence Erlbaum Associates.

Stuart, Ann. "Five Uneasy Pieces, Part Two: Knowledge Management." *CIO* (1 June 1997).

Stuller, Jay. "Chief of Corporate Smarts." *Training* 35, no. 4 (April 1998): 28-34.

"Special Focus: Knowledge Management." (special report; cover story). *Journal of Business Strategy* 19 (January-February 1998): 10-28.

"Tips for Making Knowledge Management Pay Off." *IT Cost Management Strategies Letter* 16, no. 4 (April 1997): 7-8.

Trussler, Simon. "The Rules of the Game." *Journal of Business Strategy* 19 (January-February 1998): 16-19.

Young, Ron. "The Wide-Awake Club." *People Management* 4 (5 February 1998): 46-49.

Wagner, R.K., and R.J. Sternberg. "Practical Intelligence in Real-World Pursuits: The Role of Tacit Knowledge." *Journal of Personality and Social Psychology* 49, no. 2 (1985): 436-458.

Watson, Sharon. "Getting to 'Aha!'." *Computerworld* 32, no. 4 (January 26, 1998): s1-s5.

Wiig, K.M. "Knowledge Management: Where Did It Come from and Where Will It Go?." *Expert Systems with Applications* 13, no. 1 (July 1997): 1-14.

Wiig, K.M., R. De Hoog, and R. van Der Spek. "Supporting Knowledge Management: A Selection of Methods and Techniques." *Expert Systems with Applications* 13, no. 1 (July 1997): 15-27.

Wolff, M.F. "Knowledge Management Gains Momentum in Industry." *Research Technology Management* 39, no. 3 (May 1996): 5-7.

Intellectual Capital

Aoki, R., and T.J. Prusa. "International Standards for Intellectual Property Protection and R&D Incentives." *Journal of International Economics* 35, no. 2 (1993): 251-273.

Bassi, Laurie J. "Harnessing the Power of Intellectual Capital." *Training and Development* 51, no. 12 (December 1997): 25-30.

Bontis, Nick. "Intellectual Capital: An Exploratory Study that Develops Measures and Models." *Management Decision* 36, no. 2 (1998): 63-76.

Bontis, Nick. "There's a Price on Your Head: Managing Intellectual Capital Strategically." *Business Quarterly* 60, no. 4 (Summer 1996): 40-47.

Bowes, R. "How Best to Find and Fulfill Business Information Needs." *ASLIB Proceedings* 47, no. 5 (May 1995): 119-126.

Bradley, Keith. "Intellectual Capital and the New Wealth of Nations." *Business Strategy Review* 8, no. 1 (Spring 1997): 53-62.

Bradley, Keith. "Intellectual Capital and the New Wealth of Nations II." *Business Strategy Review* 8, no. 1 (Winter 1997): 33-44.

Brooking, Annie. "Knowledge Management and Corporate Memory." In *Intellectual Capital Core Asset for the Third Millennium Enterprise*. London, New York: International Thomson Business Press, 1996.

Brooking, Annie. "The Management of Intellectual Capital." *Long Range Planning* 30, no. 3 (June 1997): 364-365.

Brown, Tom. "Ringing Up Intellectual Capital." *Management Review* 87, no. 1 (January 1998): 47-50.

Caulkin, Simon. "The Knowledge Within." *Management Today* (August 1997): 28-32.

Dearlove, Des. "From Brawn to Brainpower." *The Times* (8 May 1997): s4.

Edvinsson, Leif. "Developing Intellectual Capital at Skandia." *Long Range Planning* 30, no. 3 (June 1997): 366-373.

Edvinsson, Leif. "Visualizing Intellectual Capital in Skandia." *Skandia's 1994 Annual Report.* Stockholm, Sweden: Skandia AFS, 1995.

Gould, David M., and William C. Gruben. "The Role of Intellectual Property Rights in Economic Growth." *Journal of Development Economics* 48, no. 3 (1996): 328-350.

"A Hands on Look at Intellectual Capital." *Management Review* 87 (January 1998): 50-51.

Hyden, Steven D., Michael J. Mard, R. Wade Wetherington. "Identifying, Protecting, and Valuing Intellectual Property." *Journal of Asset Protection* 3, no. 6 (July-August 1998): 32-38.

Jeffers, Michelle. "Here Come the Consultants: Corporate America Soon Will Spend Billions on IC." *Forbes ASAP* 159, no. 7 (7 April 1997): s70.

Koenig, M.E.D. "The Convergence of Computers and Telecommunications, Information Management Implications." *Information Management Review* 1, no. 3 (September 1986): 23-33.

Koenig, M.E.D. "Intellectual Capital and How to Leverage It." *Bottom Line* 10, no. 3 (1997): 112-118.

Koenig, M.E.D. "Intellectual Capital and Knowledge Management." *IFLA Journal* 22, no. 4 (1996): 299-301.

Kurtzman, Joel. "A Mind Is a Terrible Thing to Waste." *Chief Executive* no. 112 (April 1996): 20.

Lenzner, Robert, and Carrie Shook. "Whose Rolodex Is It, Anyway?" *Forbes* 161 (23 February 1998): 100-104.

McRae, Hamish. "Small Firms Nurture Big Brains." *Director* 50, no. 6 (January 1997): 64-65.

"Measuring Training's Contribution to Intellectual Capital." *Training* 35 (March 1998): 14-16.

Miller, William C. "Fostering Intellectual Capital." *HR Focus* 75, no. 1 (January 1998): 9-10.

Mirabile, Rick. "Technology and Intellectual Capital: The New Revolution." *Human Resources Professional* 11, no. 4 (July-August 1998): 19-22.

Nahapiet, Janine, and Sumantra Ghoshal. "Social Capital, Intellectual Capital, and the Organizational Advantage." *The Academy of Management Review* 23, no. 2 (April 1998): 242-266.

Reid, Joanne. "Tom Stewart on Intellectual Capital." *Ivey Business Quarterly* 62, no. 3 (Spring 1998): 15-18.

Roos, Johan. "Exploring the Concept of Intellectual Capital." *Long Range Planning* 31, no. 1 (February 1998): 150-153.

"Skandia: The Pioneer of Intellectual Capital Reporting." *Business Strategy Review* 8, no. 4 (Winter 1997): 38-41.

Special Issue: Intellectual Capital. *Forbes ASAP* (7 April 1997).

Special Issue: Intellectual Capital. *Long Range Planning* (June 1997).

Special Issue: The Epistemological Challenge: Managing Knowledge and Intellectual Capital. *European Management Journal* 14 (August 1996): 333-426.

Stewart, Thomas A. "Brainpower." *Fortune* 123, no. 11 (3 June 1991): 44-51.

Stewart, Thomas A. "Getting Real about Brainpower." *Fortune* 132, no. 11 (27 November 1995): 201-203.

Stewart, Thomas A. "Gray Flannel Suit? Moi?" *Fortune* 137 (16 March 1998): 76-82.

Stewart, Thomas A. "How a Little Company Won Big by Betting on Brainpower." *Fortune* 132, no. 5 (4 September 1995): 121-122.

Stewart, Thomas A. "Now Capital Means Brains, Not Just Bucks." *Fortune* 123, no.1 (14 January 1991): 31-33.

Stewart, Thomas A. "Your Company's Most Valuable Asset: Intellectual Capital." *Fortune* 130, no. 7 (3 October 1994): 68-73.

Stivers, Bonnie P., Joyce Covin, and Nancy Green. "How Non-Financial Performance Measures Are Used." *Management Accounting* 79 (February 1998): 44-46.

Stuller, Jay. "Chief of Corporate Smarts." *Training* 35, no. 4 (April 1998): 28-34.

Sveiby, Karl-Erik. "Intellectual Capital: Thinking Ahead." *Australian CPA* 68, no. 5 (June 1998): 18-22.

Tapp, Lawrence G. "Management Education in Canada." *Ivey Business Quarterly* 62, no. 3 (Spring 1998): 7-9.

Tapsell, Sherrill. "Making Money from Brainpower." *Management-Auckland* 45, no. 6 (July 1998): 36-43.

Ulrich, Dave. "Intellectual Capital Equals Competence x Commitment." *Sloan Management Review* 39, no. 2 (Winter 1998): 15-26.

Wiig, Karl M. "Integrating Intellectual Capital and Knowledge Management." *Long Range Planning* 30, no. 3 (June 1997): 399-405.

Knowledge Management and the Learning Organization

Argote, Linda, Sara L. Beckman, and Dennis Epple. "The Persistence and Transfer of Learning in Industrial Setting." *Management Science* 36, no. 2 (February 1990): 140-154.

Argyris, Chris. "Teaching Smart People How to Learn." *Harvard Business Review* (May-June 1991): 99-109.

Argyris, Chris, et al. "The Future of Workplace Learning and Performance." *Training and Development* 48 (May 1994): s36-s47.

Benson, George. "Battle of the Buzzwords." *Training and Development* 51 (July 1997): 51-52.

Brown, J.S. and P. Duguid. "Organizational Learning and Communities-of-Practice: Toward a Unified View of Working." *Organizational Science* 2, no. 1 (1991): 40-57.

"The Challenge of Managing Organizational Change: Exploring the Relationship of Re-engineering, Developing Learning Organizations and Total Quality Management." *Total Quality Management* 9, no. 1 (February 1998): 109-122. In *Proquest Direct*, ABI Global (8 October 1998).

Darling, Michele S. "Building the Knowledge Organization." *Business Quarterly* 61, no. 2 (Winter 1996): 61-66.

Evers, James L. "An Interview with a Utopian Corporate Heretic." *Training and Development* 52, no. 6 (June 1998): 60-64.

Fisher, Kimball, and Mareen Duncan Fisher. "Shedding Light on Knowledge Work Learning." *Journal for Quality and Participation* 21, no. 4 (July/August 1998): 8-16.

Garvin, David A. "Building a Learning Organization." *Harvard Business Review* (July-August 1993): 78-86.

Gill, T.G. "High-Tech Hidebound: Case Studies of Information Technologies that Inhibited Organizational Learning." *Accounting Management and Information Technologies* 5, no.1 (1995): 41-60.

Goh, Swee C. "Toward a Learning Organization: The Strategic Building Blocks." *SAM Advanced Management* 63, no. 2 (Spring 1998): 15-22.

Graham, William, Dick Osgood, and John Karren. "A Real-Life Community of Practice." *Training and Development* 52, no. 5 (May 1998): 34-38.

Harvey, Michael, Jonathan Palmer, and Cheri Speier. "Implementing Intra-Organizational Learning: A Phased-Model Approach Supported by Intranet Technology." *European Management Journal* 16, no. 3 (June 1998): 341-354.

Imai, K., I. Nonaka, and H. Takeuchi. "Managing the New Product Development Process: How Japanese Companies Learn and Unlearn." In K.Clark, R. Hayes, and C. Lorens, eds., *The Uneasy Alliance*. Boston, MA: Harvard Business School Press, 1985.

Jashapara, Ashok. "The Competitive Learning Organization: A Quest for the Holy Grail." *Management Decision* 31, no. 8 (1993): 52-62.

Kermally, Sultan. "The Learning Organization." *European Management Journal* 15 (April 1997): 208.

Kim, Daniel H. "The Link Between Individual and Organizational Learning." *Sloan Management Review* 35, no. 1 (Fall 1993): 37-50.

King, W. R. "IS and the Learning Organization." *Information Systems Management* 13, no. 3 (Summer 1996): 78-80.

Levitt, B. and J.G. Marsh. "Organizational Learning." *Annual Review of Sociology* 14 (1988): 319-340.

McGill, Michael E. and John W. Slocum. "Unlearning the Organization." *Organizational Dynamics* 22, no. 2 (Autumn 1993): 67-78.

Nathan, Maria L. "The Nonprofit Executive as Chief Learning Officer." *Nonprofit World* 16, no. 2 (March/April 1998): 39-41.

Raimond, Paul. "From the Conference Scene." *European Management Journal* 16, no. 2 (April 1998): 242-245.

Reed, M. "Organizations and Modernity: Continuity and Discontinuity in Organization Theory." In J. Hassard, and M. Parker, eds., *Postmodernism and Organizations*. London, England: SAGE Publications, 1993, 163-182.

Seeley-Brown, J. and P. Duguid. "Organizational Learning and Communities of Practice." *Organizational Science* 2, no. 1 (1991).

Senge, Peter. "The Leader's New Work: Building Learning Organizations." *Sloan Management Review* 32, no. 1 (Fall 1990): 7-23.

Senge, Peter. "Rethinking Leadership in the Learning Organization." *The Systems Thinker* 7, no. 1 (1996).

Senge, Peter. "Sharing Knowledge." *Executive Excellence* 15, no. 6 (June 1998): 11-12.

Slocum, John W., Michael McGill and David T. Lei. "The New Learning Strategy: Anytime, Anything, Anywhere." *Organizational Dynamics* 23, no. 2 (Autumn 1994): 33-47.

Starbuck, William H. "Learning by Knowledge-Intensive Firms." *Journal of Management Studies* 29, no. 6 (November 1992): 713-740.

Starkey, Ken. "What Can We Learn from a Learning Organization?" *Human Relations* 51, no. 4 (April 1998): 531-546.

Tetenbaum, Dr.Toby J. "Shifting Paradigms: From Newton to Chaos: Part 1 of 2." *Organizational Dynamics* 26, no. 4 (Spring 1998): 21-32.

Tichy, Noel M. and Eli Cohen. "The Teaching Organization." *Training and Development* 52, no. 7 (July 1998): 26-33.

Turoff, R. "An Arranged Marriage: Knowledge Management and Organization Development." *American Programmer* 11, no. 3 (March 1998): 30-33.

Yamauchi, Futoshi. "Information, Neighborhood Effects, and the Investment in Human Capital: Learning School Returns in a Dynamic Context." Philadelphia, PA: University of Pennsylvania, Department of Economics, 1998.

Knowledge Cultures / Knowledge-Based Organizations

Anonymous. "The People Factor." *People Management* 4, no. 2 (22 January 1998): 38.

Blair, Jim. "Knowledge Management: The Era of Shared Ideas." *Forbes* (The Future of IT Supplement) 1, no. 1 (22 September 1997): 28.

Boland, R.J. Jr., and R.V. Tenkasi. "Perspective Making and Perspective Taking in Communities of Knowing." *Organization Science* 6, no. 3 (1995): 350-372.

Bonaventura, M. "The Benefits of a Knowledge Culture." *ASLIB Proceedings* 49, no. 4 (April 1997): 82-89.

Caulkin, Simon. "So, a Little Knowledge Is Not Quite So Dangerous." *The Observer* (28 September 1997): B10.

Darling, Michele S. "Knowledge Cultures". *Executive Excellence* 14, no. 2 (February 1997): 10-11.

Dash, Julekha. "Knowledge is Power." *Software Magazine* 18, no. 1 (January 1998): 46-56.

Davis, Stan, and Botkin, Jim. "The Coming of Knowledge-Based Business." *Harvard Business Review* (September-October 1994): 165-168.

Davis, Stan, and Botkin, Jim. "The Coming of Knowledge-Based Business." In Dale Neef, ed., *The Knowledge Economy*. Boston, MA: Butterworth-Heinmann, 1998.

De Meyer, Arnoud. "Manufacturing Operations in Europe: Where Do We Go Next?" *European Management Journal* 16, no. 3 (June 1998): 262-271.

Drucker, Peter F. "The Age of Social Transformation." *The Atlantic* 274, no. 5 (November 1997): 53-70.

Drucker, Peter F. "The Coming of Knowledge-Based Business." *Harvard Business Review* 66, no. 1 (September-October 1988): 45-53.

Grant, Robert M. "The Knowledge-Based View of the Firm: Implications for Management Practice." *Long Range Planning* 30, no. 3 (June 1997): 450-454.

Grant, Robert M. "Toward a Knowledge-Based Theory of the Firm." *Strategic Management Journal* 17 (Winter 1996): 109-122.

Hiser, Jeff. "Understanding the Value of your Employees' Knowledge." *CPA Journal* 68, no. 7 (July 1998): 56-57.

Holsapple, Clyde W. and Andrew B Whinston,. "Knowledge-Based Organizations." *Information Society* 5, no. 2 (1987): 77-90.

Meister, Jeanne C. "Extending the Short Shelf Life of Knowledge." *Training and Development* 52, no. 6 (1 June 1998): 52.

Nonaka, Ikujiro. "A Dynamic Theory of Organizational Knowledge Creation." *Organization Science* 5, no. 1 (February 1994): 14-37.

Nonaka, Ikujiro. "The Knowledge-Creating Company." *Harvard Business Review* (November-December 1991): 96-99.

Nonaka, Ikujiro. "A Theory of Organizational Knowledge Creation." *International Journal of Technology Management* 11, no. 7/8 (1996): 833-845.

Nonaka, Ikujiro and Noboru Konno. "The Concept of 'Ba': Building a Foundation for Knowledge Creation." *California Management Review* 40, no. 3 (Spring 1998): 40-54.

Orr, J. "Sharing Knowledge, Celebrating Identity, Community Memory in a Service Culture." In D. Middleton and D. Edwards, eds. *Collective Remembering*. Newbury Park: Sage, 1990, 269-189.

Ostro, Nilly. "Dynamics." *Chief Executive* no. 123 (May 1997): 62.

Powell, Tim. "Competitive Knowledge Management: You Can't Reengineer What Never Was Engineered in the First Place." *Competitive Intelligence Review* 8, no. 1 (Spring 1997): 40-47.

Rowland, Hilary, and Lynn Harris. "Doctor Know." *People Management* 4, no. 5 (5 March 1998): 50-52.

Spender, J.C. "Making Knowledge the Basis of a Dynamic Theory of the Firm." *Strategic Management Journal* 17 (Winter 1996): 45-62.

Tobin, Daniel R. "Networking Your Knowledge." *Management Review* 87, no. 4 (April 1998): 46-48.

Tsoukas, Haridmos. "The Firm as a Distributed Knowledge System: A Constructionist Approach." *Strategic Management Journal* 17 (Winter 1996): 11-25.

Waitley, Denis. "Self Leadership and Change." In *Empires of the Mind—Lessons to Lead and Succeed in a Knowledge-Based World*. William and Morrow, 1995.

Watt, Peggy. "Interview—Q & A: Where Learning Counts." *Network World* 14 (18 August 1997): I23-I24.

Webber, Alan M. "Surviving in the New Economy." *Harvard Business Review* (September-October 1994): 76.

Webber, Alan M. "What's So New About the New Economy?" *Harvard Business Review* (January-February 1993): 24.

Zuboff, S. "The Emperor's New Workplace." *Scientific American* 273, no. 3 (September 1995): 202-204.

Knowledge Mapping / The Information Audit

Bates, Mary Ellen. "Information Audits: What Do We Know and When Do We Know It?." *Library Management Briefings* (Fall 1997).

Berkman, Robert. "The Steps to Take for Conducting an Information Audit." *Information Advisor Knowledge Management Quarterly Supplement* 1, no. 3 (September 1997): 1-4.

Cortez, Edwin, and Edward Kazlauskas. "Information Policy Audit: A Case Study of an Organizational Analysis Tool." *Special Libraries* (Spring 1996): 85-88.

Cliffe, Sarah. "Knowledge Management: The Well-Connected Business." *Harvard Business Review* 76, no. 4 (July-August, 1998): 17-21.

Dietrick, Bill. "The Art of Knowledge Mapping: Where to Begin." *Information Advisor* (Knowledge Management Supplement) 1, no. 4 (December 1997): 1-3.

Gibb, F., and S. Buchanan. "The Information Audit: An Integrated Strategic Approach." *International Journal of Information Management* 18, no. 1 (February 1998): 29-47.

Hildebrand, Carol. "Guiding Principles." *CIO* 8, no. 18 (July 1995): 60-64.

Horton, F.W. Jr. "Mapping Corporate Information Resources." *International Journal of Information Management* 8, no. 4 (1988): 249-259.

Horton, F.W. Jr. "Mapping Corporate Information Resources." *International Journal of Information Management* 9, no. 1 (1989): 19-24.

Horton, F.W. Jr. "Mapping Corporate Information Resources." *International Journal of Information Management* 9, no. 2 (1989): 91-95.

Murray, B.S., and E. McDaid. "Visualizing and Representing Knowledge for the End User: A Review." *International Journal of Machine Studies* 38 (1993): 23-49.

Ostro, Nilly. "Metrics." *Chief Executive*, no. 123 (May 1997): 61.

"The Steps to Take for Conducting an Information Audit." *Information Advisor Knowledge Management* (Supplement) 1, no. 3 (September 1997): 1-4.

Skyrme, D.J. "Valuing Knowledge: Is It Worth It?" *Managing Information* 5, no. 3 (March 1998): 24-26.

Stewart, Thomas A. "Measuring Company IQ." *Fortune* 120 (24 January 1994): 24.

Stewart, Thomas A. "Mapping Corporate Brainpower." *Fortune* 132, no. 9 (30 October 1995): 209-212.

Knowledge Management and Organizational Aspects

Abecker, A., A. Bernardi, K. Hinkelmann, O. Kuhn, and M. Sintek. "Toward a Technology for Organizational Memories." *IEEE Intelligent Systems* 13, no. 3 (May-June 1998): 40-48.

Alonzo, Vincent, and Daniel McQuillen. "Best Corporate Asset: Brain Power?" *Incentive* 170, no. 1 (January 1996): 7.

Blair, Jim, and R. Hunter. "Introducing the KM Project Viability Assessment." *Research Note KM: SPA-03-5005*. Stamford, CT: Gartner Group, 1998.

Breton, Ernest J. "Creating a Corporate Brain." *Bulletin of the American Society for Information Science* 15, no. 1 (October-November 1988): 27-28.

Coleman, David. "Taking the Best Approach to Knowledge Management." *Computer Reseller News* no. 791 (1 June 1998): 111-112.

Davenport, Tom. "Coming Soon: The CKO." *Information Week* no. 491 (5 September 1994): 95.

Dove, Rick. "Managing Core Competency Knowledge." *Automotive Manufacturing and Production* 109, no. 12 (December 1997): 18-19.

Due, R. T. "The Eye of the Beholder: A Third Approach to Knowledge Management." *American Programmer* 11, no. 3 (March 1998): 26-29.

Gordon, Edward E. "How to Identify and Clone Top Performers." *Corporate University Review* 6, no. 2 (March 1998): 42-45.

Grayson, C. Jackson, Jr., and Carla S. O'Dell. "Horse and Carriage: Benchmarking and Knowledge Management." *Across the Board* 35, no. 4 (April 1998): 25.

Hedlund, Gunnar. "A Model of Knowledge Management and the N-form Corporation." *Strategic Management Journal* 15 (Summer 1994): 73-90.

Hiebeler, Robert J. "Benchmarking: Knowledge Management." *Strategy and Leadership* 24, no. 2 (March-April 1996): 22-29.

Holsapple, C.W. "Knowledge Management in Decision Making and Decision Support." *Knowledge and Policy* 8, no. 1 (Spring 1995): 5-22.

"It's What You Know—and Share—That Counts." *Training* 34, no. 2 (February 1997): 18-20.

Johnson, Donald E.L. "Knowledge Management's New Competitive Edge." *Health Care Strategic Management* 16, no. 7 (July 1998): 2-3.

Kerr, S. "Creating the Boundaryless Organization: The Radical Reconstruction of Organization Capabilities." *Planning Review* (September-October 1995): 41-45.

Malloy, Amy. "Supporting Knowledge Management: You Have It Now." *Computerworld* 32 (23 February 1998): 78.

McCartney, Laton. "Getting Smart About Knowledge Management: Managing Intellectual Resources Can Maximize Innovation and Competitiveness." *Industry Week* 247, no. 9 (4 May 1998): 30-34.

Ostro, Nilly. "The Corporate Brain." *Chief Executive*, no. 123 (May 1997): 58-62.

Orlikowski, Wanda J. "Improvising Organizational Transformation over Time: A Situated Change Perspective." *Information Systems Research: ISR: A Journal of the Institute of Management Sciences* 7, no. 1 (1996): 63-92.

Orlikowski, Wanda J. "Learning from Notes: Organizational Issues in Groupware Implementation." *The Information Society* 9 (1993): 237-250.

Quinn, James Brian, Philip Anderson, and Sydney Finkelstein. "Managing Professional Intellect: Making the Most of the Best." *Harvard Business Review* (March-April 1996): 71.

Quintas, Paul, Paul Lefrere, and Geoff Jones. "Knowledge Management: A Strategic Agenda." *Long Range Planning* 30, no. 3 (June 1997): 385-391.

Sanchez, Ron, and Joseph T. Mahoney. "Modularity, Flexibility, and Knowledge Management in Product and Organization Design." *Strategic Management Journal* 17 (Winter 1996): 63-76.

Sauer, Steven D. "Managing Corporate Knowledge Can Yield Significant Dividends." *Healthcare Financial Management* 50, no. 12 (December 1996): 31-32.

Stamps, David. "A Conversation with Doctor Paradox." *Training* 34 (May 1997): 42-48.

Stear, Edward B. "The Content Management Strategy: Don't Go to Work Without It." *Online* 22, no. 3 (May-June 1998): 87-90.

Turner, Mary Johnston. "Knowledge Management Works When Everyone's Involved." *Internet Week* no. 725 (27 July 1998): 29.

Turoff, R. "An Arranged Marriage: Knowledge Management and Organizational Development." *American Programmer* 11, no. 3 (March 1998): 30-33.

Watt, Peggy. "Knowing It All." *Network World* 14, no. 33 (18 August 1997): 117-118.

Weick, K. "Prepare Your Organization to Fight Fires." *Harvard Business Review* 74, no. 3 (1996): 143-148.

Wielinga, B., Sandberg, J., and Schreiber, G. "Methods and Techniques for Knowledge Management: What Has Knowledge Engineering to Offer?" *Expert Systems with Applications* 13, no. 1 (July 1997): 73-84.

Wilson, O. "Knowledge Management: Putting a Good Idea to Work." *Managing Information* 5, no. 3 (March 1998): 31-33.

Knowledge Management and the Information Professional

Abram, Stephen. "Post Information Age Positioning for Special Librarians: Is Knowledge Management the Answer?" *Information Outlook* 1, no. 6 (June 1997): 18-25.

Albert, Judith. "Nuts and Bolts of Knowledge Management for Information Professionals." *Proceedings of the National Online Meeting* 19, no. 1 (12 May 1998): 6-15.

Backer, Thomas E. "Information Alchemy: "Transforming Information Through Knowledge Utilization." *Journal of the American Society for Information Science* 44, no. 4 (May 1993): 217-221.

Boeri, R.J. and M. Hensel. "Special Librarians and Enterprise Knowledge Management." *EMedia Professional* 11, no. 4 (April 1998): 36.

Bowes, R. "Expanding the Information Horizon. Alternative Careers for Information Professionals." *ASLIB Proceedings* 43, no. 9 (September 1991): 271-275.

Broadbent, Merianne. "The Emerging Phenomenon of Knowledge Management." *Australian Library Journal* 46, no. 1 (February 1997): 6-24.

Broadbent, Merianne. "The Phenomenon of Knowledge Management: What Does It Mean to the Library Profession?" *Information Outlook* 2, no. 5 (May 1998): 23-36.

Chase, R.L. "Knowledge Navigators." *Information Outlook* 2, no. 9 (September 1998): 17-26.

"The Chief Knowledge Officer—A New Career Path?" *Information Advisor Knowledge Management* (Supplement) 2, no. 2 (June 1998): 1-3.

Corcoran, Mary, and Rebecca Jones. "Chief Knowledge Officers? Perceptions, Pitfalls, & Potential." *Information Outlook* 1, no. 6 (June 1997): 30-36.

DiMattia, Susan, and Norman Oder. "Knowledge Management: Hope, Hype, or Harbinger?" *Library Journal* 122, no. 15 (15 September 1997): 33-35.

Drotos, P.V. "From Online Specialist to Research Manager—Changing with the Times." *Online* 18, no. 1 (1994): 54-58.

Dysart, J.I., and Tom Davenport. "Tom Davenport on Knowledge Management: Selected Quotes." *Information Outlook* 1, no. 6 (June 1997): 27-28.

Dysart, Jane I. "The SCIP Conference for CI Professionals: Conference Coverage Focused on Knowledge-Based Strategies for Success." *Information Today* 5, no. 5 (May 1998): 23, 62, 73.

Field, Judith J. "Excellence and SLA." *Information Outlook* 2, no. 3 (March 1998): 5.

Field, Judith J. "A New Year, New Challenges, and New Opportunities." *Information Outlook* 2, no. 1 (January 1998): 5.

Field, M. "How to Dine Free at the Hilton" (Report on IBC Conference on Knowledge Management). *Library Association Record* 100, no. 3 (March 1998): 124.

Fisher, A. "So What Is the Big Fuss About?" *Library Association Record* 100, no. 4 (April 1998): 190-191.

Ghilardi, Fiona J. Mellor. "The Information Center of the Future? The Professional's Role." *Online* 18 (November-December 1994): 8-9.

Helfer, Joe. "A Practitioner's Guide to Knowledge Management." *Searcher* 6, no. 7 (1 July 1998): 44.

Hibbard, Justin. "Knowledge and Learning Officers Find Big Paydays." *Information Week* no. 686 (15 June 1998): 170.

Jurek, Richard J. "An Argument for Change." *Marketing Research* 9 (Winter 1997): 56.

"Knowledge Management: Lessons for Information Professionals." *Information Advisor Knowledge Management* (Supplement) 1, no. 1 (March 1997).

"Knowledge Management: The Third 'Era' of the Information Age." *InfoManage* 3, no. 10 (September 1996): 1-5.

Lyon, Jo. "Personal Development—Understanding Knowledge." *Information World Review* no. 125 (May 1997): 24-25.

Marshall, Lucy. "Facilitating Knowledge Management and Knowledge Sharing: New Opportunities for Information Professionals." *Online* 21, no. 5 (September-October 1997): 92-98.

Pedley, P. "The Best Placed Profession to Give Tips on Filtering." *Library Association Record* 100, no. 2 (February 1998): 82-83.

Pemberton, J. Michael. "Chief Knowledge Officer: The Climax of Your Career?" *Records Management Quarterly* 31, no. 2 (April 1997): 66-69.

Pemberton, J. Michael. "Knowledge Management (KM) and the Epistemic Tradition." *Records Management Quarterly* 32, no. 3 (July 1998): 58-62.

Peters, R.F. "Information Partnerships: Marketing Opportunities for Information Professionals." *Information Outlook* 1, no. 3 (March 1997): 14-16.

Pigott, S. "New Roles for the Information Professional." *SLA Specialist* 19, no. 9 (September 1996): 8.

Ponelis, S. and F.A. Fairer-Wessels. "Knowledge Management: A Literature Overview." *South African Journal of Library and Information Science* 66, no. 1 (March 1998): 1-9.

Prusak, Laurence. "Hiring Outside the Box." *CIO* 8, no. 18 (July 1995): 98.

Solomon, Marc. "Re-Tooling the Information Professional." *Searcher* 5, no. 3 (March 1997): 10-14.

St. Clair, G. "Knowledge Management for OPLs? Why Not?" *One-Person Library* 14, no. 9 (January 1998): 1-2.

St. Clair, G. "Special Libraries." In Maurice Line, Graham Mackenzie, and Paul Sturges, eds. *Library and Information Work Worldwide 1998*, London: Bowker-Saur, 1998, 103-120.

St. Clair, G., and L. Remeikis. "Knowledge Management: The Third 'Era' of the Information Age?" *Records Management Bulletin* no. 77 (December 1996): 13-16.

Stear, E.B., and J. Wecksell. "Information Resource Center Management (IRCM)." *Bulletin of the American Society for Information Science* 23, no. 4 (April-May 1997): 15-17.

Taylor V. "SLA Institute Focuses on Knowledge Management: A New Competitive Asset." *Library Hi Tech News* no. 150 (March 1998): 1-2.

Taylor, V. "Transform Yourself into a Knowledge Executive." *Information Outlook* 2, no. 3 (March 1998): 16.

Van Heust, G., R. Van Der Spek, and E. Kruizinga. "Corporate Memories as a Tool for Knowledge Management." *Expert Systems with Applications* 13, no. 1 (July 1997): 41-54.

Williams, Ruth L. and Wendi R. Bukowitz. "Knowledge Managers Guide Information Seekers." *HR Magazine* 42 (January 1997): 76-81.

Wleklinski, J. "Leaving the Library: An Information Professional's Odyssey." *Searcher* 5, no. 7 (July 1997): 6-10.

Knowledge Management—Issues

Adler, Paul S. "When Knowledge Is the Critical Resource, Knowledge Management Is the Critical Task." *IEEE Transactions on Engineering Management* 36, no. 2 (May 1989): 87-94.

Aghion, Philippe, and Patrick Bolton. "A Theory of Trickle-Down Growth and Development." *Review of Economic Studies*. 64, no. 2 (1997): 151-172.

Alavi, Maryam. *KPMG Peat Marwick U.S.: One Giant Brain*. Boston, MA: Harvard Business School Publishing, 1997.

Albert, S. "Knowledge Management: Living up to the Hype?" *Midrange Systems* 11, no. 13 (7 September 1998): 52.

Anonymous. "Evaluating the Value of Knowledge Capital." *CPA Journal* 68, no. 7 (July 1998): 57.

Banerjee, Abhijit. "Simple Model of Herd Behavior." *Quarterly Journal of Economics* 107, no. 3 (1992): 797-817.

Bergsman, Steve. "Corporate Spying Goes Mainstream." *CFO: The Magazine for Senior Financial Executives* 13, no. 12 (December 1994): 24.

Blair, J. "Key Issues for Knowledge Management." *Gartner Group Research Note/Key Issues K-KMGT-1650*. 1997.

Brown, C. and S. Migill. "Alignment of the IS Functions with the Enterprise: Toward a Model of Antecedents." *Management Information Science Quarterly* 18, no. 4 (1994): 371-403.

Burlton, R. "Process and Knowledge Management: A Question of Balance." *American Programmer* 11, no. 3 (March 1998): 16-25.

Chard, Ann Maria. *Knowledge Management at Ernst & Young*. Graduate School of Business, Stanford University, 1997.

CommerceNet Research Center. "Search Engines Most Popular Method of Surfing the Web." 2 June 1998. http://www.commercenet.com/research/stats/4-8-97.html.

Cropley, J. "Knowledge Management: A Dilemma." *Business Information Review* 15, no. 1 (March 1998): 27-34.

Davenport, Tom. "Known Evils: Seven Fallacies that Can Hamper Development of Knowledge Management in a Company." *CIO* 10, no. 17 (15 June 1997): 34-36.

Davenport, Tom. "Managing Customer Knowledge." *CIO* 11, no. 15 (1 June 1998): 32-34.

Davenport, Tom. "Think Tank." *CIO* 9, no. 6 (15 December 1995): 30-32.

Dove, Rick. "Building a Principle-Based Knowledge Management Practice." *Automotive Manufacturing and Production* 110, no. 2 (February 1998): 16-17.

Dove, Rick. "Knowledge Management—It's Not Just in the IT Department." *Automotive Manufacturing and Production* 110, no. 3 (March 1998): 26-28.

Due, R.T. "The Eye of the Beholder: A Third Approach to Knowledge Management." *American Programmer* 11, no. 3 (March 1998): 26-29.

Essers, J., and J. Schreinemakers. "Nonaka's Subjectivist Conception of Knowledge in Corporate Knowledge Management." *Knowledge Organization* 24, no. 1 (1997): 24-32.

"Executive Roundtable." *Information Week* (23 March 1998): 8ER-10ER.

Fahey, Liam and Laurence Prusak. "The Eleven Deadliest Sins of Knowledge Management." *California Management Review* 40, no. 3 (Spring 1998): 265-276.

Galagan, Patricia A. "Smart Companies." *Training and Development* 51, no. 12 (December 1997): 20-24.

Ghilardi, Fiona and J. Mellor. "Getting to 'Real-Time' Knowledge Management: From Knowledge Management to Knowledge Generation." *Online* 21 (September-October 1997): 99-100.

Ghoshal, Sumantra. "Changing the Role of Top Management: Beyond Structure to Processes." *Harvard Business Review* (January-February 1995): 86-91.

Graham, Ann B., and Vincent G. Pizzo. "A Question of Balance: Case Studies in Strategic Knowledge Management." *European Management Journal* 14, no. 4 (August 1996): 338-346.

Greif, Avner. "Cultural Beliefs and the Organization of Society: A Historical and Theoretical Reflection on Collectivist and Individualist Societies." *Journal of Political Economy* 102, no. 5 (1994): 912-950.

Grenier, Ray and George Metes. "Wake up and Smell the Syzygy." *Business Communications Review* 28, no. 8 (August 1998): 57-60.

"Harnessing Corporate IQ." *CA Magazine* 130 (April 1997): 26-29.

Hock, Ran. "How to Do Field Searching in Web Search Engines." *Online* 22, no. 3 (1998): 18, 22.

Hope, Kerin. "Albania Has Only 1.4 Fixed-Wire Telephones for Every 100 Inhabitants. *Financial Times* (19 February 1997).

Hunter, R. "KM in Government: This Is Not the Consulting Industry." *Research Note KM: KA 03-6492.* Stamford, CT: Gartner Group, 1998.

Jones, M. "Knowledge Management Column." *SIGGROUP Bulletin* 18, no. 2 (August 1997): 16-18.

Jordan, Judith and Penelope Jones. "Assessing Your Company's Knowledge Management Style." *Long Range Planning* 30, no. 3 (June 1997): 392-398.

Kaplan, R.S. and D.P. Norton. "The Balanced Score Card—Measures that Drive Performance." *Harvard Business Review* 70 (January-February 1992): 71-91.

Kerssens-Van Drongelen, Inge C., Petra C. de Weerd-Nederhof, and Olaf Fisscher. "Describing the Issues of Knowledge Management in R&D: Towards a Communication and Analysis Tool." *R&D Management* 26, no. 3 (July 1996): 213-230.

Knapp, Ellen. "Know-How's Not Easy." *Computerworld* 3, no. 11 (17 March 1997): L1-L11.

"Knowledge Management: Fighting the Fad." *Online and CD-ROM Review* 22, no. 2 (April 1998): 107-113.

Laberis, Bill. "One Big Pile of Knowledge." *Computerworld* 32, no. 5 (2 February 1998): 97.

Lawrence, Steve and C.Lee Giles. "Searching the World Wide Web." *Science* 280 (3 April 1998): 98-100.

Levitas, E., M.A. Hilt, and M.T. Dacin. "Competitive Intelligence and Tacit Knowledge Development in Strategic Alliances." *Competitive Intelligence Review* 8, no. 2 (1997): 392-398.

Malhotra, Yogesh. "Tools @ Work: Deciphering the Knowledge Management Hype." *Journal for Quality and Participation* 21, no. 4 (July-August 1998): 58-60.

Marshall, Chris, Larry Prusak, and David Shpilberg. "Financial Risk and the Need for Superior Knowledge Management." *California Management Review* 38, no. 3 (Spring 1996): 77-101.

Media Metrix, The PC Meter Company. "Media Metrix Reports Top 25 Web Site and Web Property Rankings for April 1998. 1 June 1998. http://www.mediametrix.com/corp/press/press_mm60.htm.

Menou, Michel J. "Studies of the Impact of Electronic Networking on Development: Report of the Mid-Project Meeting of the CABECA Survey of African Internet Use." Addis Ababa: Pan African Development Information System, 1998.

Mesdag, Martin van. "Too Much Information, Not Enough Knowledge." *Chief Executive* (May 1983): 38-39.

Milne, J. "Out One Ear, In the Other [Knowledge Management]." *Information Week* no. 31 (June 1998): 85-86.

Nerney, Chris. "Getting to Know Knowledge Management." *Network World* 14, no. 39 (29 September 1997): 101.

Osin, Luis. "Computers in Education in Developing Countries: Why and How." Education and Technology Series Paper No. 3 (1). Washington, D.C.: Human Development Department Education Group—Education and Technology Team, World Bank, 1998.

Puccinelli, B. "Messaging Is the Medium." *Inform* 12, no. 1 (January 1998): 24-27.

Ravallion, Martin, and Shaohua Chen. "What Can New Survey Data Tell Us About Recent Changes in Living Standards in Developing and Transitional Economies?" Washington, D.C.: World Bank, Policy Research Department, 1996.

Schwuchow, W. "Measuring the Information Market(s): A Personal Experience." *Journal of Information Science* 21, no. 2 (1995): 123-132.

Skyrme, David J. and Debra M. Amidon. "New Measures of Success." *Journal of Business Strategy* 19, no. 1 (January 1998): 20-24.

Slater, Derek. "Knowledge Management: Do as I Say, Not as I Do." *CIO Enterprise* 11, no. 4 (15 November 1997): 22.

Stamps, David. "Managing Corporate Smarts." *Training* 34 (August 1997): 40-44.

Stear, E.B. "Technology-Enabled Content: Threat or Opportunity." *Online* 21, no. 4 (July-August 1997): 80-82.

Willard, N. "Knowledge Management: What Does It Imply for IRM." *Managing Information* 4, no. 8 (October 1997): 31-32.

Zerega, Blaise. "Art of Knowledge Management." *InfoWorld* 20, no. 30 (27 July 1998): 61.

Zuckerman, Amy. "Are You Really Ready for Knowledge Management." *Journal for Quality and Participation* 20, no. 3 (June 1997): 58-61.

Zuckerman, Amy and Hal Buell. "Is the World Ready for Knowledge Management?" *Quality Progress* 31, no. 6 (June 1998): 81-84.

Knowledge Management and Information Technology

Allerton, Haidee E. "Thing One and Thing Two." *Training and Development* 52 (February 1998): 9.

Alter, Allan E. "Know-How Pays Off." *Computerworld* 31, no. 2 (13 January 1997): 72.

American Productivity and Quality Center. *Using Information Technology to Support Knowledge Management*, Final Report. 1997.

Bond, James. "The Drivers of the Information Revolution—Cost, Computing Power and Convergence." In *The Information Revolution and the Future of Telecommunications*. Washington, D.C.: World Bank, 1997.

Bond, James. "How Information Infrastructure Is Changing the World." In *The Information Revolution and the Future of Telecommunications*. Washington, D.C.: World Bank, 1997.

Bond, James. "Telecommunications is Dead, Long Live Networking—The Effect of the Information Revolution on the Telecom Industry." In *The Information Revolution and the Future of Telecommunications*. Washington, D.C.: World Bank, 1997.

Braga, Carlos A. Primo. "Liberalizing Telecommunications and the Role of the World Trade Organization." In *The Information Revolution and the Future of Telecommunications.* Washington, D.C.: World Bank, 1997.

Braga, Carlos A. Primo and Carsten Fink. "The Private Sector and the Internet." In *The Information Revolution and the Future of Telecommunications.* Washington, D.C.: World Bank, 1997.

Clippinger, John H. "Visualization of Knowledge: Building and Using Intangible Assets Digitally." *Planning Review* 23, no. 6 (November-December 1995): 28-32.

Clottes, Francoise. "The Information Revolution and the Role of Government." In *The Information Revolution and the Future of Telecommunications.* Washington, D.C.: World Bank, 1997.

Coleman, David. "Knowledge Management: The Next Golden Egg in Groupware." *Computer Reseller News*, no. 729 (31 March 1997): 79-80.

Davenport, Tom. "Saving IT's Soul: Human-Centered Information Management." *Harvard Business Review* (March-April 1994): 119-131.

DiRomualdo, Anthony and Vijay Gurbaxani. "Strategic Intent for IT Outsourcing." *Sloan Management Review* 39, no. 4 (Summer 1998): 67-80.

Finerty, Pat. "Improving Customer Care Through Knowledge Management." *CMA Magazine* 71, no. 9 (November 1997): 33.

Ford, Nigel. "From Information to Knowledge Management: The Role of Rule Induction and Neural Net Machine Learning Techniques in Knowledge Generation." *Journal of Information Science Principles and Practice* 15, no.4-5 (1989): 299-304.

Gallivan, M. "Value in Triangulation: A Comparison of Two Approaches for Combining Quantitative and Qualitative Methods." In A. Lee, J. Liebenau, and J. De Gross, eds. *Qualitative Method in Information Systems.* New York: Chapman & Hall, 1997, 83-107.

Gartner, Gideon. "Grappling with e.Knowledge." *Computerworld* 32, no. 1 (29 December 1997-5 January 1998): 43.

Holsapple, Clyde W. "Adapting Demons to Knowledge Management Environments." *Decision Support Systems* 3, no. 4 (December 1987): 289-298.

Kellogg, C. "From Data Management to Knowledge Management." *Computer* 19, no. 1 (January 1986): 75-84.

Kennedy, M.L. "Building Blocks for Knowledge Management at Digital Equipment Corporation: The Web Library." *Information Outlook* 1, no. 6 (June 1997): 39-48.

King, Julia. "Knowledge Management Promotes Sharing." *Computerworld* 32, no. 24 (15 June 1998): 24.

LaPlante, Alice. "Sharing the Wisdom." *Computerworld* 31, no. 22 (2 June 1997): 73-74.

Malcolm, Stanley E. "Where EPSS Will Go from Here." *Training* 35 (March 1998): 64-66.

Maurer, H. "Web-Based Knowledge Management." *Computer* 31, no. 3 (March 1998): 122-123.

Preston, C.M., and C.A. Lynch. "Report of the First International Conference on Information and Knowledge Management." *Library Hi-Tech News*, no. 102 (May 1993): 7-8.

Rischard, Jean-Francois. "Connecting Developing Countries to the Information Technology Revolution." *SAIS Review* 16 (Winter/Spring 1996): 93-107.

Sah, Raaj K., and Joseph E. Striglitz. "Sources of Technological Divergence Between Developed and Less Developed Economies." In G. Calvo, R. Findlay, P. Kouri, and J. Braga de Macedo, eds. *Debt, Stabilization, and Development.* Baltimore, MD: Johns Hopkins University Press, 1993.

Sarel, Michael. "Growth in East Asia: What We Can and What We Cannot Infer." *Economic Issues No. 1.* Washington, D.C.: International Monetary Fund, 1997.

Sawyer, S. and R. Southwick. "Implementing Client-Server: Issues from the Field." In B. Glasson, D. Vogel, P.Bots, and J. Nunamaker, eds. *The International Office of the Future.* New York: Chapman Hall, 1996.

Shen, Sheldon. "Knowledge Management in Decision Support Systems." *Decision Support Systems* 3, no. 1 (March 1987): 1-11.

Strapko, William. "Knowledge Management: A Fit with Expert Tools." *Software Magazine* 10, no. 13 (November 1990): 63-66.

Ubois, Jeff. "From Web Sites to Knowledge Management." *Midrange Systems* 10, no. 19 (28 November 1997): 24.

Watson, Gregory H. "Bringing Quality to the Masses: The Miracle of Loaves and Fishes." *Quality Progress* 31, no. 6 (June 1998): 29-32.

Wilck, Jennifer. "IT Drivers are Myriad for Chemical Manufacturers." *Chemical Market Reporter* 251 (19 May 1997): 21.

WorldSpace. "WorldSpace: The Technology." 1998. http://www.worldspace.com/text/technology.html.

Knowledge Management and Intranets

Campalans, A., E. DeVito, C. Honig, E. Koska, and E. Reid. "Exploiting Intranets for Knowledge Management and Information Sharing." *Journal of Business and Financial Librarianship* 3, no. 1 (1997): 27-39.

Cohen, Sacha. "Knowledge Management's Killer App." *Training and Development* 52, no. 1 (January 1998): 50-57.

Fishenden, J. "Managing Intranets to Improve Business Process." *ASLIB Proceedings* 49, no. 4 (April 1997): 90-96.

Fletcher, Liz. "Information Retrieval for Intranets: The Case for Knowledge Management." *Document World* 2, no. 5 (September-October 1997): 32-34.

Gardner, Dana. "Get Smart." *InfoWorld* 20, no. 14 (6 April 1998): 97-98.

Gillman, P. "Evaluating the Intranet as Part of Your Knowledge Management Strategy." *ASLIB Proceedings* 49, no. 2 (February 1997): 27-52.

"IRC Notes." *Information Outlook* 2, no. 9 (1 September 1998): 42.

"Managing the Corporate Mind." *Internal Auditor* 55, no. 2 (April 1998): 13-18.

"A Talk with Patricia Foy: Director of Knowledge Strategies, Coppers & Lybrand." *Information Advisor Knowledge Management Supplement* 2, no. 1 (March 1998): 3-4.

Knowledge Management Application Packages

Adams, Steve. "Knowledge Management." *Inform* 11, no. 10 (November 1997): 10-13.

Adhikari, Richard. "On the GrapeVine." *Information Week* no. 647 (8 September 1997): 120-122.

Angus, Jeff, Jeetu Patel, and Jennifer Harty. "Knowledge Management: Great Concept... But What Is It?: Part 1 of 2." *Information Week* (16 March 1998): 58-60.

Angus, Jeff, Jeetu Patel, and Jennifer Harty. "Knowledge Management: Great Concept... But What Is It?: Part 2 of 2." *Information Week* (16 March 1998): 62-64.

Anonymous. "Software for Knowledge Management." *Online* 21, no. 5 (September-October 1997): 96.

Blake, P., and C. Rabie. "Tooling Up for a Revolution." *Information World Review* no. 132 (January 1998): 15-16.

Bock, G.E. "Information Retrieval Tools for Knowledge Management." *Workgroup Computing Report* 21, no. 1 (USA: Patricia Seybold Group, January 1998): 3-25.

Bock, G.E. "Knowledge Management Frameworks." *Workgroup Computing Report* 20, no. 2 (USA: Patricia Seybold Group, February 1997): 3-22.

Cole-Gomolski, Barb. "Finding the Knowledge You Need." *Computerworld* 32, no. 18 (4 May 1998): 69-70.

Darrow, Barbara, and Lee Copeland. "Lotus Looks to Break Ground in Knowledge Management." *Computer Reseller News* no. 773 (26 January 26 1998): 3-6.

Davenport, Tom. "The Knowledge Biz." *CIO* 11, no. 4 (15 November 1997): 32-34.

Davenport, Tom. "We Have the Techknowledgy." *CIO* 9, no. 21 (15 September 1996): 36-38.

Fusaro, Roberta. "IBM/Lotus to Tackle Information Overload." *Computerworld* 32, no. 26 (29 June 1998): 24.

Hane, Paula J. "19th Annual National Online Meeting and IOLS '98: Knowledge Management, Search Engines Were Hot." *Information Today* 15, no. 6 (June 1998): 1, 70, 72.

Hibbard, Justin. "Ernst & Young Deploys App for Knowledge Management." *Information Week* no. 641 (28 July 1997): 28.

Hibbard, Justin. "Lotus Takes on Knowledge Management." *Information Week* no. 667 (2 February 1998): 26.

Hibbard, Justin. "Notes Goes Real-Time." *Information Week* no. 686 (15 June 1998): 28.

Liebowitz, J. "Expert Systems: An Integral Part of Knowledge Management." *Kybernetes* 27 no. 2, (1998): 170-175.

Marshak, D.S. "Organizational Knowledge Management: New Approaches from Information and PFN." *Workgroup Computing Report* 20, no. 8 (USA: Patricia Seybold Group, August 1997): 3-19.

McNamara, Paul. "Lotus Gives Knowledge Management Brain Dump." *Network World* 15, no. 26 (20 June 1998): 91.

McNamara, Paul. "Notes to Ride the Knowledge Management Wave." *Network World* 15, no. 5 (2 February 1998): 10.

Odem, Peggy, and Carla O'Dell. "Invented Here: How Sequent Computer Publishes Knowledge." *Journal of Business Strategy* 19 (January-February 1998): 25-28.

Solomon, Marc. "Knowledge Management Tools for Knowledge Managers: Filling the Gap Between Finding Information and Applying It." *Searcher* 5, no. 3 (March 1997): 10-14.

"Two Schools of Knowledge." *Information Week* no. 696 (17 August 1998): 45.

Vedel, M. "Group Therapy—Groupware." *Application Development Advisor* 1, no. 4 (March April 1998): 52-55.

Walker, Christy. "Notes 5.0 Bets Is on Track; Lotus CEO Papows Focuses on Knowledge Management." *PC Week* 15, no. 19 (11 May 1998): 19.

Walker, Christy. "New Ways to Make Data Pay: Knowledge Management Technology Improves Analysis and Decision-Making." *PC Week* 15, no. 34 (24 August, 1998): 14.

Willett, Shawn, and Lee Copeland. "Knowledge Management Key to IBM's Enterprise Plan." *Computer Reseller News* no. 800 (27 July 1998): 1, 6.

Knowledge Management–Current Initiatives

Anonymous. "Knowledge Management—How to Make It Work." *Management Today* (August 1997). 31.

Anthes, Gary H. "Learning How to Share." *Computerworld* 32 (23 February 1998): 75-77.

Ash, Jerry. "State of KM Practice Among Early Adopters." *Knowledge Inc.* (August 1997).

Buckman, Robert H., PhD. "Knowledge Sharing at Buckman Labs." *Journal of Business Strategy* 19, no. 1 (January 1998): 10-15.

Cerny, Keith. "Making Local Knowledge Global." *Harvard Business Review* (May-June 1996): 22.

Cole-Gomolski, Barb. "Corporate Strategist: Gordon Petrash." *Computerworld* 32, no. 1 (29 December 1997-5 January 1998): 49-50.

Davenport, Thomas H., David W. De Long, and Michael C. Beers. "Successful Knowledge Management Projects." *Sloan Management Review* 39, no. 1 (Winter 1998): 43-57.

David, Ian. "Doing the Knowledge." *Professional Engineering* 11, no. 11 (10 June 1998): 29-30.

Davis, Michael C. "Knowledge Management." *Information Strategy: The Executive's Journal* 15 no. 1 (Fall 1998): 11-22.

Gibson, Paul. "Knowledge Management Makes It Online: Publisher Web Sites Now Offer a Range of Long-Awaited KM Resources." *Information Today* 15, no. 6 (June 1998): 46.

Hafstad, Sissel. "The Knowledge Management Process in a Business School Environment." *Business Information Review* 14, no. 3 (September 1997): 135-140.

Hamilton, F. "Knowledge Management in the Oil and Gas Industry." *Information Management Report* (April 1997): 18-19.

Hibbard, Justin and Karen M. Carrillo. "Knowledge Revolution." *Information Week* no. 663 (5 January 1998): 49-54.

Hildebrand, Carol. "Experts for Hire." *CIO* (April 15, 1995): 32-40.

"How to Manage Knowledge" Interview with L. McKenzie, National Director of Knowledge Management with E&Y Kenneth Leventhal Real Estate Group." *Real Estate Forum* 53, no. 3 (March 1998): 92-93.

Jahnke, Art. "Share Ware." *CIO* 11, no. 18 (1 July 1998): 10.

Johnson, Donald E.L. "Making Knowledge Management a Priority." *Health Care Strategic Management* 15, no. 4 (April 1997): 2-3.

Knapp, Ellen M. "Knowledge Management." *Business and Economic Review* 44, no. 4 (July September 1998): 3-6.

"Knowledge Management: The Era of Shared Ideas (The Future of IT)." *Forbes* 160, no. 6 (22 September 1997): F 28.

Koch, Christopher. "Reap What You Know." *CIO* 10, no. 14 (1 May 1997): 118-122.

Martin, Justin. "Are You as Good as You Think You Are?" *Fortune* 134, no. 6 (30 September 1996): 142-152.

Martinez, Michelle Neely. "The Collective Power of Employee Knowledge." *HR Magazine* 43 (February 1998). 88-94.

Mullin, Rick. "Knowledge Management: A Cultural Evolution." *Journal of Business Strategy* 17, no. 5 (September-October 1996): 56-59.

Odem, Peggy and Carla O'Dell. "Invented Here: How Sequent Computer Publishes Knowledge." *Journal of Business Strategy* 19 (January-February 1998).

O'Leary, D.E. "Using AI in Knowledge Management: Knowledge Bases and Ontologies." *IEEE Intelligent Systems* 13, no. 3 (May-June 1998): 34-39.

Prokesch, Steven E. "Unleashing the Power of Learning: An Interview with British Petroleum's John Browne." *Harvard Business Review* (September-October 1997): 146-148.

Schein, Esther. "Keeping the Motor Humming with Data." *PC Week* 15, no. 6 (9 February 1998): 75-77.

Taylor, Andrew, and Tom Oates. "Technology as Knowledge—Towards a New Perspective on Knowledge Management in Electronics." *International Journal of Technological Management* 11, nos. 3-4 (1996): 296-314.

Knowledge Management and Training

Adler, Paul S. and Robert E. Cole. "Designed for Learning: A Tale of Two Auto Plants." *Sloan Management Review* 34, no. 3 (Spring 1993): 85-94.

Alonzo, Vincent. "Ernst & Young LLP." *Incentive* 172, no. 6 (June 1998): 26-27.

Bassi, Laurie J., Scott Cheney, and Mark Van Buren. "Training Industry Trends 1997." *Training and Development* 51 (November 1997): 46-50.

Calvacca, Lorraine. "Training for the Bottom Line." *Folio* 27, no. 4 (15 March 1998): 32-34.

Chaudron, David. "Global Training Gets High-Tech at Buckman Labs." *HR Focus* 75, no. 4 (April 1998): S12.

Densford, Lynn E. "General Motors University: Overseeing Training for 650,000." *Corporate University Review* 6, no. 2 (March 1998). 8-9.

Kenyon, Henry S. "Volvo University: Building a Culture of Customer Satisfaction." *Corporate University Review* (1 February 1998).

Levin, Rich. "Train at the Speed of Change." *Information Week* (8 June 1998): 1A-5A.

"Measuring Training's Contribution to Intellectual Capital." *Training* 35 (March 1998): 14-16.

Srikantaiah, Kanti. *LS 808 Knowledge Management Course Syllabus: Fall 1998*. Dominican University, Graduate School of Library and Information Science, River Forest, IL.

Switzer, John. "Managing Human Capital." *Banking Strategies* 72 (November-December 1996): 50-55.

Knowledge Management Chapters in Conference Proceedings

Addleson, M. "Languages of Possession and Participation: Traps, Tropes, and Trapezes of Organizational Discourse." Paper delivered at The 3rd International Conference on Organizational Discourse. London, England, Kings College Management Centre, July 29-31.

Bharat, Krishna and Andrei Broder. "A Technique for Measuring the Relative Size and Overlap of Public Web Search Engines. In Proceedings of the 7th International World Wide Web Conference. Brisbane, Australia: Elsevier Science, April 1998, 379-388. http://decweb.ethz.ch/WWW7/1937/com1937.htm.

Barker, K., and Ozsu, M.T., eds. Proceedings of 5th International Conference on Information and Knowledge Management. New York: ACM, 1996. Boersma, J.S.K.T. and R.A. Stegwee. "Exploring the Issues in Knowledge Management." Chapter in Proceedings of the 1996 Information Resources Management Association International Conference. Harrisburg, PA: Idea Group Publishing, 1996. Boynton, A. "How to Get Started with Knowledge Management." In *Exploring Opportunities in Knowledge Management, Knowledge Management Symposium: Leveraging Knowledge for Business Impact*, IBM Consulting Group, Sydney, 1996.

Choo, C.W. "National Computer Policy Management in Singapore: Planning an Intelligent Island." Chapter in *Forging New Partnerships in Information Proceedings of the 58th Annual Meeting of the American Society for Information Science*, Chicago, IL, October 1995. Medford, NJ: Information Today, 1995.

David, Paul A. "Knowledge, Property, and the System Dynamics of Technological Change." In Lawrence M. Summers and Shekhar Shah, eds. *Proceedings of the World Bank Annual Conference on Development Economics*. Washington, D.C.: World Bank, 1993.

Field, J. "Information + Technology + You Equals Knowledge Management." Proceedings of the 13th Annual Computers in Libraries '98 in cooperation with the Special Libraries Association, (2-4 March 1998): 60-62. Medford, NJ: Information Today, 1998.

Kappes, Sandra and Beverly Thomas. *A Model for Knowledge Worker Information Support*. Champaign, Illinois: US Army Corps of Engineers, Construction Engineering Research Laboratories, 1993.

Kappes, Sandra, Wayne J. Schmidt, and Duane D. Sears. *Document Management for the Knowledge Worker System*. Champaign, Illinois: US Army Corps of Engineers, Construction Engineering Research Laboratories, 1995.

Klempa, M.J., and J.A. Britt. "Managing Information Technology: An Acquisition/ Diffusion Contingency Model Integrating Organization Culture, Organization Learning, and Knowledge Sharing." In *Emerging Information Technologies for Competitive Advantage and Economic Development Proceedings* of 1992 Information Resources Management Association International Conference, Charleston, S.C., May 1992. Harrisburg, PA: Idea Group Publishing, 1992.

Kotnour, T., C. Orr, J. Spaulding, and J. Guidi. "Determining the Benefit of Knowledge Management Activities." In *1997 IEEE International Conference on Systems, Man, and Cybernetics*, vol. 1. New York: IEEE, 1997.

LeFaure, Skip. "The 1998 Conference of Knowledge Management and Organizational Learning." Presentation at the Conference Board Conference, Chicago: 15 April 1998.

Malhotra, Yogesh. "Knowledge Management in Inquiring Organizations." In *Proceedings of the 3rd Americas Conference on Information Systems*. Indianapolis, IN (15-17 August 1997): 293-295.

Mayer, Richard J., et al. *Design Knowledge Management System (DKMS) Beta Test Report*. Ohio: Wright Patterson Air Force Base, Armstrong Laboratory, Air Force Material Command, 1993.

Mayer, Richard J., et al. *Design Knowledge Management System (DKMS) Technology Impact Report*. Ohio: Wright Patterson Air Force Base, Ohio: Armstrong Laboratory, Air Force Material Command, 1993.

Prusak, Larry. "Managing Principal, IBM Global Services, Consulting Group." Presentation at the Conference Board Conference, The 1998 Conference of Knowledge Management and Organizational Learning. Chicago: 16 April 1998.

Remeikis, L.A. and E. Koska. "Organization for Knowledge: Developing a Knowledge Management System." In *Proceedings of the 17th National Online Meeting* New York, May 1996. Medford, N.J.: Information Today, Inc., 1996.

Skyrme, D.J. "From Information to Knowledge Management—Are You Prepared?" In Online Information 97 Proceedings, 21st International Online Information Meeting. Oxford, UK: Learned Information, 1997.

Swartz, L.H. "Implicit Knowledge (Tacit Knowing), Connoisseurship, and the Common Law Tradition." Paper presented at the faculty workshop of the University at Buffalo School of Law, Buffalo, NY, 11 April 1997.

Weiss, Andrew and Georgiy Nikitin. "Performance of Czech Companies by Ownership Structure." Paper presented at the William Davidson Institute (University of Michigan) Conference on Finance in Transition Economies. Boston University, May 1998.

Web Sites

AIAI (Artificial Intelligence)
http://www.aiai.ed.uk/~alm/kamlnks.html

American Productivity and Quality Center
http://www.apqc.org/

Awaken Technology
http://www.awaken.com

@Brint: Knowledge Management and Organizational Learning
http://www.brint.com/OrgLrng.htm

CIO Magazine Online
http://www.cio.com/archive/

Collaborative Strategies
http://www.collaborate.com/

Commercenet
http://www.commercenet.com

Decision Support System—A Knowledge-Based Approach
http://www.uky.edu/BusinessEconomics/dssakba/

Digital Systems Research Center
http://www.research.digital.com/SRC/home.html

Ernst & Young
http://www.ey.com/knowledge

Forbes ASAP
http://www.forbes.com/asap/97/0407/034.htm

Graduate School of Business, University of Texas at Austin
http://www.bus.utexas.edu/kman/

grapeVine Technologies
http://www.gvt.com

Group Decision Support Systems
http://www.gdss.com/learning.htm

Idea Exchange
http://www.sol-ne.org/ide/#know_man

Institute for Intellectual Capital Research
http://business.mcmaster.ca/mktg/nbontis/ic/

Integral Performance Group
http://knowledgecreators.com/ipg/learning.html

Intelligence Online
http://www.indigo-net.com/annexes/289/baumard.htm

The International Knowledge Management Network
http://kmn.cibit.hvu.nl

KM World Magazine
http://kmonline.com

Knowledge Associates
http://www.knowledge.stjohns.co.uk

Knowledge Construction Glossary
http://www.cs.colorado.edu/~otswald/glossaries/kc-glossary.html

Knowledge Inc.
http://www.knowledgeinc.com/quantera

Knowledge Magazine
http://www.media-access.com/publications.html

The Knowledge Management Forum
http://www.km-forum.org

Knowledge Management Group
http://www.csu.edu.au/research/sda/KMG/index.html

Knowledge Media Institute
http://kmi.open.ac.uk/~simonb/org-knowledge/

Knowledge Praxis
http://www.media-access.com/whatis.html#history

Knowledge Research Institute
http://www.knowledgeresearch.com

Knowledge Transfer International
http://www.ktic.com/TOPIC1/ABOUT.HTM

Learning-Org Dialog on Learning Organizations
http://world.std.com/~lo/

The Montague Institute Review
http://www.montague.com/review/review.html

Stanford Learning Organization Web
http://www-leland.stanford.edu/group/SLOW/

Sveiby Knowledge Management
http://www.sveiby.com.au/

The Technology Broker
http://www.tbroker.co.uk/intellectual_capital

I3 Update
http://www.skyrme.com

Videos

Data Mining for Business Professionals. Syosset, NY: Computer Channel, Inc., 1997.

Getting Out of the Box: The Knowledge Management Opportunity. Special Libraries Association, 1996.

Intelligent Agents. Syosset, NY: Computer Channel, Inc., 1997.

Knowledge Management Company. Special Libraries Association, 1997.

Sanders, Terry. *Into the Future: On the Preservation of Knowledge in the Electronic Age.* Produced and directed by Terry Sanders. American Film Foundation, 1997.

Information-Driven Management: A Thematic Model

This appendix is an extension of Chapter 3, "The Evolution of Knowledge Management." It derives from two resources:

> Koenig, Michael E.D. Information Driven Management, Concepts and Themes: A Toolkit for Librarians, Saur, K.G.,1998

> Koenig, Michael E.D. "Information Driven Management, The New, but Little Perceived Business Zeitgeist," to appear in Libri.

For the last decade and a half, the business community has seen what appears to be one fad after another. To a surprising (and greatly under-recognized) degree, however, those fads and enthusiasms are facets of and constitute one major theme —the importance of information and the skillful use of information to the success of the modern corporation. This appendix briefly reviews those concepts and attempts to show how they do indeed constitute one logical whole.

To provide context for this appendix, those business themes are briefly reviewed in a rough reverse chronological order, most recent first, of their appearance in the consciousness of the general business community. The description here is quite brief.

These themes are listed in chronological order with the most recent first.

- Supply Chain Management
- Enterprise Resources Planing (ERP)
- Information Driven Marketing
- Knowledge Management and Intellectual Capital
- Data Warehousing/Data Mining
- Core Competencies

- Business Process Re-engineering
- Hierarchies to Markets
- Competitive Intelligence
- TQM and Benchmarking
- Information Technology and Productivity
- Minimization of Unallocated Cost
- Information Technology and Organizational Structure
- Information Resource Management
- Enterprise-Wide Information Analysis
- Management Information System (MIS) to Decision Support Systems (DSS), and External Information
- Information Technology as Competitive Advantage
- Managing the Archipelago
- Information Systems Stage Hypotheses
- Decision Analysis and Expected Value of Perfect Information (EVPI)
- Data-Driven Systems Design

Supply Chain Management

Supply chain management (Brown, 1997) is the successor to just-in-time (JIT) inventory management. JIT was the concept of establishing a relationship with suppliers such that instead of the purchaser ordering and receiving materials ahead of time and then warehousing them (at considerable expense), rather the supplier delivered the needed materials "just in time." Supply chain management is simply the extension of the JIT concept to supply management in general, including one's own production and processing as well as one's relations with suppliers. The terminology "supply chain management" has much to do with the popularity of Michael Porter's (1985) "value chain," often used as a format or template for analyzing the operations of an organization.

Enterprise Resource Planning

Enterprise resource planning (ERP) (Davenport, 1998) is the name for the use of one very large (and very expensive) but modularized commercial data management package to integrate an organization's handling of its internal data. The name is confusing, a much better one would be enterprise information integration systems, or simply enterprise systems, and the latter term is beginning to be used more often. At the moment though, ERP is the buzzword. The idea behind ERP is to replace all of an organization's old legacy systems that communicated poorly with each other and that stored information in different formats, with one flexible but totally integrated system.

Information Driven Marketing (Relationship Marketing)

Relationship marketing (Bessen, 1993) is simply using information to target potential customers more precisely, tailoring services to specific customers more effectively, and individualizing communications with customers. The phrases "targeted marketing" or "individualized marketing" are probably more descriptive, but relationship marketing is the phrase that has gained popularity in the business community.

Knowledge Management and Intellectual Capital

In the early and mid-1990s there was an increasing awareness in the business community that knowledge was an important organizational resource that needed to be nurtured, sustained, and accounted for, if possible. Intellectual capital (Stewart, 1994) was the name given to the growing awareness that information is a factor of production, in a category with land, labor, capital, and energy (Talero and Gaudette, 1995). Knowledge management is the product of that awareness and the information sharing potential of the Internet, or more specifically its derivative, the Intranet.

Data Warehousing/Data Mining

Data warehousing (Darling, 1997) is the assembling of selected, filtered, and structured data from a variety of sources into one coherent assembly for the purpose of being able to find meaningful relationships within that data. Data mining is the attempt to extract useful relationships from within large bodies of data. The notion behind the enthusiasm is that if an organization can assemble and combine the data on its operations that it collects, most likely with external information as well, then an organization can discover meaningful and useful patterns in that data.

Core Competencies

The motion of core competencies (Prahalad and Hamel, 1990) is the argument that each organization has its own core competencies, areas in which the organization's performance excels. The organization should insofar as practical, focus on its core competencies and consider outsourcing/purchasing from outside, those goods or activities that are necessary to the organization's activities and are not within its area of core competencies. What is new is the recognition that information technology and communication technology is rapidly changing the balance between making it in-house, rather than buying it from an outside supplier, and making it more and more practical to outsource non-core competencies. The strategic derivative from this concept is that organizations should define themselves and their plans based on core competencies, not based on markets served and products produced.

Business Process Re-Engineering

Business process re-engineering (Davenport and Short, 1990; Davenport, 1993) was the hot topic in the business community in the mid-1990s. It simply meant redesigning the operations and the workflow of the organization to take advantage of the capabilities of electronic communications. Those capabilities, such as real-time operation and the distance independence of modern electronic information systems, permitted radical redesign and often dramatic rationalization and simplification of business procedures and systems.

Business process re-engineering acquired a bad reputation because it frequently became associated with the downsizing of organizations and the consequent laying-off of employees, which, needless to say, were very unpopular consequences. Another criticism was that, in many cases, in their enthusiasm to "right-size," a euphemism for downsize, and make themselves more profitable by reducing costs, organizations often divested themselves of key mid-level employees who took their expertise and knowledge, their intellectual capital, with them.

Hierarchies to Markets

The argument that constitutes the hierarchies and markets theme (Malone and Benjamin, 1967) is a fascinating one due to the scope of its possible ramifications, both in the political sector as well as in economics and business. The basic precept is that an organization always faces a "make or buy" choice, and improved information and communication technology tends to continuously shift the balance point to the "buy" end of the balance.

Competitive Intelligence

The notion of competitive intelligence is not new, but it has enjoyed a resurgence of interest in the business community (Fuld, 1988). This revival has mostly been driven by the increasing internationalization of business.[1] When the competition is not in the same country or the same continent, it is difficult to be aware of what the competition may be intending. That, in turn, results in the need for a more conscious and explicit effort to stay on top of things and to acquire appropriate competitive intelligence. This development is reinforced by the core competency thesis that implies the requirement to focus on the state of the art and remain equal with or ahead of competitors in your core competencies, with less reliance on natural markets. Similarly the hierarchies to markets phenomenon implies less protection and market creation by government actions, more exposure to the vicissitudes of the market and competition, and consequently a greater need for competitive intelligence.

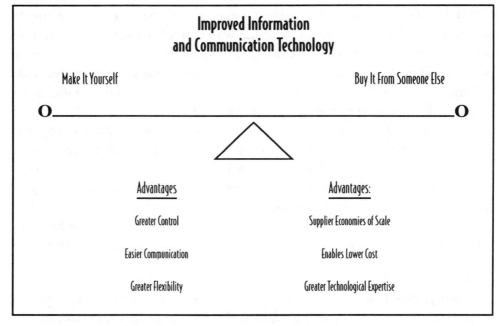

Figure C.1 Make or Buy Balance

TQM and Benchmarking

There are two basic concepts behind TQM (Walton, 1986). The most basic thrust is quality control and, in particular, enlarging the responsibility for quality control from engineers and quality-control staff to include the operators on the floor and the customers whom are being supplied. Quality becomes not just tolerances and rejection rates, but fitness for use, and as the customer perceives it. The second is precisely that of the employee involvement and the ramifications of greater involvement, not only in the quality control of the process as it exists at any particular time, but also in the role of improving the processes and the products. Also included, however, is the notion of benchmarking. Benchmarking is the process of examining any process your organization performs, finding out who else needs to undertake that same process (whether in your industry or not), then finding out who performs it best, and using that performance as a benchmark against which to compare your own performance and with which to generate new expectations and standards about what constitutes first class performance from which you can generate new ideas about how to improve your performance.

Information Technology and Productivity

A key driver of modern business thinking is that the appropriate use of information technology enhances productivity. A good example of this increased productivity is modern communications, such as telephony and email, which rely on sophisticated electronic switches to make connections instead of the manual methods used by early telephone operators.

Minimization of Unallocated Cost

The concept of minimization of unallocated cost is based on the distinction between two types of cost incurred by an organization. First, there are those costs that are directly attributable or allocable to the organization's output. Second, there are those costs which are not easily attributable and which must be treated as overhead, also known as burden, or general and administrative (G&A) costs. Basic accounting doctrine holds that the smaller proportion of unattributable cost, the better the decision-making performance of the organization (Dearden, 1978).

As information technology and information services, often treated as unallocated G&A expenses, commanded a larger and larger share of the organization expense pie, then the more the principle of minimization of unallocated cost drives management attention to the importance of information technology and information technology management (Koenig, 1987).

Information Technology and Organizational Structure

For several decades, there has been much speculation about the effect of information technology on the structure of organizations. The central theme that has emerged is that we have been far too unaware of how much the structure of organizations and bureaucracies has been shaped by the limitation of print-on-paper and the requirement to shape job and functional unit parameters around the availability of information. Information technology, however, is increasingly providing the capability to place the information where the user is, rather than require the user to go or be where the information is, and some of the resulting reconfigurations can be quite dramatic. Thomas Whisler (1970) did the seminal research and predicated that organizations would become flatter with fewer, particularly mid-level, professional jobs. Such broad generalizations, however, have fallen into disfavor. Numerous counter examples were found, for example, the insurance industry where Brophy (1985) points out that the effect of information technology has been to markedly increase the ration of professional to non-professional staff.

Information Resource Management

Information resource management (IRM) (Synnott and Gruber, 1980; Marchand, 1985) is a term that is now rather dated and has been replaced by the term knowledge management. IRM arose in the 1970s and was, to an extent, an offspring of the enthusiasm for MIS systems, discussed in a subsequent section. It was basically the recognition that information was a resource that the organization should explicitly pay attention to and manage, just as it managed finance, inventory, and personnel. The concept received additional momentum when, in the paperwork reduction act of 1980, United States government agencies were required to assign a senior administrator the responsibility of information management.

Enterprise-Wide Information Analysis

Enterprise-wide information analysis (Parker 1982, 1985) is a phrase coined by IBM in the early 1980s. The basic idea is very simple and very elegant, but it needs to be put in a contextual setting. IBM offered free courses for its customers on what it called "business systems planning," or planning for how much data processing capability an organization would need in the future.

In the late 1970s, the phrase "critical success factors" had become very popular to describe the concept that management should not merely respond to current issues and emergencies, i.e., crisis management, but should take the time to carefully analyze which factors were critical to the success of the organization, and whether or not the organization's resources were deployed accordingly.

Enterprise-wide information analysis is basically the grafting of the critical success factors notion onto business systems planning. The basic precepts of enterprise-wide information analysis are:

1. Determine what your enterprise is.

2. Determine which decisions have to be made correctly to be successful in that enterprise.

3. Determine what information is needed to make those decisions correctly.

From the above, proceed with your business systems planning and decide what information technology capabilities will be required.

MIS to DSS, and External Information

In the 1970s, there was a great enthusiasm for what were then termed MISs. As data processing systems developed, the awareness grew that most organizations had large amounts of data and information contained in electronic form. As this information was migrated to database management systems, the concept then arose that management could access this central data store to address and support management decision making.

After much enthusiasm for MIS development, a backlash of disappointment occurred when it became apparent that MIS systems were not performing as advertised, and that executives were not using them to any great extent. Gradually, it became clear that the principle reason for the shortcomings of MISs was that they contained, for the most part, the wrong information. The MIS systems were aggregations of the organization's internal transaction data, almost exclusively internal information, with minimal external information (Dearden, 1972). However, the basic MIS idea, which was to make information available to senior-level management, was a sound one. Therefore, the idea did not die, it reemerged with a new name, decision support systems (DSS). The principle changes were improvements in ease of use, not entirely coincidentally this coincided with major developments in graphical user interfaces (GUIs), and the provision of more information, particularly external information.

Information Technology as Competitive Advantage

The potential role of information technology in securing competitive advantage (Parsons, 1982; Porter and Millar, 1985) for an organization was probably the hottest topic in all business literature in the 1980s, and it remains an important theme. The thrust of the argument was that information technology, when skillfully employed, could in various ways differentiate an organization from its competition, add value to its services or products in the eyes of the customers, and secure a competitive advantage in comparison to the competition. The key point was that this thesis explicitly said that information technology was no longer a backroom support function that could be left to mid-level management to implement in their individual realms. Rather, information technology was a major strategic enabler that could secure competitive advantage and affect the success and the very survival of the firm.

Managing the Archipelago

The "archipelago of information services" is a phrase coined by Warren McFarland and James McKenney in a trilogy of articles that appeared in the *Harvard Business Review* in 1982 and 1983 (McKenney and McFarland, 1982; McFarland et al., 1983, McFarland and McKenney, 1983). The phrase archipelago of information services has become a standard phrase, which refers to the need to coordinate the activities of different information services and activities, and refers to the managerial and administrative problems caused by the dispersion of those information activities within different administrative units of the typical business organization. McFarland and McKenney pointed out various logical historical reasons why the information functions of a typical company are widely dispersed hierarchically, why common control and coordination are not easily achieved, and why the issue demands top management attention.

Information Systems Stage Hypotheses

In the last two decades, a number of stage theories postulated to help illuminate the typical patterns of growth and development associated with the increasing capability of information technology.

These hypotheses attempt to derive some order from, and more importantly to predict some order in, the development of information systems, and serve as tools for planning and for management. Given the cost of information technology and the innate order of an exponential growth that information technology shows (and with no signs of slumping over at some unpredictable point into the standard S-shaped logistic growth curve), there is a substantial degree of interest in such hypotheses and a more than average predisposition to expect that they might have some predictive value.

There are two classes of stage hypotheses, the "cyclical" and the "progressive" or "developmental." The cyclical or lifecycle hypothesis posits that there is a repetitive and predictable lifecycle of development as each major new information technology capability comes along, whether that be word processing, spreadsheets, in-house CD-ROM mastering, or Intranets. Note that the capability may be a hardware development, a software development, or any combination. The second class of stage hypothesis is that of the progressive, non-cyclical, non-repetitive hypothesis that tries to predict broad-spectrum maturational stages of overall information technology growth.

For discussion of particular stage hypotheses, please refer to Koenig (1992).

Decision Analysis & the Expected Value of Perfect Information

The term decision analysis was coined by the Rand Corporation (Menke, 1979) to describe a methodology for calculating the tradeoff between making a decision with partial information versus expending resources to obtain more information and making a decision based on more complete information. The general technique they referred to as decision analysis, and the added value obtained by making a decision based on better information they referred to as the expected value of perfect information (EVPI).

The phrase EVPI is a bit misleading, the obvious point being that one seldom has perfect information. The technique actually attempts to calculate the expected negative consequences, the dis-benefit, of making a decision based on less than perfect information, and then calculates how much that dis-benefit would be reduced if the decision could be based on better information, and whether or not that reduction of dis-benefit is greater than the cost of obtaining better information.

Data-Driven Systems Design

The importance of data-driven systems design, the key component of structured programming, is that it represents the realization that not the process, not the precise steps to be undertaken, but the information and its flow within the system is the driving factor behind systems designs (Gane and Sarson, 1979). The essential requirement of data-driven systems design is that before one begins traditional flow charting, one does a data flow analysis of the proposed system with the data, not the process, driving the system design.

The Aggregate Theme and Four Macro-Themes

These themes, taken in their aggregate, constitute what might be called a new constellation, a constellation we may perhaps call "information-driven management." As we examine that constellation, several macro-themes emerge (see Figure 2).

1. As information systems mature, the emphasis within information technology shifts from the T in technology, to the I in information.

    This macro-theme is evident in a number of themes, which are ranked below by the degree to which they represent this macro-theme.

    - Knowledge Management
    - Information Systems Stage Hypotheses, particularly the Nolan and McFarland cyclical stage hypotheses, but also the Marchand, Koenig, and Zachman progressive stage hypotheses
    - Information-Driven Marketing
    - Information Resource Management
    - Enterprise-Wide Information Analysis
    - MIS to DSS, and External Information
    - Data-Driven Systems Design
    - Supply Chain Management

From this theme, one can derive the corollary that as information systems mature, the relative importance of information technology diminishes, while the relative importance of those who know how to manipulate and manage the information itself increases.

2. Releasing the shackles of print-on-paper technology is necessary. To some degree, all of the topics share this theme. It is particularly prominent (though rarely explicitly recognized) in:

    - Business Process Reengineering
    - Information Technology and Productivity
    - Enterprise Resource Planning
    - Information Technology and Organizational Structure
    - Knowledge Management
    - Hierarchies to Markets
    - Data-Driven Systems Design
    - Information Systems Stage Hypotheses (particularly those of Koenig, and Gibson and Jackson).
    - Supply Chain Management

The lesson here is that one must be careful not to be perceived as closely tied to print-on-paper technology, which is a real danger. Instead, librarians and information professionals must be perceived as technologically au courant, and as actively implementing and embracing change.

3. Information management is important and demands top-management attention and involvement.

   This is a key element in the following themes, which are in rough order by the degree to which they support this macro theme:

   - Knowledge Management and Intellectual Capital
   - Information Technology as Competitive Advantage
   - Information Technology and Productivity
   - Enterprise-Wide Information Analysis
   - Managing the Archipelago
   - Information System Stage Hypotheses
   - Information Technology and Organizational Structure
   - Enterprise Resource Planning
   - Business Process Reengineering
   - Supply Chain Management
   - Core Competencies
   - Minimization of Unallocated Cost
   - Information Resources Management
   - TQM and Benchmarking and to some degree all of the other themes.

   The obvious point here is that information, the commodity in which we deal, and information management, the skills we deploy, are important and are becoming increasingly so.

4. External information is important and that importance is often overlooked. This theme sometimes emerges explicitly as in MIS to DSS, but more often it emerges only implicitly. The key themes are:

   - MIS to DSS, and External Information
   - Competitive Intelligence
   - Information-Driven Marketing
   - Enterprise-Wide Information Analysis
   - Data Warehousing/Data Mining
   - Decision Analysis
   - Knowledge Management

This theme is important, but it continues to be very much under-recognized. Note that in knowledge management, the hottest of the current buzzwords, external information, is downplayed and the emphasis is upon internal information, particularly the organization's tacit knowledge—the knowledge that is not in documents or databases, but that exists in the knowledge and experience of individuals, knowledge that they carry in their heads or in their personal files.

The densely interwoven relationships of the aggregate theme, information-driven management, the four major themes above, and the twenty-one base themes are displayed in Figure C.2.

A Classificatory Structure

Schema:	Macro Themes:	Themes:
Information-Driven Management	Information Management is important and demands top management attention and involvement.	• Supply Chain Management
		• Enterprise Resource Planning
		• Information-Driven Marketing
	As information systems mature, the emphasis shifts from the T, technology, to the I, information.	• Knowledge Management and Intellectual Capital
		• Data Warehousing/Data Mining
		• Core Competencies
	External information—the librarian's domain—is important and its importance is often overlooked.	• Business Process Re-Engineering
		• Hierarchies to Markets
		• Competitive Intelligence
		• TQM and Benchmarking
	Releasing the shackles of print-on-paper technology	• Information Technology and Productivity
		• Minimization of Unallocated Cost
		• Information Technology and Organizational Structure
		• Information Resource Management
		• Enterprise-Wide Information Analysis
		• MIS to DSS and External Information
		• Information Technology as Competitive Advantage
		• Managing the Archipelago
		• Information Systems Stage Hypotheses
		• Decision Analysis
		• Data-Driven Systems Design

Note: To some degree, almost every theme can be limited to the macro themes of "Information Management is Important..." and "Releasing the Shackless...". We tried to select those where the link is particularly germane.

Figure C.2 A Classificatory Structure

References

Bessen, John. 1993. "Riding the Marketing Information Wave." *Harvard Business Review* 71, no. 5 (September/October): 150-160.

Brophy, Joseph T. 1985. Presentation at the Conference Board's 3rd Annual Conference on New Opportunities in Management Information. New York: April 17-18.

Brown, Eryn. 1997. "The Push to Streamline Supply Chains." *Fortune* 135, no. 4 (March): 108-111.

Darling, Charles B. 1997. "Datamining for the Masses." *Datamation* 43, no. 2 (February): 52-55.

Davenport, Thomas H. 1993. *Process Innovation: Reengineering Work Through Information Technology*. Boston, MA: Harvard Business School Press.

Davenport, Thomas H. 1998. "Putting the Enterprise into the Enterprise System." *Harvard Business Review* 76, no. 4 (July-August): 121-131.

Davenport, Thomas H.; Short, James E. 1990. "The New Industrial Engineering, Information Technology and Business Process Redesign." *Sloan Management Review* 31, no. 4 (1990): 11-27.

Dearden, John. 1972. "MIS Is a Mirage." *Harvard Business Review* 50, no. 1: 90-99.

Dearden, John. 1978. "Cost Accounting Comes to Service Industries." *Harvard Business Review* 56, no. 5 (September-October): 132-140.

Fuld, L.M. 1988. *Monitoring the Competition: Find Out What's Really Going on over There.* New York: John Wiley & Sons.

Gane, Chris; Sarson, Trish. 1979. *Structured Systems Analysis: Tools and Techniques.* Englewood Cliffs, NJ: Prentice Hall.

Koenig, Michael E.D. 1987. "Fiscal Accountability, and the Principle of Minimum Unsprung Weight." *The Bottom Line* 1, no. 1: 18-22.

Koenig, Michael E.D. 1992. "Entering Stage III—The Convergence of the Stage Hypotheses." *Journal of the American Society for Information Science* 43, no. 3 (April): 204-207.

Malone, Thomas W.; Yates, Joanne; Benjamin, Robert I. 1987. "Electronic Markets and Electronic Hierarchies." *Communications of the ACM* 30, no. 6 (June): 484-497.

Marchand, Donald A. 1985. "Information Management: Strategies and Tools in Transition." *Information Management Review* 1: 27-37.

McFarland, F. Warren; McKenney, James L. 1983. "The Information Archipelago Governing the New World." *Harvard Business Review* 61, no. 4 (July/August): 91-99.

McFarland, F. Warren; McKenney, James L.; Pyburn, Philip. 1983. "The Information Archipelago—Plotting a Course." *Harvard Business Review* 6 (January/February): 145-156.

McKenney, James L.; McFarland, F. Warren. 1982. "The Information Archipelago Maps and Bridges." *Harvard Business Review* 60, no. 5 (September/October): 109-114.

Menke, Michael M. 1979. "Strategic Planning in an Age of Uncertainty." *Long Range Planning* 12, no. 4: 27-34.

Parker, M.M. 1982. "Enterprise Information Analysis: Cost Benefit Analysis and Data Managed System." *IBM Systems Journal* 21, no. 1: 108-123.

Parker, M.M. 1985. Enterprise-*Wide Information Management: Emerging Information Requirements*. Los Angeles, CA: IBM Corporation.

Parsons, G.L. 1982. "Information Technology: A New Competitive Weapon." *Sloan Management Review* 25, no. 1: 3-14.

Synnott, William R.; Gruber, William H. 1980. Information *Resource Management: Opportunitiesand Strategies for the 1980s*. New York: John Wiley & Sons.

Talero, Eduardo; Gaudette, Philip. 1995. *Harnessing Information for Development: World Bank Group Vision and Strategy*, Draft Document, (Washington, D.C.: The World Bank, July).

Walton, Mary. 1986. *The Deming Management Method*. New York: Pedigree Books.

Whisler, Thomas L. 1970. *Information Technology and Organizational Change*. Belmont, CA: Wadsworth Publishing Company.

Endnote

1. See discussion about "Core Competencies" and "Hierarchies to Markets."

About the Contributors

Taverekere (Kanti) Srikantaiah

Taverekere (Kanti) Srikantaiah, Director, Center for Knowledge Management at Dominican University, joined the university faculty in 1997 as an associate professor. He teaches graduate courses in GSLIS and also cross-disciplined courses with the School of Business at Dominican University. Prior to that, Kanti had a distinguished career at the World Bank where he headed varied and important assignments in the area of information management at headquarters in Washington D.C. (and also at the World Bank's field offices in Africa and Asia). Before joining the World Bank, Kanti built a strong and advanced academic foundation in the sciences as well as in the social sciences. He received his B.S. (chemistry and geology) from the University of Mysore; M.S. (geology) from Karnatak University; M.S.I.S. from the University of Southern California; M.P.A. from the University of Southern California; and his Ph.D. from the University of Southern California. He also worked at the Library of Congress as an area specialist and taught at the California State University as an associate professor. His areas of specialization include systems analysis, organizations of information, information policy, and knowledge management. Some of his research includes: several research studies and project reports at the World Bank; articles and presentations at IFLA and similar international organizations; and two prominently published books, one on systems analysis and the other on quantitative research methods.

Michael E. D. Koenig

Michael E. D. Koenig, Dean, Long Island University, was formerly professor and dean of the Graduate School of Library and Information Science of Dominican

University. He has thirty years of experience in information systems design and management. This experience includes positions as vice president of information management for Tradenet, Inc., and head of information services for Pfizer Research. He holds a Ph.D. in information science from Drexel University, an M.B.A. in quantitative methods, and an M.S. in library and information science from the University of Chicago. Koenig is the author of more than eighty peer-reviewed papers. One of his principle research focuses has been the effect of information services on organizational productivity. He is also the former president of the International Society for Scientometrics and Informetrics.

Yogesh Malhotra

Yogesh Malhotra serves as a professor of information technology and operations management on the Faculty of the College of Business at Florida Atlantic University. Before joining Florida Atlantic University in 1998, he taught at the University of Pittsburgh and Carnegie Mellon University in the areas of management information systems, information policy, and research methods. He is also the chairman and chief knowledge officer of @BRINT Research Institute, and founder of its WWW-based virtual knowledge enterprise, and the WWW virtual library on knowledge management. As an internationally known thought leader in knowledge management and other contemporary business and technology issues, he advises senior management and technology executives, delivers keynote presentations, facilitates dialog among senior executives and scholars, and serves on industry advisory panels. Over the last fourteen years, he has held executive and professional positions in select Fortune 100 companies and multinationals in global Internet/WWW, software development, banking and finance, healthcare, manufacturing, and education sectors. *Computerworld* and *Information Week* have critiqued his award-winning knowledge management initiatives as benchmarks for information professionals. His WWW-based initiatives, interviews, commentary, and analyses have been frequently profiled in publications such as *Wall Street Journal, Fortune, Fast Company, Harvard Business School Publishing, Information Week, CIO, Computerworld, Training & Development, Forbes ASAP, PC Week Executive, The New York Times, Los Angeles Times, Government Executive, Computer Reseller News, Strategy and Business*, and *Strategist Quarterly*. He has published over fifteen articles on contemporary business, technology, and knowledge management in leading scholarly and practitioner journals and conference proceedings.

Yogesh Malhotra earned his Ph.D. in business administration with concentrations in information systems and knowledge management from the University of Pittsburgh, Katz Graduate School of Business. Prior to his doctoral work, he earned the credentials of an M.B.A. and Bachelor of Engineering. By virtue of his professional experience and training, he also holds the credentials of certified computing professional and chartered engineer.

Judith Albert

Judith Albert has written about and made presentations on knowledge management for the Special Libraries Association, National Online Meeting, and Online World. Currently Research Coordinator at the Ernst & Young LLP Center for Business Knowledge in New York City, Judith was formerly knowledge coordinator at FIND/SVP, and directed information services at two leading public relations firms. She holds an M.L.S. from Columbia University and a B.A. from Yale University. Judith lives in an 1842 row house in Brooklyn with her husband Stan Stanford and three children. She can be reached at stanorjudith@worldnet.att.net.

Mark Mazzie

Mark Mazzie serves as chief knowledge officer for Barrett International and directs the global knowledge management consulting practice, as well as the internal knowledge sharing activities, within Barrett. Barrett is a global consulting firm, which concentrates on areas of knowledge management, strategic planning, and clinical research. Mark is the former chairman of the conference board's Learning and Knowledge Management Council. He frequently speaks on the topic of knowledge management and intellectual capital and has chaired conferences on these issues in North America, Europe, and Asia.

Prior to his current position, Mark directed the knowledge management program at Wyeth-Ayerst Pharmaceuticals, a subsidiary of American Home Products. He received his Master's degree from Harvard University in 1985 and an undergraduate degree in 1982 from Suffolk University in Boston.

David P. Schmidt

David P. Schmidt is associate professor of business ethics at Fairfield University where he specializes in the ethical dimensions of corporate policy and practice. He has a joint appointment with the School of Business and the Department of Religious Studies. Previously, David was the director of the Trinity Center for Ethics and Corporate Policy, a program sponsored by the historic parish of Trinity church at the head of Wall Street. In addition to teaching and researching in business ethics, David consults with Fortune 500 corporations, investment and savings banks, professional and trade associations, and universities and religious institutions. He designs and leads training programs, composes ethics codes and mission statements, and provides resources for policy making.

David is a member of the editorial advisory board of the *International Journal of Value-Based Management*. His most recent publication is "Wake-Up Calls: Classic Cases in Business Ethics." He received a B.S. from Illinois State University, M.A. degrees in divinity and public policy from the University of Chicago, and a Ph.D. in social ethics from the University of Chicago.

Mark Addleson

Mark Addleson is associate professor and director of the Program on Social and Organizational Learning at George Mason University. Before joining the university in 1994, he lived in South Africa and was head of general management at the Graduate School of Management, University of the Witwatersrand. He was also a director of and consultant to a firm of economics consultants. His areas of research and teaching include the changing frames of social and organizational thinking, collaborative technology in organizations, organizational learning, and strategic knowledge management.

Vicki L. Gregory

Vicki L. Gregory received an M.A. in history and an M.L.S. in library service from the University of Alabama and a Ph.D. in communication, library and information studies from Rutgers University. She is currently an associate professor in the School of Library and Information Science at the University of South Florida where she teaches courses in the areas of library networks, collection development, library automation, and technical services. Prior to beginning her teaching career, she was the head of the systems and operations department at the Auburn University at Montgomery Library.

Vicki is an active member of a number of professional associations, including the Special Library Association, the American Society for Information Science, the American Library Association (including the Association of College and Research Libraries, Library and Information Technology Association, the Association for Library Collections and Technical Services, and the Library Research Round Table), the Association of Library and Information Science

Education, the Southeastern Library Association, and both the Florida and Alabama Library Associations.

Steve Sawyer

Steve Sawyer is on the faculty of Syracuse University's School of Information Studies, a senior research fellow at Syracuse University's Center for Information Technology and Policy, and co-director of the Ph.D. Program in Information Transfer. His research focuses on social and organizational informatics: studying how people work together and how they use information technology. Steve holds Masters degrees in both engineering and information systems and earned his Doctorate in business administration from Boston University. He has been with the School of Information Studies since 1994 and was named "Professor of the Year" in 1997. His work appears in a range of journals, including *Information Technology & People, The IBM Systems Journal,* and *Computer Personnel.* He co-authored his first book, *Information Technologies in Human Contexts: Learning from Organizational and Social Informatics,* with Rob Kling, Suzie Weisband, and Howard Rosenbaum, which is forthcoming from Indiana University Press. Steve is a member of the ACM, AIS, INFORMS, IEEE, and USRowing.

Kristin Eschenfelder

Kristin Eschenfelder is a doctoral candidate at the School of Information Studies at Syracuse University. Her research interests include: organizational change and computing; the work life of technologists; organizational behavior and communications; information seeking behavior; information system evaluation; information policy; telecommunications policy; and research methods. She has published in the areas of informal social networks and organizational communications, the skill needs of technologists, and the United States federal government Web site management and evaluation.

Robert Heckman

Robert Heckman is a faculty member at the School of Information Studies at Syracuse University. Prior to joining the faculty, Robert worked for over twenty years in the information industry. As vice president and division head for one of the largest providers of information services to the financial industry, he led the product management, system development, and customer service functions, and was director of the company's research and consulting practice. He developed the first university course on information technology procurement to be offered in the

United States, and he recently directed three studies for the Society of Information Management (SIM) on current practices in software contracting and the management of information technology procurement. Robert's current research is focused on management of the information technology procurement function, the role played by marketplace brokers in acquiring and integrating information resources, and discovering the factors that lead people to make discretionary contributions of time, effort, or money. This interest has most recently led to investigations of discretionary collaboration among distributed information support personnel and in information technology help desk service encounters. He received his Ph.D. in information systems from the University of Pittsburgh in 1993.

Bill Crowley

Bill Crowley is a former reference librarian, public relations representative, consultant, and deputy state librarian. Following twenty-three years of "real world" experience in four states, he enrolled as a full-time student at Ohio University, earned a doctorate in two years, and spent a third year as a researcher for the university's president emeritus. He holds a Ph.D. in higher education from Ohio University, an M.A. in English from Ohio State University with a thesis in occupational folklore, an MS in library service from Columbia University, and a B.A. in history from Hunter College of the City University of New York. Bill has published and co-published in both the higher-education and library and information science literatures, addressing topics as diverse as formulating local government information policies, the status of the academic librarian in Canadian universities, legislative activism, and the competition between "library" and "information" in graduate education. He joined the faculty of Dominican University's Graduate School of Library and Information Science in 1996. Long active in professional associations, Bill served as chair of the State Library Agency Section of the American Library Association's Association of Specialized and Cooperative Library Agencies.

Sumitra Muralidhar

Sumitra Muralidhar is currently a research assistant professor in the department of microbiology and immunology at the Georgetown University Medical Center, Washington D.C. She has a Masters degree in genetics from the University of Bangalore, India, and a Ph.D. in microbiology from the University of Maryland, College Park. She worked as a post-doctoral fellow at the National Institute of Allergy and Infectious Diseases (NIAID), and later as a Research Associate at the

National Cancer Institute (NCI), both at the National Institutes of Health (NIH), Bethesda, Maryland. Her research work encompasses bacteriology, molecular virology, and more recently molecular biology of cancers, such as cervical carcinoma and Kaposi's sarcoma, which is the most common malignancy in AIDS patients. Her work has been published in peer-reviewed journals.

Curt M. White

Curt M. White, currently at DePaul University in Chicago, has been a college educator since 1978. During those years, he has taught computer science, information systems, management information systems, and library and information science courses. Curt has published over twenty articles including a textbook on data communications and computer networks. He received his Ph.D. in computer science at Wayne State University in 1986. Curt has also chaired a number of computer conferences, including the Association for Computing Machinery's Technical Symposium on Computer Science Education, and the Midwest Conference of the Consortium for Computing in Small Colleges.

Ken Black

Ken Black is director of teaching and learning technology at Dominican University. He has been at Dominican since 1985, where he was previously assistant director of the library. He has held his present position since June 1998. Ken is also an adjunct faculty member of the Graduate School of Library and Information Science at Dominican University, where he teaches the basic reference class and online searching. Ken served on the editorial board of ALA's *Reference Books Bulletin* for four years, and continues to do guest reviews for that publication. He also contributed to encyclopedias, atlases, and dictionaries. He has given several workshops on Web searching.

Vikas Sahasrabudhe

Vikas M. Sahasrabudhe received his Ph.D. in computer science from the University of California, Berkeley in 1972. He has extensive, practical experience in planning for and use of information technology for business applications, for decision support, for training and education, and for different aspects of knowledge management. His work has taken him to many countries around the world. His current interests are leveraging information technology to provide effective learning opportunities on a variety of important topics to learners worldwide (including self-learning and distance learning), using information technology for improved knowledge management, and learning about how information and technology is changing the way business gets done or will get done in the "global village." Currently, he is working at the World Bank in Washington, D.C.

Ileen Fiddler

Ileen Fiddler is a knowledge specialist at Comdisco, Inc. She has been a researcher for over ten years in various contexts and a published author in a range of venues. She earned her M.L.I.S. from Dominican University and also holds an M.A. in Ibero-American studies from the University of Wisconsin, Madison, and a B.A. in Spanish from the University of Illinois, Chicago. Her interests include the use of the Internet for information professionals, Intranet content management, and the co-evolution of technology and knowledge management. Several of her publications reflect these topics.

Bor-sheng Tsai

Bor-sheng Tsai joined the faculty of Pratt Institute's School of Information and Library Science in 1997 as an associate professor. Prior to that, he was a member of the faculty at Wayne State University's Library and Information Program for ten years. He holds a B. A. in library science from Fu-jen Catholic University in Taipei, Taiwan, an M.S. and a Ph.D. in information science from Case Western Reserve University in Cleveland, Ohio. Prior to joining the faculty, he worked as an acquisitions librarian in the National Central Library in Taiwan, and as a reference librarian in CWRU libraries. He designed a funded, computer-assisted, multilingual tutorial system for a public school in Cleveland. He is an expert in information processing and computer programming, information storage and retrieval, database management systems, networked information resources management, and microcomputer software applications and management. His research directions have been in 3-D spatial information indexing and memory management involving multimedia, imaging, 3-D graphics, and VR technologies. His research contributions were published in various library and information science journals, including *Resource Sharing and Information Networks*, *ASIS Proceedings*, *Journal of Library and Information Science*, *International Journal of Scientometrics and Informetrics*, and *International Journal of Information Communication and Library Science*. He is an active member of several library and information science associations including ASIS, ISSI, ALA, and ALISE. He is profiled in Who's Who in American Education, Who's Who in America, Who's Who Among Asian Americans, Who's Who in the East, and Who's Who in the World.

Abraham Bookstein

Abraham Bookstein has been on the faculty of the University of Chicago since 1970. He currently holds professorships in the department of psychology and the division of the humanities. His educational background includes graduate work in theoretical physics at the University of California, Berkeley, and a Ph.D. in physics from the Belfer Graduate School of Science of Yeshiva University. He has carried out research in the application of mathematical methods to the information sciences, with specialties including information retrieval, data compression and information coding, and statistical methods, for which he received the American Society for Information Science's research award.

John Agada

John Agada is associate professor at Emporia State University's School of Library and Information Management where he is director of the school's research center. He holds an M.Ed. in educational communications and instructional technology (Ahmadu Bello University, Nigeria) and a Ph.D. in library and information science (University of Pittsburgh). His research and teaching interests include international information policy and information diagnosis and customization. He has undertaken funded research projects investigating the information needs and seeking behaviors of inner-city residents. John also has authored more than thirty peer-reviewed publications.

Thomas Short

Thomas Short is a senior consultant in IBM Global Services' Worldwide Knowledge Management Market Initiative. He is responsible for developing and leading client consulting work as well as researching, writing, and speaking on the topic of knowledge management.

Thomas began consulting sixteen years ago in the area of organizational development and change. Since then, he worked on over fifty client engagements, providing knowledge management services such as solution identification, design, and implementation, as well as general business consulting services such as business process redesign, activity-based costing, team building, culture change, performance measurement, Lotus Notes strategy, and organizational restructuring to clients in a variety of industries.

He also has published articles about, spoken on, and designed and delivered training on knowledge management, the role of the Internet/Intranet in business, business process redesign, problem solving, and other business topics. Prior to joining IBM, Thomas consulted for Lotus Consulting (Sydney, Australia); Cost Reconstruction (Sydney); and Coopers & Lybrand (New York); as well as worked in private practice for himself.

Thomas attended the University of Michigan, in Ann Arbor, where he earned Bachelors and Masters degrees in industrial and operations engineering. His Masters work focused on organizational psychology and change, and included research work on a major NSF-funded project studying the impact of flexible manufacturing systems. Post-graduate education includes scenario planning and video production.

Ellen J. Ryske

Ellen J. Ryske is a senior manager with Andersen Consulting specializing in knowledge management. For the past five years, she has focused on a strategic initiative to develop the global knowledge-sharing infrastructure for the firm's technology specialists. The results include seventeen global communities of practice and a collection of Lotus Notes databases that ship thousands of knowledge items each business day. In addition, Ellen is frequently asked to discuss knowledge management concepts and practical techniques for clients seeking to establish knowledge management operations. She has managed the Technology InfoCenter since 1996.

Ellen has extensive experience in the design and implementation of business software packages, following structured methodologies and using formal usability studies. She specializes in complex systems, innovative practices and technologies, and has consistently developed high-functioning and motivated teams. She joined Andersen Consulting in 1978 after earning a graduate degree in management and a B.A. in mathematics from Northwestern University.

Theresa B. Sebastian

Theresa B. Sebastian joined Andersen Consulting in 1996 as research specialist in the Technology InfoCenter, specializing in electronic commerce. Theresa recently served on an organization-wide taskforce to review searching capabilities on Andersen Consulting's Knowledge Xchange knowledge management system. Her previous research experience includes Duff & Phelps, McKinsey & Company, Helene Curtis, and her own online research business.

Before launching her career in information science, Theresa managed operations planning units for two healthcare product manufacturers, and was a senior analyst for Baxter Heathcare. In addition, she was an adjunct faculty member and served as director of business and industry training for the College of Lake County, Illinois. She holds a B.S. in mathematics from Loyola University of Chicago, an M.B.A. in finance from DePaul University of Chicago, and an M.L.I.S. from Dominican University.

Prudence W. Dalrymple

Prudence Dalrymple became dean of the Graduate School of Library and Information Science at Dominican University in August 1997. Prior to that, she directed the office for accreditation at the American Library Association during the implementation of the 1992 Standards for Accreditation. She has taught at the University of Illinois and the University of Wisconsin and practiced as a health sciences librarian in both clinical and academic settings in Illinois. She is a Phi Beta Kappa graduate of Clark University in Worcester, Massachusetts, and holds a Master's degree in library science from Simmons College in Boston and a Ph.D. from the University of Wisconsin-Madison. She has published widely in the area of user studies and educational evaluation; two of her most recent articles appeared in *American Libraries* and the *Bulletin of the Medical Library Association*. She is the recipient of numerous honors and awards and has served the profession in a variety of leadership capacities. Prudence consulted with a variety of educational institutions in the United States and Canada. She is a distinguished member of the Academy of Health Information Professionals and was recently appointed to the National Library of Medicine's Biomedical Library Review Committee at the National Institutes of Health.

Nina Platt

Nina Platt is director of library services for the Faegre & Benson law firm in Minneapolis, Minnesota, and also served in a variety of positions in public, academic, and special libraries and as an information management consultant. Nina contributed to a number of information management publications, including *Database*, *Law Office Computing*, *Law Technology Product News*, and *Law Library Resource Exchange*. She currently writes a bi-monthly column, "Research Options" for *Law Office Computing* and is co-editor of the e-journal, *Integrated Library System Reviews* <http://www.ilsr.com/>. In addition to writing, Nina speaks on a variety of topics, including developing searchable Web sites, networking CD-ROMs, developing attorney-workproduct systems, search engines for the Intranet, cost-effective legal research (using the Internet, online services, CD-ROM), and printing effectively.

Nina received a B.S. from the University of North Dakota and an M.S.L.I.S. from Dominican University. She is a member of the American Association of Law Libraries, Special Libraries Assocation, Minnesota Library Association, and Minnesota Association of Law Libraries.

Katherine Shelfer

Katherine Shelfer is currently assistant professor at the College of Information Science and Technology at Drexel University. Her teaching interests include business information management; competitive intelligence; and the design, marketing, and evaluation of information products and services. Her research interests focus information needs analysis of entreneurs. Katherine performs strategic needs analysis and manages research projects for a number of enterprises, including technology transfer centers and business incubator facilities in several states and at Cybermark, L.L.C., a joint venture of Sallie Mae, Huntington Bancshares, and the Batelle Institute.

Anthony Debons

Anthony Debons, professor emeritus, School of Information Sciences, University of Pittsburgh joined the faculty in 1968 at which time he was asked to develop the interdisciplinary Program of Information Sciences of the Graduate School of Library and Information Science at that university. Prior to this appointment, he was head of the department of information science, following his tenure as professor and chair of the department of psychology, University of Dayton, Dayton, Ohio. This appointment, as a tenured full professor, followed his retirement as a Colonel in the United States Air Force in which he served twenty-two years. His last assignment in the Air Force was director of computers, electronic system division, Air Force Research and Development Command. He has written and edited several books, the last of which, *Information Science: An Integrated View,* won the best book award rendered by the American Society for Information Science.

Margareta Nelke

Margareta Nelke studied at the universities of Stockholm, Lund, and Copenhagen and obtained her B.A. in 1971. She graduated from the Swedish School of Library and Information Science in 1982. Margareta completed her diploma in marketing in 1990. She worked as library manager at Tetra Laval since 1983, at Alfa-Laval 1983-1989, and at Tetra Pak 1989-present. She has published many research articles and lectured at conferences in the area of information and knowledge management. Her recent publication is "Knowledge Management in Swedish Corporations: The Value of Information and Information Services." Margareta has worked on different commissions of trust in the Swedish Society for Technical Documentation (TLS). At present, she is the chairwoman of the industry's consultative group for information services within TLS.

Index

A

ABI/INFORM, 466
About.com, 258
academic institutions as research organizations, 225
Access, 414
ACP (American College of Physicians) Journal Club, 397
Adams, Deborah L., 88
adaptive methods of encoding, 322–323
Addleson, Mark, biographical information, 560
Advance Research Projects Agency (ARPA), U.S. Department of Defense, 238
Agada, John, biographical information, 565
Agarwala-Rogers, R., 182, 196
Agency for Health Care Policy and Research, 398
Agre, Phil, 123
AICPA, 110
AIDS epidemic, NIH response to, 227–228
Albert, John W., 111
Albert, Judith, biographical information, 559
Albert, S., 53
Albrow, M., 141, 147
Alic, J.A., 216
Allee, Verna, 139, 406, 415
Allen, Thomas J., 89
Alston & Bird, 413
AltaVista, 255–260
Alverson, M., 423
Amazon.com, 371
American Bankers Association, 425, 440
American College of Physicians (ACP), 397
American Home Products, 90
American Productivity and Quality Center, 8
American Society for Information Science, 8
American Society for Training and Development (ATSD), 107–108
American Stock Exchange, 111
Amoco, 9
Anerson, R.K., 391–392
animated citation map series, 298–302, 304–315 (figs.)
Annals of Internal Medicine, 397
Anthes, G.H., 41
anticipative processes, 48–51

Applegate, L., 40
Applets, 299
application and creation of knowledge, balancing, 171
archiving best practices, 43–44
Argote, L., 172
Argyris, Chris, 50, 165, 168–170
Aristotle, 206, 209
arithmetic encoding, 322, 324
Arora, Ashish, 211
ARPANET, 238
Arthur, W.B., 38
Arthur Andersen, 8, 40
Arthur D. Little International, Inc., 64, 206
article criteria in MEDLINE searches, 395
artifacts, knowledge, 355, 358, 359
    in market culture of the DTS, 191–193
artificial intelligence, 33, 41, 64–65
Artz, J., 69
ASCII code, 319, 412
Ash, Jerry, 69
Ashby, W.R., 45, 49
Ashford, S.J., 183
AskJeeves, 268
Assessing Aid Overview study, 453–455
assessment
    current state of knowledge transfer, 103
    questions for a learning environment, 415–416
    research skills, 385–387
Association for Information and Image Management, 8
Association of American Medical Colleges, 391
ASTD (American Society for Training and Development), 107–108
ATM technology, 252–253
Attorney Work Product Systems, 407, 409
audio storage requirements, 321
audits, information, 70–71
Ayerst, 90–91

B

balanced score card, 25–26
Banks, H., 28
Bannister, D., 56
Banyan Vines, 249

E

G

Gadamer, H.-G., 148, 155
Gambro, 482
Gane, Chris, 549
Garfinkel, S., 326
Gartner Group, 3, 8, 386
Garvin, D.A., 162, 175
Gates, Bill, 127, 356
Gateway, 423
Gaudette, Philip, 23, 542
GDB (Human Genome Data Base), 393
General Electric Corporation, 51, 105–106
General Motors Corporation, 9, 27
General Motors University, 27
Gephardt, R.P., 148
Germany, financial reporting in, 26
Gers, R., 216–217
Gersho, A., 324
Gerstner, Lou, 35
Ghoshal, S., 43, 51, 355–356
Gibbons, Michael, 93
Gibson, C.F., 27
GIFF formats, 324
Giga, 386
Gilbert, Carole M., 88
Giles, C. Lee, 255–256
Gill, T.G., 41, 44
Ginman, Mariam, 92
Giuse, N.B., 400
Glaser, B.G., 210
Glick, W.H., 42
global economy, 222
goals, long-term, 51
Goldhar, Joel D., 89–90
GoTo.Com, 267
GPEP report, 391
Graduate School of Library and Information Science, University of Pittsburgh, 460–462, 470
Graduate School of Library and Information Science, University of Puerto Rico, 462, 465–466, 470–471
Graham, Margaret, 79
Granat, Richard, 414
Grant, E.B., 216
graphics storage requirements, 321
Grateful Med, 392–393, 400
Gray, R.M., 324
gray literature, 207

Grayson, C.J., Jr., 378
Greer, R., 335
Gregory, J.J., 216
Gregory, Vicki L., biographical information, 560–561
Griffiths, Jose-Marie, 82–87, 92
Group Bull, 439
GroupWare, 10–11, 31, 71, 74, 155, 202, 275
    See also communication; email; listservs
Grover, R., 335
Gruber, William H., 546
Guskey, A., 202
Guyatt, G.H., 398

H

Hale, M.L., 335
Hamel, G., 50, 542
Handy, C., 42
Harari, O., 390
harnessing knowledge, 359–360
Harper, W., 210
Harrop, Peter, 431
Harvard Business Review, 548
harvesting knowledge, 358–359
Haskell, B.G., 321
Hassard, J., 148
Havelock, R.G., 460–461
Hayes, D., 49
Hayes, Robert M., 87
Haynes, R.B., 396
health care, impact of information services on, 88–89, 400
health sciences library, evolution, 391–392
Health Services Technology Assessment Texts (HSTAT), 398
Heckman, Robert, biographical information, 561–562
Hedberg, B., 44–45, 49–51
Hegelian systems, 47, 56
Hekman Library, Calvin College, 258
Hellman, M.E., 327
help desks, 10
help screens in search engines, 259–260
Hepworth, J.B., 400
hermeneutics, 148
Hershfield, A., 460–461
Hewlett-Packard, 360
Hibbard, Justin, 15–16, 24, 406–407
hierarchical management, 174–175

R

Rand Corporation, 549
Rasmussen, R.V., 163
ratio of providing information services, cost-benefit, 80–87
RDBMS (relational database management systems), 270–271
R&D innovation studies, 89–92
reading
    and productivity, 92
    time spent, business professionals', 488–489
    value of, 83–85
Reber, A.S., 208
reciprocity as motivation for knowledge transfer, 195
records management, 74, 407–408
Reed, M., 141
Reed Elsevier's LEXIS-NEXIS, 256
re-engineering, business process, 10, 28–32, 100, 543
Reference.Com, 267
reference effectiveness, improving, 217–218
referral services, 10
relational database management systems (RDBMS), 270–271
relationship marketing, 542
relationship of explicit and tacit knowledge, 11–15
relevance algorithms, 72
relevancy rankings in search engines, 258
Remeikis, Lois A., 64, 283
Rennie, D., 398, 399
repackaging information
    analysis and synthesis, 338–340
    evaluation, 344–346
    interpretation and evaluation services, 344
    locational and access tools, 343
    purpose, 334–335
    quality of, 344–345
    representational sources, 344
    symbols, channels, and media, 340–342
    types of services, 342–346
    usefulness of, 345–346
repetitive routines in factory systems, 143–144, 150
representational information sources, 344
requisite variety, 361, 423
research
    approaches of social scientists, 212–215
    cost avoidance, 84–85
    productivity, impact of information services on, 79–94

skills track, 385–387
    time spent information seeking, 86
Research Clearinghouse: The Intangibles Research Center, 109
researchers' tacit knowledge, 212–215
Research Memo Collections, 407
research organizations, 225–230
Research Policies for the Social and Behavioral Sciences, 213
research priorities at NIH, 226–227
return on information investment, 79–87
reward systems. *See* incentives, knowledge transfer
Reyes, Edwin, 459
Richardson, W.S., 396
richness or reach in communication, 27, 29
Rider, Fremont, 16
Rigney, Melanie, 439
risk-taking by management, 170
Ritzer, G., 186
Rivest, R.L., 322
Roberts, C., 162–163, 165, 172
Roderer, Nancy K., 82
Rogers, E.M., 93, 182, 196, 336–337
Rorty, R., 142
Rosenberg, W., 396
Ross, Faith V., 88
Ross, R.B., 162–163, 165, 172
routinization in organizations, 171
Royal-Dutch Shell, 361
RSA cryptosystem, 327–328
Rubenstein, Albert H., 92
rules, consequences of obedience to, 49–50
Rutledge, J., 67
Ryle, Gilbert, 205–206, 208–209, 212, 218
Ryske, Ellen J., biographical information, 566

S

Sackett, D.L., 396
Sahasrabudhe, Vikas, biographical information, 563–564
Sallie Mae, 436
Salton, G., 320
San Francisco State University, 436
Saracevic, T., 333, 338–339
Sarson, Trish, 549
Sassone, Peter G., 81
Saturn division, General Motors, 27

More Books from Information Today, Inc.

ARIST 33
Annual Review of Information Science and Technology
Edited by Martha E. Williams

Since 1966, ARIST has been continuously at the cutting edge in contributing a useful and comprehensive view of the broad field of information science and technology. ARIST reviews numerous topics within the field and ultimately provides this annual source of ideas, trends, and references to the literature. A master plan for the series encompasses the entire field in all its aspects, and topics for the annual volume are selected on the basis of timeliness and an assessment of reader interest. The newest edition of ARIST covers topics that fit within the fundamental structure as follows: Planning Information Systems and Services, Basic Techniques and Technologies, and Applications.

hardbound ISBN 1-57387-065-X
ASIS Members $79.95   **Non-Members $99.95**

Information Management for the Intelligent Organization, Second Edition
Chun Wei Choo

The intelligent organization is one that is skilled at marshalling its information resources and capabilities, transforming information into knowledge, and using this knowledge to sustain and enhance its performance in a restless environment. The objective of this newly updated and expanded book is to develop an understanding of how an organization may manage its information processes more effectively in order to achieve these goals. This book is a must read for senior managers and administrators, information managers, information specialists and practitioners, information technologists, and anyone whose work in an organization involves acquiring, creating, organizing, or using knowledge.

hardbound ISBN 1-57387-057-9
ASIS Members $31.60   **Non-Members $39.50**

Millennium Intelligence
Understanding & Conducting Competitive Intelligence in the Digital Age
Edited by Jerry Miller

With contributions from the world's leading business intelligence practitioners, here is a tremendously informative and practical look at the CI process, how it is changing, and how it can be managed effectively in the Digital Age. Loaded with case studies, tips, and techniques, chapters include What Is Intelligence?; The Skills Needed to Execute Intelligence Effectively; Information Sources Used for Intelligence; The Legal and Ethical Aspects of Intelligence; Corporate Security and Intelligence ...and much more!

softbound • ISBN 0-910965-28-5 • $29.95

Internet Business Intelligence
How to Build a Big Company System on a Small Company Budget
David Vine

According to author David Vine, business success in the competitive, global marketplace of the 21st century will depend on a firm's ability to use information effectively—and the most successful firms will be those that harness the Internet to create and maintain a powerful information edge. In *Internet Business Intelligence*, Vine explains how any company—large or small—can build a complete, low-cost Internet-based business intelligence system that really works. If you're fed up with Internet hype and wondering "where's the beef?," you'll appreciate this savvy, no-nonsense approach to using the Internet to solve everyday business problems and to stay one step ahead of the competition.

softbound • ISBN 0-910965-35-8 • $29.95

SUPER SEARCHERS DO BUSINESS
The Online Secrets of Top Business Researchers
Mary Ellen Bates • Edited by Reva Basch

Super Searchers Do Business probes the minds of 11 leading researchers who use the Internet and online services to find critical business information. Through her in-depth interviews, Mary Ellen Bates—a business super searcher herself—gets the pros to reveal how they choose online sources, evaluate search results, and tackle the most challenging business research projects. Loaded with expert tips, techniques, and strategies, this is the first title in the exciting new "Super Searchers" series, edited by Reva Basch. If you do business research online, or plan to, let *Super Searchers Do Business* be your guide.

softbound • ISBN 0-910965-33-1 • $24.95

The Extreme Searcher's Guide To
WEB SEARCH ENGINES
A Handbook for the Serious Searcher
Randolph Hock

"Extreme searcher" Randolph (Ran) Hock—internationally respected Internet trainer and authority on Web search engines—offers advice designed to help you get immediate results. Ran not only shows you what's "under the hood" of the major search engines, but explains their relative strengths and weaknesses, reveals their many (and often overlooked) special features, and offers tips and techniques for searching the Web more efficiently and effectively than ever. Updates and links are provided at the author's Web site.

softbound • ISBN 0-910965-26-9 • $24.95
hardcover • ISBN 0-910965-38-2 • $34.95

Ask at your local bookstore or order online at
www.infotoday.com

For a complete catalog, contact:

Information Today, Inc.

143 Old Marlton Pike, Medford, NJ 08055 • 609/654-6266

email: custserv@infotoday.com

DATE DUE
